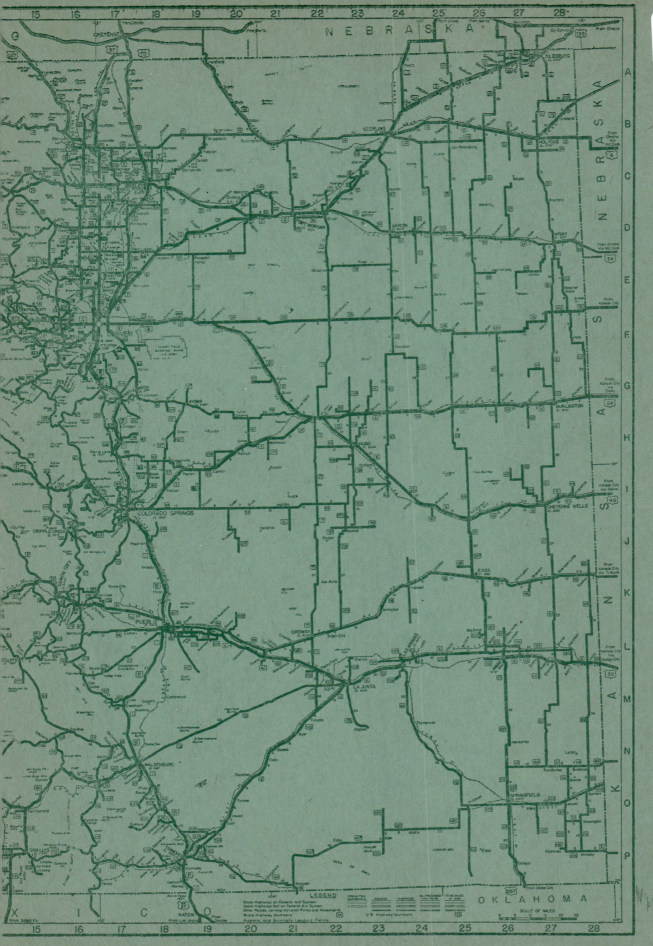

COLORADO

and

ITS PEOPLE

Denver in 1858

(Courtesy State Historical Society of Colorado)

COLORADO

and

ITS PEOPLE

A Narrative and Topical History
of the Centennial State

Edited by
LeROY R. HAFEN, Ph.D., Litt.D.
Executive Director, The State Historical Society
of Colorado

VOLUME II

LEWIS HISTORICAL PUBLISHING CO., INC.

NEW YORK

rivers which have carved deep, narrow, canyons with steep walls. Only in canyon bottoms does the elevation reach much less than 5,000 feet and some of the plateaus are as much as 11,000 feet above sea level.

Colorado has not always looked like this nor will it always present the same appearance, for the changing forces of nature are still at work. During the millions of years which have elapsed since the earth was formed this area has undergone many changes. Great seas have covered it, volcanoes have poured forth shimmering streams of molten lava, glaciers have formed and disappeared, and strange, fantastic plants and animals, never seen by man, have lived and died within its borders. All that we know of these long ago ages must be learned by a study of the rocks which contain a fascinating story for those who can read it.

The earliest rock formations which we know are those called pre-Cambrian, which were produced perhaps as much as 2,000 million years ago. Some of these are *igneous* rocks, that is, those which were produced by volcanic action and were deposited in a molten condition. Some were *sedimentary* rocks, which are made up of material derived from wear and decay of already existing rocks and deposited elsewhere, usually by water. Later action of heat and pressure has altered the character of some of these rocks and turned them into what we know as *metamorphic* rocks. No satisfactory fossil specimens have been found in the oldest levels but the presence of certain chemicals, believed to be of organic origin, suggest that some simple one-celled organisms may have been in existence. Before the close of pre-Cambrian times more advanced forms of life had developed. In the eastern and western zones of Colorado these rocks are buried under thousands of feet of later deposits, but in the central section they have been forced up by the mighty earth movements which later created the Rocky Mountains and appear on the surface in many places.

During the first part of the Cambrian period, which followed some five hundred million years ago, rock surfaces in Colorado were being eroded. Later the sea advanced from the northwest and covered all the area. Sediments were deposited on the sea floor and eventually became sandstone, shales, and conglomerates. Later heat, pressure, and recrystallization changed some of the sandstones into quartzites. The limy shells of tiny animals accumulated on the ocean bottom and, in the course of time, were consolidated into limestone. There were great advances among the shelled animals, and corals and sponges progressed.

The next period, which is known as the Ordovician, was marked by a continuation of the rock-making activity of the preceding time. Some of the limestone which was formed during this period was later metamorphosed into beautiful marble. Late in the period the land arose again and the sea retreated for a long time. During the Silurian period which followed, Colorado was a land area. It was a flat country with sluggish rivers which carved only shallow valleys as they carried their loads of eroded rock to the sea. Vegetation was scanty and of a simple type. There was little animal life on the land.

Fairly late in the following period, the Devonian, whose age is estimated at between three hundred and three hundred and fifty million years, the sea came back to the western part of the state and limestones, clay shales, and sandstones were laid down. This is sometimes called the age of fishes, for this was the most prominent form of life. Where there was still land there evolved luxuriant vegetation with many tree-like ferns.

The sea retreated from Colorado late in Devonian times but early in the Mississippian period which followed it suddenly returned. The land subsided until almost all of the state was covered by water. The principal rocks formed at this time were limestones. There were innumerable forms of invertebrate animals but there were also many fish. It was at this time that the first amphibians, animals capable of living both on land and in the water, are believed to have appeared. Late in the period the sea subsided once more, leaving Colorado a peninsula. The exposed sea floor was carved and weathered by the elements and hills and valleys were formed.

The Pennsylvanian was the next period. Once more the land was submerged and the sea covered most of the state. Later the eastern section reappeared but the western portion remained submerged. In other parts of the country where the land was exposed the lush vegetation of dense forests gave rise to great coal deposits. In the land area of Colorado a little coal was formed but it is not workable. It is to deposits of this period, however, that we owe the great oil wealth of the Rangely field.

The following period, the Permian, was a time of great changes everywhere. Tremendous crustal movements produced mountain ranges in many parts of the world and almost all of this continent rose above sea level. Much water was drained away and there was great aridity and later widespread glaciation. Under these unfavorable conditions it was impossible for many plants and animals to survive.

Next came the Triassic period, which marked the beginning of a new geological era. The estimated dates for this period are between one hundred and sixty and two hundred million years. The climate began to improve and new forms of plant and animal life appeared. Reptiles, particularly dinosaurs, replaced amphibians as the dominant animals. Small primitive mammals appeared.

Colorado was a land area during most of the Jurrasic period which followed. Late in the period there was an invasion by the sea but it did not last very long. The climate was good and there was plenty of moisture. Tremendous evolutionary progress was made. Reptiles dominated the world of vertebrate animals, both on the sea and on the land. Some were meat eaters and others fed on vegetation. Prominent among the land forms were great herbivorous dinosaurs, some of which reached a length of almost eighty feet and weighed as much as forty tons. Fine fossilized skeletons of these long dead monsters have been found in Colorado.

The next period, known as the Cretaceous and with estimated dates of from sixty to one hundred and twenty-five million years, was perhaps the most important time in all geological history for Colorado. In a large measure it is to the events of this time that we owe much of the magnificent scenery which has made the state famous and many of the great natural resources which have provided its wealth. During part of the time Colorado was a land area and part of the time it was under the sea. While the land was exposed there was an abundant plant life which gave rise to coal deposits. While the sea covered the area great sedimentary beds were laid down. Many of these were shales which in some places are over 10,000 feet thick. Limestones and sandstones were also formed. Some of the sandstones in eastern Colorado yield artesian water. Other beds provide the oil of the Florence, Boulder and Wellington fields. Some sedimentary deposits laid down at this time provide fine commercial clays.

Maroon Bells, near Aspen

Late in the Cretaceous a great mountain-making period began. It was a time of tremendous upheavals and great disturbances of the earth's crust. Rocks stretched and folded as arching occurred and elevation increased. There was much volcanic action and streams of molten rock poured from the earth or, sometimes, were trapped underground. It is to the latter that we owe the formation of some of the ores which have brought so much wealth to Colorado. Some ores were formed in later periods.

With the close of Cretaceous times the sea retreated for the last time, leaving the state divided into plains, mountains and plateaus. It must not be forgotten, however, that there were also later periods of elevation and erosion. It has taken more than fifty million years to make the topography of Colorado what it is today.

During the Eocene times which followed there was an abundant vegetation which is responsible for some of the state's coal deposits. Various sedimentary rocks were formed by fresh water deposition. Among these are tremendous deposits of oil shales. When it becomes commercially practicable to exploit these beds for the production of petroleum products they may become one of the greatest of all Colorado's mineral resources. Many old types of animal life were dying out and mammals were now the dominant form.

The following period was the Oligocene, which is characterized by sedimentary deposits, chiefly clays, sandstones, and conglomerates. The distinction between carnivorous and herbivorous, clawed and hoofed mammals was becoming more marked. Among the fossil skeletons of animals which lived at this time have been found some which would seem very strange in Colorado today. They include primitive rhinoceroses, camels, and little horses about the size of a collie.

The Oligocene was followed by the Miocene period, which in turn was succeeded by the Pliocene. During this time the deposition of sandstones, sands, gravels and clays continued. Animals assumed more and more modern forms. During most of Miocene times the climate varied from subtropical to semiarid and the flora of Colorado was different in many of its details from that of today, but by Pliocene times a temperate zone flora prevailed.

The final period which began about a million years ago is called the Pleistocene. It is also known as the Glacial or Great Ice Age. During this time the earth experienced periods of intense refrigeration. The periods of glaciation marked by ice advances were separated from each other by intervals during which the climate improved and the ice retreated. The time following the last advance of the ice is assigned to the Recent period by most geologists, but it has also been suggested that the present era may be part of the Pleistocene. There were no giant ice sheets in Colorado, but glaciation was quite intense in the mountains and we may see clear-cut evidence of this period in the great cirques carved by the glaciers, the accumulations of earth and stones, known as moraines, which they deposited, and the terraces which glacial streams cut into the valley floors which they had previously formed. After the most intensive glaciation had passed but while the climate was still cold and moist, primitive hunters whom we know as the makers of the finely chipped Folsom points entered Colorado. The remainder of the story of the development of Colorado falls in the realm of the archaeologist and the historian.

THE HISTORY OF COLORADO EXPLORATION

Colorado, with its diversity of terrain, has long been of interest to the explorer, naturalist and sportsman. Stories of the wealth of fur-bearing and big game animals were told by the early travelers of the region, with the result that trained field men started to scour the country at an early date. Dr. Hafen has given an account of the fascinating journeys of these pioneers, but I should like to mention a few who commented on the natural history of the region.[1]

The Spanish friars who laboriously made their way through southern and western portions of the state made occasional references to the animals encountered. Padres Silvestre Velez de Escalante and Francisco Atanasio Dominguez were among the first to leave a written record of travels through Colorado, in which birds, mammals

Wild Turkey Group, Colorado Museum of Natural History, Denver

and plants are mentioned. In 1776, they left Santa Fe on a long trek in an attempt to discover a northern route to Monterey, California, and they mention seeing grouse between the San Miguel and Uncompahgre Rivers on August 26. In his journal (Father Escalante's Journal, 1776-77, *Utah State Historical Quarterly,* vol. XI, page 41), Escalante tells of the terrain, and then describes animals and plants as follows: "The chain of the Tabehuachis Mountains which we have just crossed runs in a northwest course and may be about thirty leagues long and, where we crossed it, about eight or ten leagues wide. It has abundant good pasture, is very damp and has good soil for crops which require much moisture. It produces many fir trees, pinon, royal pines, small oaks, several kinds of wild fruit and in some places flax. Deer, roe deer and other animals are found

---

[1] See also Rockwell, R. B., Hist. of Colo. ornith., *Condor,* 11:24-32, maps. 1909.

here, and hens of the size and shape of domestic hens, with this difference, that they have no crest; their flesh is very tasty. About twenty leagues west in these mountains we find the La Sal Mountains, which also seem low." A few days later, September 11, he was to the northward, near the Green River, and he describes the taking of the first bison by white men in the western portion of Colorado.

> A short distance from the ravine we saw a fresh bison trail; on the plain we saw it still more clearly and that it followed the direction we were taking. By this time we were carrying few provisions, compared with the length of the journey we had to make, because of what we gave to the Sabuaganas and the Yutas. So, just before arriving at the brook, two companions left to follow the bison trail; a little after noon one of them returned saying they had found the bison. We sent other men ahead on the fastest horses, and by half past seven in the evening and after a run of about three leagues, they killed the bison and brought back a large amount of its flesh (much more than an ordinary large bull of the fields has). In order to prepare the meat so that the heat would not spoil it for us and at the same time to give the animals a rest, we stayed on the 12th in this place without traveling and we called it the Arroyo del Cibolo (bison). It rained tonight for many hours.

Anyone who has read the account of the exploration of Zebulon Montgomery Pike (1806-1807) must have been impressed with the important part played by the game animals in furthering the work of early travelers—how dependent adventurers were upon the natural resources of the state—and how, oftentimes, game animals were almost lacking in this virgin wilderness. Pike killed turkeys along the Arkansas Valley, which were badly needed for food, and later he crossed the Sangre de Cristo range in winter, and nearly starved to death because of the lack of game animals.

Thomas Say was probably the first trained naturalist to enter Colorado; he was a member of the Major Stephen H. Long expedition in 1820. They travelled up the South Platte and crossed the divide toward the present location of Colorado Springs, and then followed down the Arkansas River. Eight species of birds new to science were named as a result of this trip. John Torrey published the account of the plants collected by Edwin James, of the Long expedition. An interesting account of Say's part in Long's expedition may be found in H. B. Weiss and G. M. Ziegler's biography of Say (1931).

The expedition of Captain John C. Fremont in 1844-5 crossed the state and the specimens collected were reported upon by Spencer F. Baird in volume nine (1858) and ten (1859) of the Pacific Railroad Reports, but unfortunately, plants collected on the expedition were destroyed.

Shortly after Fremont's journey, gold was discovered and thousands of eager prospectors crowded the Colorado hills. Among them were men interested in all branches of the natural sciences and consequently, through the years, thousands of specimens have been collected which are deposited in museums of the world.

Animal and Plant Associations

The student of natural history soon learns that the distribution of animals depends upon the plant life of a given region. In one way or another birds, mammals, reptiles and insects are influenced by the enviroment available to them, and often the relationship is so close that certain animals—particularly insects—live upon one species of plant only. If for some reason the vegetation is destroyed, the animals also disappear.

The converse is true, probably, for the majority of the flowering plants are pollinated by insects or other animals, and so the vegetation is dependent upon the animals which live upon them. The yucca moth is one of the well known examples.

As a result of this interdependence of one species upon another, the natural history student thinks in terms of environment—he automatically associates an animal with a given type of habitat which is essential for its well being. We do not know why animals prefer prairies to woodlands, or timbered tracts to open savannahs—we merely accept as true the fact that certain kinds of life will be associated with other types, and so we have been able to arrange plants in more or less definite associations, depending upon many factors—soil, humidity or aridity, slope exposure, latitude or altitude—and with these plant environments we have learned to expect certain forms of animal life. In other words, each organism has a preferred ecological niche—ecology meaning the mutual relationship between animals and their environment.

Colorado, then, because of its diverse terrain, its great differences in elevation and climatic conditions, is a fascinating field for the specialist in each branch of biology, or for the average individual who is merely interested in the out-of-doors, but would like to know something of the creatures of plain and mountain.

Ecologists do not agree, and probably never will, upon the names used to denote plant habitats, associations or communities. Biologists have divided Colorado into five life zones according to elevation, with certain plant associations characteristic of each. Such divisions are not entirely satisfactory, for one merges into another with species typical of a given area encroaching into other sections.

Because of the great differences in elevation in various sections of the state, Colorado is a good proving ground for theories on various phases of distribution. As a traveler ascends mountains there is a temperature change, and consequently, also a difference of animal and plant life. A rise of one thousand feet is roughly equivalent to a journey to the northward of three hundred miles, and so when a motorist drives from Denver, a mile above the sea, to the top of 14,000 foot Mt. Evans, he has passed from the prairie or Upper Sonoran Zone, through three others, the Transition, Canadian and Hudsonian into the Alpine. In a two hour motor car journey up the mountains, he has made the equivalent of a trip northward to the Arctic Circle—for on the mountain tops, the plants, the birds and mammals are related to species which would be encountered in the far north.

The five life zones recognized in Colorado are not well defined areas, but are merely belts of certain elevations, within which are found characteristic species of trees, shrubs and flowering plants—their distribution within the zone depending upon soil, slope exposure, humidity and latitude. It should be emphasized that there is no hard or fast rule—that growing things are where you find them, but for the most part there is an association of species, so that with a little experience in a given region, a botanist is able to predict more or less accurately the forms which he will find. For instance, he knows that on the open prairies of low elevation, he will likely find buffalo grass and small prickly pear cactus; that the pinyons and cedars will clothe the more or less arid hills of low elevation, and that the cottonwoods and willows will be found along stream beds. Thus he has group plant associations which will likely be found within a given range of elevation in Colorado—between 3,500 and 5,500 feet.

The student of animal life has learned that each species of bird, mammal, reptile or insect likewise has preferred areas, that its distribution is dependent upon the types of vegetation in a given region, and consequently, he is able to predict with fair accuracy the various species which will be encountered in habitats of each elevation.

Robert Rockwell, in the *Pictorial Guide to the Colorado Museum of Natural History,* has given a good discussion of the life zones of Colorado, and has listed a few of the obvious plant associates in each area. He has covered the subject so well in a brief amount of space that I quote him as follows:

> The most obvious forms of life which characterize the various types of country are the trees and plants, and a study of any given area will reveal a more or less definite association of birds, mammals, insects, and reptiles with the characteristic vegetation of the area. For example, prairie-dogs, burrowing owls and rattlesnakes are invariably associated with the short grasses and weeds of the arid plains or rocky hillsides. Arkansas kingbirds (*Tyrannus verticalis*), western mockingbirds (*Mimus polyglottos leucopterus*), and white-rumped shrikes (*Lanius ludovicianus excubitorides*) are characteristic of the broad leafed cottonwoods along the prairie streams. Wading birds and ducks are attracted by aquatic vegetation to lakes, ponds and marshlands. Pine squirrels (*Sciurus fremonti*), dusky grouse (*Dendragapus obscurus obscurus*), and Audubon's hermit thrushes (*Hylocichla guttata auduboni*) live almost exclusively in the great evergreen forests of the higher mountains. Southern white-tailed ptarmigan (*Lagopus leucurus altipetens*) and (during the summer) Rocky Mountain pipits (*Anthus spinoletta alticola*) are found only among the dwarf willows and grassy meadows in the bleak, wind-swept regions above timber line.

For the sake of convenience and uniformity, biologists have divided the various types of country into faunal areas called "Life Zones," five of which are represented in Colorado.

 I. The Upper Sonoran or Plains Zone, which includes the lower portions of the state from about 3,500 to 5,500 feet altitude, embraces roughly the prairies of eastern Colorado and the warm valleys in the cen-

Timberline Group, Colorado Museum of Natural History

tral, southern and western parts of the state. Characteristic plant associations are:

 (*a*) pinyon (*Pinus edulis*), cedar (*Juniperus monosperma*), tree cactus (*Opuntia arborescens*)

 (*b*) buffalo grass (*Buchloë dactyloides*), grama grass (*Bouteloua*), and prickly-pear cactus (*Opuntia polyacantha*)

 (*c*) broad-leaf cottonwood (*Populus sargenti*) and peach-leaf willow (*Salix amygdaloides*)

 II. The Transition or Foothills Zone includes the rough, broken foothills separating the lower portions of the state from the mountainous portions, and ranges in altitude from 5,500 to 8,000 feet above sea-level. Characteristic plant associations are:

 (*a*) yellow pine (*Pinus ponderosa*) and scrub oak (*Quercus*)

    (*b*) Douglas fir (*Pseudotsuga taxifolia*) and blue spruce (*Picea pungens*)
    (*c*) Rocky Mountain alder (*Alnus tenuifolia*), shrub willow (*Salix Nuttallii*) and Rocky Mountain birch (*Betula fontinalis*)

III. The Canadian or Montane Zone includes the true mountainous portions of the state from about 8,000 feet elevation to over 10,500 feet. Characteristic plant associations are:
    (*a*) lodgepole pine (*Pinus contorta*) and quaking aspen (*Populus tremuloides*)
    (*b*) Alpine birch (*Betula glandulosa*) and shrubby cinquefoil (*Dasiphora fruticosa*)
    (*c*) Engelmann spruce (*Picea engelmanni*) and balsam fir (*Abies lasiocarpa*)

IV. The Hudsonian or Sub-Alpine Zone is a narrow and irregular area separating the heavily forested Canadian Zone from that portion of the higher mountain ranges lying above timberline, which, in Colorado, varies from 10,500 feet elevation to about 11,500 feet. Characteristic plant associations are: limber pine (*Pinus flexilis*) and foxtail pine (*Pinus aristata*)

V. The Arctic-Alpine Zone embraces all that portion of Colorado above timberline. Characteristic plant associations are:
    (*a*) Alpine willows (*Salix*)
    (*b*) lichens—mat and cushion plants: mountain forget-me-not (*Eritrichium argenteum*) and cushion pink (*Silene acaulis*)

The elevations stated above are only approximate, the zonal limits varying considerably. A zone will extend higher on the warmer southwestern slope of a mountain than on the cooler northeastern slope. Zonal limits are uniformly higher in southern Colorado than in the northern part of the state. Variations in precipitation, stream-flow, topography, and other factors all exert modifying influences upon the extent of the various zones.

Some birds spend their entire lives within the confines of a single zone. Others breed only in one certain zone and later migrate into or through others, while a comparatively few species—typical of which are the western robin (*Turdus migratorius propinquus*), red-shafted flicker (*Colaptes cafer collaris*), and American magpie (*Pica pica hudsonia*)—occur and breed commonly from the plains to timberline.

Rockwell's table, showing birds of characteristic habitats, lists the types of vegetation to be encountered in the various life zones, with the characteristic species of birds. Anyone interested in the birds of the west will find the following tables of value.

TYPICAL ASSOCIATIONS

TERRAIN		TYPICAL BIRD	TYPICAL VEGETATION
Dry Prairies		Burrowing Owl Mountain Plover Desert Horned Lark McCown's Longspur	Short Grass, Weeds and Cactus
Prairie Bluffs (or Cliffs)		Desert Sparrow Hawk Ferruginous Roughleg Prairie Falcon Cliff Swallow	Scattered Shrubbery and Weeds
Prairie Stream Bottoms	Cottonwoods	Red-headed Woodpecker Great Blue Heron Swainson's Hawk Rocky Mt. Screech Owl Crow Bullock's Oriole Kingbird Arkansas Kingbird Western Mockingbird White-rumped Shrike	Broad-leaved Cottonwood Black Willow Box Elder Choke-Cherry Wild Plum Wild Rose
	Shrubbery	Black-headed Grosbeak Brown Thrasher Catbird Yellow Warbler	
Prairie	Cultivated Fields	Brewer's Blackbird Western Vesper Sparrow Ring-necked Pheasant	Alfalfa Grain
	Long Grass Pastures	Western Meadowlark Lark Bunting	Long Grass and Weeds
	Farm Buildings	Barn Swallow Say's Phoebe House Finch	
Perpendicular Dirt Banks along Streams and Ditches		Bank Swallow Kingfisher	
Prairie Lakes and Ponds		Pied-billed Grebe Ring-billed Gull Forster's Tern White Pelican Ducks (13 species) Geese (2 species) American Coot Herons (2 species) Avocet Killdeer Sandpipers	Willows Cat-tails Tules Sedges Salt Grass Aquatic Plants
Marshland (Dense Cover)		Sora Virginia Rail American Bittern Wilson's Snipe	
Swamps		Red-winged Blackbird Yellow-headed Blackbird Western Yellowthroat	
Pinyon and Cedar Belt (Southern and Western Colorado)		Western Gnatcatcher Pinyon Jay Canyon Towhee Gray Titmouse Lead-colored Bush-tit Mountain Bluebird	Pinyon Cedars Tree Cactus

UPPER SONORAN ZONE, 3,500 feet to 5,500 feet elevation

TYPICAL ASSOCIATIONS—Continued

	TERRAIN	TYPICAL BIRDS	TYPICAL VEGETATION
TRANSITION ZONE 5,500 ft. to 8,000 ft.	Lower Tablelands	Virginia's Warbler Woodhouse Jay Spurred Towhee Poorwill Rock Wren	Scrub Oak
	Higher Tablelands and Foothills	Long-crested Jay Natalie's Sapsucker Lewis Woodpecker Green-tailed Towhee Plumbeous Vireo Pigmy Nuthatch Mountain Chickadee Chestnut-backed Bluebird	Yellow Pine Douglas Fir
	Canyons and Cliffs	Golden Eagle Canyon Wren Cliff Swallow White-throated Swift	Narrow-leaved Cottonwood Colorado Blue Spruce
	Mountain Parks	Sage Grouse Sage Thrasher Sage Sparrow	Sage-brush Greasewood
CANADIAN ZONE 8,000 ft. to 10,500 ft.	Forest-covered Mountains	Western Goshawk Red-naped Sapsucker Violet-green Swallow Western Wood Pewee Western Warbling Vireo Rocky Mountain Jay Lincoln Sparrow Ruby-crowned Kinglet Audubon's Warbler Audubon's Hermit 　Thrush	Quaking Aspen Lodgepole Pine Engelmann Spruce
HUDSONIAN ZONE 10,500 ft. to 11,500 ft.	Upper Edge of Coniferous Forest	Rocky Mountain Pine 　Grosbeak Rocky Mountain Creeper White-crowned Sparrow Pileolated Warbler	Engelmann Spruce Balsam Fir Foxtail Pine
ARCTIC-ALPINE ZONE Above 11,500 feet	Mountain Tops (above Timberline)	White-tailed Ptarmigan Brown-capped Rosy 　Finch American Pipit Desert Horned Lark	Arctic Willows Grassy Meadows No Trees

Only those species are included in the above list whose breeding range is largely restricted to one life zone, hence typical of it. The great majority of species breed in more than one zone, and a number of varieties breed in all five zones.

The above will serve as a brief summary of the various habitats at different elevations in Colorado, and of the species of birds which are likely to be found associated. *The Birds of Denver and Mountain Parks,* by Robert J. Niedrach and Robert B. Rockwell (Pop. Ser. no. 5, Colo. Mus. Nat. Hist., 1939) is recommended for those desiring more detail.

MAMMALS OF COLORADO

As mentioned previously, all forms of animal life have their preferred plant associations, and to the above tables could be added forms of mammals which are to be found in the listed areas. Edward R. Warren, the dean of Colorado mammalogists, mentions many of the common forms in his notes on *The Mammals of Colorado* (Pop. Ser. no. 1., Colo. Mus. Nat. Hist., 1946), and I quote him at length.

Many Colorado mammals are not at all particular as to the life zones in which they dwell, although certain species confine themselves to rather narrow limits. These prefer to live in the rather arid plains regions, in the Upper Sonoran and lowest portions of the Transition Zones. Aridity seems to be a factor in this.

On the other hand many species seem to have no preferences. The larger animals, such as elk, deer, mountain lion, bobcat, and bear wander from one zone to another, the wanderings being partly seasonable, and probably partly in search of food. Coyotes range into all our life zones; the red fox seems to be confined to the Canadian and Hudsonian for the most part, while the gray fox frequents the two zones below. The weasels, except the blackfooted ferret, range from Transition to Alpine, breeding below the latter. The ferret goes above 9,000 feet at times, but it is an open plains animal and prefers to live about the prairie-dog towns.

The shrews, except the water shrew (*Neosorex palustris navigator*) are tiny animals, secretive in their habits, which I think prefer the Canadian and Hudsonian Zones, although the dusky shrew (*Sorex obscurus obscurus*) has been taken on the summit of Pikes Peak. The water shrew, about the size of a house mouse, lives about the mountain streams and is an expert swimmer.

Not enough is known about the bats for anything very definite to be stated as to their zonal preferences. Some species undoubtedly reach the Canadian Zone, very likely the Hudsonian. Probably the little western bat (*Pipistrellus hesperus hesperus*) is confined to the Upper Sonoran, and possibly some of the smaller species of the genus *Myotis* do not go high into the Transition.

Marmots, woodchucks, or ground hogs, as they are variously called, seem to prefer the Upper Hudsonian and Alpine, but may come down even to the Transition.

The pale-striped ground squirrel (*Citellus tridecemlineatus pallidus*) is an open country animal, found not only on the plains east of the mountains, but also in the large open valleys or "parks," such as the San Luis and Wet Mountain Valleys and South Park. Another ground squirrel, the Wyoming, also called "picket-pin gopher" (*Citellus elegans*), has proved to be quite a wanderer in the past twenty-five years; at first confined to the northwest part of Colorado and that part of Larimer County east of the mountains, it has spread out eastwardly onto the plains some distance, and westwardly up into Estes Park; it has crossed such high mountain passes as Berthoud, Hoosier, and Tennessee, and extended its range until it occupies a much greater area than formerly.

The rock squirrels (*Citellus grammurus*) belong in the Upper Sonoran and Transition Zones, reaching somewhere above 7,000 feet. Their preference seems to be for rocky ground.

The various species and subspecies of chipmunks of the genus *Eutamias* range from Upper Sonoran to Alpine, the majority being inhabitants of the Canadian and Hudsonian Zones. The Say ground squirrel (*Citellus lateralis lateralis*) goes from Transition to the upper limit of the Hudsonian and probably at times wanders into the Alpine.

The Fremont or pine squirrel (*Sciurus fremonti fremonti*), the Colorado representative of the eastern red squirrel, ranges from the uppermost Transition through the Canadian into the upper limits of the larger timber, except perhaps in occasional wanderings. The tuft-eared squirrels of the *Sciurus aberti* group are confined practically to the yellow pine belt of the Transition Zone. Both of these squirrels feed largely on the seeds of pines, spruces, and firs, and their kitchen middens or refuse piles often contain so much material that one would think that they had been accumulated by many generations of the animals.

Of the several species of pocket gophers in Colorado, the chestnut-faced gopher (*Cratogeomys castanops castanops*) is probably confined to the Upper Sonoran, and the yellow pocket gopher (*Geomys lutescens*) is likewise Sonoran and lowest Transition. The several other subspecies of pocket gophers, all belonging to the genus *Thomomys,* are all Upper Sonoran and Transition with the exception of the Colorado pocket gopher (*Thomomys fossor*), which ranges from Upper Transition through Canadian and Hudsonian into Alpine, where its workings may be seen in grassy places above timberline.

One species of prairie-dog the plains' animal (*Cynomys ludovicianus ludovicianus*) limited closely to the Upper Sonoran and the very lowest Transition. On the other hand, the Gunnison prairie-dog (*Cynomys gunnisoni gunnisoni*) and subspecies may at times enter the Canadian. The white-tailed prairie-dog (*Cynomys leucurus*) is an Upper Sonoran and Transition animal.

The long-nosed deer mouse (*Peromyscus nasutus*) seems to prefer the lowest Transition and upper edge of the Upper Sonoran, while the commonest species of deer or white-footed mouse (*Peromyscus maniculatus rufinus*) and (*Peromyscus maniculatus osgoodi*) are found in all the life zones, from the Upper Sonoran to the Alpine. These mice are found on the summit of Pikes Peak, where they have as companions the

Colorado bushy-tailed rats (*Neotoma cinerea orolestes*). This animal is usually found above the Transition, though it lives in the Upper Sonoran at Grand Junction.

Kangaroo rats and pocket mice, grasshopper mice, and spotted ground squirrels are the dry ground lovers, and often they appear to prefer a sandy soil. One species of wood rat, Bailey's (*Neotoma floridana baileyi*), adheres closely to the eastern plains region, and, to the best of my knowledge, does not enter the foothills. Three other species of the round-tailed wood rats live in the Upper Sonoran. I do not think the hoary wood rats (*Neotoma micropus canescens*) or Warren's white-throated wood rat (*Neotoma albigula warreni*) range much, if any, above Upper Sonoran, while the Colorado wood rat (*Neotoma mexicana fallax*) reaches an altitude of somewhere about 8,000 feet. There are three species of bushy-tailed wood rats which remain in Upper Sonoran and lowest Transition, the pallid (*Neotoma cinerea cinnamomea*) in the northwest corner, and the Arizona (*Neotoma cinerea arizonae*) down in the southwest.

Another mouse, the cantankerous vole (*Microtus mordax mordax*), has been taken above 14,000 feet on Pikes Peak. Two other species, the Saguache meadow mouse (*Microtus pennsylvanicus modestus*) and dwarf vole (*Microtus nanus nanus*), while reaching into the Hudsonian from below, do not find in the Alpine Zone the damp or wet ground they prefer. Another species, Hayden meadow mouse (*Microtus haydeni*), is on the plains of northeastern Colorado. The little pigmy vole (*Lagurus pauperrimus*) has thus far been found in a few widely scattered localities in Colorado, and it is not easy to say what zone it prefers, but probably the Transition and Upper Sonoran.

On the contrary, the red-backed mouse (*Evotomys gapperi galei*) lives in the Canadian and Hudsonian Zones, usually in the woods about fallen logs. Muskrats go from the plains up to about 9,000 feet, perhaps a little into the Canadian.

The porcupine (*Erethizon epixanthum epixanthum*) wants timbered country, apparently preferring conifers, where he can do the most damage by gnawing the bark from the trees; sometimes he wanders down onto the plains, where he takes the chance of being put in a zoo.

The three races of cony or pika (*pee-ka*) (*Ochotona princeps*), the little fellow with the squeaky voice and no tail, may be found most anywhere in the three upper zones, where there is open ground with rock slides, and plenty of green vegetation from which to make hay.

Several species of cottontail rabbits inhabit Colorado, and between them they manage to cover the ground from Upper Sonoran into Canadian. The western white-tailed jack rabbit (*Lepus townsendii townsendii*) reaches from Upper Sonoran up into the Alpine, while the Great Plains jack (*Lepus californicus melanotis*) confines himself to the Upper Sonoran and Transition. The snowshoe rabbit (*Lepus bairdi bairdi*) is an inhabitant of the Canadian and Hudsonian Zones.[†]

THE GROWTH OF OUR KNOWLEDGE OF COLORADO PLANT LIFE
JOSEPH EWAN[*]

The earliest published account of the plants growing in Colorado was that of John Torrey. This concerned the collections of Edwin James, M.D., who with Thomas Say, naturalist, accompanied the expedition to the Rocky Mountains, led by Stephen Harriman Long. Torrey's account of the James' collections was not only the first enumeration of Colorado plant species but it represented, significantly, the first paper in America drawn up along the lines of the "natural system" of plant classification of the French botanist Jussieu which was at that time replacing the highly artificial "sexual system" of the Swedish botanist Carl von Linne—a system based on the "genitalia" of the flower or the number of stamens and pistils. Torrey presented this account, consisting of nearly one hundred pages, before the meeting of the New York Lyceum of Natural History on December 11, 1826, but it was not published until 1828, when it appeared in volume two of the Lyceum's *Annals*.[1]

Edwin James reached the summit of Pikes Peak on July 14, 1820, the first white man successfully to ascend any 14,000 foot peak in the United States. He was then twenty-three years of age. The significance of Long's Expedition and of James' plant collections for botany rests not alone upon the fact that the plant discoveries were systematically named, organized and published, but that the specimens were reasonably ample, accompanied by collection data, for its times, of fair exactitude, and that the plants have been preserved in the Torrey Herbarium now at the New York Botanical Garden. The identity of the plants forming the basis of the published records may thus be checked by consulting the original James collections.[2]

Although the region that later was to become Colorado was visited before Fremont by Alexander Gordon[3] and Adolphus Wislizenus[4], few plant specimens of their collecting were preserved. During the 1830s

---

[†] Warren's, *The Mammals of Colorado* (University of Oklahoma Press, 1942), is the outstanding work on the animals of the State.

[*] Assistant Professor, Department of Botany, Tulane University, New Orleans, La.; formerly Instructor in Biology, Curator of Botany, University of Colorado.

[1] Two shorter papers by Torrey describing the James' collections appeared in the *Annals,* volume one, previous to this comprehensive paper.

[2] Cf. Ewan in *Trail and Timberline*, no. 282: 79-84 port. (June, 1942).

[3] English gardener who collected in the Rocky Mts., Louisiana (?) and S. Carolina for George Charlwood, nurseryman and Covent Garden seedsman.

[4] Frederick Adolphus Wislizenus, *Ein Ausflug nach den Felsen Gebirgen im Jahre, 1839* (St. Louis, 1840).

Thomas Nuttall, English-born botanical explorer, one-time Professor of Botany at Harvard University, and "Old Curious" of Richard Henry Dana's *Two Years Before the Mast,* passed just to the north of present Colorado.[5]   Nuttall's collections from the high plains of what is today South Dakota and west to South Pass or what he sometimes referred to as the "northern Andes" were of pioneer importance since his published botanical studies upon them made known a flora up to that time wholly unknown.

In 1835 Colonel Henry Dodge proceeded up the Platte River to the foothills and thence south to the Arkansas River and returned to Fort Leavenworth by way of the Santa Fe trail.   No naturalist accompanied this small government expedition, however, and for this reason they made no additions to our botanical knowledge.

John Charles Fremont, "pathmarker of the West," judging by his discerning collecting in California and the Amargosa country of southern Nevada, would have made known many distinctive Colorado species discovered during his crossings of present Colorado, 1842-44, had his collections survived.   Unfortunately, Fremont's plant collections were destroyed by a flash flood that swept an encampment of his party during his return overland trip across Kansas.   Many distinctive Colorado species almost certainly taken by Fremont in traversing the state were not actually described until about twenty years later from the collections of C. C. Parry.   Fremont crossed the crest of the Rocky Mountains over Hoosier Pass and down into South Park, where he found an Indian battle in progress.   Whether he left South Park by way of historic Ute Pass or via Oil Creek is not clear from his narrative account, but his route along the Arkansas River eastward from the vicinity of Pueblo is perfectly clear from his narrative.   Nor did Fremont's last expedition to Colorado in 1853 contribute much to the progress of botanical knowledge for this state[6].

Between 1852 and 1854 the Federal Government sent out five surveying parties, stimulated by Fremont's important explorations and the interest of the public in the West, "to ascertain the most practicable and economical route for a railroad from the Mississippi River to the Pacific Ocean." One of these parties, the third government expedition to the Great Basin within ten years, directed by Captain J. W. Gunnison in 1853, explored the Rocky Mountains along the present route in part of the Denver and Rio Grande Western Railroad. Gunnison was assisted by E. G. Beckwith, as well as by such scientific men as F. Creutzfeldt, botanist, and Dr. James Schiel, surgeon and geologist.   Very few plant collections seem to have been made in Colorado.   After entering Utah the party crossed the Green River near the present town of Green River City.   They then continued westward through Salina Canyon and on to the desert near Delta, Utah.   On October 25, 1853, Captain Gunnison, Creutzfeldt, and several

---

5 Phrases such as "discovered by Nuttall in the Rocky Mountains of Colorado" (Porter & Coulter, *Synopsis,* 121. 1874) involve an oldtime generalized use of the geographic designation. For an account of Nuttall's itineraries, with a map, cf. Pennell in *Bartonia* 18:1-51 (1936).

6 Cf. Ewan in *Trail and Timberline,* no. 291: 31-37. port. (March, 1943).

other men of the party were massacred by the Sevier River Indians. Afterwards Beckwith directed the expedition westward but in the main this expedition contributed "very little to our knowledge of the natural history of the Great Basin,'" and perhaps even less to Colorado botany. *Calochortus gunnisonii,* the well known mariposa or sego lily which blooms in May along the Front Range foothills, commemorates Captain Gunnison.

It was Charles Christopher Parry who, more than all his predecessors, collected, studied and made known the plant life of Colorado. First coming to Colorado in 1861, and financing his own way with a view toward subsequent sales of dried plants to museums and subscribers to defray a portion of his expenses, Parry set out for the gold district of the Clear Creek watershed. After spending a season collecting there, he communicated his material to Asa Gray for naming. His plant discoveries were of such moment and novelty that he was encouraged to return the following year in company with two Illinois collectors, Elihu Hall and J. P. Harbour, and again the plant collections were sold. Indeed, these early Colorado specimens were the first really adequate representations to reach the museums of Europe, where they came to be studied and written about in important contemporary botanical works. Parry also took a considerable interest in the topography of the state, naming mounts Engelmann, Audubon, and Flora, as well as influencing the naming of Torreys Peak and Grays Peak, and writing an account of the subject for the St. Louis Academy of Sciences[8]. He revisited the Clear Creek country, valley of the Blue River, Middle Park, "Boulder City," and Osborn(e) Lake in the vicinity of Gold Hill. It is unfortunate that Parry took so little interest in the adequate labelling of his collections, necessitating the tedious assembling of scattered clues from his herbarium and from his widely dispersed published articles in the contemporary press and scientific journals. Parry's collections were the basis of important papers on the botany of Colorado by Asa Gray, who considered Parry the "Nestor" of Colorado botanical explorers. Surely many species, including beautiful *Primula parryi* of timberline stream borders and rivulets in the fir forests, attest to Parry's acumen as a field botanist.

Soon to follow Parry across the recently created Colorado Territory, and to strike out on new trails, were many men, who, incidental to their diverse occupations, collected native plants. Among them were financier William A. Bell, friend of General William J. Palmer, who made a few collections in the late 1860s; geologist F. V. Hayden, in 1868, and his young student field assistant John Merle Coulter; Lafayette College professor T. C. Porter, surveyor T. S. Brandegee, episcopalian rector E. L. Greene, Philadelphia amateur botanist John H. Redfield, Delaware merchantman W. M. Canby, Illinois naturalist John Wolf, agrostologist George Vasey's son George Richard Vasey,

---

[7] V. M. Tanner in *Great Basin Naturalist,* 1:58 (1940). A few vaguely labelled specimens in U. S. National Herbarium may have been taken on this expedition.

[8] For this and other Parry references cf. Ewan in *Trail and Timberline,* no. 268: 55-57, 59. port. (April, 1941).

and Iowa College teacher of Latin Marcus E. Jones[9]—all of these came in the early and middle 1870s. Based upon the collections of many of these men was the *Synopsis of the Flora of Colorado* (1874), by T. C. Porter and J. M. Coulter. This summation included the first report on the mosses of Colorado and was the product of the organizing ability of Prof. Porter who enlisted the assistance of many specialists in its preparation. Though primarily of historic interest today, the *Synopsis* is interesting especially to determine oldtime stations for plants and for its notes on the persistence of species now yielding to civilization's pressure.

Notable among the personages mentioned above was T. S. Brandegee, whose *Flora of Southwestern Colorado* (1876) enumerated the plants of a little known region and included cellular cryptogams along with the vascular plants; indeed, 79 species and varieties of mosses alone were listed therein (cf. Geneva Sayre, "Progress in the study of Colorado mosses," *Jour. Colo.-Wyo. Acad. Sci.*, 2:22 (1938).

Quite naturally the *Synopsis* was succeeded by a revision carried out by its junior author, Coulter, composed along the lines of Gray's well-known *Manual* for the Eastern United States, and retitled *Manual of the Botany of the Rocky Mountain Region* (1885). This work, conservative in its nomenclatural decisions, was the standard reference work on Colorado plants for a quarter of a century. During this period Coulter's *Manual* served alike the tourist visiting Manitou Springs, the botanist naming a Colorado specimen and the local natural history professor teaching his college class.

Notable visitors who came upon separate occasions in 1872 were Asa Gray and John Torrey, botanists of Harvard and Columbia College respectively[10]. Two prominent 14,000-foot peaks of the Continental Divide were that year formally christened their respective names. Evidently very few plant specimens were actually collected that year in Colorado by either Gray or Torrey, but the occasions brought together at different times during the summer of 1872 the botanists Gray, Torrey, Parry, and Greene in a kind of festive reunion or for Greene a first meeting. Torrey was never again to visit Colorado, for he died in 1873, but Asa Gray revisited the state in 1877, this time in the company of the English botanist Joseph Dalton Hooker. After a trip up the "Grand Canyon of the Arkansas," as the Royal Gorge was known in that period, Hooker and Gray camped out together in the Sangre de Cristo Range. From this summer's reconnaissance came a 77-page study, the "Vegetation of the Rocky Mountain Region and a comparison with that of other parts of the world" (1880). Hooker and Gray concluded that "the characteristics of the Rocky Mountain flora * * * are in no small degree negative. What this flora lacks is perhaps more remarkable than what it possesses."

---

9 Most of these personages are identified in the "Bibliography and history of Colorado botany," by Edith M. Allison (*Univ. Colo. Studies* 6:51-76. 1908), and some have been more fully noticed in my series in *Trail and Timberline* under the title "Botanical explorers of Colorado."

10 Cf. Erl H. Ellis in *Colo. Mag.*, 18:214-217 (1941).

Alice Eastwood, as the youngest teacher in East Denver High School in the early 1880s, taught over a period of a few years algebra, geometry, astronomy, chemistry, bookkeeping, drawing, Latin, American and English literature, Greek and Roman history, music and calisthenics!—courses that no one else wanted to teach! Yet, before she was thirty, she had, in her spare time, become an authority on Colorado plants. She traveled widely over the state on a pass issued by the Denver and Rio Grande Railway and collected many overlooked plant species. Her explorations about Paradox and in the San Juan Mountains and about Crested Butte in the Gunnison River watershed included notable first collections. As did other field collectors of the day, she often detrained some miles short of the town where she expected to pass the night in order to botanize along the route. Upon the occasion of Alfred Russell Wallace's visit to Colorado, Miss Eastwood accompanied him to the summit of Grays Peak[11]. After moving to San Francisco and assuming the curatorship of the herbarium at the California Academy of Sciences, Miss Eastwood published the first local flora for Colorado, a 57-page *Popular Flora of Denver, Colorado* (1893)[12].

During this period new records were accumulating from the activities of such resident naturalists, teachers and laymen as nurseryman Darwin Maxon Andrews, entomologist C. F. Baker, teacher Ellsworth Bethel, professors Cassidy, Cockerell, Cowan, Crandall, Longyear, Aven Nelson, lumberman Osterhout, and professors Payson, Ramaley, Robbins and Sturgis. James Cassidy was professor of botany at Colorado Agricultural College, Ft. Collins, from 1881 up to the time of his death in 1889. Jointly with O'Brine, Cassidy published in 1889 the first study of "Some Colorado grasses." His successor, Professor C. S. Crandall, explored many of the less visited parts of the state for plants and placed his findings in the Ft. Collins herbarium. Upon the resignation of Crandall, "an energetic and promising student," J. H. Cowan, became professor of horticulture and botany, but an early death terminated Cowan's botanical activities. At this time Charles Fuller Baker was laboratory assistant in entomology at the College Experiment Station (1892-97). In addition to his field work on insect pests and diseases he collected plant materials along with an enormous series of insects. Ten new fungi alone were described by Ellis and Everhart from Baker's first year of collecting in the vicinity of Ft. Collins.[13] Professor E. L. Greene, earlier a resident botanical collector of Colorado along with his duties as an episcopal clergyman, but at this time at Washington, D. C., identified Baker's vascular plant collections and published his records and new species under the title "Plantae Bakerianae." A large share of these records

11 Cf. A. R. Wallace, *My Life,* vol. 2, pp. 180-184 (1905). For a brief sketch of her work cf. R. C. Miller, in *Golden Gardens,* 9:3-4, 15 (Oct., 1941).

12 Undated but date of publication determined by annotated copy belonging to Ellsworth Bethel and now the property of Dr. James Waring of Denver.

13 Cf. P. F. Shope, in *Mycologia,* 21:292-96 (1929).

were made on one strenuous vacation trip to southwestern Colorado when Baker was accompanied by F. S. Earle and S. M. Tracy.

When Professor T. D. A. Cockerell arrived in Wet Mountain Valley in 1887 he began at once to collect the natural history objects about him there. Soon short papers on his findings began to appear in the British *Nature Notes* and *Science Gossip* and in the *West American Scientist,* published in San Diego, California, by Charles Russell Orcutt. In 1890 Cockerell left Colorado for a brief stay in England and Jamaica, after which he returned to New Mexico, exchanging his position as curator of the Public Museum at Kingston, Jamaica, for Professor C. H. T. Townsend's appointment on the faculty at the Agricultural College, Mesilla Park. During his residence there and later at Las Vegas, New Mexico, again as a teacher of biology, Cockerell continued his interest in plants, naming no less than 32 species and varieties during this period. After a short service as curator of the museum at Colorado College, Colorado Springs, Professor Cockerell went to the University of Colorado in 1904. There he remained as professor of zoology for the greater part of his service, until his retirement in 1935. During all these years he maintained an active interest in Colorado botany, and no person, botanist or non-botanist, published more titles, if not number of printed pages, upon the subject than he. A "naturalist" in the tradition of Alfred Russell Wallace—his friend and mentor of younger years, for whom he worked as editorial assistant in the issuance of the second edition of *Island Life*—of Bates, de Vries, and J. D. Hooker, Cockerell became internationally known for the breadth of his biological interests. From a lifetime of travel, garden cultures and critical, if vestigial, botanical collections, he leaves an array of short studies upon a myriad of topics in the fields of fossil and recent botany, plant geography, genetics and systematics,[14] along with hundreds of titles in entomology.

Francis Ramaley came to the University of Colorado in 1898 and served that institution until his retirement in 1939. Taking up every activity initiated by John Gardiner, first professor of natural history at the University of Colorado, Ramaley added several fields of interest to those already in cultivation. He created a good environment for the growth of field biology at the University through this eager interest in the library, in his willingness to serve on critical academic committees, to supervise many of its scientific activities in a personal way, to edit its publications, to participate in local and national meetings of scientific societies, and often to contribute financially to some project of the Department of Biology when funds were tardily available. His plant collections related, in the main, to his ecological studies on mountain park vegetation, sandhill and lake types. Perhaps plant ecologists would agree that his "Sandhill vegetation of northeastern Colorado" (1939) constituted his most significant contribution to that field. His founding of the Mountain Laboratory at Tolland, Colorado, in 1909—one of the first field stations of its kind in this country

---

14 Cf. T. D. A. Cockerell, "Recollections of a Naturalist," esp. parts I and IV *Bios,* 6:372-85. illus. (Dec., 1935) and 8:12-18 (Mar., 1937).

devoted to the study of mountain ecology—brought to the state both promising young students who later entered the field in various professional capacities and veteran scientists as well. When the Tolland laboratory was disbanded Ramaley worked hard for the creation of the present Science Lodge, its natural descendant in the field of mountain ecology, located near Ward in Boulder County. Of interest to the lay reader as an introduction to the subject is Ramaley's collection of essays entitled *Colorado Plant Life* (1927)[15].

The nucleus of the University of Colorado Herbarium was the collection made by J. I. McFarland in Boulder County in 1881, his searches reaching to the upper slopes of Longs Peak. His collections bear a characteristic handwriting and may be recognized, apart from the early date, by the heavy grade of paper used with the label form printed directly upon the sheets.

During the decades from 1890 to 1920 several out-of-state botanical collectors visited Colorado. In this group was Harry Norton Patterson, printer-publisher-plant collector, of Oquawka, Illinois, and son of the Georgetown, Colorado, newspaper publisher Edwin H. N. Patterson, familiarly known locally as "Sniktau." H. N. Patterson was a careful collector and discovered some "novelties" in the central part of the state, Gore Range and Middle Park, but especially about the mountains above Georgetown. As one portal of Loveland Pass stands "Mt. Sniktau," commemorating the Pattersons, father and son[16]. Another visitor was the distinguished Swiss protozoologist, Eugene Penard, who spent some time in 1891 with Boulder as a base of operations for collecting in the Caribou and Arapaho Peak country; along with the Protozoa he collected vascular plants which were studied by both European and American botanists. J. Cardwell Lees, of Middleton, England, made a small collection of plants, as one of a surveying party in extreme southwestern Colorado in 1892, in the region previously visited by Brandegee on the Hayden Survey. Early in this period William Trelease, while director of the Missouri Botanical Garden (1889-1912), visited Colorado on at least two occasions and made some collections. He studied the pollination of *Yucca glauca* in the mountains above Manitou. "Mt. Trelease" above Georgetown commemorates this distinguished American botanist. Dr. Harry Hapeman, long-time physician of Minden, Nebraska, visited the Cache La Poudre and other localities from time to time and his collections have been widely distributed. John M. Holzinger made an intensive collection of mosses in Colorado in 1896, from which sets of fifty species were distributed as "Mosses of Colorado." William S. Cooper, professor of botany at the University of Minnesota, made plant collections in the vicinity of Estes Park while still an undergraduate at Alma College and continued his studies on the alpine flora of Longs Peak region when later at the University of Chicago.

15 Cf. Edna L. Johnson, "Francis Ramaley," *Madroño,* 6:260-265. port. 1942.
16 Cf. Ewan in *Trail and Timberline,* no. 293:62-63. port. (May, 1943).

Francis Potter Daniels was employed in the summer of 1906 by the University of Missouri, Department of Botany, to collect plants in Colorado for the university herbarium. All the collecting was carried on over a period of two and one-half months in Boulder County. From this season's work Daniels published a 311-page catalogue entitled *Flora of Boulder, Colorado, and Vicinity* (1911), containing an introduction on plant ecology of the region based on Ramaley's writings. Due to the fact that Daniels proposed certain nomenclatural changes in species and varietal names therein, the work has been rather widely known and is now scarce.

The earliest mountain laboratory devoted expressly to plant environment studies and notably to transplant investigations involving reciprocal interchanges of living plants from a plains' habitat to montane or timberline ones, was that inaugurated by Frederic Edward Clements. First visiting Colorado in the late 1890s, Clements soon established a field station at Minnehaha, in upper Engelmann Canyon, on the cog-train road up Pikes Peak, calling the location the "Alpine Laboratory." Between this site, one later established at Colorado Springs, at the foot of Pikes Peak and a third, above Minnehaha, at Windy Point (ele. 12,100 ft.), Clements planned a long term series of habitat studies designed to determine the nature of measurable alterations, if any, in the morphology of the plant organism under transplantation. Though Clements firmly believed in what may be called a neo-Lamarckian interpretation of such alterations as were sometimes distinguished, in opposition to genetic explanations of today involving chromosomal effects, it may be fairly said that he assembled an impressive array of experimental data and induced much fruitful discussion. These results were published mostly in the Yearbooks or other publications of the Carnegie Institution of Washington, which supported the project for many years. Alpine Laboratory became a mecca for visiting biologists interested in experimental evolution, who came to study, confer, and collect at this beautifully situated field station. This in a way is unique for the altitudinal range it offers stretching from the plains at 5,800 feet to over 14,000 feet at the summit of Pikes Peak, or from the Upper Sonoran Life Zone (C. H. Merriam's term) to the Arctic-Alpine. Working with Dr. and Mrs. Clements and technical assistant Dr. Frances Louise Long, many university students and scientists found it profitable to join the summer staff there; among these may be mentioned William T. Penfound, Ivan Murray Johnston, C. William Penland, Lee Bonar, Stanley Cain, William S. Stewart and the writer, along with many field men of the Soil Conservation Service. Well known to the public visiting the Rocky Mountains is the attractively illustrated book *Rocky Mountain Flowers* (1920), the joint work of F. E. Clements, who wrote the text, and his wife, Edith Schwartz Clements, who contributed the colored drawings.

The twentieth century brought what might be called the Rydbergian period in the history of Colorado botany. Per Axel Rydberg, lifetime associate of the New York Botanical Garden, published his

Flora of Colorado in 1906. This book was based upon his own considerable collections, especially in southern Colorado, and upon the records amassed by Crandall, Cowan and Baker at Ft. Collins. This book lacked descriptions but contained skeleton keys to the "finely drawn" species. Indeed, it was this narrow view of the plant species that fired Clements to attempt the "transformation" of species to demonstrate that what Rydberg believed represented several distinct species were in truth no more than ecologic variants of a widely variable species reacting in different ways under unusual environmental stress. Continuing his studies on the phytogeography and systematics of the Rocky Mountain flora, Rydberg published his important *Flora of the Rocky Mountains and Adjacent Plains* (1917), followed by a second edition five years later. Though his delimitation of species is uneven, with at times tenuous characters separating them, Rydberg's work stands as the most comprehensive and definitive ever attempted upon the Rocky Mountain flora.

Three years after Rydberg published his *Flora of Colorado,* there appeared a revised edition of Coulter's *Manual.* In its preparation John Merle Coulter was joined by the veteran botanist of the University of Wyoming, Professor Aven Nelson. This *New Manual of Rocky Mountain Botany* (1909) contained workable descriptions of the species, along with full keys in the manner of the contemporary seventh edition of Gray's *Manual,* and this "Coulter-Nelson" *Manual* remains today the best introduction to the flora of the central Rocky Mountains. An inspiring, devoted teacher, Professor Nelson numbers among his students such well-known biologists as Elias Emanuel Nelson, Ernest Pillsbury Walker, J. Francis Macbride, Edwin Blake Payson, Leslie Newton Goodding, Charles William Penland, George Jones Goodman, Louis O. Williams and Alan Beetle. Today octogenarian Aven Nelson is "one of the men who has grown with the opportunities of the West, and who has made time to do more than his work of teaching."

In the tradition of Hooker and Gray's comparative study of the Rocky Mountain flora with that of other regions of the world is Theodor Holm's *Vegetation of Alpine Region of Rocky Mountains in Colorado* (1923). Bringing to the task field experience from three expeditions to the arctic, Holm tabulated and discussed the ecology and affinities of Colorado alpine species with related arctic forms of America and Eurasia. Holm believed nearly all the circumpolar species had an arctic origin, while some alpine species occurring farther south may have had a cordilleran origin in either Asia or America and still others may have had a polytopic origin, arising independently in more than one widely separated locality.

Ira Waddell Clokey, mining engineer, prepared and distributed the plants of Colorado in admirably standardized sets or exsiccatae on a very wide scale to herbaria all over the world. In this way vouchers for many critical taxonomic revisions have been placed in a large number of study centers.

Charles William Penland came to Colorado College in 1922 and since then has built up a good reference collection there of the plants of the southern part of the state. His interest in plant geography and the alpine flora, along with an opportunity for a collecting season in the Ecuadorian Andes, resulted in a comparative study entitled *Alpine Vegetation of the Southern Rockies and Ecuadorian Andes* (1941). Ruth E. Ashton prepared a descriptive handbook upon the subject *Plants of Rocky Mountain National Park* (1933), illustrated with good photographs, and widely useful over the state for the suggestive identification of the more common species. Charles H. Boissevain and Carol Davidson have provided an excellently illustrated quarto about *Colorado Cacti* (1940), while for the fancier of conifers there is Robert E. More's *Colorado Evergreens* (1943), a 48-page attractive booklet, illustrating most of the species with photographs and containing many cultural notes for the grower. Burton O. Longyear's *Trees and Shrubs of the Rocky Mountain Region* (1927), in the Putnam Fieldbook series, is a semi-popular guide to the woody flora. The Denver landscape architect M. Walter Pesman has prepared ''an easy way to recognize [over 700] Rocky Mountain wildflowers, trees and shrubs,'' entitled *Meet the Natives* (1st printing, 1942). By what may be styled self-indexing, Pesman has arranged for easy recognition the more conspicuous Colorado species, first according to habitat zones by altitude and then by color of the flower. This is a handy-to-use spiral-bound manual, full of recognition marks for the beginner.

Among the very numerous technical studies treating of special topics in Colorado botany may be mentioned those of P. F. Shope on *Colorado Rusts of Woody Plants* (1940), J. Harlan Johnson's *Algae as Rock Builders, with Notes on some Algal Limestones from Colorado* (1936), a host of ecological studies by Ramaley, Holch, Durrell, and their students, of the very recent limnological investigations involving aquatic plants undertaken by Robert Pennak, and those of Southwestern ethnobotany by Earl Morris and his colleagues.

CHAPTER II

Prehistoric Peoples[1]

FRANK H. H. ROBERTS, JR.
Bureau American Ethnology, Smithsonian Institution

COLORADO is commonly regarded as one of the younger states in the Union, a state with a relatively short history, yet within its boundaries there is evidence to show that it was one of the earliest occupied areas in North America. In the closing days of the last Ice Age when the climate was cooler and more moist than that of today and when large glaciers still lingered in the nearby mountains small groups of hunters roamed the plains east of the foothills, some even drifted westward into the San Luis Valley, following the herds of game upon which they relied for sustenance. These nomads were part of one of the first in a series of migrations from northeastern Asia that was to populate the New World with what, millennia later, Columbus mistakenly called Indians.[2] The most likely route of travel for the earliest of these movements was by way of the Bering Strait region.[3] During the last stage of the Pleistocene the lowlands bordering Bering Sea and the Arctic Coast were not glaciated and following the climax of the period, although large portions of North America were still covered by remnants of the Wisconsin ice sheet, there was an open corridor along the eastern slopes of the Rocky Mountains. Consequently it was possible for men and animals to pass from Central Asia to Alaska, eastward to the Mackenzie River and thence southward into the Northern Plains. This undoubtedly was the avenue by which the early hunters reached the area now included in the Centennial State.

FOLSOM MAN

The existence of such a people and their significance was first established in northern New Mexico, but much of the information about them has come from Colorado. In the summer of 1926 a party from the Colorado Museum of Natural History was collecting bones from an extinct species of bison at a quarry in a little valley on a small, intermittent tributary of the Cimarron River several miles west of Folsom, Union County, New Mexico. During the course of

---

[1] Contributed by permission of the Secretary of the Smithsonian Institution.

[2] The marked similarity in physical features between the American Indians and eastern Asiatics, together with certain cultural and linguistic resemblances, indicate a common heritage and there is general agreement that the Indians came from Asia. See A. Hrdlicka, "The origin and antiquity of the American Indian," in *Annual Report of the Smithsonian Institution* for 1923, pp. 481-494.

[3] Ernst Antevs, "The spread of aboriginal man to North America," in the *Geographical Review*, 25, 302-309.

the excavations parts of two finely-chipped stone projectile points were recovered from the loose dirt. Later a small, triangular piece of "flint" was found embedded in the clay surrounding an animal bone. This fragment was left in the block of earth with the bone and sent to the laboratory at Denver where the dirt was carefully cleaned from the bit of stone. The latter appeared to be of the same material as one of the points and examination showed that it actually was a part of the point. It was possible to fit the two pieces together. Here, seemingly, was good evidence of a definite association between man-made objects and an extinct species of bison.[4] Further work at the quarry in the summers of 1927 and 1928 produced more points and bison skeletons and demonstrated beyond doubt that they were contemporaneous. The investigations also revealed that the assemblage of bones and artifacts lay in what probably were the remains of an old bog or water hole. The animals had come there to drink and were surrounded, killed and butchered by the men who made the points. Above the stratum containing this material were several feet of sediments of highly restratified earth of a nature indicative of considerable antiquity. Geologists studying these deposits and the adjacent terrain considered them to be very Late Pleistocene or Early Recent in age. This indicated a much earlier occupation of the country than was previously supposed. The points differed from those ordinarily found in the region. They were thin, leaf-shaped blades without barbs or tangs and were characterized by longitudinal grooves or channels extending along

Folsom Points and Knives

(Top specimen in center column, a channel flake knife; right-hand column, fluted knives)

4 J. D. Figgins, "The antiquity of man in America," in *Natural History,* 27, 229-239.

each face from the base towards the tip. Because the scene of the excavations was known as the Folsom site, from the name of the nearby town, the points also were so designated.

Interest was quickly aroused by this find and people began to talk about Folsom Man and Folsom Culture, although little was known beyond the fact that he lived in the area at a comparatively early date and made a peculiar type of projectile point which he used in killing a kind of bison no longer in existence. It was not until several years had passed that more extensive information on the subject became available and when it did it was obtained from a site in northern Colorado. This location was discovered by Judge C. C. Coffin, A. Lynn Coffin, and C. K. Collins, all of Ft. Collins,[5] in 1924. They recognized that the points found there differed from the usual Indian arrowheads which are so abundant in that general region but did not regard them as particularly significant until the summer of 1930 when they were identified as Folsom type. Subsequent visits to the site established the fact that it actually had been a camping grounds and that other types of stone artifacts were made and used by the people who made the points. On the basis of this evidence and with the permission of Wm. Lindenmeier, Jr., the then owner, a program of excavations was initiated in the fall of 1934 by the Smithsonian Institution and was continued each summer through 1940. In addition a party from the Colorado Museum of Natural History worked there during the summer of 1935 and Judge C. C. Coffin and Major Roy G. Coffin, of Ft. Collins, carried on independent investigations throughout the years that the other groups were at the location.

The Lindenmeier Site is 28 miles north of Ft. Collins, in Larimer County, on what was known as the Lindenmeier Horse Ranch in distinction from the home ranch situated a few miles northeast of the city. It is now a part of the Warren Livestock Company holdings in that district. The remains are found on portions of the floor and the south slope of a little valley that occurs on the break between the High Plains and the Colorado Piedmont, directly east of the Colorado Front Range. As a result of erosion of part of the ridges that once bordered its southern side a large portion of the old valley has taken on the appearance of a terrace lying above an intermittent tributary to a series of creeks belonging to the Cache la Poudre-South Platte drainage. The geologic formation, commonly called the White River, consists of a thick stratum of Brulé tuff-clay overlain by a conglomerate of poorly cemented arkosic sand and gravel known as the Arikaree. The little valley was formed when water flowing from the west cut down through this conglomerate and into the top of the Brulé.

5 Roy G. Coffin, *Northern Colorado's first settlers.*

Frank H. H. Roberts, Jr., "A Folsom complex: Preliminary report on investigations at the Lindenmeier site in northern Colorado," in *Smithsonian Miscellaneous Collections,* 94, no. 4.

Excavations showed that when the Folsom people first found their way into the valley its bottom consisted of a thin layer of soil resting on the light-colored clay, while the surface of the slopes was mainly the top of the clay and scattered patches of thinly-deposited sand and gravel that had weathered from the capping conglomerate still remaining on the tops of the bordering ridges. Here and there along the bottom were small ponds and marshy places, swampy meadows with springs and succulent grasses. These attracted the game and the presence of the animals drew hunters into the area. The additional assets of raw material—quartzite nodules comprising varieties of stone commonly called chalcedony, chert, moss-agate and jasper— for use in making implements, a good supply of water, firewood, and a pleasant camping spot led to more than a casual sojourn. This was shown by the fact that between the time of the people's first arrival and their ultimate departure there developed a definite soil zone varying from a few inches in thickness on the upper slopes to a depth of two feet along the valley floor.

In the beginning numerous objects associated with the daily round of life were scattered over the top of the clay, the sand and gravel patches, and the thin layer of brownish-black earth on the valley bottom. The charcoal and ashes from the fires, stone chips from the manufacture of implements, broken tools and other artifacts, and bones from the animals used for food became embedded in the rising soil level and similar materials dropped in turn on each succeeding new surface were also buried. After the valley was abandoned by its human occupants conditions conducive to the growth of vegetation remained favorable for a time and the soil zone continued to develop. Then an era of erosion set in. Sand, gravel, and boulders were swept down from the hillsides and the grassy slopes and bottom were covered to a depth of several feet. It was during this period that the bordering ridge on the southern side disappeared, some of it contributing to the valley fill and the remainder being carried away toward the south. Water subsequently cut a broad channel in the valley bottom, removing all of the deposits along its course down to the top of the old tuff-clay but not disturbing the layers on the southern slope. The later channel, in turn, was filled with gravelly alluvium washed in from the ridges on the north and the upper part of the valley at the west. This material also covered the lower borders of the old, undisturbed layers along the southern slope and greatly increased the over-burden above the soil zone containing the bones and artifacts. After this new floor was established the valley was visited by modern Indians, possibly the Comanche or even later Cheyenne and Arapaho. In the broad bottom south of the old site are numerous tipi rings which probably date from the same late occupation.

In relatively recent years the runoff from the hillsides and upper valley formed the arroyo which now extends along a portion of the site, revealing the buried cultural stratum and evidences of the subsequent cycles of cutting and filling. Geologists studying these deposits have been able to correlate the old valley bottom and occupation level with a certain terrace of the adjacent minor streams. This terrace was traced to the main rivers of eastern Colorado and thence back up the Cache la Poudre River where it was correlated with a certain stage of glaciation in the mountains. On the basis of this and comparative studies on the continental glaciation in central and eastern United States it is believed that Folsom men entered the little valley after the climax of the Wisconsin period of the Pleistocene but still within that glacial stage. The character of the deposits also indicates that the climate in that part of northeastern Colorado was at times almost Arctic. There is evidence that strong winds blowing across flood-plain surfaces only sparsely covered with vegetation piled up dunes, while the drifting sand cut and polished the rocks and pebbles lying on the surface. Precipitation in the mountain area may have been greater, but on the plains to the east conditions probably were comparable to those of the present Canadian Great Plains. The time when this environment prevailed and the Folsom men took advantage of the sheltered Lindenmeier Valley is estimated at from 10,000 to 25,000 years ago, with the possibility that the age was nearer the latter than the former figure.[6]

Implements and artifacts found at the Lindenmeier Site, as well as those from other parts of the State, include the characteristically fluted or channelled points, fluted knives, knives made from channel flakes, ordinary knife blades, scrapers of various kinds, choppers, hammerstones, rubbing stones used in working hides, flakes with short-needlelike points on one side or end that probably were used for scratching designs on wood or bone or may even have been used for tattooing, bone beads, bone needles and awls, engraved bone disks, engraved steatite disks similar to those of bone, lignite beads, and pieces of rubbed hematite and red and yellow ocher which undoubtedly were sources of pigment. The fluted points, fluted knives, and channel flakes, however, are the only artifacts that are peculiarly Folsom and which can be considered criteria for the culture. The other forms occur throughout later horizons and in themselves are not sufficiently distinct to be identified as being from a specific cultural complex. The assemblage of implements at the Lindenmeier was found in association with quantities of cut and split animal bones. This is definite indication that the Folsom men were typical hunters depending almost entirely upon game for their maintenance and subsistence. They probably supplemented their preponderant meat diet with such "greens" and wild seeds as were available but certainly did not cultivate any vegetal food. Most of the bones were from bison, an extinct species which has been called *Bison taylori* and which was a much larger animal than the modern bison, or buffalo as it is popularly called. In addition, however, there were bones from the pronghorn or antelope, deer, rabbit, wolf, fox, large American camel, and a proboscidean, probably the mammoth. The three extinct forms,

---

6 Kirk Bryan and Louis L. Ray, Geologic antiquity of the Lindenmeier site in Colorado," in *Smithsonian Miscellaneous Collections,* 90, no. 2.

bison, camel, and mammoth, are significant because they are another indication of age. The same bison occurred at the original Folsom site, has been reported from the San Luis Valley,[7] and was associated with Folsom artifacts in other localities. Fluted points were found with mammoth skeletons at Dent, Colorado, some 40 miles southeast from the Lindenmeier.[8] The presence of modern species of fox, wolf, rabbit, pronghorn, and deer has no bearing on the problem one way

View of Excavations at the Lindenmeier Site

or the other because there has been no change in those particular forms from Pleistocene times to the present.

How Folsom Man hunted his game or what methods he used in butchering the carcass after an animal had been killed are not known. Inasmuch as the period in which he lived long antedated that of the horse in American Indian cultures the chase unquestionably had to be on foot. Greater cunning and skill, if not more actual bravery, probably were required under such circumstances than was the case when the men were mounted on horses. The type of weapon used has not been determined. The projectile points are sufficiently vari-

<hr/>

[7] C. T. Hurst, "A Folsom location in the San Luis Valley, Colorado," in *Southwestern Lore*, 7, no. 2, 31-34.

[8] J. D. Figgins, "A further contribution to the antiquity of man in America," in *Proceedings of the Colorado Museum Natural History*, 12, no. 2.

able in size to indicate that they may have been hafted on either arrow or spear shafts, but in view of the fact that evidence from other sources indicates that the bow and arrow was a late introduction in the New World it is generally assumed that these early peoples employed spears. Such being the case it was necessary for the hunter to approach very close to his prey before he could use his stone-tipped spear with success. On the basis of later customs, it may be suggested that brush shelters or blinds may have been erected close to the ponds and watering places frequented by game and the animals have been struck from ambush. This was common practice in the buffalo plains before the Indians acquired horses[9] and may well have been the survival of an ancient custom. On occasions animals undoubtedly became bogged and could be approached and a spear be driven into some vital organ with little difficulty. Also, it is possible that the hunters camouflaged themselves with wolf skins and crawled on hands and knees until close enough to the game to strike it. This technique was used by modern Plains Indians and it may well have been a traditional method. Wolves were numerous and commonly followed the herds of buffalo,[10] the latter paying little attention to them, so that such deception was practicable. Wolf bones were not only present at the Lindenmeier Site but have been found at other locations where Folsom material occurs. Hence, it is evident that skins suitable for such a purpose were available and hunting in that fashion would have been feasible.

Butchering of the smaller animals probably was not too difficult but in the case of the large bison, which were preponderant in the economy, it must have been considerable of a task. There were no mechanical aids for turning, lifting, or transporting the carcass and the skinning and cutting up of the meat must have been done at the scene of the kill. Such work had to be done by manpower alone and the only tools available for the dismembering operation were those of stone or perhaps bone. Castañeda, the chronicler of the Coronado expedition which penetrated the buffalo area in 1540, gives what probably is the closest approximation to a description of such an undertaking. He, together with other members of the party, observed Indians under conditions comparable to those of earlier centuries in that the white man's culture still had not influenced them. In his account of the skinning of bison he wrote: "They cut the hide open at the back and pull it off at the joints, using a flint as large as a finger, tied in a little stick, with as much ease as if working with a good iron tool. They give it an edge with their own teeth. The quickness with which they do this is something worth seeing and noting".[11] Mention of the use of the teeth to sharpen a stone blade has been questioned by many, but a similar custom has been reported for some of the Australian aborigines and motion pictures of them using stone knives clearly

---

9 H. E. Bolton, *Spanish Exploration in the Southwest, 1542-1706,* 230.

10 G. P. Winship, "The Coronado Expedition, 1540-1542," in *14th Annual Report Bureau of American Ethnology,* 528.

11 G. P. Winship, *ibid.,* 528.

show the practice. Hence, it seems that Castañeda did not err in calling attention to it in the case of our own Plains Indians.

The uses made of the various parts of an animal are described in other documents of the early explorations period.[12] The skins were employed in the making of tents, clothes, footgear, and rope. Sections of large intestines were emptied and filled with blood and were carried around the neck to drink from when thirsty. When the stomach was opened the chewed grass was squeezed out and the juice drunk. This furnished essential vitamins, although the Indians did not know it. The intestines also served as containers of fat and marrow and the stomachs as pitchers and vessels. The sinews were used to make thread for sewing the clothes and tents, and for wrapping shafts. The bones were split for marrow and awls were made from the fragments. The horns were cut into spoons, cups, and ornaments. The hoofs were converted into glue to aid in fastening projectile points in shafts and the brains were used in tanning and softening the hides. If such were true in the days of Folsom Man, and it most likely was, there is little wonder that most of the places where he camped are so littered with scraps and splinters of bone and that it is so difficult to obtain specimens of the latter sufficiently intact to make identification of the animal represented a certainty.

There is no evidence as to what type of habitation Folsom Man may have used. When available, he undoubtedly occupied rock shelters and caves. Most manifestations of his former presence, however, occur in open country where such natural features are not to be found. Furthermore, he probably did not settle long in one place, although he may have returned to the same locality from time to time, but followed the bison in their migrations from feeding ground to feeding ground. Consequently it is not likely that he attempted anything in the way of permanent construction, rather that he depended in the main on flimsy brush windbreaks and tents made from the skins of the bison. Traces of the places where he pitched his shelter will be extremely hard to find at this late date because a hard-packed floor and hearth, possibly some post molds, are all that would remain. That he worked in skins is indicated by the presence of bone needles, punches, and awls in his implement complex. Although no actual pieces of hide have been found it is reasonable to assume that clothing, footgear, and tents were fashioned from it. Men capable of making the highly specialized Folsom type of projectile point were sufficiently intelligent and inventive to contrive shelters and body covering from so ready a source of material. Because of the more rigorous climate during that period some such protection would have been essential.

Most of Folsom Man's energies undoubtedly were expended in the manufacture of weapons and implements needed in the killing and butchering of game, in the actual hunt, the making of tents and cloth-

[12] G. P. Winship, *ibid.*, 570: C. E. Castañeda, *tr.*, "History of Texas, 1673-1779, by Fray Agustin Morfi," in *The Quivira Society*, 6, 67: G. P. Hammond and Agapito Rey, *trs.*, "Expedition in New Mexico made by Antonio Espejo, 1582-1583, as revealed in the journal of Diego Pérez de Luxán, a member of the party," in *The Quivira Society*, 1, 120-121.

ing, and the moving of his camp. That he did now and then have time for what nowadays is called "the finer things of life" is shown by the bone beads with simple designs scratched on them, the engraved bone disks which probably were gaming pieces, and by the rubbed pieces of hematite and the ochers that supplied pigment which he possibly applied to his own person and may have used to paint decorations or marks of identification on his spear shafts and other possessions. For the most part his life unquestionably was grim and hard, as is true with most peoples dependent on a hunting economy, yet there must have been interludes of comfort and pleasure when his attention could be turned to matters other than the struggle for existence. So far as his physical characteristics are concerned Folsom Man is still an unknown person. No human remains have yet been found that can definitely be identified as his. Several skeletons purporting to belong in that category have been reported but their authenticity could not be established because no artifacts were buried with them. Once he is known, however, it is not likely that he will prove to be other than an essentially modern type of man, albeit a primitive form of Indian. He certainly will not be, nor should he be expected to be, a Neanderthaloid.

Centering in Yuma County, in eastern Colorado, but occurring over most of the western plains are types of points that have been called Yuma. The first examples were noted in collections gathered from sites where artifacts were weathering from a dark-clay substratum that has been swept clear of surface soil over large areas by the strong winds which are so common in that district. Because Folsom points and fragments from them were also picked up in the same localities the two types were at first believed to be related. On the basis of certain general similarities in outline and methods used in chipping the stone, typological studies were made in an effort to demonstrate that one derived from the other. In one case it was concluded that the Folsom followed the Yuma, was merely a Yuma with channel flakes removed from the faces. The other study reversed the process and had the Yuma the type which was developed after the custom of fluting the points was abandoned. As a result the terms Yuma-Folsom and Folsom-Yuma were used for a time. They have now been dropped by most writers, however, as later investigations have shown that the two types probably are from different complexes. Numerous unfinished and broken points from the Lindenmeier Site show clearly the method used in making the Folsom type and from these it is obvious that it was not a Yuma with channel flakes removed. The point was first roughly shaped by percussion flaking, the tip being left blunt and rounding. The channel flakes were then knocked out, probably by indirect percussion, and the point was given its final form by secondary pressure flaking around the base, sides, and the tip. It is possible that the broad, relatively flat Yumas with a lenticular cross section may have developed from the rough blanks of the Folsom type, but the chipping on the Yumas is sufficiently different to make such a postulation questionable. Most of the evidence at present available suggests that early forms of the Yuma may have been contemporary with the last of the Folsoms. Their main development, however, was later. In fact they continued to be made in some regions until almost historic times. No actual Yuma camp site has been excavated, or if one has it has never been described in print, and there is no information about the other forms of implements associated with such points. Hence it is not possible to speak of a Yuma complex or culture. In a large majority of cases where Yuma points have been found with animal bones they have been those from modern species, the buffalo rather than the extinct bison. Because of this and the other factors mentioned above it is obvious that Yuma-type points are not as significant as was formerly believed and their presence in a collection may mean little from the standpoint of age.

What eventually happened to the Folsom people is a problem still to be solved. There is an unmistakable break in the continuity of occupation in the areas where they formerly roamed. When undisturbed, their camp sites are covered with layers of earth containing no archaeological material and it is only in the higher levels that there are indications that the region was again inhabited. Some believe that the people, like the animals they hunted, became extinct and that no human beings were present until a subsequent migration brought new groups into the area. Others think that this break was only in the western plains and Southwest, that the increasing temperatures and progressive desiccation accompanying the postglacial era produced such unfavorable conditions that the people were forced to other regions where they continued to live. Later, after the environment again became more salubrious, their descendants may have returned to the former habitat where they came in contact and mingled with newer migrants drifting in from the north. In the meantime they had ceased to make the typical fluted implements, although the other forms of tools continued in vogue, and had adopted new types of projectile points. This would account for the persistence into more recent times of many kinds of artifacts present in the Folsom series and also for the sporadic appearance of older physical types among the later population. This is an interesting postulation, yet the most that can be said at the present writing is that there appears to be an hiatus of considerable duration between the Folsom and later peoples in Colorado. Whether or not this gap will be filled is a matter that only the future and much more investigation can determine. Once the archaeological record again appears, following this break, there is evidence for continual occupation into historic times.

The Anasazi

The best known of the pre-Columbian inhabitants of Colorado are those comprising the group which modern archaeologists have called the Anasazi, a Navajo word meaning the "ancients" or the "old people." Most readers probably are more familiar with the names of the two subdivisions, the Basket Makers and the Pueblos or Pueblo-Cliff Dwellers, than with the general term of Anasazi. From the evidence collected over a period of some 70 years by numerous explorers and excavators[13] it is possible to draw a rather clear-cut picture of the people, their mode of life, and the outstanding events during the 1,500 years which preceded the arrival of the Spaniards in the Southwest.

Scattered over southwestern Colorado and adjacent portions of the neighboring states of New Mexico, Utah, and Arizona, was a nomadic people dependent upon the hunt and a chance gathering of wild seeds, fruits, and plant roots for their livelihood. Their traces are meager indeed, but there are sufficient indications to warrant statements to the effect that they were present for several centuries prior to the beginning of the Christian Era. After a time they obtained corn and pumpkins and the knowledge of how to plant and cultivate them. How these products reached them is not known, but it is certain that they were introduced from Mexico as both are of Middle American origin. They probably were passed along by groups living in the northern Mexico southern Arizona region, although there is thus far no direct evidence of the routes along which they diffused into the Southwest. They were of great importance, however, as they provided the foundation for the entire structure of ensuing cultural growth. Because of its essential character agriculture imposed a more sedentary form of life upon the people. In the beginning the effect probably was not marked, but as improving knowledge and a better understanding of the art of cultivation brought larger crops it became necessary to provide storage bins for the harvest.

The Basket Makers

The first comprehensive and accurate information about the people pertains to this period in their history. That they were abandoning their former roving, hunting mode of life is revealed by the materials found in the lower levels of dry caves. The latter show that they served as temporary shelters and places for storage. In the floors of many such caves are circular or oval pits, three to five feet in diameter and in many cases lined with slabs of stone. They are the remains of lower portions of granaries. Occasionally one is found in such a good state of preservation that the pole, brush, and adobe-plaster superstructure is still in place. Some have contained corn, the kernels of which were as bright and shiny as though from a recent harvest instead of having been placed there many centuries earlier. When no longer filled with grain these granaries or their slab-lined basal portions often served as burial places. When the body of the deceased was placed in the grave, objects used in daily life were

---

[13] Much information in this field has been contributed by expeditions sent out by the State Historical Society of Colorado, the University of Colorado, the University of Denver, Western State College of Colorado, the Colorado Archaeological Society, and the Colorado Museum of Natural History.

deposited with it. This demonstrates that the people had a belief in some form of after life. The grave material supplemented by articles found in other locations in the caves furnishes information about the arts and industries of the people and the human remains tell us about their physical characteristics. The extreme aridity in Colorado and the Southwest in general has made conditions unusually favorable for the preservation of objects which otherwise would rapidly decay and as a result specimens from portions of caves where no moisture has penetrated are still in very good condition.

The artifacts show that the people were skilled makers of baskets—from which the name Basket Maker was derived—, twined woven bags, ropes, game snares, and large nets for catching small animals. Their clothing appears to have been rather simple. It is supposed that the men wore a small loin covering of the "gee-string" variety, although thus far no male body has been found with such an article in place. The women had small, apron-like cord skirts. The hair was held in place by elaborately woven head bands and the feet were protected by sandals woven from yucca or apocynum fibres. When the bleak mesa tops and canyons were swept by cold winds or occasional storms fine fur robes augmented the meager body coverings. They also served as bed coverings and when their owners died were used as shrouds. For personal adornment there were necklaces of small black seeds, of olivella shells, of various kinds of stone, and of twisted skin or fiber cords with pendants of abalone shell, stone, feathers, or a few beads. Weapons consisted of a short javelin, with the stone point hafted in a short foreshaft, hurled by means of a spearthrower or atlatl, short curved clubs of wood, clubs fashioned from elk antlers, knives of stone, and daggers of bone. The implements of their more peaceful pursuits were wooden planting sticks, wooden scoop-like objects used for digging, curved sticks employed in dressing skins, and various kinds of bone tools for service in weaving.

Not too much is known about dwellings at this stage of cultural growth. Thus far the only evidence that the people actually had domiciles is that found along the Animas River some eight miles above Durango. There, in a large cavern and on the slopes of a hillside about two miles away, were the remains of crude structures that throw some light on the problem. In erecting these habitations the builders dug into the slope of the talus or hillside, piling the earth in front to form an approximately level platform of the desired size. Upon this a roughly circular house, from ten to thirty-three feet in diameter, was placed. The walls were fashioned of wood and masonry—logs, poles, twigs, and pieces of stone of sundry shapes and sizes laid horizontally with the intervening spaces filled with mud and the surfaces chinked with mud, as is done in building log cabins. The roofs were cribbed, with each succeeding series of horizontal timbers being laid in ever smaller circles, the logs cutting across the corners of the layer below, etc., until the framework rose into a kind of dome. The finished house must have looked like an inverted bowl with a break in the contour at the juncture between the roof and walls. Where the entrance was placed or what its nature was has not been learned as yet. Inside, the floor was saucer shaped, with a fire pit near the center. There must have been some form of opening in the roof above to permit the escape of smoke, but this has not been definitely determined. Much of the floor area was taken up by storage bins which usually consisted of a subfloor part lined with stone slabs surmounted by an open-topped, roundish dome three feet or more in height. There also were mud domes without the subfloor portion and rather large jug-shaped pits with openings at the floor level. Metates or milling stones used in grinding corn usually accompanied these bins, from two to six being placed at convenient points about the room. They were either embedded in mud or were propped on stones.[14]

Houses of this type appear to have been built in rows, as close together as was practicable. They were highly inflammable and destruction by fire was frequent. In such cases the debris was levelled, a new excavation made in the bank above, and the earth spread out over the ashes of the former structure to prepare the floor for the new one. It is possible that they were a local development and although characteristic for the Durango district were not known elsewhere. Other features about the Durango sites are also somewhat different from the general pattern and the same may be true in this case. No traces of dwellings have been found in other localities but it would seem that the people must have had some sort of habitation, possibly one even more flimsy in construction so that no remains have been preserved. Some of the smaller caves were lived in from time to time, as on the Mesa Verde, yet do not appear to have been occupied continuously, since the large accumulations of refuse which would have resulted from permanent residence are lacking. In caves that did serve as temporary shelters, hearths were placed at a convenient spot on the floor and shallow ''fox-holes'' were scooped out of the earth and lined with grass to serve as sleeping places.

The skeletal remains of the people show that they were short of stature, although not pygmies, and slender in build. Their faces lacked the massive size and prominent cheek bones of the later Indians and their noses were medium to broad. Their heads tended to be long and were undeformed. Their skin probably was brown and their hair dark, with more of a tendency to be wavy or curly than in the case of the present-day American Indians. The group was not wholly uniform, however, and appears to have been a blend of at least three basic strains. It is quite possible that three different types of individuals would have been observed by visitors to the different communities. The most numerous, probably, were those with a comparative smoothness and symmetry of head form, medium to long in length, rather narrow faces which tended to be a little long, weakly developed

14 E. H. Morris, "Southwest Archaeology," in *The Carnegie Institution of Washington Year Book,* 40, 304-306.

chins and jaws, and medium to narrow noses with elevated bridge. Another group consisted of somewhat more rugged and robust people with long heads, receding foreheads and prominent brow ridges, shorter and broader faces with more noticeable cheek bones, and medium to broad noses with submedium bridge. The third, and possibly least numerous, type was composed of individuals with long although smaller heads, slightly swollen foreheads, inconspicuous brow ridges, very broad noses with flat bridges, moderately developed cheek bones and weak chins. It is not thought that separate groups comprising each of these types migrated to and mixed in the Southwest, rather that the people who spread into North America from northeastern Asia were racially mixed and that their descendants in the Southwest exhibited the differences described because of the segregation of features in occasional individuals.[15] Taken as a whole this group was predominantly non-Mongoloid in character. The Durango people seem to have varied from the general type in that their heads tended to be medium long to broad rather than long. This, in conjunction with certain differences in the material culture, may be attributable to the fact that they actually were on the periphery of the Basket Maker area and may have included individuals representative of the first wave of an incoming type which was to play an important part in later developments. This feature is considered in more detail in subsequent pages.

Modified Basket Makers

Many of the caves in which the evidence for the early stage of these people were found also contain manifestations of their progress. In the upper levels, the deposits of more recent date, are the remains of definite although rather crude houses. These show that a sedentary mode of life actually had become established and that the organization of regular communities was well under way. The remains of such villages are not only found in caves but also in the open, on the mesa tops and valley bottoms. There is some question about the origin of these houses. Some data tend to show that they were the result of constant improvements in the methods of granary construction and the attendant discovery that a reasonably comfortable dwelling of the pit variety could be built by enlarging the subsurface portion and heightening the brush superstructure.[16] It is also possible that they may have been an outgrowth from the type of structure noted above Durango, but it would seem that the granary heritage was the more logical. On the other hand the houses so strikingly suggest a relationship with the basic earth-lodge type widely distributed in both the New World and northeastern Asia that the form perhaps should

15 E. A. Hooton, "The Indians of Pecos Pueblo, a study of their skeletal remains," in *Papers of the Southwestern Expedition Phillips Academy, Andover,* 4, 355-362.

16 A. V. Kidder, "An introduction to the study of Southwestern Archaeology," in *Papers of the Southwestern Expedition Phillips Academy, Andover,* 1, 121.

be attributed to a diffusion from the Old World rather than to local developments.[17]

These houses consisted of a circular, oval, or rectangular excavation, about three feet deep and ten to twenty feet across, roofed over with a truncated pyramidal superstructure of poles, brush, cedar bark, sometimes reed mats, plaster and earth. The walls of the pit generally were reinforced by a lining of stone slabs or a wainscoting of small poles, although there are sporadic examples where the earth was sufficiently compact to hold a face and neither was used. Mud plaster was then spread over the walls. A hole in the center of the flat portion of the roof permitted the escape of smoke from the fire which was lighted in an open pit in the center of the room. Small holes were usually provided here and there in the floor for the storage of minor articles and cupboards were sometimes cut in the walls. On either side of the doorway, which usually was at the southeast side of the chamber, were slab bins for storage purposes and nearby was the milling stone for grinding meal. In most cases the doorway opened into a passageway which frequently had an antechamber or entry room at its outer end. As a rule this passage was not very long, but it was sufficient to protect the doorway from drafts and inclement weather. Several granaries of the type described for the preceding stage were built close to each dwelling. A number of such houses and their storage units were grouped in an irregular cluster to form a village. Examples of these villages are widely scattered over southwestern Colorado and occur sporadically as far north as Moffat County. Not much is known about the latter, however. The most numerous and the best studied are those in the La Plata section,[18] on the Mesa Verde, and in the Ackmen-Lowry district.[19] They are not restricted to Colorado, however, and similar remains may also be seen in New Mexico, Arizona, and Utah.

When the first of these houses were being built the people also began to make pottery. This new industry is generally considered as another introduction from the south. However, it seems that only the idea reached the area because the entire ceramic development unquestionably was local in its character. The first crude containers of clay were fashioned in basket molds and could not be called true pottery because they were not fired. They were merely dried. Eventually it was discovered, no doubt by accident, that the secret of making durable and useful clay vessels lay in firing them and from that time forward pottery assumed a major role in the material culture. Baskets became less and less important, although they continued to be made.

---

[17] F. H. H. Roberts, Jr., "Shabik'eshchee Village, a Late Basket Maker site in the Chaco Canyon, New Mexico," *Bulletin 92, Bureau of American Ethnology,* 149. The term Late Basket Maker in this publication corresponds to Modified Basket Maker as currently used.

[18] E. H. Morris, "Archaeological studies in the La Plata District, southwestern Colorado and northwestern New Mexico," *Publication 519, The Carnegie Institution of Washington.*

[19] P. S. Martin, "Modified Basket Maker sites, Ackmen-Lowry Area, southwestern Colorado, 1938," in *Anthropological Series, Field Museum Natural History,* 23, No. 3.

Other changes were also taking place. Where previously there had been but one hard flintlike variety of corn, several were now grown and kidney beans were added to the agricultural complex. Fields, however, continued to be located in the valley bottoms or on the mesa tops in places where the runoff from rains would help to irrigate them. There was a change in sandal types with those articles exihibiting extremely elaborate patterns, both woven and in color. Intricate designs were also woven into the head bands and into sashes. Ornaments were abundant. There were beads of wood, of several kinds of seeds, of shells, and of turquoise; pendants of stone, lignite, shell, and turquoise, some in the shape of birds; mosaic ornaments of shell and turquoise; shell bracelets; necklaces of animal claws, crystals; feather hair ornaments and bone pins. Toward the end of the period feather robes began to replace those made from fur and the bow and arrow came into use. Despite these important changes, however, the basic cultural pattern remained the same and there was no change in the people. They were still the Basket Makers, but to differentiate this stage from the earlier one in which the new traits were lacking they are called the Modified Basket Makers.

THE PUEBLOS

The appearance of the bow and arrow probably was associated with another factor, one which was to have a marked bearing on the future. A new group of people was drifting into the region, coming down the cordillera from the north. It was possible that they were the bearers of this different kind of weapon, although it probably preceded them through capture and trade as a diffused cultural trait. This new group did not sweep into the area as an invading horde, but it infiltrated gradually in small bands. There probably were clashes of greater or less degree between the newcomers and those already occupying the region. On the whole, however, the general tendency seems to have been toward a mixing of the old and new. Formerly it was thought that the Basket Makers were driven out to find new homes elsewhere or else were completely absorbed. In the light of recent evidence this appears not to have been the case and the old racial stock can be traced down to modern times. There is a definite Basket Maker strain in the population at Zuñi, New Mexico, and it has been noted in skeletal remains from ruined towns that long postdate the time when the Basket Makers were supposed to have disappeared.[20] Evidence for the arrival of a new element in the population is shown by the physical remains of the people. In addition to the types already described, they include a larger and more robust group with distinctly Mongoloid broad heads. Subsequent adoption of the practice of cranial deformation, a flattening of the occiput, introduced a feature which was characteristic throughout the later

[20] C. C. Seltzer, "Racial prehistory in the Southwest and the Hawikuh Zuñis," in *Papers of the Peabody Museum of American Archaeology and Ethnology, Harvard University*, 23, No. 1.

periods. It not only emphasized the broad headedness of the individuals in that category but also helped to modify the long headed characteristics of the other group. The occurrence of broad heads at the Durango sites suggests that some of that group reached Colorado at a much earlier time than previously supposed. They may represent the advance guard and very first of the new strain. In most districts, though, the date of arrival was considerably later.

The period immediately following the advent of the new people was one of cultural transition and instability. The immigrants appear to have brought little with them beyond the bow and arrow, possibly the grooved ax, and a marked capacity for cultural advancement. They took over and adapted to their own needs the material culture of the old inhabitants. The mixing of the two peoples produced a vigor which finally carried them to the high level which sedentary life reached in the Southwest. Several new features appeared. Cotton was introduced, at first probably as finished fabrics imported from the peoples in southern Arizona and northern Mexico and then as raw material to be worked into textiles. It is doubtful that much, if any, was ever grown in Colorado. Most of that used in this and later times probably was imported from the Hopi country in Arizona. Whereas the dog had been the only tamed creature previously, the turkey was now domesticated. The fowl does not seem to have been eaten, except in rare cases, but was kept for its feathers, which were used for ceremonial purposes and in the making of feather robes. The grooved ax became an important implement. There was a distinct improvement in pottery making and a decided trend toward stylistic fashions in the decorations painted on the vessels. In various districts, particularly along the Piedra River[21] and in the La Plata section farther west, the single-room semisubterranean dwellings were replaced by structures which had only slightly depressed floors rather than pits. A major portion of the house was above ground and each structure had several contiguous rectangular rooms. In some cases the walls were of pole and mud (jacal) construction, in others they were stones horizontally laid in mud mortar. These were followed by houses, a single story in height and containing six to fourteen rooms, with good masonry walls and built entirely above ground. The latter are usually called the unit type. Pit-houses continued in use for a time in some of the more isolated areas, but certain changes were made in them. The pits were dug deeper and instead of an entryway at one side a ladder extending through the smoke hole in the roof provided access to the chamber. The side passage and doorway, however, were retained in reduced size and modified form and functioned as a ventilator. These structures eventually were replaced by others of the unit type.

The building of above-ground houses containing several rectangular rooms raised a problem somewhat different from the material ones which the people had been surmounting. It became necessary

---

21 F. H. H. Roberts, Jr., "Early Pueblo ruins in the Piedra District, southwestern Colorado," *Bulletin of American Ethnology*, No. 96.

to make some provision for the religious rites and ceremonies which formerly were held in the circular semisubterranean form of house. Rather than change the rituals to fit the new dwellings each house group erected one of the old-style chambers, usually at the south or southeast side and some distance away from the "modern" domicile, where the rites could be carried on in orthodox fashion. As time went on these ceremonial chambers became more and more specialized and finally developed into what is now called the Kiva. The period in which these developments took place is designated the Development Pueblo by archaeologists. Sometimes it is broken up into an early and late stage and the divisions are called Pueblo I and Pueblo II.

The Classic Pueblo

While the changes chronicled for the Developmental Pueblo period were taking place the people lived in small villages scattered throughout the area. Then a new trend set in. The small houses began to be replaced by large communal centers. Buildings composed of many units, with second, third, fourth, and sometimes even fifth stories, were erected. These great terraced structures in many cases contained several hundred rooms. In addition it became the general practice to incorporate the ceremonial rooms in the main block of the building and to simulate their former subterranean character by filling with earth the spaces between their circular walls and the rectangular ones which enclosed them.

Reasons for the rise of these urban centers are not definitely known. They seem to have been the result of people abandoning the outlying small houses and concentrating in larger communities rather than as a consequence of a sudden and marked increase in population. Several factors probably contributed to the movement. The Southwest is subject to severe periodic droughts and one or more such occurrences may have made some districts so inhospitable that the inhabitants were forced to withdraw and join their kinsmen in places where conditions were more favorable. To avoid the occupation of too much tillable land the dwellings were consolidated and the typical apartment house of the period evolved. Furthermore, there was a constantly increasing pressure from the wilder, more nomadic Indians along the frontier of the Pueblo area. Periods of drought would greatly reduce the supplies of wild fruits, seeds, nuts, even game, and small unprotected villages with reserves of corn, pumpkins, and beans would be tempting plunder. In the Montezuma Valley north and west of the Mesa Verde, in the La Plata district, and along the Piedra, are evidences of communities which were raided and burned and their occupants slaughtered. Hence the desire to gather in populous centers for self defense no doubt was an important factor. This is particularly well shown by the ruins on the Mesa Verde, where extensive communal houses were built in large natural caverns that furnished easily defended locations, and by the protective measures taken in the construction of the houses themselves.

Cliff Palace, Mesa Verde National Park

Many of the ruins along the Mancos exhibit similar traits and the remains of the large Pueblo building on Chimney Rock Mesa above the Piedra River had numerous features that unquestionably were intended to make the place more secure.[22] Yucca House, the large ruins formerly called Aztec Springs, and the Lowry group, as well as others in the Montezuma Valley, were situated in the open and less easily defended. Yet the concentration of peoples and the nature of the buildings no doubt helped in keeping the invaders somewhat in check. There is nothing at present to indicate definitely who these enemies were, but it seems that those who were operating in the district west and northwest of the Mesa Verde were most likely Shoshonean groups working in from the Great Basin. Along the northeastern and eastern borderlands they may well have been of Athapascan stock, the advance guard of the Apache and Navajo. Those coming in from the east possibly were accompanied by people from the pillaged villages of the eastern periphery.

These large centers prospered for a time and in addition to their architectural developments showed progress in the arts and industries. A tendency toward specialization in various lines which started when the people began gathering in larger and more isolated communities reached its climax in a crystallization of definite and characteristic forms peculiar to each center. As a consequence it is possible to identify certain pottery types with certain restricted districts; to associate different styles of masonry with particular precincts; and to correlate the several kinds of Kivas with specific centers. The main economy continued to be based on agriculture, with several varieties of corn, beans, and pumpkins the chief products. The people had cotton mantles, usually plain but occasionally with elaborately colored patterns; feather string blankets, with a few of the fur ones still in use; sandals woven from yucca leaves and, early in the period, a fine cord type; undecorated head bands; turquoise beads and pendants; several kinds of shell beads; minute stone beads; pendants of stone, pottery, and lignite; and shell bracelets. They made effigies of birds and animals from lignite and hematite and fashioned mosaics of turquoise, shell, lignite, and galena. They also manufactured coiled and twilled-ring baskets, twilled rush mats, twined reed mats, and strung willow mats. Their chipping and grinding of stone was well done and their woodworking was skillful and diversified. They made black on white, black on red, polychrome, red exterior with polished black interior, and corrugated pottery. Their weapons were the bow and arrow, grooved ax, and grooved hammer. In all respects it was truly the great or classic period of the Pueblo peoples.

After a time these urban centers began to collapse. This phenomenon undoubtedly was caused by a combination of drought, greater activity on the part of the nomadic raiders, and internal discord and factional strife. A series of prolonged crop failures

22 J. A. Jeancon, *Archaeological Research in the northeastern San Juan Basin of Colorado during the summer of 1921.*

with their attendant "hard times" no doubt created trouble within each community and between the various centers. Furthermore, they may have reduced the resistance of the people to such an extent that they not only were not able to protect themselves against attack but lost all desire to do so and set out in search of better locations. The movement was not one concerted exodus. The first communities to be abandoned appear to have been those in the Piedra district. People from the Piedra proper quite likely drifted south and southwestward along the San Juan River and joined with other groups at the settlements whose ruins are seen in the vicinity of Aztec, New Mexico, and a few may even have continued on to the Chaco Canyon farther south. Inhabitants from the large houses in the tributary canyons farther east along the San Juan seem to have spread south and east into the northern Rio Grande region. In the early stages some of the settlers in the Johnson Canyon region, farther west, possibly took advantage of refuge spots along the Mancos River and its tributaries leading back into the Mesa Verde. Some may even have worked their way onto the Mesa and temporarily joined the inhabitants there, while others unquestionably went south to the communities in the Aztec cluster or on to the great Chaco Canyon towns. Refugees from the large village groups in Montezuma Valley scattered in several directions. Some travelled west into southeastern Utah, where they left numerous traces of their occupancy of the canyons and mesa tops. Others migrated south and southeast into New Mexico and a few may have gone up the Mancos and side canyons to the Mesa Verde. The villages on the Mesa held out the longest, but in time they too were deserted. A large band from there went to Aztec, where the houses had already been abandoned by their builders, but did not tarry long before moving on. Some probably reached the Rio Grande, others the Little Colorado, areas where Pueblo peoples still live. It is not possible to say which are descendants of the former Coloradans, although the Tewa have a legend of having lived on the Mesa and have place names for various features in that district. The Hopi and the Zuñi also say that the ancestors of some of their clans came from that region. Owing to the fact that there is no knowledge of the language spoken by the Mesa Verde people there is no way of checking relationships through that medium. The Hopi speak a Shoshonean dialect, the Tewa a Tanoan dialect, and the Zuñi are considered a separate linguistic stock. Hence, it does not seem likely that all three groups were derived from the Mesa Verde district. Probably only one was, but which one is the question. Archaeological evidence points toward the Tewa, although it is not sufficiently convincing to warrant the statement that the Tewa are so related. With the dispersal of the occupants of the Mesa Verde, southwestern Colorado ceased to be an Anasazi habitat, although occasional hunting parties may have drifted back into the area for short visits.

One question that is always foremost in the minds of people interested in the Basket Makers and the Pueblos is that of their age.

Fortunately there is a calendar which gives some information on this subject. It was not devised by the Indians, who had no method of recording events so that we may reconstruct them, but was a contribution by Mother Nature and was discovered through research in another field of activity. Dr. A. E. Douglass, an astronomer, in making a study of sun spots and their effects on climatic conditions in the Southwest, turned to the growth rings of trees in an attempt to obtain evidence on the occurrence of droughts and intervals of moisture. In doing this he discovered that definite ring patterns, as distinct as human fingerprints, recorded specific year groups and as a consequence devised a system whereby he can tell the year when a log was cut from a living tree. Beginning with trees whose actual cutting date was known he has been able to draw a master chart showing the characteristic rings for each year back to the second century before the Christian Era. To substantiate his own theories he was forced to use timbers from ruins for material antedating living trees and thus furnished the archaeologists with a valuable time scale. When beams are found in ruins it is possible to check their rings against the master chart and, if their outer surfaces have not been removed or damaged, tell the year of the cutting. A log occasionally was re-used and sometimes one may not have been placed in a house immediately after it was cut, but such things can be checked against the archaeological features of a site and a date is assured which closely approximates the year or years when the dwellings were erected.[23]

The tree-ring calendar has shown that the Basket Makers with the simple agriculture of corn and pumpkins were living in the area at the beginning of the third century A. D. Hence, their nomadic ancestors probably were there at about the beginning of the Christian Era, if not some centuries earlier. The pit-house-building, pottery-making Modified Basket Makers on present evidence fall within the period from 450 to 700 A. D., although further work may show that they started somewhat earlier. The Developmental Pueblo stage belongs in the span of years from 700 to 1,000 A. D., and the Classic from 1,000 to 1,300. Certainly by 1300 no Pueblos were left in Colorado. Small groups apparently returned at the time of the Pueblo Revolt against the Spaniards, 1680-1700, but only remained a few years before withdrawing again to New Mexico.

The calendar also gives interesting information about droughts. It records one in the 790's; one from 900 to 904; another about 924; a short, although severe one about 980; another in the decade 1090 to 1101; a short one at 1131; followed by another at 1217. The most severe of all was one of 23 years' duration, 1276 to 1299. Also there were intervals when conditions were not entirely favorable. The early part of the 11th century, 1005 to 1044, is an example. Moisture was noticeably below normal during this 30-year period,

---

23 A. E. Douglass, "Dating Pueblo Bonito and other ruins of the Southwest," in *National Geographic Society Pueblo Bonito Series*, 1.

yet it actually was not a drought.[24] Correlating this data with that from the archaeological researches it is apparent that the trend toward concentration in urban communities corresponds with the dry period at about 980, but the full force of the movement did not develop until the subnormal 1005 to 1044 span of years. In some sections, particularly the Mesa Verde, the main impetus came after the 1090-1101 drought. The great drought of 1276-1299 unquestionably

(Courtesy of the Denver and Rio Grande Western Railroad)

Spruce Tree House, Mesa Verde National Park

was an important factor in the abandonment of southwestern Colorado. The last construction date thus far reported from the Mesa Verde is 1274. The people no doubt continued to live there for a time, although they did no more building. As a matter of fact those who lingered until the end probably had more places in which to live than they could use.

OTHER INHABITANTS

Little is known about the people living along the mountains and throughout the eastern part of the State during the millennium and more that the Anasazi were evolving their culture. In the days

---

[24] A. E. Douglass, *ibid.*, 48-49.

when the nomadic Basket Makers were wandering along the San Juan and its tributaries, possibly northward as far as the Yampa, other nomadic hunting tribes probably roamed the slopes of the Rockies, the mountain parks and larger valleys, and the plains. Leading a vagabond life, as they did in following the game on which they depended, and establishing more or less temporary habitations they left only scattered evidence of their history. Stone implements of various kinds are widely distributed over the whole region, there are sporadic camp sites or cave shelters, and in suitable places clusters of pictographs. In many cases it cannot be determined whether they are pre-Columbian or later or to what tribes of Indians they should be attributed. To further complicate the problem, very little has been done in this branch of Colorado archaeology.

One of the few examples of work in such sites is that at Tabeguache Cave, in western Montrose County, where it was found that the original occupants had been hunters and seed gatherers and possibly were contemporaries of the original Basket Makers, or even somewhat older. After an interval of some duration in which the cave was unoccupied, they were followed by a group that grew corn and pumpkins and may have been related to the agricultural Basket Makers. They in turn were succeeded by peoples presumed to be early Utes.[25] Much remains to be learned about the earliest inhabitants, however, before they can take their proper place in the history of Colorado.

In the San Luis Valley in the region extending from the Dry Lakes and Sand Dunes southward along the east side of the Rio Grande Valley and into New Mexico, southwestward to the Rio Grande in the vicinity of Del Norte and Monte Vista, and thence southward along the hills forming the western border of the river valley to Los Pinos and on south into New Mexico, are many extensive camp sites and occasional rock shelters formerly occupied by nomadic hunters whose archaeological remains have been called the Upper Rio Grande Culture.[26] The main axis of distribution for this culture appears to have been in the region east of the river. The people killed buffalo, deer, antelope, and smaller animals. They had no agriculture and made no pottery. The distinguishing feature of their material culture is that most of the implements were made from a black volcanic stone. The projectile points have a typical long, broad and squarish stem that is set off from the body of the blade by small shoulders, usually cut at an oblique angle. The body of the blade generally is broad and rather short, with convex edges and a spoon-shaped or rounded point. Evidence has shown that the makers of these points were in the area prior to the visits of Pueblo peoples from New Mexico who came into the valley on hunting trips in the 11th century. Hence, it is obvious that the nomads occupied

25 C. T. Hurst, "Completion of excavation of Tabeguache Cave II," in *Southwestern Lore,* 11, no. 1, 8-12.

26 E. B. Renaud, "The Rio Grande Points," in *Southwestern Lore,* 8, no. 2, 33-36: "Archaeology of the Upper Rio Grande Basin in southern Colorado and northern New Mexico," *Archaeological Series University of Denver,* 6.

the valley for some time before 1000 A. D., but when they entered the region or how long they were there are questions for which there is no answer as yet. Whether some of them were still there when the Pueblos made their trips to the district or the whole group had withdrawn from the area is not known. Neither is it known who they were or what eventually became of them. That is still to be determined.

Along the western edge of the San Luis Valley are other remains in the form of ruins of small, circular and oval stone-walled houses scattered over the tops and sides of the rock promontories which jut out into the plain. These clusters of former dwellings extend from the neighborhood of the town of Villa Grove, Saguache County, on down to and beyond the Rio Grande. They are similar to other ruins found along the San Miguel, Uncompahgre, Lower Gunnison, Upper Colorado, and Yampa River drainages. The people who built them have been called the Hogan Builders.[27] They appear to have been primarily a hunting people depending for the most part on deer, antelope, and mountain sheep rather than on smaller game. In districts where it was possible to do so they raised some corn and perhaps pumpkins. They made arrowheads, knives, scrapers, spokeshaves, and hammers of stone, and used grinding stones for seeds and corn. They also had an extensive assortment of bone tools, bone and stone beads, and some pottery. The latter is interesting because in some cases it was of the Pueblo type and in others appears to have been related to or derived from forms found on the Plains. It has been suggested that these people were of Athapascan stock, possibly ancestral Apache and Navajo, and that the house remains trace the course of their migration from the north, southward into New Mexico. They may well have been the enemies who forced the early Developmental Pueblo groups south from Moffat County's frontier and have been a contributing factor in forcing the concentration of Pueblo peoples in southwestern Colorado. The Pueblo type pottery found in the Hogan sites on the Uncompahgre Plateau belongs to the late Developmental Period and indicates a date of about 1000 A. D., for the communities in that district. The occurrence of the other type of pottery in the San Luis Valley is significant as it may indicate the source of a non-Pueblo form of ware which made its appearance in the northeastern Pueblo area in New Mexico at about 1100 A. D. It is a form which seems to have been the precursor of the Navajo and Paiute pottery of a somewhat later period.

The vestiges of hogan communities, from north to south, probably chronicle the passage of several centuries from the time when their builders first entered the northwestern corner of the state until they moved on into New Mexico. That the latter took place before the beginning of the historic period is indicated by the fact that the first Spaniards to visit the San Luis Valley reported it to be a

---

[27] Betty H. and Harold A. Huscher, "The Hogan Builders of Colorado," in *Southwestern Lore,* 9, no. 2.

disputed hunting ground for the Navajo, Jicarilla-Apache, and Ute. Later it became Ute territory, although subject to raids by the Comanche.

The area east of the mountains has numerous camp sites and sporadic cave shelters extending from the Wyoming line on the north to New Mexico on the south. Many of the sites in the open are characterized by rings of stones which show where tipis were pitched. These were the stopping places of the buffalo hunting Indians who followed the herds in their seasonal migrations from south to north in the spring and summer and back again in the fall and winter. Many of these sites are pre-Columbian, others are early historic, and some date from the period of the westward expanding United States and the settlement of the country by our own people. Thus far, with a very few exceptions, it has not been determined what ones belong to the different periods nor to what tribes they should be attributed. Future archaeological work may make this clear, but at present the information is lacking.

In the southeastern part of the State, mainly in the Arkansas drainage, there are numerous stone enclosures situated on the tops of cliffs along the deep and wide canyons or on high promontories overlooking the surrounding country. They were made from large slabs or blocks of stone, used just as found, without any attempt to shape or work the native rock. Their purpose is puzzling. From their location and character it seems obvious that they are not the remains of dwellings. It has been suggested that they were ceremonial shrines or gathering places, but this does not wholly fit their character. Their positions on high points indicate that they may have served as observation posts and that is the best explanation yet offered. In form and nature they do not fit in with what is known of the culture of the Plains Indians and they are not Puebloan. Hence, it is difficult to account for them. That they were built by Indians seems certain, but when and by what Indians is a question.[28] They may be quite old or they may be relatively recent and fall into the period generally considered that of the modern Indians.

Preceding pages have briefly sketched the story of the aboriginal occupants of Colorado over a period of several thousands of years prior to the arrival of the white man. In this area the date of the beginning of the historic period is placed at 1540, the year when Coronado and his stalwart band of explorers penetrated the region. The Spaniards found many tribes of Indians, some possibly old inhabitants, others only recent arrivals from the north. The story of the Indians does not end at that time, however, but continues on into modern days as described in the following chapter.

28 E. B. Renaud, "Indian stone enclosures of Colorado and New Mexico," *Archaeological Series University of Denver*, 2.

CHAPTER III

The Indians

Edgar C. McMechen
Curator of the Colorado State Museum

WHEN one begins to delve into the story of historic Colorado Indians he is confronted at once with the assumption of the Pikes Peak gold seekers that the important tribes in Colorado history were the mountain Utes, and the Arapahoes and Cheyennes of the plains area; further, that all other tribes, excepting the Kiowa and Comanche, were visitors only on hunting or war expeditions.

The viewpoint of the pioneers is understandable since they came in direct contact with the Indians named and this contact, especially in regard to the Arapaho and Cheyenne, was short, bitter and fatal—for the Indians.

Early Occupants and Migrations

Such a conception is far from the truth. It is doubtful whether the Arapaho and Cheyenne were residents for more than one century, whereas other Indian nations can be ascribed residence for several centuries. When one speaks of "home" Indians, three tribes stand forth: the Ute, the Apache and the Comanche. Before the Comanche, a branch of the great Shoshonean family, appeared at the Spanish settlements of New Mexico at the start of the eighteenth century, they had resided for an unknown period in southwestern Wyoming and northwestern Colorado. The Jicarilla division of the Apache claimed all of eastern Colorado north to the South Platte River at least as early as the middle of the seventeenth century—probably much earlier.

Of all the tribes who once lived in this state only the Utes retain, in the Ignacio Reservation of southwestern Colorado, a small portion of Colorado soil. Leaving aside the Utes, the Arapahoes and the Cheyennes, who were removed directly by Anglo-American force, all other tribes succumbed to pressure from superior tribes with whom they came in contact; or migrated voluntarily after the introduction of the horse by the Spaniards.

The pressure stemmed primarily from the white race, and came from two directions: from the northeast, when the French introduced steel and firearms; and from the southwest when the Spaniards brought the same tools from Mexico.

The horse stimulated voluntary migration tremendously. It had the same effect upon the Indian as the iron horse had upon the whites. At once, the Indian was freed from narrow horizons. His hunting and warring range was expanded by hundreds of miles. He could transport his goods and chattels with comparative ease. Until then his only beast of burden had been the dog. Changes of habitat that formerly would have required centuries came to pass within the span of a long life.

The first great shock struck the Apache of southeastern Colorado and northeastern New Mexico and, to understand subsequent events, some background is necessary. The Apache nation constitutes the southerly group of the Athapascan family.[1] This nation was first mentioned by name by Governor Onate in 1598, although the same people probably were the Querechos of Coronado. He sent one of his captains, Vicente de Zaldivar Mendoca to the north and east of Santa Fe in 1599, who found that the Vaqueros (Apaches) were then trading with the Picuries and Taos Pueblos, selling "meat, hides, tallow, suet and salt, in exchange for cotton blankets, pottery, maize and some small green stones which they use." He found the Apache living in tents of "tanned hides, very bright red and white in color and bell-shaped, with flaps and openings * * * to drag the tent poles, supplies of meat and pinole or maize, the Indians used medium-sized dogs. Harnessed round their breasts and haunches and snarling at one another, they kept pace with their masters, who followed the roaming buffalo."[2] Onate himself visited the "Apachi" east of Pecos in 1601 and reported: "They were not people who sewed or reaped, but lived solely on the cattle."[3]

During the seventeenth century the Apaches continued to annoy the Spaniards by continual raids upon outlying settlements and Pueblo allies. The Utes also became well known to the New Mexican authorities but were, on the whole, peaceable and friendly. After the Pueblo revolt of 1664, some of the Picuries fled to an Apache settlement on the Arkansas River and built a Pueblo there, which became known as El Cuartelejo. This settlement is reputed to have been on Horse Creek, north of the river. From this name, the northern band of Jicarillas became known to the Spaniards as Cuartelejo Apaches. Juan de Archuleta, sent to bring back the fugitives, reported that the French were trading with the Pawnees to the north.[4]

This alarming news brought about efforts to make peace with the Jicarillas and thereby set up a buffer state between the Spanish dominions and the French. It was not difficult because the Jicarillas were not a warlike people. At the close of the century peace reigned between the Spanish settlements and the Jicarillas, together with their northern branches—the Carlana, who occupied southeastern Colorado below the Arkansas, and the Cuartelejo and Paloma Apaches, who lived between the Arkansas and the South Platte.

By this time the Apaches seemed destined to become sedentary Indians. Juan de Ulibarri found, during his expedition to El Cuartelejo in 1706 that some of the Jicarillas south of Raton Pass cultivated "grain, maize, corn, frijoles and pumpkins, and produced dried

[1] F. W. Hodge, *Bureau of American Ethnology, Bul. 30,* I, 63.
[2] Alfred Barnaby Thomas, *After Corondo,* 7.
[3] *Ibid.,* 7-8.
[4] *Ibid.,* 11-12.

grapes.'' North of Raton they cultivated "corn, frijoles, pumpkins and cherries.'' At El Cuartelejo, north of the Arkansas River, the fare was buffalo meat, roasting ears of Indian corn, tamales and plums. The Pawnees, with French, had just attacked Quartelejo. These Indians had just killed a white man and woman, captured fowling pieces, white men's clothes, French iron axes, guns, and the foot of a gilded silver chalice.[5]

And now, the full fury of a tornado struck suddenly upon the Apache homeland. Lured by that greatest of prizes, the horse, and the promise of booty, the Comanche swept suddenly eastward across northern Colorado and southern Wyoming, turned southward when they reached the plains and appeared east of the Spanish settlements at the beginning of the eighteenth century.

This nation is the southern branch of the Shoshonean linguistic stock. Some authorities state that they were forced south by Siouan pressure,[6] but their migration was so rapid that it resembled more the nature of a Tartar raid.

Bold, daring, and savage fighters, they attacked the more inoffensive Apaches like wolves. With them were allied, at first, the Shoshonean Utes.

When, in 1719, Governor Valverde traveled northward to El Cuartelejo, he found the various Jicarilla bands in full retreat, and, in 1748, Governor Rabal testified that the Comanche had completely driven the Jicarilla from their ancient homelands.[7] In less than fifty years, Apache civilization in Colorado was destroyed by the raiders. The resident Spanish governors, without exception, foresaw what was to come and repeatedly urged establishment of Spanish outposts to the north and east of Taos to keep the Apache as a buffer nation against expected French aggression but, at that time, New Mexico was ruled from Spain and the royal exchequer was first in the minds of the Viceroys.

With the Apache driven back upon the Spanish settlements, the Comanche now moved into full possession of eastern Colorado. On the Cimarron were (using Spanish appellations): the Cuchenac Comanches (buffalo eaters); north of the Raton mountains, or Sierra Jicarilla, were the Comanche Yupes (people of the woods); and north of the Arkansas were the Comanche Yamparica (root eaters, a name derived from their use of the edible root of the Yampa plant, *Carum gairdneri*). Apparently, not all of the Comanche had made the migration because, in 1776, Escalante reported the Comanche Yamparica still on the present Yampa River in northwestern Colorado.

The Comanche now redoubled their attacks upon the Spaniards. Their chief booty was in horses and mules, and their raids came from north, east and south. Governor Mendinueta, in 1773, pursuing Comanche raiders, accidentally surprised thirty of them driving a herd

---

[5] *Ibid.,* 17.
[6] Hodge, *op. cit.,* I, 327.
[7] Alfred Barnaby Thomas, *Forgotten Frontiers,* 58.

Little Raven

(Arapaho)

Buckskin Charley

(Ute)

Black Kettle

(Cheyenne)

Ignacio

(Ute)

of two hundred stolen horses, near the Rio de los Conejos (San Luis Valley).[8]

The weak efforts of the Spanish governors, for which they cannot be entirely blamed because the parent country refused them adequate troops and money, bade fair to lose New Mexico. However, at the critical point, Governor Juan Bautista de Anza, founder of San Francisco, was sent to New Mexico to save the situation. This able soldier and statesman, within ten years, broke the power of the Comanche and then sealed them to Spanish allegiance with a brilliant series of maneuvers worthy the best traditions of Spain's colonial rule. The first step in this strategy was worked out upon Colorado soil.

In 1779, Anza led an expedition into the San Luis Valley in pursuit of the Comanche raider, Cuerno Verde (Green Horn). This bold leader, who had hated the Spaniards since they had killed his father, had his rancherias on the Colorado plains in the vicinity of the Arkansas River.

Anza's expedition reached South Park, where he turned eastward and crossed the Sierra del Almagre south of Pikes Peak. He destroyed Cuerno Verde's home village near the present Wigwam, Colorado, learning, as he had calculated, that the Indian chieftain was then on a raid against the Spanish settlements in New Mexico. He met the Indians on their return near present Rye, Colorado, killed Cuerno Verde and his four principal chiefs. With great sagacity, he did not pursue the defeated warriors.[9]

Returning to Santa Fe, Anza set in motion a plan to make a lasting peace with the Comanches. He selected, as the key figure among his enemies, Ecueracapa (Cota de Malla), a Cuchenac Comanche, recognized by the Indians themselves as the ablest leader. At a council of northern Comanche bands at Caso de Palo, Rio de Napestle (Arkansas River) he was elected their representative.

There are some remarkable points of similarity between this able chieftain and Ouray, the great chief of the Utes, who came into prominence a century later. Each became a great peace chief. Each was a statesman of the highest order. Each was able to maintain command over the diverse bands of his nation. Neither would brook rebellion among his followers. When Toroblanco, a chief of the Yamparicas, refused to be bound by the agreement, Ecueracapa led an expedition against him and killed the malcontent.

In 1786, Anza completed a treaty with the Comanche, which provided for joint action against the southern and eastern bands of the Apache, more warlike than the now half-sedentary Jicarillas. An annual trading fair was established at Pecos, where the Comanche brought hides, meat and tallow, and horses.

Ecueracapa was appointed Commissioner General for his nation, a position similar to that given Ouray of later date by the United States government. Anza's own staff of office was loaned the

[8] *Ibid.*, 62.
[9] *Ibid.*, 67, 68.

Comanche chieftain, who sent it by special envoy to all Comanche bands as proof of his Spanish title and perogatives.[10]

Equally important was the conclusion of a treaty between the Comanche and Utes, who had broken their former friendship. Had not Mexico soon after freed itself of the strong arm of Spanish rule, this treaty might well have changed the history of Colorado.

At the close of the Eighteenth Century, some one hundred years after the great Comanche migration, the emphasis again shifted to the north. The first noticeable movement, insofar as Colorado is concerned, came from the headwaters of the Missouri and the Yellowstone. Some time prior to 1800 the Kiowa nation began to infilter the Colorado plains region. This tribe is the mystery nation of Western America, as it represents a distinct linguistic stock. Always notable raiders and savage fighters, they had been noticed in early Spanish records as early as 1732.[11] These Indians moved down from the mountains, probably under Siksika (Blackfoot) pressure and formed an alliance with the Crows. Lewis and Clarke reported them on the North Platte, while Pike, in recording the story of James Pursley, related that 2,000 Kiowas and Comanches had encamped in South Park in 1803, driven into the mountains by the Sioux.[12] The Kiowas have been close confederates of the Comanches since 1795.[13]

Closely associated with the Kiowas were the Kiowa Apaches, a small Athapascan tribe, mentioned by La Salle as the Gattacka in 1781 or '82, as living south of the Pawnees and supplying the latter with "horses which they probably steal from the Spanish in New Mexico."[14] This was seventy years before the first mention of the Kiowa. This tribe was not related to the Apaches of the Southwest.

Almost coincident with the appearance of the Kiowa in Colorado was that of the Arapaho, a plains tribe of the Algonquian family. According to their traditions they were once a sedentary, agricultural people who lived near the Red River Valley of northern Minnesota.[15] Originally, the Atsina (Gros Ventre of the Prairie) had been an integral part of this nation, but had separated to become known later as an associated band of the Blackfeet.

Thus, early in the Nineteenth Century, the Indian map of the Colorado plains region would have shown: east of the mountains and south of the Arkansas, Comanche, Kiowa and Kiowa Apache in close alliance; east of the mountains and north of the Arkansas, Arapaho and Cheyenne in close alliance. The arrival of the Cheyenne as Colorado home Indians may be dated almost with exactitude from contemporaneous reports.

10 For translation of this Treaty see Thomas, *Forgotten Frontiers.*
11 Hodge, *op. cit.,* I, 699.
12 Zebulon Montgomery Pike, *Exploratory Travels Through the Western Territories of North America* (Phila. Ed. 1810), Appendix IX to Part III, 16.
13 Hodge, *op. cit.,* I, 327.
14 *Ibid.,* I, 701.
15 *Ibid.,* I, 72.

In 1820 Major Stephen H. Long of the U. S. Topographical Engineers led an exploring expedition up the South Platte, southward along the mountains to the Arkansas, down this river to the vicinity of La Junta, where the expedition split, one party continuing to the Red River and the other returning by the Arkansas. Long reported that at the mouth of Grand Camp Creek (probably present Bear Creek south of Denver), four years earlier (1816) a band of Choteau and DeMunn traders had met with several bands of Indians: "Kiowas, Arapahoes, and Kaskaias" (probably Kiowa Apaches).

"They had assembled for the purpose of holding a trading council with a band of Shiennes (Cheyennes)." These last had been recently supplied with goods by the British traders on the Missouri, and had come to exchange them with the former for horses, "which they rear with much less difficulty than the Shiennes, whose country is cold and barren."[16]

When Long's expedition reached the Arkansas he found a band of Cheyennes living with the Arapahoes. This was the initial split that resulted in the North and Southern bands of this nation.

This highly important plains tribe of the Algonquian family derived its name from the Sioux word Sha-hi'yena. Its first authenticated habitat before 1700 was on the upper Mississippi and Red Rivers of Minnesota, where the Cheyennes lived in villages and were agricultural.[17] They were among the greatest warriors and horsemen of the plains; among the last to be subdued. Their standard for the chastity of their women was exceptionally high in Indian annals.

Cheyenne-Arapaho and Comanche-Kiowa relations were not uniformly friendly during the early years of the Nineteenth Century, but about 1840 a treaty was negotiated which established cordial cooperation. This was never broken.

Reference to migration trends of these later tribes indicates the pressure area which caused their southern movement—Minnesota. The immediate force that impelled the migrations was the great Siouan nation. However, back of this impulse again we find the white man. The French fur traders, supplying arms to the Chippewas, always at war with the Sioux, gave the former tribe that superiority of weapons which invariably prevailed. Under this pressure the Sioux, spreading westward and southward, forced weaker tribes to abandon their homelands.

The Siouan was the most populous linguistic family north of Mexico, next to the Algonquian. The name is an abbreviation of Nadowessioux, a French corruption of *Nadowe-is-iw,* a Chippewa name for the Sioux. In their own tongue the Sioux were the Dakota.[18] The Sioux were known to French missionaries by the middle of the Seventeenth Century, but their real emergence as a power was first given attention by Lewis and Clark, and by Pike during his expedition to the head of the Mississippi.

16 Long's Expedition, London Ed., II, 186.
17 Hodge, *op. cit.,* I, 577.
18 *Ibid.,* II, 577.

The Sioux spearhead that most affected migration to Colorado by the tribes already described, constituted the two great buffalo hunting divisions—the Tetons and the Yanctons—both already plentifully supplied with horses at the opening of the Nineteenth Century. The tip of the spear was the Brulè Teton, reinforced at a later date by the Oglala Teton, both of which caused the Pawnee much misery. These sub-divisions may almost be classed as Colorado Indians, as they ranged up the South Platte and as far south as the Arkansas with unimpaired freedom. On friendly terms at the time with the Arapaho and Cheyenne, they caused as much interruption to emigrant travel in northeastern Colorado as either of the other tribes mentioned.

Aside from the plains tribes and the mountain Utes, three other Indian nations should be mentioned. The Pawnees of the Platte and Republican Rivers were known to the Spaniards for two centuries because of their success in stealing horses from the Spanish settlements. Allied with the French in the eighteenth century, these raiders kept the Spaniards in a continual flurry of apprehension. Their attacks on El Cuartelejo, already mentioned, are instances. In 1819, they attacked and defeated the Spanish in an outpost near the Sangre de Christo Pass in Colorado.[19] The following year, Don Pedro de Villasur was dispatched to the Pawnee country with a large expedition in an effort to conclude peace—and learn the French strength. He and most of his command were ambushed and annihilated by these Indians near present North Platte, Nebraska.

The Pawnee confederacy consisted of four bands of Caddoan stock that lived in permanent earthen lodges, cultivated corn, beans and melons and also engaged in buffalo hunts on the plains of Nebraska, Colorado and Kansas.[20] Although no Pawnee village site has been discovered on Colorado soil, the Republican Pawnee village was close to the Colorado line, and these Indians roamed throughout eastern Colorado for more than two centuries. They warred with all tribes about them, most of the time—Sioux, Comanche, Kiowa, Arapaho, and Cheyenne, and persisted with remarkable stubbornness, although not rated highly as warriors by their neighbors. Nevertheless, when used as scouts by the United States army, they proved themselves among the finest Indian soldiery that the army has ever had. A remarkable fact about them is that they never warred against the United States government.

In extreme northwestern Colorado, extending from the Utah line eastward to the Medicine Bow Range, were located the Eastern Shoshoni. This was part of the old Yamparica range. These Indians are distinctly to be classed as "home" Indians. Being of the same linguistic stock, they mingled with the Utes. The country described, however, was recognized Shoshoni territory, and was ceded by this tribe to the government by the Fort Bridger Treaty of 1868. Mention also must be made of the Navajo, who ranged southwestern

---

[19] *Colorado Magazine*, XIV, 81-85.
[20] Hodge, *op. cit.*, II, 213.

Colorado freely as far east as Pagosa Springs until comparatively recent date.

Of all Colorado tribes, however, the Ute alone has an unbroken record of residence for more than three centuries. This great division of the Shoshonean family formerly occupied the entire central and western portions of Colorado, the eastern part of Utah, including the Utah Valley and eastern Salt Lake Valley, much of the drainage area of the San Juan in New Mexico, and at certain times, the upper Cimarron.

Ute Indian Delegation from Colorado

Standing: Warency, Shavano
Sitting: Ancatosh, Ouray, Guerro

Today, it is the sole Indian tribe still remaining, in part, on Colorado soil. Its divisions are: Tabeguache, Moache, Capote, Wiminuche, Yampa, Grand River and Uintas.[21] Of these the Moache, Capote and Wiminuches remain on the Ignacio Reservation. In 1776, Escalante encountered them from the Rio Dolores to White River, and listed the bands as: Comanche Yamparicas, Sabuaganos, Yutas, Tabeguaches and Muhuachis.

On the whole, the Ute has acquitted himself well during his historical span. Able warrior and the best rifle shot among all American Indians, his potential for damage was enormous. Yet, as we consider his long record in retrospect, his infractions were minor. It is worth reflection that three of the ablest peace chieftains in American history—Ecueracapa, the Comanche; Ouray, the Ute, and Washaki, the Shoshoni—all stemmed from Shoshonean stock, although Ouray was of mixed Ute and Jicarilla blood.

The successive steps by which the major part of Colorado's Indian population was removed from the state by the federal government reveals an entirely different philosophy than that of the Spaniard in the treatment of the Indian problem. The Spaniard,

---

21 *Ibid.*, II, 875-6.

on the whole, used conciliation and appeasement. The Anglo-American used ruthless force.

The Treaty of Fort Laramie, 1851, recognized the Arapaho and Cheyenne claim to all Colorado land, east of the Rockies and north of the Arkansas. It recognized also the Comanche-Kiowa claim to southeastern Colorado, south of that river and east of the Rockies.[22] The Treaty of Fort Wise, 1861, forced the Arapaho and Cheyenne to cede all their lands except a small reservation adjacent to the Arkansas River. But the Treaty of Medicine Lodge, 1867, transferred them to a new reservation in then Indian Territory. The above statement refers to the Southern branches of the respective tribes discussed, as the two nations by that time had split into permanent Northern and Southern divisions.

The Treaty of the Little Arkansas, 1865, forced cession of all Comanche-Kiowa lands north of the Cimarron, but the Treaty of Medicine Lodge likewise confined these Indians to Indian Territory.

The first Ute cession was encompassed at Conejos in 1863, when the Tabeguache ceded the entire San Luis Valley. However, the Moache, Capote and Wiminuche chiefs refused to sign this treaty. It was not confirmed by the United States senate, but in a practical sense went into immediate effect.

Kaneache, a Moache chieftain, who ranged from the Cimarron northward to the Cucharas and Huerfano rivers, was ringleader in the opposition. In 1866, he and his followers raided settlements along the Cucharas and upper Huerfano. Ouray, then just coming into prominence, led his band across the mountains, captured Kaneache and his band, and returned with them to the San Luis Valley, where he turned the rebels over to Kit Carson. Two years later, in 1868, the basic terms of the Treaty of Conejos were reenacted in Washington, chiefs of all Ute bands, including Kaneache, joining in the cession. The final Northern Ute separation from their homelands came in 1880, after the Meeker and Thornburg massacres. The following year General Mackenzie escorted the Uncompahgre, (Tabeguache) White River and Yampa bands to their new reservation in the Uinta Basin, Utah. Only the Southern Utes—the Moache, Capote and Wiminuche—now remain on the Ignacio Reservation.

The Eastern Shoshoni claim to present Moffat, Routt and Jackson counties was recognized in the Treaty of Fort Laramie, 1851, but the Treaty of Fort Bridger, 1868, deprived them of this territory. The Jicarilla had long ceased to be a factor when the Pikes Peak gold rush occurred, although a few remnants still were to be found in the Raton Mountains and vicinity. After many vicissitudes, these Indians finally came to rest on the Tierra Amarilla Grant in Northern New Mexico. They are of mixed blood, having absorbed much Pueblo and Ute infusions through intermarriage.

---

[22] For this and other treaties mentioned see Charles J. Kappler, *Indian Laws and Treaties.*

Thus, in less than thirty years, the Anglo-American solved the Indian problem in Colorado. It was not entirely to his credit.

Customs and Manners

Discussion of Indian life, in the space allotted, can be general only. All Indians of the United States proper, were stone age people.[23] They fashioned tools of stone for four basic purposes: to strike, to throw, to cut and to bore. They made implements of bone and wood. They built houses of stone, wood, mud or skins. They made clothing of skins or vegetal materials. They believed in a life after death, and their religious beliefs, centering upon the food problem, were strongly tinged with animism. All followed war and the chase; some practiced agriculture.

Indeed, the only basic difference was found between the nomad, following the game animals with his moveable habitations; and the sedentary peoples, living in stationary abodes, and planting crops. It was not unusual for one nation to change from the sedentary to the nomadic life, or *vice versa*. The Cheyenne and the Jicarilla Apache, as we have pointed out, are examples of this truth. Of course, all Indians made use of certain roots and wild fruits to obtain a balanced diet, or for medicinal purposes, but this cannot be classed as a true agricultural pursuit.

Excepting the Jicarilla and Pawnee all plains and mountain tribes of Colorado were nomads, living by the chase. What follows then applies to the Indians who lived in portable skin lodges, and depended for their main food supply upon the buffalo, the antelope, the elk and the deer.

The buffalo was the great game animal of the Indian. These beasts were not confined to the plains area alone, but were found in the elevated mountain parks of the state. South Park, the *bayou salado* of the French fur traders, was a famous hunting ground, frequented both by the mountain Utes, and by the plains Arapaho, Kiowa, Cheyenne and Comanche; hence a contested battle area between the tribes. The same was true of the San Luis Valley and North Park. When the animals were scarce in these parks, the Utes would sally forth upon the plains to lay in large supplies of meat. Conversely, the plains tribes visited the mountains to obtain lodge poles and buckskin.

The wedge of prairie between the Arkansas and South Platte, from the Rocky mountains into western Kansas, was one of the finest buffalo ranges in the West. This led to continual intertribal warfare on the plains of Eastern Colorado. To complicate this situation, introduction of the horse by the Spaniards resulted in innumerable horse-stealing expeditions along the base of the Rockies; so much so that early western travelers and early fur traders called this strip the "great war road" of the Indians. There are frequent

---

[23] The possible exception were the Mound Builders who had some metal implements, which may have been the result of early European contact.

references in early records to war and horse-stealing parties, not only of resident tribes, but of bands from the Pawnee, the Sioux, the Crow, the Shoshoni and the Gros Ventres.

Much of the Indians' existence was taken up by the Buffalo. Tribal hunts were staged during the summer and fall, to provide daily food and to store food for the winter months. These hunts were under strict supervision of the tribal council, and were preceded with ceremonies to propitiate the gods of the hunt. A master of the hunt was appointed, whose word was law. Certain of the older warriors were designated as soldiers to see that the inviolable rules of the hunt were followed. Each Indian brought forth his buffalo runner, a horse as wise as the Indian himself in following the buffalo and keeping his master and himself out of danger. Woe to the young brave whose eagerness led him to violate the prescribed rules. A soldier might shoot his steed from under him, break his weapons or lash him with a whip. Such punishment was never resented. With the hunters in position, the drive began. Horses carried their riders to the side of a laboring beast. The arrow sank to the feathered end and the horse drew away to find another target. Squaws, boys and untried warriors followed upon the heels of the hunters, skinning and dressing the animals. The veteran hunters took no part in this work, but the hide and the choice portion were his. The remainder of the animal was divided between the butchers in the order of their arrival. It was an easy matter to identify the Indian whose arrow dealt the mortal blow, for each warrior painted upon his arrow shafts consecutive bands of various colors, his own identification.

In skinning, the animal was turned upon its stomach, split down the back and dismembered with knives and hatchets. Nothing was wasted. The large sinews were saved for thread, used in sewing garments. The stomachs became water bags. The intestines were eaten, raw or roasted, or were stuffed with minced meat or tallow to facilitate transportation.

Upon conclusion of the hunt the entire village celebrated with dances giving thanks for success. It was the duty of the squaws to cut up and preserve the meat. This was cut into thin strips, dried on racks in the sun, or smoked over slow fires. The dried meat was then packed in rawhide bags, called parfleches, and would keep for months. Pounded into a powder with stone pestles, mixed with tallow and cherries, the meat became pemmican. This also kept for long periods. A great delicacy was the marrow.

Before the Indian obtained the horse various devices were employed to trap large numbers of buffalo. They might be driven over the edges of steep arroyos, or caught in deep snowdrifts. But artificial barriers also were constructed. An excellent description of such an event is contained in the Journal of Rudolph Friederich Kurz,[24] while acting as clerk at the fur post of Fort Union:

[24] Rudolph Friederich Kurz, *Journal*, B.A.E. *Bul. 115,* pp. 145-6. Kurz was a Swiss artist from Bern, who spent the years 1846-52 on the Mississippi and Missouri rivers, serving as clerk at Forts Berthold and Union.

"On the ground suitably chosen for the purpose, they [the Indians] throw up a widespread, circular enclosure of heavy logs and dried boughs. They leave a small opening through which the park is entered. They then set up two rows of stakes that diverge from either side of this entrance and thus form, when completed, a passageway of sufficient width for a herd to pass through. As soon as the hunters are aware of a nearby herd, one of them disguised as a buffalo, goes out to meet it, and by imitating the cry of a calf, by bellowing, by shaking his buffalo robe, and resorting to all sorts of motions endeavors to attract the attention of the animal nearest him, and then approaches by slow degrees the entrance to the park."

Curiosity then led the animals into the trap. If the hunter, however, made some bungling movement and scared the herd he lost his reputation as a skilled huntsman. Once in the entrance, hunters on horseback rushed the herd. The decoy was not permitted to leave the park until he had reached the medicine pole in the center, presented his buffalo robe as an offering and suspended various decorations. All then became quiet while the warriors killed the animals with arrows and spears. Only then the squaws entered the enclosure with knives, washed themselves in the gore, drank warm blood and proceeded with the butchering.

Skins taken in the summer and fall were immediately stretched and dried in the green state. Upon return to the village, dressing was done when convenient. The hide was pegged upon the ground, the dried flesh and fat removed with an adze-like instrument, and the hide thinned. The surface was then plastered with the brains or liver of the animal, and a warm meat broth poured over it. When dry, it was again subjected to the action of brains and broth, stretched in a frame and, while still wet, scraped with pummice stone, sharp stones or hoes until perfectly dry. If not yet pliant it was pulled back and forth over a twisted sinew, or stretched and pulled by two or more squaws.[25]

One brain was sufficient to tan the hide of any animal. Skins intended for lodges, leggings, dresses and summer moccasins were adzed on the hair side instead of the flesh side. Skins desired for bed robes, winter robes and moccasins, were taken during the late winter hunt, ending in April, when the hair was prime. This hair was not removed.

Buffalo dances formed an essential part of the hunting ritual. The dancers wore buffalo masks made of the head, with horns attached, and fastened the tails to their belts in the back. The performers imitated in the most natural manner "the way that buffaloes drink, the way they wallow, how they jostle and horn one another, how they bellow."[26]

---

[25] Reuben G. Thwaites, *Early Western Travels*, I, 312, 313.

[26] Kurz, *op. cit.*, 66.

Many tribes had a great annual buffalo dance before the summer hunt began. This was also, as was the custom in many other Indian dances, a dance devoted to the life principle of procreation, and involved unnatural practices.

The horse divided with the buffalo the most important position among all animals in the eyes of the plains Indians. He gave to the Indian an amazing mobility, greatly reduced the labor of moving camp, simplified his problem of gaining food, and speeded his war activities. The horse herds usually were four or five times in number the human occupants of the village. These animals also furnished a major article of trade, and were the most valuable chattels of the Indian. During the fur trade days a horse would bring ten tanned buffalo robes. The owners often bestowed more finery upon the animals than upon themselves. They hung their most precious articles, obtained from white traders, upon the horses' chests, and interwove eagle feathers in their manes and tails. When one considers that, for designating a coup, only the tail feathers of an eagle were used, this fact indicates the regard of the Indian for his horse. An eagle has only twelve tail feathers, and the tail of an eagle cost as much as a horse.[27] The Indians never shot one of these birds at a distance but caught it by concealing themselves in pits, covered with brush and surmounted with a piece of carrion. When the bird lit, he was seized by the legs, jerked through the cover and killed with a knife.

Horses of chieftains were liberally decorated and smeared with painted designs in red or white paint. A hand designated a coup; a hoof-print, a stolen horse. The squaws also lavished much attention upon the horses, manufacturing elaborate, overall, beaded cruppers. The Crows, among the greatest of Indian horsemen—and horse thieves—often protected their horses' hoofs with shoes of buffalo hide.[28]

The Indians seldom went without saddles, except on their hunts. These saddles were of two general types. The Sioux, Arapaho, Cheyenne, Shoshone, Kiowa and other tribes of the great buffalo plains used a saddle with high pommel and cantle of the Moorish type. This, doubtless, was derived from the Spanish saddle. More northern tribes, such as the Crow, Assinaboin, Hidatsa, Mandan, favored what is known as the Crow type. This consisted of two pads, joined by a broad, heavy leather girth. A piece of buffalo skin was used as a blanket. This made a comfortable seat and did not gall the horse. Both types were fitted with stirrups, generally made of wood. The southern type of saddle was fashioned from forked limbs of trees, or elk horns, fastened together on either side with flat pieces of wood. Over this, rawhide was stretched tight, sewed and dried. Neither pegs, nails nor mortices were used, but the saddle would stand almost any abuse. A squaw could fashion one of these saddles in a very short time.

27 *Ibid.*, 182, 183.
28 Washington Irving, *Astoria*, 225.

Many depictions by artists and illustrators representing Indian attacks upon emigrants, show the Indian shooting from under the horse's neck, apparently hanging by his heel from the cantle—or from nothing at all. The trick really was very simple—for a good horseman. The Indian on such raids always had an extra loop of rope tied about the horse's neck. As he dropped over the side he shoved his right elbow through the loop, which bore the weight of his body, and shot as though riding in a swing. Another trick of the hunt was to tie a rope around the animal's neck and let it trail thirty to forty feet in the rear. If unhorsed, the rider had a chance to grab this rope and remount before the herd ran over him.

Life in an Indian village, while novel to white men's eyes, essentially was no different than that in the white man's town. Domestic labors, games, gossip, the hundred little incidents of daily life, all were there. This eye-witness account of a Cree village by an excellent observer,[29] who had many opportunities to witness similar scenes, might be applied to all such encampments:

> Around the various campfires men and young lads smoke or else stand beside their horses; boys and girls frolic among their many dogs; children play with puppies as though they were dolls, or carry them like babies on their backs beneath their blankets; the women employ themselves with their chattels, their tent poles, and their beasts of burden * * * There is a confused din of voices calling, beating of drums, strokes of an ax, crash of a falling tree, whinnying of horses, shooting of guns, and howling of dogs * * *. The place is enlivened by human figures; men walking about with majestic mien, some actively engaged, some idle; youths at their games, girls carrying water, women trudging in with wood, cleaning and scraping hides; horses grazing or tethered near their owners' tents, saddled for use; a multitude of dogs eager to steal something, chasing one another about, scampering away with some old bone, a piece of leather, or an ill-smelling rag * * *. There is no strife, no oath is ever heard.

> The incessant drum-beat, the howling of dogs, neighing of horses, now and then a loud call, are the only sounds that come across the sandbank from that village. There are neither harsh tones of dispute nor conflict, neither glad notes of song or yodel. Only the tattoo of the drum resounds, from beside a sickbed, the music of the montebank, not denoting joy. An Indian's ideal of enjoyment in the home is a feast; tobacco smoking is his diversion; dancing, his excess of indulgence in pleasure.

No Arabian sheik in his desert oasis ever was more hospitable than the Indian to visitors. The arrival was taken to the lodge of

---

[29] Kurz, *op. cit.*, 226, 227.

the chief, or of a leading warrior. The squaw busied herself at the fire, prepared meat, or a stew, and served the guest. The ritual of pipe-smoking followed and only then did the business of the visit come under discussion. The white trader hastened to make himself the guest of some celebrated soldier, placed his goods under that individual's protection and then relaxed with the knowledge that they were safe. Fur traders usually made rich gifts to some soldier of their acquaintance for this reason. At Fort Pierre, Kurz saw a soldier shoot a dog instantly as he was lifting his leg against a pile of goods.

Indian etiquette was strict and demanded that certain forms be observed. A party from one village did not ride unannounced into the village of another tribe. First, a messenger was sent to announce the impending visit. If this was from a friendly tribe, an appointment was made for the visit. The messenger returned, the waiting party opened parfleches, and the cylindrical rawhide containers used to carry feather bonnets. Beaded costumes were donned, bonnets adjusted, faces painted. Then, with measured pace, the visitors filed toward the village and were welcomed with loud shouts and many feasts.

On the other hand, the approach of an enemy threw the village into a turmoil. When this attack was not a complete surprise, it was usually heralded by outlying pickets, kept upon high hills in plain view of the village. Upon discovering an enemy the sentinel galloped forward and backward, then crosswise. But if the discovery was that of a buffalo herd, the pickets rode slowly up and down in a straight line, often throwing dust in the air.[30]

In either case pandemonium reigned. The council of chiefs and head men hurriedly assembled in the council lodge to plan the defense against an enemy. Warriors and young men leaped upon their horses and rode forward to reconnoiter, women shrilled and scolded children, dogs howled, weapons were taken from the tripods that stood before every lodge.

However, such contacts were accidental. The Indian always preferred the ambush, the night attack before dawn, the stealthy approach and rapid retreat with the enemy's horse herd bunched before. The Indian was brave, but he did not believe in useless sacrifice. War to him was a stratagem, a wily ruse, and success indicated craft and skill. Neither was it a credit to shoot an enemy at long range and ride away. To gain full acclaim and honor from the tribe, he must touch the body of an enemy. This represented the acme of courage and daring. Even though he merely touched a foe and inflicted no damage, this fact was counted a coup and could be recorded by another eagle feather, or painted symbol on his robe.

A war party, returning from a successful foray, always sent a runner ahead to announce the results and to allow suitable preparation for its reception. A mile or more from the village the war party

_____
30 *Ibid.*, 185.

halted, and waited until messengers brought to them their articles of personal finery and decoration. Much time, sometimes half-a-day, passed before each warrior was sufficiently painted and decorated to suit his fancy. Then with drumbeat and slow, measured pace, the war party rode toward the village. As they approached, mounted riders, women and children streamed forth. They shouted in glee at sight of the scalps waving from poles and lances carried aloft, or wailed and keened at news of the dead who did not return. The raiding party maintained perfect decorum. Upon the date set for the war dance, the whole village gathered about, women, children and dogs on the fringe, the elders seated in a circle at some distance from the medicine and scalp poles. At the base of these sat the medicine men in masks of bear or wolf, thrumming upon their drums. A low chant began and swelled. Maidens with blackened faces entered the circle to chant a victory song. Then, mounted on his favorite charger and bearing proudly aloft his lance, with scalps depending therefrom, some fortunate brave would ride slowly into the circle, curvetting his horse. In loud tones he would recount his feats, tell of the enemy killed, of the scalps taken, while the elders nodded solemnly in approval. Ending his harangue, he would wheel his horse violently, dash at full speed from the circle and head for the horizon as though overcome with modesty.[31]

Aside from hunting, war and horse-stealing the men did little because they considered labor beneath their dignity. Success in the theft of horses ranked high and due honor was accorded the raider. His feats in this respect were as carefully recorded as coups upon a human foe.

Around the village the warrior kept his weapons in order, made ornaments for his hair, took care of his horses and spent hour after hour telling tales of his exploits. The young boys and untested men listened to these deeds of glory with unwearying eagerness. It was in this manner that the elders instructed male children in tribal ethics and the warrior's code. Indians never punished their children physically, especially boys, as it was believed that this would break the martial spirit.

Indian women's duties were arduous and back-breaking, yet they knew no other life. Any woman who induced her mate to perform recognized women's labor was immediately unbraided by the other women, who scorned her for trying to turn her husband into a woman. Breaking camp and packing, raising the tipis, hauling wood, skinning and butchering the prey, tanning hides, making clothing, digging herbs and roots, cooking, caring for the children were among her multitudinous duties. The children alone were a tax upon her strength, since the Indian woman frequently nursed children until they were eight to ten years old.

A woman's recreation included chatting, gossiping, singing, dancing, painting and adorning herself, gambling and love affairs. She

---

[31] George Frederick Ruxton, *Life in the Far West,* 46-50. The scalp dance described here was witnessed by Ruxton in South Park. It was a Ute ceremony.

Cheyenne Indian Village

(Diorama in State Museum, Denver)

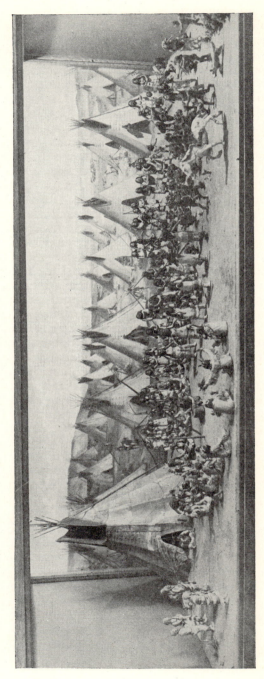

Ute Scalp Dance

(Diorama in State Museum, Denver)

had no voice in council and was not admitted to the council lodge with rare exceptions. In the Crow tribe, however, the women took voice in all discussion of tribal affairs and wielded great influence.

The marriage status was easily arranged and easily broken. An element of purchase entered into all negotiations for matrimony under the guise of presents. When the bargain was completed, man and maid simply went away and set up housekeeping. Among some tribes, notably the Navajo, a formal betrothal and ceremony by the shaman were included.

Polygamy was practiced to a large extent. A warrior taking more than one wife contrived to accumulate sisters, if possible, as this lessened the chance of discord. Women who left their husbands for new suitors generally were not pursued as this was deemed beneath the dignity of the injured husband. There were instances of conjugal vengeance, however. On the other hand, the warrior could cast aside the wife at his pleasure. This was noticeably so with the Sioux. The more successful hunter, indeed, needed more wives to take care of the skins he brought in. Mothers guarded their young daughters with vigilance until they were about fourteen, when the girl was considered ripe for marriage. The Indian dandy was a feature of all tribes. His beautifully tanned and beaded buckskins, his elaborate decorations and paint, his feather fan, marked him. The warrior looked with scorn upon this version of the modern "wolf," but these handsome young men were not without their conquests.

All Indians were passionate and desperate gamblers, men and women alike, and would stake lodges, horses, weapons, clothes upon a moment's notice. Men would sometimes bet their wives upon a turn of chance. Among the common gambling games none was more popular than "hand." This was merely the Indian version of "button, button, who's got the button?" It was played by two opposing groups seated in lines upon the ground. The object to be hidden might be a bit of wood, bone or stone passed back and forth by the group "in hand." To confuse the guessers, the party "in hand" would chant, yell, beat upon dry poles to make a loud noise and confuse the opposition. The excitement often became so intense that perspiration would roll from the faces and shoulders of the contestants.[32]

A favorite woman's game was double-ball, a sort of shinny with two balls fastened together with a thong. Dice was played with plum stones, pieces of bone or stones, marked with dots, transverse lines or triangles, and placed in a basket. The leader took this basket in one hand, shook it, bounced it sharply upon the ground and caught the dice as they fell. Upon the number of dots, lines or triangles uppermost, depended the amount won.[33]

A favorite game of the men was the arrow-game, in which turns were taken in shooting at a peeled wand or arrow. But to men and women alike, the grand passion was horse-racing.

---

[32] Washington Irving, *The Adventures of Captain Bonneville*, 265.
[33] Rufus Sage, *Rocky Mountain Adventures*, 181.

The basic food among both the plains and mountains Indians of Colorado was meat. Indians preferred the red meat of buffalo, elk, deer, antelope, mountain sheep. Fish and birds were not eaten unless no other food was available, while the Navajo never touched fish because spirits of certain ancestors dwelt therein.

To balance the diet the women gathered many kinds of roots, chokecherries, wild plums and berries. Among the southern Indians of Colorado, including the Utes, fruit of the yucca, mesquite beans and pinon nuts were added. This vegetal food, as well as dried meat, was pulverized in stone mortars with stone pestles.

Due to their close contact with the Pueblos, the Jicarillas employed a far greater range, including true agricultural crops. Major Long mentions the use of "intoxicating beans" by the Kiowa in 1820. This was the mesquite bean, from which the tribe mentioned had brewed an intoxicating liquor.

The buffalo Indians of the western plains understood the principles of agriculture but disdained to practice it. They preferred to enjoy its benefits through theft or trade. However, the river tribes who lived in permanent earth or grass lodges—the Siouan Hidatsa, Mandan, Omaha, Oto, and the Caddoan Pawnees, for illustration—were adepts as Indians go. They planted corn, pumpkins and melons along the sides of ravines, cultivated the soil with wooden or bone hoes, stored corn by burial underground. This crop usually was gathered before it was quite ripe, boiled, cut from the cob and dried. Hominy is an Indian invention. Pumpkins were cut into strips, dried in the sun and then woven into mats for convenience of transport. Women and children cultivated the crops among the nomadic tribes. Major Long reported: "Some of the young females were accompanied by a jolly young man as a protector."

Great ingenuity was displayed by the Indian in the manufacture of implements from almost any material at hand. Common stone implements, produced by a slow and painful process of chipping, flaking or grinding, included spear and arrow-points, axes, hammers, mauls; scrapers, fleshers and knives; drills, paint slabs, war-clubs and pipes. The jewel of great price was the pipe of Catlenite, or the red pipe-stone from the great quarry in Minnesota. The distance to which these pipes traveled through trade-routes, as well as the presence of various sea-shells, especially the prized nacre, testifies to the ability of the Indian as a trader.

Bones of animals and birds were widely used as implements, particularly in the manufacture of fleshers, awls, perforating tools and beads.

Wood was employed in the manufacture of saddle frames, perforators, platters, spoons, stirrers, spear shafts, lodge-poles. The latter were, preferably, slender lodge-pole pines twenty feet or more in length. When not supporting the lodge, these were fastened in bundles, on either side of a horse, crossed over the neck and tied. Behind the animal, the bundles were held in place by rawhide thongs and held tipi covers of buffalo hide, woven willow baskets in which very young children rode, chattels and traps of the women. The common term for this conveyance was *travois,* derived from the French fur trappers. The conveyance was in use when the Spaniard first penetrated the Southwest and the only draft animal was the domestic dog. Wood also was used as the basis for baby-carriers, covered with soft buckskin, elaborately decorated with quill or beadwork, and carried upon the mother's back. The plains tribes were not basketmakers, but had a very crude type of pottery. The Pah-Utes, however, made excellent baskets, while the mountain Utes of Colorado, during their early history, made baskets of inferior technique to a lesser degree.

The Indians were excellent tanners, especially the Utes. For lodge-covers the tough, durable buffalo hide was sought. The favorite skins for articles of clothing were those of the deer and the antelope. Well-plaited ropes, kept pliable with grease, were made of buffalo hide, although horse-hair also was used. Parfleches of rawhide, painted in geometrical design, were manufactured to carry food, articles of clothing, beadwork or gifts. The Indian was an inveterate ''giver,'' although a gift carried a strong moral obligation to return the favor.

Like all primitive races, the American Indian had an instinctive genius for color harmony. Nowhere was this employed to better advantage than in quill and beadwork. Before the introduction of manufactured beads by white traders, the Indians used dyed porcupine quills. This involved great skill and produced beautiful effects. The first Spaniards coming to the New World introduced large, glass Venetian beads. The small beads on dress and moccasins today first became available through traders about one hundred years ago. Beads of native material made by the Indians themselves, and pendants, charms and plaques were made of shell, birds' bones, certain seeds, elk teeth, eagles' claws and bear claws. The Pueblos far surpassed the nomadic tribes in this craft, a very old one as evidenced by beautiful inlays of turquoise in native jet (cannel coal) found in prehistoric ruins.

Geometrical designs prevailed among all plains and mountain tribes, based upon the rectangle and triangle. The Sioux, particularly, evolved complex designs. However, the Northern Sioux, Missouri River tribes, the Caddoan Pawnees were addicted to floral design. Environment largely determined this.

Indians are all fond of personal adornment and each Indian had his small buckskin paint bag. Mineral paints were ground on small mortars. Ochre, hematite, kaolin and copperas were commonly used, but, in addition, many varieties of vegetable dyes were employed.

Smoking was an important factor in the Indian's social and ceremonial life and was entirely indigenous. This contribution alone has affected the entire world. The peace pipe, stem pointed alternately to the cardinal points of the compass, to mother earth and those above, has inaugurated every treaty made between Indian and white.

The Indians worshipped a supreme deity, residing in the sun.

Their religion was strongly tinged with animism. Animals and birds possessed souls as well as men. No hunt was inaugurated without propitiating the gods of the hunt; the bear, the wolf, the coyote, the mountain lion. Early in life the young man preparing himself to become a warrior would retire to a solitary place where, by fasting and self-mortification, he induced dreams and visions. The first beast or bird that appeared to him in his hallucinations became his personal medicine and remained so during the remainder of his life.

The Indian had an extensive mythology, built of legends of origin, good spirits, demons, miraculous events, which were passed down orally. Many of these tales had the beauty of Hellenic myths. Many dances, both ceremonial and social, were practiced by the nomadic tribes, but these never attained the elaborate ritual and the rhythmic perfection of Pueblo and Navajo dances. One of the most widespread ceremonial dances was the Sun Dance. In early days, the torture feature, through which the candidate for warriorship must pass, was practiced. The young brave was suspended from the medicine pole by buckskin thongs, slipped beneath the muscles of chest or back; or buffalo skulls were tied to wooden splinters inserted beneath these muscles. Before he could win the status of warrior he was compelled to break loose from these fetters. This torture sometimes resulted fatally. The rite was rife with mysticism, with the effort of primitive minds to understand and interpret the wonderful and often terrifying manifestations of nature. About 1880, the United States government stopped practice of the torture feature.

Music was an essential feature of these dances. Among the musical instruments employed, as among all primitive peoples, the drum was most important. Drums ranged from the one-side drum, known as a tambourine, to the large medicine and ceremonial drums, closed at both ends. The essential feature was the rawhide surface. War and signal whistles were made from the wing-bone of the eagle or turkey. Flutes were used, the Ute having two: one a wooden flute used in love-making, the other a bone flute used in the Sun Dance. The Utes also employed a rude fiddle, consisting of a notched stick, resting upon a resonator. The noise produced by rubbing this with a second piece of wood to imitate the growl of the bear, was realistic. This instrument, called a *morache,* was employed in the Bear Dance, symbolic of that animal's awakening after the winter hibernation; hence a ceremony symbolical of awakening life. This dance was peculiarly Ute. Bull-roarers, flat sticks whirled rapidly through the air on a string to produce a humming noise, were universally used, as well as rattles of gourds or rawhide.

The plains and mountain tribes did not have the gentile system. Their societies were military or social in character and often derived their names from animals. In every phase of Indian life the shaman, or medicine man, wielded great power. He was the agent that exorcised evil spirits and drove them from the bodies of the sick; he was the healer, with his herbs, his vile concoctions, his mystic chants; he was the invoker of favor from the gods of the chase; he could cast out evil spells. The medicine man was not entirely a monte bank. The Indians well understood the curative properties of certain herbs and roots: those that healed wounds; that served as emetics. He practiced rude surgery and bone setting. In all these arts the medicine man was supposedly a master.

A remarkable instance of this is related in the William N. Boggs manuscript[34] (State Historical Society records). Boggs, an associate of William W. Bent, part owner and builder of Bent's Old Fort on the Arkansas River, tells of a Cheyenne medicine man, called by the whites, "Lawyer," who found Bent with throat swollen by an infection. The latter's Indian wife had managed to keep the trader barely alive by feeding him broth through a quill. Lawyer gathered sand burrs, strung them on a piece of sinew, coated them with buffalo tallow and forced the string down Bent's throat with a stick, barbs pointing upward. Waiting until the tallow had melted, he jerked the string forth and removed the infected tissue. Colonel Bent recovered.

When we come to the final analysis, in justice we must admit that the American Indian has made a tremendous contribution to civilization. In general, he has been judged by two erroneous standards, both of which are based upon false emotional reactions. The first of these is the Fenimore Cooper conception of the noble redman. This conception was carried to ridiculous heights. After all, the white man found the Indian endowed with certain admirable qualities: hospitality, valor, ingenuity, a code of ethics to which he was faithful. But he was still a savage. The other conception was that the Indian was a diabolical fiend. The true judgment must be that he was merely a human being, reacting, according to his standards, quite naturally when deprived of his homeland and his means of livelihood. He learned, the hard way, that treaties, especially with the American, were made only to be broken and that, in white man's eyes, he had no rights.

Today, we have come to realize that civilization owes a great debt to the Indian. Among the few contributions he has made, we must acknowledge the impression he had made upon world agriculture and world trade. He gave to the world corn, potatoes and tobacco, to name only a few. In time to come his contribution to cultural life, especially to the arts, will be equally recognized.

---

[34] Manuscript of William M. Boggs, *Colorado Magazine,* VII, 45-69.

CHAPTER IV

The People of Colorado

COLIN B. GOODYKOONTZ
Professor of History, University of Colorado

WHO are the people of Colorado? In general, they are a blend—or at least a conglomerate—of many nationalities; they represent in their ancestry all parts of the United States and Europe—and to this extent at least are typically American. What are the ingredients? Take a big helping from the Middle West; add New Englanders and Southerners galore; season with Spanish-Americans from the Southwest; stir in a goodly number of English, Scotch, Irish, Welsh, Swedes, Germans, and Canadians; make room for some Slavs, Italians, Dutch, French, and Greeks; mix together in a mile-high melting pot, and the product is a thoroughly American compound. Not that the process of fusion has been completed; on the edges, more or less unassimilated, are many hundreds or even thousands of Indians, Negroes, Mexicans, and Japanese—many of whom perforce live a life somewhat apart from that of the great mass of the people of the state.

The United States has been called a "nation of nations," and perhaps, as Joaquim Nabuco, sometime Brazilian ambassador to this country, once said, its greatest contribution to civilization has been the way in which it has made it possible for people of many diverse and often antagonistic nationalities to live together peacefully in a new homeland and to form, through their voluntary fusion, a new race of mankind.[1] In this process Colorado has shared fully.

POPULATION

As to the number of its people, Colorado has never ranked high among the states of the Union. Its population according to the census of 1860 was 34,277. This figure needs an explanation. What is now Colorado was in that year divided among the four territories of Kansas, Nebraska, New Mexico, and Utah. What was called the Territory of Colorado in the 1860 census was really only the western end of the Territory of Kansas; it was bounded on the north by the fortieth parallel, on the south by the thirty-eighth, and on the west by the "summit of the Rocky Mountains." This was the most important part of the Pikes Peak country at the time, since it embraced such "cities" and mining camps as Denver, Golden, Russell Gulch, Central City, California Gulch, Tarryall and South Park.[2] That part of present-day Colorado which lies north of the fortieth

---

[1] Joaquim Nabuco, "The Share of America in Civilization," *American Historical Review,* XV, 54-55.

[2] *Population of the United States in 1860; Compiled from * * * the Eighth Census* (cited hereafter as *Eighth Census (1860): Population*), 548.

parallel and east of the continental divide was then in Nebraska, and was included in the Nebraska census reports for 1860. Its population (Boulder, Gold Hill, Platte and Cache la Poudre Valley settlements) numbered 1,401.[3] The San Luis Valley was a part of Taos County, New Mexico, and contained in 1860 more than 2,500 inhabitants (Conejos, 1,512; Culebra District, 1,029).[4] The land west of the continental divide was then in Utah, but no returns for the "Colorado" mining camps on the western slope (Breckenridge, French Gulch, and Negro Gulch) were included in the published Utah report for 1860;[5] their population may be estimated conservatively at three hundred in the summer of that year. Thus the total population, known and estimated, of what is now Colorado was around 38,500 in 1860. But whether we take the figures for the restricted or the enlarged Colorado, it stood in 38th place among the states and organized territories, with only four lower in rank.

So uncertain was the future of Colorado during the decade between 1860 and 1870 that its population in the latter year was not much larger (39,864)[6] than it had been ten years earlier—and this despite the fact that by 1870 the four parts of the "Colorado" of 1860 had been put together to form the present political and geographical unit. In rank it had dropped to 41st place, but there were six other western territories below it. The decade of the 1870s by way of contrast was one of rapid growth: there were nearly two hundred thousand people in the new state in 1880 (194,327), and it had moved up to 35th place in the line. The population of Colorado more than doubled in the next ten years (413,249 in 1890); passed the five hundred thousand mark for the first time in 1900 (539,700); was slightly more than a million in 1930 (1,035,791); and totaled 1,123,296 in 1940. In relation to the other states, Colorado was in 31st place in 1890, 32nd in 1900 and again in 1910, and in 33rd according to each of the three succeeding census reports. In 1940 its population was slightly less than that of Nebraska on the one hand, but a little more than that of Oregon on the other. Perhaps the only practical significance of this ranking in relation to other states is the size of the delegation in the House of Representatives and the number of votes in the Electoral College. Under the present apportionment Colorado has four seats in the House. But if Colorado's rank is low, it can point with pride to the increase in its share in the total population of the nation. Comprising little more than one-tenth of one per cent in 1860, it had more than eight-tenths of one per cent of the total in 1940.

PLACE OF BIRTH: FOREIGN-BORN

As to place of birth, the population of Colorado has always been predominantly native—less so than the Old South, more so than the

[3] *Ibid.,* 559.
[4] *Ibid.,* 571.
[5] *Ibid.,* 574.
[6] *Ninth Census (1870),* I, 328.

industrial East—and has always shown a distribution by national origins much like that of the nation as a whole. This was evident in the first census in Colorado. In spite of the fact that gold camps usually attract a heterogeneous crowd and draw the adventurous from far and near, only 7.7 per cent of those caught by the census takers in the Kansas part of the Pikes Peak country in 1860 were not natives of the United States.[7] For the whole country in that year the percentage of the foreign-born was nearly twice as large, or 13.2 per cent.[8] The figure for Colorado rose to 16.5 per cent in 1870 and to 20.4 per cent in 1880. This was the highest point reached and may be explained by the Leadville mining boom of the period. The percentage of those of alien birth dropped slightly in 1890 (20.3 per cent); since then each census has shown a figure lower than that of the one that immediately preceded: 16.9 in 1900, 16.2 in 1910, 12.6 in 1920, 9.6 in 1930, and 6.3 in 1940. The figures for Colorado have varied more than those for the nation during the same period. Considerably less in 1860, more from 1870 to 1910, the percentage has been slightly less since 1920. Colorado has shared with the nation in the downward trend of the last three decades.

The Percentage of the Foreign-born in the Total Population

	Colorado	United States
1860	7.7	13.2
1870	16.5	14.4
1880	20.4	13.3
1890	20.3	14.7
1900	16.9	13.6
1910	16.2	14.7
1920	12.6	13.2
1930	9.6	11.6
1940	6.3	8.8

So far as numbers go there has been little cause for any anti-foreign agitation on the part of the native-born in Colorado. This is especially true since the state has always been sparsely populated. Indeed, in the 1870s, 1880s and 1890s, when those of the foreign stock were relatively most numerous, the empty state was fairly crying for settlers and workers.

---

[7] All Colorado population figures in the census of 1860 apply only to that part of the territory between the 38th and 40th parallels and east of the continental divide. The percentage of the foreign-born was approximately the same north of the 40th parallel (*i. e.,* in Nebraska). In Gold Hill 76 out of 490 were of alien birth; in Boulder City, 10 out of 177; in the Boulder Creek settlements, 6 out of 159. Statement based on an examination of photostatic copies of Nebraska census of 1860 in Library of State Historical Society of Colorado (S.H.S.C.).

[8] Summary of foreign-born in population, 1850-1940, in *Sixteenth Census (1940), Population,* II, Part I, 19.

Population per Square Mile

	Colorado	United States[9]
1860.............	0.3	10.6
1870.............	0.4	13.4
1880.............	1.9	16.9
1890.............	4.0	21.2
1900.............	5.2	25.6
1910.............	7.7	30.9
1920.............	9.1	35.5
1930.............	10.0	41.2
1940.............	10.8	44.2

Nor has there ordinarily been much cause for alarm among the natives over the origins of the aliens in the state. In general, local trends have followed those in the nation. Up to 1900 the foreigners came mainly from the north and west of Europe; since then there have been more from the south and east of that troubled continent.

In 1860, when the total number of foreign-born in Colorado—by which of course is meant only the Kansas end of the territory—was 2666, British America, especially the part we know as Canada, stood first with 684 persons;[10] Ireland was a close second with 624; the various German States came next with a total of 567, while England with 353 and Scotland with 120 were respectively in fourth and fifth places. Twelve other European countries were represented, but those who had been born within the British Empire made up more than two-thirds of the total.[11]

Ten years later, in 1870, the general distribution was much the same, except that the sons of Erin were the most numerous among the foreign-born (1685), followed closely by Germans (1456) and English (1359). Farther down the list, in order, were Canadians (753), French (209), Scotch (188), Swedes (180), and Welsh (165). More than four thousand of the 6599 aliens listed that year had been born under the Union Jack.

In 1880 first place among the foreign-born was held by those who had come from England (8799), with Ireland in second rank (8263) and Canada fourth (5785); the German Empire, which had only recently come into existence through the union of many German principalities and kingdoms, was third (7012). Scotland and Wales had contributed respectively 1673 and 1212 persons. In this year for the first time the Chinese stand fairly high in the list of foreign-

---

9 *Statistical Abstract of the United States, 1944-45,* 5.

10 The figures on the number of foreign-born in Colorado have been taken from *Sixteenth Census (1940), Population,* II, Part I, 711.

11 At Gold Hill in "Nebraska" 20 of the 76 foreign-born in 1860 were from the various German states; 15 were from England, 12 from Ireland, and 9 from Canada and Nova Scotia. In Boulder City 6 of the 10 of alien birth were from British North America. From photostats of 1860 census in Nebraska (S.H.S.C.).

born, being in ninth place with 601 listed. Here was a situation out of which trouble might arise—and so it did. So far there had been little cause for conflict among the various nationalities or between the foreign-born and the natives. To be sure, there was the usual chaffing and bragging; men too deep in their cups might engage in brawls occasionally; the Irish and the Welsh might "let off steam" by a jolly good fight now and then—all this was only what was to be expected in a frontier community where animal spirits ran high. But the appearance of the Celestials in increasing numbers, and exaggerated tales of the hordes to come, injected a disturbing element into the population. There were really not many Chinese in Colorado, but their presence created disturbances in 1880 quite out of proportion to their numbers—but more about this presently.

In 1890 former residents of Germany stood first among the foreign-born in Colorado (15,151). The English were a close second (14,407), and they with the Irish, Canadians, Scotch, and Welsh made up about half of those of alien birth (42,322 out of 83,990). The number of Swedes in Colorado was also increasing rapidly. In 1870 there had been 180 of these transplanted Northlanders; the number rose to 9,659 in 1890, and they then held fourth place among the foreign-born.

In 1900 as in 1890 the four top places were held by four nationalities of Northern Europe: Germans, English, Swedes, and Irish, in that order. But signs of the impending change in the character of immigration, the shift from the North and West to the South and East of Europe, were already appearing. Italy and Austria in 1900 took sixth and seventh places in the list, and Russia was in ninth place.

The census of 1910 gave clearer indications of this change: first place was still held by Germany, but Italy and Russia were respectively in the second and fourth ranks. England, Ireland, and Canada had each declined both in the number of their nationals represented and in their order in the list. For the first time Greece and Japan appear with significant numerical contributions (more than two thousand for each), while those of Mexican birth (2,543) ranked above these two.

In 1920 Russia was first in numbers (16,669) and Italy was second (12,579); Germany had dropped to third place (11,992) and Mexico had risen to fourth (10,894). Ten years later (1930) Mexico held first place, with Russia second and Italy third. In 1940 Russia was back in first, with Italy second, Germany third and Mexico fourth. It should be noted in passing that Russia's high standing in the list was due in part to the presence in Colorado of several thousand German-Russians, who, although they had been born in the Czar's empire, were German rather than Russian in blood.

By way of summary, it might be pointed out that three sections of the British Empire, Canada, Ireland, and England, had respectively held first place among the foreign-born in the census reports for 1860, 1870, and 1880; the German Empire was first in 1890, 1900, and 1910; since 1920 this distinction has gone to Russia twice (1920 and 1940) and to Mexico once (1930). Canada which led off with first place in 1860 dropped to fourth in 1870 and 1880, to fifth in 1890 and 1900, and to seventh in 1910. Ireland's ranking was second in 1860, first in 1870, second again in 1880, third in 1890, fourth in 1900, and since then has dropped, by stages, to tenth in 1940. England went from fourth in 1860 to first in 1880, down to second in 1890, back to third in 1910, and since then has held sixth place. Those of German birth occupied either third or second place from 1860 to 1880, first rank from 1890 to 1910, and since then, through the census of 1940, have been in either third or fourth place. The Russians, by which is meant of course those born in Russia, do not appear prominently in the list of foreign-born until 1890; in that year they were in thirteenth place. By 1910 they were in fourth place, in first in 1920, down to second in 1930, and back in first in 1940. The shift in the ranking of the Italians is a good indication of the changing character of immigration to the United States. In 1880 they were in fourteenth place in the list in Colorado; they were in seventh place in 1890, sixth in 1900, and from 1910 to 1940 they held second place three times and third place once.

PLACE OF BIRTH: NATIVE-BORN

The native-born in Colorado, exclusive of those born within the state, have come mainly from a compact block of states extending from New York and Pennsylvania on the east to Kansas and Nebraska on the west. In 1860 Ohio stood first in the number of transfers to the Pikes Peak country; Illinois, New York, Missouri, and Indiana followed, in that order.[12] But all parts of the country—New England, the deep South, and the Pacific Coast—were also represented.

In 1870 three significant changes appeared with respect to the place of origin of the native-born in the new territory: New Mexico took first place; Colorado itself was second; and there was a general decrease in the number of those who had come from the eastern states. The first of these changes is to be explained by the shifting of the boundaries of Colorado. In 1860, when the San Luis Valley was a part of New Mexico,[13] very few of the inhabitants of Colorado had been born in New Mexico. Exact information is not available from the published census reports, since all of the Coloradans who had been born in the Territories, of which New Mexico was one, were lumped together to make a total of 107.[14] In 1870, after the present boundaries of Colorado had been established, most of the Spanish-speaking population in the southern end of the territory probably reported New Mexico as their place of birth; the figure was 8,229.

[12] As usual, this generalization based on the census of 1860 applies only to the region between the 40th and 38th parallels. In Boulder City the numerical order was New York, Missouri, Illinois, Ohio, and Iowa.

[13] LeRoy R. Hafen, "Status of the San Luis Valley, 1850-61," *Colorado Magazine*, III, 46-49.

[14] *Eighth Census (1860): Population,* lxi, lxii.

FOREIGN-BORN IN COLORADO: Place of Birth

1860	1870	1880	1890	1900	1910	1920	1930	1940
Canada 684	Ireland 1,685	England 8,799	Ger. Em. 15,151	Ger. Em. 14,606	Ger. Em. 16,908	Russia 16,669	Mexico 13,125	Russia 11,185
Ireland 624	Ger. St. 1,456	Ireland 8,263	England 14,407	England 13,575	Italy 14,375	Italy 12,579	Russia 12,979	Italy 8,352
Ger. St. 567	England 1,359	Ger. Em. 7,012	Ireland 12,352	Sweden 10,765	England 12,926	Germany 11,992	Italy 10,670	Germany 7,017
England 353	Canada 753	Canada 5,785	Sweden 9,659	Ireland 10,132	Russia 12,757	Mexico 10,894	Germany 9,988	Mexico 6,360
Scotland 120	France 209	Sweden 2,172	Canada 9,142	Canada 9,797	Sweden 12,445	Sweden 10,112	Sweden 8,328	Sweden 5,844
France 103	Scotland 188	Scotland 1,673	Scotland 4,339	Italy 6,818	Austria 11,581	England 9,584	England 6,892	England 4,706
Wales 38	Sweden 180	Wales 1,212	Italy 3,882	Austria 6,354	Canada 9,562	Canada 7,660	Canada 5,848	Canada 4,194
Sweden 27	Wales 165	France 825	Austria 2,912	Scotland 4,069	Ireland 8,710	Ireland 6,191	Yugosl. 3,650	Austria 3,226
Mexico 25	Switz. 140	China 601	Wales 2,082	Russia 2,938	Scotland 4,269	Austria 5,722	Irish F. St. 3,184	Yugosl. 2,239
Switz. 25	Mexico 129	Switz. 551	Denmark 1,650	Denmark 2,050	Denmark 2,755	Scotland 3,357	Scotland 2,877	Irish F. St. 2,120
Denmark 16	Denmark 77	Austria 544	China 1,447	Wales 1,955	Mexico 2,543	Denmark 2,823	Poland 2,488	Scotland 1,883
Neth. 16	Austria 66	Denmark 507	France 1,328	Switz. 1,479	Greece 2,270	Yugosl. 2,109	Austria 2,468	Denmark 1,847
Norway 12	Poland 49	Norway 354	Russia 1,306	France 1,162	Japan 2,245	Czecho. 1,953	Denmark 2,375	Poland 1,796
Belgium 11	Norway 40	Italy 335	Switz. 1,255	Norway 1,149	Wales 1,989	Poland 1,867	Czecho. 1,714	Greece 1,049

Those born in Colorado, as reported in the census of 1870 (6,277), were obviously, except for some of the Spanish-Americans, mainly the children of those who had come to the Pikes Peak country since 1858. The drop in the number born in such eastern states as Ohio, New York, Illinois, and Missouri, reflected the return movement from the Rocky Mountains after the first excitement of the gold rush had died down. As pointed out above, after adjustments have been made for boundary changes, the population of Colorado in 1870 was only about one thousand more than it had been in 1860.

The next decade, 1870-1880, was a period of rapid growth. There were nearly five times as many people in Colorado in 1880 as there had been in 1870, and the grant of statehood in 1876 was one of the ways in which the nation took cognizance of this change. As to the state of origin, Colorado itself had taken first place according to the census of 1880; the percentage was not high, only about 13 per cent of the total, but it grew with each succeeding census until in 1940 about half the people in the state had been born within its limits. Another tendency was the decline in the relative numerical importance in Colorado's population of people from the Atlantic seaboard states on the one hand and on the other the increase in the number from middle western states, such as Missouri, Kansas, and Nebraska. From 1910 to 1930 Missouri was second only to Colorado as the birth place of Coloradans; in 1940 Missouri dropped to third rank while Kansas went into second place. Illinois, which had been in second place in 1890 and again in 1900, had dropped to sixth in rank in 1940. Noteworthy also in recent years has been the increase in the number of people who have moved from Oklahoma and Texas to Colorado. In 1920 these two states were respectively in the twelfth and thirteenth ranks in this category; by 1940 they had risen to eighth and ninth places. In general the states to the east and south of Colorado have contributed many more people to its population than have those to the west and north.

As to mobility of population, Colorado stands well above the national average. According to the census of 1940, 22.5 per cent of the people in the United States were living in some state other than that of their birth. But in that year 36.4 per cent of those who had first seen the light of day in Colorado had gone elsewhere to live; on the other hand 49.9 per cent of those living in Colorado had come in from some other state.[15] Colorado had gained more than it had lost: the in-migrants numbered 119,518, of whom 62,631 had come from contiguous states and 56,887 from the non-contiguous; the out-migrants were 110,406 in number, more than two-thirds of whom (80,115) had moved to non-contiguous states.[16]

DISTRIBUTION BY AGE, SEX, AND MARITAL STATUS

As to the distribution of the sexes, Colorado has always had more males than females. In 1860 the disproportion, as might have been expected in a new mining community, was excessive: 2,061.2 males for every 100 females in the Kansas end of Colorado. Obviously there were very few women in any of the new camps in Colorado, almost none in those that were most isolated. In California Gulch there were 2,000 males to 36 females; in South Park the numbers

---

[15] *Statistical Abstract of the United States, 1944-45,* 31.
[16] *Sixteenth Census (1940), Population: Internal Migration, 1935-40,* 17.

NATIVE-BORN IN COLORADO: Place of Birth

1860	1870	1880	1890	1900	1910	1920	1930	1940
Ohio 4,125	N. Mex. 8,229	Colo. 26,363	Colo. 79,486	Colo. 151,681	Colo. 233,516	Colo. 317,506	Colo. 419,563	Colo. 524,417
Ill. 3,620	Colo. 6,277	N. Y. 15,593	Ill. 28,196	Ill. 33,824	Mo. 50,729	Mo. 62,799	Mo. 65,769	Kansas 78,837
N. Y. 3,492	N. Y. 2,771	Ill. 12,993	N. Y. 23,964	Mo. 31,188	Ill. 49,964	Kansas 55,045	Kansas 63,849	Mo. 64,002
Mo. 3,312	Ohio 2,045	Mo. 12,435	Ohio 23,806	Iowa 24,960	Iowa 44,276	Ill. 51,432	Neb. 47,702	Neb. 57,714
Ind. 2,587	Ill. 1,805	Ohio 11,759	Mo. 21,952	Ohio 24,824	Kansas 37,356	Iowa 45,253	Ill. 46,940	Iowa 41,946
Ken. 1,861	Mo. 1,595	Penn. 11,387	Iowa 20,008	N. Y. 22,320	Ohio 30,573	Neb. 38,848	Iowa 45,556	Ill. 41,076
Penn. 1,405	Penn. 1,552	N. Mex. 9,501	Penn. 20,005	Kansas 20,864	Neb. 24,643	Ohio 26,026	N. Mex. 27,596	N. Mex. 26,182
Mass. 1,400	Iowa 1,308	Iowa 7,520	Kansas 13,265	Penn. 19,734	N. Y. 23,802	Ind. 20,974	Ohio 20,544	Okla. 25,520
Wis. 1,204	Ind. 808	Ind. 5,231	Ind. 12,596	Ind. 14,535	Penn. 23,596	Penn. 20,055	Okla. 18,201	Texas 19,597
Conn. 980	Ken. 656	Kansas 4,011	N. Mex. 9,331	Neb. 11,681	Ind. 21,219	N. Y. 19,515	Ind. 18,082	Ohio 15,733
Va. 868	Wis. 633	Wis. 3,910	Wis. 7,051	N. Mex. 10,222	Wis. 12,085	N. Mex. 16,212	Texas 16,525	Ind. 14,765
Tenn. 813	Mass. 618	Ken. 3,786	Mich. 6,844	Wis. 8,874	N. Mex. 11,992	Okla. 14,295	Penn. 16,090	Penn. 12,775
Mich. 806	Mich. 528	Mich. 3,654	Ken. 6,049	Mich. 8,094	Mich. 11,049	Texas 13,353	N. Y. 14,215	N. Y. 10,983
Iowa 797	Va. 467	Mass. 3,638	Neb. 5,661	Ken. 7,146	Ken. 10,103	Wis. 11,333	Ken. 10,681	Ark. 9,962

were 10,519 and 91; in the valley of the Platte 3,704 and 10. In Denver the disproportion of the sexes was not so great: 4,140 to 609; in Golden it was 893 to 121.[17] At Gold Hill, over on the Nebraska side of the line, there were 423 males and 65 females; in the Boulder Creek settlements the numbers were 238 and 86.[18]

---

17 *Eighth Census (1860): Population,* 548.
18 Photostats, census of 1860, Nebraska, in S.H.S.C.

Ten years later the ratio of males to females, although still abnormal, had dropped to 165 to 100; in 1880, at a time when the Leadville boom was on, the ratio rose to 198.1 to 100. Since then the curve of disproportion has dropped still further, at first sharply and latterly more gradually. In 1940 there were in the state 102.6 males for each 100 females; in the same year the ratio for the United States was 100.7 to 100.

Males per 100 Females

	Colorado	United States[19]
1860.	2,061.1	104.7
1870.	165.0	102.2
1880.	198.1	103.6
1890.	146.7	105.0
1900.	120.9	104.4
1910.	116.9	106.0
1920.	110.3	104.0
1930.	105.1	102.5
1940.	102.6	100.7

The Colorado population was abnormal also in the early days in its age distribution. In 1860 the occupants of the Pikes Peak mining camps were mainly young men. Of the 34,277 persons listed in the Colorado census of 1860 there were 770 under ten years of age, 1,313 between ten and twenty; 18,143 between twenty and thirty; 10,806 between thirty and forty; 2,712 over forty, eleven of whom were over seventy. A sampling of age groups in California Gulch showed that of the first 197 persons listed in the census returns there was no one under eighteen, and only five who had attained the age of fifty or over. The first two hundred counted in the South Park included no one under seventeen, but there were 52 over forty.[20] Of the 455 whose ages were noted at Gold Hill, 38 were under twelve and 17 over fifty.[21]

As the years passed and normal family life was established, the number of children increased at one end of the life span, while at the other the young grew old and the old grew older—or died. The 1940 census showed a pattern of age distribution much like that of the whole country, but with two significant deviations. Colorado had fewer between the ages of ten and fifty-five, and more over fifty-five. Why? Is it the wonderful climate that has added to the length of years? Or is it due to an old age pension system more generous than that of many of the states in the Union? Whatever the reason, those who believe that Colorado is too conservative in its political and social outlook may perhaps find here a partial explanation.

[19] *Sixteenth Census (1940), Population,* II, Part I, 694.
[20] Census of Arapahoe County, 1860, from typed copy in S.H.S.C.
[21] Photostats, census of 1860, Nebraska in S.H.S.C.

Age Distribution in 1940

	Colorado	United States[22]
Under 5	8.6%	8.0%
5–9	8.3	8.1
10–14	8.7	8.9
15–19	9.1	9.4
20–24	8.5	8.8
25–29	8.2	8.4
30–34	7.5	7.8
35–39	6.8	7.2
40–44	6.3	6.7
45–54	11.7	11.8
55–59	4.7	4.4
60–64	3.9	3.6
65–69	3.1	2.9
70–74	2.3	2.0
Over 75	2.3	2.0

As to marital status, the population of Colorado in 1940 did not deviate greatly from the national average. Since a slightly smaller percentage of Coloradans were single, it followed that somewhat more were married; the number divorced, both among men and women, was above the average for the country as a whole.

Marital Status (15 years of age and over)[23]

	Colorado		United States	
	Male	Female	Male	Female
Single	31.4%	22.5%	33.2%	25.8%
Married	61.9	63.1	61.2	61.0
Widowed	4.7	12.0	4.3	11.5
Divorced	2.0	2.4	1.3	1.7

RURAL AND URBAN

As was to be expected in a new and sparsely settled state, the population of Colorado, at least until the turn of the century, was more rural than urban. In 1860 about 14 per cent of the "Peakers" lived in "cities" (communities of 2,500 or over). The percentage dropped to 12 in 1870, a result of the temporary decline in mining on the one hand and the increase in agricultural activity on the other. After that the number of city dwellers grew until it crossed the half-way line in 1910 (50.3%). The percentage dropped back a bit in

22 *Sixteenth Census (1940), Population*, II, Part I, 10, 697.
23 *Statistical Abstract of the United States, 1944-45*, 45, 46.

1920, was slightly above the middle point in 1930 (50.2%), and again in 1940 (52.6%). In the United States the curve of urbanization has gone steadily upward since 1860 (from 19.8% to 56.5%); in Colorado the trend has likewise been upward, but in an irregular manner. Less urbanized than the average of the nation in 1860, Colorado went ahead in 1880 and remained so through 1910. It fell below the national average of city dwellers in 1920 and has remained slightly below in the census reports of 1930 and 1940.

Urban Population, 1860-1940

	Colorado	United States[24]
1860.............	13.9%	19.8%
1870.............	11.9	25.7
1880.............	31.4	28.2
1890.............	45.0	35.1
1900.............	48.3	39.7
1910.............	50.3	45.7
1920.............	48.2	51.2
1930.............	50.2	56.2
1940.............	52.6	56.5

MISCELLANEOUS CHARACTERISTICS[25]

Coloradans with criminal tendencies—there are such alas!—have a little more respect for life but a little less regard for property than the average law breaker in this country: they commit fewer murders and assaults but engage in more robberies, burglaries, larcenies, and thefts.

Crime Rates: Offences Known to Police in Urban Communities, per 100,000 Population, 1943

	Colorado	United States
Murder, non-negligent manslaughter	4.46	4.77
Aggravated assault	27.0	49.7
Robbery	67.5	45.3
Burglary, breaking or entering	488.7	300.9
Larceny, theft	1,261.4	829.4
Auto theft	194.0	187.8

Residents of Colorado who steal should not plead ignorance: they have been in school somewhat above the national average. In 1940 of all persons in the United States between the ages of 5 and 24, 57.7 per cent were in school; in Colorado 60.4 of this age group were

---

[24] *Sixteenth Census (1940), Population*, II, Part 1, 18.

[25] All data in this section have been taken from *Statistical Abstract of the United States, 1944-45*, 80, 83, 99, 226, 231, 274-75, 405.

Air View of Fort Collins, Showing the State College of Agriculture

so engaged. At the same time the median year of school completed for persons 25 years of age and over in the United States as a whole was 8.4; in Colorado it was 8.9.

On the other hand Coloradans might plead a greater degree of economic necessity since their average per capita income is below the national average. In 1941 when the figure for the United States was $693.00, in Colorado it was $620.00. Two years later (1943) the national average rose to $1,031.00; that of Colorado went up to $950.00. These figures would indicate that the inhabitants of the Centennial State should not—and they do not—pay income taxes as high as those paid by the average citizen of the United States. In 1941 Colorado, with .85 per cent of the population of the country, filed .69 per cent of the returns, received .66 of the net income, and paid .61 per cent of the tax.

Individual Income Tax Returns, 1941

	Colorado	United States
Average net income per return	2,161.48	$2,271.13
Average tax per return	130.81	148.06
Tax per capita, total population	20.73	28.87

Two certainties, we are told, are death and taxes. The "grim reaper" takes a slightly heavier toll per 100 of the population in Colorado than on the average elsewhere in the United States. From 1935 to 1939 the average in death-registration states was 11.0 per thousand; in Colorado it was 12.1. In 1943 the national average was 10.9; in Colorado it was 11.0.

If you are a Coloradan you are less likely to die of heart disease, cancer, tuberculosis, diabetes, or intercranial lesions of vascular origin (which is a long way of saying a "stroke"), than the average of your fellow countrymen; but beware of pneumonia, influenza, nephritis, and accidents.

Death Rates per 100,000 Population for Leading Causes of Deaths, 1943

	Colorado	United States
Diseases of the heart	274.3	318.3
Cancer and other malignant tumors.......	122.4	124.5
Intercranial lesions of vascular origin	83.1	95.0
Nephritis	75.5	74.1
Pneumonia and influenza	86.2	67.3
Accidents, excluding motor vehicles	75.1	56.1
Tuberculosis	40.5	42.6
Premature births	29.0	25.8
Diabetes mellitus	18.1	27.1
Motor vehicle accidents	18.5	17.8

At this point we may again ask the question: "Who are the people of Colorado?" Statistically, they are quite normal Americans. In comparison with their fellow countrymen, they are a little more "native," a trifle less urban, a bit more masculine, and a shade grayer. But the tables and charts behind these generalizations are too impersonal: Coloradans are first of all living men and women, boys and girls, with emotions, prejudices, beliefs, many of which are the product of their immediate social heritage, their racial and family backgrounds. The various groups presented above in numbers and percentages have all made their contributions to the richness and variety of life in a typical American state.

PERCENTAGE OF FOREIGN-BORN IN POPULATION

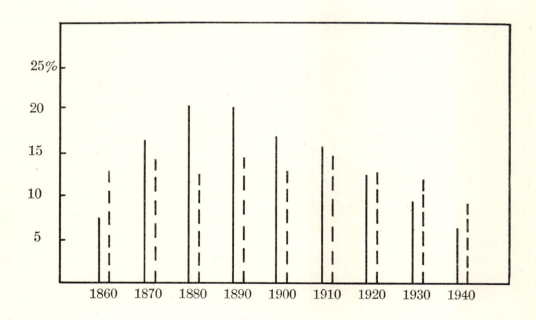

PERCENTAGE OF POPULATION
LIVING IN CITIES OF 2500 AND OVER

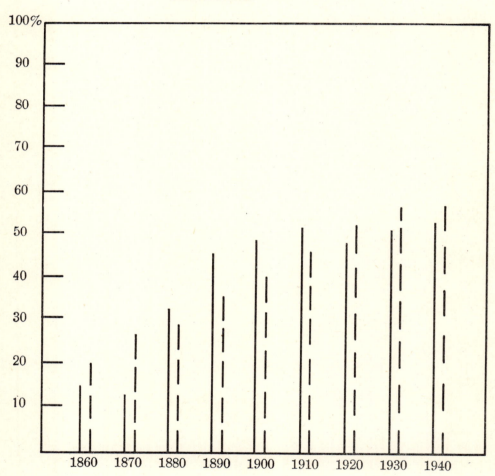

NUMBER OF FOREIGN-BORN IN COLORADO

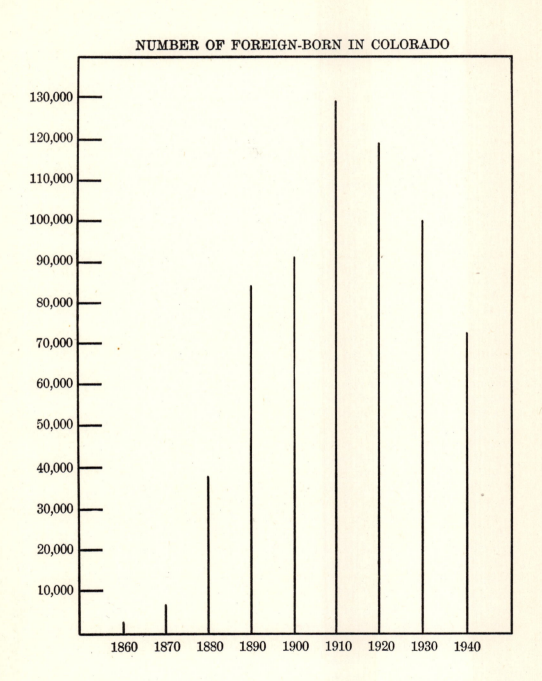

THE INDIANS

The first inhabitants of Colorado were the Indians. The principal tribes of the region when the whites came were the Arapahoes and Cheyennes on the plains and the Utes in the mountains, all told probably not more than 15,000 in number. Their warlike defence of their homes and hunting grounds retarded only slightly the white advance. Sand Creek, Beecher Island, and the Meeker Massacre are words which in Colorado history suggest an irrepressible conflict. Defeat for the red men was followed for most of the survivors by monotonous and depressing reservation life and a low economic and social status. In 1940 there were 1,360 Indians left in Colorado, 499 of whom were listed in Montezuma County and 402 in La Plata. There were at the same time 195 in Denver, and smaller numbers, ranging from 2 to 25, in 16 other counties. Many, probably most, of those scattered about the state had so completely taken up the white man's mode of life that they were hardly distinguishable from other citizens. It was not so with those on the reservations in Southwestern Colorado. There were two of these: the Southern Ute agency at Ignacio in La Plata County and the Ute Mountain sub-agency at Towaoc in Montezuma County.[26] "How have the mighty fallen!" exclaimed a man who went to live among these reservation Utes as missionary. They wore the white man's garb, spoke or at least understood a little English, farmed a bit but leased more of their land for grazing purposes, raced their horses for sport, and gambled a good deal for small stakes. Memories of the old culture were kept alive in the Bear Dance and the Sun Dance. The former had been intended to signalize the awakening of the bear from hibernation and the return of spring; the latter was a ceremony of worship for the sun, the personification of the Great Spirit.[27]

It would not be strange if these remnants of a once proud and powerful tribe, as they compared their present humble and miserable condition with the wild freedom of the old days, should reach the conclusion that the Great Spirit had turned his face from them. But they have only to look at a map of the state to see how the memory of Indian tribes and leaders has been kept alive in place names.[28] Among the counties of Colorado are Arapahoe, Cheyenne, Kiowa, Yuma, and Ouray; towns with Indian names include Manitou, Niwot, Ignacio, Saguache, and Amache; other geographical names with Indian connotations are Ute Pass, Uncompahgre Peak, Pawnee Creek, and Arikaree Creek. And then there are on the map the names of white men, such as Meeker, Kit Carson, and Chivington, who are remembered largely because of their relations, friendly or otherwise, with the Indians. So far as Colorado is concerned, it has not been true

[26] L. F. Schmeckebier, *The Office of Indian Affairs,* 303.

[27] James Russell, "Conditions and Customs of Present-Day Utes in Colorado," *Colorado Magazine,* VI, 104-112.

[28] On place names in Colorado see two articles by LeRoy R. Hafen in *Colorado Magazine,* VIII, 48-60, and IX, 170-183.

that "the only good Indian is the dead Indian." Still honored in the state are those Indian leaders, such as Ouray and his wife, Chipeta, Ignacio, and Buckskin Charley, who used their influence to bring about friendly relations between their people and the whites.

SPANISH-AMERICANS

The first men and women of European descent to settle in Colorado were the Spanish-speaking people who had moved north

(Courtesy Pueblo Chamber of Commerce)

Pueblo City Hall and Auditorium

from New Mexico. Some were white, although in many families intermarriage with the natives had introduced an Indian strain. Spanish interest and activity in the upper Rio Grande Valley went back to the time of Coronado. The settlements around Santa Fé were established in the days of Oñate—just about the time that Jamestown was founded in Virginia. The New Mexico community was far removed from Mexico City, the center of political and cultural activity in New Spain. For two hundred years New Mexico was largely isolated from the rest of the world. Early in the nineteenth century a change came. In 1807 Captain Zebulon Pike of the United States Army appeared with his ragged band, a portent of the hundreds of Anglo-Americans who were soon to arouse the New Mexican communities from their century-old quiet.

One sign of renewed activity in New Mexico was an advance of settlers up the Rio Grande into what is now the state of Colorado in the 1840s and 1850s. Although this movement into new lands represented essentially a normal advance into an adjacent frontier area, it may have been stimulated by the disturbances in New Mexico following the American occupation by General Kearny at the time of the War with Mexico.[29]

However that may be, new settlements were made in the San Luis Valley and on the east side of the mountains as far north as the Arkansas River (*Napeste* to the Spaniards). From that day to this Spanish influence has been strong in this part of Colorado. It is shown conspicuously in the place names of the region. Such peaks and mountain ranges as the La Plata, San Miguel, Blanca, and Sangre de Christo remind us of the Spanish explorers, miners, missionaries, and soldiers who early visited this country and left behind these musical appellations. In addition to the Rio Grande, the Huerfano, Cucharas, Las Animas, La Plata, Florida, Dolores, and Conejos are streams with Spanish names. A few of the many towns and cities whose names are redolent of old Spain are Pueblo, Trinidad, Antonito, Los Cerritos, Durango, Del Norte, La Junta, Los Pinos, San Pablo, and La Plaza de los Leones (later known as Walsenburg). Many of the counties in southern and western Colorado have Spanish names: Las Animas, Alamosa, Archuleta, Dolores, Otero, Conejos, Costilla, Baca, Mesa, and San Juan.

These Spanish-Americans—and it should not be forgotten that after 1848 they and their descendants were citizens of the United States—were a simple people in the early days, largely unlettered, and, according to Anglo-American standards, not too industrious, progressive, or efficient. But they enjoyed a life in which work was for *mañana* while the *fiesta* and *fandango* were for today. True, they raised cattle, sheep, and goats on a small scale; they farmed in a primitive manner, using ox-drawn iron-tipped wooden plows which barely scratched the surface of the small plots of ground on which they raised a little corn, some pumpkins, beans, and peppers. They were content to raise only what they needed; their farming operations did not greatly disarrange the life cycle of the region. The native trees and shrubs and the tall grasses in the valleys remained largely undisturbed. They did not overgraze the pasture land or stir up much of the soil for the wind and rain to carry away.

Among these people in southern Colorado and New Mexico in the early days the family was of the patriarchal type. In addition to the parents and children a normal household might include grandparents and unmarried or widowed aunts. The adobe houses were built around courtyards for safety and privacy. The families tended to cluster in villages which were significant more as cultural and social centers than as places for barter and trade. The larger towns were in addition centers of local government.

---

[29] Louis B. Sporleder, "A Day and a Night on Spoon River," *Colorado Magazine,* IX, 102.

Since the dominant religion among these people was Roman Catholic, holidays were essentially holy days. During Holy Week the Penitentes,[30] members of a secret society of flagellants which had developed in New Mexico, lashed themselves and, at least until the close of the nineteenth century, chose one of their number to carry a heavy cross and submit to crucifixion: death might or might not be the fate of the one who took the part of Cristus. The ceremonies at Christmas were more cheerful but still primarily religious. On *La Noche Bueno* (Christmas Eve) there was often an allegorical or religious play (*auto sacramental*) which told the story of the birth of Christ. The New Year was introduced by a midnight mass, followed shortly by the serenading of the "Manueles" of the community —those who bore the sacred name of Manuel, Spanish for Emmanuel or Messiah. On January 6 came the Feast of the Three Kings or Wise Men with a dramatization of the visit of the Magi to the Christ child. Several weeks later there might be another *auto, El Niño Perdido,* on the visit of the boy Jesus to the temple. Weddings were naturally festive occasions, with elaborate ceremonies; and in addition each community had an annual celebration in honor of its own particular saint.[31]

Men who knew at first hand the quiet unhurried life of these friendly folk and who were later annoyed by the noise and rush of a mechanized existence looked back to the good old days in southern Colorado with nostalgia.[32] The contrast in social values between the Latin and the Anglo-American way of life has often been pointed out. As one writer put it recently: "The Anglo-American is the servant of time; to the Latin there is time for everything. The Anglo-American is practical and wants organization. The Latin-American is theoretical and individualistic. The Anglo-American is supreme in science, because he places economic well-being and wealth above everything else. The Latin-American is supreme in human relations; friendship is the most important element in his life. To the Latin-American work is an auxiliary of life, not the main objective."[33] Colorado is the richer for having had within her borders even so little of this Latin influence.

At most there were only a few thousand of these Spanish-speaking people in what is now Colorado at the time of the gold rush. But they formed an important element in the population of the territory, and they had such prestige as came from priority in settlement. Some

[30] There are many articles on the Penitentes. One of the first writers to bring them to the attention of Anglo-Americans was Charles Lummis in his *Land of Poco Tiempo.* The article by Aurelio M. Espinosa in the *Catholic Encyclopedia,* XI, 635, gives a careful summary.

[31] Olibama Lopez, "Pioneer Life in the San Luis Valley," *Colorado Magazine,* XIX, 161-167. Cf. Nina Otero-Warren and John P. Flores, "Christmas in New Mexico," (mimeographed pamphlet issued by Tom L. Popejoy, State Director of Educational Division, W.P.A., Santa Fé).

[32] Louis B. Sporleder, "La Plaza De Los Leones," *Colorado Magazine,* X, 28-38.

[33] Daniel T. Valdes, "The Spanish-Speaking People of the Southwest," (mimeographed bulletin WE-4, June 25, 1938; Henry W. Hough, State Supervisor of Workers Education; W.P.A. Program of Education and Recreation of the Colorado State Department of Education).

of their leaders, notably Casimiro Barela, were active in state politics and held important places in the government. Most of the older people among them spoke and read Spanish rather than English; hence from 1877 to 1899 the laws of the state were printed in Spanish as well as in English.[34]   There were also a few Spanish-language newspapers. In 1875 the Trinidad *Pioneer* introduced a Spanish section, which in 1876 became *El Exporador*.[35]   In the 1870s a Walsenburg paper also had a Spanish section. In 1946, according to the standard guide to newspapers, there appeared to be only one newspaper in Colorado printed in Spanish; it was *El Heraldo del Valle* of San Luis.[36]

Inasmuch as these Spanish-Americans are native-born citizens of the United States, it is impossible from the published census returns to get precise figures as to their numbers. One estimate made in 1924 was that there were about 35,000 Spanish-Americans in Colorado.[37]   Of these there were thought to be about 16,000 in Las Animas County, with its chief city at Trinidad; about 9,000 in Huerfano County, with its county seat at Walsenburg; perhaps 5,000 in the San Luis Valley, particularly in Conejos and Costilla counties; in the San Juan country they were most numerous in Archuleta and La Plata counties; they could also be found in Denver, and in Pueblo and other parts of the Arkansas Valley. Throughout southern Colorado they have represented a fair cross section of society. In the San Luis valley most of them have been engaged as farmers or ranchers either on their own lands or as laborers or tenants on the lands of others. In the mining counties along the eastern base of the Sangre de Christo range (Huerfano and Las Animas) a considerable number have found employment in the coal mines. In Pueblo they have found work in the steel mill. In the towns and cities of this part of the state they have been well represented in the learned professions and various commercial activities.

MEXICANS

Another Spanish-speaking group in Colorado is the Mexican. This term is sometimes inaccurately applied in the Southwest to all those whose mother tongue is Spanish. It is properly applied only to those who have come from the Republic of Mexico or to their children.[38]   It does not necessarily tell anything about a person's race. Citizens of the Republic of Mexico may be Indians or whites

---

34 Cf. Colorado Constitution (1876), Art. XVIII, Sect. 8.

35 Douglas C. McMurtrie and Albert H. Allen, *Early Printing in Colorado*, 285.

36 N. W. Ayer & Sons *Directory Newspapers and Periodicals, 1946,* 128. In Henry W. Hough, Ed., "Americans with Spanish Names," (Bulletin No. 11, Colorado W.P.A. Workers Service Program), 18, there is a reference to a Spanish language newspaper in Trinidad, *El Faro,* and to *La Verdad* in Denver, as of 1942.

37 R. N. McLean and C. A. Thomson, *Spanish and Mexicans in Colorado* (pamphlet, 1924), ix. Valdes, "Spanish-Speaking People of the Southwest," estimates the Spanish-speaking population of the San Luis Valley at 15,000.

38 For discussion on this point see Valdes, "Spanish-Speaking People of the Southwest."

or any one of various degrees of intermixture.   Among the masses
of the people the Indian strain is predominant.

Between 1900 and 1930 more than a million Mexicans moved into
the United States.   Most of them came as laborers because of higher
wages here and other economic and social advantages.   It is estimated
that three hundred thousand of them went to California, where they
have been employed in the fruit industry; half a million are thought
to have gone to Texas, where they have worked in the cotton fields.
The number who have come to Colorado is estimated at 45,000.
They have found work mainly in the beet fields, and to a smaller
extent in factories, smelters, and on the railroads.   In general they
have had to take a position near the bottom of the social and economic
scale.

It is in the beet fields that they have made their chief contribution to the economic life of Colorado and indirectly have presented
to many communities in the state some of their most serious social
problems.   The successful growing of sugar beets requires intensive
cultivation and, so far, a great deal of hand labor.[39]   Ordinarily the
seeds are sown generously and then thinned so as to get the proper
stand of beets.   Then the plants must be cultivated, and finally
topped after they have been dug.   This is hard, monotonous work,
poorly paid.   Very few native-born Anglo-Americans will stoop to
this sort of work.[40]   The Mexicans with their lower living standards
have been willing to do it; hence they have been brought in for this
purpose.   Under the contract labor system that has been in general
use the beet laborer enters into an agreement to do the necessary
work on a certain tract of beets at so much per acre.   Not only the
father of the family but his wife and their children who have passed
the age of toddlers work in the fields.   The more children there are
in the family the larger the tract it can care for; the number of
acres per family will run from 20 to 40, with 25 as an average.   In
addition to the money payment for this work, the contract usually
contains a stipulation that there shall be provided by the grower a
habitable house with an adequate supply of water.   These houses
are often small, cheerless shacks, meagerly furnished.[41]   If reproached
for failure to provide decent living accommodations, the grower may
say: "It's only a Mexican family; they don't expect anything better,
and they wouldn't take care of it if they had it."   To which the
Mexican might reply that "there is no incentive to neatness and
cleanliness when forced to live in hovels not fit for human habitation."
Another serious problem in the beet fields is that of school attendance
by the Mexican children—many of whom, it must not be forgotten,
are native-born citizens of the United States.   Indifference on the
part of some of the parents and the urgent need for help from the
children in the fields at the times of thinning and topping, result

[39] T. F. Mahony, *Problem of Mexican Wage Earner* (printed pamphlet, 1930).
[40] Paul S. Taylor, *Mexican Labor in the United States Valley of the South Platte Colorado,* 103.
[41] *Ibid.,* 162.

in many absences from school. Moreover, work in the beet fields is seasonal. Even if the houses in which the workers live in summer could be heated adequately in winter, there is nothing to do in the fields, and so there has been a tendency for the beet workers to flock to such cities as Denver and Pueblo after the fall harvest. There they stay until spring. Overcrowding in slum areas, appeals for poor relief, and adjustments in school attendance are some of the social problems presented by this seasonal shift in habitations. There are also religious problems. The leaders in the Roman Catholic Church, of which the vast majority of these people are adherents, point out that because of the conditions of life both in summer and winter it is difficult to care adequately for their spiritual needs.[42]

According to the census figures, there were 6,360 persons in Colorado in 1940 who had been born in Mexico. They were to be found in all counties save ten. In each of 18 counties their number exceeded one hundred. Weld had the largest number (1,042); Pueblo was second (1,009); and Denver third (955). Other counties with more than 200 each were Otero (495), Las Animas (319), Prowers (318), Larimer (242), and Morgan (221). As is apparent from the location of these counties, the Mexicans were to be found mainly in the beet-growing sections of the Platte and Arkansas valleys. But their wide distribution in the state (*e. g.*, 75 in Mesa County, 102 in Routt, 104 in Huerfano, 106 in El Paso, and 168 in Fremont) indicates that not all of them were employed in the beet fields; some had found work on railroads as section hands or at mines, smelters, and factories as day laborers.[43]

Occasionally there has been an outburst of anti-Mexican sentiment. During the depression of the 1930s the combination of a labor surplus and a long list of poor on the relief rolls led to a movement to restrict the number of Mexicans entering and living within the state. Governor Ed. C. Johnson in April, 1936, called out the Colorado National Guard, proclaimed martial law along the southern boundary, and gave orders that automobiles, busses, and trains entering Colorado from New Mexico be stopped, searched, and that all aliens likely to become indigents be turned back. "If they do not have money or means of support, do not let them pass," the Governor is reported to have said.[44] Within a few days the ban was removed. In addition to protests against this action on constitutional grounds, there was strong objection by religious leaders for humani-

[42] T. F. Mahony, "Catholic Work Among Mexicans," Address at Fifteenth Session of the National Conference on Catholic Charities, New Orleans, November 12, 1929. Mimeographed copy in Denver Public Library. For this and many other references on the foreign-born in Colorado I am indebted to Miss Ina T. Aulls of the Western History Division of the Denver Public Library.

[43] Stuart Cuthbertson, "The Problem Presented by the Spanish-Speaking People of Colorado," in *Proceedings of the Northern Colorado Conference on Problems of the Spanish-Speaking People * * * Greeley * * * 1942* (mimeographed pamphlet), estimated that the Spanish-speaking population of Colorado in 1942 was between 80,000 and 90,000, and was increasing rapidly.

[44] *Rocky Mountain News,* April 20, 1936.

tarian reasons and by beet growers for practical considerations.[45] A few years later under war-time conditions special efforts were made to induce Mexicans to come in for the beet season. Arrangements were made by which several thousand *braseros* (strong arms)— they are now referred to as expert farm workers—were brought up in the spring to work in Colorado, Wyoming, and Nebraska, with the understanding that they would return to Mexico in the autumn.[46]

ENGLISH

As was pointed out above, the non-American groups most in evidence in Colorado in the early days were the British. Of these, the English call for consideration first. So strong was the English influence that one writer said in 1892 that Colorado might be termed "England beyond the Missouri, for in proportion to its population, in no other American state is there a greater number of English immigrants or a greater amount of British capital."[47] This writer estimated that the stocks and bonds of the railroads of Colorado were owned in England to an amount of £15,000,000 or more; and that the investments in mines, smelters, land, irrigation projects, breweries, and hotels added at least another £10,000,000 sterling.

Men born in England were often active in the management of these business enterprises. Dr. W. A. Bell of Manitou, formerly of Bournemouth, England, was one of the most successful of the promoters of railroads and ranches in Colorado; E. T. Jeffery, sometime president of the Denver and Rio Grande Railroad Company, was born near Liverpool; the Earl of Dunraven once held a claim to a large tract of land in Estes Park; another land owner of British origin was T. J. Livesay, who had an extensive sheep ranch in southern Colorado. James Duff from London organized the Colorado Mortgage and Investment Company (the "English Company"), and brought in English capital for irrigation projects in northern Colorado and the building of the Windsor Hotel in Denver. In this connection mention should be made of the Cornforth brothers, Birks and Joseph T., natives of Cheshire, who offered in their grocery and fruit stores in Denver English delicacies to the "carriage trade."

Some of the Englishmen in Colorado were "second sons" or "remittance men" who had come to America for adventure and who lived on their payments from home and such additional money as they made from their own ventures in ranching or mining[48] These scions of great families were most in evidence in the Valley of the Platte, in the vicinity of Colorado Springs ("Little Lunnon"), and in the Wet Mountain Valley. Many, perhaps most, of the English eventually became citizens of the United States, but even so they

45 *Ibid.,* April 26, 1936. Cf. *Denver Catholic Register,* June 20, 1935.

46 As samples of newspaper articles see Colorado Springs *Gazette,* August 7, 1942; *Bent County Democrat,* May 21, 1943; *Rocky Mountain News,* January 1, 1944; Longmont *Times-Call,* March 29, 1945; Denver *Post,* April 1, 1945.

47 T.T., "The English in Colorado," *The Coloradoan,* I, (November 15, 1892), 6.

48 Clarice Richards, "The Valley of the Second Sons," *Colorado Magazine,* IX, 140-146.

retained a liking for English customs. Those from upper-class families stopped work for tea at five and "dressed" for dinner at eight, no matter how plain the fare. Some of them rode to the hounds and gave a sporting touch to the Pikes Peak country. One newspaper article referred to the Wet Mountain Valley as "the half-way heaven of Englishmen." Why? "Here come high bred gentlemen and scions of nobility to lead a primitive and pastoral life * * *. Almost any day during the sporting season you may encounter a lord in the roughest sort of a rig, out with a 'scatter gun' and a brace of 'small dogs.' They are so common, these lords and baronets, that our democratic bosoms scarcely thrill at the sight of one any more." In general, the English clung to an urbane mode of life that set them somewhat apart from their neighbors in a community that inevitably shared fully in the crudities of American life as intensified in the frontier environment. Mr. S. Nugent Townshend, who traveled through Colorado in 1876 with an eye open for former residents of the "old country," said that he had observed among these transplanted Englishmen "no deterioration of home manners, culture or ideas." The reason was that they were "exclusive," an easy matter "in these beautiful solitudes."[49] Like many other transplanted groups in Colorado, the English organized for social and benevolent purposes: two of their early societies in Denver were the St. George's Benevolent Association and the Albion Club.

With the passing of the years the number of the English in Colorado has greatly declined. But those that are left are well distributed over the state: in 1940 61 of the 63 counties contained two or more persons who had been born in England. Denver of course stood first (2,001), with El Paso second (317), and Boulder third (264).

SCOTCH, WELSH, AND CORNISH

Among the foreign-born in Colorado the Scotch, while never near the top in numbers, have held a fairly even line with respect to their percentage of the whole. When there were 120 of them in the Colorado of 1860 they comprised 4.5 per cent of those of foreign birth; they reached their highest percentage in 1890 (5.2) with a total of 4,339 persons. By 1940 the figures had declined to 2.7 per cent and 1,883 persons. In the latter year they were to be found in all but eight of the counties of the state, with the largest numbers in Denver (720), El Paso (114), and Weld (87). In the closing decades of the nineteenth century there was an active Caledonian Club in Denver, one of whose projects was the erection of a statue to Robert Burns in City Park.[50] There were for a time similar organizations in Leadville and Cripple Creek.[51]

Another British group which was prominent in the early history of Colorado was the Welsh. Experienced in mining in the old country,

49 S. Nugent Townshend, *Colorado.* 59.

50 Denver *Republican,* January 16, 1893; January 19, 1902.

51 Denver *Times,* July 15, 1899.

they were especially valuable members of many Rocky Mountain communities. In the hard-rock mining country they were conspicuous in the boom days at Central City, Georgetown (named for George Griffiths, a man of Welsh extraction), Idaho Springs, Silver Plume, Gold Hill, Leadville, and Silverton. They also worked in the coal mines and were numerous in the 1880s at Erie in Weld County, at Coal Creek in Fremont County, and New Castle in Garfield County. And as has been true with most racial and national groups in Colorado they had a goodly representation in Denver. Wherever they were present in sufficient numbers they formed a distinct cultural group. Social and gregarious, they united in such societies as the Cambrian, which was organized in Denver in 1883. Religious by nature, they established Sunday schools. Good singers, they organized glee clubs and choral societies. One of the old institutions among the Welsh was the Eisteddfod, a literary and musical festival.[52] Many such gatherings were held in Colorado during the hey-day of Welsh activity, some purely local, others on a state-wide scale. Hundreds of participators and auditors assembled for these contests. Prizes might be offered for the best original poem or essay, written in Welsh of course; or for the best grand chorus, or the best vocal or instrumental solo, or for the best painting. For example, at the Grand Eisteddfod held in Denver in 1896 a prize of $300 was offered for a Welsh poem of not less than three thousand nor more than five thousand words on the subject "Eangden, Dyfuden, Uchelden."[53] A prize of $1,000 and a gold medal were offered to the grand chorus of 140 to 150 mixed voices that would render best the following selections: "Hark to the Deep Tremendous Voice," from Haydn's Seasons, and "Lullaby of Life," unaccompanied, by Henry Leslie. For the best landscape painting in oil of the entrance to City Park in Denver there was offered a prize of $50. These are only a few of many aspects of literary and artistic achievement which these curious people sought to reward. How strange to offer prizes for poems, and paintings, and songs! What about the biggest pig, or the best jar of pickles or mincemeat?

In 1890 there were more than two thousand natives of Wales in Colorado. The number decreased as mining declined in importance. As their numbers dwindled, it became increasingly difficult for the survivors to keep alive the old associations, and they were gradually merged in the general population. According to the 1940 census the Welsh were well distributed over the state, with the largest number in Denver (164); Boulder County was next with 66, while El Paso was third (48).

Closely akin to the Welsh were the Cornish. Some of them had come to Colorado directly from Cornwall, while others had come by way of the Lake Superior copper mines. Like the Welsh, they as

---

[52] Evan Williams, "History of the Welsh People of Colorado." (Original in Welsh; there is a typed copy of the English translation in the Western History Division of the Denver Public Library.)

[53] *Program of the Grand Eisteddfod * * * Denver * * * September * * * 1896.* (Illustrated pamphlet.)

a group were experienced miners. The census reports give us no clue as to their numbers, since they were English in birth. But they were easy to identify because of their peculiar language and customs. We know that there were many of them in Central City and other Gilpin County mining towns in the 1880s and 1890s. One resident of Central City mentioned in his reminiscences the many "robust, stout-chested, pink-cheeked lads from the tin mines of Cornwall;" another "who came to Central City in 1885, said afterwards that it had then seemed to him that 'the majority of the population was Cornish.' "[54] The Cornish were a desirable element in the population. The men were industrious; the women were excellent home makers. They comprised nearly half of the membership of the local Methodist Church; its choir, so it is said, was especially good because of its "rich Cornish voices."[55] With the decline of hard-rock mining in Gilpin County and the coming in after 1900 of Italian and Austrian miners from the Tyrol,[56] who would work for less, the Cornish drifted away; probably many of them moved to Denver.

IRISH

More numerous than the Welsh and Cornish in Colorado, the Irish added much to the zest of life. In 1890 when Colorado had 83,990 residents of foreign birth, more than 12,000 of these were from Ireland. Nearly five thousand of these Irish were to be found in Denver, where they made up about one-sixth of the foreign-born population of that city. Many of them retained a lively interest in their native land and took an active part in supporting various movements for home rule in Ireland or reform in the land laws. Denver newspapers through the 1870s and 1880s contain many references to meetings of such organizations as the Denver Land League, the Irish National League, the Irish Agitation Club.[57] But however much they may have loved the "old sod," they were fast becoming Americanized; they had also an Irish Political League in Denver, which aimed, according to one pronouncement, to "promote a political ascendancy over ward bummers and to secure election to office of good men."[58] There were also the usual benevolent or protective associations, whose aims were to furnish social contacts and a form of social security among the people of Irish ancestry. In 1884 there was organized in Denver the St. Patrick's Mutual Benevolent Society.[59] The Ancient Order of Hibernians was also well represented in Denver and other parts of Colorado.

---

[54] Lynn I. Perrigo, "The Cornish Miners of Early Gilpin County," *Colorado Magazine*, XIV, 93.

[55] *Ibid.*, 97.

[56] Denver *Post*, October 7, 1900.

[57] For examples see *Rocky Mountain News*, December 25, 1879; December 19, 1881; January 12, 1882; February 4, 1884.

[58] *Ibid.*, February 10, 1884.

[59] *Ibid.*, April 9, 1884.

The Irish were active in the business and professional life of the state. Among the Colorado mining engineers of Irish origin were Philip Argall from Belfast and Thomas J. Waters from Kings County. Too much should not be made of names, but such designations of mines and mining districts as Robert Emmet, Maid of Erin, Kilkenny Boy, and Shamus O'Brien suggest an appeal to Irish luck. In the field of industry two of the outstanding figures were the Mullen brothers, J. K. and D. W., natives of County Galway; their Colorado Milling and Elevator Company was long one of the leading enterprises of the sort in the Rocky Mountain area. James Archer, native of Armagh, helped establish the Denver Gas Works and the Denver Water Works in the early 1870s. Martin D. Currigan from Roscommon and Michael McIntyre from County Donegal were two men prominent in building and construction activities in Denver in the latter part of the nineteeth century.[60] Another native of Ireland, Thomas M. Patterson, made a great impression on the state, not only as lawyer and politician, but also as editor and owner of the *Rocky Mountain News*.

The census of 1940 distinguished between those born in Ulster or the North of Ireland and the natives of the Irish Free State; there were many more of the latter than the former in Colorado. From North Ireland had come 398; from Irish Free State, 2,120. More than half of the latter were to be found in Denver.

GERMANS

Since the gold-rush days the German element has been active in the development of Colorado. So numerous were the people of German descent that for twelve years (1877-1889) the laws of Colorado were printed in German as well as in English and Spanish. There were also some attempts to plant German colonies in Colorado. Best known of these, although not successful, was the German Colonization Society which, under the leadership of Karl Wulsten, tried in 1869 to establish a cooperative community in the Wet Mountain Valley south of Canon City.[61]

In communities where the Germans were sufficiently numerous they organized turnvereins and singing societies. In the turnvereins the emphasis was on gymnastic exercises; they were also centers of German language, culture and institutions. The Denver Turning Society was organized about 1865, and was admitted to the North American Turnerbund in 1868. A Turner hall was built for its use in 1873; it was soon outgrown and replaced by a larger one in 1890.[62] The membership of the Denver Turnverein in that year stood at 330. Leadville had its Turnverein too; its Turner hall was built about 1880, with Charles Boettcher, later a prominent capitalist, on the

---

60 *Ibid.,* March 17, 1895.

61 J. F. Willard and C. B. Goodykoontz, *Experiments in Colorado Colonization,* 29-133.

62 Robert Barth, "History of the Denver Turn Verein," in *Souvenir des Denver Turnvereins* (1890), 99-135.

building committee. The Germans also organized in singing societies or maennerchor; there was one of these in Denver and another in Central City during the 1880s.[63]

Because of the number of the German-American societies and lodges in Colorado an attempt was made to secure some union among them through a German-American Central Verein which was formed in Denver in 1891. Its announced objects included these: the promotion of the interests of public welfare in general and of German-Americans in particular; the cultivation and maintenance, besides English, of the German language; the diffusion more generally of rational ethics and ideas of life; the resistance most resolutely of every infringement of the social, civil, and political rights guaranteed by the Constitution of the United States; and the opposition to all class and sumptuary legislation.[64]

The German influence was strongly "liberal" whenever puritanical or "blue laws" were suggested with respect to the use of liquor or the observance of Sunday. In 1879, for example, when there was agitation in Denver for laws limiting personal freedom in these respects there was organized "The Liberal German-American Citizens Society," whose announced purpose was to work for the election of city officials who were "liberal and fair minded."[65] The *Rocky Mountain News* supported the German stand, saying editorially: "We may as well say plainly that the strait-jacket Yankee Sunday will not take in this cosmopolitan Western town."[66]

The Germans also used their influence to have instruction in "turning" or gymnastics introduced in the public schools of the state. The Colorado legislature passed a law in 1877 which made the teaching of German, Spanish, and gymnastics obligatory in schools on petition of twenty or more citizens.[67] A few months later it was admitted that the law, at least so far as it applied to physical education, was a dead letter, partly because of the difficulty in securing competent instructors. Ultimately, whether through German or other influences, physical education became a well-recognized part of the curriculum of the schools.

From the early 1870s until World War II Colorado had one or more German newspapers. The first one appears to have been the *Colorado Journal* started in 1872;[68] another was the *Colorado Post*, which began in 1879. In commenting on the appearance of the latter publication, the *Rocky Mountain News* made the observation: "Few are aware that nearly a third of our people are Germans."[69] The columns of the *News* recorded the appearance of two other German

63 *Rocky Mountain News,* January 19, 1884; June 1, 1884.

64 *Platform und Constitution des Deutsch-Amerikanischen Central-Vereins von Arapahoe County. Gegrundet den 2 Mai, 1891* (pamphlet), 5.

65 *Rocky Mountain News,* August 19, August 29, September 9, 1879.

66 *Ibid.,* September 10, 1879.

67 *General Laws of Colorado,* 1877, Chap. XCII, No. 2523, Sect. 77.

68 Douglas C. McMurtrie and Albert H. Allen, *Early Printing in Colorado,* 259.

69 *Rocky Mountain News,* July 13, 1879.

papers in 1884: a daily called the *Staats Zeitung,* and a weekly known as the *Denver Herald.* Many of these were of short life, but the *Colorado Herald,* which claims it was established in 1866, was the one which apparently lasted longest.[70]

The list of the names of men of German birth or descent who have taken an active part in the economic, political and cultural life of Colorado is a long one. Among the names familiar to Coloradans are those of Wolf Londoner, an early-day merchant in Denver; George Tritch, founder of a well-known hardware firm; Fred Walsen, after whom Walsenburg was named; Philip Zang and Adolph Coors, founders of breweries; Max Kuner, one of the founders of the Kuner Pickle Company; Luther Kountze, banker, and Charles Boettcher, financier and builder of sugar factories. In the realm of artistic achievement one of the great names in Colorado is that of Albert Bierstadt, whose famous landscape, "Storm in the Mountains," was painted near Georgetown.[71]

Especially significant in the relations between the whites and the Indians in Colorado were the services of Charles Adams, who had been born as Karl Adam Schwanbeck in Germany. After coming to the United States he had fought with the Union Army during the Civil War, had continued in military service in Indian fighting after the war, and then was put in charge of the Ute Indian agency at Los Pinos; while there from 1872 to 1874 he won the confidence of Chief Ouray. Although he was no longer in the Indian service, he was called upon by the government immediately following the Meeker massacre (1879) to attempt to secure the release of the white women and children who had been taken captive; this he was able to do with the help of his friend Ouray.[72]

In 1940 there were people of German birth in every one of Colorado's counties. Denver headed the list with 2,829; the other counties with two hundred or more were Pueblo (352), El Paso (350), Jefferson (315), Weld (312), Arapahoe (211), Larimer (207), and Boulder (204).

GERMAN-RUSSIANS

Also German in their cultural background, although listed as natives of Russia, were the German-Russians. They are the descendants of people who had gone from Germany to Russia as colonists in the latter part of the eighteenth century on the invitation of Catherine the Great. There were enough of them to keep alive their language and culture in the Volga Valley where they settled, but not enough to secure for themselves a good and happy life. They and their children began to look for new homes. Some went back to the German fatherland; some went to Brazil or Argentina; still others

---

[70] In N. W. Ayer & Sons *Directory* for 1946, 121, the date of the establishment of the *Colorado Herald* is given as 1866: it is not listed in McMurtrie and Allen, *Early Printing in Colorado.*

[71] W. R. Hentschel, *The German Element in the Development of Colorado,* 3-11.

[72] LeRoy R. Hafen, "Charles Adams," *Dictionary of American Biography,* I, 39.

came to the United States. The first of these people came to America in the 1840s, but the migration did not begin on a large scale until after our Civil War. Because of their agricultural background, they naturally turned to the more or less vacant lands of the West. They settled in Iowa, Nebraska, the Dakotas, Colorado, California, and other western states and territories.

In Colorado the German-Russians settled mainly in the beet-growing areas of the Platte Valley. They were on the whole poor people on their arrival in this country and consequently were willing to take disagreeable and poorly paid work. They were thrifty and industrious, however, and many of them have lifted themselves far up the social and economic scale. In 1940 Weld County had 2,473 natives of Russia, Larimer 1,288, Morgan 823, and Logan 777. Probably most of these "Russians" were German-Russians. In religious affiliations some are Lutherans, but many are Congregationalists. The reason for this rather strange association is historical: when some of the early German-Russians reached America without any strong denominational affiliation they settled near some German Congregational churches in Iowa, whose ministers began to work among them; Congregational polity was sufficiently flexible to make room for them and the Congregational missionary boards gave financial support.[73]

SWEDES

Another substantial element in the population of Colorado has a Swedish background. There were nearly ten thousand Swedes in Colorado in 1890. Many of them had come from the parish of Ryssby in the province of Smaland. Among the first were eight families who took adjoining homesteads in Left Hand Valley to the southwest of Longmont, at a new Ryssby, between 1869 and 1871. This became a Swedish center in northern Colorado. By 1873 the Ryssby settlement included 14 families who had taken up two thousand acres of land. Soon a church was organized. Then, following a Swedish custom, a tract of land was bought and set aside for the support of the minister. Each man in the congregation contributed labor for farming or work on the irrigation system. Later a church was built, modeled in design after the parish church in old Ryssby. With the passing of the years the congregation declined in numbers and the church was finally abandoned. However, in 1924 the survivors and the descendants of the Ryssby colonists met for a memorial service; this was so successful that the practice of having an annual summer meeting at the old Ryssby church has been continued. In commemoration of this early Swedish settlement the State Historical Society has erected at Ryssby a marker, which recites the story of the origin of the colony and the building of the church.[74]

---

[73] Emma D. Schwabenland, "German-Russians on the Volga and in the United States," 133-135. (Typed thesis in University of Colorado Library.)

[74] Esther Gunnison Kingdon, "Ryssby, the First Swedish Settlement in Colorado," *Colorado Magazine,* X, 121-130.

For some reason the Swedes in Colorado have had a tendency to settle in the towns and cities. In 1890 Arapahoe County, in which Denver was the most important community, contained about one-half of the Swedish-American population of the state. In 1930 the seven cities in Colorado with a population in excess of ten thousand contained more than one-half of those listed as Swedes. Concentration in towns and cities has made it easy for the Swedes to unite for religious and social purposes.[75] The church has usually been the center of their institutional life. There are Swedish churches in the larger towns and cities of Colorado along the eastern base of the mountains from Greeley in the north, through Loveland, Longmont, Boulder, and Denver, to Colorado Springs and Pueblo. Another agency through which the old culture is kept alive is the Swedish Day Society. Founded in 1929, its purpose is to continue an interest in Swedish customs and to promote a better understanding among the Swedes and their descendants. Newspapers have also contributed to these ends. There were at least two Swedish papers in Colorado in the 1880s: the *Colorado Posten* and the *Svenska Korrespondenten.* The latter has survived as the *Western Nyheter*.[76] The Swedes in Colorado have been thoroughly Americanized; practically all of them speak English. Their interest in the old country is purely sentimental.

In 1940 there were in Denver 2,427 natives of Sweden; the other counties with two hundred or more each were Weld (598), Pueblo (268), Jefferson (257), El Paso (256), and Boulder (242).

DUTCH

Natives of the Netherlands have appeared in small numbers in every census report for Colorado beginning with 1860. The number for that year was 16; in 1870 it was 17; in 1880, 115; and in 1890, 192. Then came an ambitious colonization scheme which, had it succeeded, would have added quickly several hundred Dutch to the population of Colorado. In 1892 the Holland American Land and Immigration Company of Utrecht sent to the San Luis Valley a party of about 350 men, women and children from the Netherlands. It was understood that they would engage in agriculture on land which the Holland Company had purchased. This first group, so it was said, was "but the vanguard of over two thousand Holland farmers and their families who will settle in the sunny San Luis valley before another year rolls around." They were a picturesque crowd. We are told that

> Although a few of the colonists dressed in the prevailing mode, the greater portion wore their native costumes. The trousers of most of the men fitted tightly around the waist and bulged like balloons over the hips, the bulges being accounted for by two overlapping pockets in which were

[75] C. A. Carlson, *Northmen Who Went West,* 49-58. (Pamphlet.)

[76] *Western Nyheter* is listed in N. W. Ayer & Sons *Directory* for 1945; the name appears as *Western News* in the 1946 edition.

carried a large assortment of miscellaneous articles. The peaked cap was the favorite head gear. Both men and women wore wooden shoes, or "klumpen," which caused them to walk pigeon-toed and to waddle. These shoes, which had cost about thirty cents, or thirty-five cents if painted frills were added, were warm and serviceable. For ordinary wear the women had white lace caps, stiffly starched. Most of them also possessed distinctive national or provincial head dresses, dresses, and aprons * * *. The children were kept painfully clean, and were noticeably polite and agreeable. Many of the boys, aged twelve to twenty, smoked long black cigars, while their fathers smoked small pipes, and all the colonists, even the smaller children, drank huge amounts of beer.[77]

Among these people, many of whom were men of substance and all of whom presumably shared in the traditional Dutch virtues of thrift and industry, there was soon great dissatisfaction over the conditions they found in their new home.[78] There had been misrepresentations about the climate and economic opportunities; there had been mismanagement on the part of some of the agents of the company; an epidemic of diphtheria took a heavy toll among the children during the first winter. The experiment failed, and soon the Dutch scattered. Some went to the Platte Valley in Logan County where the Holland Company was making a second attempt at colonization; this venture met with no more success than the first. The Dutch settlement in the vicinity of Crook, in Logan County, was abandoned in the autumn of 1893. Some moved to near-by towns; some went to Iowa; others returned to the old country. One evidence of the failure of this experiment in colonization is the slight increase in the number of the natives of the Netherlands in Colorado in 1900 as compared with 1890; 192 in 1890 and 260 in 1900. In 1940 there were 683 persons of Dutch birth living in 47 of the counties of Colorado: Denver was first with 389; Arapahoe was second with 54; and Weld was third with 26.

ITALIANS

Although there were some sons of sunny Italy among the Fifty-niners and other early settlers in the Pikes Peak country, the number of Italians in Colorado was not great enough to attract attention until the decade of the 1880s. According to the census of 1880 there were 335 natives of Italy in the state; in 1890 the number was 3,882. Many of them had come to America in response to propaganda designed to secure cheap labor for western mines, smelters, and railroad construction gangs. Wages were higher than in the old country but methods of payment and working conditions were often

[77] Dorothy Roberts, "A Dutch Colony in Colorado," *Colorado Magazine,* XVII, 231-232.
[78] Denver *Republican,* December 18, 1892, for dispatch from Alamosa describing the discontent of the Dutch.

unsatisfactory, causing a great deal of dissatisfaction among the transplanted Italians. In April, 1882, it was reported that there were five hundred discontented Italian laborers loitering in the Platte river bottoms of Denver, nursing grievances against the railroad contractors who had misrepresented working conditions and cheated them. The Italian consul in Denver was quoted as follows: "It is a shame the way my countrymen are treated here in Colorado. The majority of them come here with good intentions to work for the support of themselves and families in Italy—but they are defrauded out of so much of their money that it is impossible for them to send the amount of money home that they desire."[79]

Perhaps Colorado wasn't so bad after all. At any rate, many of the men sent for their families and took out their naturalization papers. Relief came also through the formation of protective and benevolent associations. The first one for the Italians in Denver was organized in 1884. In commenting on the establishment of this society the *Rocky Mountain News* pointed out that as the members of the various racial and national groups came to know one another better they became more independent and self respecting and thus made better citizens.[80] From time to time there are references in the Denver papers to such organizations as the *Circolo Italiana* and the *Societa de Mutuo Soccoro e Fratellanza Italiana*.[81]

One of the outstanding cultural leaders among the Italians in Colorado was Angelo Noce,[82] who came to Denver in 1882, and who in 1885 began the publication of *La Stella*, an Italian-language newspaper. For lack of adequate patronage this paper had to suspend publication after about four years. Several other Italian papers have been founded in Colorado and at the present time there are two survivors, *Il Risveglio* in Denver and *L'Unione* in Pueblo.[83]

Among Italians old-world memories and customs have been kept alive, in part through religious pageants and homage to great men. They have generally celebrated the discovery of America by Columbus; and, indeed, Angelo Noce appears to have been largely responsible for the passage of a law in 1907 setting aside October 12 as a legal holiday.[84] Another great day for Denver Italians is the celebration in August in honor of San Rocco, a patron saint; there is usually a parade with floats and religious exercises at Mount Carmel Church.

The religious activities and interests of Italians in Colorado naturally bring to mind Mother Frances Xavier Cabrini, who was made a Saint by the Roman Catholic Church in 1946. Founder in Italy of the order of Missionary Sisters of the Sacred Heart of Jesus, she

---

[79] *Ibid.,* April 20, 1882.

[80] *Rocky Mountain News,* October 7, 1884.

[81] *Ibid.,* January 5, 1885.

[82] Angelo Noce gathered material for a history of Italians in Colorado; much of this material, with his permission, was incorporated in G. Perilli's *Colorado and the Italians in Colorado.* Noce's manuscript is in the possession of the State Historical Society of Colorado.

[83] N. W. Ayer & Sons *Directory* for 1946, 121, 127.

[84] G. Perilli, *Colorado and the Italians in Colorado,* 14.

came to the United States in 1889 with the approval of Pope Leo XIII to work among the Italian immigrants. Denver was one of the cities where she labored and it was there that she founded the Queen of Heaven Orphanage.[85] Her elevation to the sainthood is noteworthy not only because she was the first citizen of the United States to be so honored, but also because of the unusually short time that had elapsed between her death (1917) and her canonization.

The Italians in Colorado are to be found mainly in the industrial centers and coal mining camps. In 1940 Denver was credited with 2,339 natives of Italy; Las Animas County was second with 1,185; Pueblo was a close third with 1,179. The descendants of these men and women who were born in Italy number many thousands; in 1931 it was reported that Denver alone had in it approximately 15,000 Italians.

The Slavic Peoples

The changing character of immigration into the United States by the opening of the twentieth century is reflected not only in the increase in the number of Italians in Colorado, but also in the growing number of those who had come from central and eastern Europe, from Poland, Austria, Russia, and the Balkans. Although there was no state of Poland between the final partition of that unhappy land in 1795 and its revival at the end of World War I, there was a strong sense of Polish nationalism and it was easy to identify the Poles in America. There were 272 of them in Colorado in 1890, 620 in 1900, and 2,483 in 1910. The largest number in any one community in Colorado was in the Globeville district in Denver, where they found employment in the smelter until it was closed, and then at the stockyards, and in the packing plants. The center of their religious life was St. Joseph's Roman Catholic Church, which had been consecrated in 1902.[86]

Poles in America have been proud of the share of two of their fellow countrymen, Count Casimir Pulaski and Thaddeus Kosciuszko, in the American War for Independence. From time to time Denver Poles have had celebrations in commemoration of the death of General Pulaski at the Battle of Savannah in 1779.[87] Poles have also followed with keen interest the fortunes of Poland in the European turmoil. In World I their sympathies were strongly on the side of the Allies, because of their hope that the defeat of the Central Powers and the triumph of Woodrow Wilson's program as announced in his Fourteen Points would be followed by the restoration of Poland; and so it was. World War II was precipitated by the invasion of Poland by Hitler's hordes; and again the Poles in America pledged their

---

[85] Sister M. Lilliana Owens, "Frances Xavier Cabrini, Foundress of Queen of Heaven Institute," *Colorado Magazine*, XXII, 171-178.

[86] Denver *Republican*, August 29, 1902.

[87] *Rocky Mountain News*, October 6, 1942.

loyalty to American principles and hoped for the revival of an independent Poland.[88]

Prior to the census of 1920 there was no indication as to the number of men and women in Colorado who had been born in either Czechoslovakia or in Yugoslavia. Before World War I those countries, both known as "succession states," had been part of Austria. From Austria had come to Colorado, according to the census of 1910, no fewer than 11,581 persons. By 1920 the figure for Austria had dropped to 5,722, a result, in part at least, of the appearance on the map in 1919 of Czechoslovakia, which was set down as the birthplace of 1,953 persons, and of Yugoslavia, from which had come 2,109 individuals. The Czechs in Colorado in 1940 were to be found mainly in the industrial and mining centers: Denver, 255, and Pueblo, 167. The same was true with respect to the distribution of the natives of Yugoslavia: Pueblo, 886; Denver, 252; Lake County (Leadville), 152.

In 1900 there were only 2,938 natives of Russia in Colorado; by 1910 the number had increased to 12,757. It was 16,669 in 1920, but had dropped to 11,185 in 1940. As pointed out above, some of these Russians were German-Russians, people who were Russian only in the sense that they had been born within the Czar's dominions. It is also clear that at least a few hundred of those listed as Russians in the census reports through 1920 were natives of Latvia, Estonia, and Lithuania. How many are left, after these subtractions, who may properly be called Russians cannot be stated with precision— but there were probably still several thousand. In 1940 there were 3,675 natives of Russia in Denver, most of whom presumably were Slavs from Russia proper. In 1942 "Slav Day" was celebrated in Denver. According to newspaper reports three thousand Russians, Serbs, Czechs, Poles, and other Balkan racial groups met in City Park and pledged their loyalty to American principles.[89]

JEWS

Some mention should be made of the Jewish contribution to the life of Colorado, but this is a topic which does not lend itself readily to statistical treatment. A dispersed people without a national homeland, the Jews came to America from many countries in Europe. So far as census reports go, they cannot be distinguished from others who were born in Russia or Poland, in Germany or England. Then, too, many of this group, which is quite as much religious as racial, were native-born citizens of the United States at the time of their arrival in Colorado.

Jews, along with those of other races and faiths, participated in the gold rush to the Rockies. By 1861 their number in Denver had increased sufficiently to lead to the formation of a Jewish

[88] See article by Frank L. Rhoades, "Poles Hope to Celebrate Soon," *Rocky Mountain News,* July 9, 1944.

[89] *Rocky Mountain News,* June 22, 1942.

Cemetery Association. In 1872 a Denver lodge of B'nai B'rith was instituted; this was followed shortly by the organization of Temple Emanuel, which through the years has been the best known of the Jewish synagogues in Colorado. New life was infused into this religious organization in 1889 with the coming of a young rabbi, William S. Friedman,[90] who soon became and who long remained one of the religious and social leaders of the state—a man to whom all those of good will in all creeds and faiths were proud to do honor. His record of achievement is too long to set down here; but it is not out of place to refer specifically to what is generally recognized as his greatest memorial, the National Jewish Hospital.[91] Distressed over the almost helpless and miserable state of so many people who had come to Denver in search of relief from tuberculosis, but who were without adequate financial means to secure food and shelter, Dr. Friedman was largely instrumental in founding a sanitarium, which for years has had a distinguished record for public service. Although founded by and administered by Jews, it is open to all irrespective of faith who need its help and qualify under its rules for admission.[92]

In Colorado, as elsewhere in the nation, Jews have tended to gather in the cities. The one notable attempt to plant a Jewish colony in a rural community—at Cotopaxi in Fremont County—ended in failure. It was in 1882, at a time when thousands of Jews who had fled from persecution in Russia were seeking refuge in America, that Emanuel H. Saltiel, owner of a silver mine at Cotopaxi, sought to found an agricultural colony near his mine. Ostensibly an humanitarian project, it appears to have been a selfish scheme on the part of the promoter and one that resulted only in disappointment to the unfortunate victims of an ill advised experiment.[93]

Jews have always stood high in the business and professional life of the state. Among the names that come to mind quickly in this connection are L. H. Guldman of the Golden Eagle store in Denver, Wolfe Londoner, an early-day mayor of Denver, David May, founder of the May Company, and the Guggenheims of mine and smelter fame.[94] To Otto Mears, "pathfinder of the San Juan," who was of "mixed English and Jewish stock," Colorado owes much for

---

90 In the Western History Division of the Denver Public Library there is a large volume of newspaper clippings on Jewish activities in Colorado, with particular attention to Rabbi William S. Friedman.

91 Samuel Schaefer and Eugene Parsons, "A Brief History of the National Jewish Hospital at Denver," *Colorado Magazine,* V, 191-198. References to the hospital in Denver newspapers are numerous; see, for example, Denver *Republican,* December 11, 1899; Denver *Times,* November 17, 1901.

92 William S. Friedman, *Modern Methods of Fighting Tuberculosis: * * * Address * * * Atlantic City, New Jersey, July 28, 1905.* (Pamphlet.)

93 Dorothy Roberts, "The Jewish Colony at Cotopaxi," *Colorado Magazine,* XVIII,. 124-131.

94 Joseph E. Smith, "Jewish Builders of Colorado," *Intermountain Jewish News,* September 15, 1939.

his services in the economic development of the southern part of the state and in the maintenance of friendly relations with the Indians, notably with Ouray.[95]

CHINESE

Chinese who had been attracted to America by the opportunities in the California gold fields soon made their way into other parts of the Far West as new mining camps were opened up. There were apparently none in Colorado in 1860 and only seven in 1870. But by 1880 the number had risen to 601. The coming of even so few Celestials to the region provoked protests in some quarters. They were cheap, peaceable, and industrious workers and were favored by some employers over men of any other nationality. Some were employed on the road-beds of the new railroads; others were hired as gulch miners by companies which were reworking the placer mines; a few had jobs as laborers and wood cutters around the mines and smelters. Opinion differed as to whether they were a desirable or undesirable element in the population.[96] Some stressed the need of the state for cheap labor and said there was room for all;[97] others, who objected to their competition, tried to drive them away. At Caribou on the Middle Boulder a group of Chinese brought in by the Nederland Mining Company was escorted out of the camp one day in April, 1874.[98] In Leadville the unwritten law grew up that no "Chinaman" should be allowed within the city limits.[99] In 1879, when the South Park Company replaced some Italian laborers in its coal mines at Como with Chinese, there were at once protests both there and elsewhere in the state.[100] The company explained and defended its action, but an anti-Chinese spirit was rising. The agitation of the period led to violence in the autumn of 1880.

For several months the *Rocky Mountain News,* at this time a Democratic party paper, had been carrying on what might fairly be called an anti-Chinese campaign. It was partly political: President Hayes was under fire from Democrats because of his veto of a Chinese limitation bill; and Garfield, Republican candidate for President, was accused of supporting a cheap labor policy.[101] It was partly moral and social: the *News* frequently ran articles describing the vile conditions that prevailed in Denver's "Chinatown," on Sixteenth

[95] LeRoy R. Hafen, "Otto Mears, 'Pathfinder of the San Juan'," *Colorado Magazine,* IX, 71-74.

[96] Central City *Register,* January 14, 1874, reported that about 150 "Celestials" were at work near Camerontown, each making on an average from $1.00 to $2.50 per day. "If such results are sufficient to induce Chinese cheap labor, there is room for several cargoes of them in Colorado, and in places where they will interfere with no one. As they spend but little with our trade, they are of but little use, but we cannot see that they do any harm."

[97] The Territorial Legislature in 1870 adopted a resolution favoring Chinese immigration to the territory: *General Laws, Joint Resolutions * * * 1870,* 134.

[98] *Rocky Mountain News,* April 2, 1874.

[99] *Ibid.,* September 24, 1879.

[100] *Ibid.,* November 22-27, 1879.

[101] *Ibid.,* October 23, 27, 29, 1880.

Street, between Wazee and Blake.[102]   The charge was made that the Chinese were operating vicious opium dens, gambling joints, and houses of prostitution.   The underground tunnels and rooms in the district only added to the suspicion.   "A more horrible place can scarcely be imagined than these dens, filthily dirty," said the *News* in one story.[103]   The death of an eighteen-year-old white lad who had, so it was alleged, become an opium addict, added fuel to the flames.[104]   This tragic occurrence, according to the *News,* had finally stirred the city authorities to attempt "to suppress the villainous dens which provide the means for this horrible habit."   There were other articles pointing out the bad effects the Chinese had had on California and predicting similar results in Colorado unless steps were taken to check their movement into the state.[105]   There was hardly a day, so it was said, that some of the "pig-tails" did not enter Colorado.   "Keep out John Chinaman, the pest of the Pacific Coast," became the slogan of the nativists.[106]

Perhaps it did not come as a result of these articles, but soon there was an "incident."   A row started between a white man and a Chinese,—perhaps over a laundry bill,—a mob gathered, and on the night of October 31, 1880, the Chinese in Denver were driven from their homes and places of business, some buildings were burned and one Chinese was killed.[107]   The city authorities quickly restored order and escorted the Celestials back to what the *News* contemptuously called their "washee houses."[108]   The riot may have had a wholesome effect upon the Denver Chinese.   At any rate the Denver *Tribune* a few months later had this to say: "The Heathen Chinee in our midst has improved wonderfully since the riot last fall, and is gradually transforming himself from a keeper of an opium joint to a boss of a Sunday School."[109]

Hop Alley, as Chinatown was known locally, long remained one of the "sights" of Denver.[110]   There the Chinese lived quietly, both among themselves and with their neighbors; it has been said that "not once in its colorful history has Denver's Chinatown been embroiled in a tong war."   But once a year, on the Chinese New Year, there would be noise enough; the exploding firecrackers, so it was reported, made the American Fourth of July sound tame by comparison.

102 For example, *ibid.,* March 28, 1880.

103 *Ibid.,* October 21, 1880.

104 *Ibid.,* October 9, 1880.

105 *Ibid.,* October 31, 1880.

106 *Ibid.,* October 23, 1880.

107 The Chinese legation in Washington protested to the State Department because of this incident.   For correspondence, with sworn testimony, see *Papers Relating to Foreign Relations of the United States * * * 1881,* 318-337.

108 *Rocky Mountain News,* November 4, 1880.

109 Denver *Tribune,* April 6, 1881.

110 "Denver's 'Hop Alley' 'fell' Friday before the advance of the army of 'social betterment.'   The city building department * * * ordered razing of the buildings in the once glamorous Chinatown."   Denver *Post,* June 14, 1940.

The number of Chinese in Colorado apparently reached its high point about 1890. The census report for that year showed that 1,447 residents of Colorado had been born in China; the number dropped to 581 in 1900 and to 320 in 1910. Since 1920 the number of Chinese in the state, both native and foreign-born, has ranged between 200 and 300.

Chinese nationals in America have usually taken a lively interest in what went on in their old homeland. Many of them, including those in Colorado, contributed in various ways to the origin and success of the Chinese Revolution. It is a matter of local interest that at the time the revolt against the Manchu dynasty broke out in October, 1911, Dr. Sun Yat Sen, father of the revolution and later first president of China, was in Denver soliciting among his countrymen support for the projected rebellion. Because of this coincidence a special stamp issued in 1942 in commemoration of China's five years of resistance to Japanese aggression was first put on sale in Denver.[111]

JAPANESE

The number of Japanese in Colorado was negligible throughout the nineteenth century: none in 1880, ten in 1890, and 48 in 1900. Then came a rapid increase: the number for 1910 was 2,300, most of whom (2,245) had been born in Japan. The number in 1920 was 2,464, of whom 1,762 had been born in Japan. The number of Japanese in Colorado in 1930 was 3,213, but only 1,389 had been born in Nippon. Of the 2,734 Japanese in the state in 1940, 1,869 were native-born and 865 foreign-born. They were engaged mainly in agriculture, especially of the intensive sort, and were located largely in the Platte and Arkansas valleys.

One effect of the outbreak of war between the United States and Japan in December, 1941, was the great increase, temporarily at least, in the number of Japanese in Colorado. For reasons of national security the federal government in the early part of 1942 began to move out of certain parts of the Pacific Coast states all persons of Japanese ancestry, including those who were native-born citizens of the United States. Temporary relocation centers were established in several western states. In Colorado there was one known as the Granada Relocation Center at Amache. It was opened in the summer of 1942 and by the spring of 1943 had more than 7,500 residents. Two-thirds of them were citizens of the United States and at least one-fourth were professed Christians, members of the major Protestant denominations. They represented a fair cross section of Japanese-American life: there were among them rich and poor, learned and ignorant, professional men and day laborers.[112]

Since the government had no desire to work unnecessary hardship on these people, most of whom were innocent victims of circumstances entirely beyond their control, arrangements were made for

[111] Hazel C. Arnold, "Sun Yat Sen in Denver," *Colorado Magazine,* XIX, 197.
[112] "Amache Colorado. Granada Relocation Center." (Mimeographed pamphlet.)

the release of some of them from the camp. Permission to leave was granted to those of unquestioned loyalty who could get jobs in the communities to which they intended to go or who had sufficient funds to insure that they would not become public charges. This policy, together with some voluntary migration from the Pacific Coast before the relocation policy had been put into effect, resulted in a great increase in the number of Japanese in Denver, Boulder, and some other Colorado towns. In Denver the number of Japanese increased seven-fold between 1940 and February, 1944. Of the 2,310 Japanese in Denver in 1944, 27 per cent were foreign-born and 73 per cent were citizens of the United States.[113] At the University of Colorado in Boulder scores of loyal Japanese and their families were assembled to give instruction in the United States Navy's Oriental Language School.

In spite of the demonstrated loyalty of the great majority of American-born Japanese a movement was launched in the summer of 1944 to secure an amendment to the Colorado constitution denying to aliens ineligible for citizenship the right to own land in the state. After a spirited campaign, in which several of the churches came out strongly on the side of tolerance, the amendment was rejected by a majority of more than 10,000 votes. It is noteworthy that the ballots of the absentee soldiers, which were counted separately, were also mainly in the negative.[114]

With the end of the war and the closing of the camp at Amache, many of the Japanese who had been brought to Colorado returned to their old homes. It seems likely, though, that because of the generally friendly attitude that has been manifested to the Japanese in Colorado during the war years, the next census will show some increase in the number of those of that racial group. Although many American-born Japanese have become Christians, Buddhism is still strong among them. There is in Denver a Japanese Buddhist Church which is said to be the only one of that faith between New York and Salt Lake City.[115]

NEGROES

The Negro population of Colorado has never been large. In 1870, the first census year after emancipation, there were 456 Negroes in Colorado. The number rose slowly from 2,435 in 1880 to 11,453 in 1940. It has remained at about that point since then: 11,828 in 1930 and 12,176 in 1940. While the number of Negroes in the state has increased slightly in recent years, their percentage in the total population has decreased. In 1890, 1.5 per cent of Colorado's population was black; in 1920 it was 1.2 per cent, and 1.1 per cent in 1930 and again in 1940. Lack of economic opportunity and competition with

---

113 C. W. Jackson, *A Study of the Japanese Population of the City and County of Denver*, 2.

114 *Rocky Mountain News,* November 9, 26, 1944.

115 Writers' Program, W.P.A., *Colorado,* 137.

Mexicans for the low-priced jobs are probably the reasons why so few Negroes have come to Colorado.   More than half of those in the state live in Denver.   They are employed mainly as laborers, waiters, household servants, chauffeurs, porters, janitors, hod-carriers, and in

Cutter Hall, Colorado College, Colorado Springs

similar poorly paid menial tasks.   Probably the most important occupation for Negro men is that of Pullman porter.   Colorado's laws forbid racial discrimination, but it exists to a certain extent in practice.   In Denver, for example, there is no legal residential segregation, but public opinion has caused most of the Negroes to seek homes in the Five Points district, an area of run-down houses between Twenty-fourth and Thirtieth Streets.[116]

There have been enough Negroes in Colorado to support Negro newspapers since the 1880s.   In 1946 there were three in the state: in

116 Ira De A. Reid, *The Negro Population of Denver, Colorado,* 3.

Denver there were the *Colorado Statesman* and the *Star;* in Pueblo, the *Western Ideal.*[117] All three are weeklies with small circulation which voice the protest of their people against racial discrimination.

AMERICANS ALL

Now after all this has been written about the various races and nationalities, each of whom has made some contributions to the social and cultural life of Colorado, it should not be forgotten that ever since the gold-rush days the state has been overwhelmingly "American," or, more accurately, "United States." The unusual, the picturesque, the transient in our cultural scene should not blind our eyes to the usual, the commonplace, and the permanent. Granted that you can find a "little Italy" in North Denver, a flavor of Poland in Globeville, or that "in Crested Butte you are in Austria,"[118] the America of today is everywhere about us. This is so evident that it seems unnecessary in this chapter on "The People of Colorado" to do more than make a casual reference to the most important of all the cultural influences in this region, those that have come from the Middle West and the Atlantic Coast.

Black and White, Oriental and Occidental, Latin and Anglo-American, Slav and Swede, Celt and German—all have had an opportunity in Colorado to demonstrate their acceptance of the Biblical statement that of one blood God hath made all nations. It is not always easy. The so-called minorities are becoming increasingly resentful at such discrimination as exists; the under-privileged are voicing indignant protests at injustice in economic and social opportunity. Obviously reform in such matters should come through education and an enlightened public opinion rather than through violence or futile legislation. An appreciation by each of the worth of the other is essential. In recent years an important contribution towards such an understanding has been the annual International Folk Festival held in Denver.[119] Representatives of twenty or more different racial and national groups meet together to show through song and pageant what each has accomplished culturally and what each has contributed to American life. But at the end they all unite in saying "I am an American."

117 N. W. Ayer & Sons, *Directory* for 1946, 121, 127.
118 "Childe Herald," "Ideas and Comments," *Rocky Mountain Herald,* February 17, 1940.
119 *Rocky Mountain News,* May 22, 1942.

CHAPTER V

History of Agriculture

ROBERT G. DUNBAR

Associate Professor of History, Colorado A. & M. College

MOST of the pioneer farmers of Colorado came from the humid East. Inasmuch as they were unaccustomed to farming in a region of less than twenty inches of annual rainfall, they had to adjust their humid-country agricultural techniques and institutions to their new environment. This involved failure, experimentation, poverty, discouragement, perseverance, and eventual success. It is a story of epic proportions.

IRRIGATION

The first farmer-settlers, however, did not have to make these adjustments. They were Spanish-Americans from arid New Mexico; they moved up the Rio Grande Valley and settled on the Culebra and Conejos Rivers in the southern part of the San Luis Valley. Shortly after their arrival, they began to dig ditches and to transplant the irrigation institutions which they had known in New Mexico. On April 10, 1852, the settlers on the Culebra commenced the San Luis People's Ditch, which has the distinction of being the oldest ditch in Colorado in continuous use. The San Pedro Ditch on the same stream dates from the same month. West of the Rio Grande, Lafayette Head's colony began the diversion of the Conejos in 1855. Four ditches on this river have appropriations dating back to this year; eleven date back to 1856.[1] These Spanish-American canals, designed to irrigate small plots of land, were narrow and short. Annually, those who lived under each ditch elected one of their number to serve as ditch superintendent in order that the ditches might be kept in repair and their waters diverted equitably. Irrigating was done by means of the check and border system. Small rectangular areas were enclosed by little banks of earth and the basins so formed were flooded to a depth of two or three inches.[2] Indeed, the fifty-niners might have learned something concerning semi-arid agriculture from these San Luis Valley irrigators, but geographical

[1] Alvin T. Steinel, *History of Agriculture in Colorado* (Fort Collins, 1926), 177-178; Francis Cheetham, "The Early Settlements of Southern Colorado," *Colorado Magazine,* V (1928), 5-7. The Hatcher Ditch on the Purgatoire River was constructed and used in 1846-1847, but abandoned in 1847. A. W. McHendrie, "The Hatcher Ditch (1846-1928): The Oldest Colorado Irrigation Ditch Now in Use," *Colorado Magazine,* V (1928), 81-95.

[2] Frederick H. Newell, *Report on Agriculture by Irrigation in the Western Part of the United States at the Eleventh Census: 1890* (Washington, 1894), 106-107; Colorado Territory, *Session Laws,* 1866, pp. 61-64; Interview with H. H. Griffin, Fort Collins, Colo., March 30, 1946.

isolation and cultural differences blocked interchanges of techniques and ideas.

The fifty-niners came from the wet country east of the Missouri River. They came to mine gold, but soon some of them decided that money could be made by supplying the mining communities with provisions. After a number of years, they were joined by men like the Union colonists, who came specifically to farm and who also found their markets in the mountains. In the valleys of the South Platte and its tributaries, these provisioners of mining camps worked out by trial and error the techniques and institutions of an irrigation society.

David K. Wall was the first of the fifty-niners to irrigate. Using the experience which he had gained as an irrigator in California, in 1859 he diverted the waters of Clear Creek at Golden over two acres of garden and cleared two thousand dollars.[3] That fall several parties began to dig ditches, taking water from Boulder and Bear creeks. The first recorded diversions from the St. Vrain and the Cache la Poudre date from 1860. On the Big Thompson the earliest priority dates from November, 1861. In short, within three years after the initial gold rush, one or more irrigation ditches had been taken out of nearly all the principal streams of the upper South Platte Valley.[4]

The irrigation system of this part of Colorado was constructed by five types of agencies: individuals, partnerships, community cooperatives, corporations, and irrigation districts.

Most of the ditches of the sixties were built by individuals or partnerships. They were short and small, confined for the most part to the river bottoms. The Big Thompson Ditch, for instance, was "some 8 miles long, covering a narrow strip of land, seldom more than a mile in width along the river bottom, and amounting probably to less than 3,000 acres, being almost entirely hay land of the second bottom."[5] Sometimes the farmers were aided in their construction of these early ditches by surveyors from the mining camps. Many of the ditches on Boulder Creek and the Big Thompson were dug under the direction of Hal Sayre, who later became a prominent mining engineer.[6]

The best known of the community enterprises were the two canals built by the Union Colony in the eighteen-seventies. The first canal, Greeley No. 3, was commenced as soon as the colonists arrived and was enlarged in 1871, 1872, and 1873. It was a river bottom ditch, taken out of the south side of the Cache la Poudre, and was designed to water the lots and gardens of the town of Greeley. Greeley Canal No. 2 was the revolutionary one. Not only was it the first large canal built by community effort in Colorado, but it was also the first

---

[3] *Rocky Mountain News,* February 22, 1860; Steinel, *op. cit.,* 180-182.

[4] Colorado State Engineer, *Second Biennial Report,* 1883-1884, Appendix, 4-59.

[5] John E. Field, "Irrigation from Big Thompson River," U. S. Office of Experiment Stations, *Bulletin 118* (Washington, 1902), 20.

[6] John E. Field, "Development of Irrigation," *History of Colorado,* ed. by Wilbur F. Stone (5 vols., Chicago, 1918-1919), I, 492; William N. Byers, *Encyclopedia of Biography of Colorado* (Chicago, 1901), 120.

built to water extensive areas of bench land.[7] It was started in the fall of 1870 on the north side of the river. During the first irrigating season, it proved to be too small and it was enlarged in 1872 and in 1877. When completed, it was 36 miles long and 32 feet wide on the bottom. In 1878 the farmers who were using No. 2 organized the Cache la Poudre Irrigating Company and purchased the canal. Since then it has been known as the Cache la Poudre Canal.[8] Another community effort was the Platte Water Company's ditch built by the citizens of Denver in the sixties to irrigate the city. In addition, some of the early canals in Boulder County were neighborhood enterprises.

The corporation era of canal building in the area under consideration began in 1879 with the organization of the Larimer and Weld Irrigation Company to complete the construction of the big Larimer and Weld Canal, which had been started the previous year. This company was a subsidiary of the Colorado Mortgage and Investment Company, which had been organized by English capitalists to develop investments in Colorado. The English Company, as it was called, furnished most of the capital and the chairman of the board of directors. This canal was constructed under the direction of E. S. Nettleton, the same engineer who built Greeley Canal No. 2. More than fifty miles in length, it remains to this day the largest irrigation system in the Cache la Poudre watershed.[9] The English Company likewise financed the construction of two other big canals, the Loveland and Greeley Canal, a diversion of the Big Thompson, and the High Line Canal, a diversion of the South Platte above Denver. The North Poudre Canal was built in the years 1881-1884 by the North Poudre Land, Canal, & Reservoir Company, with financial assistance from The Travelers Insurance Company. By 1885, the canal network of the South Platte-Cache la Poudre triangle was nearly complete. Consequently, the irrigation district law of 1901 found application only on the periphery of this area.

Even before the completion of these canals, it was realized that the stream flow was insufficient to supply all of them. The need for additional supplies was particularly apparent during the drier years. After 1887, the development of the late potato industry around Greeley made imperative a late supply of water in the Cache la Poudre Valley. Accordingly, in the eighteen-eighties irrigators began to search for supplemental supplies of water, first by the construction of storage reservoirs, later by means of pumping and trans-mountain diversions.

---

7 Robert G. Hemphill, "Irrigation in Northern Colorado," U. S. Department of Agriculture, *Bulletin 1026* (Washington, 1922), 3.

8 Richard J. Hinton, "A Report on Irrigation and the Cultivation of the Soil Thereby with Physical Data, Conditions, and Progress within the United States for 1891," *Senate Ex. Doc. No. 41,* 52nd Congress, 1st Session, Pt. I, 138-140.

9 Pauline Allison, "The Founding and Early Years of Eaton, Colorado," *Colorado Magazine,* XVIII (1941), 54; David Boyd, *A History: Greeley and the Union Colony of Colorado* (Greeley, 1890), 201-203.

The first reservoirs were natural lakes, such as Highland Lake, northeast of Longmont, and Warren Lake, southeast of Fort Collins. The former was used by L. C. Mead and C. A. Pound in the seventies for irrigation purposes.[10] The first artificial reservoirs in the Cache la Poudre Valley date back to 1883-1884 and form part of the North Poudre canal system. Windsor Reservoir and Terry Lake, the two big reservoirs near Windsor and Fort Collins, were started in 1890 and in 1891, respectively. Construction of the Cache la Poudre Reservoir got under way in August, 1892. So active were the reservoir builders in the eighteen-nineties that at the turn of the century E. S. Nettleton referred to the Cache la Poudre Reservoir system as "the most complete system of storage in the United States."[11] A similar development occurred in the other valleys.

The hunt for water extended to the sub-surface. Pumping for the purpose of irrigation began in 1889, when E. F. Hurdle dug a well in the Lone Tree Creek bottoms, east of Eaton, and irrigated eighty acres from it.[12] This method of irrigation, however, increased slowly in popularity. In 1909, the census-takers found only 79 irrigation pumps in the entire South Platte Valley; twenty years later that number had increased to 334. The drought of the 1930s gave a great impetus to pump irrigation, and in 1939 the pumping plants in the valley numbered 1,897.[13]

The most spectacular phase of the search for supplemental water has been the hunt for water on the other side of the mountains in the watersheds of the Colorado, North Platte, and Laramie Rivers. The first transmountain diversion was the Cameron Pass Ditch, a transfer of water from the North Platte River to the Cache la Poudre watershed. This ditch has an appropriation dated July 30, 1882. The first sizable diversion, however, was the five-mile Skyline Ditch, which was dug in 1892-1894 to take water from the Laramie River to one of the Poudre Valley canal systems. Seventeen years later (1909-1911) the construction of the Laramie-Poudre tunnel under Green Ridge precipitated a series of lawsuits with Wyoming. Even before this, in the years 1902-1904, the indefatigable water-hunters had notched the Continental Divide and built the Grand River Ditch to make the first diversion from the Colorado River. But the Grand River Ditch was only a trickle compared to the amount which might be diverted. The irrigators began to survey and to dream, but this

---

10 William E. Pabor, *Colorado as an Agricultural State* (New York, 1883), 90.

11 Edwin S. Nettleton, "The Reservoir System of the Cache la Poudre Valley," U. S. Office of Experiment Stations, *Bulletin 92* (Washington, 1901), 7; C. E. Tait, "Storage of Water on Cache la Poudre and Big Thompson Rivers," U. S. Office of Experiment Stations, *Bulletin 134* (Washington, 1903), 18-51.

12 *McClellan* v. *Hurdle,* 3 Colorado Court of Appeals Reports, 431 (1893); William E. Code, "Use of Ground Water for Irrigation in the South Platte Valley of Colorado," Colorado Agricultural Experiment Station, *Bulletin 483* (Fort Collins, 1943), 27; Steinel, *op. cit.,* 232.

13 William E. Code, "Construction of Irrigation Wells in Colorado," Colo. Agr. Ex. Sta. *Bulletin 415* (Fort Collins, 1935), 5; U. S. Census, Thirteenth Census, 1910, *Agriculture,* VI 227-232; Sixteenth Census 1940, *Irrigation of Agricultural Lands,* Colorado, 25. Statistical figures used in this chapter, unless otherwise indicated, are taken either from the U. S. census reports or from Colorado, *Agricultural Statistics,* 1924-1943.

was a job for the national government. In 1933 a group of men in Greeley organized and the next year they presented plans to the Bureau of Reclamation for the Colorado-Big Thompson Project to divert 310,000 acre-feet under the Continental Divide to the South Platte Valley. The Northern Colorado Water Conservancy District was created on September 20, 1937; the next year the Bureau started construction, and on June 10, 1944, the thirteen-mile tunnel was "holed through." The search for water goes on.[14]

The construction of the network of canals and reservoirs was indeed a difficult adjustment, but even more difficult was the adaptation of humid-country institutions and customs to the semi-arid environment. As F. H. Newell wrote fifty years ago,

> The development of irrigation is not merely the result of a succession of victories over physical or material obstacles. In our country these form but a part—and, unfortunately, often a relatively small part—of the difficulties encountered by the irrigator. By far the most vexatious and expensive impediments to be removed have been those arising from the inapplicability of our laws and customs to the conditions prevailing within the arid region. Every instinct acquired through generations of life in a humid country seems to rebel against the methods of the irrigator, and every tradition of law is in direct opposition to the proper employment of the natural waters. These instincts and traditions have had to be laboriously demolished, usually after severe struggle, and the series of contests appears a never-ending one.[15]

The water law which the settlers brought with them was the common law doctrine of riparian rights. It limited the use of stream waters to the owners of the river banks and prohibited such use as would diminish or alter the stream flow. It denied the users any proprietary right in the water and recognized only a usufructuary right in it. Obviously, such a legal principle was ill-fitted to the needs of Colorado farmers.

In the mountains the miners were following a legal doctrine that had evolved in the mining camps of California. This doctrine recognized the right of both riparian and non-riparian owners to divert the waters of a stream for beneficial use and gave priority of right to the individual who had made prior diversion or appropriation.

---

14 Burgis G. Coy, "The Laramie-Poudre Tunnel," *Transactions of the American Society of Civil Engineers,* LXXV (1912), 724-749; Northern Colorado Water Conservancy District and Colorado-Big Thompson Project, *Progress Report,* January, 1946; Colorado State Engineer, *Seventh Biennial Report,* 1893-1894, p. 16; Colorado Water Conservation Board, "Report on Irrigation Practices, Laramie River in Colorado, Larimer County, Colorado," July, 1941, Mimeographed; Tait, *op. cit.,* 27-28, 34-35; George J. Bancroft, "Diversion of Water from the Western Slope," in the *Colorado Magazine,* XXI, 178-181.

15 David Boyd, "Irrigation near Greeley, Colorado," U. S. Geological Survey, *Water-supply and Irrigation Paper 9* (Washington, 1897), 9. The introduction is written by Frederick H. Newell, later first Director of the Reclamation Service. See also on institutional adjustments, Olaf F. Larson, "Man-land Adjustment Processes in Weld County, Colorado," (Unpublished Ph.D. thesis, University of Wisconsin, 1941), 184-206.

These principles became known in time as the doctrine of prior appropriation. They applied to water a principle of the public land policy: first in time, first in right.[16]

This doctrine slowly superseded the older one. The first Territorial legislature enacted a law which recognized the right of non-riparian owners to a share of the stream flow, but which failed to mention the matter of priority.[17] This omission, however, was remedied by a later legislature.[18] Meanwhile, the doctrine of prior appropriation became the custom of the river bottoms, though not an unquestioned one.

In 1876, the framers of the state constitution transformed custom into constitutional law in these words:

> The right to divert the unappropriated waters of any natural stream to beneficial uses shall never be denied. Priority of appropriation shall give the better right as between those using the water for the same purpose. (Art. XVI, Sect. 6.)

In this manner Colorado became "the first State to incorporate the doctrine of appropriation in its constitutional law."[19]

Nonetheless, it was not until 1882 that the Colorado Supreme Court had an opportunity to give a clean-cut decision. The case was *Coffin et al,* v. *Left Hand Ditch Co.* The Court's language was clear and direct:

> We conclude, then, that the common law doctrine giving the riparian owner a right to the flow of water in its natural channel upon and over his lands, even though he makes no beneficial use thereof, is inapplicable to Colorado. Imperative necessity, unknown to the countries which gave it birth, compels the recognition of another doctrine in conflict therewith. And we hold that * * * the first appropriator of water from a natural stream for a beneficial purpose has, with the qualifications contained in the constitution, a prior right thereto, to the extent of such appropriation.[20]

So definite was Colorado's leadership in the abrogation of riparian rights that the doctrine of prior appropriation became known as the Colorado system. Later, through constitutions, statutes, and decisions, it was adopted by the other Rocky Mountain states—Utah, Wyoming, Montana, Idaho, Nevada, Arizona, and New Mexico.[21]

---

[16] Ralph H. Hess, "An illustration of Legal Development—the Passing of the Doctrine of Riparian Rights," *American Political Science Review,* II (1907), 15-31.

[17] Colorado Territory, *Session Laws,* 1861, 67-69.

[18] Colorado Territory, *Revised Statutes,* 1868, 364.

[19] Hess, *op. cit.,* 29.

[20] 6 *Colorado Reports,* 447 (1882).

[21] Walter P. Webb, *The Great Plains* (New York, 1931), 431-439; *Preservation of Integrity of State Water Laws,* Report and Recommendations of Committee of the National Reclamation Association, October, 1943, 22-44.

The people of Colorado not only took the lead in the formulation of a new legal system, but also in the creation of an administrative system for the supervision and control of the waters of the state. This innovation grew out of a quarrel in the Cache la Poudre Valley between Fort Collins and Greeley. The summer of 1874 was dry, and there was not enough water to go around. The Fort Collins farmers, higher up on the river, used so much water that there was insufficient water for Union Colony's two ditches. The colonists protested that their prior rights were being disregarded, and a convention was held at a school house between the representatives of the two communities. At that meeting it was proposed that a river commission be appointed to allocate the water equitably, but the Fort Collins group was hesitant to recognize the doctrine of prior appropriation and the meeting broke up without reaching any agreement satisfactory to the Greeley farmers.[22]

Although a heavy rain the following week filled the Poudre with water, the Greeley colonists continued to feel the need of some kind of water administration. Soon they were joined by others on the St. Vrain, and a convention was held in Denver, December 5-7, 1878, to suggest legislation to the second general assembly. The upshot was that in 1879 and 1881 the legislature of Colorado created machinery for the administration of the streams of the state and for the determination and adjudication of priority rights. It was the first attempt in the United States "to assert public control over the division of streams used in irrigation."[23]

The Acts of 1879 and 1881 provided for the division of the state into water divisions and water districts. They especially created three water divisions and ten water districts. The first nine districts were located in the South Platte Valley, which became Division No. 1. Today there are seventy water districts and seven water divisions. The Act of 1879 created the office of water commissioner, one for each district. The principal task of this official is to divide the water in the streams among the appropriators according to their prior rights. To head the organization, this legislation created the office of state engineer. Divisional superintendents were added in 1887.

No problem was more unfamiliar to the Platte Valley settlers than the measurement of water. Particularly exaggerated were their ideas concerning the amount of water in the rivers and the duty of that water. Yet the development of a stable agriculture depended upon an accurate assessment of the water resources of the state. Therefore, one of the principal duties of the state engineer was to measure the flow of the streams used for irrigation, and in 1882 the first incumbent established a gauging station in the Cache la Poudre River.[24] Not less important was the development of measur-

22 *Greeley Tribune,* July 15, 22, 1874; Boyd, *Greeley and the Union Colony,* 119-120.
23 Elwood Mead, *Irrigation Institutions* (New York, 1903), 143-147; Colorado, *Session Laws, 1879,* 94-108; 1881, 119-122, 142-161; Boyd, *Greeley and the Union Colony,* 121-123; *Fort Collins Courier,* December 14, 1878.
24 Colorado State Engineer, *First Biennial Report,* 1881-1882, pp. 16-20.

ing devices to enable the water commissioners and the ditch riders to allocate accurately the water from the streams and ditches. The 1879-1881 legislation decreed that each ditch taking water from a stream should be provided with a measuring device. Although the Italian module was widely used for a while, the rectangular weir was favored by E. S. Nettleton and became the most popular measuring device until the development in 1915-1926 of the Parshall Measuring Flume by Ralph L. Parshall and others working at the Colorado Agricultural Experiment Station in cooperation with the United States Department of Agriculture. Common in the early days for use in ditch company laterals was the dividing box, but this also is giving way to the Parshall Flume.[25]

The same generation that worked out the doctrine of prior appropriation, the public administration of waters, and the first measuring boxes evolved the characteristic organization of the cooperative ditch company, in which shares are owned by the farmers in proportion to their water rights. When the corporations entered the irrigation field, there arose the question of non-farmer control and monopoly of waters. The English Company in particular charged a royalty for the privilege of using the water carried by the High Line Canal. The farmers, led by the Grange, secured the passage of an anti-royalty law, and the Supreme Court in *Wheeler* v. *The Northern Irrigation Company* supported the agrarian viewpoint. Consequently, most of the corporation-owned irrigation systems passed into the hands of the water-users.[26].

Although irrigation began in the Arkansas Valley somewhat earlier than in the South Platte, its development was slower. Irrigated farms on the Huerfano furnished Denver with provisions in 1859, and in the same year the settlers at Fountain City took a ditch out of Fountain Creek. The first cooperative ditch of any size was the Arkansas Valley, commenced in 1861 and nicknamed the Cornmeal Ditch because the men who built it lived mainly on cornmeal. Settlers on Fountain Creek in the early seventies were concerned over priority rights, while farther down the river George W. Swink, J. W. Potter, William Mathews, Asahel Russell, and others built the Rocky Ford Ditch, which a few years later was to water the first melon patches.

Individual and cooperative effort, however, was not sufficient to build the big canals which the topography of the valley made necessary, and corporations built many of them in the eighties and nineties. The big Fort Lyon Canal, which takes water out of the north bank of the river above La Junta, was built by a corporation, as were the Lake, Bessemer, Amity, and Bob Creek Canals. The latter was an enterprise of T. C. Henry, who dreamed of a great canal extending from Boone to the Kansas line. He organized the Colorado Land and Canal Company and began construction in 1890. Although he

[25] Louis G. Carpenter, "On the Measurement and Division of Water," Colo. Agri. Exp. Sta., *Bulletin 13* (2nd ed.; Fort Collins, 1891), 3-39; Boyd, *Greeley and the Union Colony*, 110-112.

[26] Steinel, *op. cit.*, 207-209; Hemphill, *op. cit.*, 26-27.

did not reach his goal, he spent about $350,000 and dug a ditch 74 miles long, which opened up to cultivation the rich agricultural lands around Ordway and Sugar City. It made use of numerous reservoirs, including the big Twin Lake Reservoir in the mountains below Leadville.[27]

The Arkansas Valley has also searched for water on the Western Slope and has made no less than six diversions. The largest of these is the Independence Pass Tunnel, constructed in 1933-1935.[28]

Corporate effort likewise constructed much of the canal network in the San Luis Valley. Here again T. C. Henry built some of the largest of the canals. This man came to Colorado in 1883, after making a reputation by growing winter wheat in Kansas.[29] He immediately became interested in irrigation and in addition was able to interest the Travelers Insurance Company. Acting as the agent of this company and occasionally of other financial interests, T. C. Henry built no less than eleven ditch systems in Colorado: the Grand Valley and Montrose Canals on the Western Slope; the North Poudre, Fort Morgan, and Pawnee Canals in the South Platte Valley; the Fort Lyons Extension, Bob Creek, and Otero Canals in the Arkansas Valley; and the Rio Grande (formerly Del Norte), Empire, Monte Vista (formerly Citizens'), and San Luis Canals in the San Luis Valley. Of these, the San Luis ditches were the largest. Started prior to Henry's entrance into the valley, they were completed by him during the eighteen-eighties in a grandiose manner. The Rio Grande, or Del Norte as it was originally called, was the largest canal in the United States at the time of its construction. A fifth big ditch, the Farmers' Union, was commenced in 1887 and was built by the farmers themselves. By 1890 the present skeleton of canals had been completed.[30]

Because of the controversy over the Rio Grande and the "Embargo of 1896," reservoir construction was delayed until after 1907. The Rio Grande and Santa Maria Reservoirs were completed in 1913; two years later there were 16 in the valley. More recently the hope of its people for supplementary water has centered in the Wagon Wheel Gap Project of the Bureau of Reclamation.[31]

The largest irrigation systems on the Western Slope have been built by the national government. The first project of the Reclamation Service in the state, and the second in the nation, was the Uncompahgre Project, which involved the diversion of the water of the

[27] Joseph O. Van Hook, "Development of Irrigation in the Arkansas Valley," *Colorado Magazine*, X (1933), 3-11; A. P. Stover, "Irrigation in the Arkansas Valley, Colorado," U. S. Office of Experiment Stations, *Bulletin 119* (Washington, 1902), 287-298; Field, "Development of Irrigation," *op. cit.*, I, 494-495; Hinton, *op. cit.*, 147-148.

[28] Colorado State Engineer, *Biennial Reports, Twenty-eighth,* 1935-1936, p. 19; *Thirty-second,* 1943-1944, p. 16.

[29] James C. Malin, *Winter Wheat in the Golden Belt of Kansas* (Lawrence, 1944), 66-79.

[30] U. S. Supreme Court, *Kansas* v. *Colorado, Transcript of Record,* October term, 1905, No. 7, pp. 694-716; Newell, *op. cit.,* 127-131.

[31] National Resources Committee, *Regional Planning,* Pt. VI, The Rio Grande Joint Investigation in the Upper Rio Grande Basin in Colorado, New Mexico, and Texas, 1936-1937 (2 vols., Washington, 1938), I, 67-68; Colorado State Engineer, *Eighteenth Biennial Report,* 1915-1916, p. 64.

Gunnison through a six-mile tunnel to supplement the water supplies of the Uncompahgre River. After an unsuccessful effort on the part of the state to make the diversion, the Reclamation Service undertook in 1904 to complete it. In a gala celebration on September 23, 1909, President William Howard Taft opened the headgate of the tunnel, but the first water for irrigation did not flow through it until July 6, 1910. The project, however, has not been entirely a blessing. Because its cost was underestimated and the amount of irrigable land was overestimated, the farmers of the valley have found repayment difficult.[32]

The second undertaking in Colorado by the Reclamation Service was the Grand Valley Project. The first ditch to take water out of the Colorado River near Grand Junction was the Pioneer Canal, constructed in March and April, 1882. The Grand Valley Canal was started the same year, but little progress was made until Matt Arch organized the Grand River Ditch Company in 1883 and interested T. C. Henry in the project. Henry built the canal in 1883-1884, but the farmers opposed capitalist control of their water supply, and in 1894 the entire gravity canal system north of the river passed into the hands of the Grand Valley Irrigation Company, a farmer-owned cooperative ditch company. Inasmuch as there was still irrigable land above and north of this system, enterprising community builders began to agitate for a canal system to water it. In 1905 they organized the Grand Valley Water Users' Association, and after nearly a decade of controversy the Grand Valley Project was undertaken by the Reclamation Service. Construction, which commenced on October 10, 1912, included the building of a roller crest diversion dam and the sixty-five-mile-long High Line Canal, from which irrigation water was first used in 1916. In 1922-1927, the Bureau of Reclamation reconstructed and rehabilitated the irrigation system of the Orchard Mesa Irrigation District, south of the river. Seepage has been a big problem in this valley, and in 1915 the Grand Valley Drainage District was formed to cope with it.[33]

The diversion of the streams of Colorado had its repercussions in those states which border Colorado and which likewise use these streams for irrigation. Kansas was the first to protest and to sue Colorado for over-appropriation of the waters of the Arkansas River. This was in 1901. The United States Supreme Court gave an inconclusive decision in 1907, and litigation was renewed by Colorado in 1928. This led to a second decision on December 6, 1943. In both instances, the court failed to find evidence that Kansas had been

[32] U. S. Department of Interior, 1937 Repayment Commission, "Transcript of Hearings on Federal Reclamation Projects in Colorado," (Ms., Colorado A & M College Library), 104-194; U. S. Reclamation Service, *Ninth Annual Report,* 1910, p. 99; Steinel, *op. cit.,* 527-539.

[33] Mary Rait, "Development of Grand Junction and the Colorado River Valley to Palisade from 1881 to 1931," (Unpublished M.A. thesis, University of Colorado, 1931), 18-20, 127-142; J. H. Rankin, "The Founding and Early Years of Grand Junction," *Colorado Magazine,* VI (1929), 41-44; A. P. Stover, "Irrigation in the Grand Valley, Colorado, 1901," U. S. Office of Experiment Stations, *Bulletin 119,* 265-286.

greatly injured, and the second time it suggested that the two states settle their controversy by means of an interstate compact.[34]

Next in time was the dispute with Wyoming over the diversion of the water of the Laramie to the Cache la Poudre Valley. Wyoming brought suit in 1911, and in 1922 the judges limited Colorado's appropriation of the Laramie to 39,750 acre-feet of water. Twice since then Wyoming has sued Colorado for violation of the court's decree, and each time, in 1936 and in 1940, the court sustained its original decision.[35]

Litigation of interstate disputes over water proved so expensive and unsatisfactory that Coloradans sought another method to settle them. It was Delph Carpenter of Greeley, who first suggested they be settled by interstate compact. Not only did he originate the idea, but he fought for its application and negotiated the first three agreements. The first agreement was between Colorado and New Mexico over an allocation of the waters of the La Plata River. It was signed on November 27, 1922, and after ratification by the two states and Congress became effective in 1925. The Colorado River Compact was negotiated among the seven states of the Colorado River Valley, and, although it was signed three days before the La Plata agreement, it did not go into effect until 1928. It apportioned 7,500,000 acre-feet to the Lower Basin and a like amount to the Upper Basin states of Colorado, Utah, New Mexico, and Wyoming. Other compacts have been negotiated for the South Platte, Rio Grande, Republican, and Costilla Rivers. Early in 1945, the governors of Kansas and Colorado appointed a commission to negotiate a compact for the Arkansas River.[36]

DRY FARMING

Another adjustment, aside from irrigation, was dry farming, which is farming by means of drought-resistant crops and moisture-conserving tillage practices in regions of less than twenty inches of annual rainfall. Its origins are multiple and obscure. Within the United States it appears to have originated quite independently in Utah, California, Washington, and the Great Plains area. One of the cradles of the adjustment on the Great Plains was in Saskatchewan, Canada, where Angus Mackay chanced to discover summer-fallowing in 1885, and the Canadian government established the Indian Head experimental farm three years later. During the same decade Hardy W. Campbell, a settler in Dakota Territory, experimented with dryland grain culture and worked out a set of techniques that became known as the Campbell System. Likewise in the 1880s the Kansas

---

[34] 206 *U. S. Reports*, 46-118; 320 *U. S. Reports*, 383-400; Colorado State Engineer, *Thirty-second Biennial Report*, 1943-1944, 30-31.

[35] 259 *U. S. Reports*, 419-497; 260 *U. S. Reports*, 1-3; 286 *U. S. Reports*, 494-510; 298 *U. S. Reports*, 573-586; 309 *U. S. Reports*, 572-582.

[36] Colorado State Engineer, *Biennial Reports, Twenty-first*, 1921-1922, pp. 16-26; *Twenty-second*, 1923-1924, pp. 40-46; *Twenty-ninth*, 1937-1938, pp. 22-43; *Thirtieth*, 1939-1940, pp. 21-29; *Thirty-second*, 1943-1944, pp. 25-27, 30-31; Ralph Carr, "Delph Carpenter and River Compacts between Western States," *Colorado Magazine*, XXI (1944), 5-14.

Agricultural Experiment Station commenced the search for drought-resistant wheat, which was accompanied in the next decade by the importations of Russian wheats and alfalfa by Mark Carleton and Niels Hansen.[37]

Eastern Colorado was first settled by farmers in the years 1886-1889. The middle eighties was a period of abundant rainfall on the Plains; and the Dakotas, western Nebraska and Kansas, and eastern Colorado were settled with a rush. With few exceptions these farmers came from the humid areas farther east. Not only were they unfamiliar with farming in an arid climate, but the railroads, newspapers, states, and townsite companies had convinced them that the Great American Desert was a myth and that the Great Plains were as humid as the prairie states. Eastern Colorado became known as the rain-belt. Consequently, the first settlers used the tools, seed, and techniques which they had brought from the wet country. As was customary on the American frontier, corn was most commonly planted as a first crop. The first yields were satisfactory—then came the drought of 1890, beginning in 1889 and culminating the next year in a general crop failure. Many of the settlers left. Others stayed, but to survive the winter they needed assistance. Provisions, coal, and clothing were sent by communities in the irrigated valleys. Some of the business men of Denver organized a relief committee, which collected and shipped materials to Logan, Phillips, Washington, and Yuma counties. A similar committee in Colorado Springs supplied Kit Carson County. The state legislature joined in this relief work by appropriating $21,250 for seed grain.[38]

The crops were good in 1891, still better in 1892. In fact, 1892 was one of the best crop years in the history of the area. Spring wheat yielded well, and Akron's implement dealers took orders "for over three carloads of self-binding harvesters."[39] Produce shipments out of the counties were large. Between November 9, 1892, and February 9, 1893, 58 cars of wheat, 21 cars of corn, 10 cars of barley, 6 cars of rye, and 7 cars of broom corn were shipped out of Burlington.[40]

Unfortunately, the next year was dry and the year following that occurred the severe drought of 1894. The buffalo grass did not start that spring southwest of Burlington, H. G. Hoskin recalled fifty years later. The weather man recorded 8.42 inches of precipitation at

37 John A. Widtsoe, *Dry-Farming* (New York, 1912), 351-365; Paul de Kruif, *Hunger Fighters* (New York, 1928), 33-66; F. J. Alway, "Some Soil Studies in Dry-Land Regions," Bureau of Plant Industry, *Bulletin 130* (Washington, 1908), 17-28; Hardy W. Campbell, *Campbell's 1907 Soil Culture Manual* (Lincoln, 1909), 306-308; Malin, *op. cit.,* 179-187, 206-207.

38 Robert G. Dunbar, "Agricultural Adjustments in Eastern Colorado in the Eighteen-Nineties," *Agricultural History,* XVIII (1944), 42-47; *Rocky Mountain News,* January 2, 3, 5, 6, 8, 1891, and April 26, 1891.

39 Akron *Pioneer Press,* July 8, 1892.

40 Burlington *Republican,* February 25, 1893.

Burlington, 8.13 inches at Akron, 10.34 inches at Yuma, and 6.59 inches at Holyoke. Only 1934 was as dry.[41]

Again there was an exodus. A young girl in Burlington wrote her grandparents that ''A great many people have left the country, in fact nearly all that could get away, for there are so many mortgages that compel people to stay; a few families left in the night.''[42]

(Photo by Colorado A. & M. College Photo Shop)

Contour Listing, Southeastern Colorado, April 13, 1936

Kit Carson County, which had a population of 2,472 in 1890, had only 1,580 ten years later. Some of these ''okies of 1894'' emigrated to the irrigated valleys. Those who remained again needed relief. In February, 1895, the *Denver Republican* organized a charity drive that provided Sedgwick, Phillips, Yuma, Kit Carson, Washington, Morgan, Logan, and Arapahoe Counties with clothing and foodstuffs. In Kit Carson County, the county commissioners provided coal and seed wheat. In addition, some assistance was received from the East.[43]

[41] R. J. Martin and E. Corbin, editors, *Climatic Summary of the United States* (Washington, 1930), sec. 23, 7-17.

[42] Colorado State Historical Library, C. W. A. Interviews, Mss., Pamphlet 350, Document 44, Leila Shaw to Cyrus and Lydia Shaw, August 11, 1894.

[43] *Denver Republican,* February 1, 3, 5, 6, 8, 1895, March 12, 1895; Dunbar, *op. cit.,* 49-50.

It was this rough treatment by two droughts that brought about the first trials with dry farming. At first they were not very numerous, because most of the settlers made another adjustment— they went into stock-raising, not large herds but medium-sized herds of less than 300 head. Crop-raising became secondary to cattle-raising. To aid in these adjustments the state of Colorado in 1893 established at Cheyenne Wells the first dry-land experiment station in the United States; its influence, however, was not felt for another decade.[44] The Burlington railroad acquired a farm near Akron to demonstrate the value of the Campbell system. Of the two aspects of dry farming, Campbell emphasized the moisture-conserving tillage practices of deep plowing, frequent cultivation, and sub-soiling with a sub-surface packer which he invented in 1885. In August, 1895, the Akron *Pioneer Press* reported that "Quite a number of farmers in this vicinity are preparing to subsoil their ground this fall."[45] Outside Denver the next spring Robert Gauss, editor of the *Denver Republican,* began tests with drought-resistant plants. At Parker, E. R. Parsons was preparing for his later advocacy of dry farming in the issues of *The Western Farm Life.*

The first decade of this century witnessed a lively interest in dry farming. In 1905 the United States government created the Office of Dry-Land Agriculture Investigations; and the next spring its director, E. C. Chilcott, established a number of dry-land experiment stations in North Dakota, South Dakota, Nebraska, Kansas, and Texas. In 1907 he organized one of these stations at Akron.[46] In the same year the first of the International Dry Farming Congresses was held in Denver.

These years coincided with the second migration of farmers into eastern Colorado. They continued the adjustment of the 1890s, but with greater interest in dry-farming techniques. Whereas they brought with them their wet-country corn planters, they soon replaced them with listers and planted red amber cane and squaw corn. Those who planted wheat planted the winter variety. There was a lively discussion in the local press concerning the Campbell system, and some of the more enterprising farmers tried it out. Here and there a farmer summer-fallowed. Nearly all of them derived a supplemental income from dairying, selling their cream to the cream stations or trading their butter to the local stores for provisions.[47]

This adjustment was upset by several wet years and the price of wheat during World War I. Now occurred a third influx of unadjusted settlers. They broke up the pasture with tractors, discs, and plows and planted it to winter wheat. For instance, the acreage of

[44] *Sixth Annual Report of the Colorado Agricultural Experiment Station* (Fort Collins, 1894), 27, 31-32; Widtsoe, *op. cit.,* 366-367.

[45] Akron *Pioneer Press,* April 5, 26, 1895, July 26, 1895, August 9, 1895; *Denver Times,* December 31, 1894.

[46] U. S. Department of Agriculture, *Annual Reports,* 1906, pp. 236-238; Steinel, *op. cit.,* 559-562.

[47] Interviews with Mrs. Gertrude Morrow, Kanorado, Kan., April 4, 1940; Fred Johnson, Wray, Colo., June 24, 1940; and W. H. Molison, Burdette, Colo., August 18, 1941.

wheat in Washington County increased from 31,000 in 1917 to 175,403 in 1920. Corn also became an important crop. Most of the older settlers sold their stock, and eastern Colorado became a grain-raising area.

This situation lasted until the long drought of the 1930s, which ran its course from 1931 to 1939. The year 1934 was similar to 1894—7.67 inches of annual rainfall at Burlington, 10.61 inches at Yuma, and 8.83 inches at Cheyenne Wells. The plowed-up fields began to march, and eastern Colorado, particularly the southeastern counties, became a part of the Dust Bowl.[48]

This drought, like those of the nineties, had a tremendous impact upon the farming communities of the unirrigated plains. Again there was emigration, again there was relief, again there occurred an acceleration of the processes of adjustment. Stock-raising again became the dominant form of economic activity, but not to the same extent as earlier. Crop-raising continued to be important, and for the first time dry-farming techniques became nearly universal. This was particularly true of moisture-conserving practices. Under the added stimulus provided by national agricultural legislation, summer-fallowing, after thirty years of recommendation and discussion, became common. A few farmers took the advice of the technicians and terraced their wind-blown slopes, but at least in Kit Carson County most of them were "terrace-shy." More popular were strip farming and contour listing. In the aforementioned county, the county extension agent reported that in 1936, 957 farmers summer-fallowed, 414 strip-farmed, and 230 experimented with contour listing. Progressive farmers like Rell Morrow in Kit Carson County and C. T. Peacock in Lincoln County acquired basin listers and placed moisture-containing dams in their lister rows. Out of this drought situation grew the present soil conservation movement. The first soil conservation demonstration projects in the state were created in 1935 in these dry-land areas, and in the same year a soil conservation association was organized in Kit Carson County.[49]

Paralleling this popularity of moisture-conserving practices has been the increased use of drought-resistant plants. The adaptation of the winter wheat industry dates back to the second wave of settlement when Turkey Red wheat was introduced. This was the best adapted winter wheat until the early 1920s, when it was supplanted by Kanred, which was introduced into the state in 1918. In 1920 the agricultural experiment station brought in a carload, and the extension service distributed it to the farmers of eastern Colorado. Kanred's supremacy in turn was challenged by Tenmarq in the middle thirties. At the same time, grain and forage sorghums dis-

[48] Works Progress Administration, Division of Social Research, *Areas of Intense Drought Distress, 1930-1936*, Series 5, No. 1 (Washington, 1937), 29-31; U. S. Weather Bureau. *Climatological Data*, Colorado Section, XXXIX (1934), 52.

[49] Colorado Extension Service, "Annual Reports of the County Extension Agents of Baca, Kit Carson, Washington and Yuma Counties for 1935, 1936, and 1937," (Unpublished material, Colorado Extension Service, Fort Collins, Colorado).

placed corn as the principal forage crop. The most popular of the grain sorghums have been Improved Coes and Highland Kafir, which were originated at the Akron Dry-Land Field Station by J. F. Brandon and D. W. Robertson. This station has also developed Brunker oats and two varieties of adapted barleys.[50]

All these adjustments were encouraged by the United States Department of Agriculture, the Colorado Extension Service, and the

(Courtesy Greeley Chamber of Commerce)

Cutting Oats in Colorado

Colorado Agricultural Experiment Station, but the campaign was not without opposition. As late as 1937 the extension agronomist reported:

> In Logan County, the practice was followed of encouraging farmers to plant local adapted seed. In certain instances where farmers insisted that seed from other states was just as good, the county agent furnished seed for * * * side by side demonstrations with excellent results in encouraging farmers to use their home grown seed.[51]

---

[50] Interviews with Alvin Kezer, Fort Collins, Colo., July 3, 1946, and with David W. Robertson, Fort Collins, Colo., July 19, 1946; *Western Farm Life,* June 15, 1920.

[51] Colorado Extension Service, "Annual Report, Extension Agronomy Work, January 1, 1936 to January 1, 1937," (Unpublished material, Colorado Extension Service, Fort Collins, Colo.), 13.

While the farmers of Colorado were experimenting with irrigation and dry farming, they were also experimenting with the most adaptable and profitable crops to raise in the valleys of the South Platte, Arkansas, Rio Grande, and the Colorado Rivers.

SOUTH PLATTE VALLEY

The first crop harvested in the South Platte Valley by the fifty-niners was dry, wild hay, which was cut in Boulder County during the winter of 1858-1859 and hauled by ox-teams to the mining towns of Black Hawk and Central City.[52] For many years after that, haying was the principal industry of the upper Platte Valley.

Some corn was raised in 1859, and a few heads of wheat were grown by accident that year. The next year wheat was sown and harvested by the Wellman Brothers in Boulder County and by S. W. Brown, A. H. Miles, and A. C. Hunt near Denver. Eight years later when W. R. Thomas made his memorable survey of the farms of the Platte valleys, spring wheat, oats, barley, corn, and potatoes were the most popular cultivated crops. Of these, corn was the least popular because it was early decided that corn was not well adapted to this area. According to Thomas' estimate, the St. Vrain Valley that year produced 21,673 bushels of wheat, 2,075 bushels of corn, 31,023 bushels of oats, barley and other grains, and 2,800 bushels of potatoes.[53]

Wheat, oats, and wild hay remained the prevailing crop pattern until repeated croppings caused a decline in the productivity of the soil. In the Cache la Poudre Valley this occurred about 1880. Farmers first tried alternating corn with wheat; when that rotation proved unsatisfactory, they tried alfalfa, which enriches the soil with nitrates.[54]

The culture of alfalfa was introduced into Colorado by Jacob Downing in 1863. A lawyer by profession and a farmer by avocation, in 1861 he joined the First Regiment of Colorado Volunteers and campaigned against the Confederacy in New Mexico. While in the southern part of this state, he acquired about two ounces of alfalfa seed from a farmer across the border in Old Mexico. This seed he planted in the yard of his Denver law office in the spring of 1863. It flourished, and a few years later, perhaps in 1867, he imported from California some seed which he sowed on his Green Mountain ranch near Golden. Notwithstanding the scoffings of his neighbors, he soon had 400 acres planted to alfalfa. California was also the source of the seed which L. K. Perrin received in the mid-sixties and of that which J. C. Feebles imported in the fall of 1871 and

---

52 *History of Clear Creek and Boulder Valley, Colorado* (Chicago, O. L. Baskin & Co., 1880), 391.

53 *Ibid.,* 389; Daniel W. Working, "Agriculture," *History of Colorado,* edited by James H. Baker and LeRoy R. Hafen (5 vols., Denver, 1927), II, 623-629; U. S. Department of Agriculture, *Monthly Report for August and September,* 1869, pp. 295-297; Steinel, *op. cit.,* 50, 447-448.

54 C. A. Duncan, *Memories of Early Days in the Cache la Poudre Valley* (Fort Collins, n.d.), 45-46; Nettleton, *op. cit.,* 11-13.

distributed widely. Likewise the first alfalfa sown in 1872 by the Union Colonists came from California. As said earlier, the plant did not win universal acceptance until the 1880s.[55]

The first attempt to develop a specialized crop in north central Colorado was made by the horticulturists, who were able by 1909 to develop a sizable apple industry. The first fruit trees were set out in 1862, when William Lee planted 125 apple, pear, peach, and plum trees on a little island in Clear Creek. This orchard was greatly expanded in 1864, just before the great flood of that year. Most of the trees were washed away, but some of them were retrieved and transplanted on higher ground. Also in 1862, according to Ansel Watrous, the historian of Larimer County, Abner Loomis planted 500 apple trees in Pleasant Valley. The settlers along the Big Thompson set out fruit trees in 1863, and in 1866 a nursery salesman from Kansas inaugurated fruit-raising on the St. Vrain. After the initial successes in the sixties, extensive planting began in the seventies. J. S. McClelland, who for many years operated one of the most productive orchards, set out his first trees in 1876 on his farm south of Fort Collins. In 1894 the *Rocky Mountain News* declared that "the apple is the king fruit of Northern Colorado," and in 1909 Boulder, Jefferson, and Larimer counties produced 552,824 bushels of apples. Thereafter, this area declined in apple production. Only in southeastern Larimer County is the commercial apple industry important today.[56] Here also has developed an important sour cherry industry. Benjamin Harris was the pioneer grower of cherries around Fort Collins. He grew the Early Richmond and English Morello varieties. As a result of Harris' successes, J. C. Evans and his son Charles got a carload of English Morellos from New York in the fall of 1897 and set out the first commercial cherry orchard in the vicinity of Fort Collins. Cherries, however, did not become popular until about 1915, when C. L. Harvey planted some of the orchards near Terry Lake. In the same years cherries became an important crop around Loveland. In 1939, Larimer County produced 54 per cent of Colorado's cherry crop.[57]

The first agricultural products of the state to become famous outside Colorado were the Greeley potatoes. The Union colonists raised their first potatoes in 1870, but the industry did not become a big thing until the discovery of the value of alfalfa. When it was discovered that the planting of potatoes on alfalfa sod greatly increased their yield, the acreage was expanded and the Greeley merchants began to seek out-of-state markets. In 1886 a number of them organized the Greeley Mercantile Company and the next year

[55] Steinel, *op. cit.,* 411-417.

[56] Colorado State Board of Horticulture, *Annual Reports,* XIV (1902), 101; C. S. Crandall, "Fruit Interests of the State," Colo. Agr. Exp. Sta., *Bulletin 17* (Fort Collins, 1891), 3-12; *Rocky Mountain News,* January 1, 1894; Ansel Watrous, *History of Larimer County, Colorado* (Fort Collins, 1911), 143.

[57] Colorado State Board of Horticulture, *Annual Reports,* XII (1900), 78-80; Watrous, *op. cit.,* 144; Interviews with Charles R. Evans, Fort Collins, Colo., July 24, 1946 and with Mrs. C. L. Harvey, Fort Collins, Colo., August 23, 1946.

sent a man to Texas to develop a market there. He was successful, and within a few years the principal markets outside of Denver and the mountain towns were in Texas and Oklahoma. In the early nineties Greeley "spuds" were also shipped to Kansas, Nebraska, Iowa, California, and to some cities of the Old South.

The heart of the potato district was north of Greeley under Canal No. 2 and the Larimer and Weld Canal, and the reservoirs of these systems were built to supply late water to this crop. Early potatoes were not popular, and most of the fields were planted to a late variety. The average size of these fields was 40 acres, in which potatoes were rotated with wheat and alfalfa. Machine diggers and planters were introduced in the 1890s, and on each farm appeared a potato cellar or dugout which to this day is a characteristic feature of Colorado's potato-raising areas.

For three decades Weld County's production expanded. The 611,582 bushels produced in 1887 became 2,821,285 in 1899. In 1909 the census-takers counted 5,857,691 bushels; and then in 1911 came a disease. At the time, the specialists were not able to identify it, but now they believe it to have been the psyllid yellows. In 1911 the crop was almost a total loss, and the epidemic recurred each year until 1915. Weld County's potato production dropped to 2,455,170 bushels in 1919, and in the next decade it lost its primacy as a potato-producing district to the San Luis Valley.[58] In recent years, however, the county has regained much of its former productivity.

The lamb-feeding industry originated in the vicinity of Fort Collins. The *Fort Collins Express* chronicled its inception in these words:

> Will Bennett and Jim Prout returned from New Mexico in the early part of the week with a band of 1,100 sheep. They were caught in the blizzard near Walsenburg, Colo. and could not proceed upon their journey for a week. The sheep were herded about three miles from town and they had to hire three Mexicans to guard them constantly.[59]

That was in November, 1889. No lambs to speak of had been fed in Colorado before this incident. The Bennett brothers had gone to New Mexico to obtain lambs for their feeding pens at Paxton, Nebraska, in the corn-belt. By chance, a blizzard marooned them in southern Colorado until the lambs were so weak that it was feared that they could not survive a trip to Nebraska. Thereupon it was decided to winter them near Fort Collins, feeding them alfalfa hay

---

[58] J. Max Clark, "Potato Culture near Greeley, Colorado," U. S. Department of Agriculture, *Yearbook 1904* (Washington, 1905), 311-322; E. H. Grubb, *The Potato* (Garden City, 1912), 363-372; Carl H. Metzger, "Growing Potatoes in Colorado," Colo. Agr. Exp. Sta., *Bulletin 412* (Fort Collins, 1934), 7-14; Leslie B. Daniels, "Controlling Colorado Potato Pests," Colo. Agr. Exp. Sta., *Bulletin 437* (Fort Collins, 1937), 4; Boyd, *Greeley and the Union Colony*, 152-155; *Rocky Mountain News,* January 1, 1894, *Field and Farm,* September 24, 1892, July 6, 1895, October 17, 1896.

[59] *Fort Collins Express,* November 23, 1889.

and some corn. When the lambs were sent to the Chicago market the next spring, they not only sold well, but the last two cars topped the market. In this manner was born one of the largest industries of northern Colorado.

The Bennett brothers not only repeated the experience, but they were soon joined by others. Six thousand lambs were fed in Larimer

(Photo by Colorado A. & M. College Photo Shop)

Lambs Feeding Near Fort Collins, December 9, 1924

County during the winter of 1891-1892; 30,000 in 1892-1893; 40,000 in 1893-1894; 60,000 in 1894-1895; 80,000 in 1895-1896; 128,000 in 1896-1897; 193,000 in 1897-1898; 210,600 in 1898-1899. Weld County fed 15,000 in 1895-1896; 40,000 in 1896-1897, and 73,000 in 1898-1899. Within a decade lamb-feeding had become a major industry. It continued to grow until the people of northern Colorado could boast that more lambs were fed there than in any other district in the United States. For instance, in 1925 northern Colorado fed 1,250,000 lambs, which was 31 per cent of the lambs fed in the United States and 78 per cent of those fed in Colorado. In recent years Weld County has fed more lambs than Larimer.

The first lambs were nearly all obtained in New Mexico—direct descendants of the original Spanish sheep in the Southwest or the offspring of these sheep and American Merino rams. Later, lambs were shipped in from the ranges of Idaho, Utah, Montana, and Wyoming. They were purchased in the fall, fattened on alfalfa and corn, and shipped to Chicago in the spring. Long trains left Fort Collins on spring Tuesdays to arrive in Chicago for the next Monday's market. Sometimes shipments were made to New York, and in 1901 Beach & Foy shipped 5,000 head direct to England. After World War I, the market shifted partly to Denver.

The business, though generally lucrative, has always been speculative, so that several black seasons spot its history. Such were the feeding seasons of 1920-1921 and 1929-1930.[60]

The sugar beet industry in Colorado originated on the Western Slope, where the first sugar factory was built at Grand Junction in 1899. The next year two factories were built in the Arkansas Valley, and in 1901 the first factory in the South Platte Valley was built at Loveland. Thereafter construction was rapid. Factories were constructed at Eaton and Greeley in 1902, at Fort Collins, Longmont, and Windsor in 1903, at Sterling in 1905, and at Fort Morgan and Brush in 1906. Seventy-nine thousand acres were planted to sugar beets in the valley in 1909, and in that year Colorado became the leading beet sugar-producing state in the union. Later, factories were established at Brighton (1917), Fort Lupton (1920), Ovid (1926), and Johnstown (1926).

This rapid development of the sugar industry in Colorado was the culmination of many years of interest, promotion, and experimentation. Peter Magnes of Littleton grew the first sugar beets in Colorado in the 1860s. In the next decade a group of Denver business men organized the Colorado Beet Sugar Manufacturing Company, but it did not get beyond the organizational stage. Newspapers and magazines participated in the discussion. Then in the late eighties the movement gathered momentum. The newly established agricultural experiment station at Fort Collins began experimentation which was paralleled in the 1890s by many private efforts. The factories constructed at Grand Island, Nebraska, and at Lehi, Utah, exerted not a little influence, while the passage of the protective Dingley tariff of 1897 seems to have given the encouragement needed to transform dreams into reality.

The sugar factories brought to this area increased land values, growth of towns, a more diversified agriculture, and labor problems. To obtain the labor needed to hoe, thin, and harvest the beets, the sugar companies imported German-Russians from Nebraska, Japanese from California, and Spanish-Americans from the southern part of the state. In 1909, of the 10,724 beet workers in northern Colorado, 5,870 were German-Russian, 2,160 were Japanese, and 1,002 were Spanish-American. Ten years later the German-Russians had become

60 Lowell Clarke, "Lamb Feeding in Colorado," *Eighteenth Annual Report of the Bureau of Animal Industry, 1901* (Washington, 1902), 275-278; Denver *Daily Stockman,* February 1, 1898; *Rocky Mountain News,* January 1, 1894, January 1, 1899; *Field and Farm,* June 1, 1901; Interview with Charles R. Evans, July 24, 1946.

owners and renters, and the Spanish-Americans and Mexicans were supplying most of the beet labor.[61]

The greatest concentration of dairy cattle in the state is in the South Platte Valley, where there is the greatest concentration of people. Dairying started there in the early days. W. R. Thomas in his journey through the valley noted the pioneer dairies. In the Big Thompson Valley he noted that J. J. Ryan had made 7,500 pounds of cheese from 35 cows. In 1871 or the year after, R. Q. Tenney of Fort Collins obtained a Jersey bull and a heifer from the East and

Cattle on Farms   (Courtesy Greeley Chamber of Commerce)

Scene near Greeley

established his Victor Dairy. Until about 1890 the industry remained a household industry; in that year there were only eight cheese factories and eleven creameries in the state, but ten years later there were 79 creameries and cheese factories, of which 41 were in the Platte Valley. In 1901-1902 the first condensery was built at Fort Lupton, but as Denver and the other cities have grown, emphasis in this area has been more and more on the sale of whole milk. About the time of World War I, the Holstein was the most popular dairy breed with the Jersey a preferred second.[62]

Another development, of more recent years, has been the mechanization of agriculture in this valley as elsewhere in the state. The first horse-powered farm machinery brought into Colorado by the

[61] "Beet-sugar Industry in the United States," *Senate Doc.* 22, 61st Congress, 1st Session, 3-23; "Immigrants in Industries," *Senate Doc.* 633, 61st Congress, 2nd Session, Pt. XXV, vol. II, 112-116; Steinel, *op. cit.,* 281-308.

[62] J. A. Rait, "Dairy Marketing Survey in Colorado," Colo. Ext. Service, *Bulletin, Series 1, 151-A* (Fort Collins, 1919); Colorado Dairy Commissioner, *Annual and Biennial Reports,* 1889-1890, pp. 11-12; 1899, pp. 16-19; 1901, p. 8; Ansel Watrous, *Rollin Q. Tenney* (Fort Collins. 1921), 11.

fifty-niners were mowers, some of which were in the Clear Creek Valley as early as June, 1860. The first threshing machine was hauled across the plains in 1861 and was apparently used that fall.[63] The McCormick Harvester Company appointed an agent in Denver in 1869, and new reapers were shipped in either that year or the one following.[64] Horses continued to supply the motor power on northern Colorado farms until World War I, when tractors began to supplant them. This power revolution first affected the dry-land area, and only during the past fifteen years has it transformed agriculture in the irrigated sections. Small tractors have become common, as have combines, motorized mowers, and motorized buck-rakes. Machinery is also beginning to transform beet culture, and during World War II mechanical thinners and harvesters were used in the valley.

ARKANSAS VALLEY

The Arkansas Valley is known for its cantaloupes, its alfalfa, its sugar beets, and its vine seed industry. Corn and onions are also important crops.

The father of the Arkansas Valley melon industry was George W. Swink, who came to Rocky Ford in 1871. Perhaps he grew watermelons and cantaloupes in 1874; we are certain that he grew them in 1875 under the newly constructed Rocky Ford Ditch. For many years Swink grew mostly watermelons. In 1878 his harvest was so good that he called in his neighbors and some of his friends from La Junta and offered them all the watermelons they could eat. They ate a wagon load. The next year he repeated the invitation, and in this manner Rocky Ford's Melon Day originated.

The first Netted Gem cantaloupes to be raised around Rocky Ford were grown by J. W. Eastwood and J. E. Gauger in 1885, and the next year George Swink followed their example. It was this variety with a silver-colored netting and a green meat that made Rocky Ford famous.

As in the case of most of Colorado's produce, the first markets were in the mining towns, each individual shipping his own produce. Until 1894, they shipped in barrels and boxes; in that year they originated the standard crate, which has been adopted wherever melons are raised in the United States. Two years later they shipped their first produce to mid-western markets and organized the Melon Growers' Association of Rocky Ford, with Swink as president. Nearly all the growers belonged to this organization. In 1897 they shipped 121 cars eastward, some of them reaching New York, and the next year they so overexpanded their membership and acreage that the market became glutted. The setback, however, was only temporary.[65]

[63] Steinel, *op. cit.,* 50; Working, *op. cit.,* 585.

[64] William T. Hutchinson, *Cyrus Hall McCormick* (2 vols., New York, 1930-1935), II, 458-459.

[65] P. K. Blinn, "Development of the Rockyford Cantaloupe Industry," Colo. Agr. Exp. Sta., *Bulletin 108* (Fort Collins, 1906), 3-16; U. S. Supreme Court, Kansas v. Colorado, *Transcript of Record,* October term, 1905, No. 7, pp. 908-909; Steinel, *op. cit.,* 469-470; Rocky Ford *Enterprise,* September 7, 1893; October 4, 1894; October 1, 8, 22, 1896; *Field and Farm,* March 20, 1897; July 20, 1901.

At the turn of the century the district around Ordway in Crowley County began producing cantaloupes, and carlot shipments from Ordway were made for the first time in 1903. In 1909 the Rocky Ford district shipped 1,129 cars, and in 1914 the two districts combined supplied the market with 2,674 cars. The city consumers' preference for pink-meated fruit brought about a shift from the Netted Gems to the more popular varieties. In 1915, 80 per cent of the Rocky Ford cantaloupes were still the older variety, but ten years later Netted Gems had ceased to be of commercial importance.[66]

The seed industry of the valley grew out of the cantaloupe industry. By 1899, seed-growers were supplying melon-growers in Texas, Florida, Georgia, and other southern states. This industry grew until in 1925 it was estimated that the Arkansas Valley produced 95 per cent of the cantaloupe seed grown in the United States and 90 per cent of the cucumber seed. Seed growing also developed in the South Platte Valley, where Henry Lee was the pioneer seedsman, and on the Western Slope. In 1929 Colorado ranked fifth among the states in flower and seed production, being exceeded only by California, Idaho, Michigan, and Montana.[67]

The most important crop in the Arkansas Valley is alfalfa. According to a letter which George Swink wrote to D. W. Working in 1901, its culture there dates back to 1868, when George Gilbert planted some seed near Pueblo. Swink himself introduced it into the Rocky Ford region in 1877, and that same spring E. R. Sizer of Las Animas sowed a four-acre field. Declared the Las Animas *Leader* on May 23, 1879: "The conviction is gradually obtaining that alfalfa will succeed here. Mr. Merritt * * * is putting in four acres this spring."[68] In 1924, 42 per cent of the irrigated land in the valley was devoted to this crop.[69]

All the agriculture in the valley is in some measure based upon this leguminous plant. It is used in rotation with sugar beets, cantaloupes, and grains. In the 1890s it became the basis of a lamb-feeding industry similar to that of northern Colorado. On January 1, 1925, 265,000 or 16 per cent of the lambs on feed in Colorado were in this valley. Also in the 1890s the farmers began to raise alfalfa for sale. The water superintendent of division no. 2 reported on December 1, 1900: "There has recently sprung up a market for Arkansas Valley alfalfa in St. Louis and Kansas City, and owing to the reasonable rates made by the railroads, alfalfa shipped to these

66 O. W. Schleussner and C. W. Kitchen, "Marketing and Distribution of Western Muskmelons in 1915," U. S. Department of Agriculture, *Bulletin 401* (Washington, 1916), 31-38; N. D. Sanborn, "Harvesting and Marketing Cantaloupes and Honey Dew Melons in the Arkansas Valley of Colorado," Colo. Agri. Exp. Sta., *Bulletin 312* (Fort Collins, 1926), 9-11; *Rocky Mountain News,* January 1, 1904.

67 *Colorado Agricultural Statistics, 1935* (Denver, n.d.), 125.

68 Joseph O. Van Hook, "Settlement and Economic Development of the Arkansas Valley from Pueblo to the Colorado-Kansas Line, 1860-1900," (Unpublished Ph.D. thesis, University of Colorado, 1933), 306; Steinel, *op. cit.,* 416.

69 Thomas H. Summers and E. D. Smith, "An Agricultural Program for the Arkansas Valley of Colorado," Colo. Ext. Service, *Bulletin 239-A* (Fort Collins, 1925), 24.

cities is yielding the farmers of the district $6.00 per ton net.''[70]
Eight years later the valley became the cradle of an important alfalfa
milling industry.

The birth and growth of this industry were related by Floyd M.
Wilson, its founder, in a letter to the writer, dated July 19, 1946:

We first learn of the milling of alfalfa in Colorado in
1907 when Senator Harry Casaday of Boulder and Herman

(Courtesy Greeley Chamber of Commerce)

Barley Threshing Near La Salle

Kooser of the Missouri Pacific lines organized the Colorado
Milling Company. This Company built its first mill at Niwot,
Boulder County. In the spring of 1908, Floyd Wilson, who
had formerly been associated with Casaday and Kooser in
the Niwot mill, organized the Denver Alfalfa Milling and
Products Company with headquarters at Hartman, Prowers
County. The building of the Hartman mill was closely followed by another at Wiley, and in 1909 a third mill at Bristol.
Bryan Haywood of Denver, who was associated with Fred
Best, came into the Arkansas Valley in 1910 and built alfalfa
mills at Kornman (now Wilson Junction) and McClave. Other
pioneer alfalfa millers include Cora R. Strain, Ray Strain
and James P. Campbell who operated successfully many

---

[70] Colorado State Engineer, *Tenth Biennial Report,* 1899-1900, p. 74.

years in the alfalfa acreage lying north of Lamar in the May Valley and Big Bend districts.

The next few years brought many mills in the upper Arkansas Valley at Fowler, Cheraw, Ordway, Crowley and King Center. The mill at Fowler was operated by Gus Trent and George Boyd, but later owned by Andy Wadington, who made the Fowler mill famous for pea green alfalfa. The Auckland mill at King Center was noted for high quality alfalfa, most of which was grown on the Auckland farms. About 1914 John Thatcher of Pueblo built alfalfa mills at Avondale and Vineland, which operated successfully for many years. The Amity Land Company, under the management of Mr. W. S. Partridge, in seeking an outlet for their alfalfa tonnage erected a large plant at Holly, near the State line. In 1916 Henry Grout, of Trinidad, and B. F. Tucker of Lamar, interested capital to erect a mill at Hoehne, which later passed into the hands of the Denver Alfalfa Company. Otto Weiss, a pioneer feed manufacturer of Wichita, who first learned of the nutritive value of alfalfa during his boyhood days in Germany, did much to introduce the milling of alfalfa in the United States. Mr. Weiss crossed the Colorado-Kansas line and came into Colorado in about 1918 and built a model mill in Bent County at Ft. Lyon. * * *

Between the years 1912 and 1916 many small mills were built in Northern Colorado at Bijou, Severance, Ault, Kersey, Iliff, Keensburg, Weldona, Goodrich, Hillrose, East Lake and Mead, but these mills did not survive the economic upset following World War I. The cattle feeding industry in Northern Colorado had a prior claim to the alfalfa, and the mills produced less and less tonnage until they were finally closed down. Modern mills will again some day be built in Northern Colorado, as the tonnage and climate will afford prosperous operations.

In the early part of 1930 the process of dehydrating alfalfa was introduced in Illinois. The first dehydrator in Colorado was built at Wiley in 1939 by the Denver Alfalfa Company. Later dehydrators were installed at Hartman, Bristol, Wilson Junction, McClave, Johnstown and more recently a dehydrating plant has been completed at LaSalle. The dehydrating process has to do with drying the alfalfa fresh from the fields soon after cutting. This drying process is usually under about 1800° Fahrenheit. Science has proven that this process preserves the vitamins and carotene which oftentimes are depleted in alfalfa that is suncured and stacked.[71]

George Swink was also the father of the sugar-beet industry. It was he who in the early nineties imported seed from Germany, dis-

---

[71] See also "Floyd M. Wilson and the Alfalfa Milling Industry," *Colorado Magazine,* XXI (1944), 100-101.

tributed it among his neighbors, and sent samples to Washington for testing. It was he who attended a sugar beet convention at Grand Island, Nebraska, and interested Henry T. Oxnard, president of the American Beet Sugar Company, in sugar manufacturing in the valley. In 1900, this company built a factory at Rocky Ford, and the same year the National Sugar Manufacturing Company built one at Sugar City. Factories were also constructed at Holly and Lamar in 1905, at Swink in 1906, and at Las Animas in 1907. In 1925, 31,733 acres of sugar beets were harvested in the Arkansas Valley compared to 155,409 acres in the South Platte Valley.[72]

Since 1927, onions have been an important crop in Otero and Pueblo counties. At that time the Sweet Spanish or Valencia variety was introduced, and within a few years the valley outstripped the Western Slope in production. This was the valley's second experience with this crop, onion-raising as a commercial enterprise having been started in 1878 with seed imported from Sonora, Mexico, and in the year 1899, Otero County produced 2,557 bushels of onions, which is more than the census has recorded in recent years.[73]

At one time the Upper Arkansas Valley was the premier fruit-growing district of the state. The first fruit trees were set out in Fremont County in 1867 by Jesse Frazier, who orginated the Colorado orange apple. In 1888 he had the state's largest bearing apple orchard, and his harvest was estimated at 15,000 bushels. Other early growers were W. A. Helm, W. C. Catlin, B. F. Rockafellow, and James A. McCandless. The latter originated the McCandless pear.[74]

Farther up the valley, near Buena Vista, the lettuce-raising industry of the state originated in 1918. That year G. D. Isabel rented ten acres of land and planted it to lettuce. The harvest was good and the financial return high. In succeeding years others joined him until by the mid-twenties the industry had mushroomed in each of the mountain valleys. In 1925, one of these valleys—the Eagle Valley—shipped 683 cars of lettuce in addition to 125 cars of mixed vegetables.[75]

SAN LUIS VALLEY

The San Luis Valley has had a varied and interesting crop history. In its south, the first settlers, the Spanish-Americans, grew for their subsistence corn, wheat, beans, peas, and red peppers. In its north, in Saguache County, pioneer Otto Mears in 1867 sowed 200 acres of wheat and harvested 60 bushels to the acre. That year he brought the first mower, reaper, and threshing machine into the

[72] Steinel, *op. cit.,* 304-307.

[73] E. J. Allen, "A Progress Report on Onion Investigations in the Arkansas Valley," Colo. Agr. Exp. Station, *Press Bulletin 75* (Fort Collins, 1931), 1-2; Van Hook, "Settlement and Economic Development of the Arkansas Valley," 312.

[74] Crandall, *op. cit.,* 12.

[75] R. A. McGinty, "Head Lettuce in Colorado," Colo. Agr. Exp. Sta., *Bulletin 283* (Fort Collins, 1923), 2-16; R. A. McGinty, "High Altitude Vegetable Growing," Colo. Agr. Exp. Sta., *Bulletin 309* (Fort Collins, 1926), 3-8; G. A. Peterson, "Lettuce, Peas and Cauliflower at Buena Vista, Colorado," *Market Growers Journal,* XLIII (1928), 786-788.

valley.[76] Nevertheless, it remained largely a winter range for cattle and sheep until the 1880s, when, following the construction of the big canals by T. C. Henry, it was settled by farmers of North European stock.

T. C. Henry sought to repeat here the successes with wheat which he had had in Kansas. Beginning operations in the spring of 1884, he planted great fields. His North Farm, located six miles north of Monte Vista, contained 7,000 acres, and his South Farm, south of the Rio Grande, contained 3,000. So extensive were his operations that the *San Luis Valley Courier* in June, 1889, thought that he would soon have "the third greatest wheat field in America." Once again T. C. Henry became one of the big wheat-growers of the nation.[77]

His neighbors followed his lead; spring wheat and oats became the standard crops of the valley. The land was easily cleared by dragging a railroad rail across the ground and by burning the chico brush after it had been raked into windrows. Oftentimes the virgin soil was not plowed and the grain was drilled in directly. To water their fields, the settlers developed a unique system of irrigation, known as subirrigation. Water was applied through numerous trenches in such abundance as to raise the water table of the porous soil to the level of the plant roots. The first yields were good— sometimes between 40 and 60 bushels an acre—and flour mills were built at Del Norte, Monte Vista, Hooper, Mosca, Alamosa, La Jara, and Conejos. Nevertheless, seepage and repeated cropping impoverished the soil, and within a decade some farmers were abandoning their farms and others were seeking a system of rotation. Some tried summer-fallowing, but more found the answer in field peas, and out of this crop grew a new agricultural era.[78]

In 1901 or 1902 someone discovered that ripened field peas could take the place of corn in the fattening of lambs. As a result, there developed in this valley a lamb-feeding industry somewhat different from those in the other valleys. The animals were not fed in feed-lots, but were turned into fields of ripened peas early in the fall and shipped to market before New Year's Day. Many of the lambs were not shipped in, but obtained from the mountain pastures surrounding the valley. The business grew rapidly, and the 16,000 lambs fed in 1902 became 320,000 in 1905.[79]

[76] Sidney Jocknick, *Early Days on the Western Slope of Colorado* (Denver, 1913), 19; *Pioneers of the San Juan Country* by Sarah Platt Decker Chapter, Durango, Colo., (Colorado Springs, 1942), I, 40, 237.

[77] U. S. Supreme Court, Kansas *v.* Colorado, *Transcript of Record,* October Term, 1905, No. 7, p. 707; *San Luis Valley Courier,* June 26, 1889.

[78] C. E. Siebenthal, "Geology and Water Resources of the San Luis Valley, Colorado," U. S. Geological Survey, *Water-supply Paper 240* (Washington, 1910), 26-28; J. Garnett Holmes, "Soil Survey of the San Luis Valley, Colorado," U. S. Bureau of Soils, *Field Operations, 1903* (Washington, 1904), 1100-1118; Ralph H. Brown, "Monte Vista: Sixty Years of a Colorado Community," *Geographical Review,* XVIII (1928), 274-275; *Rocky Mountain News,* January 1, 1899.

[79] *Field and Farm,* September 14, 1901; Pueblo *Chieftain,* January 1, 1907; July 7, 1908; *Rocky Mountain News,* January 1, 1906; Colorado State Engineer, *Thirteenth Biennial Report,* 1905-1906, p. 168.

About this year the San Luis Valley farmers made another discovery—that hogs also could be fattened on peas and sold at a premium. Sometimes they were turned into the fields directly; other times they followed the lambs and salvaged the peas which the lambs had shelled. After fattening they were shipped usually to the West Coast, to markets in Los Angeles and San Francisco. This industry, however, experienced a temporary reverse in 1912-1913, when a plague of cholera scourged the valley. It was part of a nation-wide epidemic which killed 6,738,283 hogs during the year ending March 31, 1913. In the San Luis Valley the county agent reported that "Dead hogs were strewn over the fields and along the canals and highways everywhere." The farmers were reluctant to believe that it was hog cholera, but early in 1913, Dr. George H. Glover, head of the veterinary department at the agricultural college, was called into the valley. At a meeting held in Monte Vista on February 1, 1913, it was agreed to organize the Monte Vista Hog Growers' Association in order to hire a veterinarian and to eradicate the contagion by vaccination, quarantine, and destruction of the dead animals. Meetings were held in the other towns, and five other organizations were formed. They employed two veterinarians, and within five months the epidemic was checked and brought under control. The industry regained its earlier vigor, and in 1924, 89,808 hogs were shipped from the valley.[80]

For various reasons, in the late twenties sweet clover supplanted field peas as the basis of the valley's agriculture. A root-rot disease had reduced the acreage and yield of peas, and the extension service urged a shift to clover. So vigorously did one county agent conduct this campaign that he became known by the sobriquet of Sweet Clover Stewart. This change brought about a marked decline in the hog industry and altered the system of lamb-feeding. Many of the sheep are no longer pastured on the mountain ranges during the summer months, but are kept in the valley as farm flocks to pasture on sweet clover and to be sent to market in late August and September.[81]

Today the potato industry dominates the economy of the San Luis Valley. This industry has always centered in Rio Grande County, where the gravelly soil of an alluvial fan is particularly suitable for potato culture. Although a Scotch gardener by the name of R. C. Nesbit is credited with its initiation, it was another Scotchman, Roderick A. Chisholm, who first made the county potato-conscious. In 1889, he entered a national contest sponsored by the *American Agriculturist* and won with a yield of 847½ bushels to a measured acre. In a decade or so the valley began to rival the Greeley district, and in the early 1920s surpassed its rival in pro-

---

[80] L. M. Winsor, "First Annual Report of the Agent for the San Luis Valley, State of Colorado, from * * * December 2, 1912 to * * * June 30, 1913 (Unpublished, Colorado Extension Service, Fort Collins, Colo.), 5-19; Thomas H. Summers and E. D. Smith, "An Agricultural Program for the San Luis Valley of Colorado," Colo. Ext. Service, *Bulletin 267-A* (Fort Collins, 1927), 52-57; Pueblo *Chieftain,* December 3, 1905; Interview with George H. Glover, Fort Collins, Colo., June 26, 1946.

[81] Harvey C. Skoglund, "A History of San Luis Valley, Colorado," (Unpublished M.A. thesis, Colorado State College of Education, 1941), 171; Interview with T. G. Stewart, Fort Collins, Colo., May 17, 1946.

ductivity. The standard rotation became potatoes, peas, and grain, and later sweet clover usually took the place of peas. The harvest was sorted and bagged by Spanish-Americans, and some of it was stored in thick-walled, adobe-brick potato cellars, which were built above the ground to avoid the high water table. Nor did the industry cease to expand. In the decade 1924-1934, its harvest increased from 5,455,312 bushels to 9,256,900 bushels. In 1939 the harvest of the valley was considerably reduced, but in 1944 Conejos, Costilla, and Rio Grande Counties produced more than ever before. In that year, Rio Grande County alone raised 5,941,520 bushels.[82]

Until a decade ago the most popular variety was the Brown Beauty potato. Chisholm had made his record with them, and in 1929 L. G. Shutte raised them and set a new record of 1,145.17 bushels to an acre. In the 1930s they lost favor and were replaced in the seedbins by the Red McClures.[83]

The unrelenting search for an agriculture adapted to the cool nights and the one-hundred-and-ten-day growing season of the San Luis Valley led in the early twenties to the development of a vegetable industry which in 1942 exported 1,334 cars of pod peas, 968 cars of cauliflower, 385 cars of lettuce, and 609 cars of mixed vegetables, in addition to some cabbage, spinach, and broccoli. The lettuce industry started around Creede in 1920 or 1921 and shifted quickly down the valley to South Fork and Del Norte, where it owes some of its origin to the efforts of a county agent and three Smith-Hughes teachers. Conejos County specialized in pod peas, and Costilla County in cauliflower. Commercial cauliflower was first raised in this county in 1923 by two Japanese on land owned by the Costilla Estates Development Company.[84]

WESTERN SLOPE

The agricultural history of the Western Slope has likewise been a story of experimentation and adaptation. The first settlers believed that they could raise fruit in the Grand Valley and along the North Fork of the Gunnison. Consequently, the story of these valleys from the Year One of their settlement concerns the fruit industry. This is not true of the Uncompahgre, for the first farmers in that valley went into general farming to supply the mining towns of Ouray and Telluride, and, although the valley had its fruit boom, its agriculture has always remained more diversified than that of the other two valleys.

The Ute reservation was thrown open to settlement in September, 1881, and that fall Samuel Wade, after having visited the North Fork

[82] Ralph H. Brown, "Geography of a Portion of the San Luis Valley," *Scientific Monthly*, XXVII (1928), 492-501; Steinel, *op. cit.*, 431.

[83] Metzger, *op. cit.*, 14; Skoglund, *op. cit.*, 168.

[84] Colorado State Engineer, *Thirty-first Biennial Report*, 1941-1942, p. 474; McGinty, "Head Lettuce in Colorado," 6; McGinty, "High Altitude Vegetable Growing," 7-8, 22; T. C. McPherson, San Acacio, Colo., to R. G. Dunbar, May 21, 1946; Interview with T. G. Stewart, May 17, 1946.

of the Gunnison, returned to his home in Missouri to get some fruit trees. Four years later he related the story in this manner:

> On the first of September, 1881, E. T. Hotchkiss, myself and others came into the Valley of the North Fork and while making a stay of only one day, I discovered thorn apple and buffalo berry growing luxuriantly and in abundance. Therefore, with this evidence before me, I became strongly of the belief that many varieties of fruit might be grown here and resolved at once to make the trial. The following spring I brought with me from the State of Missouri, an experimental bill of fruit trees and plants, together with some forest trees. This consisted of 200 apple trees of the following varieties: Winter Winesap, Genette, Ben Davis, Maiden's Blush, Early Harvest, Hislop, Transparent, and Sylvan Crabs; 10 Bartlett Pears, 10 Early Golden Apricots, 20 Early Golden York Peaches, Hale's Early Crawford, Early Stump, the world-old Mixen Cling; 200 cherries, Morrell variety; 5 Osage quinces; 100 grape vines, Concord and Delaware; 1,000 blackberry plants of the Kittatines and Lawton varieties; 100 Turner and Mammoth Cluster raspberries; 12 Red Dutch Currants; 50 Houghton gooseberries; 500 silver leaf and soft maple trees, with quite a bill of the ornamentals.[85]

These trees were shipped to Gunnison by railroad and hauled across Black Mesa on sleds. The snow was so deep that sometimes the sleds would be several feet above the tandem mule team. Wrote Wade, "after shoveling snow for about three weeks * * * I succeeded in getting onto my ranch (now Paonia), on the 21st day of April, 1882." These were the first trees planted on the North Fork. The next spring when a nursery salesman from Colorado Springs came into the valley, four of the settlers bought trees and started nurseries.[86]

On the Colorado, the first plantings were made likewise in the spring of 1882 by Elam Blaine with stock brought from Fremont County by Gideon Frasier. Settler Blaine set out both apples and peaches. In the beginning peach orchards were more numerous around Grand Junction and Fruita than farther up the valley at Palisade, where apples were more popular. In 1891 the Grand Junction growers originated Peach Day, which was held each September during the peach harvest. In 1895 William Jennings Bryan was present. However, a series of severe winters and spring frosts favored the protected area around Palisade and led, about 1900, to a reversal of this situation. Consequently, in 1904 Grand Junction discontinued Peach Day.

There was much experimentation with varieties during the early years. Out of more than a hundred varieties of apples, the Jonathon

---

[85] Quoted from the *Colorado Farmer*, November 12, 1885, in Steinel, *op. cit.*, 507-508.
[86] Colorado State Board of Horticulture, *Annual Reports*, VI (1891), 98-99; Ezra G. Wade, "Early Days at Paonia," *Colorado Magazine*, IV (1927), 67-70.

and the Winesap emerged the most popular. Among the peaches, the Elberta soon became the favorite. In January, 1904, the Palisade *Tribune* declared that four-fifths of the peach trees to be planted in the Palisade district that year would be Elbertas.

The market for the first decade was in the mining towns and in the irrigated communities of the Eastern Slope. In 1891 some growers organized the Grand Junction Fruit Growers' Association to provide for more orderly selling of their crop. At first they selected one of their number as salesman for the entire association, but in 1897 they employed a full-time manager. This association apparently shipped the first fruit out of the state in 1892, when it sent berries to Omaha and Kansas City. Out-of-state shipments became common in the mid-nineties.

The popularity of Colorado fruit in out-of-state markets, the prizes which it received at various fairs, the advertising given the area, the high prices—all led to a fruit boom lasting from about 1901 to 1911. Realtors sold orchards in ten-acre tracts, would-be fruit growers came from the East, and land values climbed to fantastic figures. Late in 1908 a six-acre peach orchard near Palisade sold for $24,000. Production was high during these years. In 1909 the apple crop of Mesa County totaled 980,273 bushels, and its peach crop added up to 286,992 bushels.

The boom collapsed in the years 1912-1915. Some of the most important contributing factors were: (1) destructive late spring frosts; (2) competition with Washington apples; (3) a seepage of irrigation water which permeated the soil with alkali; (4) fall in prices; and (5) too numerous broods of codling moth. The codling moth menace became so great that the cost of spraying from eight to eleven times a season became uneconomical. The apple growers began to pull out their trees, and the lower Grand Valley gradually shifted to dairying, early potatoes, pinto beans, poultry, grain, tomatoes, and sugar beets. The *coup de grâce* to the apple industry was given in 1926 when an interpretation of the federal Pure Food and Drug Act required that spray materials be removed from fruit previous to packing for shipment. By 1939 Mesa County's apple crop had been reduced to 13,024 bushels. Experience had proved that the apple industry was not adapted to the Grand Valley.[87]

On the other hand, the peach industry has proved itself adapted to the upper Grand Valley, and after a decade or so of decline its acreage increased rapidly in the thirties. Whereas in 1925 there were 234,558 peach trees in Mesa County, in 1935 the federal census recorded 544,851 trees and in 1940, 728,891. The industry, however, was seriously threatened in the thirties by the peach mosaic disease. Although it appeared in the forepart of the decade, it was not identified until 1935. It was then checked by destruction of the infected trees: 32,163 were destroyed in 1935, 10,945 in 1936, and 3,517 in 1937.

[87] Rait, "Development of Grand Junction and the Colorado River Valley," 27-30, 37-84; E. P. Sandsten, *et al.* "A Fruit Survey of Mesa County," Colo. Agr. Exp. Sta., *Bulletin 223* (Fort Collins, 1917).

Marketing has been one of the most consistent problems of the peach grower. The first marketing association organized in the Palisade district was the Palisade Fruit Growers' Association in 1903. This was followed in 1906 by the organization of the Palisade Peach Growers' Association, which experimented with a community packing house. In 1923 the present-day cooperative United Fruit Growers' Association appeared. Nevertheless, cooperation among the growers was difficult, and the annual drop in prices as the bulk of the peaches came on the market was often disastrous. Dissatisfaction led in November, 1938, to the organization of a committee of fifteen growers, which after determining the wishes of the peach-raising communities, obtained the passage of the Colorado Agricultural Marketing Act of 1939. Acting under the authority of this law, the growers adopted in the summer of 1939 a marketing agreement which provided for grade and size regulation, price posting, weighing and inspection stations, and advertising and sales promotion. At the same time, they elected a board of control, charged with the responsibility of recommending annually to the state director of agriculture the regulations to be enforced. This organization was immediately effective in maintaining prices throughout the harvest. During World War II prices were high and production expanded. The 914,628 bushels shipped from Mesa County became 1,396,401 bushels in 1943 and 1,444,870 bushels in 1945. A boom resulted comparable to that of forty years before.[88]

In the North Fork country of Delta County, apples became the leading fruit crop. Until 1902 the fruit of this valley had to be hauled twenty to thirty miles by wagon to Delta for shipment. In that year the Denver and Rio Grande built to Paonia, the North Fork Fruit Growers' Association was organized, and the district entered the boom period. Although it participated in the collapse, by the 1920s it had become the premier commercial apple-raising district in the state.[89]

The principal potato-raising district on the Western Slope was formerly in the valley of the Roaring Fork in Garfield and Pitkin counties. Here pioneer William M. Dinkel planted two acres of potatoes in 1882—the first year of settlement—and harvested 200 sacks to the acre. Encouraged by this success, the next spring he planted seven acres, and in 1891 he shipped the first carload of potatoes out of the valley. This business venture was a failure, and the commercial era had to wait until toward the end of the decade. As in the Greeley and San Luis districts, the Roaring Fork was a late potato district; the growers favored the Peachblow variety. This area, which catered to the hotel and dining-car trade, hit its

---

[88] Colorado Extension Service, "Annual Reports of Extension Work in Mesa County, 1934-1941," (Unpublished material, Colorado Extension Service, Fort Collins, Colo.); Mary Rait, "Development of the Peach Industry in the Colorado River Valley," *Colorado Magazine,* XXII (1945), 247-258; Colorado Director of Markets, "Eighteenth Annual Report, July 1, 1939-June 30, 1940," mimeographed, 3-16.

[89] Wilson M. Rockwell, "The Fruit Utopia of the North Fork of the Gunnison," *Colorado Magazine,* XV (1938), 89-98.

peak production about 1909, and since World War I the Uncompahgre Valley has raised more potatoes.[90]   In 1938 the entire Western Slope potato industry was threatened by an epidemic of bacterial ring rot, which was first observed near Olathe in the summer of 1937. This disease later became epidemic in the other potato-raising areas of the state.[91]

The farmers of Colorado have been harassed by pests and diseases other than those which have troubled the potato, fruit, and swine industries. Grasshoppers appeared as early as 1861 and reappeared in 1862, 1864, 1865, 1866, and 1867. Their visits were particularly destructive in the years 1873 through 1876. J. Hetzel of Longmont made a device for destroying them, but it was not very practical. They reappeared in 1895 after the drought of 1893-1894 and again in the mid-thirties. The lamb-feeding industry suffered losses from hemorrhagic septicemia and in the early twenties from paratyphoid dysentery. In addition, there have been frequent losses from storms, especially hail. The eastern half of the state lies in a belt of high hail frequency, and, although the hail storms are generally local in their devastation, sometimes they have damaged large areas. "On one occasion in 1928 a single hailstorm caused over $2,000,000 damage to fruit and sugar beets."[92]

FARMERS' ORGANIZATIONS

Whether in distress or in success, the Colorado farmers have generally worked as individuals. Aside from their ditch companies, it was not until the twentieth century that any appreciable number of them participated in associational effort. The first agricultural association was formed by a group of real estate promoters. It was the Colorado Agricultural Society, organized on March 28, 1863, to sponsor an agricultural fair, which was held three years later in the fall of 1866. This fair and those which followed it were held in Denver. In 1869 a fair was held at Boulder, and the next year some people of the Arkansas Valley formed the Agricultural Society of Southern Colorado. The present state fair dates from October 4, 1887.

The founding of Greeley and the organization of the Patrons of Husbandry by Oliver Hudson Kelley gave considerable impetus to organizational activity among the farmers. On December 23, 1870, the colonists organized a Farmers' Club to exchange information and experiences, and their action was imitated. Three years later there were ten of these clubs in the South Platte Valley. By that time some members of the Clear Creek Valley Farmers' Club had organized

[90] Ivah Dunklee and W. M. Dinkel, "A Pioneer of the Roaring Fork," *Colorado Magazine,* XXI (1944), 189-195; E. R. Bennett, "The Colorado Potato Industry," Colo. Agr. Exp. Sta., *Bulletin 117* (Fort Collins, 1907), 4-5.

[91] William A. Kreutzer, *et al.,* "Bacterial Ring Rot of Potato," Colo. Agr. Exp. Sta., *Press Bulletin 94* (Fort Collins, 1941), 1; Carl H. Metzger, "A New Potato Disease in Colorado," *Amer. Potato Journal,* XV (1938), 225-230.

[92] Hoyt Lemons, "Hail in American Agriculture," *Economic Geography, XVIII* (1942), 368.

on February 8, 1873, the territory's first Grange. This one Grange had increased to 44 before the territorial organization was effected on January 27, 1874. R. Q. Tenney of Fort Collins was chosen Master. Among its initial projects was the organization of a cooperative buying service. Seventy-two years later the Grange was still a vigorous and influential organization with a membership of 9,112.

In the next decade the Farmers' Alliance appeared in the South and West. The first chapter was organized in Colorado in 1885, and a state organization was effected in 1889. Here as elsewhere the Alliance movement did not survive the Populist revolt of which it became a part.

The Farmers' Alliance was succeeded by the Farmers' Educational and Cooperative Union, popularly known as the Farmers' Union. The first local was organized in Colorado in 1907, and the next year a state organization was created. In 1940 it had the honor of having its president, James G. Patton, chosen head of the national organization.

The Colorado Farm Bureau grew out of an organization created by the extension service. It was formally organized in March, 1919, and the next November it sent two delegates to Chicago to assist in the formation of the national federation.[93]

As agricultural production exceeded the demand of the mining communities and the farmers became dependent upon out-of-state markets for the sale of their produce, they began to organize cooperative commodity marketing organizations. The first to be organized was the Grand Junction Fruit Growers' Association in 1891. The Melon Growers' Association of Rocky Ford and the Colorado Honey Producers' Association were other organizations of this decade. In 1907 a specialist of the agricultural experiment station was able to find over thirty such groups in the various valleys of the state. Nevertheless, it was not until the short depression following World War I that the present-day large marketing associations came into existence. Eventually all of them were organized under the Cooperative Marketing Act of 1923, which became law through the efforts of Governor William E. Sweet and the farm organizations. The very successful Colorado Potato Growers' Exchange grew out of seven local cooperatives which were organized in the San Luis Valley and on the Western Slope in 1921-1922 and which employed a single selling agency. The Exchange was formed in July, 1923, as the sales agency of 20 local associations with 2,000 members and was the first state-wide cooperative organization in Colorado to be formed on a commodity basis. The Colorado Wheat Growers' Association was organized in 1920, the Mountain States' Beet Growers' Marketing Association in 1923, and the Colorado Bean Growers' Association in 1925.[94]

---

[93] *Proceedings of the Second Annual Session of the Farmers' State Alliance and Industrial Union of Colorado, Held at Pueblo, Colorado, November 25th and 26th, 1890* (Trinidad, 1891), 12; Steinel, *op. cit.*, 54-61, 67-72, 342-381; Working, *op. cit.*, 606-615.

[94] Steinel, *op. cit.*, 323-341; *Market Growers' Journal*, LVIII (1936), 244.

The Role of the National Government

The role of the national government in the state's agricultural development is difficult to over-estimate. It provided the initial funds which enabled the state to open Colorado Agricultural College in 1879 and to establish the Colorado Agricultural Experiment Station in 1888. It was also responsible for the creation of the Colorado Extension Service. The first agricultural extension work in the state dates back to the first farmers' institutes held at Fort Collins, Longmont, and Del Norte in the fall and winter of 1879-1880. The first county agent was employed by Logan County in 1912 with the assistance of the United States Department of Agriculture. He was D. C. Bascom, a teacher of agriculture in the Logan County High School. Definite funds for extension work were allocated by the Smith-Lever Act of 1914, and in that year the present Colorado Extension Service was set up. Thirty-two years later, Dr. Charles A. Lory, who served twice as its Acting Director, told the writer that he thought one of the most important developments in Colorado agriculture during the previous forty years was the acceleration which the extension service had given to agricultural change and improvement.[95]

In the thirties came the "action programs" of the New Deal. The wheat control program of the Agricultural Adjustment Act was organized throughout the state by the extension service in July-August, 1933, to be followed by the corn-hog and sugar beet programs. In 1935 Congress created the Soil Conservation Service, and in 1937 the state legislature passed the Colorado Soil Erosion District Law which enables farmers to form soil conservation districts to conserve and improve their land resources. The first district was created in Moffat County in December, 1937, and was named the Great Divide Soil Conservation District. On July 15, 1946, there were 63 such districts in the state, a plurality of them being in the Arkansas Valley.[96] Another Congressional act which has meant much to Colorado farm people was the Rural Electrification Act of May, 1936. The first REA cooperative in Colorado was the Grand Valley Rural Power Lines, which began to supply electric power around Grand Junction and Fruita in 1937. By June 30, 1943, there were 19 of these cooperatives, supplying 13,748 customers. At that time, 44.5 per cent of Colorado farms were electrified, compared to 11.2 per cent in 1934. This increase has meant among other benefits a lightening of the farm household routine. In 1939 the Rural Electrification Administrator reported:

> Adaptation of electricity to household duties in the farm homes of Colorado has taken place rapidly. A typical sys-

---

95 Interview with Charles A. Lory, Estes Park, Colorado, May 18, 1946; J. H. McClelland and Blanche E. Hyde, *History of the Extension Service of Colorado State College, 1912-1941* (Fort Collins, 1941), 13-56; Ruth J. Wattles, "The Mile-High College: The History of Colorado A&M" (Mss. Colorado A&M College Library).

96 Soil Conservation Service, "Soil Conservation in Colorado," (Mimeographed pamphlet issued by region six, Albuquerque, N. Mex.), 11-15; Colorado State Engineer, *Thirty-second Biennial Report,* 1943-1944, pp. 35-36; Fort Collins *Coloradoan,* July 16, 1946.

tem survey shows that 86 percent of its members have radios, 92 percent have electric irons, and 75 percent have electric washing machines. Modern bathroom facilities have been installed in more than 20 percent of these homes. A third of the farm kitchens now have electric refrigerators, and 38 percent of the farm women served by the system clean their rugs and furniture with electric vacuum cleaners.[97]

The federal government has helped in still other ways. Its land policy encouraged agricultural settlement and a regime of farm-owned, family-sized farms. Although tenancy has increased, in 1940 less than three-eighths of Colorado's farms were tenant-operated. Beginning in 1896 the federal government provided rural free delivery. The first route in the entire Rocky Mountain region was established at Loveland in November of that year.[98] Rural free delivery and the telephone began the breaking down of rural isolation, a process which was continued by the automobile and the radio.

It is now nearly a hundred years since the establishment of the first permanent agricultural settlements. A third generation of farmers is cultivating the soil of Colorado; the two previous generations have toiled, tested, and tilled well. They not only adapted an agriculture to an arid environment, but also they created, in common with the range livestock men, the basic business of the state.

---

[97] Rural Electrification Administration, *Annual Reports,* 1937, pp. 109-112, 115; 1938, pp. 137-138, 188-189; 1939, pp. 180-183, 352; 1943, p. 19. The quotation appears on pages 180-181 of the 1939 report. See also, Merton N. Bergner, "The Development of Fruita and the Lower Valley of the Colorado River from 1884 to 1937," (Unpublished M.A. thesis, University of Colorado, 1937), 94-95.

[98] "Annual Reports of the Post-Office Department for the fiscal year ended June 30, 1897," *House Doc.* 4, 55th Congress, 2nd Session, 104-115.

CHAPTER VI

Progress of Education in Colorado

INEZ JOHNSON LEWIS
State Superintendent of Public Instruction

THE BEGINNING OF COLORADO'S SCHOOLS

ONE of the most dramatic chapters in the history of Colorado is the story of development of the state's educational system. It is a story of aspirations, hope, and faith. It is a record of changing ideals and it exemplifies the human side of progress. The educational system reflects the economic and social development of the state from the early days to the present. The groundwork laid in the past is the basis for our present achievement. The faith and courage of the pioneers in developing the state is worthy of our lasting gratitude.

The early settlers in Colorado came in search of gold. The report of new discoveries of the yellow metal had spread throughout the country. It brought a mighty throng of gold seekers to the Rocky Mountain region. They came from many states and from all walks of life. Among them were men of business ambition, scientists, farmers, and those of the professions. Their religious faith came to them by way of the Puritan and the Cavalier. In the group were Methodists, Baptists, Presbyterians, Catholics, and a sprinkling of Quakers. It is from this heterogeneous group that Colorado has a heritage rich in its broad range of tradition and culture.

The early organization of schools in Colorado is significant of the pioneer conditions as well as the aims and purposes of the people who came west. Government was unstable. The times were exciting, contentious, primitive. The confusion and competition in the location of mines demanded the establishment of courts of law to regulate procedure in fixing the boundaries of mining claims and the protection of the rightful owners. Lawyers were needed to untangle the complicated legal questions affecting the entire industry.

Most people had come to Colorado to stay only until they "struck it rich"; but when the mining industry began to assume great proportions, they began to think of Colorado as a permanent place where they had a future. They began to think of it as a place where they could remain and be happy and prosperous. The prospects were alluring, so many decided to build homes; and typical of all the pioneers, preparations were made for the establishment of schools. The demand for schools met a response of willingness to pay rates and other moneys for maintenance. The lack of housing was no obstacle. Rooms were rented, log houses were built, dance halls were utilized during the daytime, and in one case a tent was the housing solution.

The first school of the territory was opened in Denver in 1859, and was housed in a log cabin. O. J. Goldrick was the schoolmaster. "The hut had a flat roof which was a great conductor of snow and rain, much to the dripping discomfort of the dear little urchins during wet weather." The school was supported by subscription from the parents. The tuition was three dollars a month per pupil, and Mr. Goldrick boarded around. This private school was the only educational institution in the "Pikes Peak country" at that time. Historians depict Mr. Goldrick as a colorful personage—well educated, with one degree from Dublin and a Master's Degree from Columbia University.

The school reopened in 1860 and was called the Denver Union School. Mr. Goldrick stayed in the profession, and in 1862 he became superintendent of Arapahoe County schools and served two years. He was employed to organize the first public school in Denver in 1862.

While the first school of the territorial days was in Denver, it is Boulder County that boasts of having the first schoolhouse. This was the first house which was built specifically for school purposes. We are told that Mr. Abner R. Brown, a former Iowa teacher, was the first schoolmaster. He came to Colorado, passing through Boulder in the summer of 1860. Evidently his mining venture was not successful, for he returned to Boulder and opened a private school in a two-room cabin. He later built the schoolhouse by subscription. The school moved into the building in the fall of 1860.

Miss Indiana Sopris opened a private school on Eleventh Street, Denver, in May, 1860. She was the first woman to teach in the territory. Miss Wood's Denver Seminary opened October 3, 1860, and Miss Lydia Ring's School opened also in October, 1860. She taught private school until the public schools were organized and then became principal of the West Denver Schools. In 1861, there were four private schools in Denver, F. B. Steinberg maintaining one in a log hut in West Denver. Mr. N. A. Baker also taught a private school in Denver, in 1862. Tuition to his school was paid in gold dust.

In 1860, a school was held in a tent in Golden. In 1862, Pueblo opened a private school. While the schools were private, provision was made that children who could not afford to pay be extended opportunities to attend.

Pioneers followed the rivers; so in Larimer County, one of the first seventeen counties in Colorado, pioneers settled along the Big Thompson, Cache la Poudre, Little Thompson and St. Vrain rivers. Some of these first settlers were trappers seeking beaver skins. Until the early '60s there were few children—so few that schools were not feasible and patient mothers taught their children. In 1864 Mrs. Albina Washburn taught a private school in the Big Thompson Valley. In 1866 Mrs. Elizabeth Keyes taught a private school in Fort Collins, but it was not until 1870 that a public school building was built there.

The beginning of public education in Colorado dates from the Territorial Legislature in 1861. This first legislature made provision for the levying of both a district and a county tax. In 1862, the first tax-supported schools were organized. Two districts were formed in Denver. East Denver was known as District Number One and West Denver as District Number Two. A board of education was elected by each district and a two-room school in each was opened in rented buildings in December.

The first district in Pueblo was organized in 1866, and a two-room adobe building was erected on the site where the Centennial High School building now stands. In 1873, a one-room brick building was opened on the south side, soon followed by a four-room building.

In 1867, a district was organized on the southern boundary of the Territory in Las Animas County, in the town of Trinidad. The first teacher was George Broyles.

El Paso County in 1868 had organized six districts, and the first school was opened in what was then Colorado City. Before 1875, Colorado City had one graded school with some high school subjects offered.

The counties of Bent, Clear Creek, Custer, Huerfano, and Fremont each had a one-room building of frame, log or adobe in 1876. Weld County had several such schools.

The biennial reports of the Superintendent of Public Instruction of the Territory show that in 1871 there were 160 districts organized and 120 schools established. The census gave 7,742 persons of school age (between 5 and 21) and 4,357 were enrolled in public schools. In two years the number of districts had increased to 243, with 180 schools and 125 schoolhouses. The census figure had increased to 14,417 and the enrollment to 7,456. It is recorded that in 1877 there were 313 districts and 219 schoolhouses. The census had increased to 21,612, with an enrollment of 14,085, the school age having been set in the constitution at 6 to 21.

The first school law, broad and inclusive, was passed by the first legislative assembly, held in Denver in 1861. This assembly created the office of Territorial Superintendent of Common Schools and the appointment was made by the governor—the salary was $500 per year. Mr. Curtice was the first Superintendent and he published the first school laws.

In 1865, the school laws were amended and the Territorial Treasurer became ex-officio Superintendent of Public Instruction. He received $100 per year.

In 1870, the assembly amended the statutes so that the governor, with the consent of the legislature, appointed a Superintendent of Public Instruction at a salary of $1,000 a year. This law remained in effect until Colorado was admitted into the Union in 1876.

In 1862 the legislature set aside certain mineral lands to be held in perpetuity for the use and benefit of schools. The results were insignificant, since few claims located made any contribution to the State School Fund. In 1866, the legislature made it a misdemeanor to jump claims that had been set apart for the schools, or to fail to relinquish such claims as had been exempted. It also provided for the sale and leasing of school claims, and the investment of the proceeds in United States bonds. This proved to be the basis for the permanent school fund for which provision was made in the state constitution.

Colorado was admitted to the Union in 1876. The new state constitution required that all territorial laws be kept until they either expired or were repealed by the General Assembly. This

(Courtesy Pueblo Chamber of Commerce)

Central High School, Pueblo

continuity of the statutes tended to stabilize the transitional period from the territorial school to the fully tax-supported school. Steps toward modernizing and standardizing the schools marked the transitional period and the public school system began to compare favorably with those of the older states. With the adoption of the constitution, public education was put on a firm foundation.

The office of state superintendent was created by the constitution and very shortly there were twenty-five counties that had county superintendents.

There were 21,962 children of school age in the state and 14,434 were enrolled in the schools. By this time there were 341 school districts and schoolhouses had been constructed in 217 of these districts. Teachers had been employed in all districts where the number of children warranted.

High schools had been organized in Denver, Pueblo, and several other larger towns. In addition to the elementary and secondary schools, several institutions of higher learning had been founded.

Today, Colorado has reached the Biblical age of three score and ten years. This period has been one of tremendous achievement. From a school population of 21,962 in 1876, the school census has grown to 289,167 in March, 1945. From a simple curriculum, Colorado has developed a broad range of offerings equal to any in the country. The expansion of the state's system has extended in two directions— downward and upward—so that it now includes the kindergarten, elementary, high school, and junior college, as well as other provisions for adult education. While Colorado's public schools were housed in log cabins in the beginning, today she has a magnificent array of school buildings with an estimated value of $100,000,000.

Colorado's great school system has not come without conflict, challenge, and combative effort. From the beginning of statehood, members of school boards have often been elected by big majorities on economy issues alone. In later campaigns in these same districts where economy had previously been the issue, voters, with equal gusto, have approved increased levies for new buildings, better equipment, and more services. Bond issues have been voted down by big majorities, only to be carried by a nearly unanimous vote at a later election. Often consolidation has been accomplished after spirited contests. More generous financing of education has come about only after years of study and effort on the part of the people when they realized the close relationship between education and the finding of a solution to society's problems.

The Growth of Schools in the Early Days

Many human interest stories of the struggles made by the Superintendents of Public Instruction and the County Superintendents of the pioneer days are contained in the reports filed in the State Department of Education. Early superintendents revealed definite leadership and had a philosophy of education which was comparable to that of the great educators of the day. The territorial superintendent of 1869, Columbus Nuckolls, advised the "Honorable Legislature of the Colorado Territory" that "the increasing population of our Territory renders it imperative that our school system receive attention." He also notified the legislature of "the propriety of making the office of the school superintendent a separate and distinct office as our population and large increase of children in the Territory seem to demand that the office of the school superintendent be a separate office."

Two years later, in his message to the governor and the legislature, W. C. Lothrop, territorial superintendent, wrote: "No one familiar with the history of our Republic can doubt that the free school system is the safeguard of our liberties. There is no subject relating to the prosperity and improvement of a community, which more imperatively demands the services of all good and true citizens in its behalf, than that of the education of all classes."

He was also aware of the economic value of education. Said he in an elaborate statement: "Good schools will attract families of wealth and culture to our flourishing Territory   *   *   *. General education increases the value of all property and promotes its security. Taxes raised for the purpose of education are like vapors which rise only to descend again in fertilizing showers, to bless and beautify the land   *   *   *. Knowledge as well as wealth is power, and as our wealth as a Territory is rapidly increasing, we require the conservative force of popular education to regulate that power." As a man of judgment, he deplored for the sake of economy "cheap school-houses, cheap teachers, and short terms."

Two years later another leader, Horace M. Hale, then territorial superintendent, warned: "If Colorado is to keep pace with her sisters in the educational advancement of her children the friends must work." He urged: "Organizations must be formed, conventions called and attended, institutes established; and to these ends sacrifices are to be endured."

Aside from the splendid leadership of the state superintendents, the story of early education in Colorado reveals that there have been many able men and women who have served as county superintendents. We are indebted to them for the story of the difficulties and a description of the early efforts of the people in the mining camps, towns, and country sections to educate their children. It is from the county superintendents' reports of this early period that we learn of shifting populations, lack of security, and unsettled conditions. Always they deplored the indifference of the people, the lack of uniformity in textbooks, and the absence of equipment. They have described in detail the primitive log houses, the long distances, the mode of travel, and the general hardships of pioneer life in the far West.

It was not until 1877 that every county in the state of Colorado elected a county superintendent who was willing to enter upon the duties of the office. Soon after the beginning of their terms the state superintendent sent the following instructions concerning "the careless, unbusinesslike way in which districts are kept in many instances." He wrote: "By the authority vested in me by the school law, I hereby instruct you to make it a part of your official duty to examine the books of the secretary and treasurer in all districts to see if said books are properly kept and the funds properly accounted for."

In 1882 the Department of Education expressed its dependency upon the county superintendents for the supervision of public education in each county. The state superintendent wrote: "At the head of the school work in each county stands the county superintendent. The office may be made very effective in the school work but in order to do this, its importance and dignity must be recognized." The state superintendent complained of the small salaries—$800—of these worthy county officials. He contended their services were worth $1500. He expressed his appreciation: "As a class, the county superintendents of the state are a careful, earnest class of men and if other school officers were as faithful in the performance of duty and the guarding of school interests, many of our schools would be in a better condition.''

It is by careful evaluation of the continuous stories that came from all parts of the state that we see the slow but steady improvement, based upon the interest and demands of the people.

In 1873, a leader in education wrote a description which would be discouraging to one of less faith. The report reads as follows: ''Number of teachers employed in the winter, 2; in the summer, 1. Highest salary paid per month, $85; lowest $30. Number of days the school was taught during the year, 140. Average cost of tuition for each pupil per month, $1.27. No school libraries in the district. No maps, no furniture, no nothing.'' Also later, in 1881, this same county reported: ''incapable and careless secretaries.'' The picture of this county (Fremont) represents an example of the great contrast between the pioneer days and the present. This county, which in 1873 reported ''no maps, no furniture, no nothing,'' now supports excellent high schools, teachers, and equipment. It has one of the best high school systems in the West.

It is from the county superintendents that we learn of the earliest efforts in grading schools. It was in 1878 that a county superintendent saw the need of a high school in his county. At the same time, we learn of the type of school and its curriculum which would be wholly out of keeping in the school of the same county today. For instance, the county superintendent wrote: ''In District No. 3 I have Tuesdays and Fridays taught a select school (four young men and five girls over fifteen years of age) in mathematics and geometry, algebra first and second grade, logarithms, English grammar, natural history, geography, and astronomy.''

Not only did those friends of education contend with such discouraging factors as indifference and lack of equipment, but we find also that the Indians still roamed over territory where people had founded their homes. The Indian scare had its effects, as revealed by the superintendent of Grand County. ''I have been informed that the district secretary left the county during the Indian excitement here and left no district report whatever. I have made as full and correct report as I can under existing circumstances, and I hope you will make due allowance for deficiencies.'' The following year the same superintendent wrote: ''The Indian troubles last fall, as well as this fall, interfered with school matters. The district and county treasurers were away from here at the time the report should have been made, and came back in the midst of the Indian outbreak.''

A year later from the southwestern part of the state came this report: ''On the fourteenth of May, 1880, news which caused great excitement reached Mancos, stating that the Indians were on the warpath. Everyone hurried to the schoolhouse for protection. A log stockade had been built around the schoolhouse large enough for the wagons, horses, and people. It was completed all but the entrance which was never closed. The Indians, however, never reached there, so the people returned to their homes."

Mining excitement was still the basis for unsettled conditions in 1879. From Weld County we hear: "The excitement at the mine has caused many of our school officers to leave the county in a hurry and this haste has often worked disaster to the accounts." Also at this time, the county superintendent of Clear Creek County described the effects of mining booms. "In this mining region the population is continually shifting from one place to another as the excitement prevails here and there. In consequence, as in District 2, certain districts become depopulated almost entirely, while in other places communities will suddenly spring into existence and be capable of maintaining a large school within a few weeks after the first settlements there."

One county superintendent of the plains, while not disturbed by Indians and mining booms, was harassed by incorrect reports. The county superintendent of Pueblo County complained in 1879: "Many of the reports have been returned for correction and came again in worse shape than before. If future generations should call to see this report please refer them to me for explanation." However, he was consoled as he said: "In the work in the schoolroom I think there has been great improvement. My system of rigid examinations for teachers has shut out many fossils who kept school to the exclusion of teachers and in their stead we have those who feel an interest in their work."

The devotion to the cause of education is manifested here by the Pitkin County Superintendent, who received the sum of $47.80 for the year. In his report of 1881 he stated: "A school festival was held in Ashcroft, the proceeds of which and donations amounted to $230.10. Have tried to interest the people of Independence Camp in school matters but thus far have failed. Shall foot it over the trail (25 miles) next week. I hope to make a rustling among the dry bones." Another example of this same devotion in the face of untold difficulties is the reply which was given to one of the questions asked in the 1880 report from the state superintendent. The question was: "What is your compensation for the year?" The reply was: "Seventy-five dollars out of pocket."

The period 1883-1884 presented a much happier picture, in spite of the fact that many districts were lacking in uniform textbooks, the proper equipment, and the proper housing. A change, while very gradual, was significant. In Custer County we find: "Most of the schools in this county, for the last year, have been ably conducted by a class of teachers well qualified for their work, and many of them are using the latest methods and textbooks in their schools, while every teacher in the county needs one or more educational journals * * *. All the districts except two have schoolhouses and those two use very comfortable rooms donated by the patrons. We are taking steps toward holding a teachers' institute the coming year."

In the early '80s, the schools of Larimer County were in a "prosperous" condition. The county superintendent offered a constructive suggestion as to legislation. "I am a strong advocator of changing the date of our annual census. My reason for so doing is to protect our small-town schools. During the winter months you will find one-fourth of the pupils that are enrolled in the town schools are listed in other districts and we derive no benefit from the apportionment of school funds. The time I should recommend would be January of each year."

In 1883, Delta County was created from a portion of Gunnison County and had three organized districts. Delta, the county seat, "is contemplating the erection of a brick schoolhouse." Districts No. 1 and 2 had employed teachers with first grade certificates. The county superintendent regretted that the teachers had to contend with a great variety of textbooks.

Educational Trends Portrayed in Colorado

It is impossible to isolate the history of education in Colorado and not become conscious of the educational philosophies and patterns of administration in other states. There has always been an interplay of influence among the states of the social and economic events of the country.

The period closely following the Civil War not only witnessed achievements in industry and the heroic development of the West, but also witnessed the great increase of interest in cultural pursuits throughout the country. In 1870, the Metropolitan Museum of Art was granted a charter. Three great colleges were founded — California, Cornell, and Minnesota. In 1864 Colorado Seminary, now the University of Denver, was founded. The bill creating the University of Colorado was signed by the governor on November 7, 1861, but the institution was not opened until the next decade. Colorado College at Colorado Springs was established in 1874. Events like these were evidence of the growing interest in education throughout the country, and Colorado was a part of the great movement to create institutions of higher learning and was affected by the great movement in the country as a whole.

It has been the practice of educational leaders of the various states to compare the achievements of other states with their own. Apparently this has been the custom through the years and they have used these comparisons to stir the citizens of their own state into action for better things or pointed to their own accomplishments with considerable pride. This is revealed in the report of Horace Mann in the *Common School Journal* of 1839, when after a visit to New York he returned to Massachusetts and made his report.

Mr. Mann revealed that the "average length of schools in New York for the year 1837 was a little more than seven and one-half months," whereas the terms in Massachusetts were less than 7 months. While Horace Mann desired longer terms in Massachusetts, he said "the common school system of New York is of recent origin. * * * It was established so late as 1812. Owing to this fact, it is worthy of remark that the people of that state have enjoyed one great advantage over the people of Massachusetts. They have been exempted from the immense labor of forever boasting of their ancestors and have had more time to devote to their posterity."[1] This sly rebuke is interesting, but at the same time, Mr. Mann was very proud of the fact that Massachusetts did not support public education "in part" but that the schools in his state were entirely free.

There is no doubt but that Horace Mann influenced the thinking of the early educators in Colorado. In discussing the value of education in a democracy he wrote in the *Common School Journal* of 1839: "A voter is a public man. He is a member of government. He officiates indirectly in three distinct departments—judicial, legislative, and executive. * * * That intelligence and effort are the only support and stability of free institutions, was a truism a long time ago. If free institutions have any other security we should like to know it." He expressed a deep-seated and abiding faith in education as the great equalizer of the conditions of mankind. His unshakeable faith in the capacity of the individual for development has influenced the setting of aims and purposes of educational programs through the years, and Colorado has been a follower, in the main, of the idea that education is the safeguard of our liberties.

Since the time of Horace Mann, other educational leaders have emerged to direct the thinking as to educational theories—curricular content, the measuring of intelligence, organization, and administrative practices. Among them are Dewey, Terman, Thorndike and Bagley.

John Dewey, in his writings, "hunts down and exposes those elements in our educational thought and practice which violate his conception of a democratic society." He believes that the public school is the chief remedy for the ills of organized society. Social efficiency is more important than mere knowledge.

Terman was one of the pioneers in the revision and improvement of the tests for intelligence. He also has contributed among other fields of measurement — group intelligence and achievement tests. Many schools have profited in organization by Terman's work.

College and university teachers have included a description of the philosophies of these able educational thinkers in the various college courses in the state, and teachers have imbibed from their teachings and directed many activities according to their chosen leaders in educational philosophy.

In the development and growth of an educational system there is inevitably a meeting of different views in conflict; the opposing views of education have wielded a tremendous influence in challenging thought, to the end that there has been a merging or at least a

---

[1] *The Common School Journal*, I, 81 (March 15, 1839).

softening of the extreme ideas on modern educational programs. For example, the matter of discipline is a problem on which educators have long disagreed.

Horace M. Hale, who wielded a tremendous influence in the adoption of the constitution of the state of Colorado, was of the opinion that "two-thirds of the poor schools are poor from lack of government. * * * The teacher that fails in this respect, fails in his calling. One of the most important parts of a child's education is the acquirement of habits of punctuality, order, systematic study, neatness, and obedience to the law * * * and where the infringement of the rules of the school may incur suspension or expulsion, there is little need of bodily punishment; yet, it often happens, even here, that the parents or guardians are so indifferent and shiftless in regard to the welfare of their children or wards, that it would be more in accordance with Christian duty to punish the lad into subjection than to turn him into the streets to become a vagabond or criminal."[2]

Mr. Lothrop, a predecessor of Mr. Hale, also was of the opinion "certainty of punishment is the first necessity. * * * Now school punishment is not vengeance. Its object is training. * * * For instance, when a boy persists in coming late to school; when a boy is impertinent; when a boy, by willful idleness, accumulates book-punishments until the work comes to a dead-lock—these and similar cases require the rod."[3] This necessity of strict discipline is a hold-over from the austere method of the New Englanders in their early history. They believed in "rigorous discipline, firmness of purpose, and hard work." Their objectives were academic scholarship, mental discipline, moral character, and civic morality.

The idea that rigid discipline is to be extracted even at the expense of the "rod" has changed with the years and Colorado today has enacted into laws a different and humanizing plan for control of the schools, to the extent that "it shall not be lawful for any person having the care or custody of the child * * * to torture, torment, cruelly punish * * *."

Today, education is a story of attitude toward living. It concerns itself with wielding an influence upon the national welfare. The school today accepts the child as a complex organism and intends to develop him mentally, physically, emotionally, and socially. The philosophy of the right of the child was written into the Children's Charter at the White House conference on "Child Health and Protection" in 1931.

Today, the school through discovery of the child's individual abilities tries to prepare him for life by making the school a "part of life." The teacher now studies the child as an individual. The teacher has techniques to do this. Standard tests indicate his level of achievements. Physical examinations indicate the need for treat-

---

[2] Report of County Superintendent Hale, to Superintendent Lothrop, December 18, 1871, in *First Biennial Report, Supt. of Public Instruction*, 104.

[3] *Ibid.*, 13.

ment. The guidance department encourages him in the direction his talents may indicate. The visiting teacher advises with parents concerning all problems which affect the school life of the child.

In issuing the Elementary Course of Study in 1936, the State Department of Education set up these objectives:

First: health—mental and physical.
Second: the development of understanding social relationships.
Third: the development, on the part of the individual, of the ability to participate in social activities.
Fourth: the development of activities conducive to human relationships with a sense of personal responsibilities.
Fifth: the development of clear thinking, based on wide information that will aid the individual in analyzing social situations.
Sixth: the development of habits and skills that are necessary for intelligent living.

The curriculum of today is a definite break with the past.

The Growth of the State's Sense of Obligation to Childhood

The story of education in Colorado shows that as progress has been made in the development of an efficient program, there has been an ever-increasing regard for the appreciation of the individual child as a member of society. His attendance at school, his physical welfare, and his whole capacity for development have become objectives in services to be rendered by the educational program.

In 1876, when Colorado became a state, the constitution provided that the General Assembly should enact laws for compulsory education for children between the ages of six and eighteen years. The state's right to do this was based on the assumption that if the child is to receive instructions and training at the expense of the state, the state has a right to be assured of his attendance. This is in contrast to the territorial period when, even though schools were maintained by taxation, attendance was voluntary. This provision concerning proposed compulsory laws in the constitution, no doubt, was, in part at least, the result of the efforts of the state superintendent.

In 1871 the superintendent urged the Assembly to provide some regulation affecting school attendance.

It is a lamentable fact, that so large a proportion of persons of school age fail to reap the highest advantages of our public schools, and grow up in comparative ignorance. Compulsory education is commended by many of the leading educators, as the only practicable remedy for this defect in the American system of instruction. The want of school-rooms sufficient to accommodate all, is one great obstacle in this Territory, but that is being gradually overcome. When sufficient accommodations are provided, it may then be necessary to pass laws compelling all persons of school age to attend school some portion of each year; but as great differences of opinion exist upon this subject, I deem it one worthy the careful attention of educators and legislators.

Some officials did not have faith in the efficacy of school legislation for compulsory attendance. This is indicated by the report of the state superintendent of 1878. He says:

> Compulsory education in America is no longer an experiment. It is a well-proven failure. The theory is unassailable; the practice—well, perhaps it is yet too soon to apply adjectives to the practice—for no American community has been found which could be induced to practice it. Compulsory laws have been enacted by some eight or ten states, most of them under conditions far more favorable to the execution of the law than exists in Colorado. * * * It is claimed—doubtless with truth—that in certain localities the moral effect has been helpful; beyond that it is a dead letter. * * * If American experience has settled anything during the last ten years, it has established the fact that *education* cannot be made compulsory in the United States.

Perhaps this pessimistic note is somewhat justified, inasmuch as the school population of the state at that time was 21,612, whereas the average daily attendance was 8,141. For a number of years the attendance rate was low, and no effective machinery had been devised for enforcing compulsory attendance. But there were those who continued their efforts to enforce attendance, as is shown in the new gold camp of Cripple Creek, where in 1894 three truant officers were employed at $90 a month. The most effective agency, however, for compulsory attendance was to be the child labor legislation. As early as 1889 the legislature provided that no child under fourteen years of age might be gainfully employed during the time school was in session in his district. Then in 1911 came the Child Labor Law. This law regulates the employment of children under fourteen, and in general has been effective in protecting the rights of the children to attend school.

In some cities the truant officer is being supplemented by the trained case worker in pupil behavior. The change of title has had a wholesome effect. However, the visiting teacher idea has made little progress as yet in small communities.

Colorado, since the early days of her statehood, has developed a considerable degree of social consciousness. The sense of the state's obligation has been crystallized in legislation which provided for increased services to the individual child. In 1919, the Child Welfare Bureau was created. This bureau later became a division of the State Department of Education. The local districts may provide "educational services for physically handicapped children—crippled, blind, deaf and hard of hearing, defective speech, cardiopathic, tuber-culosis, or otherwise physically handicapped." The act of 1945 divides handicapped children into two groups: (*a*) those able to be transported to school; (*b*) those able to be taught only in their homes or in hospitals. Services under this particular act are paid for by state funds and are under the direction of the State Superintendent of Public Instruction.

The statutes further protect the "physical child" by making it mandatory that the "teachers or principal in every public school, or where there is no principal, the county superintendent, shall during the first months of school test the sight, hearing, and breathing of all pupils in his charge. * * *" In case that "any child is found to be defective such parent or guardian shall be notified of such defect."

There has been a further gradual development of health services and today many of the schools in Colorado have the assistance of public health nurses, as shown by the following: Fourteen rural areas have the benefit of nursing services in the schools. In the urban centers there are a total of thirty-two nurses employed to protect the health of the children.

Colorado's interest in the conservation of childhood has not only expressed itself in legislation giving responsibilities to school authori-ties, but also charges parents, guardians, and the lay public with responsibilities, as is shown here:

> It shall be unlawful for any person having the care or custody of any child, wilfully to cause or permit the life of such child to be endangered, or the health of such child to be injured, or wilfully to cause or permit such child to be placed in such a situation that its life or health may be endangered, or wilfully or unnecessarily to expose to the inclemency of the weather, or wilfully to abandon such child, or to torture, torment, cruelly punish, or wilfully and negligently to deprive of necessary food, clothing, or shelter or in any other manner injure such child. * * * It shall be unlawful for any person or persons to give or sell cigarettes to any person or persons under the age of sixteen years.

QUALIFICATIONS OF TEACHERS AND STANDARDS OF CERTIFICATION

The question of the qualifications of the early teachers of Colorado was a matter which received very little attention. Teachers were scarce, and the influences of the frontier were not conducive to demands for scholarly attainments. Colorado paralleled other states in this. In the early Colonial days, academic qualifications ranged from a standard of only a knowledge of the "three R's" to those of the educational accomplishments of the college graduate. It was a generally accepted theory, though, that those who were to teach the little ones needed only to know how to read, write and cipher. This was true in Pennsylvania.

Virginia demanded "ability to read and write" plus "good life and conversation." Teachers were also to be "sound in the doctrines of the church."

In New Jersey, the governor demanded that the teachers obtain a "license." The qualifications were "good character, loyal principles, religious faith."

The Carolinas demanded "church affiliations."

While Massachusetts had no certification standards as set by any state agency, we find that their standards were high. These standards were set by the community. We are told that as early as 1648, schoolmasters were college graduates, and Massachusetts has always demanded "competence" in teachers.

In the early days of Colorado, the county superintendent had sole discretion in granting certificates. From the beginning they showed an intelligent appraisal of their responsibility and of the importance of examination as a means of securing good teachers. Examinations were described as written or oral. One county superintendent in 1871 was of the opinion that "In order to have instruction thorough, well-qualified teachers are indispensable. No person, in my opinion, no matter how extensive his knowledge of the higher English branches, nor how well versed he may be in the dead languages, nor how many old certificates he may have, is qualified to instruct a common school, who cannot pass a simple examination in the common English branches."

Two years later another county superintendent explained: "In my examinations, while I used great discretion in selecting those to whom I grant certificates, I realize the importance of a more thorough and rigid examination."

A state superintendent had found "great variety of methods and degrees of severity prevailed" in granting certificates. It often happened that a second-grade certificate in one county required a higher degree of scholarship than a first-grade in an adjoining county.

As a result of the variety of methods and different standards that prevailed in the various counties, the State Board of Education instructed the State Superintendent of Public Instruction to issue uniform questions to all the counties. This was a voluntary act on the part of the State Board of Education and it was not until 1881 that the legislature made it a duty of the State Superintendent of Public Instruction to issue the questions.

In general, the law relative to the issuance of the certificates remained the same for a period of over forty years, except that the legislature made certain requirements in regard to particular subjects. Also during this time, various first-class districts had been given the privilege of holding their own examinations and granting certificates according to their own standards.

Before the enactment of a more extensive certification law in 1923, neither college credits nor professional training was required by the statutes for teaching in the public schools of Colorado. The following quotation from the statutes indicates the limited educational preparation which the state demanded before 1923:

> * * * The county superintendent shall meet all persons, of not less than eighteen years of age, desirous of passing an examination as teachers * * * at which time he shall examine all such applicants in orthography, reading, writing, arithmetic, English grammar, geography, history and Constitution of Colorado, civil government, physiology, natural sciences, theory and practice of teaching, and the school law of the state. If the applicant is to teach in a school of high grade, the examination shall extend to such additional branches of study as are to be pursued in such school.

In addition, the law also required the applicant to be of "good moral character."

The progress which Colorado has made in raising standards for eligibility for teaching since the passage of the law of 1923 is shown by the following steps:

Beginning with the school year 1925 teachers applying for examinations must have completed in addition to four years of high school work (or its equivalent) at least three (3) quarter hours of college credit.

Beginning with the school year 1927 the requirements were raised to twenty-five (25) quarter hours of college credit with five (5) quarter hours in Education.

Beginning with the school year 1931 the requirements were raised to ninety (90) quarter hours of college credit including thirty (30) quarter hours in Education.

In 1933 the State Department of Education in order to raise the standards of teachers secured the passage of a bill which eliminated one of the three yearly county examinations.

In 1937 the Department secured the passage of a bill which eliminated all county examinations and placed the authority for the issuance of certificates in the State Department of Education, with the exception of those issued by the state teachers colleges as provided by law. Also the State Department of Public Instruction ruled that the right of first-class districts to issue special certificates, for the teaching of special subjects only, was not affected by the new certification law.

Moreover, in the interest of more adequate standards for state certificates, to the end that Colorado would have better teachers, the State Board of Examiners on June 14, 1937, passed a resolution that would rescind existing rulings concerning requirements for applicants from outside the state who possess a diploma of graduation from an out-of-state standard two-year normal school. This action was effective September 1, 1937. (The rulings rescinded did not refer in any way to four-year college graduates who had an A.B. or equivalent degree. The Graduate Temporary Certificate is issued to applicants who hold the four-year college degree.)

Beginning September 1, 1937, one five-year Non-renewable Elementary Temporary Certificate might be granted to applicants for Colorado state general certificates who have completed, over and above graduation from a four-year high school, a minimum of 135 quarter hours of college credit earned in one or more accredited colleges, including 30 quarter hours in Education, 6 quarter hours of which must be in Practice Teaching. In lieu of the Practice Teaching credit, three school years (27 months) of successful teaching experience may be substituted when properly certified to the State Superintendent of Public Instruction.

Under rulings of the Board of Examiners in April, 1942, the number of Non-renewable Elementary Certificates that may be issued to an individual was changed from one to two. However, no Elementary Life Certificate may follow the Non-renewable Temporary Certificate.

State, County, and District Administration

In the early days society's problem was simple. People lived in a simple economy. Education was a small undertaking in comparison with the problems of running an adequate school system today.

In the first schools, teachers were the only employees. An administrator was not necessary. The school was governed by the town hall meetings. Pure democracy was in operation. Through the years the administration of education became complex. It was an extensive undertaking. The problems of finance began to appear. Proper distribution of funds on particular bases became objects of discussion. Differences of opinion arose. In view of the need for executive assistance it is difficult to understand why school administrators were not created until two hundred years after the establishment of the first public schools. Like many of the features of public education the office of the state school executive officer has been one of evolution.

New York was the first state to provide a state school executive. It did so in the year 1812. Nine years later the office of the state executive was abolished, and the secretary of state acted *ex officio* as superintendent of schools. It was not until 1854 that the office of public instruction was again created. This official became the commissioner of education in 1904. Maryland had a state superintendent of public instruction in 1826, but Maryland also abolished the office and it was not re-created until 1868. The state of Vermont had a state official of an executive nature in 1827, but did not create a permanent state officer until 1845.

Colorado followed the zigzag operations of the other states when it came to its state executive officer. It abolished the executive office of superintendent of common schools in 1865, and the territorial treasurer became *ex officio* head of the territorial school system. In

1870, the territorial legislature provided for the office of superintendent of public instruction at a salary of $1,000.

When Colorado became a state in 1876, the new constitution provided for the office of state superintendent of public instruction. Among the powers and duties of the state superintendent are:

> He shall decide all points touching the construction of the school laws, which may be submitted to him in writing by any school officer, teacher, or other person in the state, and his decisions shall be held to be correct and final until set aside by a court of competent jurisdiction, or by subsequent legislation. * * * He shall have general supervision of all county superintendents of the public schools of the state. He shall prepare and have printed * * * laws relating to the schools. He shall furnish blanks, forms, registers, courses of study, and pamphlets as shall be necessary. * * * He is *ex officio* state librarian. * * * He apportions the public school income fund. * * * He acts as chairman of the state board of education and chairman of the state board of examiners.

His responsibilities were further increased by the law of 1935. He became chief executive officer of the State Department of Education, which consists of the following divisions: (1) Division of Administration, (2) the State Board of Examiners, (3) the State Historical Society of Colorado, (4) the State Library, (5) Bureau of Home and School Service, and (6) State Board for Vocational Education.

The state constitution also provided for the creation of the office of county superintendent of schools. Among his duties are: He shall

> exercise a careful supervision over the schools of his county. * * * Make an annual report to the state superintendent of public instruction * * * examine the accounts of the district officers to see if such accounts are properly kept and all district funds properly accounted for * * * keep in a good and substantial bound book a record of his official acts and all other matters required by law to be recorded * * * obey the legal instructions and decisions of the superintendent of public instruction.

The Colorado school system is organized for administrative purposes on the district plan. Colorado accepted the plan of dividing its counties into administrative units, as did practically all of the northern and western states. The district not only suited the ideals and needs of the New Englanders, but also served well the people of the pioneer days. The process of organization was a simple one. Populations were small and the school was a community undertaking. The school reflected the simplicity of the life of the people it served. Economic security depended upon individual enterprise and social life was restricted.

Through the years the American people have registered their approval of the school district as a unit of administration. Its value lies in the fact that it represents the great strength of democracy as well as many of its defects.

The population of districts in the United States ranges from a few persons to the great population centers of the large cities.

Colorado has many district organizations. It has first, second, and third class districts, so classified according to population. These districts are a governmental unit and are regarded as agencies of the state.

It has produced a high school system by making a high school district of the county. The law also creates what is known as the union high school district by permitting the merging of districts into a so-called union high school district for high school purposes.

In the realm of controls, the constitution of Colorado has provided for the creation of boards of education. The boards of the various districts are elected by the people, and they "shall have control of instruction in the public schools of their respective districts." They are composed of honest, sincere, capable citizens serving without pay. The constitution and the statutes have given them almost unlimited powers. The high place which Colorado occupies among the systems of the country has been achieved under the management of school boards.

Some modern problems of the school boards are these: an efficient budget; the best quality and broad range of services for money available; the teaching load, the size of classes and the number of hours a teacher is to work; cooperating with local agencies in the use of the school plant; keeping the school program abreast of the times so as to meet the needs of pupils in attendance; an impartial evaluation of the program and its effectiveness. To serve well, boards must become entirely conscious of the social and economic changes that have occurred in the country, the state, and the local community.

The school board has the responsibility of keeping the public informed as to the school's progress, as well as its needs. It should have an efficient method for the selection of teachers and should adopt a long-time building program with the consent of the community.

ADMINISTRATION OF CITY SYSTEMS

The slow development of the position of city superintendent parallels the development of that of the chief state school officer. The office of the city superintendent was established first by Providence, Rhode Island, in 1836. Twenty-five cities had by 1861 created the office of the city superintendent of schools. Only three more cities— Albany, Washington and Kansas City were added before 1870, making a total of twenty-eight.

American cities are concerned with many matters. The people are occupied in manufacturing, transportation, building, structural and architectural services, besides general merchandising and the trade services. Hence the management of the city school system must be so planned as to serve heterogeneous groups under its jurisdiction. The interdependence of economic groups in centers of population offers a good basis for securing the support of public schools.

The city is a special form of district organization. It is found in practically all sections of the United States. As a rule, the city district enjoys special powers and privileges granted to it by the state legislature. It has a more complicated school organization than do the town and country schools. Though it is a part of the state educational system, it is, nevertheless, somewhat independent.

The city systems throughout the United States represent educational efficiency at its best. They have provided better buildings, better equipment, higher standards of instruction, and a broader range of services. In a large measure, the board of directors of city systems have delegated executive powers to their city superintendent of schools and the city superintendent has proved his worth through the years. As a leader of teachers and supervisors, he must have the characteristics of statesmanship. He represents both the public and the school and so plays the part of a harmonizer. He provides the leadership which guides the school in the direction it should go. The cities and towns of Colorado have attained a high standard of instruction. Many rank among the best in the country. Their superintendents, who have been elected by the local school boards, are trained leaders for executive work.

Today, the programs operating in the cities and towns are of wide range in offerings. Some of the more highly developed systems not only have provided kindergarten, elementary and secondary divisions, but also have extended their services to adult education. Colorado now boasts of junior college systems located at Trinidad, Pueblo, Grand Junction and Sterling, and there are continuation schools located at Lamar and La Junta.

The City of Denver serves as a splendid example of a well organized and well administered school system. It is superior in organization and in quality of instruction and in its social benefits to the community. The control of the schools is vested in a board of education of seven poeple elected biennially for overlapping terms at a general election in the City and County of Denver. The board of education of the city is fiscally and politically independent. The executive officer of the board is the City Superintendent of Schools. Upon the superintendent's administrative staff are four assistant superintendents and a director of instruction and research. The various departments consist of:

Art	Military Science and Tactics
Health Education	Music
Health Service	Pre-school and parent education
Home Economics	Publications
Industrial Arts and	Pupil Personnel
Special Services	Research
Libraries	Vocational Education

The system consists of fifty-eight elementary schools, ten junior high schools, five senior high schools, the Emily Griffith Opportunity School and the Evening Vocational High School.

Under the head of Business Management come the divisions of school lunch rooms, supplies, transportation, pupil personnel, operation and maintenance. The number of employees is approximately 2,200, of which about 1,600 are classroom teachers.

Services offered by the Denver special schools include:

Help for crippled children. The Boettcher School offers classes in the elementary and high school grades to children who are so crippled that they cannot make satisfactory progress in schools for normal children. Some cardiac cases are included in this group. About 200 children are enrolled.

Classes for the deaf and hard-of-hearing. These are housed in the Evans School, and offer instruction in Lip Reading as well as regular school work. High School pupils with the hearing handicap go to regular high schools but are tutored in their work in the Evans School for the Deaf and Hard-of-Hearing.

Classes for visually handicapped. Pupils who are visually handicapped and cannot do regular school work attend a special class at the Evans School. About eleven pupils are enrolled.

The Denver city schools supervise summer playgrounds. They maintain them at forty-four centers in the city and in 1945 the aggregate attendance was 612,463.

As has already been stated, many American city school systems were maintained without the leadership of a city superintendent until in the seventies. Denver got off to a good start under the able leadership of Aaron Gove, who was elected superintendent in 1874 and served through June, 1904. He demonstrated his statesmanship by assisting in drafting the resolutions which influenced the legislature in providing public education for the state of Colorado. He showed his professional spirit by assisting in organizing a teachers' association.

Each decade in Colorado's history has made its own contribution. The territorial government had provided for tax supported schools, so Denver and other towns in the state continued in a general way under the pre-statehood laws. Denver's public education began in 1862, when District No. 1 elected its first board of education and a rented building solved the housing problem.

Colorado had not yet become a state when the Arapahoe School was dedicated in 1873 and when Dr. R. G. Buckingham, president of the board of education, urged consolidation of the districts and organization of evening classes for adults.

One of the interesting facts in school history is that Denver had a high school graduating class in 1877, and that Horace Irving Hale was the valedictorian of the class. He later became General Irving Hale of military fame.

In 1878 the state superintendent reported: "All the graded schools in the state have high school courses open to all, while Denver is the only place sufficiently populous as yet to require a high school with a full and entirely distinct faculty."

Superintendent Gove was head of a city school system that showed in 1878 a school census of 3,754, and today there is a membership of 52,000. Denver's school plant, which began with the Arapahoe

East Denver High School

School, dedicated in 1873, has expanded to a plant of 58 elementary schools, 10 junior high schools, 5 senior high schools, the Emily Griffith Opportunity School, the Charles Boettcher School, the Administration Building, and the warehouses. These are valued at $23,000,000— a record of 73 years of aspiration, determination, faith, sacrifice and vision.

Emily Griffith Opportunity School. "For all who wish to learn" is the inviting message placed above the door of the Emily Griffith Opportunity School. The invitation to enter has been accepted by thousands of men and women from all walks of life.

The word "opportunity" which meets the traveler has kindled a desire to overcome the obstacles to happiness and security. The Emily Griffith Opportunity School, the most unique feature of the Denver Public School System, is what its name signifies—an opportunity for every man or woman to attend classes to receive instruction in the courses of study for those who were denied the privileges of a formal education in early youth. But the Emily Griffith Opportunity School was intended not only to serve those who had been underprivileged in their early years, but also to serve those who wanted to study for the sake of self-improvement, to satisfy the hunger for knowledge, to gain more vocational efficiency, or even to learn a new way of making a living.

The spirit of the school is expressed in the message of Charles Greene, Superintendent of the Denver schools, who wrote:

> Opportunity School is for you. * * * To give you the help you need, when you need it, is what the Emily Griffith Opportunity School attempts to do. If you are a worker, you are welcomed without charge to Opportunity's classes. If you are an employer looking for trained help, Opportunity will set up the kind of courses you want given. If you are a housewife or a citizen or anyone else, Opportunity will study your needs and help you.

> Opportunity School has no fixed curriculum, and no entrance requirements, has no interscholastic athletics and no academic atmosphere. If you wish one course, you are not required to take other courses to balance the program. * * *

> In a fast-changing world with shifting social requirements and changing vocations, the Emily Griffith Opportunity School stands ready to help you do your work better or get new work. Opportunity School also offers you courses that will enrich your leisure hours. Opportunity School is for you.

The spirit as expressed by Mr. Greene has permeated the school since its doors opened on September 9, 1916. At first the school offered only a few classes, such as typing, spelling, stenography, telegraphy, American history, and subjects for foreigners. As the years have gone on, there has been a continuous increase in the number and the kinds of courses offered. There have been full-time courses as well as short units, but the curriculum at the school is intended to meet the needs and interests of individuals.

At the opening, the authorities expected an enrollment of about 200, instead they came 2,398 strong. By 1920, the enrollment had increased to over 7,000, and in 1945, 15,000 students were in attendance during the year.

The Emily Griffith Opportunity School is a unique institution playing an ever-increasing part in the educational life of the community. It was founded twenty-nine years ago as a part of the public school system of Denver. This great institution came into being as a result of the efforts and vision of Emily Griffith. She was a teacher with a "heart and a soul." She loved folks. She believed in them. She thought the individual was one who had a right to live his life to its full capacity, and believed that the right of an education was his rightful heritage. She held that because an individual was handicapped in his youth as far as securing an education was concerned, he should not be compelled to go on through life and continue to be bound by the early lack of schooling.

By attending Opportunity School a young man can acquire more skill in any trade in which he is engaged. Any young man or woman can acquire skill in salesmanship. All business men and women have an opportunity to learn more about business management and business practices. The young housewife may learn scientific plans of homemaking. The automobile owner may learn to "fix his car." The desire for cultural attainment may be satisfied in the arts, for the young or old who like beauty for beauty's sake may go and learn how to make a vase, draw, paint, or even make a new hat.

Adults in Denver need never feel they are too old to learn. They have in their midst an educational institution to which they may go and study any one of a wide range of subjects to any extent they desire. They need not work for credits. They are not required to spend an entire day nor to attend continuously. The school serves the individual. This is the one great idea that separates it from any of the traditional adult education schools.

Emily Griffith is great in her vision and her affection for humanity. During her eighteen years of service there, she was the Opportunity School. While Emily Griffith today has retired to her mountain home, the school is still operating under the warmth of her influence.

Since its founding, Opportunity School has had the cooperation of the chambers of commerce, service clubs, and business, as well as women's organizations. On account of its digression from the traditional school, it attracted the attention of educators and industry throughout the nation. Other cities and towns have attempted to build "likewise," but it is the Opportunity School of Denver that has given the idea of adult education its greatest stimulus.

Rural Education and Consolidation

In spite of the tremendous stride in the development of an excellent school system in Colorado, it is found that the least satisfactory schools in the state are in rural areas. In spite of the idea of equal opportunity, as expressed in the state constitution, it is found that many schools are located in districts with low valuations; while others have sufficient property but with small numbers of students in attendance. Neither of the two situations is satisfactory nor produces a proper basis for an excellent school. It is readily seen that low valuations necessitate high levies, and even with high tax levies a standard school cannot be maintained with small attendance. A modern school should be sufficiently large to present an opportunity for class organization—sufficiently large in numbers for competitive as well as cooperative activities.

The rural school problem is a social and economic problem even more than an educational one. The rural school is inseparable from the social and economic problems of the country people. The little red schoolhouse is in a sociological setting which only the use of modern machinery and good roads can change. The development of roads and the electrification of the farm and the home undoubtedly show the way to the creation of larger school units.

Today, we live in a new world—a day of which the grandfathers of the present generation scarcely dreamed. The great changes that have come about in living and industry have made the farmer a part of the social revolution. Good roads and the automobile have made it possible for the rural school to render a broad range of services to the community as a whole.

It was after 1900 that rural school improvement became an active program in the State of Colorado. Educational leaders of the state had become familiar with the consolidated schools in some of the eastern states, but because of the great distances in Colorado the plan did not immediately take hold of the imagination of the people. In general it was not easy to convince Colorado farmers that the transportation of children was a practical thing; and it was equally difficult, in many instances, to convince people, not only in rural areas but also in urban centers, that the education of the country children was necessary for the common good.

Nevertheless, because of the persistence of leaders the Appleton Consolidated School became a reality under the law of 1909. This school is situated in the open country, seven miles northwest of Grand Junction. It was reported with considerable pride that a competent architect was employed previous to erecting the building. The local authorities had vision enough to secure three acres of land with water right. In the school year of 1917-1918, there was an attendance of 184, with 48 in attendance in the high school grades. C. G. Sargent, County Superintendent of Mesa County, who led the crusade for this consolidation, reported that "agriculture and manual training are taught and this school has won honors in boys' and girls' clubs. For the past two years one of the girls in this school has been the state champion in the canning club."

Following the Appleton organization was the consolidation in 1911 which became the Fruitvale School, also in Mesa County. The local authorities provided trained and experienced teachers. In this school, pupils may now pass from the first grade to the twelfth grade as they do in the best city schools. This same school boasted a strong department of home economics. Mr. Sargent also reported in his bulletin of 1918 that "because of the high degree of efficiency of the home economics work, the Fruitvale School has been approved for federal aid under the Smith-Hughes Law."

The Cache la Poudre School became the next consolidation, in 1913. It was located near Fort Collins, and was made by uniting five whole districts and two large portions from adjoining districts. Three hundred children were accommodated by this consolidation. The wisdom of the local authorities was there shown by the fact that the site consists of five acres of good land with water right. Six buildings were abandoned and were replaced by buildings of brick and stone costing $30,000.

The report reveals that the transportation at the Cache la Poudre School was done by seven horse-drawn vans. The transportation has been "a complete success," notwithstanding the fact that there were only dirt roads over which the route was traveled.

By this time the good people of the San Luis Valley became interested in consolidation and have made a notable record in its achievement. The average elevation in the San Luis Valley is 7,600 feet above sea level. In spite of long winters and considerable snow, transportation has been a complete success. The first consolidation in this valley was the LaJara School in 1914. From 1914 to 1922 was a notable period of expansion in consolidation history, not only in this single area of Colorado, but throughout the United States.

The LaJara School District was formed by the consolidation of three districts—"Two one-teacher schools and one with three were abandoned." The LaJara School cost $35,000. Even at this early period it boasted of a water system, a domestic science laboratory, and a community auditorium. There were three hundred children in attendance. The transportation was a combination of two large Studebaker busses and one horse-drawn van in which twenty-five children who lived near the school rode. Mr. Sargent says this was the first district in Colorado to attempt auto transportation on a large scale. The success of the LaJara School proved to be the inspiration for the later consolidations in this valley.

The later consolidations in the San Luis Valley in order of their organization were: Sargent, in 1916; Hooper and Center, in 1917; Del Norte and Monte Vista, in 1918; and Blanca, in 1922.

The Sargent School, situated eight miles from Monte Vista, was named for C. G. Sargent, who made such a great record in his leadership in the early days of the consolidation movement. This school, after completion of consolidation, served 250 farm homes. One of the finest systems of transportation in the country has been in operation in this district. Twelve large autobusses were in use, and 350 children were transported daily. One of the unique features of this school was a modern nine-room home for the superintendent and an equally modern eleven-room teacherage. The Sargent Consolidated School System also boasted of a garage as a part of the school equipment.

The Hooper School is an illustration that county lines are not a barrier to consolidation. Of this school Mr. Sargent says: "This, too, is a very excellent school." The style of architecture is different in that the school is built in the form of a quadrangle.

The Center Consolidated School, of Saguache County, was not dedicated until March, 1920. Its plan and architectural beauty made it one of the finest in the state.

Del Norte, one of the oldest settlements in the state, abandoned eleven districts to create the Del Norte School, which is located in the City of Del Norte. It is recorded that Del Norte School was organized by a nearly unanimous vote. The Del Norte building cost $150,000.

Monte Vista is one of the finest of its kind in the state. This school in 1921 employed thirty-two teachers and had in attendance more than 900 children—162 of these were in the high school. The senior high school was erected at a cost of $175,000.

The Blanca School District followed the blazed trail, and Blanca became a consolidated school in 1922.

The early reports on consolidation also describe the New Raymer School, in Weld County, about sixty miles from Greeley. This is a centralized school, which means that the small schools in a single district were abandoned and a school site was selected in the center of the district. This district comprised 162 square miles. Before the centralization there were eleven one-teacher schools scattered over these 162 square miles. The building cost $30,000, and the enrollment in 1918 was 205.

Pueblo County reported that the Avondale School near Pueblo was a going concern in 1914.

During this expansion period, the consolidation movement was carried on at a vigorous pace by the County Superintendent of Schools in El Paso County. She had previously evaluated the problem of comparative distances between the distances of the eastern states and those wide stretches of territory in Colorado. While she had observed that El Paso County was more than twice the area of the State of Rhode Island, she was convinced that by cooperative effort of various communities consolidation would be effected to the advantage of all communities concerned. During this time, sixteen consolidations were completed and new buildings erected.

One of the first accomplishments under the law of 1909 was the expansion of the Ellicott, Yoder and Miami schools by the addition of contiguous territory. Also, at this time came the erection of the Hanover, Squirrel Creek and Drennan schools. Later, followed the Alta Vista and Edison, both of which were planned to serve as community centers.

One of the outstanding achievements of the consolidation movement was the Lewis Consolidated at Monument, which also has served as a community center for an extensive area, and has maintained a wide range of offerings. The building is one of the best this period produced.

At the beginning of this vigorous period of consolidation activities, was the organization of the Union High School at Calhan. This school provided the first high school privileges in the northeast part of the county. A union high school is, by nature, a consolidation of districts for high school purposes only. Later the elementary school at Calhan became a consolidated district, as did the Eastonville and Table Rock schools. During the consolidation years,

El Paso County has made an outstanding record inasmuch as 98% of the children in El Paso County live in areas where they may attend high school and live at home.

The people of the Falcon area also caught the vision of greater educational facilities by eliminating many of the small schools and providing transportation to a central point and erecting a creditable building at Falcon. It is recorded that the Fountain district was joined by a contiguous district on the north, thus becoming the first consolidated school under the old law. However, under the new statute Peyton, perhaps, led the way in the march of consolidation.

As far as can be determined, the Peyton School was the first in the state to serve a complete, warm lunch at the noon hour for all children, free of charge. This hot lunch plan was a community activity under the direction of the principal.

One of the many interesting activities carried on in the county was the annual song festival. It first was held on April 23, 1920, at Stratton Park, in Colorado Springs. On various occasions, as many as 3,000 rural children took part in this musical event. Splendid work was done in chorus training, and as the plan developed, bits of opera and classical music were performed in a creditable way. The county festival was an inspiration to the extent that there were at one time as many as thirteen orchestras in the consolidated schools of El Paso County.

The other accomplishments of this period were: (1) the inauguration of the health clinics; (2) the organization of the teachers' and directors' association; (3) the county traveling library; and (4) Educational Day, at which time the Chamber of Commerce entertained the school directors of the county and a part of the day was set aside for the visiting of the Colorado Springs schools.

El Paso County more nearly approached the supervisory plan from the county office than any other in the state. There were employed in the office a deputy, a director of high schools, and two assistants, which made it possible for the superintendent to correspond with all the children of the county. The correspondence department was inaugurated about 1915. Letters and compositions were sent every two weeks to every student beyond the third grade in the county system. The plan resulted in improvement of the English work; and, what was more important, it gave the county superintendent an opportunity to contact the home directly through the medium of a letter.

The achievement in consolidation in the counties already mentioned is only a part of the picture of the consolidation movement in Colorado. Since those early days, consolidations have taken place in all portions of the state—in the mountains, the valleys, the irrigated sections and on the prairies. Much progress has been made in the creation of better buildings, better equipment, and improved transportation facilities.

In 1921, Colorado had 146 consolidated schools, located in 38 counties, with an enrollment of 29,000. The period of consolidation between 1909 and 1921 is a record achievement. Today, the consolidated schools are examples of the advancement and the ideals of equal opportunity for the children of the state. Their superiority over the old plan cannot be questioned.

Consolidation has not come without effort. There was always that natural resistance to change which had to be overcome. Sentiment played a great part in opposition. The matter of increased cost was also a source of hostility. Those in charge of campaigns for consolidation had to be convincing that a high school education is just as desirable and necessary for country children as it is for children who live in the cities and towns.

Communities had to be convinced of the social value of the consolidated school. The value of a good school plant was shown—the possibility of getting better-trained teachers and the assurance of better business management. Great pains were taken to show the increased advantage of a fuller curriculum. Art, music, health instruction, and vocational training, including homemaking, agricultural, and farm work, were all a part of an enriched curriculum which could become a part of a consolidated school, but which could have little part in the little one-teacher school.

Consolidation in Colorado has now reached a period when its superiority is not questioned by those living in the districts of consolidated schools. People have become loyal and satisfied, and one seldom, if ever, hears of complaints concerning "increased cost."

Since the expansion period in consolidation, it should be noted that there has been a continuous if limited uniting of territory and the elimination of small districts in the state. A new act of 1935 permitted the dissolution of some districts by the vote of the people, and many districts were annexed by the county superintendent, as was his responsibility when a district had not maintained a school for a period of three years. But the vigorous movement of consolidation of the earlier period should be revived.

While the impact of the depression years and the demands of two world wars discouraged and delayed consolidation to a great extent, the postwar period should witness the greatest consolidation trend yet experienced in the state. There are in Colorado many districts that now comprise the small school areas which should be organized into larger units. Some of the now consolidated districts should become larger than they now are by the annexation of some of the contiguous territory which is now maintaining inadequate schools. In many parts of the state there are isolated groups of districts with the same topographic features, which should be led into a single cooperative plan for consolidation.

One of the great rural social problems which faces the United States today is that of maintaining a happy prosperous civilization on the farms of the nation. Without some great agency, such as an excellent school system, it is thought by many that the agrarian way of life as we now know it will pass into large-tract commercial farming by individuals and companies on the one hand, and farm tenantry on the other. Perhaps this is idle speculation, but, in any event, the necessity of making provision for the development of a rich social and economic life is essential for the safety of our country.

Growth of the High School System

The evolution of the high school is one of the most impressive chapters in the sweep of the development of education in our country. Public education in 1800 was concerned mainly with the rudimentary study of reading, writing, arithmetic, English, and spelling.

The first public high school was established in Boston in 1821 "to furnish boys who did not intend to go to college with the means of completing a good English education, to fit them for active life, or qualify them for eminence in private or public station." However, the high school movement spread slowly because of opposition to levying a tax for high school purposes. A supreme court decision in the state of Michigan sustained the legality of levying a tax for supporting high school instruction. This decision gave an impetus to the movement, and since 1880 high schools have multiplied rapidly. There has been an amazing development. In 1890, there were 2,256 high schools; in 1900, 6,500 high schools; in 1910, 10,213 high schools; and in 1926, 21,700 high schools with 3,757,466 students.

Colorado shared in the idea that education above the elementary school was necessary. Since the constitution had fixed the school age from six to twenty-one years, the establishment of a program of education beyond the elementary grades was freely accepted. Boulder had previously established a high school in 1872. The same type of school was provided in Denver in the autumn of 1874. In these schools the ninth grade was added to the elementary school and the tenth, eleventh, and twelfth grades were successively added—the four forming the high school system. The first graduation exercises in Colorado were held in 1876 in Boulder. The following year the East Denver High School had a graduating class of seven.

The rapid evolution of secondary education in Colorado is indicative of the great industrial development of the state in these years. The cattle industry, mining, railroad building, and the development of irrigation systems were factors which brought prosperity to the state. The development of Colorado's educational system is a reflection of this prosperity. This rapid expansion is shown by the fact that in 1884 the high schools in the towns of Denver, Pueblo, Leadville, Gunnison, Trinidad, Georgetown, Golden, and Boulder were on the accredited list of the State University.

By 1887, there were twelve counties in the state which were maintaining high schools. The year 1888 saw the organization of the Grand Junction and the Monte Vista High Schools. In 1890, high schools were organized at Saguache and Montrose, and in 1893, at Fruita and Rocky Ford. By 1896, high schools were established at Silverton, Canon City, Florence, South Canon City, and Ridgway. By 1898, schools were organized at Wheatridge and in Hinsdale,

Ouray, Costilla, and Gilpin Counties. From 1887 to 1900 there was an increase of thirty-two counties which were carrying on programs at the secondary level. There were nine county high schools, four union high schools, and fifty-nine district high schools in 1904. Cheyenne County's first high school was organized in 1907. This school later provided a plan of dormitories for the housing of boys and girls who lived at too great a distance to be served by horse and buggy transportation.

The people's determination to provide high school privileges for the children of the state is shown by the fact that at the present time there are twenty-four county high school systems and thirty-one union high school districts, besides those in first, second, and third class districts.

It is gratifying to observe that Colorado ranks well above the average among the states of the Union in providing high school privileges. According to the figures issued from the United States Office of Education in 1940, this state ranked tenth in the per cent of persons twenty-five years and older who completed one year or more of high school, and ranked eighth in the per cent of persons twenty-five years and older who completed one year or more of college. An army poll of over seven million men reveals the interesting fact that it ranks eleventh in the Union on percentage of army enlisted men who have had four years or more of high school.

How Colorado has Financed Her Schools

From her territorial days, Colorado has, in the main, supported her schools by property tax. Through the years the people have been willing to tax their homes, farms, businesses, and industries so that their children might become educated. The schools have derived their support from two main sources—the district and the county. In addition to these, there are lesser funds derived from forest reserve rentals, certain fines, fees, forfeitures, etc. The income from these sources, however, is relatively small. The state has contributed only a small amount of money since it could use only the income from the permanent school income fund which accrued under the Federal Land Grant Act of 1875, when the United States turned over to the state of Colorado public lands equivalent to one-eighteenth the area of the state. Grave difficulties have resulted from this arrangement. Many local districts have been unable to furnish funds, even with high levies, to support a good school. The depression years emphasized the inequalities which ensue when local property taxes are the main support of education. The most challenging question in the '30s became "How to provide more adequate funds for an educational program?"

The various reports sent to the governor and the legislature not only describe the situation, but also indicate the efforts which were made to revolutionize Colorado's plan of school support. Below are excerpts from various messages to the governor by the state superintendent of public instruction.

In referring to the depression, the state superintendant said in the biennial report of 1930-1932:

These two years have been difficult years * * *. Another serious trouble, emphasized by times such as these, is that through crop failures farmers and other citizens living in these relatively poor school districts are unable to pay their taxes, and, as a consequence, school terms have been shortened, educational supplies seriously curtailed, and other needs of an efficient school have not been made possible * * *. Additional sources of support other than the *ad valorem* property tax should be found for the support of public schools. It is urged that a serious effort be made by the present Assembly to find such sources, and thereby relieve the farm and home owner of their present excess burden of taxation for the support of the government."

In the 1932-1934 report the superintendent again pointed out the great need for additional sources of school support.

You will note that our schools have not escaped the blasting effects of the economic depression. I am of the opinion that at no other time within the history of Colorado has the administration of educational affairs been attended by such precarious situations in regard to its finances. By reason of great loss in valuations among the various districts of the state, we are face to face as never before with the bewildering problem of producing sufficient funds to give the children of Colorado an adequate education, which is their rightful inheritance. In many instances, the length of the school terms have been shortened. In all instances, salaries have been materially reduced, and in many districts, school warrants cannot now be cashed by the teachers. There is no doubt in my mind but that these conditions are resultant partly from our economic depression, but in addition to the economic depression which has caused drastic losses in the school program, Colorado has been laboring for a number of years with an antiquated taxing system which is wholly inadequate to meet the school needs of the present day. We must have new sources of support for public education—the old source has broken down * * *. As a result of the property taxing system, coupled with the district system, Colorado has all sorts of educational standards. There is a wide spread between the best and the poorest schools in the state.

The report of 1934-1936 continued to call the attention of the legislature to the plight of education.

There is evidence on all sides that Colorado needs to reconstruct her plan of financing education. In the main, the great burden of supporting education rests upon property and it is hoped that in the near future property will be partially relieved.

The last two years have witnessed the merging of our state from the distress of a national economic depression * * *. The payment of delinquent taxes in many districts has stimulated activities which have tended to offset the effects of the neglect during the worst days of the depression.

In spite of our return to a degree of prosperity, many of our districts have continued to bear losses in property valuations; therefore, I am of the opinion that it is only a question of time when Colorado must seek additional sources of income if she is to maintain a creditable educational system.

These messages were effective to the extent that the people of the state became conscious of the state's obligation toward the schools. The messages set in motion the development of methods of organization for study of the state's needs in the way of refinancing her public school system. Causes of the great inequalities of the school's services were studied by members of the legislature, by the Colorado Educational Association, by service clubs, by social and political organizations, and by many interested individuals. The contention that the school is the exclusive responsibility of the local districts met challenging arguments, and there was some question as to whether the legislature under the constitution had the power to levy state taxes for schools and apportion the money to the local districts. Those advocating the state's responsibility requested the appropriation of funds for a test case. In response to this request the legislature appropriated certain funds to local units on the basis of the average daily attendance for the school year ending June 30, 1935. In its decision the supreme court ruled that the legislature had full power to levy state taxes for the benefit of local school districts and to distribute funds according to patterns set by the legislature.

Finally, in 1936, the people approved an amendment to the constitution providing for an income tax. The original purpose of this law was to relieve the property tax burden. This new tax, however, did not relieve the school situation because Colorado needed additional funds. In 1937, the legislature appropriated to the schools the revenues accruing from the state income tax for the years 1937 and 1938, but in 1939, 65% of this revenue was diverted to the General Fund of the state. Since that time, the appropriation to the Reserve for County General School Funds has been continued at 35%. This revenue seemed to reach a peak in 1944 after a gradual increase since enactment of the income tax laws. In October, 1945, there was apportioned to schools from this source $2,037,272, for an average of $7.04 per child on the school census. One year previously the amount was $2,110,767, or $7.24 per child.

The first Equalization Law was passed in 1943. It provided for a minimum classroom unit of $1,000 in the elementary schools and $1,333 in the high schools. The State School Equalization Fund consisted of 15% of the income tax collections. This law was amended in 1945, increasing the state support to a minimum of $1,200 for elementary classroom units and $1,500 for high school units. At a special session of the legislature in the same year, 1945, the law was further amended to the extent that it increased the size of the class-room units to $1,800. This law made it mandatory that three-fourths of each classroom unit shall be the minimum salary for each eligible teacher in the state of Colorado.

This special session brought to a reasonably successful conclusion a decade of continuous efforts by friends of education to convince the citizens of Colorado that the state should bear a larger share of the cost of the public school system. While Colorado had expressed her ideals for equal opportunity of educational services in the state constitution, there has been a lag between her ideals and the actual practice.

Public education in Colorado is the state's biggest business. The state, county, and district school authorities employ thousands of people. The great mass of employees include administrators, teachers, business managers, librarians, nurses, clerks, bookkeepers, custodians, bus drivers, and mechanics, besides those employed in the building trades and in the continuous repair activities. This army of servants of Colorado's schools has in its charge the educational program designed for the number recorded in the school census. The various levels of the educational program range from the kindergarten through the junior college.

The operation of the public school system is not only the state's biggest business—it is the most important business. It is Colorado's greatest enterprise in human relationships. It subscribes to the idea that universal education is the greatest defense of a free government.

The Impact of Wars and Depressions

Revoluntionary innovations were brought about by World War I. These great social and economic changes were felt by all the peoples of the earth in the realm of human relationships. The terrible experiences of World War I developed some intelligence as to the necessity of the peoples of the earth learning to live together. Out of the chaotic conditions came a glimmer of realization that there could be developed a plan for the welfare of the people of the world. Our own national liabilities in health and lack of equal opportunity for education were brought to the fore.

Research reveals that many countries provided legislation for the betterment of the masses of the people. Different and conflicting views as to what constituted a program for the general benefit of society have developed in recent years. But out of the conflicting views there has come a general agreement in regard to the necessity of providing for: (1) equal opportunity for education of all the children of all the people; (2) health as a national asset; (3) the individual—chief asset as a national resource; (4) the school—the chief agency of the state for the betterment of society; (5) the school curricula broadened to include a plan for the development of social understandings; (6) demand for adult education.

The decade following World War I was a period of general prosperity. Business flourished for some time, but in the late '20s there began to appear signs of what developed into America's greatest depression.

During the years of the depression, the federal government provided funds for the maintaining of schools for some of the rural districts. In the main, however, Colorado was able to maintain her schools even though at a lower level of efficiency. Teachers' salaries were decreased, even though school enrollments increased. The federal government also assisted Colorado, as it did other states, in maintaining certain projects.

The State Department of Education cooperated with the federal government by sponsoring many activities of an educational nature. These activities proved invaluable in the state's time of need. The W. P. A. and the P. W. A. made many improvements and constructed public school buildings in rural sections. The State Department sponsored the adult educational program. The scope of the program was wide and the range of activities included citizenship and Americanization classes; vocational, general, and academic subjects; the arts were not neglected. Hundreds of men and women were rehabilitated and were led into a state of mind where they had a new lease on life as the result of study and recreational activities. The recreational division rendered a service which was intended to decrease crime and juvenile delinquency. The State Library sponsored an extensive program and the activities of the library were revived. The service of the delivery of books was initiated by the Book Mobile and served the entire state. Other valuable projects were those of the nursery schools, hot lunches, child care for children of working mothers, and the N. Y. A. program.

Hardly had the American people begun to feel some relief from the effects of the depression, when World War II became a reality. The war complicated the daily lives of all people. The country's industries were turned to colossal production. Winning the war became the great objective.

Twelve million men and women were taken out of civilian life to fight the battles against aggression. Even though millions of our youth were removed from industry and agriculture, our country produced more than ever before in the way of food, machinery, war equipment, and transportation facilities. The cooperative effort and success of production is the most perfect illustration in the history of mankind of democracy's efficiency when geared to a common cause.

All schools in Colorado were geared to the war effort. On account of the serious shortage of farm labor, many of the high school programs were arranged so that the high school students were able to help with farm crops in the spring, the summer, and the fall without serious loss of high school credit. During the summer of 1943, hundreds of high school boys and girls were employed in war production, and because of the attractive wages, many of them remained on the jobs instead of returning to school. To combat this serious loss in high school attendance, school authorities, in cooperation with other agencies, planned and carried out a "Back to School Campaign" in 1944. The campaign was a success, as a large percentage of the youth returned to finish their courses.

The schools of Colorado also assisted the Office of Price Administration in distributing the ration books. The task was performed by the school teachers in record time and in a most efficient manner. In many instances, the older pupils assisted the local teachers in this serious and important undertaking.

During the war period, the collection of waste paper became one of the school activities of the children of Colorado. Federal authorities were outspoken in their gratitude for the efficient service rendered.

One of the most important campaigns was the scrap iron drive. There was enthusiasm and splendid effort in this undertaking. During the Liberty Ship Salvage Contest, which closed in October, 1942, there were collected 4,026,579 pounds of scrap iron by the pupils.

County and local superintendents of the state provided the type of leadership in the schools' part in the War Savings Program which resulted in the sale of over a million dollars in War Savings Stamps and Bonds by boys and girls.

During the war years, attention was given to health programs. A handbook concerning the health of Colorado's children, prepared by the State Department of Education and the State Board of Health, proved to be an excellent guide in health instruction. Home economics teachers emphasized nutrition. Home nursing was taught in many of the schools as a means of maintaining health, particularly in areas where the war had taken both the doctors and nurses. As part of the general health program, the State Department of Education encouraged rest periods and adequate school lunches for all children.

The high school authorities of Colorado arranged what were known as "pre-induction courses," in accordance with the war needs, in which science and mathematics were stressed. Also, vocational practical competence was emphasized in activities that required skillful use of the hands.

Colorado, in common with other states, suffered a shortage of teachers. It was apparent from the beginning of the war that drastic action would be necessary if the schools of the state were to be kept open in all areas. Many teaching staffs of Colorado's schools became depleted as teachers withdrew not only to enter the armed forces, but also to assume positions in war production. The serious teacher shortage created an emergency; therefore the governor issued a proclamation which was the basis of the issuance of emergency certificates. In spite of the issuance of war-time certificates, many of the one-teacher schools closed, and even in the large systems some departments were forced to suspend services for the duration.

In the field of transportation, the keeping of school busses in operation was a difficult task. The limited number allotted to the states and the wearing out of school bus equipment often challenged the local school authorities. Generally speaking, transportation was maintained throughout the war even in the face of many difficulties.

The winning of the war brought its postwar problems. The lowering of the draft age created an adult education problem. There was the postwar taxation load and the task of adjusting the returned veterans to the trades, industry, agriculture, and the professions. There was the emotional upheaval affecting the home, the school, and the adult population in many instances. How to keep children happy, hopeful, and enthusiastic became the schools' responsibilities. Some of the products of the war were fatigue, fear, suspicion, and hate. The schools were urged, therefore, to provide additional means of recreation, rest periods, and other welfare activities which would make for physical and mental well-being.

In view of this social and economic scene, educators throughout Colorado are assisting in creating postwar educational programs for all whose education has been interrupted by service in the armed forces and by the needs of war industries. New standards of scholarship have been adopted and state and local administrative machinery has assisted in accommodating those boys and girls who were taken away from their classes. All possible aid is being given to those who wish to return to high school and enter college.

These years call for a gradual constructive re-evaluation of the place of education in the life of a people. The appearance of the atomic bomb, with its stunning effect on all the world, has developed a realization of the interdependence of all peoples. That the educators are aware of their responsibility is shown by the program prepared for a conference on "International Education in Colorado Secondary Schools." The discussions at the session held February 1, 1946, included such topics as "The Social Studies Teacher in the Atomic Age," "Techniques of International Education Developed by United Nations Organization Committee," and the "Role of Secondary Schools in International Education." The value of this conference is expressed in the following letter to the State Superintendent of Public Instruction, from a social science teacher in the Denver schools.

My dear Mrs. Lewis:

What a very worthwhile conference we had yesterday. It is wonderful to look back over the last twenty years and see the growth in the interest in International Relations, among school people here in Denver, and throughout the entire state.

When your sister* and I had our two clubs back in those days, and were carried away with the vast possibilities for student and teacher growth in this field, little did we realize our dreams would come true so soon, and that not only through the clubs but also in the curricula, would all phases of international understanding and goodwill be carried all over the state to our children of every age and every origin. I think it is just thrilling! It makes one think that pioneering is very, very much worthwhile, and it sends us on into another day, another year with the hope that we may be strong enough and scholarly enough to meet the challenge which faces us.

We started, as you know, first here in Denver as a little group of International Relations Clubs at the same time Colorado Springs and Fort Collins did. Then, we planned not only regional meetings, but finally with the help of the Foundation for the Advancement of the Social Sciences at Denver University, we began to invite clubs from all over the state to meet us there in State Conferences each spring. This kept up till the recent war years, but again this spring we shall meet at the Denver University campus and discuss not only the U. N. O. but also the best possible plans for teaching international cooperation in our classrooms. The clubs pointed the way, now it is the classroom research and study which will make it possible for all the children in every school to get a taste of the importance of all peoples of the earth working together for a lasting Peace, and for One World.

I am not gloomy as I face the future and attempt to look down the years ahead. I feel the task is enormous but not impossible. I feel that the united efforts of the teachers of America, and the teachers around the world, can, and will, make this all come true. If implanted in the minds of little children is the ideal of fair play, comradeship, based upon mutual understanding and love, and a desire to really know and to really appreciate the children of other lands, I feel that future will not be marred by the awful scars of another war. It is only when children grow up that jealousy, greed, and misunderstanding take hold of them, and worst of all, intolerance! We teachers, however, can, in time, wipe this out by extending our teaching of international cooperation and understanding into the educating of the adult groups in our various communities. There is where a great part of the need lies. There is so much to do and so many tools with which to do it, that it seems that we cannot fail. * * *

---

*Lillian M. Johnson, Chairman Social Science Department, Colorado Springs High School.

I believe we in Colorado will continue, even in a much more effective way than we have in the past, to spread the doctrine of goodwill and better international understanding throughout our schools.

Sincerely yours,

VIRGINIA HARDIN STEARNS.

The above letter not only shows the trend of our educational philosophy but also exemplifies the faith of the teachers of Colorado in free and universal education as the basis for the continuance of American democracy, and as the foundation of international understanding and world peace.

CHAPTER VII

History of Religion in Colorado

MARTIN RIST[1]

LONG before the arrival of the white men in this region the Indians who roamed the plains and scaled the mountains had their own religious beliefs and practices. Christianity first entered this region along with Spanish explorers as early as the 16th century. Father Padilla, who was with Coronado's expedition, crossed a corner of Colorado, and later was killed by Indians whom he had tried to convert. From time to time other Catholic Christians, French as well as Spanish, penetrated this area, but left no lasting signs of their faith. Priests who attempted to convert the Pueblo Indians had little or no success.

Much later a group of Mormons spent the winter of 1846-47 at Pueblo and built a cabin for their religious services. However, with the end of winter they pushed on to the Salt Lake Valley. Near Conejos the Church of our Lady of Guadalupe was built by Spaniards from New Mexico in 1858. This, the first permanent Christian structure in the territory, was a memorial of migrations from New Mexico.

More significant developments occurred shortly in the vicinity of Auraria and Denver and the mining cities in the mountains during early days of the gold rush. A Cherokee Baptist preacher, John Beck, arrived in June, 1858, but he came as a gold seeker, not as a seeker of souls. But on November 16, 1858, George W. Fisher, a Methodist lay preacher who was a wagon maker by trade, arrived with a party that included Gen. William Larimer, one of the organizers of the Denver City Town Company. These two invited everybody they met to attend a church service on the following Sunday, November 21. Since the weather was inclement, the meeting was held in one end of a double cabin belonging to Jack Jones and John Smith. The attendance was small; two women (squaws of the owners of the cabin) and six or eight men in addition to the Rev. Fisher, Gen. Larimer, and his son who relates the incident. He writes that old-time songs were sung under the leadership of Mr. McLane from Omaha, and an earnest sermon was preached by the Rev. Mr. Fisher from an appropriate text. During the services a gambling game was in progress in the other end of the cabin. On the following day Gen. Larimer, in behalf of the company, gave some church lots to the preacher, and offered other lots to a preacher in Omaha. The rival Auraria Town Company made similar inducements for church buildings in January, 1859, but it was some time before any churches were erected.

[1] Professor of Religion, Iliff School of Theology.

The early preachers preached wherever they could find a place for a meeting, in private homes, dance halls, saloons, gambling rooms, store buildings, or the open air. Somewhat later, in December, or in February, 1859, the Rev. Mr. Fisher preached to a company of 75 men under some cottonwoods in front of the Smith cabin. Later, on April 14, he preached in an unfinished building near 15th Avenue and Larimer Street, with the congregation sitting on joists or standing up where they could.

In June of this same year the Rev. Mr. Porter of the M. E. Church, South, preached a sermon in Mountain (Central) City. On

"Our Lady of Guadaloupe," the First Church in Colorado

June 12 Rev. Lewis Hamilton, a Presbyterian minister, preached in the unfinished Pollock Hotel in Auraria. Acting on the advice of Horace Greeley, who heard him preach, he then went to Gregory Gulch and Central City, preaching in the open, and on to Tarryall, Fairplay, and other places. A member of Greeley's party (A. D. Richardson), tells about an open air meeting he witnessed, possibly one of Hamilton's, in June. He saw "several hundred men in the open air attending public religious worship. They were roughly clad, displaying weapons at their belts, and represented every state in the Union and almost every nation on earth. They sat upon logs and stumps, a most attentive congregation, while the clergyman upon a rude platform preached from the text: 'Behold, I bring you tidings of great joy.' It was an impressive spectacle—that motley crowd of goldseekers among the mountains, a thousand miles from home and civilization, to hear the good tidings forever old and yet forever new."

The first Protestant denomination to effect an official and permanent organization was the Methodist Episcopal Church. In April, 1859, during the session of the Kansas and Nebraska Conference in Omaha, Bishop Scott, realizing the religious needs of the gold country, appealed for volunteers to serve in the Pikes Peak and Cherry Creek Mission. After some deliberation, Rev. Wm. H. Goode, an experienced preacher and missionary, together with a young man, Rev. Jacob Adriance, volunteered.

Accordingly, after an arduous 28 days' journey of 600 miles, the two reached Denver on June 28, 1859, and immediately posted notices of services to be held in the Pollock Hotel on the following Sunday. Goode preached in the morning and Adriance in the afternoon, each to a small congregation. They set out for the Gregory diggings on the following day, stopping en route at Golden to hold a service in a gambling tent. In a few days they reached their destination and posted notices of a Sunday service. In addition to posting notices, Goode writes that they early formed the practice of making the rounds of the diggings, ranches, houses, booths, liquor stands, and gambling houses inviting all they met to attend. But the best method for obtaining a crowd was to "sing them up" at the beginning of a meeting, and in this young Adriance with his good voice was a decided asset.

The Rev. Mr. Porter, who had preceded them to Central City, graciously stepped in the background, and on Sunday, July 10, Goode preached in the open street to a large and attentive audience. In the afternoon a love feast was held on a mountainside. This was attended by a good group who "sang the old hymns, wept over their shortcomings, and shouted for joy as they related their experiences of a personal salvation." At the close 35 were accepted into membership in the church, and on the next day the Central City M. E. Church was organized, with the local elder from Denver, G. W. Fisher, as their pastor.

They soon returned to Denver, where they organized the Denver City Mission, August 2, 1859. This was later called the Lawrence Street M. E. Church, and still later Trinity. By this time there were a number of children in Auraria and Denver, enough to warrant the establishment of Mr. O. J. Goldrick's Union Day School, which opened on October 3. On November 3 the following announcement appeared in the *Rocky Mountain News:* "A union Sunday School for the children of Auraria and Denver will be held every Sunday at 3 o'clock P. M., at the home of Preachers Fisher and Adriance, near Cherry Creek. It is particularly requested that parents and guardians will endeavor to have their children attend the school regularly and punctually. Books and children's papers will soon be furnished to the scholars. The school will not only be a union school for both towns, but a union of all denominations."

This notice was signed by George W. Fisher, who had returned to Denver for the winter, Lewis N. Tappan, Jacob Adriance, D. C. Collier, and O. J. Goldrick. Mr. Collier was chosen to be the superintendent of this first Sunday School in the Territory. Twelve children attended the first Sunday (as compared with twenty enrolled in the day school), but the attendance grew. The establishment of churches with their own Sunday Schools soon made this interdenominational endeavor unnecessary, and in June, 1860, it merged with the Methodist Sunday School.

As may be seen by referring to the sketches of the separate denominations, other churches in addition to the Methodist were soon established in Auraria and Denver and in the mining camps. In addition, in 1860 the Presbyterian, Rev. Lewis Hamilton, organized an interdenominational church in Central City. Also, on June 3, a Mr. George Walker started a union ''Sabbath School,'' as he termed it, in Nevada. He was superintendent, and there were two classes for children and one for adults. A feature of this school was the library to which he contributed the few books he had brought with him from Brooklyn. By the end of the summer, however, the Methodists, who had developed a strong work in this area, had taken most of the students and teachers, ''which they had a perfect right to do,'' according to the magnanimous founder.

Such were the rude beginnings of organized religion in the pioneer period. The times were rough, and many of the gold seekers and other settlers were also rough. Furthermore, a large percentage had no idea of making this their permanent home, and as a result were disinterested in contributing to any permanent institutions, including churches. On the other hand, many of the pioneers, as in Colonial days, were men and women of considerable ability and vision, and made notable contributions towards the development of the institutions that mark our present culture. In some cases denominational headquarters had the foresight to give aid in the form of missionaries and monetary assistance so that permanent church organizations might be established, but in other instances the authorities were blind both to the needs and the opportunities of this region. It might be said in passing that this is to some extent true today.

However, as a result of both local initiative and the direction of bishops and home boards, by the close of 1860 the following churches were organized in Denver: M. E. Church, M. E. Church South, Protestant Episcopal, Roman Catholic, Baptist, and Presbyterian. Two, the M. E. Church South and the Roman Catholic, had their own places of worship. Several of these denominations were also represented by organizations in Central City and elsewhere, and in addition there was Hamilton's independent church in Central City. Also, members of the Jewish faith had organized a cemetery association and even though they had no synagogue or rabbi they celebrated their main religious festivals.

While the growth during the next decade was not spectacular, nevertheless there was growth. According to the census of 1870 there were 55 religious organizations in the Territory by this time, distributed among the denominations as follows: Baptists, 5, Christians, 2, Congregationalists, 4, Protestant Episcopal, 9, Jewish, 1, Methodists, 14, Presbyterians, 6, and Roman Catholics, 14. At this same time there were 47 religious edifices in the Territory. As would be typical of a frontier section the percentage of church members to the total population was considerably less than in the older, more settled regions of the country; this is a situation which, to a lesser degree, obtains today in Colorado. Even so, the vigor of our religious groups in the early, formative days, the remarkable ability of their leaders, and their influence upon the state as a whole, have been a significant factor in the history of Colorado. This may be seen in part by sketching the history of the separate denominations. It will be noted that the larger denominations, on the whole, were established first, the smaller groups later. Also, that very soon after statehood, in some instances before, foreign language groups were numerous enough to organize their own congregations and build churches. For the most part these groups now use English in their church services, but in some instances foreign languages are still used for the benefit of the older generation.

METHODIST EPISCOPAL CHURCH. The beginnings of Methodism in Denver and Central City have already been related. Shortly after the establishment of churches in these places other ministers began to arrive and organized churches and Sunday Schools in the various settlements, so that in 1860 the Pike's Peak and Cherry Creek Mission was made a district of the newly organized Kansas Conference. Rev. (later Col.) J. M. Chivington, a picturesque pioneer preacher, was appointed as presiding elder. On July 10, 1863, the Rocky Mountain Conference (later named the Colorado Conference) was organized in Denver with Bishop E. R. Ames presiding. This conference was composed of 8 preaching circuits, with a circuit usually consisting of a number of preaching points. Ten preachers, in addition to the bishop, were in attendance. Among them were Oliver Willard (the capable brother of the famous Frances E. Willard) and the celebrated "Father" John L. Dyer, the dauntless circuit rider who was known as the Snow Shoe Itinerant since in winter time he made his circuit through the mountains on rough skis, called snow shoes, of his own devising. At this time there were circuits and churches in Pueblo, Canon City, South Park, California Gulch (Leadville), St. Vrain, Denver, and Central City, with a total of 241 members, 33 probationers, and 449 Sunday School scholars.

The Methodists claim to have been the first Protestants to establish work not only in the places mentioned, but also in the San Luis Valley, the Arkansas Valley, the San Juan Valley and elsewhere. This was due in part to the appointment by the annual conference of preachers to relatively large areas as their circuits under the supervision of presiding elders, who were responsible for a larger district, and in part to the ability and perseverance of these pioneer preachers. As a result of this combination Methodism was able to enter a place and establish a church almost as soon as it was settled.

The camp meeting was an important feature of frontier religion, especially among the Methodists. Accordingly the first camp meeting in this region was held by the Methodists in Pueblo in 1866. A second, on the edge of Colorado City (Springs) the following year was somewhat exciting; since the Indians were on the warpath, thirty of the men brought their firearms with them and formed a guard against a surprise attack which, fortunately, did not occur.

The versatility of the frontier preacher was illustrated by the resourceful Rev. B. T. Vincent, pastor of Central City in 1863, and later of Blackhawk and Nevada as well, before being assigned to Denver in 1866. Having experienced the difficulty of obtaining a regular supply of Sunday School literature, in January, 1864, he began to publish the *Rocky Mountain Sunday School Casket,* edited and largely written by himself. It circulated among churches other than those under his immediate supervision. In 1868, however, with the coming of the railroad which assured a regular supply of Sunday School literature from the East, this, the first magazine in Colorado, suspended publication.

The Conference of 1863 adopted a resolution to establish an institution of higher learning. As a result of this sponsorship, not to mention the liberality of Gov. John Evans, a pioneer Methodist layman, Colorado Seminary opened its doors to students on Nov. 14, 1864, in a building that had been erected in Denver. After a few precarious years the institution became more firmly established, and in 1880 changed its name to the University of Denver.

By 1884 the development of the church was so marked that Denver was chosen as an episcopal residence, with Henry White Warren as the first resident bishop. A leader of rare vision and energy, he was in part responsible for the expansion and development of Methodism during his long term of residence, which ended in 1912. A widower, he married Mrs. Elizabeth Iliff, the widow of the cattle king, a staunch Methodist. Realizing the need of a school for the training of ministers for this region, Mrs. Warren founded and liberally endowed the Iliff School of Theology in 1892 as a part of the University of Denver. At a later date it became a separate institution. Other resident bishops in turn were F. J. McConnell, Charles L. Mead, Ralph Cushman, and Wilbur Hammaker, each of them worthy successors of Bishop Warren.

Save for one period, the growth of the denomination in the state has been steady. In 1906 there were 220 churches with 24,380 members, in 1916, 236 churches and 38,584 members. In 1926 the number of churches had dropped to 217, partly through consolidation of small churches, but the membership had risen to 46,474. However, during the next decade the number of churches dropped to 148 and the membership to 36,932, less than in 1916. This was in part due to the depression, in part to other factors. However, during the past ten years the number of churches has risen to 210 and the membership to 56,106. This, of course, included the churches and members of the M. E. Church, South as a result of the merger in 1941, but even so is a remarkable increase. At present there is a great deal of emphasis in the state on youth work, with numerous institutes and camps, all of which augurs well for the future.

METHODIST EPISCOPAL CHURCH, SOUTH. The Southern branch was not far behind the Northern in the early days; indeed, in some respects it was ahead. Mention has been made of the Rev. Mr. Porter who was preaching in Central City before the arrival of Goode and Adriance in July, 1859. In June, 1860, another preacher from the South, Rev. William Bradford, organized a society in Denver and built a suitable chapel. However, with the outbreak of the Civil War he and many of his flock left for the South, and in 1862 their chapel was sold to the Episcopalians. In 1871 Rev. A. A. Morrison reorganized the Denver Church, which now is known as St. Paul's. Naturally the Southern Church has never been very strong in Colorado. In 1906 there were but 15 churches with 1,465 members; by 1936 there were 17 churches and 2,736 members. Its history from 1941 on is that of the combined church.

FREE METHODIST CHURCH. Apart from the Negro Methodist churches, discussed elsewhere, the other branches of Methodism have not had much strength in Colorado; in fact, no record of some, such as the Methodist Protestant, can be found. There is at least one Wesleyan Methodist Church in the state, located in Denver. The Free Methodist Church was organized in Denver on August 19, 1883. By 1906 there were 20 churches in the state with but 433 members, and in 1936 there were but 13 churches and 437 members.

PROTESTANT EPISCOPAL CHURCH. Rev. John Kehler, an Episcopal minister, arrived in Denver in January, 1860, and conducted services soon after his arrival, possibly in Goldrick's school house. Before long a church, called The Church of St. John's in the Wilderness, since it was the only Episcopal Church within 700 miles, was organized, with a temporary vestry selected on February 19. On his episcopal visit the following year, Missionary Bishop Joseph C. Talbot suggested that Central City would be a better location for a permanent church. However, on his return in 1862 he advised the purchase of the chapel which had been abandoned by the M. E. Church, South at the outbreak of the War. This was done, and the chapel was suitably furnished. Other churches were established in quick succession at places such as Central City, Nevadaville, Empire, Golden, Pueblo, Littleton, and Georgetown, with missions at Greeley, Canon City, and Trinidad.

Bishop George M. Randall arrived as missionary bishop on June 11, 1866. An exceptionally good choice for the position, he was in no small measure responsible for the spread of the denomination in the Territory. Among other contributions, he succeeded in inducing a number of able ministers to come to the region. Under his administration several parish schools were founded in places where the public schools were either inadequate or non-existent. Also, Wolfe's Hall, a high school for girls, was built in Denver on or about 1867; Jarvis Hall, a high school for boys, was founded in Golden in 1868; and Matthews Hall, a theological seminary, was established in Golden in 1872. With state aid the church founded a School of Mines in Golden in 1870, but in 1874 this was turned over to the Territory.

Despite all these visible signs of growth, when Bishop J. F. Spalding was assigned missionary bishop in 1874 there were but two self-supporting parishes in the Territory, Denver and Central City. During his energetic and farseeing episcopate, which lasted until 1902, the work was consolidated and placed on a firmer basis, so that in 1885 Colorado ceased to be missionary territory and was made into a diocese. Additional churches and missions were established in the state, and the membership grew steadily. In 1878 both Jarvis Hall and Matthews Hall were destroyed by fire. The former was rebuilt, but in 1881 was turned over to the state to be used as an industrial school for boys. Years later a seminary, St. John's, was organized in Greeley, but it was closed in 1933. In 1880 a cathedral Romanesque in style and costing $115,000, was begun. In the following year St. Luke's Hospital in Denver, one of the finest in the state, with an excellent school for nurses, was established. In 1897 the Mission of Transfiguration in Evergreen was founded. This beautiful place has become a national as well as a state center for Episcopalians.

Bishop Spalding was succeeded by Bishop Charles S. Olmstead in 1902. In the following year the cathedral was ruined by fire, and it was not until 1911 that the new one, a splendid Gothic structure, was ready for church services. The period from 1902 was one of steady expansion. Many churches and rectories were built, and a number of parish houses, and the membership increased steadily. Under the next two bishops, Irving Johnson (retired Nov. 1, 1938), and Fred Ingley, the work of the church has progressed in all areas. In 1936 there were 82 churches and missions in the state, with 14,401 members, while in 1945, the latest date for which figures are available, this had increased to 84 churches and missions and 19,661 members of all ages.

Among the independent Episcopal institutions in the state is the Order of St. Anne, which established a house in Denver in 1929. At present this order operates a home for convalescent children caring for as many as 40 at a time, and is also in charge of a summer camp in Indian Hills for underprivileged children.

It is of interest to note that there is an Episcopal church for negroes in Denver with a negro rector, the Church of the Holy Redeemer, with 361 members, as well as a negro mission in Colorado Springs.

BAPTIST CHURCH (NORTHERN BAPTIST CONVENTION). Apart from the Negro churches and a number of independent groups, most of the Baptist churches in the state are connected with the Northern Baptist

Convention. Baptists were to be found among the first pioneers in Colorado. It is possible that Mr. George Walker who founded a "Sabbath School" in Nevada, near Central City, on June 10, 1860, was a Baptist; at any rate, his song leader, a Mr. Sunderland was "a good Baptist brother." However, the first Baptist Church in the

First Baptist Church, Denver

state was founded in Denver, on Sept. 25, 1860, as the Rocky Mountain Baptist Church, with Elder James Ripley as pastor. It met in the Court House, and had a Sunday School with nearly 100 members. Despite this auspicious start, the church went out of existence during the next year.

The first permanent Baptist Church was organized in Golden on or about Aug. 1, 1863. Later, on Dec. 27, 1863, a meeting was held in Denver under the direction of Rev. Walter M. Potter, a representative of the American Baptist Home Missionary Society. A committee was appointed, and on May 2, 1864, the First Baptist Church of Denver was organized with the Rev. Mr. Potter as the pastor.

Zion (Negro) Baptist Church was incorporated Nov. 7, 1865, but not until 1881, when Calvary Baptist Church was founded, was there another Baptist Church in the city.

However, churches were soon established in other places, such as Canon City, Golden City, Central City, and Colorado City. Accordingly the Rocky Mountain Baptist Association was organized in Denver on Sept. 21, 1866, representing 6 churches with a combined membership of but 159.

Other churces were added in ensuing years, so that other associations were formed, the Southern Colorado in 1872, the Gunnison Valley in 1886, the San Luis Valley in 1895, the Southwestern in 1895, the Midland in 1896, and the Southeastern in 1899. By 1890 the total membership had reached the 5,000 mark.

In 1890 the cornerstone of the Colorado Woman's College was laid. This had been chartered by the Baptists in 1888. However, with the panic of 1893 building operations were suspended and the structure was not completed until 1909. In recent years this fine school has had a remarkable growth.

The church expanded steadily in all parts of the state, so that by 1926 there were 122 churches and 24,166 members. These figures, however, shrank to 99 churches and 20,496 members by 1936, a shrinkage due in part, no doubt to the depression. But at present 108 churches are reported with 30,548 members, a very significant increase in members. For a number of years the Baptist Church in Colorado has been divided into two factions, the "fundamentalists" and the "modernists." This division has been more sharp than that of other denominations in the state, and for a time threatened to be serious; but apparently the difficulties have been largely overcome.

PRESBYTERIAN CHURCH IN THE U. S. A. As has been noted above, Rev. Lewis Hamilton, a Presbyterian minister, was preaching in Auraria and Denver as early as June 12, 1859, when he preached in the Pollock Hotel. Soon afterwards he went into the mountain camps and diggings holding services in the open air. He went back to his home in Lima, Ohio, where his church had granted him a six months sick leave, but before long he returned to Colorado and in 1860 founded a union church in Central City. Like many other pioneer preachers, he found it necessary to supplement his income with other work; in his case he found employment in a grocery store.

The first Presbyterian Church in this region was founded by Rev. Alexander Taylor Rankin, Sept. 2, 1860, with 8 charter members. Services were held in a house on Larimer St. He made a preaching tour of the mining camps, and left for the East in December. A more permanent organization was effected by Rev. A. S. Billingsley from the Board of Home Missions who took over the work of his predecessor in April of 1861 and organized the First Presbyterian Church on Dec. 15 of that year in International Hall. This church, with its name changed to Central, is now located at 17th Ave. and Sherman St. It became a "mother" church, giving aid in the formation of new congregations. From the beginning it has been a leader in Colorado Presbyterianism, and at present is the largest Presbyterian church in the country.

On Jan. 18, 1862, Rev. Lewis Hamilton organized a Presbyterian church in Central City. Presumably this was an outgrowth of his union church. Rev. Simon Cort was made the elder of the Rocky Mountain region, and was very effective in the development of the denomination in the Territory. The Presbytery of Colorado was organized in Denver on Jan. 10, 1862, but failed to obtain the recognition of the General Assembly. By 1869 there were six organized Presbyterian churches in the Territory, two in Denver, and one each in Central City, Blackhawk, Boulder Valley, and Santa Fe, with a total membership of not more than 150. By 1890 there were four Presbyteries in the state and 5,902 members, making this the second largest of the Protestant bodies. In 1926 there were 132 churches and 27,090 members, but apparently as a result of the depression this middle class church had but 94 churches and 19,950 members in 1936. However, as the result of an energetic program the number of churches is now up to 125 with a membership of about 30,000.

The Presbyterian Hospital in Denver, opened about 20 years ago, is one of the leading hospitals of the region. On June 8, 1891, Westminster University of Colorado was incorporated, and before long a building costing $200,000 was erected. For a number of reasons it was not possible to make this a going institution, and finally, in Oct. 16, 1917, the project was abandoned. The property was sold to the Pillar of Fire Church and is used to house their Belleview College.

UNITED PRESBYTERIAN CHURCH OF NORTH AMERICA. This denomination was the product of the union of the greater part of two synods, the Associate Synod and the Associate Reformed Synod, in 1858. In 1873 the board of publications of the united church received a request for Psalm books from a group that had settled near the mouth of the Big Thompson River in the vicinity of Greeley. Shortly afterwards Rev. S. B. Reed was appointed to go to Colorado Territory to explore the possibilities for work there. He arrived at Evans in July, 1874. At this time Evans was an important station of the Union Pacific from Cheyenne, and the population was so rough that the town was called Devil's Round-up Camp. On Sept. 5 of this same year he organized a church at Evans with 32 members, no doubt the group that had made the earlier request for Psalm books. The First United Presbyterian Church in Denver was not founded until June 3, 1883. At present there are 11 churches in Colorado, all but three on the Eastern slope, with 2,781 members, as compared with 9 churches and 1,798 members in 1906, 15 churches and 2,707 members in 1916, 10 churches and 2,467 in 1926, and 10 churches and 3,548 in 1936. The reasons for the gains and losses during the past twenty years can not be ascertained.

SYNOD OF THE REFORMED PRESBYTERIAN CHURCH OF NORTH AMERICA. This group, going back to the old Covenanters of Scotland, had 3 churches and 278 members in Colorado in 1936, which may be compared with 4 churches and 255 members in 1906. Nothing has been learned of their history in Colorado.

ROMAN CATHOLIC CHURCH. According to the 1946 reports, the Roman Catholic Church, with 171,033 members, is easily the largest single denomination in the state, although the Protestants as a whole are the larger group. In some areas of the state the Catholics predominate, especially among the Spanish-American population and in certain districts of Denver, Pueblo, and other larger centers. In this connection, it is noticeable that about two-thirds of the membership is urban, the other one-third rural. However, at present the Catholic Church has been developing a program for increasing its work in the rural areas.

As for institutions, such as schools of all grades, orphanages, homes of various kinds, and hospitals, no other denomination in the state begins to approach the work of the Catholic Church; indeed, it is doubtful if all together can equal it. For in Colorado there are 2 Catholic seminaries, 2 colleges, 23 high schools, 56 elementary schools, 6 orphanages, 3 homes, and 17 hospitals. Furthermore, there are camps for boys and for girls and other institutions which do not appear in the report. In addition, there are 36 separate establishments for religious orders for women and 26 for men, including one abbey. The state is now an archdiocese, with the cathedral in Denver, divided into two dioceses, the Denver and the Pueblo. In all there are 118 parishes. Over all there is an archbishop, a bishop, and 330 priests. Certainly, this is a remarkable growth over a period of 88 years of organized activities in the state.

As has been noted above, Catholicism was introduced into this region in the days of the Spanish explorers and conquerors. Furthermore, reference has previously been made to the Catholic Church at Conejos, built in 1858, which was probably the first permanent Christian edifice in the state. In the spring of 1860 the Vicar Apostolic of Territory East of the Rocky Mountains, Bishop J. P. Miege, of Leavenworth, Kansas, came to Denver to explore the possibilities of establishing a congregation and building a church. Soon after his arrival he conducted services in the home of Mr. Guiraud, a French Catholic merchant, at 15th Ave. and Market St. Thus the Catholic church in Denver began in a home, as was the case with other denominations. Furthermore, like his Presbyterian and Methodist predecessors, Bishop Miege visited the various mining camps, holding services wherever he went. On his return to Denver a church association was formed, with Judge G. W. Purkins as president, and plans for a church building on Stout St. near 15th Ave.

were laid. At about this time the "Pike's Peak" Region, including Denver, was united with the Santa Fe diocese, and was accordingly transferred to Bishop J. B. Lamy.

Bishop Lamy soon sent two very able men to Colorado from Santa Fe, the Very Rev. J. P. Machebeuf and Rev. J. B. Raverdy. While en route to Denver they held mass for some Mexican Catholics in Pueblo, but no resident priest was stationed here until 1872. They also found some Catholics in Colorado City (Springs) where they celebrated mass. They reached Denver on October 29, 1860, where Father Machebeuf found 200 Catholics among the 3,000 residents. He reorganized the group, stimulated the building of the church, and was able to celebrate the midnight Christmas mass in the new structure.

In the meantime he began his celebrated trips among the mining camps and settlements, conducting mass and establishing churches wherever he went. Among his able assistants were Father Raverdy and Father Robinson. Like some of his Protestant colleagues in pioneer Colorado, he was a man of rare ability, devotion, and energy, and is deservedly called the apostle of Catholicism in the state. Among the early churches established were Central City, 1863, Trinidad, 1865, Golden City, 1863, Walsenburg, 1869, and Colorado Springs, 1876. However, there was not a settlement in the state which was not regularly visited by Father Machebeuf or one of his assistants.

In 1863 he started the far-reaching Catholic educational system of the state by establishing a school. In the following year three sisters came to Denver at his invitation and instituted St. Mary's Academy. Some time later, in 1873, St. Joseph's Hospital was established in Denver. In the meantime, in 1868, in recognition of his great services, Father Machebeuf was made Vicar Apostolic of Colorado and Utah and was consecrated bishop.

In the 1880s the church enjoyed a remarkable growth in every way. Accordingly, in 1887 the Diocese of Denver was formed, with Father Machebeuf as the first diocesan bishop. As a tangible proof of the results of his leadership, at the time of his death in 1889 there were 49 churches, including the cathedral in Denver, 53 chapels, 85 mission stations, and 40,000 baptized Catholics in the state. In the following year his capable assistant, Father Raverdy, who had been appointed his vicar general, passed away. With the death of these two great priests the first phase of Colorado Catholicism ended.

The pioneer bishop was succeeded by Bishop Matz. In 1887 a young priest, Father William O'Ryan, appeared in Denver. He was destined to have a distinguished career of more than a half century in this city, with a host of friends both within and outside the church. He was a leader in organizing the various charities of the city, Catholic and non-Catholic, into the Charity Organization Society of Denver, an early fore-runner of the Community Chest. In 1891 Loretto Heights College for girls, an outgrowth of St. Mary's, was organized, and in 1883 Regis College for boys was opened. In 1907

St. Thomas Seminary, the diocesan seminary for the training of priests, was founded.

By the end of the century it was increasingly apparent that the old cathedral was inadequate. Accordingly, in 1900 a new site at Colfax Ave. and Logan St. was purchased, and plans for a new cathedral were made. However, progress was slow until the arrival of a new rector, Rev. Hugh McMenamin, in 1908. Under his energetic leadership money was raised and the building of the superstructure was begun, so that by 1921 the magnificent cathedral, the church of the Immaculate Conception, was completed. Raised to the rank of monsignor, Father McMenamin is still the rector of the cathedral which he helped to build.

In 1924 another notable institution, the national *Register,* was developed by Father Matthew Smith, a monsignor since 1933, from a local Catholic paper. Today, with a national circulation of over 700,000 per week, serving 32 archdioceses and dioceses, it is no doubt the most widely read of any religious newspaper in the country, if not in the world.

Bishop Tihen succeeded Bishop Matz in 1917. During his episcopate notable advances were made in every area of activity. A significant achievement was the reorganization of the Catholic Charities in Denver under Monsignor Mulroy, so that the Denver system is considered to be a model for the entire country. In 1926 another significant institution, the Holy Cross Abbey at Canon City, was founded.

Bishop Urban Vehr became the episcopal leader in 1931. So marked was the growth of the church under his direction that Colorado was made into an archdiocese on Nov. 15, 1941, and he was consecrated as archbishop in a ceremony that may be called the high point of Catholicism in Colorado. At the same time a diocese was formed in Pueblo.

Comparative figures of growth over a period of years may be of interest. In 1889 there were 40,000 Catholics in the state; this number rose to 117,435 by 1906, a striking increase; dropped to 104,982 in 1916; but rose to 125,757 in 1926; to 140,797 in 1936; and to 171,033 in 1946. It is estimated that in 1906 more than 50% of the people who were members of some religious body in the state were Catholics; in 1916 this had dropped to 40%; in 1926 to 33%; but by 1936 had risen to about 40%. About two-thirds of the Catholics in the state may be classified as urban, one-third as rural. However, it should be noted that the Catholic Church, as vigorous as it was in pioneer days, is making a determined effort to win the country-side as well as town and city.

CONGREGATIONAL AND CHRISTIAN CHURCHES. On Aug. 23, 1863, a Congregational Church was founded in Central City, and on July 17, 1864, a second one was established in Boulder. In the winter of 1863-64 Mr. Samuel Cushman, an active member of the Union Sunday School in Denver, went to Boston and appealed for help in founding a church in Denver. As a result, in February of 1864 a Rev. William Crawford was sent to Denver by the American Home Missionary Society, and in October the First Congregational Church of Denver, with 12 charter members, was formed. For several years the congregation was without a church house, but on Oct. 25, 1870, its edifice was completed. By 1868 there were enough churches to form the Congregational Conference. Among its distinguished moderators was the late Wm. E. Sweet, later a governor of Colorado and a national figure in Congregationalism. Another well-known Congregationalist was Rev. Myron Reed, who became pastor of the First Church in Denver in 1884. He soon attracted attention throughout the state and nation as an outspoken exponent of the "social gospel" and friend of the laboring men.

One of the excellent colleges of the state, Colorado College in Colorado Springs, is under the auspices of the church, having been founded by the Congregational Conference in 1874.

It is noteworthy that the denomination has been effective in ministering to the Germans who migrated to Colorado; at one time one-fifth of the Congregational churches in the state were German.

In 1931 the Congregational Church was merged with the Christian (not to be confused with the Disciples of Christ). However, this scarcely affected the Colorado situation, since there were few members of this denomination in the state at the time of the merger. In 1926 there were 91 Congregational Churches in Colorado with 13,561 members; in 1945 there were 73 churches and over 14,000 members.

DISCIPLES OF CHRIST (sometimes called CHRISTIAN). This distinctly American church, founded by Thomas and Alexander Campbell in the early part of the 19th century, is one of the stronger Protestant denominations in the state, with 67 churches and 15,406 members in 1947.

In the 1870s a group of Disciples, among them Governor Routt and his family, decided to organize a church. At first they had no minister, but were able to obtain one in 1875. Furthermore they had no meeting place of their own for some time. In 1880 they used the chapel of Brinker Institute, and in December, 1881, the Central Christian Church was incorporated as a result of their efforts. The Rev. M. D. Todd became the pastor, lots were purchased where the Majestic Building is now located, and a church was built. In 1902 the congregation moved to its present structure at 16th Ave. and Lincoln St. Other early churches were established in Boulder, Colorado Springs, and Golden. The Golden Church was founded in the following manner. On or about 1877 a young evangelist, Rev. Bertie Stover, who was but 18 years of age, came to Colorado for his health. While in Golden he held preaching services, and succeeded in establishing a church in this city before he succumbed to his disease.

CHURCHES OF CHRIST. This denomination represents a conservative branch of the New Testament Church associated with the Campbells. It is quite congregational in organization, and among other features it does not permit the use of instrumental music in church services. The first congregation of this denomination in Colorado was founded at Colorado Springs in 1901; a second was formed in Pueblo in 1905, and a third in Denver in 1908. According to the investigations of one of the ministers, these were the only three congregations in the state as late as 1920, with a total membership of but 100. However, in 1936 there were 20 churches and 809 members, while at present there are 54 churches throughout the state, with about 30 ministers and 2,500 members. Over one-half of the members are from the South. This remarkable growth since 1920 is largely due to the support given by a wealthy layman, Mr. George Pepperdine of Los Angeles, who has extensive mercantile interests in Colorado. There are 8 churches in Denver, one a Negro church.

UNITARIAN CHURCH. The Unitarian Society in Denver was organized June, 1871, as a result of the visit of Rev. L. E. Beckwith of Boston, who stayed to be the first pastor. Other Unitarian churches were founded at Greeley, 1880, Colorado Springs, 1891, Fort Collins, 1897, and Pueblo, 1898. Today there are but three, at Denver, Colorado Springs and Fort Collins (federated with the Congregational Church) with a total membership of 486.

UNIVERSALIST CHURCH. This church was organized in Denver in 1890, and has occupied its present building at Colfax Ave. and Lafayette St. since 1898. Apparently the only church of this denomination in Colorado, it has been a missionary project from the beginning. At present its membership is about 150.

REFORMED CHURCH IN THE UNITED STATES (formerly GERMAN REFORMED). According to one account, in May, 1871, a number of Germans, members of the German Reformed Church, formed an association for worship in the German language, bought an organ and hymn books, and met regularly every Sunday. Thus this denomination had its beginning in Colorado. It was never very strong in the state, despite its early start; in 1926 but two churches were listed. In 1934 this denomination merged with the Evangelical Synod to form the Evangelical and Reformed Church, and in 1946 the new denomination united with the United Brethren to form the Evangelical United Brethren Church.

EVANGELICAL UNITED BRETHREN CHURCH. This denomination, largely composed of people of German extraction is the result of the union in 1946 of the Evangelical Church and the Church of the United Brethren in Christ.

The first Evangelical Church in Colorado was a mission in Pueblo, founded in 1883, but this had a short life. In 1888 German speaking people migrating from Canada and Nebraska organized an Evangelical congregation at Leroy, 22 miles southeast of Sterling. In 1891 the First Evangelical Church of Denver, now located at 33d and Josephine Sts. was founded.

The United Brethren beginnings in Colorado were somewhat different. In 1869 the Board of Missions sent a missionary, Rev. St. Clair Ross, who soon established a church in the Platte Valley, about 12 miles north of Denver. In a short time churches were also founded in Niwot and Denver. In 1872 the pastors of these three churches formed the Missionary Conference of Colorado.

The united church has 49 churches in Colorado at present with a combined membership of 6,150, with each denomination showing a steady gain over previous reports.

LUTHERAN CHURCHES—Missouri Synod. It is fairly certain that the first Lutheran Church in Colorado was established at Westcliffe (Blumenau) in 1870. On March 1, of that year, a colony of 100 families, including a number of German Lutherans, arrived from in and near Chicago to settle in the Wet Mountain Valley. One of the group Mrs. ("Grossmutter") Gottlieb O'Graske, Sr., wrote a letter to the president of the Missouri Synod requesting a pastor. As a result of this request Rev. J. Hilgendorf, then stationed at Omaha, was sent out in the fall of 1872 to investigate. He first stopped at Denver where he looked up some Lutheran families, and then went on to Blumenau, where he preached on two successive Sundays, and organized a church of 14 families. Next he went to Pueblo, preaching there, and on his return to Denver he organized a church, St. John's, with a congregation of 11 families. In 1873, the next year, a permanent pastor was assigned to the Denver church, and shortly afterwards one was sent to the Blumenau church.

These two pastors conducted a preaching tour in the San Luis Valley, organizing a church at Del Norte. Other pastors arrived and conducted missions in various parts of the state before the end of the century and organized a number of churches. At present this denomination is in a flourishing condition in Colorado, with 46 pastors, 77 Congregations and Preaching Stations, 8,140 confirmed members, 16 parochial schools, and hospitals at Wheatridge, Alamosa, and Monte Vista.

AMERICAN LUTHERAN CHURCH. The church at Bethune in eastern Colorado, organized in 1926, may be the oldest in the state, while St. Paul's, in Globeville, founded in 1926, is the oldest in Denver. At present there are 20 churches in the state with 2,715 confirmed members.

EVANGELICAL LUTHERAN AUGUSTANA SYNOD OF NORTH AMERICA. Probably the first church of this synod to be organized was the one at Ryssby, near Longmont (now abandoned), which was founded in 1878. Some six months later a home missionary organized the Augustana Church in Denver. In 1945 there were 12 churches in the state and 3,201 confirmed members. The Augustana Church of Denver operates the Augustana Home for working girls.

WISCONSIN SYNOD. In 1933 a church at Sugar City joined the Wisconsin Synod, thus marking the entry of this group into the state. In 1936 there were 8 churches and 477 confirmed members, in 1945 there were 27 "preaching stations," including missions as well as churches, and 725 confirmed members.

UNITED DANISH EVANGELICAL LUTHERAN CHURCH. The Danish Lutherans founded a church in Denver in 1893, and soon afterwards completed a building. In 1936 there were 3 churches and 431 members. From the beginning in Denver their services were in the English language.

NORWEGIAN LUTHERAN CHURCH. In 1885 a missionary from St. Louis organized the Emmanuel Lutheran Church, now located at 34th Ave. and Lafayette St. In 1946 there were 9 churches with about 1,600 confirmed members in the state.

UNITED LUTHERAN. The United Lutheran Church was introduced into Colorado at Colorado Springs in 1884. At present there are 10 churches in Colorado, with 3 in Denver, and 2 new missions which have been started in this city. The combined membership is about 1,000.

SEVENTH DAY ADVENTIST DENOMINATION. This denomination, characterized in part by the observance of Saturday as the Sabbath and by the ardent expectation of the second coming of Christ and the establishment of the millennium, was first established in Denver in 1880 with a church at the corner of 23d and Lawrence Sts. The pastor of this church, Rev. E. R. Jones, also held a number of tent meetings. This first church is now occupying a building, once Congregationalist, at 11th and Kalamath.

The Colorado Conference was established in 1883, with churches at Boulder, Longmont, Hillsboro, and Loveland, in addition to Denver. Within a few years, due to the evangelistic fervor of the leaders and people, the denomination was established in the leading centers of the state, with 49 churches and 2,311 members by 1906. A high point was reached in 1926 with 63 churches and 3,169 members. This was followed by a decline with the figures of 1936 approximating those of 1906. However, there has been a marked increase in the past decade, for at present there are 63 churches with 4,790 adult members (over 15 years of age) in the state.

Colorado is a part of the Central Union Conference, which maintains the following institutions in Colorado: Porter Sanitarium, a modern hospital located in Denver; the Colorado Sanitarium in Boulder; and Campion, an academy three miles south of Loveland for boys and girls.

CHURCH OF THE NAZARENE. This denomination, organized in 1887 on the principles of John Wesley, had but one church in Colorado in 1906. This may have been Olivet church at Kirk in Eastern Colorado. The first church in Denver was founded in 1908. The growth of the denomination in the state was slow at first, but by 1926 there were 39 churches with 1,728 members. By 1946 the number of churches and members had practically doubled, with 68 churches and 3,326 members reported.

CHURCH OF GOD (Anderson, Ind.). This denomination, organized in 1880, entered Colorado in 1887. In this year Evangelist D. S. Warner held a series of meetings in the Methodist Church at 14th and Lawrence. These were followed by meetings in homes, including that of Mr. Wm. Speckels at 52 Lowell Blvd. These home meetings were followed by the organization of the Church of God at W. 34th Ave. and Vallejo St.

In the past decade this church has had a remakable growth in Colorado, for in 1936 there were 16 churches with 894 members, while at present there are 25 churches and 1,317 members.

CHURCH OF GOD (Cleveland, Tenn.). This denomination, not too different from the other by the same name, came to Colorado in 1942, and now has three churches in the state, 1 in Denver, 1 in Colorado Springs, and 1 in La Junta, with a total membership of about 100.

ASSEMBLIES OF GOD. This orthodox, millennial group, was organized in 1914 as The General Council of the Assemblies of God. It has had a marked growth since its entry into Colorado. There were but 11 churches in 1926 with 817 members. This jumped to 63 churches and 2,841 members in 1936, while at present there are about 100 churches with an estimated membership of 5-6,000. They have a Camp Meeting Ground near Littleton, and have purchased the site for another one near Grand Junction.

INTERNATIONAL CHURCH OF THE FOURSQUARE GOSPEL. Founded by ''Sister'' Aimee Semple McPherson in Los Angeles in 1927, this denomination stresses divine healing and the second coming. The first church to be established in Colorado was in Sterling. In 1936 there were 19 churches in the state, with 863 members, while in 1946 there were 22 churches, with over 1,000 members.

PILLAR OF FIRE. The Pillar of Fire, a denomination which originated in Colorado, was founded by Mrs. (later Bishop) Alma White, the wife of Rev. Kent White, a Colorado Methodist minister. On occasion she occupied her husband's pulpit, and with Champa St. as a base of operations they carried on vigorous evangelistic campaigns in Denver and the surrounding territory, working among the underprivileged and the unchurched. Following her husband's death Mrs. White assumed leadership. Feeling that the Methodist Church had departed from its original teachings and was becoming "modern" in its doctrines she organized the Pentecostal Union, on Dec. 29, 1901, to supervise the missions that had been established. Soon this became an independent movement with Bishop White as its leader. On Oct. 6, 1917, the name was changed to Pillar of Fire.

In 1936 this denomination had 46 branches with 4,044 members in 15 states and the District of Columbia, with schools, radio stations, and printing plants. In Colorado, Belleview College (which since 1919 has occupied the building of the former Westminster University) and radio station KPOF are among its visible assets. Also, most of the branches in the state have day schools which meet the state educational requirements.

In 1906 there was but one branch in Colorado with 163 members, in 1916 there was still but the one unit in the state, but by 1926 there were 7, with 474 members, in 1936, 9 with 858 members, and now in 1947 there are 14 branches and 2 missions, with the number of members not given. Bishop Alma White died recently, but her son, Bishop Arthur K. White, is a capable successor. This denomination provides an interesting case study of the way in which religious groups originate and develop.

SALVATION ARMY. The Salvation Army has been established in Denver for a considerable period of time. In 1906 there were 13 corps and 432 members, in 1936, 14 corps and 1,397 members, and in 1946, 10 corps, with the membership total unavailable. In Denver there is a home that is conducted by the Army, also the Booth Memorial Hospital for unwed mothers.

VOLUNTEERS OF AMERICA. The Volunteers of America were established in Colorado around 1899. At one time there were several stations in the state, but at present there is only the one in Denver, which has a staff of 8 officers with 137 adherents. It conducts an emergency guest home for women and children in Denver and a summer camp for underprivileged children on Lookout Mountain.

CHURCH OF CHRIST, SCIENTIST (CHRISTIAN SCIENCE). This denomination, organized in 1879 by Mary Baker Eddy, was not in existence when Colorado was first settled. However, it soon reached the state, for in 1885 a Mr. Bradford Sherman of Chicago taught a class in the home of Mrs. Charles L. Hall in Denver. By 1888 an organization was formed, and in 1891 the interest had grown to such an extent that a church was incorporated. During that year a building was begun at Logan St. near 18th Ave. These quarters proved inadequate, and in May, 1904, the congregation moved to its present home at 14th Ave. and Logan St.

Mrs. Ella Peck Sweet started the churches in Colorado Springs and Canon City, and supplied in Pueblo. Another church was organized in Grand Junction, so that by 1895 there were five churches in the state. In this year the impersonal pastor system was used, with two readers from each congregation. Since this plan did away with the necessity for a personal pastor, the growth of the church throughout the state was facilitated, so that by 1906 there were 20 churches and 1,489 members. This rose to 39 churches and 3,088 members in 1936. At present there are 5 churches in Denver and 4 reading rooms. The current number of churches in the state and their membership cannot be ascertained. The success of this and other divine healing groups in this state to which many health seekers have come is significant.

EASTERN ORTHODOX CHURCHES. In 1896 a Russian Orthodox church was organized in Denver, by a group of Russians who, for the most part, had come to America from Austria-Hungary. In 1906 there were three Russian churches in the state with 725 members, but by 1936 the combined membership had dropped to 403. In 1930 the Denver congregation, located at 47th Ave. and Logan St., changed its name to the Russian-Serbian Orthodox Church, in recognition of the number of Serbians who had become members.

In 1906 there were 13 Greek Orthodox churches in Colorado with 2,180 members, but by 1936 there were but 2 churches with 737 members. The Denver congregation now at 6th Ave. and Pennsylvania St., was organized in 1908. In 1912 Archimandrite Isaias Paschopoulos came to Denver from his monastery in Greece to become the pastor of this church. Under his leadership the local church prospered. At the time of his death (1947) there were 450 families in his parish, according to the newspapers, but it is probable that the actual membership does not exceed 500.

SOCIETY OF FRIENDS (QUAKERS). The Society of Friends has been represented in Colorado for more than 70 years. At present there are 14 meetings in the state, with about 1,000 members, all of the Orthodox group. The Denver meeting has about 200 members, and at this time has a Methodist theological student for a pastor. It was begun in the 1880s, but as late as 1893 the meetings were held in a tent. Later they rented a more suitable place in North Denver, and in 1899 built their present meeting house.

MENNONITE CHURCH. Around 1890 a group of Mennonites from Kansas built a sanitarium in the neighborhood of La Junta for health seekers of their denomination and organized a church. Later this sanitarium was closed and another one was built in La Junta together with a general hospital. There is also a nurses' school connected with this hospital. The denomination also operates a Mission Home in Denver for the use of student nurses completing their training in Denver hospitals and for Mennonite girls who are working in the city. There are churches in La Junta, E. Holbrook (near La Junta), Manitou, Denver, Limon, Thurman, and Pueblo, and a Spanish mission in La Junta, with a total membership of 580. In 1906 there were 3 churches and 169 members, in 1936 there were 5 churches and 484. Bishop E. M. Yost, who supplied some of this information, makes his home in Denver.

The Mennonite Brethren, a collateral denomination which developed in Russia in the middle of the 19th century, was established in America after 1874, with centers in Kansas and Oklahoma. There are but two congregations in Colorado, one at Joes, the other at Vona, with a combined membership of 70.

CHURCH OF THE BRETHREN (DUNKERS). Members of this German denomination came West from Pennsylvania, but little information concerning their organization in Colorado is at hand. In 1906 there were but 6 churches with 339 members, while in 1926 there were 12 churches with 1,427 members. A slight decline is noted for the next decade. The latest report, for 1944, lists 11 congregations in Colorado and 1,371 members.

CHRISTIAN REFORMED CHURCH. The Denver church was organized in 1907 by a group of Hollanders from Grand Rapids, Michigan, with Rev. Ivan Dallen as pastor. In 1936 there was a total of 4 churches in Colorado with a combined membership of 899. Though small in numbers, the group supports a parochial school and the Bethesda Sanitarium in Denver.

NEGRO CHURCHES. Although the Negroes belong to a number of denominations, including certain that may be termed white for lack of a better name, in view of their special history they may be considered separately. Negroes entered the Rocky Mountain region along with the white explorers, traders, miners, and settlers, some as slaves, others as freemen. Capt. Clark, of the Lewis and Clark expedition, had a Negro servant and interpreter named York. Negro slaves were to be found at Ft. Bent, the Gregory mines, Estes Park, and other places. A number were connected with the fur trade, for they were able to get along with the Indians better than were the white men. Apparently the free Negroes outnumbered the slaves, and of course in a short time all were free.

Many of the Negroes who came here had a vital interest in religion. Early in the history of the Methodist Church in Colorado this was recognized, and a proposal was made to provide a special ministry to them, but apparently without any tangible results. It is known, however, that "Aunt" Clara Brown, a freedwoman, was associated with the Union Sunday School which was founded by two Methodist preachers in Denver on Nov. 6, 1859.

It is probable that the earliest Negro church to be established was Zion Baptist in Denver. It is possible that a group had been holding meetings under a Baptist circuit rider as early as 1863. At any rate, by Nov. 7, 1865, Zion Church was incorporated. For a period of time their meetings were held in a dug-out along the Platte River, but a more suitable building, at 20th Ave. and Arapahoe St., was erected in 1877.

The African M. E. Church was not far behind—indeed, it claims priority, but apparently without good reason. In July, 1868, Rev. J. M. Wilkerson came to Denver from Omaha by way of Cheyenne and organized the A. M. E. church in Denver with 18 members. This is now called the Shorter A. M. E. Church, in honor of a pioneer bishop. By 1887 there were 23 churches of this denomination which had been established in Colorado, Kansas, Wyoming, New Mexico, and Montana. Six of these were in Colorado, at Denver, Pueblo, Colorado Springs, Leadville, Boulder, and Trinidad. In this year the Colorado Annual Conference, comprising the 23 churches in the territories named, was held in Denver.

But not all Negroes belong to these two groups. Other Negro denominations, such as the Colored M. E. Church and the Churches of God in Christ, were established. Still others belonged to white denominations. In some cases, as with the Methodist, the Episcopal, the Presbyterian, and the Adventist, a few separate congregations for Negroes were formed. In other cases the Negroes became associated with white congregations. At present, although there is no Negro Catholic congregation in the state, the Roman Catholic Church is making a serious effort to attract Negroes to certain of the existing Catholic churches. In one instance a Catholic week-day religious school was conducted in the basement of a Colored M. E. Church. In 1939 there were six branches of the "Father" Divine cult in Colorado, but in 1946 there was but one, and that mixed in membership, at Colorado Springs. This indicates that the Negroes of Colorado are not too greatly interested in strange cults.

According to a survey made in 1946, there were 12,176 Negroes in Colorado. Of these, 11,234 are located in the cities of the state, and of this number two-thirds live in Denver. There are 51 Negro churches in Colorado, with 8,677 members. Accordingly, at least two-thirds of the Negroes are church members, a high percentage.

The following table, prepared from statistics gathered by Dr. Daniel G. Hill in 1946, shows the distribution of the Negro churches by denominations, with their membership. It does not include those Negroes who are affiliated with the Roman Catholic Church, Christian Science, and so on, since these do not have separate churches for Negroes in Colorado.

Denomination	Churches	Membership
Baptist	13	4,055
African M. E.	9	2,651
Church of God in Christ	15	602
Protestant Episcopal	2	493
Methodist	3	328
Colored M. E.	2	213
Seventh Day Adventist	2	200
Presbyterian	1	125
Church of God	1	30
Pentecostal Church	1	..
Church of Christ	1	..
"Father" Divine	1	..
	51	8,677

The growth and development of the Negro church in Colorado, despite the obvious difficulties and handicaps, is indeed a tribute to their race.

CHURCH OF JESUS CHRIST OF LATTER DAY SAINTS (MORMONS). A group of Mormons, including convalescents from the Mormon Battalion and immigrants en route to Utah, spent the winter of 1846-47 at Pueblo. In November, 1877, seventy converts from Georgia and Alabama, led by Elder John Morgan, organized a branch in Pueblo with Daniel R. Sellers as president. The group soon went on to the San Luis Valley and settled near Conejos. Here they organized the San Luis Stake in 1883. Missionaries began their work in Northern Colorado in 1896, under Apostle John W. Taylor, and on Jan. 3, 1897, the Denver Branch was organized. This was made a stake on June 30, 1940. At present there are three stakes in Colorado, plus the Western States Mission, with 27 wards and branches and 6,968 members, as compared with 22 units and 6,945 members in 1936. However, at present an energetic missionary program throughout the state is underway.

REORGANIZED CHURCH OF JESUS CHRIST OF LATTER DAY SAINTS. This denomination, with headquarters at Independence, Mo., is fairly well represented in Colorado. In the late '70s or early '80s Missionary Henry Kemp went from Independence to the Western Slope where he organized a number of branches. Later on branches were established in the eastern part of the state. The Denver branch, one of the earliest of these, was organized by James Cassall, a traveling apostle, in 1889 with 22 members. This congregation now numbers 680. In 1936 there were 11 units with 1,630 members, not a great increase over 1926 or 1916. However, according to an unofficial report, today there are 17 branches and 4 missionary groups, with approximately 3,000 members. This is the result of an aggressive missionary effort.

JEWISH ORGANIZATIONS. In 1860 members of the Jewish faith formed a cemetery association. In addition they began to celebrate the main yearly festivals, Passover, New Year, and the Day of Atonement, before any synagogue was founded. However, the first permanent institution was that of the fraternal organization, the Independent Order of B'nai B'rith, on April 7, 1872, in Denver. Two months later Temple Emanuel (Reformed Jewish) was organized. In 1889 the young William S. Friedman arrived as rabbi, and during his pastorate of fifty years or more he was both a religious and civic leader in Denver. The present temple was dedicated in 1899. The first orthodox congregation was Ahava Amunoh, founded in 1877 by H. Plonsky. This synagogue ceased to exist in 1903, but some of its members founded Shearith Israel. H. Plonsky, dissatisfied with the orthodox congregation he had founded, established the conservative Beth Ha Medrosh Hagodol in 1892. In 1902 Rabbi Charles Hillel Kauvar became rabbi, and has served in this capacity ever since. Other congregations were formed in other parts of the state, so that by 1906 there were 13 in all, with 853 heads of families listed. In 1916 there were only 7 synagogues, but with 2,356 heads of families listed. In 1926 this rose to 22 synagogues and 18,950 Jewish people all told, in 1936 to 23 synagogues and 20,116 Jewish people. At present there are 15 synagogues in the state, 10 in Denver, 2 in Colorado Springs, 2 in Pueblo, and 1 in Trinidad, with about 20,000 Jews in all. Accordingly, during the past 20 years the Jewish population in the state has been stationary, while the great growth occurred in the period between 1906 and 1926.

Among the institutions, apart from the synagogue schools, are the following: The National Jewish Hospital, founded in 1898 as a project of the national B'nai B'rith; The Jewish Consumptive Relief Society, just west of Denver, founded in 1904 to aid indigent consumptives; The Ex-Patients' Home for Tuberculars; The National Home for Jewish Children; and the *Intermountain Jewish News*.

BUDDHISM. There are two Buddhist "churches" in Colorado, one in Denver, the other in Ft. Lupton, but each has a number of branches. The Ft. Lupton church has branches at Platteville and Keenesburg, while the Denver church has branches in Wyoming and Nebraska as well as in Colorado. In Colorado the following branches have their own buildings: Brighton, Longmont, and Alamosa-La Jara (the building is at La Jara), whereas the rest, Greeley, Blanca, Swink, Rocky Ford, and Ordway-Crowley, have no buildings as yet. The Ft. Lupton church has one priest who ministers to more than 50 families; the Denver church has two priests and a youth worker and ministers to about 200 families in the state. Very shortly the Denver church will erect a new building at 1943 Lawrence St., and may change its name to the Tri-State Buddhist Church. The Denver church, probably the oldest organized group in the state, was founded by Rev. Ono around the year 1912. Both the Ft. Lupton and Denver groups are connected with the national Buddhist Mission of North

America, of the Shin sect, with headquarters in San Francisco. The first church in the country was organized in San Francisco in 1905.

OTHER GROUPS. Colorado, and Denver in particular, has been a center for a number of sects and cults, some stressing healing, some theosophical in nature, and some radically apocalyptic. Among these are Divine Science, with two recent off-shoots, Mental Science and the Institute of Religious Science, the "I Am" group, Bahaism, the Brotherhood of the White Temple, and the Witnesses of Jehovah. In addition, a number of evangelists have established independent tabernacles or other places of worship (including store fronts). These are usually quite fundamentalistic in character. Also, there are a number of community churches, in cities as well as in villages and the country-side, which are interdenominational or non-denominational in character, but frequently depend upon the established denomination for their preachers.

CHAPTER VIII

The Literature of Colorado

LEVETTE J. DAVIDSON
Professor of Literature, University of Denver

EVERYTHING that has ever been written about Colorado and judged worthy of preservation is, in one sense, a part of the literature of Colorado. By common definition, however, predominatingly factual works are assigned to the field of history; and literature is restricted to verbal expressions that appeal imaginatively and emotionally, thus winning the reader by their artistry to vicarious participation in the lives of others. But the distinction is often difficult to make. Much that will be discussed here lies somewhere near the borderline between factual reporting and artistic creation.

The literature of Colorado has been built by succeeding generations of writers as they have attempted to communicate what they have seen, heard, done, read, felt, thought, and dreamed in or about the area now designated as the state of Colorado. Some of these authors satisfied their own generation, but were soon forgotten; others created works that still have beauty or significant meaning when measured by current standards. Considerable attention will be devoted to the history of literary expression in Colorado from the beginnings; the greater emphasis, however, will be upon those writings which vividly portray the characteristics and the accumulated traditions of the region.

The early writers were, for the most part, only visitors or temporary residents. They were so impressed by what they saw or by the unusual events in which they participated that they put down descriptions and records for the folks back home to read. These works present a mixture of historical data and of literary art. With the establishment of permanent settlements in the Rockies and on the plains, local authors tried to express in such literary forms as poetry and fiction their reactions to the more peculiar aspects of life about them. As time went on, serious Western writers depended for their reader appeal less upon the exploitation of regional differences and more upon the artistic revelation of those universal aspects of human experience which are shaped by special backgrounds, of course, but are basic everywhere.

Colorado has, nevertheless, made its greatest contribution to American literature up to now by the share its authors have had in the creation of works that reflect succeeding periods of the Westward movement, that embody frontier experiences, that communicate something of the impact of the Rocky Mountains upon the souls of men. With less than a century of continuous occupation by English-speaking peoples, Colorado has inspired a library of books that are worthy of systematic description and some critical discussion. Here and there volumes have emerged that should be treasured by everyone who wishes to reconstruct imaginatively the dramatic careers of those who built the West. Many a Colorado author has created beautiful and memorable word pictures of our romanitic past and of our inspiring natural surroundings. Fewer and less successful have been the attempts to deal realistically with contemporary problems.

The Beginnings

Long before the coming of the white man the Indians of the mountains and the plains had developed an oral literature consisting of myths, legends, and entertaining tales that were handed down from one generation to the next.[1] Many of these were told to the fur trappers and traders, to the explorers, and to the early adventurers in the West. Later on such anthropologists as A. L. Kroeber, G. A. Dorsey, and George Bird Grinnell systematically collected what they could still find among reservation Indians.[2]

Those myths and legends which have been written down in English indicate the Indian's dependence upon and appreciation of nature, his naive attitude toward the supernatural or the mysterious, and his tendency to repeat a few simple folk patterns and motifs. Many are the stories of the beginnings of things, of legendary events connected with places, and of culture heroes and pranksters. Although representative of a lower stage of civilization than that of Greek mythology, the tales of the Utes, the Arapahoes, and the Cheyennes amply repay the reader who takes the trouble to look them up.[3]

Campfire tales were, also, one of the chief methods of entertainment and of exchange of information and experience among fur traders, exploring parties, early Western travelers, and pioneer settlers. Most of these yarns are now lost, but a few are to be found scattered through old books, the files of early newspapers, and the manuscripts, diaries and reminiscences of our forerunners.[4] Even today oral narration flourishes at the reunions of old-timers and around the mountain campfires of vacationists. The modern yarns may be more sophisticated and more influenced by print than the ones which trappers spun at their annual rendezvous from 1825 to 1840, but they too reflect the attractions and the hardships of outdoor life in the Rockies.

[1] Vera Campbell, *Myths and Legends of Colorado*. Greeley, 1924.

[2] Stith Thompson, editor, *Tales of the North American Indians* (with bibliography). Cambridge, Mass., 1929; Hartley Alexander, *Mythology of All Races,* X "North American." Boston, 1916; and Reports of the U. S. Bureau of Ethnology.

[3] Two fine research collections of Western writings, containing practically all of the works mentioned in this history, are located in Denver: the library of the State Historical Society of Colorado, in the State Museum building, and the Western History Collection of the Denver Public Library. Both are administered by well-trained and efficient librarians.

[4] Cf. Hiram M. Chittenden, *The American Fur Trade of the Far West,* New York, 1902 and 1935; Sabin, *Kit Carson Days;* and L. J. Davidson and Forrester Blake, *Rocky Mountain Tales,* University of Oklahoma Press, 1947.

Popular themes for early Colorado storytellers included battles with hostile Indians, sufferings from near-starvation or terrific storms, the big catches of beaver, thrilling buffalo hunts, struggles with wounded bear, the escapades of outlaws, Indian massacres, fortunate or unlucky prospecting trips, the feats of stagecoach drivers, pony express riders, and freighters, and the foolish behaviour of greenhorn or tenderfoot. Occasionally, an old-world tale of magic, of witches, or of princesses was passed along by the Spanish-speaking settlers of the San Luis Valley or the Walsenburg district. These, together with the Indian myths and legends, provide exotic touches. The more common fare was made up of buckskin yarns, personal adventure stories, and tall tales of the wonders of nature. Such stories grew naturally out of the occupations, the interests, the beliefs, and the personalities typical of the age. Unfortunately no Colorado Chaucer has as yet appeared to rework this raw material into a literary masterpiece.

The first formal writings to describe the Colorado region were the official records of government explorers; these were supplemented by the reports of curious travellers.[5] Too often these early volumes lack literary appeal; but from them one may glean passages that portray quite vividly the wonders and the terrors of the new land, as well as many a heroic struggle against great odds in snow-covered mountains or far out on desert plains.[6] More literary than the reports of the expeditions of Pike, Long and Fremont were the books by such travellers through what later became Colorado as George F. Ruxton, Francis Parkman, Thomas Jefferson Farnham, P. St. George Cooke, Rufus B. Sage, and Lewis H. Garrard. Before the discovery of gold in Colorado in 1858, Western adventurers usually by-passed the region; the Santa Fe trail and the Oregon and California trail carried most of the traffic to the south and to the north, although Bent's Fort on the Arkansas was a popular stopping place during the '40s and the trail between the Platte and the Arkansas just east of the mountains was well known.

Farnham seems to have been the first after Pike to explore the upper reaches of the Arkansas. In his *Travels in the Great Western Prairies, the Anahuac and the Rocky Mountains and in the Oregon Territory* (Poughkeepsie, 1841) he gives enthusiastic descriptions of the scenes which he encountered while crossing the mountains in 1839, on his way from Santa Fe to Ft. Hall by way of Brown's Hole. Parkman's *The Oregon Trail* (N. Y., 1849) treats briefly his journey from Fort Laramie to the Arkansas, in 1846. Rufus B. Sage, in his *Scenes in the Rocky Mountains* (Philadelphia, 1846), waxed enthusiastic over the joyous emotion of freedom which he experienced in *Bayou Salade,* now South Park, Colorado. At times he interrupted the prose narrative of his far wanderings to break into romantic

5 Henry R. Wagner, *The Plains and the Rockies, A Bibliography of Original Narratives of Travel and Adventure, 1800-1865.* Revised by Charles L. Camp, San Francisco, 1937.

6 Cf. selections in Levette J. Davidson and Prudence Bostwick, *The Literature of the Rocky Mountain West.* Caxton Printers, Caldwell, Idaho, 1939.

verse. In spite of his wordy and sentimental style, Sage succeeds in giving the reader a good picture of many phases of frontier life, such as the rendezvous of the mountain men, the liquor traffic with the Indians, the sufferings of winter travel, and the westward moving emigrant trains, which grew in number during the forties.

One of the most readable of the early narratives of adventure is Garrard's *Wah-To-Yah and the Taos Trail* (Cincinnati, 1850). As a youth of seventeen the author joined a caravan headed by the fur trader St. Vrain, and followed the Santa Fe Trail to Bent's Fort on the Arkansas and then on to Taos. His pictures of the Rocky Mountain trappers, the Mexican rancheros, the Cheyenne Indians, and the life on the frontier have rarely been equalled. Phillip St. George Cook's *Scenes and Adventures in the Army* (Philadelphia, 1856) is a semi-literary work by a U. S. Army officer, including descriptions of Longs Peak, Pikes Peak, and Bent's Fort, as well as a dialogue between himself and a "Friend" on the curses of civilized life and the delights of outdoor existence. Well-written, also, is Colonel Randolph B. Marcy's account of his adventures as a soldier and guide in the Rockies. Although not published until later, his *Thirty Years of Army Life on the Border* (N. Y., 1866) vividly communicates numerous aspects of life in the Rockies before the gold strike; especially noteworthy is the story of his winter expedition in 1857-58 from Fort Bridger to New Mexico to secure relief for Colonel Johnston's army.

Ruxton's *Life in the Far West (Blackwood's Magazine,* 1848; Edinburgh and London, 1849), although in fictional form, is based upon the author's travels in the Rockies in 1846-47, which he had previously described in *Adventures in Mexico and the Rocky Mountains* (London, 1847). His novel tells the romance of La Bonte, a trapper, who rescues Mary Brand, the sweetheart of his youth, and her family, who have been pursued by hostile Indians while the family is passing through the mountains on the way to the Pacific Coast. The plot is merely the thread on which Ruxton strung his authentic and vivid pictures of the mountain men, including the well-known Bill Williams, Kit Carson, Jim Bridger, and the Sublettes. He managed to include most of the places and experiences common to the lives of the trappers, traders, and scouts during the thirties and forties.

Another early work of fiction touching on Colorado is Theodore Winthrop's *John Bent* (Boston, 1861). Although not published until later, it was written before the Civil War, in which the already popular Eastern author lost his life. The book contains a thrilling Cooper-like description of the pursuit by the hero and the narrator of two desperate characters who had kidnapped Ellen, the heroine, from a Mormon train camped at Fort Bridger. The romantic recapture took place in Luggernel Alley, which seems to be the fictional counterpart of the Canyon of Ladore in northwestern Colorado.

Shorter tales of adventure with scenes in the Colorado Rockies are to be found scattered through the volumes devoted to the careers of famous Western characters; these began to appear in the late fifties. Outstanding examples are the campaign biographies of John Charles Fremont, in 1856; T. D. Bonner's *Life and Adventures of James P. Beckwourth,* 1856, which is full of wild Indian romances and battles; and the hero-worshipping *Life and Adventures of Kit Carson, the Nestor of the Rocky Mountains,* 1858, by DeWitt C. Peters.

Fictional treatments of Rocky Mountain life before 1858 are even more romantic than the versions furnished by adventure-seeking travelers or sensational biographers. Commercially minded story-tellers wished to capitalize on the new interest in the Far West, but they had little or no first-hand contact with the supposed settings of their stories. No one could take seriously today such cheap thrillers as Percy B. St. John's *The Trapper's Bride, a Tale of the Rocky Mountains* (N. Y., c. 1845). In chapter one we find the trappers assembled at Fort Bent, on the Arkansas River. "But Pierre loved the flower of the Eutaw, the lovely young Moama," with whom he elopes to Brown's Hole. Then we see the aroused "Eutaw Village," with "The Chase" following. Emerson Bennett's once popular *The Prairie Flower; or Adventures in the Far West* and *Leni-Leoti,* its sequel (Cincinnati and St. Louis, 1849), are not much better. They were the forerunners of our modern pulp paper magazine fiction, selling an artificial Wild West to those who prefer thrills to the truth.[7]

The Gold Rush Era (1859-1869)

The discovery of gold in the South Platte in 1858 and the Pikes Peak gold rush of 1859 aroused the curiosity of the whole nation. Many books were written to satisfy the demand for information about the new diggings.[8] Guidebooks were hastily prepared for sale to emigrants; but they made no pretenses to literary style. Newspapers and magazines carried letters written to homefolks by the Argonauts or by special correspondents sent out to view the new discoveries and the life which sprang up around them. Within a decade a score or more books appeared with at least a few chapters devoted to the Colorado scene. Some were compilations by correspondents of their newspaper articles.

Among the most popular of these volumes were Horace Greeley's *An Overland Journey from New York to San Francisco in the Summer of 1859* (N. Y., 1860), Henry Villard, *The Past and Present of the Pike's Peak Gold Regions* (St. Louis, 1860)—supplemented in 1904 by *Memoirs of Henry Villard, Journalist and Financier—,* Samuel Bowles, *Across the Continent* (Springfield, Mass., 1866) and *A Summer Vacation in the Parks and Mountains of Colorado* (Springfield, 1869), Demas Barnes, *From the Atlantic to the Pacific Overland* (N. Y., 1866), Bayard Taylor, *Colorado, A Summer Trip*

---

[7] L. J. Davidson, "Early Fiction of the Rocky Mountain Region," in *The Colorado Magazine,* X, 161-172.

[8] L. J. Davidson, "Books Concerning Colorado (1859-1869)," in *The Colorado Magazine,* V, 64-75.

(N. Y., 1867), Albert D. Richardson, *Beyond the Mississippi* (Hartford, 1867), James F. Meline, *Two Thousand Miles on Horseback* (N. Y., 1867), Silas Seymour, *Incidents of a Trip Through the Great Platte Valley* (N. Y., 1867), and A. K. McClure, *Three Thousand Miles Through the Rocky Mountains* (Philadelphia, 1869). These books are journalistic in style, not very deep, but vivid in the description of booming frontier settlements, of the excitement in the mining camps, and of the wonders of Rocky Mountain scenery.

A readable account, in letter form, of the usual adventures incidental to the overland journey is *A Trip to Pike's Peak and Notes by the Way* (Chicago, 1861), by C. M. Clark, M.D. Quite shocking but verified by a contemporary item in the *Rocky Mountain News,* Cherry Creek, Kansas Territory, May 14, 1859, is the *Thrilling Narrative of the Adventures, Sufferings and Starvation of Pike's Peak Gold Seekers on the Plains of the West in the Winter and Spring of 1859,* by Daniel Blue, "one of the survivors" (Chicago, 1860). Fortunately not many of the emigrants had to undergo such tragic hardships.

British travelers soon stopped off in their travels in order to see the Wild West, later including in their books somewhat distorted versions of life in Colorado Territory. It is amusing to read such accounts as those given by Maurice O'Connor Morris in *Rambles in the Rocky Mountains* (London, 1864), William Hepworth Dixon in *New America* (Philadelphia, 1867), and F. Barham Zincke in *Last Winter in the United States* (London, 1868). Evidently the "natives" enjoyed telling tall tales to their English cousins.

Local publishing began with the first issue of the *Rocky Mountain News* on April 23, 1859. This pioneer Denver newspaper, which has continued through the years, was owned and edited by William N. Byers and various associates until 1878. Its early columns contain much verse, humor, and other semi-literary materials. On its presses were printed most of the books and pamphlets issued in Colorado during territorial days. Much near-literary material was included, also, in the *Western Mountaineer* and the *Colorado Transcript,* edited by George West in Golden, and in the papers of Central City and other mining camps. By browsing through the yellowing files of these old journals, one comes about as close as is now possible to reliving in imagination the experiences of the pioneer settlers.

Although early Colorado imprints were chiefly of the utilitarian variety, some remarkable works of a literary nature were produced.[9] Other volumes were sent to Omaha or Eastern cities better equipped to handle book work. Even though the place of publication is not given, Denver may claim the distinction of being the subject of the first work of popular appeal to be issued locally, a forty-four page, paper bound pamphlet entitled *Denver City and Auraria, the Commercial Emporium of the Pike's Peak Gold Region in 1859.* Its unsigned "History of the Settlements on Cherry Creek" is dated

9 Douglas C. McMurtrie and Albert H. Allen, *Early Printing in Colorado.* Denver, 1935.

January 1, 1860; and its three page "Beauty and Advantages of Location—Commercial Importance" may be regarded as the ancestor of the now extensive "tourist literature" devoted to "Colorful Colorado."[10]

Further evidence that the pioneers wished to have their deeds recorded in durable print is present in two other early works: Ovando J. Hollister's *History of the First Regiment of Colorado Volunteers* (Denver, 1863) and J. E. Wharton's *History of the City of Denver from the Earliest Settlement to the Present Time; to Which is Added a Full and Complete Business Directory of the City* by D. O. Whilhelm (Denver, 1866). The first, written by a member of Company F during the victorious New Mexico campaign against the Confederates, is full of personal experiences, told partly in diary form. The second contains an informal record of early events in Denver, frequently drawn upon by later historians. Ned E. Farrell's *Colorado, the Rocky Mountain Gem; as It Is in 1868* (Chicago, 1868) is a curious guide to every county in the territory, by a Central City writer. *Outposts of Zion* (Cincinnati, 1863), by Reverend William H. Goode, contains an interesting description of his pioneering missionary journey to Colorado in 1859.

Numerous books were published concerning the mines and mining conditions in Colorado and about the opportunities for railroad development in the region. Some of these volumes contain somewhat literary accounts of the history of important developments or impassioned pleas for recognition of the commercial possibilities latent in the Rockies. The following are outstanding: William Gilpin, *The Central Gold Region* (Philadelphia, 1860; reissued with additions, in 1873, as *Mission of the North American People*), a grandiloquent plea by Colorado's first territorial governor-to-be for a Pacific Railroad, supported by arguments in a field now called "geo-politics"; Ovando J. Hollister's dependable *The Mines of Colorado* (Springfield, Mass., 1867); and William A. Bell's account of his experiences while engaged in the survey for a southern railway to the Pacific, *New Tracks in North America* (London, 1870). Although the descriptions are brief, the pictures in Alfred E. Mathews *Pencil Sketches of Colorado* (N. Y., 1866) and *Gems of Rocky Mountain Scenery* (N. Y., 1869) make them much-sought-after volumes.

More definitely literary is Lawrence N. Greenleaf's *King Sham and Other Atrocities in Verse* (N. Y., 1868). The bulk of the work is on conventional topics in rather weak verse, appealing no longer except as a curiosity; but Greenleaf was Colorado's first important poet, composing tirelessly for Denver newspapers in the sixties and seventies, for Fourth of July celebrations, for Masonic functions, etc. Some of his humorous pieces are still amusing, especially the "Pike's Peakers of '59." Another curious testimonial to the popularity of verse in the pioneer settlements is a twenty-five page paper-bound

[10] A facsimile reproduction of this pamphlet is included in Nolie Mumey's *History of the Early Settlements of Denver*. Glendale, California, 1942.

pamphlet with the following title page: "Pike's Peak. A Poem. Delivered before the St. James Library Association, Central City, Colorado, on Friday Evening, April 20, 1866. By B. B. Wade, Esq. Central City. Printed for the Association. Collier and Hall, 1866." The quality of the composition is no higher, however, than that of the annual "New Year's Greeting," prepared by local poets for the *Rocky Mountain News* and other papers and distributed by newsboys to their patrons. These effusions were sometimes witty; and in their comment upon regional and national affairs, they managed to convey much of the spirit of the times.

Before the building of the railroads to Colorado, conditions in the territory were not favorable for local magazines; but one pioneer in this field managed to survive through five volumes—from January, 1864, to October, 1868. This serial, the *Rocky Mountain Sunday School Casket,* was edited by Reverend B. T. Vincent, first in Central City and then in Denver.[11] Although its main function was to provide Sunday School news notes, lesson plans and other religious materials, it also included didactic verse and fiction in the Horatio Alger tradition. When the approaching railroad made more easily accessible the standard Sunday School aids prepared by Methodism back East, Reverend Vincent terminated the publication of the *Casket,* Colorado's first magazine.

THE ERA OF DEVELOPMENT (1870-1900)

With the coming of the railroads in 1870, to connect Colorado with the rest of the nation, the territory—which became a state in 1876—began a great period of rapid expansion. New mining enterprises, population increases, a greater margin of wealth and leisure, and more settled conditions were influences favorable to the development of a regional literature. During the next few decades permanent additions were made by Coloradoans or by writers about Colorado to Western history and description, biographical and autobiographical works, fiction, poetry and such miscellaneous prose forms as humor, personal essay, and scholarly discussion. Newspapers and magazines, as well as books and pamphlets, multiplied in order to satisfy both local and world-wide interest in the people, the events, and the places connected with the spectacular new life in Colorado. Much of the writing was journalistic or strictly utilitarian; but some of the works are still full of interest and delight.

As outlets for literary expression several magazines were started during the last three decades of the century. Usually their careers were brief, even shorter than those of the many newspapers that opened up and, before long, closed down in the booming or declining mining camps, cow towns, and trading centers scattered over Colorado. In addition to the religious journals, mining reviews, agricul-

---

[11] L. J. Davidson, "Colorado's First Magazine," in *Colorado-Wyoming Journal of Letters,* February, 1939, 47-52. The only known file of the *Casket* is in the library of the State Historical Society of Colorado.

tural magazines and numerous other publications that served special clienteles, the most important of the periodicals were *The Colorado Monthly,* Denver, 1871-74; *Out West,* Colorado Springs, 1872-74; *Inter-Ocean,* Denver, 1880-82; *The Great Divide,* Denver, 1889-94 and Chicago, 1894-96; *The Commonwealth,* Denver, 1889-91; *The Rocky Mountain Magazine,* Pueblo, 1889-1907; *The Cactus,* Pueblo, 1891-92; *The Colorado Magazine,* Denver, 1893-94; *The Tourney,* Ft. Collins, 1894; and *Outdoor Life,* Denver, 1898-1932 and, thereafter, Mount Morris, Illinois.[12]

The contents of these early magazines are indicative of the literary taste of the times. Early issues of the *Inter-Ocean,* for example, published articles celebrating the attractions and the history of various parts of Colorado, many poems, stories "For the Little Folks," "Chronicles of Frontier Days: The Haunted House on Vinegar Hill, by Fat Contributor," a sketch of the life of Tabor, a bitter political attack upon "Brick" Pomeroy, and a serialized novel by the journalist O. H. Rothacher, entitled "The Man With A Mine."

Usually the literary magazine was a focal point for a group of writers. Perhaps the most famous of the journals, in this respect, was *The Great Divide,* whose chief contributors were Stanley Wood, Patience Stapleton, Fitz Mac (Fitzjames McCarthy), Cy Warman, Lute Wilcox, and W. F. Hornaday. Their romantic fiction and sentimental or humorous poetry is unappealing today; but many of the articles are full of Western human interest. Although this magazine claimed a "circulation of 20,000" in the first issue, March 1889, it moved to Chicago in 1894, soon after the silver panic; there it failed, after two years of struggle. *The Commonwealth,* a solid sort of a monthly, also started in Denver in 1889; but it transferred to Chicago after twenty issues, for according to its editor, "it outgrew its environments and sought, at the center of Western thought and progress, the opportunities which a provincial town could not afford." Although it planned to remain "essentially a Western magazine" and although it continued to draw upon Colorado writers, it failed to make a permanent place for itself in its new location.

The literature of travel in Colorado was augmented during the seventies and eighties by the publicity booklets and the guides designed for tourists over the new railroads and by the books published by visitors, after they had returned home. A curious example of the former type is *Summering in Colorado* (Denver, 1874), an anonymous book describing sights along the recently opened Colorado Central Railroad, and illustrated by photographic prints of the scenery, pasted in at appropriate places. Frank Fossett's *Colorado* (Denver, 1876) was the first of the complete guides to all parts of the state. In the nineties, promotional booklets, elaborately illustrated, were widely distributed by such cities as Colorado Springs, Cripple Creek, Denver, Leadville, and Glenwood Springs.

[12] Cf. L. J. Davidson "The Colorado Monthly," in *The Colorado Magazine,* XVI, 137-142, and "Out West, A Pioneer Weekly and Monthly," in *The Colorado Magazine,* XIV, 135-142.

Perhaps the most eloquent of the travelers was Helen Hunt Jackson, who became a resident of Colorado Springs during the last ten years of her life. In her *Bits of Travel at Home* (Boston, 1878) are enthusiastic descriptions of Rocky Mountain landscapes. The books by the journalist Ernest Ingersoll, *Knocking Round the Rockies* (N. Y., 1882) and *The Crest of the Continent* (Chicago, 1885) are more fun to read, for they include humorous accounts of people and places encountered by the author while accompanying U. S. geological and geographical surveys in 1874 and 1877 and while vacationing with his wife among the mountains of Colorado in 1884. Books of impressions by European visitors continued to appear during this period, including Rose Kingsley's *South by West; or Winter in the Rocky Mountains* (London, 1874) and her famous father's account of their extended visit in Colorado Springs, printed by his wife in *Charles Kingsley, His Letters and Memories of his Life* (London, 1877).[13]

Highly entertaining is Isabella L. Bird's *A Lady's Life in the Rocky Mountains* (London, 1879). Most of the book is concerned with the English lady's stay in the Estes Park region, where she climbed Long's Peak with the aid of "Mountain Jim." An experienced traveler, she did get around in Colorado and recorded vividly her impressions of frontier life in the Rockies. Later editions of her book carry on the title page a cut illustrating her costume, which she described as "a half-fitting jacket, a skirt reaching to the ankles, and full Turkish trousers gathered into frills which fall over the boots,— a thoroughly serviceable and feminine costume for mountaineering and other rough travelling in any part of the world."

Autobiographical and biographical works are, perhaps, the best among the books devoted to the life of the Colorado pioneer. One of the finest of these is Howard Louis Conard's *"Uncle Dick" Wootton, the Pioneer Frontiersman of the Rocky Mountain Region* (Chicago, 1890), because the personality and the career of "Uncle Dick" are preserved therein, in spite of the somewhat clumsy way in which Conard put down the story. "Uncle Dick" had lived the life of a trapper, hunter, freighter, scout, rancher, store keeper, and toll road builder. He had seen the Indian and the fur trader replaced by rancher and townsman. His reminiscences should be read by everyone interested in Colorado history and literature; unfortunately, they have never been reprinted and copies are quite rare.

Other books of this type include John L. Dyer's *The Snow-Shoe Itinerant, an Autobiography* (Cincinnati, 1889), the story of a mountain circuit rider of the Methodist Church; Isaac H. Beardsley's *Echoes from Peak and Plain* (Cincinnati, 1898), most of which is a factual history of Colorado Methodism; Alexander Major's *Seventy Years on the Frontier* (Chicago and N. Y., 1893), with its stories of

---

[13] Many other descriptive works may be found by consulting the card catalogs of the Library of the State Historical Society of Colorado and of the Western History Collection of the Denver Public Library.

freighting, stagecoach business, and the pony express; and General D. J. Cook's *Hands Up; or, Thirty-five Years of Detective Life in the Mountains and on the Plains* (Denver, 1897), compiled by John W. Cook, son of the early-day scourge of Rocky Mountain outlaws. Also good reading are the volumes by Colonel Henry Inman: *The Old Santa Fe Trail* (N. Y., 1897) and (with "Buffalo Bill," William F. Cody), *The Great Salt Lake Trail* (N. Y., 1898). They include among other things many stories, more or less reliable, of events that took place on Colorado soil in the early days.

Cy Warman

Part fiction and part fact are the contents of Alice Polk Hill's *Tales of the Colorado Pioneers* (Denver, 1884; revised but not improved in 1915 as *Colorado Pioneers in Picture and Story*). With a good sense of humor and an eye for human interest Mrs. Hill put down the anecdotes that she collected from the old-timers whom she met in her travels over the state, thus preserving glimpses of the personal history of Colorado. More obviously an attempt at local color writing in *New Colorado and The Santa Fe Trail* (N. Y., 1880), by A. A. Hayes, Jr., who toured the West, collecting material for his magazine contributions. Cy Warman, also, used Colorado backgrounds and events for his *Frontier Stories* (N. Y., 1898). Although he stressed the sensational events, there is much of realism in his descriptions.

Cy Warman deserves inclusion, also, in a discussion of Colorado novels published before 1900. As an engineer on the Denver and Rio Grande Railroad and as a railroad reporter and publicity writer he gained the background not only for his *The Story of the Railroad* (N. Y., 1898), a contribution to the Appleton series called "The Story of the West," but also for such novels as *The Express Messenger* (N. Y., 1897) and *The White Mail* (N. Y., 1899). Another writer who found good fictional materials during a few years' residence in Colorado was Mary Hallock Foote. While residing in Leadville with her husband, a mining engineer, she got the inspiration for two of her novels: *The Led-Horse Claim* (Boston, 1882) and *John Bodewin's Testimony* (Boston, 1886).[14]   Less readable today is Helen Hunt Jackson's *Nelley's Silver Mine* (Boston, 1887). This author's *Ramona* (Boston, 1884), a Western classic, was written at least in part in Colorado although it deals with the Indian Mission period of California. Not to be taken seriously are the dime novels of the eighties and nineties; but their stories of Carson, Buffalo Bill, Indian chiefs, and other picturesque Western characters are collector's items now. Quite entertaining to the student of popular taste in fiction is, for example, Edward L. Wheeler's *Deadwood Dick, Jr., in Denver; or Cool Kate, the Queen of Crooks* (No. 584, Vol. XXIII, Beadle and Adams, N. Y., 1888).[15]

During the period under discussion the Rocky Mountains continued to inspire poetic impulses in nearly all observers. More and more of them attempted to put into words their emotional responses to the majestic landscapes and to the epoch-making efforts of human beings to turn this vast region into a dwelling place for man. Unfortunately the subject proved too much for most of the would-be poets to handle. Usually they ended up in verbose rantings, sentimental prettiness, or didactic echoings of the Psalmist's "I will lift up mine eyes unto the hills, whence cometh my help." Nature was so overpowering that, for them, it seemed also to obscure the significance of the people and of the events.

The most useful guide in this field is the anthology compiled and edited by Francis S. Kinder and F. Clarence Spencer, *Evenings With Colorado Poets* (Denver, 1894, and revised, 1926). Most of the authors represented were magazine poets; but a few did publish volumes that have survived. Among these books are T. O. Bigney's *A Month With the Muses* (Pueblo, 1875), containing extravagant stories of frontier life in rocking-horse verse, such as "The 'People's Court'—a Tale of Quartz Hill in 'Fifty-Nine' "; Thomas N. Haskell's *Young Konkaput, the King of Utes, a Legend of Twin Lakes* (Denver, 1889), a long and didactic treatment of "The Indian question in the United States," inspired by the Meeker massacre of 1879, with a Christianized Indian as the hero of its romance; and Cy Warman's *Mountain Melodies* (Denver, 1892), including his widely quoted "Creede," with its refrain, "It's day all day in the day-time, and there is no night in Creede." Worthy of mention, also, are H. L. Wason's *Letters from Colorado* (Boston, 1887), with its poems about

---

[14] For Mrs. Foote's apology for the omission of the rougher elements of Leadville life cf. L. J. Davidson, "Letters from Authors" in *The Colorado Magazine,* XIX, 122-126.

[15] Many other works of fiction, too numerous to mention here, are described or listed by Irene Pettit McKeehan in "Colorado in Literature," *Colorado: Short Studies of its Past and Present,* University of Colorado, 1927, 141-202.

localities in the Western part of the state; Stanley Wood's *Rhymes of the Rockies* (Chicago, 1898), including a Swinburnian ode on the "Homes of the Cliff Dwellers"; and James Barton Adams' *Breezy Western Verse* (Denver, 1899). As a special writer for the *Denver Post,* Adams turned out entertaining material that resembled that of James Whitcomb Riley and, at other times, that of Bret Harte.

A few of the best poems about Colorado were written by famous Americans who resided elsewhere. While on a brief visit to Colorado in 1879, Walt Whitman wrote "Spirit That Formed This Scene"; and Katherine Lee Bates composed "America the Beautiful", so it is said, after looking from the top of Pikes Peak in 1893. Longfellow's "The Cross of Snow" was based upon a Colorado landscape which the poet had heard about but never seen. Frémont, under somewhat of a shadow in his later years, expressed his sorrow in a poem entitled "On Recrossing the Rocky Mountains in Winter after Many Years."

The verse which Eugene Field composed during his Denver period (1881-83), while serving on the *Tribune,* helped to fill his newspaper space, along with much humorous prose. A selection of this prose made up his first book, or pamphlet, *A Tribune Primer* (Denver, December, 1881). Some of his poems—including those about Red Hoss Mountain, to be identified with Gold Hill, Colorado,—later appeared in *A Little Book of Western Verse* (1889); others were assembled from the columns of the newspaper by a fellow worker, Joseph G. Brown, and published as *A Little Book of Tribune Verse* (N. Y., 1901). Field never took the West very seriously; but he did find in Colorado abundant subjects upon which to practice his talents for satire and burlesque. A large part of his verse is characterized by the sentimentality about children which once made him famous. His Denver stay has been remembered chiefly on account of the practical jokes and hoaxes which he perpetrated on friends and enemies alike. Such was his dressing up and pretending to be Oscar Wilde, shortly before Wilde was to arrive for a lecture in Denver, and his pranks with "Bill" Nye when the latter came down from Laramie to visit the *Tribune,* to which he had contributed humorous sketches.

Among the books of a miscellaneous nature which appeared in Colorado during this period were those by L. B. France, a Denver attorney who cultivated fishing and the personal essay as hobbies. His *Mountain Trails and Parks in Colorado* (Denver, 1887) is the record of a summer's camping trip. *Mr. Dide, His Vacation in Colorado and Other Sketches* (N. Y., 1890) includes fiction as well as personal narrative. Another nature book is the curious volume *On the Plains and Among the Peaks; or How Mrs. Maxwell Made Her Natural History Collection,* by Mary Dartt (Philadelphia, 1878). After exhibiting in Boulder and in Denver the stuffed birds and animals which she had shot and skinned in the Rockies, Mrs. M. A. Maxwell took her collection to the Centennial Fair in Philadelphia. The questions asked by visitors to the exposition led her to publish this account of her experiences, which were truly remarkable for a woman of her day.

Another book that was published in response to public curiosity was *The Ute War, A History of the White River Massacre* (Denver, 1879), by Fred J. V. Skiff and Thomas F. Dawson, editors on the staff of the Denver *Tribune* at the time of the Meeker Massacre. Their book is based upon contemporary newspaper accounts, and belongs to journalistic writings rather than to literature. Today it is valued chiefly for its rarity, although it is, also, a source work for historians.

During the last decades of the nineteenth century, it is evident, books about Colorado and by Colorado authors were produced in ever greater numbers. The above discussion includes the names of the outstanding works; dozens of others have been omitted. By 1900 the publication of a new book in Colorado or elsewhere by a native of this state was not particularly noteworthy unless the writing was above average in quality. The provincial period of literary culture ends when national standards are used in measuring the success of local writers.

Twentieth Century; Historical Writings

One of the leading motives of Colorado writers during the first two decades of the new century seems to have been a desire to further record the story of frontier days in the Rockies. The files of the *Sons of Colorado* (Denver, 1906-08) and its successor *The Trail* (Denver, 1908-28), for example, contain many interesting articles of an autobiographical nature by old-timers. Life in Central City and along the overland trail are the themes of two delightful books privately printed by Frank Crissey Young, *Echoes from Arcadia,* (Denver, 1903) and *Across the Plains in '65* (Denver, 1905). Other volumes of reminiscences include Robert McReynolds, *Thirty Years on the Frontier* (Colorado Springs, 1906), *Life of Tom Horn, Written by Himself* (Denver, 1904), Eugene F. Ware, *The Indian War of 1864* (Topeka, 1911), Sidney Jocknick, *Early Days on the Western Slope* (Denver, 1913), Irving Howbert, *Indians of the Pike's Peak Region* (N. Y., 1914) and *Memories of a Lifetime* (N. Y., 1925), Milo L. Whittaker, *Pathbreakers and Pioneers of the Pueblo Region* (Pueblo, 1917), William H. H. Larimer, *Reminiscences of General William Larimer and His Son* (Lancaster, Pa., 1918), and C. C. Davis, *Olden Times in Colorado* (Los Angeles, 1916). Each of these books succeeds in giving to the reader the flavor of unique experiences.

History of a more formal nature, also, was produced in great quantity. Perhaps the most valuable of the early volumes is Jerome C. Smiley's *History of Denver* (Denver, 1901). It is well-written and well-illustrated by one who had witnessed much of what he described; but, alas, the author did not list his sources and he neglected to provide an index. Smiley's *Semi-Centennial History of the State of Colorado* (Chicago, 1913), accompanied by a volume of biographical sketches of citizens "acquired exclusively by representatives of the publishers," was but one of such projects by which expensive works got into print. Present students are much indebted to both the histories and to the biographies for information that otherwise would have been lost. The *History of Colorado* by William N. Byers, which occupies the first 167 pages of *Encyclopedia of Biography of Colorado* (Chicago, 1901), is, unfortunately, fragmentary in nature; but it indicates what Byers might have accomplished had he set himself to the task when he was a decade or two younger.

Wilbur Fish Stone's *History of Colorado* (Chicago, 1918), containing one volume of history and several of biographical sketches, is also valuable.[16] It does not, however, supplant the four volume work by Frank Hall, *History of the State of Colorado* (Chicago, 1889-95). Although Hall sometimes allowed prejudice to color his accounts of the political affairs of the state, his volumes are readable and rich in detail. He was able to draw not only upon his long experiences as a Colorado newspaper man and office holder but also upon such pioneer histories as the series prepared by W. B. Vickers and his associates throughout the state: *History of the City of Denver, Arapahoe County, and Colorado* (Chicago, 1880); *History of Clear Creek and Boulder Valleys, Colorado* (Chicago, 1880); and *History of the Arkansas Valley, Colorado* (Chicago, 1881). Other early volumes are Will C. Ferril's *Sketches of Colorado* (Denver, 1911), Ansel Watrous' *History of Larimer County, Colorado* (Fort Collins, 1911), and the many booklets issued by ambitious communities throughout the state, telling of their past accomplishments and of their future prospects. *The Story of Colorado* (Chicago, 1924), by Arthur Chapman, a former Denver journalist and author of the well-known poem *Out Where the West Begins,* was designed for use in the schools of the state.

The History of Colorado (Denver, 1927; three volumes of text and two of biographical sketches), prepared under the supervision of the State Historical and Natural History Society of Colorado and with the editorial direction of James H. Baker and LeRoy R. Hafen, marks the transition from historical writing based largely upon reminiscences to that dependent primarily upon research methods.[17] Since 1924 *The Colorado Magazine,* edited by Doctor Hafen, the state historian, has provided a medium for the publication of source materials and of scholarly articles. Doctor Hafen's one volume *Colorado, the Story of a Western Commonwealth* (Denver, 1933), and *Colorado, a Story of the State and its People* (Denver, 1943) by Doctor Hafen and his wife, Ann W. Hafen, are dependable and readable introductions to the romantic and significant events, backgrounds, and personalities in Colorado's past.

---

16 "Colorado Literature," Stone, I, 877-890, was written by Eugene Parsons, perhaps the first to attempt a record of the accomplishments of Colorado authors.

17 The brief but stimulating account of "Literature and the Arts," Baker and Hafen, is by Edgar Carlisle McMechen, long connected with Colorado's cultural life and now Curator of the State Museum.

Worthy of mention, also, are the following more highly special-ized books: Emma F. Langdon, *The Cripple Creek Strike, 1903-1904* (Victor, 1904), *Prose and Poetry of the Livestock Industry* (Denver and Kansas City, 1905), Arthur J. Fynn, *The American Indian as a Product of Environment* (Boston, 1907), S. M. Frazier, *Secrets of the Rocks* (Denver, 1907), W. C. Whitford, *Colorado Volunteers in the Civil War* (Denver, 1906), Alvin T. Steinel and D. W. Working, *History of Agriculture in Colorado* (Fort Collins, 1926), Edgar C. McMechen, *The Moffat Tunnel* (Denver, 1927), James F. Willard, *Records of Union Colony* (Boulder, 1918), James F. Willard and Colin B. Goodykoontz, *Experiments in Colorado Colonization* (Boulder, 1926), and Archer B. Hulbert's several volumes in *Overland to the Pacific Series,* published by the Denver Public Library and the Stewart Commission of Colorado College.   More popular in appeal is George F. Willison's story of early days in Denver and in Leadville, *Here They Dug the Gold* (N. Y., 1931). Designed for juvenile readers were such books by E. L. Sabin as *Buffalo Bill and the Overland Trail* (N. Y., 1914), *The Great Pikes's Peak Rush* (N. Y., 1917), and *On the Overland Stage* (N. Y., 1918). Of more permanent worth is Sabin's two volume *Kit Carson Days, 1809-68, Adventures in the Path of Empire* (Revised edition, N. Y., 1935).

BIOGRAPHY AND AUTOBIOGRAPHY

Akin to history but even more definitely a part of the literature of Colorado are the biographical and autobiographical works which appeared in great number after 1900.   These range in style from the somewhat formal studies like Thomas F. Dawson's *Life and Character of Edward O. Wolcott* (N. Y., 1911) to Gene Fowler's *Timberline* (N. Y., 1933), a sensational account of the careers of Fredrick G. Bonfils and Harry H. Tammen, founders of the *Denver Post.*   In the traditional pattern of biography are William Howlett, *Life of the Right Reverent Joseph P. Machebeuf * * * First Bishop of Denver* (Pueblo, 1908); Edgar C. McMechen, *Life of John Evans* (Denver, 1924); Thomas R. Garth, *The Life of Henry Augustus Buchtel* (Denver, 1937); and the more recent book about W. J. Palmer, John Fisher's *A Builder of the West* (Caldwell, Idaho, 1939). Elmer Ellis, *Henry M. Teller, Defender of the West* (Caldwell, Idaho, 1941) and LeRoy R. Hafen and W. J. Ghent, *Broken Hand, the Life Story of Thomas Fitzpatrick* (Denver, 1931) are scholarly works based upon extensive research.

Reflecting the more sensational side of Western life are William MacLeod Raine's *Famous Sheriffs and Western Outlaws* (N. Y., 1929), David Karsner's *Silver Dollar, the Story of the Tabors* (N. Y., 1932), Evelyn Walsh McLean's *Father Struck It Rich* (N. Y., 1936), and Frank Water's biography of Winfield Scott Stratton, *Midas of the Rockies* (N. Y., 1937).   Equally readable but less highly colored are the following autobiographies: *The Pioneer Photographer* (Yonkers-on-Hudson, 1929) and *Time Exposure* (N. Y., 1940) by

William H. Jackson, Clarice E. Richards' *A Tenderfoot Bride* (N. Y., 1924), R. B. Townshend's *A Tenderfoot in Colorado* (London, 1923), Emma Shepard Hill's *A Dangerous Crossing and What Happened on the Other Side* (Denver, 1924), Anne Ellis' *The Life of an Ordinary Woman* (N. Y., 1929), L. C. Gandy's *The Tabors* (N. Y., 1934), and Gene Fowler's *Solo On Tom Toms* (N. Y., 1946).

The most widely advertised figure ever to be associated with Colorado was "Buffalo" Bill, the great showman. It is improbable that he himself made as much Western history as is credited to him in *Memories of Buffalo Bill* (N. Y., 1919), by Mrs. Cody and Courtney Ryley Cooper, or in Colonel William F. Cody's *An Autobiography of Buffalo Bill* (N. Y., 1920), or in the dozen other volumes devoted to his glorification. But the debunking process is carried almost too far in *The Making of Buffalo Bill* (Indianapolis, 1928) by Richard J. Walsh and Milton S. Salsbury. Somewhat controversial, also, are the accounts given by Judge Benjamin B. Lindsey and Harvey J. O'Higgins of the Judge's Denver career in *The Beast* (N. Y., 1940). Philip C. Van Cise, in *Fighting the Underworld* (Boston, 1936), told his version of how he, as District Attorney, fought the bunco gang which had its headquarters in Denver in the early twenties. Likewise, Barron B. Beshoar's biography of John R. Lawson, *Out of the Depths* (Denver, 1942), is a sincere and worthwhile book; but not everyone accepts without demur his interpretation of the labor struggles in Colorado coal fields.

DESCRIPTIVE WRITINGS

Rocky Mountain scenery and the delights of outdoor life in Colorado have been championed by the pens of many authors. Their books portray in word and in picture the tourist attractions and the less well-known beauties of the state. Some works are for armchair travelers; others are guides to be followed by the more active. In the former class are Mae Lacy Baggs, *Colorado, the Queen Jewel of the Rockies* (Boston, 1918); John T. Faris, *Seeing the Far West* (N. Y., 1920), parts of which are concerned with Colorado; Charles Hansen, *My Heart in the Hills* (Philadelphia, 1925); Courtney Ryley Cooper, *High Country, the Rockies Yesterday and Today* (Boston, 1926); and David S. Lavender, *One Man's West* (Garden City, N. Y., 1943). Of interest to juveniles, especially, is Deric Nusbaum's *Deric in Mesa Verde* (N. Y., 1926).

Although designed for use by travelers through the state, the following volumes are also good for leisurely reading and permanent reference: Eugene Parsons, *A Guidebook to Colorado* (Boston, 1911); Lilliam Rice Brigham, *Historical Guide to Colorado* (Denver, 1931); and *Colorado, A Guide to the Highest State* (N. Y., 1941), compiled by workers of the Writers' Program of the W. P. A.

Most famous of Colorado nature writings are those by Enos Mills, long associated with Estes Park. While managing Long's Peak Inn and serving as a guide to mountain climbers, nature lovers, and vacationists, he prepared many magazine articles and books. Although romantic in style, they are based upon an extensive and close observation of nature's ways and upon an intimate knowledge of the region which the government later set aside as Rocky Mountain National Park. His first volume was *The Story of Estes Park and A Guide Book* (Denver, 1905). Those containing nature essays and narratives of personal adventure out of doors include, among others, *Wild Life in the Rockies* (Boston, 1909), *The Spell of the Rockies* (Boston, 1911), *The Rocky Mountain Wonderland* (Boston, 1915), and *The Adventures of a Nature Guide* (Boston, 1920).

LATER FICTION

Romance continued to dominate Colorado fiction during the first quarter of the twentieth century. Hamlin Garland, famous for his naturalistic stories of Midwestern farm life, was unable to break away from stereotyped conceptions of Western love and adventure in the books which grew out of his visits to the Rockies. Among his ten Western romances are *Her Mountain Lover* (N. Y., 1901), *The Captain of the Gray-Horse Troop* (N. Y., 1902), *Hesper* (N. Y., 1903), *Cavanagh, Forest Ranger* (N. Y., 1910), and a collection of short stories, *They of the High Trails* (N. Y., 1916). Although these volumes contain mountain backgrounds and characters from mining camps, Indian reservations, and national forests, they fall far short of depicting the true West.

No one, however, should use the test of conformity to reality when evaluating the popular fiction appearing in Western pulp paper magazines and in books by such authors as Emerson Hough, Zane Grey, and William MacLeod Raine. During some forty years, Raine has produced over seventy widely-selling volumes. This type of writing is designed for the entertainment of unsophisticated readers who desire a quick escape into the realm of exciting physical action where characters are definitely good or bad. Here men live on galloping horses, with smoking guns in their hands; the women are sweet and plucky, but in need of masculine protection. The backgrounds and the occupations are far removed from those characteristics of our present urbanized, mechanized and complicated, international culture.

Other romantic novels, with Colorado settings and by popular Colorado authors include the following, most of them historical: Robert Ames Bennet, *A Volunteer With Pike* (Chicago, 1909); Courtney Ryley Cooper, *The Cross-Cut* (Boston, 1921); Will Irwin, *Youth Rides West* (N. Y., 1925); Clifford Sublette, *The Golden Chimney* (Boston, 1931); and Forbes Parkhill, *Troopers West* (N. Y., 1945).

More true to life in their pictures of the early days when the open range cattle industry was at its height are the books by Andy Adams. His *The Log of a Cowboy* (Boston, 1903) is a Western classic, even though it lacks the love interest requisite for success as the basis of a Hollywood "cow opera." After ten years of work on cattle ranches in Texas and along the cattle trails, Adams moved to Colorado. For a short time he engaged in mining, during the Cripple Creek excitement; but he spent his last years in Colorado Springs, writing. Except for *The Log of a Cowboy* his books are not widely read today; full of authentic cowboy and cattle lore, their appeal is limited because they lack skillfully contrived plots

Andy Adams

and convincing women characters. Worth-knowing, in addition to *The Log of a Cowboy,* are *The Outlet* (Boston, 1905), *Cattle Brands, a Collection of Western Camp-Fire Stories* (Boston, 1906), and *Reed Anthony, Cowman* (Boston, 1907).

Some of the best novels of Colorado life have been written within the past decade. Dorothy Gardiner's *The Golden Lady* (N. Y., 1936) is a skillful although somewhat sensational portrayal of "the epic of Colorado mining as told through the life of Vannie Swenk, child of the Leadville Lily." Still earlier, William M. John's *Seven Women* (N. Y., 1929) gave a satirical picture of small town life in Southern Colorado. *Second Hoeing* (N. Y., 1935), by Hope Williams Sykes, is a strong novel of the Colorado sugar beet country, centering about Hannah Schrissmiller, who was determined to rise above the level of her immigrant parents. Frank Waters has succeeded in demonstrating the strange fascination that gold mining has over men, in the person of the leading character of his novel, *Below Grass Roots* (N. Y., c. 1937). A former Denver journalist, Clyde Brion Davis, has utilized Colorado backgrounds in some parts of his recently successful books, including *The Anoited* (N. Y., 1937) and *The Great American Novel* (N. Y., 1938).

Many other writers of fiction have been connected with Colorado in one way or another. Although Denver was the early home of Wilbur Daniel Steele, his literary career has been centered elsewhere. One of the best of his short stories, "The Man Who Saw Through Heaven," may have been inspired by Wilbur's memories of his father's teachings in the Department of Religion of the University of Denver and of his own visits to the University's astronomical observatory. The most widely circulated short story to come out of Colorado life is, in all probability, Chauncey Thomas' "The Snow Story" or "Why the Hot Sulphur Mail Was Late." It tells, in the Jack London manner, of a terrific storm on Berthoud Pass and a terrific fight between a desperado and the mail carrier. Although a typical murder mystery in plot, Brett Halliday's *Murder Wears a Mummer's Mask* (N. Y., 1943) is of special interest to Colorado readers because the detective, Michael Shayne, solves this case in Central City during the festival season in the old opera house.

Modern Poetry and the Drama

Poets in great numbers have continued to appear in Colorado down to the present. Many of them have published only in magazines and newspapers, or have issued volumes at their own expense; as with poets everywhere, only a few have been able to find a commerical market for their wares. The following anthologies may be used as guides, for even the less well-known have been included: Francis S. Kinder and F. C. Spencer, *Evenings with Colorado Poets* (third edition, revised, Denver, 1926); David Raffelock, *The Echo Anthology of Verse* (Denver, 1927); and *Colorado Poets,* edited by the House of Henry Harrison (N. Y., 1935), with a "Foreword" by Nellie Burget Miller, who was appointed Poet Laureate of Colorado in 1923 by the then Governor of Colorado.

The following volumes of poetry are deserving of special recommendation because of their use of Western materials: Thomas Hornsby Ferril, *High Passage* (New Haven, 1926), *Westering* (New Haven, 1934), and *Trial By Time* (N. Y., 1944); Lillian White Spencer, *Arrowheads* (New York, 1929) and *Pageant of Colorado* (Denver, 1927); Mrs. Clyde Robertson, *Yellow Witch;* and Ann Woodbury Hafen, *Quenched Fire* (Denver, 1937). Space does not permit the listing of the works of many other Colorado poets who have excelled in their chosen fields but have been less influenced by definitely Western scenes and traditions.

The writing and the appreciation of poetry have been encouraged during recent years by the Poetry Society of Colorado and the Colorado Poetry Fellowship. *Timberlines,* published several times a year by the latter group, provides an outlet for Colorado writers and contains news of Fellowship activities. The Colorado Authors' League, the Denver Women's Press Club, and the Pen Women of Colorado are other organizations interested in stimulating authorship, although their chief concerns are in other fields than poetry.

Also of help to local writers have been the sessions of such institutes as the Writers' Conference of the University of Colorado and the Regional Writers' Workshop of the University of Denver. From time to time semi-literary magazines have appeared in Colorado, such as the *Garden of the Gods Magazine* (Colorado Springs, 1902-06) and the *Echo* (Denver, 1923-28); but their life span has usually been short. Practically all of the literary production of this region is still shaped for Eastern markets. The *Author and Journalist,* however, is a Denver monthly with a national circulation. Quite a few Colorado writers have been very successful in writing for popular magazines for women and for juveniles; other writers contribute to outdoor journals and the pulp-paper "Westerns." A few appear regularly in *The Saturday Evening Post, Harpers,* etc.

The same dependence upon Eastern leadership prevails in the field of the drama. For a comprehensive study of the early period one should consult Melvin Schoberlin's *From Candles to Footlights: A Biography of the Pike's Peak Theatre, 1859-1876* (Fred A. Rosenstock, Denver, 1941). Some plays, it seems, were written in pioneer days for the local stage; but they have not been preserved. Early dramas by Colorado authors that are still remembered include Lute Johnson's *Sheep,* Stanley Wood's *Brittle Silver,* and a thriller entitled *Down the Black Canon.* Later, Eugene Walters, while working as a Denver journalist, wrote *The Easiest Way* (Hartford, 1908), based upon a popular Denver summer stock theatre and a vacation resort in the mountains. The greatest Broadway success by a Colorado author has been the Puckish *Harvey,* by Mary Coyle Chase, which was a continuous "sell-out" in the 1944-45 and '45-46 seasons. Denver audiences also enjoyed her earlier plays: *Me, Third* and *Sorority House.* The former was produced by the W. P. A. Federal Theatre Project in Denver, and the latter, by the University Civic Theatre of the University of Denver.

In conclusion it may be said that the literature of Colorado has been the product of one of the younger states of the Union, one that has been relatively sparse in population. Nevertheless, the quantity and the quality of the writings about Colorado are such as to attract the attention of any serious student of American literature. For those who wish to know the rich human experiences that have accompanied the development of this region, the writings mentioned here are indispensable.

CHAPTER IX

Journalism in Colorado

Edwin A. Bemis

Managing Director, Colorado Press Association

THROUGHOUT the ages, the almost insatiable desire to know what is going on in his environment has been an important characteristic of the human being. From the first records, through petroglyphs and cave man pictures, on down through records on papyrus, the town crier, and journals, there is immutable evidence of the fact that man must have news.

There is little evidence so far as I know as to when news, as we know it, was first written for the enlightenment of the human being, but undoubtedly the petroglyphs were the first, and since we find such petroglyphs in certain spots in Colorado, we can presume that these were the forerunners of the newspapers of Colorado, even though they have little resemblance to the news dispensers of today.

Man and his newspaper are as inseparable as the moon and the stars. Wherever man has invaded new frontiers, his newspaper has followed him, has entertained him, has amused him, and has been the tie between him and the loved ones and friends back home. The newspaper perhaps assuaged his lonesomeness or kept him so well informed about the world he had left, that he was content and eager to push on into the unknown frontier.

Newspapers have a two-fold purpose: recording information about the activities of people in general, and carrying on various types of crusades. That the newspapers have done a tremendous job in both cannot be denied, if one will but take the time to examine the files.

What the newspapers have meant to Colorado throughout the years cannot be measured in dollars and cents; but it is not doubted that they played one of the most important roles of any industry in the development of the West.

So, it is not surprising that the history of the newspapers in Colorado starts with the advent of the gold seekers in 1859. Although there were Spanish settlers in the San Luis Valley prior to that date, I can find no record that a newspaper was published there at that time.

Thus, the history of the press in Colorado begins with that dramatic episode in which two newspapers made a race for the honor of being first in the region. And the newspaper which captured the honor was winner by only 20 minutes! The story is as follows:

John L. Merrick, of St. Joseph, Missouri, had followed the rumors of gold, bringing with him the first newspaper press to enter Colorado. This machine already had a notable history behind it, and was destined to serve more papers in the Territory of Colorado than any similar piece of equipment. Its known story begins with the Mormons, who used it to print a newspaper advancing their opinions in Independence, Missouri. Their entire two-story establishment was razed by an angry mob in 1833, and the press unceremoniously thrown into the Missouri River. Years later it was fished out and rehabilitated; sold to a Mr. Riddenbaugh, it served the *St. Joseph Gazette,* founded in 1845. From the *Gazette,* Merrick purchased it in 1858, and loaded it into a covered wagon, bound for paperless gold regions at Pikes Peak.

It seems that Merrick started for Pikes Peak in advance of the Byers party, which consisted of William N. Byers, Thomas Gibson and Dr. George C. Monnell of Omaha. Merrick reached Denver first and to that extent was the pioneer publisher; but the superior energy of Byers enabled him to get out the first paper ever published in the Rocky Mountain region. Merrick issued a paper on the same day, but just 20 minutes later. Both were rather crude specimens of typography, especially as compared with the well printed papers now circulating in the state. Byers issued the *Rocky Mountain News,* and Merrick, the *Cherry Creek Pioneer.* That issue of the *Pioneer* was the one, lone, solitary issue from Merrick's press. Before he could collect himself sufficiently to get out another one, Byers had bargained for the sorry little outfit and consolidated it with the *Rocky Mountain News.*

The *Intermountain Press* for January, 1923, describes the race between Merrick and Byers as follows:

As a matter of fact both papers appeared on the evening of Saturday, April 23, 1859, in the midst of a driving snow storm. But a self appointed and excited committee of citizens, rushing back and forth between the two offices, decided that Byers, with the first issue of the *Rocky Mountain News,* had produced a finished paper about twenty minutes before Merrick could hand out a completed copy of his *Cherry Creek Pioneer.* By this narrow margin the *News* won the honor of being the first newspaper printed in Colorado. Merrick made no further effort to compete with Byers. The first issue of his paper also was the last. He then traded his printing outfit to Tom Gibson, an associate of Byers, for $30 worth of provisions, and headed for the "diggins." When he returned to Denver, broke, in a few months, he took a job at the case in the office of the *Rocky Mountain News,* and worked there off and on during 1859 and 1860. "At the first alarm of war (Civil War)," to quote the exact words of Byers, "he hurried to the states, and enlisted in one of the earliest volunteer regiments organized in Illinois. He served

ROCKY MOUNTAIN NEWS.

THE MINES AND MINERS OF KANSAS AND NEBRASKA.

VOL. 1. CHERRY CREEK, K. T., SATURDAY, APRIL 23, 1859. NO. 1.

Rocky Mountain News.

WM. N. BYERS & CO.,
Editors, Publishers and Proprietors,
CHERRY CREEK, K. T.

TERMS.—Five Dollars per annum, in advance. Single Copies for Mail, 25 cents.

RATES OF ADVERTISING;

Business Cards, (5 lines or less) 1 year,	$12 00
1 square, three months	10 00
1 " six "	15 00
1 " one year,	20 00
One quarter column, three months,	25 00
" " " six "	40 00
" " " one year,	60 00
One half column, three months,	40 00
" " " six "	60 00
" " " one year,	100 00
One column. three months,	70 00
" " six "	100 00
" " one year,	150 00

Having an excellent assortment of job type and materials, we are prepared to do all kinds of

JOB PRINTING,

with dispatch, in the best manner, and on reasonable terms.

BUSINESS CARDS.

A. F. PECK, M. D.
PHYSICIAN AND SURGEON,
Cache-a-La-Poudre, Nebraska.

WHERE he may at all times be found when not professionally engaged or digging gold.
n1tf

HERNDON HOUSE.
Omaha City, Nebraska.

MILLER & RICHARDSON,
PROPRIETORS.
n1tf

JOHN H. SAHLER. JOHN HUGHES.
SAHLER & CO.,
BANKERS, COLLECTORS, LAND AND GENERAL AGENTS,
OMAHA CITY, : : : : NEBRASKA.

THE OPENING OF JAPAN.

The present age is signalized by the rapid succession of striking events in the history of divine providence. Nations and continents which had maintained a rigid exclusiveness, or had been enveloped in unbroken obscurity, are now brought into friendly communication with the rest of the world, and doors are opening for the introduction of the gospel where heretofore it has not been allowed a foothold.

Scarcely had the news of the opening of China to the commerce and Christianity of the Western world reached us, when tidings came that a treaty with the United States, granting the fullest privileges, had been ratified by the Emperor of *Japan*.—This empire is composed of several islands the largest of which is about eight hundred miles in length, some of the others being larger than Great Britian, and has a population of about forty millions. In consequence of the commercial rapacity and fraud of the Portugese, whose enterprise opened a trade with Japan in the sixteenth century, and of the intrigues of the Jesuits who followed in their train, a fierce persecution arose against the Christians, that did not cease till every thing bearing the name was extirpated. For over two centuries the empire has been closed against the nations of Christendom with the exception of theDutch, who have been allowed a few privleges.

A little over four years ago, Commodore Perry of the United States navy was sent to Japan, and succeeded in negotiating a treaty. In consequence of that treaty, the first that had been made with any western country, Mr. Townsend Harris, a gentleman who had spent many years in the East, was appointed Consul-general of the United States. Though at first regarded with no favor by the Japanese authorities he soon gained their good will, and at length obtained permission to visit Jeddo, the capital city, and had an audience with the Emperor, the first obtained by any foreign minister. While at the capital, he received the kindest attentions from all classes. During his residence of about two years in the country, Mr. Harris has exhibited the principles of Christianity as far as he was able, statedly observing the Sabbath, refusing to make or receive visits, or to transact business on that day.

In the meantime he was able to arrange the articles of a treaty with the emperor,

ALPHABETICAL CONUNDRUMS.

Why is the letter A, like a meridian? Because it is the middle of day.

Why is the letter B, like a hot fire? Because it makes oil boil.

Why is the letter C, like the ocean? Because it makes the "sea."

Why is the letter D, like a fallen angel? Because by associating with "evil" it becomes Devil.

Why is the letter E, like the end of time? Because it is the beginning of eternity.

Why is the letter F, like death? Because it makes "all," fall.

Why is the letter G, like wisdom? Because it is the beginning of greatness and goodness.

Why is the letter H, like the dying words of John Quincy Adams? This is the end of earth.

Why is the letter I, like the American Revolution? Because it is the beginning of independence.

Why is the letter J, like the end of spring? Because it is the beginning of June.

Why is the letter K, like a pig's tail? Because it is the end of pork.

Why is the letter L, like a young lady giving away her lover to another? Because it makes over a lover.

Why is the letter M, like the first glass of rum? Because it is the beginning of misery.

Why is the letter N, like a newly-married woman? Because it is the end of maiden.

Why is the letter O, like a courageous woman in disguise? Because it makes her a hero.

Why is the letter P, like two winds meeting? Because it makes air pair.

Why is the letter Q, like a king? Because it is attached to the Queen.

Why is the letter R, like a treaty ratified? Because it is the end of war.

Why is the letter S, like the end of hogs? Because it is the beginning of sausages.

Why is the letter T, like a victory? Because it is the end of conquest.

Why is the letter U, like fragrance? Because it is the centre of the "bud."

Why is the letter V, like two extremes? Because it is the beginning of vice and virtue.

Why is the letter W, like a dying christian? Because it is the end of sor-

THE WORLD WITHOUT A SABBATH.

What would it be? Labor without rest; care without solace; probation without preparation; a night without day.

To the *laboring man*, the loss of the Sabbath would bring unceasing toil without increased compensation, and a consequent wasting of physical strength which would soon wear out the machinery of life. It would rob him of the allotted period for mental and spiritual improvement, and for home duties and enjoyments.—Brutalized in mind, body, and association, he would sink to the level of the serf, be the sport of capital, and end his days in heathenism.

To the *family*, the Sabbath lost would entail the loss of the *home day*—the day of domestic re-union, instruction, worship, and charity. Family government would lose its tone; family joys would die out; domestic purity would be imperiled—for the two oldest institutions in the world are interlinked—and family piety would become extinct.

To the *church*, a lost Sabbath would involve the loss of its solemn assemblies, its godly ministry, its day for edification and action, its season for domestic and associated instruction of the young, and its antetype of the "rest that remaineth for the people of God." An Arctic winter—without light, or heat, or food—is but an emblem of the state of the Christian world without the Sabbath and its ordinances.

A *state* without a Sabbath must be without liberty. To a free state the Sabbath brings the support of some of the most powerful elements of self-government. It inspires respect for law, divine and human. It fosters the sense of omnipresent Deity, and of man's dependence and accountability. It engenders a lively conscience, more potent to restrain from crime, than all legislative or judicial guards. Its educational force, through the pulpit, the Sabbath school and the fireside, quickens the intellect and moulds the heart of a nation. It gives the weekly occasion for illustrating the equality of man before God, and of inculcating the great lesson of human brotherhood. It is the foe of despotism, and the ally of freedom. The nation that has the Sabbath may dispense with armies and tax-gatherers for their support; no nation on the globe without the Sabbath, or with only a profane holiday in its stead, has free institutions or dare disband its standing ar-

COMMUNICATIONS RECEIVED BY THE NEBRASKA IMMIGRATION SOCIETY.

MONROE, N. T. Nov. 30, 1858.

DEAR SIR: The Circular of the Nebraska Immigration Society of which you are Secretary has been received, and I will cheerfully give any information that I can, at any and all times. In regard to his country:

First. Labor is worth from $1 to 2$ per day.

Second. The soil is similar to the prairies of Illinois; perhaps a little more sandy.

Seventh. Wood is plenty; in fact this is one, if not *the* best timbered counties in the Territory. The timber consists of Black Walnut, Ash, Elm, Cedar, and Cottonwood; the latter predominates.—Water is also abundant. The following streams run east and west through the county:

Platte River, Loup Fork, Looking-Glass Beaver, Shell, and Maple Creeks. (Lime stone has been found.)

Tenth. Elk, Deer, Antelope, Ducks, Geese, Quails, and Turkeys are found in abundance.

Owing to the newly settled character of this country, the remainder of the questions are not applicable to this country, but I will make a few remarks on the settlement of the country, and chances for Immigrants. This country was first settled in May, 1857, by a company of persons from Oneida county N. Y. They started this town—MONROE. In June, a company of Mormons settled in the western part of the county and started the town of Genoa. In July, a few persons from Florence, started the town of Cleaveland, in the eastern part of the county. In Aug., of 1857, the county seat was located here, and the county organized. Since when, the emigration has been gradually, settling up the country; but still there are good chances for emigrants to get good claims on the direct route to the new gold region, plenty of good claims can be had in this immediate vicinity for the mere taking. The land is principally prairie, as level as the city of Omaha; yet perfectly free from swamps, the streams are all clear and pure. We have had very little ague for a new country. There is an excellent ford across the Loup Fork, at this place and a good ferry at Genoa.

Respect. Yours,
L. GERARD

YANKEE VISIT TO CARLYLE.

The Rev. Theodore Clapp, of New Orleans, in an autobigraphy, gives the following account of his introduction to the "Great Censor of the Age," Thomas Carlyle. Having received letters from Mr. Bancroft, the American Ambassador at the English Court, he called at the door of his residence. A lady, with a very intelligent appearance, received the visitor. "I have called this morning, he said, "to see Mr. Carlyle; is he at home?" She replied, "Mr. Carlyle has just entered his study, and no *gentleman* can see him this morning. If the Queen of England should now call and request an interview, it would not be granted." The Doctor asked if she could oblige him by taking a written message to his study. An affirmative answer was given, when he wrote with a pencil the following words:

"Dear Sir: No *gentleman*, but a *man* is at your door—a Unitarian, a Yankee, a Democrat, and a radical, all the way from the banks of the Mississippi; a careful reader, and a great admirer of Mr. Carlyle, and begs the favor of a short interview, which must be granted *now*, or never this side of the grave."

The letter of introduction was sent with this unique note. Directly the invitation came, "walk up sir; I shall be happy to see you."

We copy Dr. Clapp's account of this interview:

"I was received in the most kind and unceremonious manner. The topics on which we conversed were so numerous that I have not room even to mention them. The colloquial style is plain, easy and unaffected, and bears no resemblance to that of his later writings; has none of those qualities commonly called transcendental. Our conversation was protracted till afternoon. Though I rose several times to depart, he insisted on my staying longer so earnestly that I acceded to his wishes. Much of the time was spent in answering his inquiries concerning the statistics of the United States, the peculiarities of our government, laws, manners, schools, churches, literature, &c. He professed to be much gratified with the information which I gave him in regard to these subjects."

CAUTION TO SORGHO GROWERS.—The Independence (Iowa) *Guardian* gives an account of the destruction of seven head of cattle belonging to I. G. Freeman,

First Issue of Rocky Mountain News

his term with credit and gained promotion. When mustered out he (Merrick) returned to his former home in Leavenworth, Kansas, and secured a commission in a Kansas veteran regiment. About the close of the war he was provost marshal of Leavenworth, where, while in the active discharge of his duty, he was killed in a street brawl."

During those early days, there was much competition between Auraria and Denver. Auraria was on the south side of Cherry Creek and Denver, on the north side. When Byers established the *News,* in order not to be considered as favoring either side, he established his newspaper office over the edge of Cherry Creek, the dividing line. The office remained there until the famous flood of May 20, 1864, when the building and equipment were caught in the flood. Byers immediately went to work on a new building at 269 Larimer Street, where the paper was published until 1897. In 1898, while construction work was going on, parts of the old *Rocky Mountain News* press were dug from the sands in Cherry Creek near the Platte River. They are now in the State Historical Museum.

There was a great deal of romance in connection with the *Rocky Mountain News* during its early day struggles, too much to be mentioned here.

The temper of the time may be shown by the fact that one of the first questions Byers asked an employee was if he could handle a gun, and "a printer who was handy in this respect stood high with the proprietors of the paper, even though he had a multitude of shortcomings as a compositor." Byers' own weapons were "never far from the editorial desk."

These were not idle precautions. The editor's open warfare against the lawlessness and violence of the pioneer underworld won him many enemies in that quarter. On July 31, 1860, following a printed attack upon the notorious Criterion saloon—spoken of as a criterion of everything bad—a number of desperadoes who made their headquarters there decided that it was time to do something about this troublesome foe. Therefore, primed with liquor and "righteous indignation" they raided the *News* office and seized Byers. When his men rallied to his defense with guns, the fearless editor quieted them and went calmly off with his captors, who took him to the Criterion. The ruffians were for killing him without more ado, but the owner of the place, Charlie Harrison, was a lodge brother of the editor. He therefore took the prisoner into a back room and sent him out a rear entrance.

Back at his office, Byers barricaded the building, preparing for an attack that was not long in coming. The desperadoes, discovering Harrison's action, swept down upon the *News* in full force, led by two particularly vicious characters named George Steele and Carroll Wood. For several hours a state of siege prevailed, until Steele, tiring of indirect methods, made a one-man attack. Lashing his horse to speed past the office, he fired two ineffectual shots into the building. The return fire—buckshot sent by Jack Merrick—wounded Steele seriously. He rode away, only to run into a force of the honest element of the town, who were rushing to Byers' aid. The town blacksmith and hangman, "Noisy Tom" Pollock, blew Steele's brains out with a charge of buckshot.

William N. Byers
Founder of the "Rocky Mountain News"

Steele's companions fled, but the aroused populace rounded them up with more vigor than ceremony. Wood was banished, and many of his satellites followed him from the camp. Harrison, the ringleader who had saved Byers' life, later was killed while engaged in activities on behalf of the Confederacy during the Civil War.

On another occasion, Byers was challenged to a duel, then the favorite method of settling difficulties in the gold camp. He replied contemptuously: "To any who may feel like calling us out, we have only to remark that you are wasting our time by sending us challenges or other belligerent epistles. You may murder us, but never on the so-called 'Field of Honor' under the name of a duel."

The story of early Colorado newspapers, however, is not limited to Denver. As a matter of fact, the population center of "the Pikes Peak Country" shifted to the Central City area when gold was discovered there in the spring of 1859. After Byers' partner, Gibson, had secured Merrick's press, he took it to the Clear Creek gold regions to start the *Rocky Mountain Gold Reporter and Mountain City Herald*, the first newspaper in the mountains. It suspended publication at the end of the first summer. Almost all of the miners, unfamiliar with Rocky Mountain weather, fled the area after the first heavy snow in early autumn. With them went Gibson, promising that he would return to Mountain City the following year. Instead, he remained in Denver to provide Byers with serious competition. Gibson's equipment was sold to George West, a young printer.

West had arrived at the Cherry Creek settlements in June, 1859, to find both towns in a flurry of excitement. Great gold discoveries had been made in the mountains, and three nationally known journalists, Horace Greeley, Albert D. Richardson, and Henry Villard had just completed a report of the "diggins"—a report eagerly awaited by gold seekers in every section of the country. Byers of the *News* was searching frantically for help to put out an extra; George West and two printers who had arrived with him thus earned their first mountain dollars.

Not satisfied with the job of printer, young West selected Golden as a promising town for a journalist. With the press that once had printed articles from the pen of Mormon Prophet Joseph Smith, he began running off the *Western Mountaineer*, taking on the subscription list of the late *Rocky Mountain Gold Reporter*.

Of the four papers started in the region in 1859, one press had served to print three of them. The one-time Mormon Washington hand press seemed to have a jinx attached to it. It could never stay long in one place. The *Mountaineer* gave up in December, in spite of having the most brilliant staff of any territorial paper, including, as Religious Editor, Albert D. Richardson, famous *New York Tribune* writer; and, as military editor, Thomas Knox, later to edit *Leslie's Illustrated Weekly*. The press was sold to the *Canon City Times*.

In the spring of 1860, Canon City had a dozen people and only one saloon; but about 500 people arrived, and the *Times* was established. The first issue was dated September 8, 1860. A few months after the acquisition of the old press, the paper became a semi-weekly and proudly described the town's rapid progress. An item from the *Times* of May 20, 1861, says, "Abe Lincoln subscribes to *Canon City Times*. Among the distinguished names that have been added to our subscription list is that of Abe Lincoln, the famous rail-splitter."

But like its predecessors that were run off on the "Wandering press," the *Times* proved a temporary venture. Soon after, it was sold and moved to the new mining camp of Buckskin Joe near Fairplay. The town of Buckskin Joe had depended on a single mining lode and when that lode began playing out, the town soon became a ghost town. The press that had served 5 papers in 5 towns in less than 3 years returned to Denver, where it was placed in storage pending new adventures in Boulder County.

The *Miner's Register*, a tri-weekly, made its appearance in Central City, July 26, 1862. It was issued by Alfred Thompson, who brought the equipment from Glenwood, Iowa. The paper prospered, and on April 9, 1863, David Collier, with two other employees, Hugh Glenn and George A. Wells, bought the *Register*. Later, Wells bought out Glenn, and Wells in turn sold his interest to Frank Hall, who became one of the state's historians.

G. M. Laird, who had worked on the old *Register* under Hall, started the *Evening Call* several years later, which resulted in a consolidation of the two papers. This is still operating as the *Register-Call* and is edited by Laird's son, Rae L. Laird. I shall tell of G. M. Laird later.

In this story, I am making no effort to bring in every individual newspaper that started publication during these early years, although any complete history should include them all. What I want to do is to high-light some of the interesting incidents which have happened.

The *Colorado Transcript,* General West's second attempt to establish a paper in Golden, was successful. His daughter-in-law and her husband, carrying on the same paper today, represent the best in Colorado tradition. One paper published continuously by the same family for 75 years is a record that few other publications in the United States can equal.

The number of papers in Colorado gradually increased each year. From the *Rocky Mountain News* of September 11, 1867, we obtain the following:

> Nebraska has but two daily newspapers—Of the number weekly published in the state we are not informed. The territory of Colorado has five daily newspapers, eight weeklies and two monthlies, one devoted to Sunday schools and the other to temperance. We believe the people of Colorado sustain more newspapers and support them better than does any other western state or territory of the same size. The fact is highly credible to the intelligence and industry of our people.

In the summer of 1867, a stimulus to press organization was given Colorado newspapermen when Illinois editors organized an elaborate excursion to the west. The *Colorado Tribune* provided an advance account in its issue of September 25, 1867, as follows:

> For some months past the subject of an editorial excursion from Illinois to the Rocky Mountains, has been agitated in the newspapers of Illinois, and is now in a fair way of being accomplished.
>
> A convention was called in Jacksonville; an organization formed, committees were appointed to take charge of the details, until finally the arrangements are completed, and a hundred and fifty knights of the goose-quill start on their tour from Chicago on the 7th of October—expecting to be gone for two weeks.
>
> The talent and observation they bring with them, combined with the means they possess to make public what they see and think of the countries they visit, make the trip a gigantic advertisement—to be read by the entire population of Illinois——

They will advertise the Union Pacific R. R. and tell all about the towns along the route, of North Platte—its few busy weeks; the capping of its fountain of life and its rapid return to a primitive existence; the birth of another infantile town and its use by the forces drawn from its elder brother, and in turn its speedy relapse and decay, while the third steps into view as at present the fastest city of the age. They will advertise these places, write their histories and predict the future of Cheyenne, as well as how it was built in a night, and how it grew to be a city before the grass was trodden down.

Denver was not included in their original route, but we understand that the party is quite unanimous in desiring to visit us, and also our cities in the mountains.

We shall be glad to see all the stage coaches of the two overland lines chartered to meet the party at Cheyenne and bring them to Denver.

They are to come in a special train from Chicago, and will travel by day only, the train switching off and resting at night.

Mr. H. M. Kinsley, the well-known excursion commissary, has been employed to subsist the party, which it is expected will consist chiefly of game to be killed on the way. For this important service he is to receive the sum of two dollars per diem for each "excursher," this to be exclusive of "extras."

An artist is also to be employed to make sketches of the principal scenes along the route, while a printing press, with a staff of typographers and other materials, is expected to produce a twenty column daily newspaper during the absence of the party.

In addition to all the foregoing, Adjutant General Haynie of Illinois, has agreed to provide all the "excursers" with a first class Enfield rifle and "Equipments" with "forty rounds" each, from the State arsenal, to be used in "self defense," against any hostile or uncivilized foe, of whatever shape. A platform car, with a field howitzer and experienced gunner, will also constitute a feature of the excursion. They will thus be prepared for any emergency, and should any occasion arise requiring the use of arms, a good account will be given of the weapon which is said to be less mighty than the pen.

It was four years before the Colorado publishers began to plan a similar organization and excursion. However, we have been unable to find more than two references to the idea of organizing during the next several years and this was a brief mention in 1871 and again in 1874. No records have ever been found to prove whether or not the publishers did organize. Not until 1878 was there a permanent organization set up, and this has operated continuously to the present day.

From the "History of the Colorado Press Association," comes the following:

Meanwhile new chapters were being written in the story of Western journalism. The Wandering Mormon press that Merrick had brought across the Plains, was dragged out of storage in Denver in 1866 by D. G. Scouten. He took it to Valmont in Boulder County to print the *Valmont Bulletin.*

The *Rocky Mountain News* reported May 2 of that year:

"Our merry friend, D. G. Scouten, alias 'The Orderly,' has become the sole editor and proprietor of the sparkling little sheet published in Boulder County, the *Valmont Bulletin.* He has a large circulation among the farmers of that populous county, making his paper a valuable advertising medium for our merchants who desire to secure their patronage, which amounts to thousands of dollars a month. Scout will be down in a few days, and his pockets should be filled with Denver advertisements for his paper."

Scouten, however, had plunged into a furious battleground—known in the '60s as the "battle of the B's." Three towns were fighting for county supremacy—Boulder, Burlington, (south of the present site of Longmont), and Bugtown (the rivals' name for Valmont). Burlington, like Boulder, was made up of a few rough log cabins, shingled with mud, and boasted a small frame hotel. Ambitious Bugtown, with the first newspaper, was now after the county seat.

Boulder citizens decided that they also must have a newspaper; they found an editor, W. C. Chamberlain, but had no press. So when the "merry Mr. Scouten" came into Boulder one night in April, 1867, for a few drinks, he found the Boulderites strangely friendly, and very anxious to "set him up" to one after another. Scouten was not one to resist such gracious hospitality, and soon was enjoying the deep sleep of the man who had had too much.

The Boulder men hitched up a team, drove to Valmont, loaded the old press and type on the wagon, and brought it to the county seat. The equipment consisted of the old Washington hand press, an imposing stone made of wood, and two stands of type cases. When Scouten revived, he accepted the coup, and went to work for the new *Boulder Valley News* as a printer. The old press, described by one man who worked on it as "Very dangerous by the poor light in those days," served several papers in Boulder. Finally it was sold again and carried down to Elizabethtown, New Mexico.

Quoting from Jerome C. Smiley's *Semi-Centennial History of Colorado,* of 1913, we learn that:

The closing out of the *Canon City Times,* in the winter of 1861-62, left the southern part of Colorado Territory without a newspaper. In 1868, four years before the arrival of the first railroad, the void was filled with Pueblo's *Colorado Chieftain,* founded by Dr. Michael Beshoar and Sam McBride. Dr. Beshoar had had newspaper experience, while McBride was a practical printer who had been in the employ of George West in Golden. In the following year, Dr. Beshoar moved to Trinidad, but continued his newspaper work, traveling between the two towns by horseback.

It was learned from biographical files in the State Historical Society of Colorado Library that the *Chieftain* was sold by its founders to Captain J. J. Lambert, an army man stationed in the Arkansas Valley at Fort Reynolds, eight miles east of town. This was in 1869. Three years later, with the Denver & Rio Grande Railroad building into Pueblo, Lambert converted his paper into a daily. The captain continued at the helm of the *Chieftain* until 1903, piloting it through sometimes difficult, sometimes exciting times. Although not very profitable at the time, the *Chieftain's* attractive typography and excellent news coverage gave it the appearance of a bonanza. As a result, numerous enterprising publishers rushed to the steel town to start papers, most of which proved dismal failures.

In the early days, there were times when it was difficult to get newsprint across the plains. Newspapers were printed on wrapping paper or almost anything that could be gotten. This critical paper situation was responsible for the establishment of a paper mill at Golden. It was known as the Golden Paper Mill and was built either late in 1868 or early '69 by Oscar Barber. Apparently, the mill was designed to manufacture wrapping papers and was not equipped for newsprint in its earlier years. On occasions, the newsprint supply was tied up at eastern railway terminals due to shortage of cars and storms, and now and then, this forced a number of Colorado newspapers to print their issues on the wrapping paper which was manufactured at Golden. By 1871, the mill was manufacturing newsprint. However, we have no record of how long the paper mill operated, but it is presumed that it did not last very long.

About this time, Horace Greeley's name came into the journalistic history of Colorado. In 1870, with the backing of the *New York Tribune's* editor, the Union Colony was organized to settle in Colorado. The present site of Greeley was chosen upon the recommendation of William N. Byers, editor of the *Rocky Mountain News.* While the first cabins were being erected, there was talk of a newspaper. October 19, 1870, the *Rocky Mountain News* announced, "Mr. Meeker of Greeley will probably issue the first number of his newspaper, the Tribune of the West, the last of this week." Meeker was later the central figure in the famous Meeker Massacre. The first issue of the *Greeley Tribune* was dated November 16, 1870. Alice Polk Hill, in *Pioneers in Pictures and Story,* says:

The masthead for the newspaper was prepared from a photo-engraving of Greeley's illegible handwriting. When the paper later was changed from a weekly to a daily, the post office authorities insisted that the word "daily" be inserted. But when the historic old masthead was replaced by one in Roman type, to conform to the order of the post office department, protests from the community poured in. To satisfy both government and citizens, the word "daily" was prepared in a "reasonable facsimile" of the famous scrawl, and the unusual trademark of the paper was restored.

One of the famous men of Colorado who was an editor but was little known as such, was Otto Mears. Most people remember him as a great pioneer builder, which he was, but he also established and edited a newspaper. From the *Colorado Editor* of July, 1937, we find that "Saguache had grown into a busy and prosperous point after the construction of the toll roads to the Arkansas Valley and to the San Juan." Mears, to advertise the San Luis Valley, had started the *Chronicle* at Saguache in 1872, writing editorials, boosting the soil, the climate, the wealth to be had in farming and manufacturing; as a result, the population had grown in the town and valley. Mears built many mountain highways, including the Million Dollar Highway. He established railroads and was one of the leaders in the construction business.

One of the interesting episodes in his life was in the capture of Alfred Packer, the famous man-eater. Mears was operating a general merchandise store at Saguache. While Packer was purchasing something in the store, Mears noted a Wells-Fargo draft in the possession of Packer and he recalled that Wells-Fargo had been robbed. Mears became suspicious. He remembered too that the five men that Packer was supposed to have slain also had some Wells-Fargo drafts and Mears assumed that he had taken these drafts from the bodies of the men he had slain. He communicated this information to an officer and Packer was picked up. He later confessed.

Getting back to the papers in Boulder County. W. C. Chamberlain was employed to edit the paper in Boulder, after it was moved from Valmont. He published the paper, then called the *Valley News,* in Boulder until the fall of 1868, when it gave place to the *Boulder County Pioneer,* started by Dr. E. J. Horton. The *Pioneer* turned against the townspeople and their interests and the merchants and subscribers withdrew their support and forced the paper into the sheriff's hands. The stockholders regained possession and leased it to Robert H. Tilney, who changed the name to the *Boulder County News.* This was in the autumn of 1869. Tilney had come to Colorado in 1865 and worked for the *Mining Journal* at Black Hawk. Later he was employed on the *Register* at Central City. In April, 1870, he left the *Boulder News* and was out of the printing business for two years. In 1872, he took a job on the *Rocky Mountain News* as a printer. The *Boulder News* changed hands on several occasions from then until 1874, when the paper was sold to Amos Bixby and Eugene Wilder. In 1875, Otto H. Wangelin bought the *Rocky Mountain Eagle,* established in Boulder in September, 1873, by Webb Morris. Wangelin started the *Colorado Banner,* of which he was editor and owner until February, 1878, when Robert Tilney returned to Boulder and purchased a half-interest. In January, 1880, Wangelin sold out to Tilney. February 18, he established the weekly *Boulder County Herald,* which on April 17, became a daily, Boulder's first daily newspaper.

The mining camp of Sunshine had a newspaper, *The Courier,* started May 1, 1875, by J. B. Bruner and J. W. Cairns. June 30, 1877, the ownership was changed to Bruner and Hawkins; November 3, that year, to Bruner and Shedd; and on August 2, 1878, it passed into full possession of William G. Shedd, who removed it to Boulder where soon it was consolidated with the *Boulder County News.*

Longmont was laid out in 1871 by the Chicago-Colorado Colony, which was organized at a meeting February 22, 1870, in Chicago, by persons interested in making new homes in Colorado. The Territory's first newspaper man, William N. Byers, assisted an executive committee to select 30,000 acres in the St. Vrain region and to locate a townsite. The old town of Burlington was moved across the St. Vrain to the new town of Longmont, named for Long's Peak which rises directly west from the town. Longmont was incorporated January 7, 1873.

The first newspaper was the *Sentinel,* published by Lowe & Hall, started in July, 1871. The next year this was changed to the *Longmont Press,* with E. F. Beckwith, proprietor, and later on, F. C. Beckwith, associate editor. In May, 1877, the *Longmont Post* appeared, the owners being the Longmont Printing Company, with W. L. Condit, editor. The *Post* became, in course of time, the *Valley Home and Farm,* with the beloved W. E. Pabor, excellent journalist and gifted poet, as editor. Again it was changed, this time to the enduring title of the *Longmont Ledger,* which is still published as a weekly.

One of the interesting characters in the History of Colorado Journalism is that of Jesse S. Randall, who for a great many years owned and edited the *Georgetown Courier.* Born on April 23, 1848, Randall, as a 14 year old boy, went to work on an Iowa newspaper to learn the printing business. In 1869, he came to Georgetown to take care of his father, who had come a year previously but who had become ill. However, his father lived for many years and died in Georgetown when he was within two months of reaching 102 years of age. When Jesse Randall arrived at Georgetown, he found that his father had arranged for him to take charge of the printing department of the *Colorado Miner.* He went to work immediately upon his arrival. Governor John Evans of Colorado was financially interested in the paper. On June 30, 1869, Morris E. Wood, a nephew of Governor Evans, changed the paper to a daily. However, the following October, it was discontinued as a daily for lack of patronage. Another famous man of Colorado was also interested in the Georgetown *Miner*. He was Senator Edward O. Wolcott. Wolcott, after participating in the Civil War, graduated from the Harvard Law School in 1871. He then came to Colorado and taught school in Central City, and later went to Georgetown. In April, 1873, he became associated with Alex Cree in the *Colorado Miner* and succeeded the Rev. Weiser as editor. The *Miner* was changed from an evening to a morning paper.

Randall was with the Georgetown *Miner* until 1875, when he left the paper and opened a job shop in Georgetown. Two years in the job printing business gave him the funds and opportunity to establish a newspaper, *The Courier,* the first number of which came out May 24, 1877.

Jesse Randall was a crusader for decency; he made enemies and they were powerful. The fight against him extended to Washington, but one by one he licked the "giants." From the April, 1938, issue of the *Colorado Editor* we read:

William A. Hamill came to Georgetown in 1867 seeking his fortune. His sister was the wife of Joe Watson who built the first fine residence in the town. It still stands, now known as the Alpine Lodge, containing works of art purchased in Europe, a spacious, dignified mansion in the midst of large grounds ornamented with a fountain of classic design.

"Bill" Hamill occupied a cabin in the rear of the Watson house. He made a fortune in mining and was superintendent of the celebrated Terrible Mine at Silver Plume for the English owners. Entering politics he became the boss of Clear Creek County, and rode rough shod over all opposition. With reason he claimed he carried the county in his vest pocket. What the Republican ring put over, under his leadership, caused such widespread indignation that he began to lose ground and the fight against him, led by Jesse Randall, started in 1882.

The county convention was to be held in the court house at Georgetown, the county seat. The delegation from Idaho Springs came up to get Hamill's scalp. To keep them out, he had a blacksmith place two strong iron hooks on the sides of each door, and in these were bars of two-by-fours. The boss, who wanted to be United States senator, held his hand picked convention behind locked and barred doors. The Idaho Springs delegates held a separate convention at the famous old Barton House, since they could not break into the court house.

Hamill swore he controlled the Republican party in Clear Creek County and he would continue to control it.

Further, he ordered that there should be no Democratic ticket filed, and therefore no Democratic candidate for office.

In those days the politicians did not file the ticket until the last minute to make it legal. Agreeable to the Boss's orders, County Clerk Ben C. Catren, Sr., closed his office early Saturday afternoon to prevent the Democrats from filing their ticket, and disappeared. After a frantic search for him, the Democrats sought Sheriff John C. De Votie, the only candidate elected on the Democratic ticket in the election in 1880, and the sheriff with plenty of witnesses went to the court house, broke a window in the clerk's office and laid the document on Catren's desk.

The *Courier,* which has been staunchly Republican, gave all details of the high handed proceedings and denounced both the closing of the court house and the attempt to shut the Democrats out of the election. It attacked Hamill and waged warfare on him and all his works. It exposed the machinations of the ring and bluntly charged Hamill had been running too high and pleaded for his downfall. The result was, Clear Creek County that had been going 700 Republican majority at every election, elected by 600 majority every Democrat, filling every county office, for the first time in history, with Democrats, and completely changed the political complexion.

Chairman E. Foster of the Board of County Commissioners, Catren and other Republican leaders told Jesse Randall they were going to run him out of the county for not supporting the Republican ticket and immediately started a boycott that was financially disastrous.

Jesse Randall can afford to chuckle about it now, but it was a mighty serious business then.

"Do you know," he says, "they even fired cannon at me? Yes, sir, it is a fact. Remember the Alpine Hose House directly across the street from the Courier building? Well, Hamill had donated the 1,209 pound fire bell that hangs in the seventy feet high tower and those whiskered, red hatted, blue-shirted volunteers were fond of him, naturally. When he ordered a celebration of some kind to be held with cannon in front of the hose house, their's not to question why, their's but to do without a murmur of surprise.

"The cannon were hauled to the hose house and pointed directly at the Courier office. Hamill knew what would happen, all right. He ordered several shots fired. Bang! went the cannon, and bang! went my window glass. The building rocked with the vibration. Again and again the shots were fired. What could I do to stop 'em? The boys were just celebrating and the cost of glass to a boycotted editor meant nothing to General Hamill."

Jesse Randall passed away at Georgetown on January 24, 1939, six months after the death of Mrs. Randall.

He was a close friend of the late U. S. Senator Henry M. Teller and of nearly every famous character of the Colorado mining camps. He was the only man in whom Louis Dupuy, French nobleman, would entrust his identity. The two built the Hotel de Paris of Georgetown which became famous throughout the United States in the '70s and '80s.

Another of his friends was President U. S. Grant, who spent several hours with the editor during his visit to Georgetown in 1873.

During his lifetime the veteran editor collected much material connected with the history of his era which he later gave to the Denver Public Library, the State Historical Society and the library of the state Supreme Court.

Around 1872, Henry C. Brown, later famous as the Brown Palace Hotel builder, took over the *Denver Tribune*. It had been produced on a hand press and was limited in its influence as well as in its circulation. Brown moved the *Tribune* into his three-story building on the corner of 16th and Market Streets. During its brilliant but relatively brief career, it was one of the most influential organs of the entire West. In this hectic period of personal journalism, the leading journals almost always were Republican in politics. The slogans and sectionalism of the Civil War remained long after the surrender of General Lee. Colorado, both Territory and State, was a Grand Old Party stronghold for years. A notable exception to the rule that all successful papers had to espouse the Republican Party cause was George West's *Transcript*.

The Democrats attempted to add to their list of papers, but Byers gleefully reported in the *Weekly Rocky Mountain News*, November 3, 1875:

> One more unfortunate weary of breath, rashly importunate, goes to its death. So young and so fair, too! Not a woman, this time, but a newspaper—the *Evening Sentinel*. Its creditors probably outnumber its mourners ten to five. The *Sentinel* was started on the "moral support" of the Democratic party. And it died of that. It takes a good deal to kill one of these things—That is, a paper of that kind; but it will soon famish on "moral support," mighty soon, if it has nothing else to live on. Nearly every Democrat in town, who can write at all, has contributed something to its columns. It is surprising how many people there are in Denver who have a lot of stuff in them aching for expulsion, who imagine it to be a faculty for journalism. The proprietors of the *Sentinel,* personally, are very clever men, and the death of the paper is not so much due to lack of ability on their part, as to the malpractice of the accoucheurs of the Democratic party, who brought the thing into the world. Next!

And a month later Editor West in Golden regretfully reported the death of another struggling enterprise (*Golden Transcript,* December 22, 1875):

> The *Denver Democrat* has at last yielded to the inexorable decree of fate. It has battled long and bravely against its stern and uncompromising adversary—poverty—but has been compelled to succumb to his repeated blows. Stanton, while you survey its ruins let the proud reflection cheer you, that in falling "you fell with your back to the field and your face to the foe." Democratic party is now without an organ or journalistic exponent in the capital of Colorado—Three newspapers in one year; that should be holocaust enough. The furies ought to be appeased with that sacrifice. There is one refuge for the Democracy, remaining in the bosom of the *Transcript.*

One of the outstanding events in Colorado in the 1870s was the opening up of the rich San Juan Mountains area. At Del Norte, Colorado, gateway to this section of the Territory and to the San Luis Valley, the *San Juan Prospector* began publication. Another newspaper praised the issue highly, and pointed to the fact that it was issued in the "about-to-be-famous" mining district.

One of the most spectacular early day editors was Cy Warman, who edited the *Candle* at Creede. Probably the thing best known about the *Candle* was the poetry written by Warman, and I presume the most notable of his bits of poetry is familiarly known as "It's Day All Day In The Daytime and There Is No Night in Creede." Here is the poem, which was written in 1892:

> Here's a land where all are equal—
>   Of high and lowly birth—
> A land where men make millions,
>   Dug from the dreary earth.
> Here meek and mild-eyed burros
>   On mineral mountains feed—
> It's day all day in the daytime
>   And there is no night in Creede.
>
> The cliffs are solid silver
>   With wond'rous wealth untold,
> And the beds of the running rivers
>   Are lined with the purest gold.
> While the world is filled with sorrow,
>   And hearts must break and bleed—
> It's day all day in the daytime
>   And there is no night in Creede.

George M. Laird, who was editor of the Central City *Register-Call* for 58 years prior to his death in April, 1936, was a man who held more closely perhaps than any other man the fabulous, glittering history of the "Little Kingdom of Gilpin."

But the great story of his town and county, a romance of gold, and the men and women, big and small, who sought it, is not dead with him. For George M. Laird was a newspaper man of the old school, an editor in the best of the pioneer tradition, and in the files of his newspaper, the *Register-Call* of Central City, Gilpin County, is the day-by-day chronicle of the life of one of the world's most famous gold camps.

He had been active in newspaper work for 75 years, had been editor and proprietor of the *Register-Call* for 58 years and was proud of the fact that his paper never had missed an issue during the early days when at times it was difficult to get newsprint and supplies.

As a boy, he sold newspapers on the streets of Chicago, then learned the printing trade in the Freeport, Illinois *Bulletin* office from 1863 to 1866, and came to Colorado in May, 1872, to work at Black Hawk in the office of the *Daily Journal,* conducted by George Collier.

At that time, the *Daily Register,* with Collier and Hall as editors and publishers, and the *Daily Herald,* of which Frank Fossett was editor, were published in Central City.

After the *Journal* suspended publication, following the election of 1872, Mr. Laird worked as a substitute printer on the *Register* in nearby Central City, later becoming foreman of its composing room.

In 1876 he installed a job printing press in Central City and with Den Marlow as a partner, began publication of the *Daily Evening Call,* a five-column, four-page paper which was printed one page at a time on an old Gordon press operated by foot power.

In May, 1878, Laird & Marlow purchased the *Register* at sheriff's sale, combined it with their paper and brought into being the *Register-Call.*

Mr. Laird, foremost authority on the history and development of Gilpin County, where gold was discovered in 1859 to start the great rush of miners to Colorado, was an enthusiastic patron of the movement which restored the old Central City Opera House, Colorado's "Cradle of the Drama." Mr. Laird was present at the opening of the Opera House in 1878.

In 1878, when the town of Ouray became the center of the San Juan area on account of the discovery of important silver deposits, two brothers named Ripley bought the *Canon City Times* and hauled equipment to Ouray. During the year 1878, the little paper struggled along and often complained of lack of advertising patronage. In 1879, vigorous competition was provided for the *Times* when Dave Day founded his *Solid Muldoon.* Dave Day was a reckless, sarcastic type of writer. While the paper gave a complete news coverage, he carried a great deal of the barroom type of stories. His characterization of the State Legislature in 1879 under the column, "Muldoon's Primer," is an example of his style. The following appeared in *Colorado, The Centennial State,* by Percy Stanley Fritz:

Is that a Salvation Army?

No, my Child, that is a Band of Horse Thieves.

What are they Doing that they look so Excited?

They are Suspicioned by the People, and are Debating a Motion to Investigate the Charges.

What is an Investigation?

Investigation, my Child, is a preparation of Self-amalgamated Whitewash introduced by the Colorado Legislature in the Latter part of the 19th Century.

What is a Legislature?

In Colorado it is a conglomeration of Rural and Metropolitan Asses elevated by Misguided Suffrage to positions intended by the Constitution for Brains, Honor and Manhood.

Advertising copy furnished by advance agents was usually consigned to the wastebasket while the editor wrote his own copy. When a theatrical company, managed by Sam T. Jack, and featuring Jennie Lamb was scheduled for Ouray, the *Muldoon* published this announcement:

> Oh Jennie Lamb is coming,
> She is flying o'er the track,
> With twenty lovely Jennies
> And a solitary Jack.

Ouray's opera house was packed.

After Day had moved his presses and plant to Durango in 1892, his blistering comments resulted in forty-two libel suits pending at one time. Towards the end of his career, scathing criticisms of a court decision brought a $300 fine for contempt; he refused to pay the fine, and for ten days edited the *Democrat* from a jail cell, continuing to attack the judge in every issue.

During the free-silver controversies of the early '90s, when any attack on the white metal was considered treason to Colorado, Dave was a victim of a practical joke. Day was serving as Commissioner of Indian Affairs, and an investigation of Indian problems was under way. Francis E. Leuppe, assistant Commissioner of Indian Affairs, came to Durango, and the two spent the day in Ignacio. Day had an appointment in Navajo Springs that evening and complained to the Commissioner that he had lost his entire day and had not written a line of editorial copy for the next day's *Democrat*. Leuppe said he would edit the issue for him, if the editor would print his articles.

Dave replied that he would give the foreman instructions to honor the copy, and he added, "I don't care what you write."

The next day's issue caused consternation in Durango. The leading editorial was captioned, "A Confession Wrung from Conscience." Intended as a joke on Day, it repudiated silver and included all of the "gold bug" arguments. The Associated Press sent it over the country, it was widely quoted, and the editor was an "untouch-able" in his home town for a month.

The same year that Day founded the *Solid Muldoon,* Carlyle Channing Davis, more familiarly known as "Cad," began his news-paper work in Leadville. He had come to Denver in 1876, hoping to improve his health, and went to work as editorial writer for the *News.* When the stories of the Leadville silver discoveries reached the capital city, Davis joined with John Arkins, a printer on the *Tribune,* to grubstake another printer, James Burnell.

The latter, after twenty-four hours' investigation, wired back: "Greatest silver camp on earth: but better for a newspaper than for silver." Quickly the three men organized the "Chronicle Publishing Company," with Arkins as editor, Davis as business manager, and total capital of $3,000. Transportation costs for machinery were prohibitive, but Davis succeeded in getting an entire printing plant transported from St. Louis in a sealed car billed "emigrant household goods." Necessary items of this kind commanded a greatly reduced rate. At Colorado Springs, he stayed up one entire night, and in the early morning secured receipted expense bills, before ordering a transfer of the "iron foundry" to wagons. The local agent raged but Davis had outsmarted him.

Lumber for the Leadville office cost hundreds of dollars, and brick for the chimney could have been shipped in by mail for consider-ably less money than it actually cost. The first issue of the *Chronicle* was off the presses on January 29, 1879. According to Davis' account, an edition of 9,000 was completely sold out, although at first he had anticipated only 500 sales. Davis had a tendency to exaggerate figures, but at any rate, the paper was an astonishing success.

The New Year's edition of the Leadville *Carbonate Weekly Chronicle* appeared first in 1880. Printed on calendar book-paper, and profusely illustrated with half-tones, Davis contracted to have it printed at the plant of the *New York Graphic.* He ordered a run of 60,000, to the amazement of the Graphic office, and sold the papers at 50 cents a copy. He made a profit of $7,500 in spite of the heavy costs. However, Leadville was not the first town to have a fancy annual edition; the *Colorado Miner* in Georgetown brought out a book-paper edition in August, 1875. In ten pages with sixty-five illustrations, it was the finest typographical specimen put out in Colorado up to that time.

Davis bought out his two partners on the *Chronicle* during the first year after the successful venture was launched. By 1883, the *Chronicle* had absorbed the presses and equipment of six competing papers. The secret of his success, he said, was simple: "I did unto others what they would have done unto me, and I 'did it fust.' That was all."

He included on his staff some of the top newsmen in the United States, for he could pay high salaries. Among them was John Bonner, author of *Child's History of the World,* and the first editor of *Harper's Weekly;* Robert Gauss, who later served the *Denver Repub-*

lican as editorial writer for twenty-nine years; Henry Butler, editor of the paper for more than thirty years; Charley Vivian, who founded the Benevolent Order of Elks; James McCarthy ("Fitz Mac"); Major Henry Ward; and many more.

Colorado Territory's first newspapermen's organization was started in 1867, the year of the visit of the Illinois editorial expedition. It was the Denver Press Club, started by grocery merchant Wolfe Londoner, who always enjoyed the companionship of the gentlemen of the press. He maintained a "cyclone cellar" in the basement of his store where representatives of the Fourth Estate gathered to enjoy the liquid refreshments cached therein. And the reporters and columnists stopped once a day at Londoner's store to pick up the day's gossip.

The early Press Club was an informal group. Its only officer, Londoner, was elected executive by common consent. The only apparent requirement for membership was to be on Wolfe's visiting list. In addition to evening meetings, largely devoted to political arguments and shop talk over the card tables, the club held excursions to near-by lakes and attended in a body the annual masked ball of the Denver Turnverein.

While Londoner was not a publisher, but rather a Denver merchant, the editors always went to his establishment and visited his wine cellar. Drinks were always available to the publishers when they came to Denver. Londoner was in attendance at all conventions and tours of the newspaper publishers and at one time issued a publication called the "Wine Cellar" for the editors.

Press organization of a more serious type began in 1871. This was five years before Colorado was admitted to statehood, and eight years prior to the beginning of the present organization. It was the year that the *Boulder County News* was suffering from lack of news, that Colorado Springs was being laid out, and rapid increase in population was indicating the beginnings of the boom that was to make Colorado important. The *Rocky Mountain News* for July 8, 1871, announced:

> The publishers of daily and weekly newspapers in Colorado will meet in Denver at 10 o'clock A. M. Saturday, July 15, to complete the formation of a Publisher's Association, to adopt a constitution and by-laws and to discuss such matters pertaining to the business as merits their attention. A full attendance is desired.

The meeting was held in the editorial room of the *News,* on Larimer Street between Fifteenth and Sixteenth.

In 1874, another feeble attempt was made to organize an association, but the files of the newspapers do not show that it was successful. Not until 1878 was a permanent organization formed and it was the beginning of the present Colorado Press Association. With the exception of the panic year of 1893, the Colorado Press Associa-

Colorado Editorial Association Meeting at Denver, January, 1922

tion has never missed an annual session, and that year was passed due to the changing of the meeting time from late fall of 1892 until a time soon after the first of January, 1894.

During the early years of the Association, long trips were a part of the annual convention. On one occasion, the publishers went to Portland, Oregon. Another time, they went to New Orleans. One of the trips took them to Chicago. On other occasions they went through Colorado. The first post-convention trip was in 1878, when, following the first meeting, the delegates went to Central City. It was on that trip that the train was derailed between Black Hawk and Central City and one or two cars hung over a precipice. However, no one was injured and the delegates walked the rest of the distance from the train to Central City. By the time they were ready to return that evening, the track had been cleared and they came back to Denver without difficulty. Of course, in those days the railroads provided free transportation for these trips. Otherwise they would not have been taken.

The story of Eugene Field is a long and an interesting one. Probably he was the most unusual of the unusual early day editors in Colorado. Joseph G. Brown in the *Colorado Magazine* of March, 1927, tells of a number of interesting side-lights in connection with Field. Brown worked with him for two years. Gene was managing editor of the old *Denver Tribune* and it was during the time he was a busy editor of this paper that he wrote much of his poetry.

Field was elected official poet of the Colorado Press Association at its meeting in Denver, July 12, 1881. For the next annual convention which was held in July, 1882, Field wrote the poem "Chipeta," later famous throughout the West. Field, incidentally, dashed it off only two hours before the convention opened, having previously decided not to write a poem at all because of the press of work in the *Tribune* office. The poem appears in the *Denver-Tribune* of July 12, 1882. At the association's annual meeting, July 10, 1883, Field was elected treasurer. He resigned when he left the *Tribune* and Colorado, during this same year.

William M. Arkins, a nephew of Col. John Arkins, a publisher of the *Rocky Mountain News* in the early days, wrote recently about some of the things which happened in the early days. In speaking of Field, Arkins said that one of the habits of Field while sitting at his desk was to kick the wall with the toe of his shoe. He finally kicked the plaster off in that particular spot. On several occasions after that they replastered the hole, but invariably, Field would kick it out again.

Arkins said that Field always had a row of red ink bottles across the back of his desk. Not for a long time did they know why he had so many little red ink bottles, but it seems that a friend of his who drank about as much as Field did would go into Field's office when no one was around, pull out a flask, and fill the ink bottles with whiskey. Finally, someone happened to walk in while Field's friend was filling the bottles, and it was then realized why he seemed to need so much ink on his desk. Just how Field drank the whiskey out of these ink bottles was not told, but apparently he had a system.

J. G. Brown writes in the *Colorado Magazine:*

It was well known among all of his friends that Field had no idea of the value of money or purpose of economy. The man with the bank account was an important personage in his eyes. Reckless in his generosity, he never saved or thought of saving a dollar. With money in his pockets he gave loose rein to his mania for buying books or fantastic gimcracks for himself or his friends, or else squandering in social rounds with his fellows, after first his family expenses were provided for.

[Brown continues with the following]:

Field's familiar mention of Perrin's saloon warrants the rehearsal of a widely circulated story, of which there are two versions as to location and exactness of detail. The variation is that of quantity and quality—a single drink of whiskey, or bottles of champagne for the crowd, the story of the latter originating in Kansas City. Both have appeared in print, but I know that I have the true story. Perrin's saloon was located on Lawrence Street near Seventeenth in Denver, one of the most convenient as a popular resort of newspaper men and their convivial friends. Incidentally I have met 'Gene Field there, though not frequently. It was his habit, and in accord with his liberal disposition to "treat" any acquaintance he might find there or who might drop in for a drink. Often when a friend or group of persons offered the courtesy to him he would decline, saying, "No, boys, this is on me—drinks for the crowd;" and then, to the bar-keeper: "Westley, set them up on me." For such transactions there were many charges on Field's ticket.

One night following such a transaction, Westley Perrin called Field to the bar and gave him a sound verbal drubbing for his method of beating him out of cash customers, ending by demanding that Field pay something on his bill. As usual Field declared he was broke, but gave assurance that he would "make it all right." Whereupon Westley held up Field's bill of $31.25 before his eyes, Field remarking, with a smile, that it was a very pretty piece of paper.

"Gene," said Westley, "do you know what I am going to do with this bill?"

"Why, no; keep it as a souvenir, I suppose."

"Here's what I shall do," Westley said, as he tore it in two and then into many small pieces. "Now, Gene, your bill is paid and you don't owe me a cent, but please don't try to run up any more bills especially when you order for men who would pay me cash."

"Well, West, that is good and kind of you and I thank you more than I can tell."

"Well, now, Gene, it is time for me to close, and for you to go back to your work. Come, I must lock the door."

Field ran his hands down into his trouser pockets and swaggered up and down in front of the bar.

"What are you staying for, Gene, when I tell you I will be fined if I don't lock up right away?"

"Why, I am waiting for my due."

"You've got much more than your due; what more do you ask?"

"Don't you know?" answered Field in a tone of commanding assurance, "Don't you know that it is a custom among gentlemen that when a customer pays his bar bill that the barkeeper must set them up?"

The bottle and glass appeared on the counter; Field took his drink and departed with a cheery "Good Night."

Gene was always pulling tricks on his friends; some of them were rather disastrous and others only created fun. One of the disastrous ones was in connection with an old friend who had come out to Denver to introduce a new device of his own invention for extinguishing fire, a sort of hand grenade. He had appealed to Field, his only acquaintance here, to aid him in promoting his enterprise. Through Gene's influence, permission was obtained from the authorities to place an empty cabin upon a vacant lot, ignite the structure in the presence of a multitude, including the fire department and city officials, and then demonstrate the efficacy of the new device in extinguishing the fire. That the intensity of the flames was increased by every grenade that was thrown into them, and that an entire wagon-load was sacrificed in a futile effort to check their progress, astonished all except one of the spectators. The practical joker of the *Tribune* had tampered with the bottles, substituting coal oil for the chemicals they were supposed to contain.

Sniktau was a name well known to the early journalists. The *Colorado Magazine* of June, 1928, has a complete story on E. H. N. Patterson, who was the Sniktau referred to. Many people did not know who Sniktau was. Patterson was working with his father in publishing the Oquawka, Illinois, *Spectator,* when the news of the gold discoveries in 1858-59 reached that state and Patterson could not resist the temptation to go west. He arrived with the vanguard of the Pikes Peak emigration in the spring of 1859. Sniktau was a name given to Patterson when he was with the miners who went to California in '49 and the word means "equal to any emergency."

Patterson came to Denver, not as a prospector, nor a journalist, but as a law-maker. Having reached the diggins known as Left Hand in the course of his prospecting above Boulder, he was recognized by his comrades as superior in intellect and experience and was accordingly requested to represent them in the Constitutional Convention being assembled to frame the laws for the future "State of Jefferson." The State of Jefferson was no more than an abortive dream, but the convention was Sniktau's introduction to the press of the region then represented by the *Rocky Mountain News* of Denver and the *Western Mountaineer* of Golden. Soon his interesting and chatty letters were appearing in both papers and his Indian nom de plume became a household word in the territory. After roving up and down the state for sometime, he finally disposed of his interests in Illinois and settled in Georgetown as editor and proprietor of the *Colorado Miner.*

Ansel Watrous was one of the outstanding crusading editors of the earlier days. While I do not have an extensive history of him, I note that he founded the *Ft. Collins Courier* in 1878, and in spite of threats of death for himself and dynamite for his newspaper plant, he waged a vigorous campaign against the underworld. The better element backed him in Ft. Collins and he won the fight to clean up the town. The *Courier* consolidated with the Ft. Collins *Express* and was known as the *Express-Courier* until 1945, when the name of the paper was changed to the *Coloradoan.* Watrous died in Ft. Collins, August 5, 1927.

At one of the conventions of the association which was held in Denver, February 21, 1888, one of the speakers was Roger W. Woodbury of the *Golden Transcript, Denver Tribune* and *Denver Times.* He finally purchased the *Denver Times* and the paper operated for many years. He made one statement in his talk to the publishers at that convention which I should like to quote:

> Suppose I should say that the *Denver Republican* and the *Rocky Mountain News,* after having their type set by machinery, will be printed, folded, wrapped and addressed and delivered to every post office in the state in a minute of time or that they should be instantly printed in every town and city and automatically delivered to subscribers at the instant of printing. The wonderful developments in electricity of which no one can yet tell the why should warn us that that impossibility may no longer exist.

Of interest, of course, is the fact that Woodbury was foretelling the invention of facsimile broadcasting by radio. While at this time it is still in an experimental stage, there will probably be certain types of daily spot news items which will be broadcast in the future, but it is my opinion that this can never supplant the local newspapers in the towns away from the metropolitan centers.

Going back to the *Rocky Mountain News,* I have an interesting story from my friend, William M. Arkins, and I shall give it to you as he wrote it to me:

> I have forgotten the year, but it was when certain persons representing the Republican Party secured an option

on the *Rocky Mountain News* for $400,000.00. The sum of $10,000 was paid down and the option read that the balance had to be paid IN CASH.

The night the option was expiring I sat with my Uncle and A. M. Stevenson on the Stout Street side of the Albany Hotel bar room. A. M. Stevenson had a certified check for $390,000.00 and wanted Uncle John to take it and close the deal. Just before the clock struck twelve, Stevenson asked Uncle John to take the check but he refused. He said he didn't know of an easier way of making $10,000.00. As the clock struck twelve Uncle John said: "Well, I'll buy a drink." The option had expired because they had not lived up to the terms—CASH. Stevenson told me some years later that he was of the opinion that T. M. Patterson had talked Col. Arkins out of selling. At that time, Col. Arkins had an option on the old *Chicago Times*.

The foregoing history has dealt mainly with the earlier years leading up to the turn of the century. Since that time there have not been as many stories of a spectacular nature regarding the newspapers as was characteristic of the pioneer days, but all of them have had their interesting careers dotted with unusual happenings.

While the *Rocky Mountain News* throughout all of these years has been, and is yet, under the able direction of Editor Jack Foster, a very great factor in all phases of social and industrial activity in Colorado, the *News* has not always had the field to itself. Newspapers have come and gone. Not until 1892 did anything appear which in any way became effective competition.

On August 8, 1892, the *Denver Post* was founded. It was launched by a group of men who incorporated the Post Publishing Company. They were Hugh Butler, George D. Herbert, Caldwell Yeaman, R. T. McNeal, H. C. Jackson, I. C. Crose, and M. J. McNamara. The Board of Directors at that time included George D. Herbert, W. P. Caruthers, A. B. McKinley, Charles J. Hughes, Jr., and Platt Rogers. The first issue was published at 1744 Curtis Street in the basement of the old Curtis Theater. The paper was issued daily except Sunday. It was a Democratic sheet and stood for the principles of Grover Cleveland who was then very unpopular in Colorado and apparently that policy wrecked it. Publication was suspended on August 29, 1893. On June 22, 1894, the Post Printing Company was again incorporated; this time by H. Y. Anderson, William Cavanaugh, and Frank J. Medina, Jr. The paper was then called the *Evening Post* and was published at 1734 Curtis Street. The depression of that time reduced the paper to straitened circumstances but publication continued until October 28, 1895, when the paper and property were purchased by Frederick G. Bonfils and Harry H. Tammen. On November 4, 1895, the Post Printing Company was incorporated for a third time. This time the incorporators were Frederick G. Bonfils, Harry H. Tammen and Carl Litzenberger.

The plant was then moved to 1019—16th Street, and remained there until April, 1907, when it moved to its own building on Champa Street.

When Bonfils and Tammen bought the *Denver Post,* they inaugurated a type of journalism not hitherto known. With banner headlines, plenty of color, and a well developed kind of showmanship, the *Post* grew into a newspaper with a tremendous reader interest and one of the best money making newspaper properties in the United States. A great many features and some books have been written about the *Denver Post* and its editors, and any attempt to give a complete story about it here would make this chapter too long. For those who want to follow its entire history, we respectfully refer them to the books and stories written about the *Post.*

Many reporters and writers who have gained fame were at one time employed by the *Denver Post.* Gene Fowler, author of *Timberline,* was one of them; Paul Harris, founder of Rotary International, was another. Although it would be difficult to list all of them, there should be mentioned Julian Hawthorne, Hallie Erminie Rives, H. H. Van Loan, Mary McLean, Otto Floto, Frances Maull, Winifred Black, Alice Rohe, Arthur Bennett, Walter Juan Davis, and Polly Pry.

No story of the Denver newspapers would be complete without mention of the fight between the *Denver Post* and *Rocky Mountain News* in 1926, when the Scripps-Howard organization bought the *News.* Then was staged a want-ad drive in which both papers competed for the want-ad business by offering all sorts of premiums and inducements. At that time, the *Rocky Mountain News* was putting out the *Denver Times,* an afternoon paper in competition with the afternoon *Post.* This brought out a morning edition of the *Denver Post* to compete with the *Denver Rocky Mountain News.* The fight went on for many months but finally both sides realized that nothing was being gained and they decided to talk it over. The result of the consultation was an agreement to suspend the *Morning Post* and the afternoon *Times.* This suspension took place in November, 1928, leaving the morning field to the *Rocky Mountain News* and the afternoon field to the *Denver Post.*

H. H. Tammen died July 19, 1924, and F. G. Bonfils died February 2, 1933. Following Bonfils' death, William Shepherd was managing editor and carried on until February, 1946, when Palmer Hoyt, editor of the *Portland Oregonian* and former director of the Domestic Branch of the Office of War Information, accepted an invitation to take over the paper. He was made publisher and editor.

Lute Wilcox, who for many years was editor and publisher of *Field and Farm,* an outstanding agricultural and stock paper published in Denver, but which suspended several years ago, wrote the following incident in his life in 1916 and it was published in the August *Colorado Press* of that year:

> The first time they sent me out in Denver to get a piece of news I came near flunking and giving up the profession as

a regular occupation for the remainder of my life. In fact I thought it would be my last night on earth, for I had been assigned to interview a tribe of Ute Indians which had just arrived from the White River country. They had encamped, as the city editor said, somewhere up Cherry Creek among briars and brambles. It was all a confounded uncertainty and no one around the shop could say just where it was, and as for my tenderfooted self I had never heard of Cherry Creek for I had only been here a day or so and had not taken much of a chance on getting lost in a city of 15,000 wild and woolly white folks, to say nothing about a band of man-eating redskins with no appreciation of the courtesies that go with high breeding and all that.

The bewhiskered boss who prided himself on the fact that he was a pretty good Indian himself said I could get a saddle pony over across the street and that I had better hike out. It was then after nine by the Dutch clock which allowed none too much time to get the story in the morning paper. The first side closed at midnight and old Salty would be calling for copy before the other reporter came in with his half-column of stuff.

The old hassayamper who helped saddle the bronk said he had once seen a passel of Utes and knew all about injuns, good and bad, but he had never seen any good ones until they were dead. The best of them were a blood-thirsty lot who just "doted on a tender young tenderfoot just like your-self," he remarked as he gave me a quick once over and hoped I would get there before supper was done. I was to go up Sixteenth Street until I got out of town, turn south on Broadway and take the trail to the left when I came to the bridge. The Ute camp would be found somewhere two or three miles up the creek among the cottonwoods. "Be dead shore you bring the hoss back," he added as a fond farewell and I thought there was a tone of personal solicitude in his voice as he said this.

The midsummer night was misty and chilly enough for September in this balmy climate and seemed altogether unsalubrious to a lunger who had come out all the way from Cleveland to get his health back. I found the trail where the old man said it was and in fifteen minutes a great ki-yi ahead in the loaming, about where the Country Club is now located, assured me I was on the right steer and by the smell borne on the gentle breeze I knew the pony and I were on the proper scent. I knew also by the fever chills up and down my back that we were going south and presently the camp fires were seen burning holes in the darkness.

Suddenly the bronk gave a start as a hand reached out and caught the bridle. A gruff voice like that of Beelzebub asked what I wanted. I knew enough to say that I was a

Tribune reporter and desired to see the chief. "I am Curtis, the interpreter," replied the man, "and I will take you in to Colorow. Go easy with him and don't try to kill anybody in camp. You see these injuns are powerful afeered of the palefaces and we mustn't skeer 'em." I promised to be good and felt pretty chipper when on reaching the village a big buck stepped up and stuck out a friendly paw saying, "How." All I could do was to grunt back, "How yourself?" The interpreter gent said it was Colorow and before the old fellow could give me a punch in the slats I handed him a Punch cigar and as it was a real five-center he gleefully stuck it into his facial orifice, turned on his heel and disappeared in the darkness in the regulation J. Fenimore Cooper way while I was still digging around for a match.

Curtis remarked dryly that "Injuns don't talk much nohow," and I felt a little disappointed when he added that the interview or whatever it might be called was over. The ki-yi and the dogs made more of a racket than ever and I realized that it was time to be disappearing. I passed Curtis the remaining cigar, remarking, that I knew his street down town. Then like the king's army I turned around and marched right back again, stopping a spell at the bridge to catch my wind, kill time and frame up a story for the boss. When I rode into the livery barn on Holladay Street the old chambermaid greeted me with a Missouri smile and essayed the remark, "I knowed you'd git tru hunky-dory," whereupon I asked him to sign a receipt for the horse and to send the bill to the office. A minute later I bustled into the editorial sanctuary and wrote a two-column interview with Colorow which even Jo Ward would have accepted at space rates on a dull day. Leastwise Tom Dawson put it over, for editors were not very finicky in those cheerful days, and besides we had scooped the *News*.

Wilcox died in Denver, January 16, 1947, at the age of 90. He had been inactive in the publishing field for many years on account of being totally blind. In his later years he was one of the leaders in organizations for the blind and was recognized as one of Colorado's outstanding men in this type of humanitarian work.

Only once in the history of Colorado journalism has any newspaper been censored. During some labor troubles between the coal miners in the Walsenburg area and the CF&I, in late 1921, J. F. Coss was editing the *Walsenburg Independent*. Coss wrote many biting and forceful editorials favoring the coal miners and he was also against the Colorado Rangers, who were the state police, and were under the command of Col. Pat J. Hamrock. The Rangers were sent into Walsenburg to try to quell the disturbance and to help maintain peace and order, but apparently, their presence incited the antagonism of that area, and as a result, Coss carried on a barrage of criticisms and news stories about the unlawful activities of these Rangers.

The situation around Walsenburg became very tense, until finally, the County Sheriff asked the then Governor Oliver H. Shoup to send in troops, which he did.

In defending the laborers and the citizens against the military and the Rangers, Editor Coss kept on writing bitter editorials, and with the encouragement of other newspapers in the state, he soon found that he was causing the governor and others some embarrassment. Consequently, with the issue of December 2, 1921, the *Independent* was put under strict censorship and could not get out an issue until all copy had been read by a representative of the governor. Joseph E. Moorhead, a newspaper man who was private secretary to Governor Shoup, was charged with the job of checking all copy under this censorship plan. This censorship ran for seven weeks, after which the trouble subsided and troops were withdrawn. On several occasions during this time, the lives of Editor Coss and members of his family were threatened, but at no time were they harmed. This is the only instance in which the freedom of the press has been violated in Colorado.

The next year, Editor Coss ran for the State Senate and was elected to a four-year term. He left the *Independent* as editor on November 24, 1923, and later moved to Denver.

Throughout the history of the newspaper business in Colorado, one can find countless instances of the constructive work done by the newspapers for Colorado industries and its people. We would fall far short of covering the complete history if we attempted to enumerate the work done by the newspapers individually. It cannot be doubted that the newspapers in Cripple Creek, Creede, Leadville, Aspen, Ouray, Silverton, Telluride, Durango, Boulder, Idaho Springs, Georgetown, Central City, Breckenridge, and other mountain towns have carried on a relentless fight to protect the metal production in these areas and have always crusaded for better markets and better prices for the minerals.

Newspapers in the plains towns have carried the fight for the agriculturists and the stock growers. In the Grand Junction and Canon City areas, the newspapers have given much help to the fruit industry. In the resort towns, the newspapers have always encouraged the tourists and have publicized the scenic beauties of the state. In Denver, Pueblo and some other towns, industry has had the backing of the newspapers, and the publishers can look back with much satisfaction to the part they have played in the development of this great state.

During both World War I and World War II, the publishers did a magnificent job in selling War Bonds and in leaving to posterity an almost perfect record of the men and women who went into service and the part these people played in the winning of both wars.

Prominent in the newspaper industry in the past few years have been such men as Walter Walker, editor the *Grand Junction*

Sentinel, a leader in the Democratic party and who flew to Washington to be sworn in to serve as U. S. Senator for a few hours; Col. L. C. Paddock of the *Boulder Camera,* who was known for his unusual editorial style; T. E. Nowels, for a long time publisher of the Colorado Springs *Gazette & Telegraph;* Frank S. Hoag, of the Pueblo *Star-Journal and Chieftain;* Roy Ray, editor of the Windsor *Poudre Valley* and for several sessions a member of the State Legislature; Eugene T. Hogue, editor the *Eaton Herald,* who carried on a long, running editorial battle with Roy Ray, even though the two were the closest of personal friends; Edward D. Foster, editor the *Greeley News* and other papers, author of the Penny Ante Column, and later Commissioner of the State Board of Immigration and Director of the State Planning Commission; Charles H. Leckenby, editor the *Steamboat Springs Pilot,* secretary of the Moffat-Tunnel Commission since it was created, and author of a book *The Tread of Pioneers;* Dell W. Gee of the *La Jara Gazette;* Guy U. Hardy, *Canon City Daily Record* and for years a member of Congress; Charles Hansen, editor the *Greeley Tribune* and the father of the Grand Lake Diversion Project, and many others. In this list should be a number of other publishers who have outstanding records but it is not possible to include them all here.

There have been several monthly publications issued in the interests of the newspaper publishing industry in Colorado. The first one of which there seems to be any copies available was the *Ink Spot,* issued in 1901. Only two copies are available at this time and they are in possession of the Denver Public Library. Next came the *Colorado Press,* issued by Guy U. Hardy of the Canon City *Daily Record.* This publication ran from February, 1914, until February, 1920. In April, 1919, the *Intermountain Press and Printer* was launched by Ed Foster and George Haubrich. This publication continued until April, 1926, when it was absorbed by the *Colorado Editor,* a publication which was started with the April number of that year by the Colorado Press Association with Edwin A. Bemis as editor.

As noted previously in this article, the newspaper publishers organized the permanent Colorado Press Association in 1878. It remained mostly a social organization until about 1920 when the publishers began to see the need for the establishment of a central business office and the employment of a full-time manager. This plan was not activated until late in 1922 when it was definitely decided to have a full-time manager. The Board of Directors of the Colorado Press Association employed a manager at its meeting, February 10, 1923, and the association has continued under that plan to the present time.[1]

---

[1] Edwin A. Bemis, author of this article, was selected to manage the Colorado Press Association at this time. At a meeting of publishers at Greeley on September 23, 1922, while he was still president of the Colorado Press Association, he agreed to undertake the work. Official action was taken by the board of directors of the association on February 10, 1923, employing him as of March 1, 1923, more than four months after he actually took over the job. At the time of the publication of this book he is still the association manager.

Upon invitation of the regents and the president of the University of Colorado, the Colorado Press Association opened its business office on the campus at Boulder on July 1, 1926, and operated from the Extension Division. This arrangement gave the newspapers many advantages because the facilities of the University in research and library were at the disposal of the publishers. This plan continued until July 1, 1945, when the office was moved to the campus of the University of Denver.

On May 1, 1946, there are 25 daily newspapers and 154 weekly newspapers in the state of Colorado, many of which are nationally famous. Their total valuation was approximately $20,000,000.

Thus have the newspapers recorded the history of Colorado and have documented the many achievements of the citizens who have built this great state—as they have written history in all civilized countries. They have perpetuated the knowledge of events, ambitions, and the hopes of man through the power of the pen, ink, and newsprint.

CHAPTER X

Banking and Monetary Problems

GEORGE L. ANDERSON

Associate Professor of History at Colorado College, and member of the faculty from 1934 to 1945*

A BASIC feature of the history of large nations is the intricate interplay of local and national processes and institutions. True of almost every phase of political and economic history, this generalization is particularly noticeable in the development of banking and financial institutions. Almost inevitably banking practices and agencies of national scope reach out to the relatively immature communities of a new state and exert an influence that must be taken into account by the historian. Just as inevitably, the economy of a state initiates developments that ramify in an amazingly complex fashion especially if it is an important producer of materials regarded as indispensable to the financial and monetary system not only of the nation but of the world at large.

The impact of these diverse forces upon a state is particularly important during the period of growth from economic infancy, when bank credit and business leadership must come largely from the outside, to a stage of economic maturity when these can be supplied to a considerable degree from within its borders. During this period banking institutions and facilities are of paramount importance. They provide the most direct, the most sensitive, and the most inclusive connecting link with the older, more mature, and more highly developed sections of the nation. Within the newer region the banks became the focal points for the mobilization and investment of capital whether it was of local or distant or foreign origin. Of unquestioned validity even when note issue was the primary foundation of banking, these considerations apply with even greater force when the supplying of credit became the principal function of a banking institution. The rapid economic development of Colorado occurred at about the time that this change in the banking institutions of the nation was coming to completion. This fact is of considerable importance in analyzing the banking and currency history of the state.

INFLUENCE OF MINING UPON BANKING

The nature of the mineral frontier exerted tremendous influence upon the development of banking in Colorado. Just as the problems of settlement and adaptation were not the same for the agricultural frontier when it left the forested areas and trenched upon the plains,

---

* After Dr. Anderson began the writing of this chapter, he accepted and now holds the position of Associate Professor of History at the University of Kansas.

so the problems of banking in a mining state were different from those of predominantly agricultural or industrial states. In Colorado the banking problems arising out of the mining industry were super-imposed upon those produced by agriculture, industry, and expensive transportation facilities. Moreover the banking and financial problems of many agricultural communities in Colorado are not in any way comparable to those of agricultural communities farther to the east. Although direct information is not available, the extremely costly character of privately financed irrigation projects and the large invest-ments of capital in irrigated lands must have exerted considerable influence upon banking activities in communities where large areas of land were under irrigation. But it was the mining industry's emphasis upon speed which provided one of the most direct and inclusive influences upon Colorado banking. An unidentified writer in *Hunt's Merchant's Magazine* in 1854 called attention to the impact of rapid economic development upon banking activities. "The more rapid the development of the natural resources of a region," he said, "the greater are the *apparent* benefits resulting from a bank expansion, and the greater are the *real* evils resulting from a bank contraction."[1] For the history of banking in Colorado the important words in this quotation are not the italicized ones, nor those that refer to contraction and expansion; it is the reference to the speed with which natural resources are developed and the relation of the rate of speed to banking problems that provides a key to understand-ing the history of banking and monetary problems in the state.

It will be generally admitted that in an age when the business of the world was founded to some degree upon gold and silver and the circulating media of the world consisted of these metals or their representatives, no natural resource could be susceptible of more rapid exploitation than the deposits of precious metals. Whether it was placer deposits or refractory ores made very little difference; the premium was upon speed. The fast moving "rushes" to new strikes, the continuous activity in the mining towns, and the feverish schemes of promoters bear testimony to the emphasis upon speed. The ghost towns contain mute evidence of the efforts to extract the greatest possible quantity of specie in the least possible period of time. One result of this emphasis upon speed was the creation of an atmosphere of impermanence and evanescence which seemed to permeate most mining communities. A competent, contemporary observer undoubtedly had this characteristic in mind when he wrote,

> It [mining] has founded states, attracted population, enlarged the boundaries of civilization; and it has done this work in a careless and lawless way without much regard for the future. All other parts of society springing from it, are gradually becoming systematized and consolidated, but the primitive industry remains in a primitive condition. Estab-lishing everything else it has not established itself.[2]

1 "Condition of the Banks," XXXI (1854), 94.
2 Rossiter W. Raymond, *The Mines of the West*, 6.

Banking, with its emphasis upon security, stability, and regularity, could not help but be influenced by an environment that did not possess any of these qualities and by a people who did not prize them.[3]

The Shortage of Capital

The emphasis upon speed, so characteristic of mining psychology, was related to the desire for adequate transportation facilities and to another significant phase of the background of banking and monetary developments: the problem of outside capital investments in the state. Those who were interested in mining as well as in transportation did not heed the advice of some of their contemporaries that it was probably better to build more slowly and securely. They wanted rapid development of the resources of the region. It was clear to all that large supplies of outside capital were essential. It was invited to flow in.

The elaborate news-editorial entitled "Eastern Capital" that appeared in the Colorado Springs *Gazette* on May 6, 1876, may be used as an illustration of the appeal that was made. The editor undertook to inform eastern capitalists of the disadvantages of investing their surplus funds in their own localities while at the same time pointing out the extremely profitable nature of investments in Colorado. Attention was called to the large amounts of idle and unproductive capital in the East, to the unsatisfactory character of land and railroad investments, and to the generally depressed state of business in the eastern section of the country. By contrast Colorado was pictured as an investor's paradise. Money loaned on real estate security would yield from ten to fifteen per cent annually without involving the slightest risk. Better security could be had on eighteen per cent loans in El Paso county than on seven per cent loans in the East. Enterprises were open where an investment of from one to two thousand dollars would yield from thirty to fifty per cent within a year. Trade in and with the mining districts would yield good returns. Careful husbandry in the sheep and cattle business never failed of success. Even mining had been reduced to a business of nice calculation and by prudent management would always be profitable and often immensely productive. The erecting of smelting works would be sure to pay and the development of the coal beds along the route of the Denver and Rio Grande Railway could not fail to yield largely.

The three subsequent issues of the *Gazette* contained follow-up stories reprinted from other territorial newspapers: a Denver *Times* statement of the general arguments; a La Plata *Miner* summary of the profitable opportunities awaiting investors in mining and merchandising in the San Juan country; and a Central City *Register*

---

[3] In a letter to the Colorado Springs *Gazette,* January 16, 1875, "Money Lender" after asserting that the people of Colorado felt under no obligation to pay their bills said, "The banks may justly be held responsible for a large share of this difference between the business men of the East and of the West."

item which called attention to the unprecedented activity, extraordinary profits, increasing confidence, and universal disposition to work the mines as legitimate undertakings that were becoming characteristic in the area that it represented.[4]

In addition to issuing many printed invitations to eastern capitalists to invest in Colorado the laws of the state were adjusted to make investment more attractive.[5] There was no maximum interest rate fixed by the state. Laws concerning the collection of debts favored the creditor over the debtor. No adequate regulation of banking practices was established during the first three decades of statehood. The failure of the state to provide for adequate supervision and inspection of banks operating under state laws prior to 1908 is eloquent if not direct evidence of the fact that the political leaders of the state acquiesced in the development of ''financial banking.''

Residents of eastern states came to Colorado with the overt intention of becoming the representatives of eastern capital that was seeking investment in the state. A conspicuous example is General William J. Palmer. Following the conclusion of the Civil War he wrote a letter to an uncle which may be taken as a statement of his reasons for making Colorado the center of his railroad building activities. Writing from St. Louis, on August 20, 1865, he said:

> Young men without money can only make a fortune by connecting themselves with capitalists. The heaviest of these reside in the East where they can look after their own affairs. But the best place to invest capital is in the West. Eastern capitalists must therefore have representatives here to attend to their interests if they wish to invest heavily in the West. Such representatives, if able and correct, must acquire great wealth and influence with their distant principals—to a greater extent and more rapidly than if they lived in the East where the capitalist can judge for himself.[6]

To these formal or direct attempts to induce eastern capital to flow into the state there must be added the less tangible influence of the wealthy tourists and travelers who became interested in Colorado's possibilities as a result of a visit or tour. Of the same character, but probably of greater importance, were the well-to-do health-seekers suffering from illness and forced to seek not only a new home, but a new center of business activity. Only a careful study can reveal the contributions made to the financial development

[4] There is some reason to believe that the *Gazette* was carrying on a campaign to interest Eastern investors. As early as January 15, 1876, a column of mining notes supplied by the Colorado Springs Mining Agency had appeared. In the items for that issue attention was called to the growing interest in the East in the gold and silver mines of Colorado and to the likelihood of large amounts of capital flowing in during the year.

[5] Leon W. Fuller, *The Populist Regime in Colorado,* unpublished Ph.D. thesis, University of Wisconsin, 1933, 7-9. This study places a great deal of emphasis upon the role of outside capital in the development of the state.

[6] Quoted in John Fisher, *A Builder of the West* (Caldwell, Idaho: Caxton Printers, 1939), 127.

of the state by those who came with the bleak prospect of a few months or at most a few years of life remaining to them, only to survive for long periods of time and to make available to the state capital funds, mature business leadership, and valuable connections with eastern firms.

Not only was eastern capital invited to enter the state in many direct and indirect ways, but it was not to be discouraged nor frightened into leaving. One of the most frequently repeated arguments in opposition to the Populist campaign and administration of Governor Davis H. Waite was the statement that his election would be followed by a withdrawal of capital from the state; that Colorado would be set back ten years in its business development; that investors would boycott a state that was likely to indulge in visionary political and legislative experiments.[7] During the panic of 1893 the newspapers that favored the free coinage of silver, but opposed the Populist regime of Governor Waite, found it necessary to admonish their readers not to go too far in their demands for relief. An early version of the "prosperity is just around the corner" argument is contained in the following,

> Keep cool and make a determined and dignified fight for free coinage. Don't go into the calamity howl business and make Colorado ridiculous in the eyes of her enemies and ruin her credit abroad. Three years from now our state will be more prosperous than ever.[8]

PROPOSED REMEDIES FOR CAPITAL SHORTAGES

The consistent attempt to induce eastern capital to seek investment in the state does not constitute the sole evidence of shortages of capital, circulating currency, and bank credit. During the early period of mining activity the establishment of private mints in Denver and elsewhere in the territory to produce gold coins and thus provide a more satisfactory circulating medium, plus the constant interest of members of Congress from Colorado and of newspaper editors in expanding the facilities of the Denver mint after it became a branch of the United States mint, reflect something more basic than pride in the mineral resources of the state.[9] Following the early days of the panic of 1873 the Georgetown *Miner* argued that the government should order coinage to be undertaken at the Denver mint because the scarcity of currency was the worst result of the financial panic in the East. Only the low grade ores could be sold because buyers could not get sufficient amounts of currency to

---

[7] Fuller, *op. cit.*, 56-57. One business and banking leader presumably remarked that a Populist victory would put "Colorado on the same footing with Kansas." In general the Republican arguments in 1892 were to the effect that the state should support the party of protection and sound finance and thus realize its destiny as the Pennsylvania of the West.

[8] Pueblo *Chieftain*, July 27, 1893.

[9] A good description of the private mints and allied subjects is contained in LeRoy H. Hafen, "Currency, Coinage and Banking in Pioneer Colorado," *Colorado Magazine*, X (1933), 81-90.

buy the better grades and the banks could not help them. Coinage at the Denver mint would eliminate high charges for shipment of the bullion to Philadelphia and would render Colorado independent of "Eastern Money-Hoarders." The writer suggested a private establishment to put money in circulation if the government did not act promptly.[10]

The issuance of fractional currency and scrip by the private banking firms and express agencies in Denver during the early years of Colorado Territory and the resort to the more sophisticated, but comparable clearing house certificates during panic periods attest to the shortage of circulating notes.[11] An interesting approach to the problem from the point of view of credit rather than circulating currency was suggested in Greeley in 1874. It was proposed that the town organize a loan and trust company, borrow money in the East, with the entire assets of the town company pledged as security, at a lower rate than individual borrowers could secure and then reloan it to the people of the community at twelve per cent a year. The Colorado Springs *Gazette* discussed the proposal approvingly and suggested that other communities could profit by adopting the Greeley method. In another column, however, it was reported that the Greeley town trustees had negotiated the loan at one and one-fourth per cent per month and were making funds available on real estate security at one and one-half per cent, the end of two per cent per month in Greeley.[12]

The frequent announcements in the press of the shortage of money indicate that a real problem did exist. On one occasion the shortage in Colorado was attributed to stringency in the "general money market."[13] Again it is noted in connection with some local situation. Thus in one instance a rancher offered some fine Spanish merino bucks and cashmere goats for sale, but owing to the prevailing scarcity of currency, he proposed to take cattle and brood mares in exchange for them.[14] A simple statement that "Money seems to be tighter than ever" is used on another occasion.[15] Again it is the shortage of capital that is singled out as the principal obstacle to the expansion of business.[16] A more interesting variation is the advocacy of self-sufficiency in order to prevent the outflow of money. In words reminiscent of mercantilistic literature one newspaper reminded its readers on two widely separated occasions that the

[10] Reprinted in the Colorado Springs *Gazette,* October 25, 1873.

[11] Hafen, *loc. cit.,* Frank Hall, *History of the State of Colorado* (Chicago: Blakely, 1890), III, 168. P. P. Wilcox and Co., C. A. Cook and Co., Clark, Gruber and Co., and the Denver agent of the Overland Express, Amos Steck, are listed as having issued scrip. A full summary of the activities of gold-buying firms, the issuance of scrip, the proposed Bank of Colorado, and the early banking institutions is contained in chapters II and III of Fred R. Niehaus, *Development of Banking in Colorado* (Denver: Mountain States Pub. Co., 1942). This booklet contains the most complete account of the history of banking in Colorado.

[12] Colorado Springs *Gazette,* March 13, 1874.

[13] Pueblo *Chieftain,* October 15, 1868.

[14] *Ibid.,* December 18, 1869.

[15] Colorado Springs *Gazette,* June 20, and November 21, 1874.

[16] Denver *Tribune* quoted in Colorado Springs *Gazette,* May 2, 1874.

shortage of currency in Colorado was due in part to the export of money for goods that could just as well be produced within the borders of the state. In commending the men who were going to build a flour mill in Pueblo the *Chieftain* remarked that $30,000 was sent out of southern Colorado during the month of December, 1874, in payment for flour. Almost twenty years later the same newspaper praised the president of the Denver and Rio Grande Railway for ordering the purchase of Colorado-made goods wherever possible because such a course would build an empire that no British, Indian, Australian, or even New York mandate could seriously affect. The writer added the assertion that Pueblo was sending out too much money in payment for California fruits, Kansas poultry, eggs, and butter, and outside flour.[17]

In other discussions of the currency shortage there is a curious mixture of popular economics and basic principles. Thus in October, 1868, the editor of the Pueblo *Chieftain* confessed that the extreme scarcity of money in Pueblo was a topic of universal comment and the cause of considerable distress, but it wasn't because business wasn't good nor men honest. It was because the supply of circulating money was wholly inadequate.[18] But in June of the same year the editor had indicated his awareness of the basic causes of the monetary stringency. The pertinent remarks are,

> Everybody wants money * * *. Now how do we expect to get it except by an increase in the value of our real property, the bettering of our markets, the development of our natural resources, and the increase of our business. Business and trade make money, and consumption and demand make business and trade. What will bring these things then will bring money to the hands of every man.[19]

In the same vein, but about a decade later, another editor found it possible to express considerable pride in the stability of Colorado banks. Discussing the broader problem of currency and credit, he said,

> The condition of our moneyed institutions is certain to become still better now that the current of exchange is setting steadily in favor of greater ease in the money market. For about the first time in our history, we are producing more than we are consuming—selling more than we are buying. This must tell soon in favor of greater ease in the money market.[20]

There is even a hint in this account that it is not the supply of currency in the nation *per se* that was of determinative importance

17 Pueblo *Chieftain,* February 10, 1875; July 31, 1893.
18 *Ibid.,* October 15, 1868.
19 *Ibid.,* June 1, 1868.
20 Colorado Springs *Gazette,* October 20, 1877.

to Colorado, but the volume of business activity plus moneyed institutions—banks—of a stable character to make the national supply of currency effective in the economic life of Colorado.

INTEREST RATES

The interest rates charged by money lenders in a region are a good index to the available supply of capital and credit. The evidence on this point is quite conclusive: the interest rates in Colorado have been high throughout its history. There are statements to the effect that during the eighteen-sixties interest rates in Denver varied from five to twenty-five per cent per month. The ruling rate on commercial paper at banks was three to five per cent per month. During 1873 the interest rate according to the Colorado Springs *Gazette* was two and a half to three per cent per month.[21] These rates seem to have prevailed over much of Colorado during the next several years. By 1877 it was remarked that the rates were a little more than half of those in effect three years earlier.[22] That rates were not uniform throughout the state during the eighteen-eighties is indicated by evidence cited by Justice William S. Jackson of the Colorado Supreme Court in his monograph on "Banking in Colorado Springs" (1942) to the effect that the prevailing rate in that city was ten per cent per annum, whereas the rate in Pueblo and Central City was between twelve and eighteen per cent, and in Gunnison it was still twenty-four per cent.[23] During the period 1893 to 1897 it cost the Denver merchant as much to borrow $1,000 as it cost the Boston merchant to borrow $2,600.[24] Governor John F. Shafroth suggested a maximum limit of twelve per cent a year during his term as governor and as late as 1920 Colorado was second only to Texas in the number of banks reporting that they were charging that much or more.[25]

THE SILVER QUESTION

Although it is not the current fashion to treat the silver question in Colorado as a subordinate phase of the larger problem of inadequate supplies of bank credit, liquid capital, and circulating currency, to do so will permit the placing of emphasis upon the more fundamental and universal rather than upon the more superficial and provin-

---

[21] February 1, 1873.

[22] *Ibid.,* August 4, 1877.

[23] Justice Jackson bases his conclusion on unpaid promissory notes taken by the El Paso County Bank in the eighteen-eighties and nineties. The writer has seen two notes in a collection of Caulfield material, one dated July 24, 1882, made out to the Stockgrowers National Bank of Pueblo, and the other dated September 1, 1882, to Meyer and Stewart, wholesale grocers in Gunnison. A good deal of information on the adjustment of interest rates to the credit standing of individual borrowers is contained in a set of instructions prepared by Joseph A. Thatcher, president of the First National Bank of Central City, for the guidance of employees during his absence in Europe. Herbert O. Brayer, editor, "Boom-Town Banker—Central City, Colorado," *Bulletin of the Business Historical Society,* XIX (1945), 67-95.

[24] A. D. S. Gillett, using Bradstreet material in *Sound Currency,* VIII (1898), 183-184.

[25] *Cong. Record,* 63 Cong., 2 Sess., LI, 14727; *Report of the Comptroller of the Currency for 1920,* 130.

cial aspects of the question. Many business and political leaders of the state were well aware of the decisive importance of the national and international ramifications of their "peculiar" industry. The abandonment of silver for monetary purposes by European nations and the closing of the mints of India to silver coinage received a great deal of attention in the press of the state, in the addresses of political leaders, and in the reactions of the public in general. Even the frequently expressed view that the decreased use of silver as a monetary metal was the result of a conspiracy hatched in Great Britain, if not historically sound, at least exempts the people of Colorado from the charge that they were provincial in their outlook and near-sighted in their search for the causes of their dilemma. Moreover the subordination of silver to the larger question of inadequate financial resources in a new and rapidly developing mineral region excludes the possibility that the whole free coinage campaign was simply a device by which the silver magnates, presumably resident in Colorado and other western states, hoped to add to their personal fortunes.[26]

It is difficult to escape the conclusion that the support of free coinage in Colorado came from the wrong people if it was an attempt to vote dollars into the pockets of the state. This is particularly the case if the investment of eastern and foreign capital in the mining industry of the state was as large as is generally assumed. In that event the most ardent and vehement support of silver should have come from eastern capitalists who owned and operated the mines and smelters and from their representatives in Colorado instead of from those who professed to represent the agricultural and laboring classes of the state. Indeed if two widely current points of view are accepted: that the silver mines were largely owned and operated by eastern capitalists and that the silver movement was largely an attempt to secure a federal subsidy for the silver industry, then it appears that the people of Colorado were engaged in a crusade to put money into the pockets of their alleged betrayers and exploiters who were just as ardent in their efforts to close their pockets to the gift.

Until further light is thrown upon the subject it is safer to assume that the leaders of Colorado who were prominent in the fight for free silver wanted it primarily for the purpose of enlarging the nation's stock of circulating currency, an enlargement which it was fondly hoped would be reflected very directly in Colorado. This was the position taken by Henry M. Teller, Davis H. Waite, John Bell, Charles S. Thomas, John F. Shafroth, and in a much more recent period by John A. Martin. Frankly accepting the quantity theory of money they wanted silver used as a monetary metal in order to provide a volume of currency that was proportionate, in their judgment, to the increased volume of business both locally, nationally, and internationally. Professor Fritz has pointed out that only the increased production of gold, a good deal of it from Colorado mines, prevented

---

[26] For a similar and earlier statement of the view that the silver agitation was largely due to an inadequate supply of circulating currency see Percy S. Fritz, *Colorado, The Centennial State* (New York: Prentice Hall, 1941), 349 ff.

a contemporary demonstration of the soundness of the position taken by the men mentioned above and that the monetary legislation of the nineteen-thirties provided convincing if belated evidence that they were on the right track.[27]

The increased coinage of silver advocated by many of the leaders of Colorado might not have accomplished the objectives that they had in view. It is conceivable that it might have intensified rather than solved the evils of which they complained. But there was a certain naturalness in the advocacy of silver coinage by Coloradans. It would benefit a leading industry of the state. The tremendous possibilities inherent in the expansion of bank credit had not been realized in the nation generally, much less in a new region with inadequate banking facilities. Moreover there seems to have been a real prejudice against an expansion of currency based upon anything but coined money. Increased issues of banknotes, and to some extent even of greenbacks, and increased reliance upon credit instruments were denounced almost as vigorously as increased coinage of silver was advocated. It was natural therefore that the answer to monetary problems should be sought in the realm of a larger volume of coin. In addition the inadequacy of Colorado's financial resources became apparent at a time when the state was producing in relatively large quantities a metal that historically had been coined and used as money. Thus a new region had not only the imaginative desire, but the physical means as well, to relieve the monetary stringency not only for Colorado, but for the world generally.

The failure of eastern capitalists who had invested heavily in Colorado silver mines and their representatives in Colorado to join the Populist and Democratic political leaders and the people of Colorado in the agitation for the increased use of silver can be explained on either of two possibilities, neither of which have been sufficiently explored by the historian. The first is that the profits from the silver industry derived more largely from the organizational and promotional period, that is, from the sale and re-sale of stock in mining companies, than from the operational aspects of the industry. The second is that silver mining and smelting had not kept pace with other industries in technological developments, thus causing it to fall behind its competitors so far as profitable operation was concerned. It may well be that the silver mining industry of Colorado would have been eclipsed during the decade of the eighteen-nineties even if the white metal had been fully utilized in the monetary structure of the nation.

GENERAL FEATURES OF COLORADO BANKING

All of the evidence cited in support of the point of view that the financial and monetary resources of Colorado were not in the earlier period of her history commensurate with her rich endowment of mineral resources and the insistent pressure for their speedy develop-

---

[27] *Colorado, The Centennial State,* 359-360.

ment serves the collateral purpose of underlining the importance of the banking institutions of the state. In a study of limited scope it is obviously impossible to mention the establishment of each banking institution. Nor does any particular value attach to the listing of the first banks in particular communities. An analysis based upon the persistence of specific institutions would have greater significance. Thus of the one hundred and forty-three banks in operation in Colorado in 1942 only four were established during the decade 1862-1871; and only eight others were established prior to 1881. Statistical analyses unhappily conceal more than they reveal by burying the unusual in the average. But even if this were not the case the statistical data are not available for a careful and complete study of Colorado banking institutions. In the first biennial report of the state bank commissioner, Henry M. Beatty remarked, "There have never been any records kept concerning the state and private banks that were of any value, or that were at all accurate—in fact, very little was known concerning them."[28] Information is not available which would make it possible to ascertain the total number of banking institutions that have been established in the state during its history. If the history of banking in Colorado Springs affords a clue to conditions throughout the state it may be safe to conclude that approximately four times as many banks have been established as had survived until 1942. In the study previously cited, Justice William S. Jackson has shown that three banks seem to have been the optimum number required for Colorado Springs during the period of its greatest growth and that currently there are four banks in the city. But there have been established since 1872 in Colorado Springs eleven distinct banking institutions.

The statistical data collected and published by the Comptroller of the Currency do reveal some interesting features of the banking history of Colorado. In 1897 the state ranked thirteenth among the states on the basis of per capita banking power, the total of capital, surplus, undivided profits, and circulation. Only the Middle Atlantic states, the New England states, and California, exceeded Colorado in this respect. If the comparison be confined to the per capita of total resources of national banks Colorado in 1897 ranked fifth, being exceeded only by Massachusetts, Rhode Island, Connecticut, and New York. In 1910 Colorado was first among the nine western states in per capita of bank resources. It may be worthy of note that in 1897 the per capita of bank resources was given as $78.29, whereas in 1910 it was $250.65, a significant indication of the rapidity of development that occurred in the decade and a half that followed the panic of 1893. In 1897 Colorado was second in the nation in the ratio of dividends to capital, reporting a ratio of 6.53 per cent. That this was not a temporary feature of Colorado banking development is indicated by the fact that in 1920 Pueblo reported the highest percentage earned on capital stock of any reserve city in the nation, 55 per cent. In

[28] *Report of the Colorado State Bank Commissioner, 1909*, 8.

second and third places were Birmingham, Alabama, with 39.77 per cent, and Atlanta, Georgia, with 38.84 per cent. The Denver banks did not languish for profitable investment, reporting that they had earned 27.86 per cent on their capital; and that the opportunities for investment were statewide is indicated by the fact that the Colorado banks as a whole ranked sixth among those of the states of the union with a reported earning on capital of 24.55 per cent.

On the basis of the number of deposit accounts per thousand of population Colorado ranked third among the states in 1920 with 320 accounts in comparison with the 393 accounts reported by Wyoming, 327 by Oregon, 319 by Utah, and 193 for the nation as a whole. In 1925 Colorado was second to Nebraska among the western states so far as the per capita of individual deposits was concerned. The figure for Colorado was $285.44 as compared with $369.13 for the nation as a whole.

If the scattered items just noted serve to indicate that Colorado banking had reached some degree of mature development by 1920, the special report made by all of the banks of the nation on April 28, 1909, in connection with the studies of the National Monetary Commission, reveals the extent to which Colorado had relied upon the national banking system. For purposes of comparison, only the data for the nine western states (North and South Dakota, Nebraska, Kansas, Montana, Wyoming, Colorado, New Mexico, and Oklahoma) will be used. So far as national banks were concerned Colorado supplied ten per cent of the number, twenty-one per cent of the total resources, fourteen per cent of the total capital, nearly twenty-four per cent of the individual deposits subject to check, and sixteen per cent of the national bank circulation that was outstanding. But in the field of the state banks Colorado supplied less than three per cent of the number, approximately three per cent of the total resources, two per cent of the capital, and less than three per cent of the individual deposits subject to check. It seems clear that the average state bank in Colorado was very much like the average state bank in the other western states. But with the national banks the case is quite different. Those in Colorado were larger, possessed larger total resources, and attracted a larger volume of individual's deposits subject to check.

It is reasonable to conclude from these percentages that the banking problems of Colorado were not the same as those of other western states. It is also fair to conclude that whatever the particular needs of Colorado may have been they could best be served through the national banking system. It is possible that the feature of the national system that made it particularly popular in Colorado was the requirement of regular reports and examinations which, in the minds of eastern investors and depositors, rendered national banks safer than the less regulated and not so carefully supervised state banks. Although it cannot be demonstrated completely, the circumstantial evidence points to the conclusion that it was the national banks rather than the state banks that provided the connecting link between eastern investors of capital and the Colorado enterprises in which they were interested.

The relationship between banking institutions and the primary economic activities of the state is the most significant criterion for

Clark, Gruber and Company Mint, Denver, 1860

singling out specific individuals and institutions for discussion. In Colorado two general features of this development are particularly important: the close connection between banking on the one hand and mining and railroad construction on the other and the development by certain individuals involved in these activities of bank chains. Because these two features are interwoven and interrelated no attempt will be made to separate them. Of the first it may be said that expensive transportation facilities capable of hauling large quantities of bulky machinery, food, fuel, and all of the accessories of living were essential to the success of mining enterprises. The unrestrained enthusiasm with which every additional unit of the Denver and Rio Grande Railway was greeted as it penetrated the remote corners of central and southern Colorado and more importantly the reasoned conclusions of competent citizens of remote towns that their future was dependent upon the railroad attest to the importance of transportation.

But the railroads could not be built without the use of outside capital and once built the whole impact of the completed task hit at once. Agricultural communities might evolve gradually over a period of years absorbing each advance in transportation more slowly and even if the boom collapsed the land remained to attract a new wave of investors. But in a mineral region there was no cushion to absorb either the impact of precipitate availability or the shock of sudden exhaustion of the principal resource. There is scarcely anything in the business world that is so final as a mining shaft that will no longer yield a profit. Likewise there is scarcely an industry that erects so many and so obvious monuments to its exploitative character. The mining promoter can rarely bury his mistakes; they are all too frequently in plain view of the rubber-necking tourist as well as the eastern investor who is failing to receive a dividend.

Some Important Denver Banks

Just as the banking institutions of England had one root in the shop of the goldsmith so the early banks of Colorado had one source in the office of the bullion buyer. The history of the private mint of Clark, Gruber and Company is well known. The firm originated in Leavenworth, Kansas, as a private banking house composed of Austin M. and Milton E. Clark, and E. H. Gruber. Becoming interested as gold buyers they entered the banking field in Denver and Central City, Colorado, and Salt Lake City, Utah.[29] In April, 1865, the firm furnished the nucleus of the First National Bank of Denver. Among the officers and stockholders of this institution, the first national bank organization in Colorado, were Jerome B. Chaffee, prominent political leader and actively associated with the mining industry; Henry J. Rogers; George T., A. M., and M. E. Clark; C. A. Cook, another resident of Leavenworth, who with his partner J. P. Sears came to Denver in 1859, established a wholesale provision house, became a gold buyer and eventually a banker; Eben Smith; and Bela M. Hughes.

The ramifications of the First National's banking connections throughout Colorado became quite complex. Two of the stockholders organized the private banking firm of George T. Clark in Georgetown. In 1867 David H. Moffat was made cashier and in 1880, following the retirement of Chaffee, became president of the First National. At various times in his career Moffat was a director and later president of the International Trust Company of Denver, an institution which united in its board of directors practically all of the outstanding bankers of Colorado, and president of state banks in Aspen, Victor, Hot Sulphur Springs, and Cripple Creek. The location of these banks plus his associations with Nicholas C. Creede and his large holdings in the Little Pittsburgh Consolidated Mining Company indicates the

29 Niehaus, *Development of Banking in Colorado,* 15 ff.

interest of Moffat in the mining development of the state. In addition, after 1884 he was president of the Denver and Rio Grande Railway Company. A few years earlier Moffat, with Charles B. Kountze and John Evans, had incorporated the Denver and New Orleans Railway. Later Moffat was instrumental in the promotion and construction of the Florence and Cripple Creek Railway and a large stockholder in the Denver Tramway Company. In 1902 Moffat organized the Denver, Northwestern and Pacific Railway, commonly known as the Moffat Road, with the object of developing the resources of northwestern Colorado and of giving Denver a direct route to the Pacific Coast.[30]

This last enterprise not only illustrates the close relationship between banking institutions and transportation developments, but it indicates conclusively that by the opening of the twentieth century the banking power of Colorado as mobilized in one of its most powerful institutions was not adequate to the demands of heavy financing. In a Senate debate in November, 1913, Charles S. Thomas reviewed the generally accepted version of Moffat's efforts to finance the Denver and Northwestern both in New York City and abroad. According to this account Moffat had invested his personal fortune of nearly ten million dollars in the project and was on the point several times of signing the formal contract for additional financial aid,

> When some mysterious and invisible influence always intercepted the arrangement about the time it was to be consummated. The Union Pacific Co. on the north and the Rio Grande and Gould interests on the south, through their banking connections all over the world, were the upper and nether millstones that ground the promoters of that enterprise to powder between them, in consequence of which the original promoter of the road, whose name it bears, beginning with an amount of wealth that would easily make him the wealthiest man in the state of Colorado ended in virtual bankruptcy.[31]

Beyond its importance as a feature of the history of the First National Bank of Denver and of Moffat's career as a Colorado financier, the story as told by Senator Thomas illustrates the control that outside banking groups exercised over the economic development of the state. The upper millstone of the story was the Standard Oil-controlled National City Bank of New York, which was represented on the Union Pacific directorate by James Stillman and Edward H. Harriman. The latter was also a director of the Colorado Fuel and Iron Company, a Rockefeller subsidiary. The nether millstone was the Morgan-controlled National Bank of Commerce, which in 1908 furnished two members of the directorate of the Atchison, Topeka, and Santa Fe, one to the Union Pacific, two to the Colorado Fuel and Iron Co., and in addition included George J. Gould, who was a director of the Colorado Midland Railway Company, and chairman of

[30] Fritz, Colorado, *The Centennial State,* 394-398.
[31] *Cong. Record,* 63 Cong., 1 Sess., 6021.

the board of directors of the Denver and Rio Grande Railway Company.

Another of the Denver banks that originated in an early day private banking firm is the Colorado National Bank. In November, 1862, Luther Kountze, a member of a banking family with so many connections in New York, Ohio, Nebraska, Wyoming, and Colorado that one newspaper called them the "Rothschilds of the West," arrived in Denver to establish a banking business. The Denver house was in charge of Luther Kountze until 1864 when a brother, Charles B. Kountze, and a brother-in-law, W. B. Berger, joined the firm. In 1866 the private bank whose major business had been buying gold and dealing in coin, exchange, and treasury notes became the Colorado National Bank. Although favorably known throughout the Territory and later the state, the Colorado National apparently did not become the center of a group of banks in Colorado.[32]

A newer trend in banking activities and connections is reflected in the banking chain established by Gordon Jones of Denver. The banks included in the chain in 1913 were The Delta National Bank, First National Banks of Hotchkiss, Hugo, Littleton, Elizabeth State Bank of Elizabeth, Colorado and Elbert County Bank, Elbert, Colorado, later Colorado Bank & Trust Company at Delta and Pierce State Bank at Pierce, Colorado. The majority stock of each of these banks was owned by a corporation controlled by Gordon Jones, who also owned a substantial interest in the United States National Bank of Denver.

At the same time, Jones organized the Colorado Cattle Loan Company which made loans on livestock in country districts where he controlled the country banks. These loans were made usually for 180 days and were discounted by a New York bank at a rate of interest from $\frac{1}{2}$ to $\frac{3}{4}$ of that borne by the note of the livestock producer. This business was very profitable and about 1916 The United States National Bank itself established a Livestock Loan Department and commenced making direct loans to livestock men as well as rediscounting this kind of paper for all their country bank correspondents.

Although there is little information concerning the career of Gordon Jones he seems to have played a role of considerable importance in the banking history of Colorado and of the nation. He had been engaged in the banking business in Missouri, beginning in 1887, and for a number of years prior to coming to Colorado had been a bank examiner in that state. He was the principal author of Colorado's banking law of 1907. In 1912 he represented Colorado on the American commission to a European conference on banking and monetary problems. At that conference he was honored with a position of responsibility on the most important committee. Returning to the United States he took an active part in preparing the program for the convention of country bankers that met in Boston, in October,

[32] The Pueblo *Chieftain,* February 18, and August 18, 1869, recommended that its readers patronize the Colorado National.

1913, and became the temporary chairman of the convention as well as a member of a small committee that was delegated to present the views of the convention before the Committee on Banking and Finance of the United States Senate. Following the establishment of the Federal Reserve system Jones took an active part in launching the tenth district.[33]

Apparently the principal business of the Jones banks was the making of agricultural and livestock loans. The loans made by the country banks were for considerable periods of time. This long term paper was taken by the United States National Bank in Denver and made the basis for a ninety day loan to the smaller bank. Then the ninety day paper was rediscounted with a reserve bank. Thus the city bank member of the chain was able to make a portion of its credit available to the customers of the country banks in the group. Information derived from the reports of the Comptroller of the Currency indicates that the business of the chain was conducted very conservatively. This impression is confirmed by a statement made by Jones to the Senate Committee to the effect that in the Panic of 1907 the United States National Bank of Denver started with a forty per cent reserve and ended with a fifty-two per cent reserve, simply by limiting loans and renewals to local customers and regular correspondents. It seemed regular practice for the bank to keep some forty-five per cent of its deposits as a reserve either in the bank or with reserve agents and correspondents in New York, Chicago, St. Louis, Kansas City, and San Francisco.

BANKING IN COLORADO SPRINGS

In addition to Denver there are at least two other cities that can claim the distinction of being important financial centers in Colorado: Pueblo and Colorado Springs. The latter has been known particularly as the headquarters of a great many mining companies, the focal point for the investment of much outside capital, and for its association with a large number of railway enterprises.[34] The banking institution in the city with probably the most far reaching and complex ramifications is the First National Bank, including the several banks that were merged with it during its history.[35] The most important of these was the El Paso County Bank founded in October, 1873, as a successor to the W. B. Young Banking Company that had been forced to liquidate. The partner holding the majority interest as well as the president and cashier was William S. Jackson, Sr., who was at the time of the founding of the bank secretary-treasurer of the Denver and Rio Grande Railway Company and was later to serve

[33] *Hearings Before the Committee on Banking and Currency on H.R. 6837 (S. 2639), Senate Doc. No. 232,* 3 volumes (Washington: Government Printing Office, 1913), III, 2247, 2248, 2259-2281. Hurshel E. Underhill, *The Kansas City Federal Reserve District* (Spaulding Moss Co.: Boston, 1941), 50-51. 61, 64.

[34] Fuller, *op. cit.,* 248-250.

[35] The best account of banking in Colorado Springs is the unpublished manuscript of Justice William S. Jackson, "Banking in Colorado Springs."

as receiver of it and as its president. As receiver Jackson was in constant touch with the English, Dutch, and Scotch bondholders of the company and with the New York bankers who represented them. The occasion for much of the correspondence was the financing of new lines in order to eliminate the threatened competition of the Union Pacific and Colorado Midland.[36] Jackson took part in the founding of the Denver National Bank in 1884, was on the first board of directors and continued as a director for twenty-seven years. He also was one of the incorporators and on the first board of directors of the International Trust Company of Denver in 1891.

The El Paso County Bank became a national bank in 1900 and continued as an independent institution until it was consolidated with the First National Bank in 1916. The First National in its own right was nearly as old as the El Paso Bank. It was founded in 1874 by B. F. Crowell, Irving Howbert, H. A. McIntyre, S. M. Saunders, C. B. Greenough, G. A. Stewart, W. B. Young, and F. L. Martin. After Howbert became one of the leading officers of the bank in 1878 it began to grow more rapidly and to participate more widely in the business development of the state. Several of its officers and directors became stockholders in the International Trust Company of Denver. Howbert was instrumental in the construction of the Colorado Springs and Cripple Creek Shortline Railway. J. J. Hagerman, president of the bank in 1891, had been a president of the Colorado Midland Railway Company. A. E. Carlton, who was financially interested in the First National, was an active participant in the mining developments in the Cripple Creek-Victor area, in the reduction mills at Colorado City, and was president of at least two other national banks, the First National of Canon City, and the First National of Cripple Creek. Spencer Penrose and Eugene P. Shove, leaders in the development of low grade porphyry copper companies, were also directors of this bank.

The banking development of Colorado Springs illustrates both the diversity of financial activity in the state and the contribution of the smaller cities to the growth of Denver as the financial center of the region. The Colorado Springs National Bank, founded in 1907, has been conspicuous in the financing of mercantile, livestock, and agricultural activities. This has been especially true under the leadership of W. R. Armstrong and O. E. Hemenway. In an entirely different field H. A. McIntire, after participating in the organization of the First National Bank of Colorado Springs, followed the mineral frontier, opening banking houses in the mining towns of the mountains. Sometime in 1875 he became the proprietor of a banking house in Rosita which he committed to the care of H. T. Blake, who, it was said, "can run a bank or keep a hotel with equal facility." The next year McIntire resigned the presidency of the First National Bank of

---

36 William S. Jackson, "Railroad Conflicts in Colorado in the Eighties," *Colorado Magazine,* XXIII (1946), 3-28; "The Record *vs.* Reminiscence" by the same author in *The Westerners Brandbook, 1945,* edited by Herbert O. Brayer, (Denver: Bradford-Robinson Printing Co., 1946), 55-91.

Colorado Springs in order to make his home in Lake City, where the Hinsdale County Bank of which he was one of the founders was being reorganized as the First National Bank of Lake City. It was reported that the stockholders of the Lake City bank were men of great wealth, that increases in the paid-up capital would keep pace with the enlarged demands for money, and that the men who founded the bank were also the incorporators of the San Juan Railway Company, with a capital stock of $1,500,000. That the ramifications of McIntire's banking interests were far reaching and not too sound may be concluded from the fact that by April, 1878, he was debtor to his banks for considerable sums and had borrowed largely in Del Norte and Denver on the basis of his bank stock.[37]

The banking business launched in Colorado Springs in August, 1873, by James McFerran, formerly of Chillicothe, Missouri, followed somewhat the same pattern, but was operated more soundly. The Peoples' Bank of Colorado Springs that was founded by McFerran was a private banking enterprise which conducted a general banking business. Following the mineral discoveries in and around Leadville, McFerran, with two other citizens of Colorado Springs, organized the Miners Exchange Bank of Leadville. In 1887 the Peoples' Bank was sold to the El Paso County Bank, but before the sale took place two sons-in-law of McFerran, who were to become active in the banking life of Colorado, had received their training. One of them, George W. Trimble, participated in 1884 in the establishment of the Denver National Bank. The second, A. V. Hunter, became president of the First National Bank of Denver in 1911, following the death of David H. Moffat.[38]

PUEBLO BANKS

Pueblo was the point of origin of at least two banking chains that had extensive connections throughout the state of Colorado. Both of them had their origin in the banking house established by John A. and Mahlon D. Thatcher in January, 1871, with Jeff Raynolds in charge. Originally the Thatcher Brothers had operated a mercantile firm in Pueblo, but the need for banking facilities at some place nearer than Denver prompted them to establish the bank which in June, 1871, was incorporated as the First National Bank of Pueblo. The Thatcher banking chain included at one time or another directorships in two Denver banks: the First National, and the International Trust Company; the presidency of six national banks: The First Nationals of Pueblo, Florence, Rocky Ford, Silverton, and Trinidad, and the Montrose National Bank of Montrose; and the presidency of at least five state banks: the Minnequa Bank of Pueblo, the Pueblo Savings Bank, the Bent County Bank of Las Animas, the Miners and Merchants Bank of Lake City, and the Miners and Merchants Bank

[37] Colorado Springs *Gazette,* September 26, 1874, November 13, 1875, April 11, 1877, and April 13, 1878.

[38] Colorado Springs *Gazette,* April 26, July 19, and August 2, 1873; Jackson, "Banking in Colorado Springs," 1, *et passim.*

of Ouray. The location of these banks suggests a distribution of interest between the mining activities of the mountains and the farming and livestock activities of the Arkansas Valley. That Mahlon D. Thatcher was also interested in railway construction is indicated by his close connection with the Pueblo and Arkansas Railway Company in 1878, and later with the Atchison, Topeka, and Santa Fe.

The other banking chain that originated in the Thatcher Bank in 1871 was that of the Raynolds Brothers. In November, 1874, Jefferson and F. A. Raynolds purchased the Stockgrowers Bank of Pueblo from O. H. P. Baxter, Henry W. Cresswell, and Charles Goodnight. At that time Jefferson Raynolds was the manager of the Stockgrowers Bank and F. A. Raynolds was the proprietor of the Fremont County Bank of Canon City. In December, 1874, Charles B. Lamborn, president of the Central Colorado Improvement Company, actively interested in the Denver and Rio Grande Railway Company, and secretary-treasurer of the South Pueblo Flouring Mill Company, joined the Raynolds Brothers in their banking enterprises. For a time at least the banks were known as Raynolds, Lamborn, and Company. F. A. Raynolds proved to be the most active member of the firm. In rapid succession he became president of the Fremont County Bank of Canon City, established a bank at Rosita and assumed the presidency of it in 1876, became the silent partner in the banking firm of Zollars, Eshelman and Company of Leadville in 1878, and the president of the bank when it nationalized as the First National Bank of Leadville in 1879, and in the same year established the Custer County Bank at Silver Cliff. In 1880 and 1881 banks were established by F. A. Raynolds in Buena Vista, Alpine, and Saguache. A biography written in 1881 asserts that he was the youngest national bank president in the United States at that time and that a majority of the banking business of the state, exclusive of Denver, was transacted through his chain of banks. Although F. A. Raynolds was an officer of the Canon City and San Juan Railway Company, the dominant reason for the founding of the banks seems to have been the demand for banking facilities arising out of new discoveries of gold and silver.[39]

It is possible to cite a great many other illustrations of the close relationship that existed between the banking interests of Colorado and the building of its railroad system, the exploitation of its mineral resources, and the development of its agricultural industry. The list of examples would include the banks founded by J. B. Wheeler in Manitou, Colorado City, and Aspen; the Buckingham banks in Greeley, Longmont, and Boulder founded by Charles G. and W. A. Buckingham during the period 1874-1877; the active participation of John Evans in the affairs of the Denver and South Park Railway and later in the Denver, Gulf, and New Orleans; the election of H. A. W. Tabor to the presidency of the First National Bank of

[39] B. F. Rockafellow, "History of Fremont County," in *History of the Arkansas Valley* (Chicago: O. L. Baskin and Co., 1881), 670-671.

Leadville; the interest of M. A. Lowe of the Chicago and Rock Island Railway in the formation of the Exchange National Bank of Colorado Springs; and the interest of O. H. P. Baxter in the irrigation development of the state. Because of the scarcity of direct information it is possible that many of the most significant relationships have not been mentioned, but the ones referred to are sufficiently important to justify the conclusion that the bankers of Colorado provided much of the business leadership of the state during its period of rapid growth and development.

Laws Relating to Banking

Another index to the growing maturity of the banking structure of a state is the increasing interest which political leaders and agencies of the state take in the functioning of the banks individually and as a group. This interest usually takes one of two forms: increasing rules and regulations with agencies provided to enforce them; and public discussions of banking problems by political leaders, editors, and interested citizens. Perhaps it is because of the very close relation to the welfare of the people whom they serve that almost everyone feels that banks are vested with such a degree of public interest that government is under obligation to charter them, supervise and regulate them, and terminate them if need be. For the same reason periodic reports are required of them, meagre though they may be in revealing the true character of the bank to its patrons. Moreover, banks are required to open their books to examiners to such a degree and to conduct their business so constantly in the eye of the government that it is almost safe to conclude that they are viewed as being public utilities rather than private enterprises.

During the Territorial period, legislation enacted in 1868 and modified in 1870 gave legal sanction to the formation of banks. The free banking law of Colorado was enacted in March, 1877, by the first state legislature. It provided a means by which banking firms could be organized without the necessity of securing specific authorization from the legislature. The provisions of the law were similar to those of other states. The most glaring defect was the failure to provide for adequate supervision and inspection. Except for legislation relating to the liability of stockholders and limiting the amount of a bank's funds that could be loaned to a single borrower, no important changes were made until 1907.

In 1893 Governor Davis H. Waite proposed an improved form of bank inspection, but it was not until fourteen years and two panics later that the necessary legislation was enacted. The banking law of 1907, written to a considerable extent by Gordon Jones, established the office of state bank commissioner and provided for the closer supervision of the state banks of Colorado.[40]   In spite of the obvious merits of the law it did not go far in the matter of supplying personnel for thorough examinations nor did it require that adequate information be disclosed to the public. A rigid requirement of secrecy renders the information collected by the state bank commissioner of little value to the historian.

Although the reports of the state bank commissioner refer on many occasions to the need for additional legislation the changes since 1907 have not been many. Early in 1909 an attempt was made to pass a carefully drawn state guaranty law. Because of the opposition of the Colorado Bankers' Association an individual guaranty law was substituted for the general measure. The intent of the new proposition was to require that each bank set aside one per cent of its deposits until a ten per cent fund had been accumulated and deposited with the state treasurer. This fund was to be used on a *pro rata* basis for the benefit of the unsecured depositors in the bank in event of failure. Although many sound arguments were marshalled on behalf of the proposal it failed of adoption in the legislature.[41] Sounder requirements with respect to incorporation, the bonding of all employees who have the care, custody, or control of funds, reserves against deposits, and minimum capitalization limits were enacted into law in 1911, 1913, 1927, and 1929. In the *Fourteenth Annual Report of the State Bank Commissioner* (1920) Grant McFerson commented that the National Association of Supervisors of State Banks considered the Colorado bank law "workable, and in some points superior to that of many other states."[42]

BANKING VIEWS OF POLITICAL LEADERS

If eruption on the journalistic and political levels is some indication of popular reaction and opinion, then it must be concluded that the people of Colorado did not become critically aware of their banking agencies and institutions until after the panic of 1893. If the newspapers that the writer has seen are a fair sample banking questions were discussed very infrequently in the press of the state. The record of Colorado's representatives and senators is equally meagre prior to 1893. It is possible that preoccupation with the silver question absorbed the time and attention that otherwise would have been invested in discussions of banking. On the general monetary ques-

---

[40] Niehaus, *op. cit.,* 43-46; Appendix A of the study by Professor Niehaus contains a copy of the law of November 7, 1861, which incorporated the Bank of Colorado, the general banking law of March 14, 1877, and the law of April 13, 1907. The book also contains convenient summaries of the changes that have been made in the banking laws of Colorado. *The Digest of State Banking Statutes* issued by the United States National Monetary Commission, *Senate Doc.* No. 353, 61 Cong., 2 Sess., 83-96, briefs the several laws enacted prior to 1910 and provides comparative tables. An interesting feature of the National Monetary Commission was the presence of two men from Colorado on it, Henry M. Teller, and Robert W. Bonynge. Texas was the only other state to be similarly represented.

[41] George E. Barnett, *State Banks and Trust Companies Since the Passage of the National Bank Act,* National Monetary Commission Report, *Senate Doc.* No. 659, 61 Cong., 3 Sess., 327-329.

[42] Page 17.

tion there seems to have been almost complete agreement among the political leaders of the state on two general principles: the supply of circulating currency was inadequate and the federal government, not the banks of the nation, should control the volume of currency. Thus on January 7, 1886, while discussing the silver question Representative George G. Symes remarked that he had little but praise for the national banks. "They form," he said, "the best banking system and the best banks of issue we have ever had in this country, but they should not be allowed to control the financial policy of the government."[43] A few months later in almost identical words Senator Thomas M. Bowen praised the banking system of the country for furnishing the best bank currency that the nation had ever had and "next to silver and gold coins and United States Notes the best we can ever hope for." But he warned of one fatal defect—the power wielded by the banks to regulate the volume of money.[44]

But the success of the Populist Party in 1892 brought an entirely different type of person into Congress to represent the state. The speeches of John Bell are characterized by frequent references to the banks in connection with his remarks on the silver question. The West was debt-ridden and oppressed for lack of sufficient currency. The people of Colorado were paying two dollars in value to the East for every dollar that they had borrowed. The depositors in savings banks belonged to the sloths and dolts of the country because they would not invest their savings in business activities. In the same speech in commenting on the banks, Bell said,

> The curse of our present system is found in the domination of the banks. * * * We have too many banks now. There are in the country two or three banks in every crossroad town. This is because of the enormous profits in banking."[45]

At the next session of Congress Bell expressed violent opposition to a bill which proposed to repeal the ten per cent tax on state banknotes. It was an effort, he said, to replace gold and silver with bank currency and to delegate to banks the exclusive right to issue and control the currency of the country. It was a "herculean effort on the part of the bank power to crown with shining glory the aspirations of the banking world to secure the alliance of this republic with the European banking oligarchy."[46] On later occasions Bell charged that New York bankers had conspired to produce the panic of 1893 in order to force the repeal of the Sherman act,[47] and that financial bills in Congress were "fathered by the banks, made by the banks, and for the banks, and for the banks alone."[48] In December, 1899, he

43 *Cong. Record,* 49 Cong., 1 Sess., XVII, 796.
44 *Ibid.,* 2171.
45 *Ibid.,* 53 Cong., 2 Sess., XXVI, 840-841.
46 *Ibid.,* 53 Cong., 3 Sess., XXVII, 43-44.
47 *Ibid.,* 54 Cong., 2 Sess., XXIX, 2284.
48 *Ibid.,* 56 Cong., 1 Sess., XXXIII, 589.

objected to having a banker occupying the position as head of the
Treasury Department; he protested giving the banks bonds at par
when they were worth a premium in the market, and against allowing
banks to use government deposits without paying interest on them.
He argued that the control of the volume of currency should be
vested in the government and not in the banks.[49]   To Bell as late as
1902 this last point was the vital one.   He asserted that it had been
the nub of the debate over silver throughout the eighteen-nineties.
After remarking that he had never discussed "the silver question on
the stump or anywhere else," he continued,

> We all realized that the point at issue was not whether you
> should have silver, or gold, or paper. The issue was shall we
> have an abundance of Government money issued and con-
> trolled by the Government for all the people or bank paper
> controlled by the banks for the banks. * * * The whole
> philosophy of the silver question is that gold, silver, and
> paper issued by the Government is safer than mere bank
> promises to pay. * * * The question at issue still is whether
> you should have money issued by the Government in full
> and necessary quantity or whether you should leave it to the
> banks of the country to issue the currency and contract it or
> expand it at will.[50]

To some degree at least Congressman Bell reflected the thinking
of the people who favored the free coinage of silver and the issue of
an abundance of government currency.   The criticism of the banks
is strong evidence of the important role that banks were coming to
play in the economic life of Colorado.   The confidence that men acting
through the channels of government could be trusted to do what men
acting through the channels of business could not be trusted to do
illustrates a naiveté which Bell shared not only with the Populists
and Progressives of his day, but with the progressives and liberals
of a later generation.

The role of Senator Henry M. Teller in the silver controversy
has been analyzed and described in considerable detail in a comparatively recent biography,[51] but very little seems to be known concerning his attitude toward banking agencies either state or national.
During the struggle over the repeal of the Sherman Silver Purchase
Act in 1893, he digressed momentarily to assert that he had always
voted against the continuation of national banks as banks of issue.
He expressed the point briefly and directly, "I believe as banks of
deposit they have had some value, but as banks of issue none.''[52]
He was critical of the failure of eastern banks to honor the drafts of

[49] *Ibid.,* 590-591; 1792-1794.
[50] *Ibid.,* 57 Cong., 1 Sess., XXXV, 3477-3483.
[51] Elmer Ellis, *Henry Moore Teller, Defender of the West.* (Caldwell, Idaho: Caxton Printers, 1941), chs. XIII, XIX and XXI.
[52] *Cong. Record,* 53 Cong., 1 Sess., XXV, 1021.

their western correspondents who in turn had to close their doors because they could not draw money that was rightfully theirs. But then in words that closely resembled those of John Bell, he said,

> I am not moved against the national banks by prejudice or passion. I hold that banks properly conducted are helpful agencies of commerce and business. Whenever banks confine themselves exclusively and wholly to legitimate banking business, they may become valuable agents, I repeat, of commerce and trade; but when they attempt as they have done on more than one occasion, to dictate the policy to be pursued in public affairs, they have been absolute failures every time.[53]

So far as the present writer is informed Senator Teller did not discuss banking problems in the Senate again until fifteen years had elapsed. But upon the central issue his attitude remained the same: "The furnishing of money by the government to its people is not a banking business. It is an exercise of sovereign power, just as the coining of gold and silver." But the nation, he continued, had turned the control of money over to the banks on the theory that Congress could not be trusted. In effect, he commented, "What we have said we were unable to do we have turned over to the banks to do."[54]

Earlier in the same session when a resolution to investigate the deposit of funds in New York banks during the panic of 1907 was under consideration, Senator Teller expressed a much milder view toward the large banks of the East than he had in 1893. He asserted that the trouble in 1907 was all in New York; that Denver banks had $11,000,000 on deposit in New York banks that they could not get. But it was their own fault. They could have deposited their funds in St. Louis or Chicago banks. He admitted that the deposit of bank funds in New York caused over-loaning and over-trading, but it was precisely because the New York banks needed help that he thought the Secretary of the Treasury was wise in helping them and thus indirectly help the people of the West who were just as much interested in the integrity of New York banks as the people of New York. And then as if to provide an obituary notice for the banking system, he said,

> Mr. President, I think we have a vicious system of finance. I expect it will continue. I have no idea that there will be any change in it for years to come. It is a system which has been condemned by the wisest financiers of the world. It has been condemned in this country by men who have given thought and attention to it. Yet we are likely to

---

53 *Ibid.*, 1066.
54 *Ibid.*, 60 Cong., 1 Sess., XLII, 2029-2030.

go on in the same way and if we do we shall have the same trouble.[55]

The period when Colorado leaders, political and financial, exerted the greatest influence upon national banking legislation began in 1913 when John F. Shafroth, former governor and largely responsible for major improvements in Colorado's banking code, and Charles S. Thomas, also a former governor, represented the state in the Senate and participated actively in the establishment of the federal reserve system. The former as a member of the Senate Committee on Banking and Finance occupied a strategic position both in the preliminary hearings and in the Senate debate that fruited in the passage of the federal reserve act. His views on banking and currency reflect the fact that in four decades of statehood Colorado had developed a considerable degree of financial maturity. While retaining his devotion to the cause of the free coinage of silver and avowing that he had no apologies to make for having supported silver in 1896 when the country needed more currency, he was able at the same time to declare his belief that as a result of the careful thought that had gone into banking legislation there had been "consummated the most perfect banking system so far as individual banks are concerned that the world has ever known."[56] In view of his ardent defense of the federal reserve system and of his expressed hope that all state banks would come into it, it is probable that he viewed the system as the capstone of the nation's banking structure. There is considerable reason to believe that the feature of the federal reserve system that Shafroth regarded as most commendable was the possibility of expanding the circulating medium whenever business conditions required it. Although both Shafroth and Thomas supported the federal reserve legislation and played important roles in securing its enactment they continued to believe that the free coinage of silver would have been a sounder solution and would have eliminated the necessity for so much legislation on banking.[57]

In one of the most amazing demonstrations of political consistency on the part of the leaders of a party John A. Martin and to a lesser extent Alva Adams chose to stand on the same ground in 1933 and 1934 that Shafroth and Thomas had stood on in 1913, and Bell and Teller had occupied in 1893. As one reads the speeches delivered by Martin over national radio chains or in the House of Representatives he feels that forty years of history have been turned back and the great debate on silver is again echoing in the halls of Congress. The same references to the historic role of silver as a monetary metal; the same comparisons of production of silver with that of gold. India, China, and the countries of South America; the crime of 1873; the plot of the national bankers to force the repeal of the Sherman act by creating an artificial stringency; the bitter denuncia-

[55] Ibid., 1025. In connection with the debate Teller stated that he was interested in banks, "Not financially to any extent, but as an attorney in several banks." Ibid., 1026.

[56] Ibid., 63 Cong., 2 Sess., LI, 14,962; 14,966.

[57] Ibid., LI, 1126.

tion of Wall Street; and the principal actors — Seyd, Cleveland, Carlisle, McKinley, Bryan, and Bland, all appear in their appointed places in the pageant. Colorado in sixty years had become a mature state; Denver had become the financial center of an entire region; silver was no longer the chief industry of the state; sixty years of change and development, but the gold standard was still the root of all evil. The depression, Martin argued, was largely due to a money famine. In chagrin he resigned from an important committee assignment because his colleagues refused to adopt his resolution directing the American delegation to the London Economic Conference to work for the international remonetization of silver at the old ratio of sixteen to one.[58]

DENVER AND THE DISTRICT FEDERAL RESERVE BANK

The final and probably the most important test of the degree to which the financial system of a state, or more specifically in the case of Colorado, the banking power of Denver, has reached a mature stage of development is the extent to which it can meet the financial demands not only of the immediate community, but of the tributary area which surrounds it.[59] As early as 1876 the delegate to Congress from Colorado, Thomas M. Patterson, had claimed for Denver a unique position in the Rocky Mountain region. He said,

> The topographical and geographical situation of Denver, its centrality to the mining sections of the Rocky Mountain region with reference to its railroad system, developed, completed, and under construction, establish the fact that the mint at Denver is an economical and essential element in the system proposed by the bill. * * * Arizona and New Mexico, Wyoming and Montana, and Utah are by nature and by the skill and energy of man have become tributary to it in all their mining interests. * * * Denver is the true entrepot of all this section.[60]

Professor Fuller in his analysis of the Colorado character has concluded that the objective of Coloradans during the period to 1893 was a great intra-continental community tied to the rest of the nation by railroads, and founded upon mineral and agricultural resources with Denver as the metropolitan center for 500,000 square miles of western country.[61]

The adoption of the federal reserve system in 1913 and the effort made by the business leaders of Denver to secure one of the

[58] *Ibid.,* 73 Cong., 1 Sess., LXXVII, 2749-2752; 5902-5904; 73 Cong., 2 Sess., LXXVIII, 4179-4181; 10,124-10,130.

[59] Mildred L. Hartsough, *The Development of the Twin Cities (Minneapolis and St. Paul) As a Metropolitan Market* contains an excellent analysis of the importance of the financial function as a test of metropolitan development. Chapters VI and VII are particularly helpful.

[60] *Cong. Record,* 44 Cong., 1 Sess., IV, 4985.

[61] Fuller, *op. cit.,* 6.

district banks affords the most convenient point from which to survey the banking progress of Colorado during the first half century of its banking history. The decentralization of banking reserves plus the possibility of securing additional currency by presenting commercial paper to the federal reserve bank of the district were not inconsistent with the objectives of Coloradans who had for several decades been asking for some method of expanding the currency supply of the nation. Moreover several prominent political and financial leaders of Colorado had contributed largely to the movement that fruited in the establishment of the federal reserve system. Charles MacA. Willcox was one of the officials of the National Citizens League for the Promotion of Sound Banking which devoted itself to winning popular support for the Aldrich bill. Robert Bonynge, member of Congress from Colorado, 1903-1909, and also a member of the National Monetary Commission, was active in the work of the League in Colorado. Another organization interested in changes in the monetary system of the nation, but from quite a different point of view was the United States Monetary League. Among its active members in Colorado were J. N. Stephens, Moses Hallett, Arthur E. Pierce, James A. Best, and D. A. Rankin, all of Denver; Morton Alexander of Arvada; H. R. Pendery, of Leadville; and E. E. T. Hagen, of Holyoke. Resolutions of the organization, read into the *Congressional Record* on March 14, 1908, by C. W. Hamlin, of Missouri, were condemnatory in violent language of pending currency bills, contained many references to the national bank trust, and favored gold, silver, and greenbacks as the circulating medium of the nation.[62]

With the passage of the federal reserve act accomplished the next task was the designation of from eight to twelve cities as the sites of federal reserve banks. A Reserve Bank Organization Committee composed of the Secretary of the Treasury, the Secretary of Agriculture, and the Comptroller of the Currency was given the responsibility of making the selections. Of the cities within the area that was later to comprise the Tenth Federal Reserve District four cities filed briefs in support of their claims: Denver, Omaha, Lincoln, and Kansas City, Missouri. The committee that presented the argument on behalf of Denver was composed of Gordon Jones, chairman, A. V. Hunter, George B. Berger, Joseph A. Thatcher, T. A. Cosgriff, W. T. Ravenscroft, Frank A. Bancroft, Richard H. Malone, Fred P. Johnson, Carl A. Johnson, Morrison Shafroth, and Charles A. Haughwout.

The brief of this committee was based upon the assumption that there would be only eight federal reserve banks instead of twelve. It was also assumed by the committee that seven of these had been located: New York City, Chicago, Boston, St. Louis, New Orleans, San Francisco, and the seventh within a triangle formed by a line drawn from Atlanta to Philadelphia, thence to Cincinnati, and back to Atlanta. Thus the problem of the Denver committee was not

---

[62] 60 Cong., 1 Sess., XLII, 3331.

merely that of competing with Omaha, Lincoln, and Kansas City. Denver was in competition with every large financial center of the nation that had not yet received a reserve bank. Within the region she was in competition with every would-be reserve bank city from Dallas and Ft. Worth on the south to Minneapolis and St. Paul on the north and between the St. Louis-Chicago line on the east and San Francisco's territory on the west. The committee speaking on behalf of Denver was striving to make their city the financial metropolis of a third of the nation's area.

The boundaries fixed by the Denver committee were to be approximately the 100° on the east and the eastern boundary of Washington, Oregon, and Nevada on the West. The region between these lines, it was asserted, possessed unique characteristics. It was thinly populated. The kinds of crops and methods of farming were different. The customary practices of business were not the same. The changes in time zones coincided approximately with the proposed boundaries of the district. In anticipation of the claims of other cities the committee pointed out that St. Paul and Minneapolis belonged logically together with Omaha in the Chicago district; that Kansas City was tied to St. Louis, and that Ft. Worth and Dallas could best be served from New Orleans. None of these cities, it was argued, should be excluded from its proper district in order to give it the remaining reserve bank, particularly since such a course would deprive,

> this vast and distinctive Rocky Mountain Region of a Federal Reserve Bank and force it to do business with a Federal Reserve Bank from 600 to 1,000 miles away, and necessarily out of touch with, and not responsive to, the peculiar and distinctive needs of this vast Rocky Mountain region.[63]

From the point of view of the Denver Committee it was logical to conclude that this region, some 700 miles in width and 1,200 miles from north to south whose geographical center is Denver, could best be served by locating a federal reserve bank in Denver. Attention was called to the fact that Denver was the greatest railway terminal between the Missouri River and the Pacific Ocean, being served by twelve railroads and one hundred and forty-eight passenger trains each day leaving only a small part of the proposed district more than fifteen hours distant; it was an administrative center and fiscal headquarters of the Western Union Company and of the Mountain States Telephone and Telegraph Company; it was a recognized western center of fire insurance companies; the headquarters of the principal sugar beet companies of the country; the favorite diversion point for the shipment of California fruits and vegetables to eastern markets, as well as the shipping point for locally produced alfalfa hay, potatoes, and melons, all requiring financial arrangements by Denver

---

[63] "Briefs of the Denver Chamber of Commerce and Denver Clearing House Association," *Location of Reserve Districts in the United States, Senate Doc.* No. 485, 63 Cong., 2 Sess., 129-130.

banks. Denver was the center of the grain business of the proposed district which amounted annually to $30,000,000, and rested on the control by Denver firms of the principal elevators in Colorado, Utah, and Idaho, and of the grain trade of western Kansas and Nebraska. It was a strategic point for the directing and financing of the movement of cattle from south to north—an activity that brought $28,000,000 worth of cattle to the Denver market in 1913. The loca-

United States Mint, Denver

tion of a branch mint and of a sub-treasury in Denver was an important factor in the plea of the committee. Finally it was pointed out that the banks in the proposed district regularly carried in the six Denver Clearing House banks an average aggregate balance of $16,780,000; that the volume of cash collections sent by the Denver Clearing House banks in 1913 to other banks in the proposed district amounted to $287,620,000; and that the out-of-town cash business handled in 1913 by the Denver Clearing House banks for their customer banks totalled $289,500,000.[64]

In a careful study of the formation of the Tenth Federal Reserve District it has been pointed out that three factors were of paramount importance in influencing the Organization Committee to select Kansas City, Missouri, as the site of the district federal reserve bank rather than Denver. These factors were:

[64] *Ibid.*, 131-142.

(1) adequate ability and sufficient resources for the organization of a strong bank; (2) ease of access from the chief points within the district to permit the prompt transmission of funds and discount applications; and (3) commercial and banking relations already established and capable of successful organization.[65]

Clearly Denver could not meet these tests to the same extent as Kansas City. Moreover it was doubtful if the member banks in the proposed Denver district could have raised the minimum capital requirements for a federal reserve bank. Indeed the Denver Committee attempted to discount this handicap in advance by filing a list of private subscribers who had agreed to make up the anticipated deficiency. Of considerable importance was the fact that of the banks of the proposed Denver district those located in western Texas, Kansas, and Nebraska, protested unanimously against the location of the reserve bank in Denver. Idaho banks preferred a western connection either at Portland or San Francisco; Montana banks preferred Minneapolis or Chicago; while those in Arizona preferred San Francisco. Texas banks wanted the reserve bank located in a Texas city or in Kansas City or St. Louis. Curiously enough the banks of New Mexico seemed to prefer Lincoln or Omaha to Denver. In the poll of the banks of the proposed Denver district Denver received 136 first place votes, 112 of them from Colorado and 12 from Wyoming. Of the Colorado banks 37 gave Kansas City as a second choice and 26 selected Omaha. Kansas City was clearly the dominant financial center of the region and was awarded a federal reserve bank to serve a district which included the entire State of Colorado.[66]

If Denver did not win the reserve bank contest the presentation of her claim by the committee served to call attention to the fact that by 1913 she had become a financial center of considerable importance. Moreover Denver did win substantial consolation prizes. The Denver National Bank was one of five banks chosen to execute the organization certificate of the Federal Reserve Bank of Kansas City. Soon after the decision with respect to the location of the principal bank of the district had been reached Denver in company with three other cities asked for branches. This application was viewed favorably and as a result the Denver Branch, Federal Reserve Bank of Kansas City, was officially opened in 1916 to serve the member banks of Colorado and New Mexico. The branch operates in much the same fashion as the parent bank, having a similar organization and possessing the same banking powers, subject of course to the rules and controls set up by the parent bank. In addition, the bankers of Denver have played an important role in directing the affairs of the Federal Reserve Bank of Kansas City. Gordon Jones was chosen as a member

---

[65] Underhill, *Kansas City Federal Reserve District,* 54.

[66] *Ibid.,* 54-55. As early as February 24, 1870, the Pueblo *Chieftain,* had referred to Kansas City as the commercial metropolis of the entire region between the Missouri and the mountains.

of the first Board of Directors. In the period 1914-1938 six other Denver men have been elected to the directorate, a number exceeded only by Kansas City, which during the same period furnished a total of ten directors.

From the first relatively small and simply operated private banks that had their origin in the early period of the mining rush the banks of Colorado have developed into an increasingly important feature of the financial system of the region and nation. They have come together in their own organizations to promote or to facilitate their own interests and activities: clearing houses and the Colorado Bankers Association. They have been subjected to an increasing amount of competition not only from building and loan associations, finance companies, small loan brokers, and credit unions, but also from federally sponsored and financed corporations operating in the fields of agriculture, housing, and industry. To meet competition and to win new customers many banks have installed personal loan departments with attractive quarters and furnishings. Service charges have become a regular feature of the operation of Colorado banks. The banks of the state have participated creditably in the financing of three major wars and have survived the shock of severe panics and the depression periods that followed them. Most of the private banks have incorporated either under state or national charters. The weaker banks were eliminated during the 1920s and 1930s either through failure or by consolidation with other banks. The fact that the number of banks has remained practically the same during the period 1937-1940 suggests the conclusion that after approximately eighty years of growth and change and adjustment the banking system of Colorado has achieved a considerable measure of stability.

CHAPTER XI

The Labor Movement

Oliver M. Dickerson
Professor of History, Colorado State College of Education

THERE have been three phases in the development of labor ideals in Colorado. The first was a bitter struggle for recognition; the second was one of slow growth accompanied by legal regulation of working conditions; and the third has been a period of rapid expansion of labor organizations.

The Fight for Recognition

Organized labor made its first bid for recognition in Colorado's first industrial plants, its mines.

General Mining Conditions

Colorado received its first important influx of settlers following the discovery of gold. At first this was placer mining like that in California, but it was not long before it was evident that Colorado mining was a hard rock proposition involving large capital investment, mills, heavy machinery, steam engines for power, and much day labor. The mines were discovered in regions essentially without population, where everything for human comfort had to be brought in from the outside and even the working population recruited and imported like an army of occupation.[1]

The earlier mines produced fortunes for many Colorado pioneers, who took pride in spending their wealth to develop the towns where they had struck it rich. Later mines became the property of non-residents whose sole interest was profits to be spent in places other than the villages that developed around the mouths of their mines. Thus the mines in some areas took on many of the aspects of the factory town at its worst. The mine, the machinery, the shaft house, the houses, the stores, the boarding houses were frequently company property. When a miner got a job he also got a place to live. When he lost his job he had to move. The company was the government; and the only government in the locality was run by the company. If there was a school the company supplied it.

Under such conditions there could be no normal population free to select its own occupation, plan its own homes, build and support

---

[1] Wilbur F. Stone. *History of Colorado.* 4 vols. (Chicago, 1918), I, ch. 12; testimony of T. J. Osgood of the Victor American Coal Co., *Report of U. S. Com. on Industrial Relations,* Senate Doc. 415, 64th Cong. 1st Ses. (Govt. Printing Office, Washington, 1916, U. S. Ser. No. 6935), VII, 6422-6458.

its own schools and churches and develop a local community according to its own ideals.

Coal mines in Colorado also grew up in areas without previous population. Coal was abundant near the surface, and in many areas could be reached by drifting into a side hill or by opening a shallow shaft. Coal was necessary to keep the mines and smelters running and it soon became essential for home heating and for railroads. The coming of the Colorado Fuel and Iron Company at Pueblo increased the demand for coal, especially in the southern district near Trinidad.

Coal mining was even less social in a democratic sense than metal mining. Coal mines require title to a considerable acreage of land. Thus they were more widely separated than most metal mines. The coal company owned all the land and erected all the buildings permitted about the mines. In spite of laws to the contrary, company stores were operated like exchanges at military posts, and the miners were paid in orders on the company store.[2]

While metal miners were largely Americans recruited from the restless west, coal miners were chiefly recruited from Mexico and southeast Europe. Their mutual suspicion of each other, their inability to understand each other readily, and their varying folk ways made any attempts at local organization difficult. There was little danger of labor unions springing up indigenously among them. This made them easy to manage. Their lack of knowledge of English made it difficult to instruct them concerning dangers in Colorado mines—they could not read directions and signs. They were a hazard to each other and to themselves. Accident rates were abnormally high, especially in the Las Animas field where conditions were worst.[3]

To add to the hazards of coal mining in Colorado, many of the mines are dry. Colorado is a semi-arid country. Powdered coal in a dry mine creates a fire hazard unknown to the damp mines of the east. In many cases there was no way of remedying this condition as water was not available for sprinkling. Some of the coal catches fire readily, giving off explosive or deadly gases. Coal was cheap and miner's wages were low. In addition much of Colorado coal is lignite and does not store. This made coal mining a seasonal industry with a large demand in winter and unemployment for miners in summer.[4]

---

[2] This is admitted by many witnesses including officers of the chief mining companies, in their testimony before the U. S. Industrial Commission. In some cases stores were run by a wholly owned subsidiary company to evade the law. Osgood testified that the profits in the Victor American stores were 20 per cent, that the stocks were turned six times a year, that miner's four-room houses cost $700 to $800 and rented for $2.00 a room or $96.00 a year. Ibid.

[3] James Dalrymple, Colorado State Coal Mine Inspector, testified before the Industrial Commission that in the years 1911, 1912, 1913, the deaths in the Colorado mines were 6.35, 7.055, 8.60, respectively, per 1,000 miners employed. These rates are more than twice the comparative rates for the entire United States in the same years. Ibid., 6463.

[4] Testimony of E. H. Weitzel, manager of the fuel department of the C. F. & I. before the Industrial Commission, that the dust was so dry that it would explode about a car that was being loaded from the flame of an open lamp. Ibid., 6729.

Scenes at Leadville Strike, 1896

The miners had grievances similar to those of laborers generally—hours of work, pay, working conditions. But more serious than these were their desire for an improvement in basic living conditions, a right to own their own homes, freedom to trade where they pleased, right to employ their own doctor, choose their own place and form of worship, and to live generally as free American citizens. In most other areas one could usually secure these by merely shifting his place of employment.

In Colorado mining camps there seemed no way of attaining these basic ends except by controlling the local community. This involved a direct conflict between miners and mine operators. There was no surrounding neutral community population to which both could appeal and which could operate as a moderating influence upon unreasonable demands of each. Under such conditions almost direct civil conflict flared and continued to break out into open disorder until the development of the rest of the state made possible the evolution of mining codes and inspection of machinery by which the state government could correct the most unwholesome conditions.[5]

BEGINNINGS OF UNIONISM

There were no organizations among the earlier miners. In 1878 the coal miners at Erie formed a union chartered by the Knights of Labor. In January, 1879, the miners at Leadville organized a group calling itself the Miners Cooperative Union and also received a charter from the Knights of Labor. A second assembly developed in the same area with a membership of 85 in 1885. In two years it had a membership of 600 and also was given a separate charter by the Knights in 1889.[6]

LABOR TROUBLES IN THE METALIFEROUS MINES

The first serious strike in the state was at Leadville, called by the Miners Cooperative Union on May 26, 1880. There had been considerable variations in working conditions. Some mines demanded nine hours work, while other mines operated on an eight hour schedule. The trouble started at the Chrysolite mine where the manager had issued some irritating regulations about smoking and talking while at work. Soon the strike took the form of a demand for an increase in pay and a uniform eight-day at all mines. Citizens of Leadville organized to preserve order, troops were called out, some strikers and the editor of their paper, *The Crisis,* were ordered out of town.

[5] Percy S. Fritz, *Colorado the Centennial State* (New York, 1941), 368. One of the fairest statements on this is the testimony of James McDonald, a Methodist minister in the Hastings area before the Industrial Commission. *Op. cit.,* 6767-6780. Eugene S. Gaddis, superintendent in charge of social work in the whole area of the C. F. & I. gives even more damaging testimony. *Ibid.,* 8487-8493. The Congressional Committee to investigate the Colorado strike, reported March 2, 1915, that it found conditions thoroughly un-American in much of the southern field. *House Document* 1636, 63 Congress, 3rd Session, U. S. Serial No. 6889, pp. 37-40.

[6] Stone, *op. cit.,* I, 837.

On June 17 there was a compromise on an eight-hour day. This ended the activity of the unions sponsored by the Knights of Labor.[7]

The next organization to make a bid for labor leadership in Colorado was the Western Federation of Miners, which established a central organization at Butte, Montana, May 15, 1893. There were delegates present from fifteen local unions; four of these were from Colorado—Aspen, Creede, Ouray, and Rico—all metaliferous miners. Within ten years this organization had increased its membership from 15 unions with 2,000 members to 165 unions and 48,000 members. Most of these were in the metaliferous mines.[8]

In January, 1894, many of the mines in the Cripple Creek area sought to reduce wages from $3.00 to $2.50 for an eight-hour day. A mass meeting was called at Anaconda; John Calderwood took the lead. The miners agreed to demand the former $3.00 for eight hours of work and to call strikes in all mines that did not follow this schedule. The mine owners decided to fight it out. They controlled the Sheriff, who at once enrolled 1,200 deputies. Some of these were recruited from other areas—50 from Colorado Springs and 100 from Denver. All of these deputies were armed and apparently paid by the mine owners.

The striking miners established an armed camp on Bull Hill, where they could maintain themselves and not be on company property. Governor Waite, of "bloody bridles" fame, was sympathetic to the miners' cause. He refused to use the militia to coerce the miners as was then the custom in most states. When all attempts at compromise failed and there was danger of serious disorders, he called out the entire National Guard and proceeded to prevent any more conflicts between miners and deputy sheriffs. Soon after, a compromise was agreed to by which the miners received $3.00 for an eight-hour day. The whole disturbance had lasted from February 2 to June 10. There had been considerable disorder and several persons had been killed. A Colorado Springs grand jury indicted 37 of the miners for various crimes. The Adjutant General of the state appeared as their defense attorney; masked men kidnapped him from his hotel and tarred and feathered him. None of the arrested miners were convicted. The trouble had not ended—it only slumbered.[9]

Two years later similar troubles developed in the Leadville district, which had now become a stronghold for the Western Federation of Miners. There had been wage cuts in this district similar to those in the Cripple Creek district. In preparation for possible trouble the mine owners had perfected their organization and had entered into a secret agreement not to deal with any one union. About 65% of the miners were receiving $3.00 per day, others were paid less. May 25, 1896, the union demanded that the $3.00 wage be made uniform, as several mines had intimated that they could no longer

[7] *Ibid.,* I, 838-840; Fritz, *op. cit.,* p. 368.
[8] Fritz, *op. cit.,* 369.
[9] Stone, *op. cit.,* I, 840-845.

Scenes at Leadville Strike, 1896

pay that rate if others paid less. The strike immediately closed all of the mines. There was open warfare between the striking miners and the armed strike breakers imported by the mine owners. The Coronado mine was attacked and its surface property destroyed. This time the governor was friendly to the owners and called out the National Guard to protect the property of the mines. The strike failed and the men finally returned to work on the owners' terms. By attacking and destroying property the miners had made themselves unpopular.[10]

In 1899 trouble broke out anew at Lake City among Italian laborers who had been imported to work the mines. The immediate difficulty was over an order requiring all single men to live and board at the company dormitory. The Italians insisted on their right to feed themselves. Again there were disorders. Troops were called out and the Italians were forced to leave. In the final settlement the company agreed that men could live where they pleased. The disturbance had lasted only about a week and people had not taken sides actively.[11]

In 1901 there was a local strike at Telluride over an attempt to introduce a piece work system entirely unsuited to the varying ore conditions of Colorado gold mines. The mine owners secured non-union miners and opened their mines. Disorder and bloodshed followed and most of the non-union men were driven from town. A few weeks later a compromise was agreed to with a wage scale that was satisfactory to all.[12]

In 1902 the Western Federation of Miners extended its organization to include workers in smelters, the manufacturing end of the metal mining industry. In February, 1903, there were strikes in the Portland and Telluride mills accompanied by sympathetic strikes in the mines at Cripple Creek. Troops were called in, compromises followed.[13]

Up to this time serious labor troubles in Colorado had been confined to the metal mining industry and in that to the mountain area of the state. In 1903 the Western Federation of Miners organized the Denver Mill and Smelters Union 93. Men had been worked ten and twelve hours a day, but living in a large city they could have normal home life. In July, 1903, a demand was made for a uniform eight-hour day, which was refused and a strike followed. Globe and Grant smelters stopped work. For the first time in Colorado an attempt was made to use court injunctions to break a strike through a sweeping order issued by Judge Dixon of Pueblo. A special session of the legislature was also called to consider the issue of an eight-hour day, but failed to arrive at a constructive solution. Finally there was a compromise settlement.

---

10 Fritz, *op. cit.*, 369-370; Stone, *op. cit.*, I, 845-847.
11 Stone, *op. cit.*, I, 847-848.
12 *Ibid.*, 849-850.
13 *Ibid.*, 850-851.

About the same time serious labor difficulties had been developing in the mines at Idaho Springs, where gold miners were receiving only $2.75 for nine hours work. The union demanded eight hours. There was violence, explosives were used, a "Citizens Protective League" was organized, determined to deport the union men. Judge Owen attempted to check the mob activities of the League without much success. The mines re-opened with only non-union men, but paid $2.75 for eight hours.[14]

In the Cripple Creek district the Western Federation of Miners, remembering their previous experience in calling a strike with the local peace officers against them, had taken care to see that their friends held all of the important local offices. Starting in 1901 they attempted to make the area a closed shop by systematically forcing non-union men to leave the district or join the union.

The strike in this area in 1903 started as a sympathetic strike in support of the efforts of the smelter workers to enforce their demand for an eight-hour day at $2.25. It quickly developed into a life and death struggle between the Western Federation of Miners and the Mine Owners Association. The latter imported strike breakers to operate the mines closed by the strikers. The latter, forced out of their company owned homes, established armed camps so located as to enable them to patrol roads leading to the mines so as to exclude the imported strike breakers whom they described as "armed foreign invaders." The mine owners black-listed all union men and supplied the non-union men with cards. No mine or mill operator would employ a man without the non-union card nor would they lease any house or place to do business to any person without such a card. Here was another type of closed shop with a vengeance. Strikers retaliated with published lists of "scabs" circulated in the Colorado mining areas to prevent the strike-breakers from securing work elsewhere.

Disorders developed into serious violence. Mine owners set up a "Citizens Alliance." Both sides set up propaganda agencies which quickly made the Cripple Creek strike a national issue. Leading newspapers and periodicals sent in "observers" and "reporters." The articles which they wrote reflected their own prejudices. They added more heat than light to the issues involved.[15]

Governor Peabody and the state administration were Republicans and cooperated closely with the mine owners. Attorney General Miller and Adjutant General John Chase were sent to Cripple Creek to investigate. They advised that the National Guard be used. As soon as these were sent in they were so distributed as to constitute a military occupation of the area.

By proclamation the governor declared Teller County to be in a state of insurrection. The military proceeded to arrest mine leaders without warrant, miner's newspapers were suppressed, writs of habeas

[14] *Ibid.*, 854-856.
[15] Editorial, *Arena*, XXXII, 187-194: J. W. Mills "The Economic Struggle in Colorado," *Ibid.*, XXXIV, 1-10, 119-128, 248-264, 379-399, 485-495, 605-619; XXXV, 150-158, 467-476; Ray Stannard Baker, "Reign of Lawlessness in Colorado," *McClure's Magazine*, XXIII, 43-47.

corpus for the release of prisoners held by the military were refused by General Chase and this action was later upheld by the courts. Small concentration camps were established, a form of summary hearing was set up and men ordered deported from the state, and the orders were executed by the military.[16] It was such an unusual proceeding in a democracy and so contrary to the average American's

Company L, Colorado 1st Infantry, on Strike Duty, Cripple Creek, November, 1903

concept of the meaning of the Bill of Rights that it excited national concern. The action might be technically legal but people did not like that kind of law.

It was election year. Roosevelt was embarrassed by the turn affairs had taken in Colorado. Peabody was a candidate for re-election. Alva Adams, a Democrat, ran against him on the military government issue and was declared elected on the face of the returns. The General Assembly, however, declared Peabody elected, who promptly resigned, leaving the Lieutenant-Governor to serve the full term. The political result was to alienate a large section of the labor vote permanently from the Republican party. The "labor vote" is still Democratic as a result of this episode.

---

16 Fritz, *op. cit.,* 272-273; Stone, *op. cit.,* I, 856-857.

With the military regime set up by Governor Peabody the Western Federation of Miners as an organization was driven from the state. The long series of strikes to organize the workers in the metaliferous mines of Colorado had come to an end. The industry, however, was a loser. It was a sick industry. Too many mines were unprofitable. Never again have labor relations in that industry been a serious problem.

Coal Mine Organization Strikes

While the struggle between the Western Federation of Miners and the Mine Owners Association had run its tragic course a similar trouble was developing in Colorado's coal mining areas. The coal miners had not joined the Western Federation and took no part in its strikes other than to express sympathy and contribute to relief funds. The coal miners belonged to the United Mine Workers of America.[17]

Conditions in many Colorado Coal mines were bad, especially in the southern district. The mining law of 1901 was largely ignored. Company stores, payment in store script, forced contributions to school funds to compensate the company for local taxes upon company property, forced payment to company physicians in amounts sufficient to yield a profit to the company, were too common. Many miners were forced to live in houses rented from the company or board at company boarding houses.

Probably the worst complaints had to do with conditions within the mines affecting health and safety. These varied from mine to mine: sometimes it was dust, sometimes gas, sometimes exposed or dangerous machinery or electric wires, sometimes lack of proper timbering or even timber by which walls and roofs could be made safe. Accident rates were much too high. It was charged that 500 miners had lost their lives in the mines of Las Animas County alone because of inadequate safety regulations.

The first strike in 1903 was largely for organization purposes. On August 14, the United Mine Workers sent open letters to the governors of Colorado, New Mexico and Wyoming and addressed generally to the people of these states, calling attention to the grievances of the coal miners. This gave the matter wide publicity and was followed by a visit to the governor with a list of specific complaints concerning conditions in the state, and asking his cooperation in calling a conference with the mine owners for September 11.

Most operators refused to attend. The fact that the Victor and the C. F. & I. mines were owned by John D. Rockefeller Jr. gave national interest to the situation. A convention of the United Mine Workers met at Pueblo on September 24 and issued a formal list of five specific demands based upon the provisions of the state laws of

[17] George W. Brayfield, "A Brief History of 50 years Progress of Colorado Labor," 50th Anniversary Edition, *Colorado Year Book,* (Colorado Federation of Labor, Denver, 1945), p. 17.

1901.[18] This was ignored by the owners, and John Mitchell on behalf of the miners called a general strike in the Colorado coal fields effective November 9. Organizers were sent into the field and soon reported enrollment of members in large numbers: 6,500 in Las Animas County, 1,700 in Fremont, 1,700 in Boulder, and 450 in Huerfano.[19]

Difficulties were quickly adjusted in the northern field. Mitchell came personally to Trinidad to direct operations. The mine operators resorted to tactics that had just succeeded in the metal mines: imported strike breakers, armed guards and action by court. As most of the houses occupied by the miners were company owned, an effort was made to drive striking miners from their homes—they would be needed to house the imported strike-breakers. At Hastings the town marshal attempted to wreck the shanties of the Victor mines; the Italian women living in them resisted. Other acts of violence followed. Finally, on March 23, 1904, the governor sent in troops. These at once clamped on a rigid censorship of telephone, telegraph and press and began a systematic program of deportation of Mine Workers' agents, officers and organizers, including the famous "Mother Jones" (Mary Harris). Troops were withdrawn June 11, 1904. The strike dragged on and was finally terminated temporarily by the union releasing its members to find work where they could.[20]

Obviously the strike had been very expensive and unprofitable to the mine owners. The Victor American attempted to recoup its losses by damage suits against the United Mine Workers. The first suits asked damages of $85,000, including $25,000 for expenses of armed guards. Later, additional suits totalling $491,000 were filed, including $75,000 for expenses of armed guards and $320,000 for alleged damages to mines. The suits were not pressed, but their size and character explain why labor unions object to incorporation under conditions that might make them liable to damage suits.[21]

Conditions in the coal mines remained unsettled. Probably the real difficulty was that the price received for coal was insufficient to pay adequate wages and make the improvements about the mines that should have been made. A new strike broke out in the northern mines in 1910 and dragged on until 1913, when it spread to the southern field where the Rocky Mountain Fuel Company and the Victor American were the big producers of coal for the Colorado Fuel and Iron Company. Vice-President Hayes of the United Mine Workers personally came to Colorado to direct operations. As before there was a preliminary convention of miners; this time at Trinidad on September 15, 1913, which set forth specific demands. These included recognition of the union, an eight-hour day, right to trade

---

[18] These were Chapter 55, regulating the payment of labor by corporations, and Chapter 91, regulating the weighing of coal.

[19] Stone, *op. cit.*, I, 869-72.

[20] *Ibid.*, 872-873.

[21] *Ibid.*

where they pleased and enforcement of Colorado's mining laws. The strike started on September 23.

To meet the problem of evictions and to provide shelter for the striking miners, ten colonies or camps were established near the various coal mines on land leased for the purpose. Thus the miners were temporarily housed in their own homes and theoretically entitled to the legal safeguards surrounding other American homes. The largest camp was at Ludlow, eighteen miles north of Trinidad on the road to Walsenburg. As the striking miners had to be fed as well as housed, the camps provided a convenient means of seeing that this was done.

From the beginning the struggle took on many of the aspects of the Spanish Civil War. The contending parties were not strictly Colorado factions. The Rockefeller millions were represented on one side and the united power of the organized coal miners on the other. Both were prepared to spend vast sums to win. Each sent in forces to participate in the Colorado battles.

The mine owners at once resorted to tactics that had succeeded in 1903, and 1904. Armed guards and strike breakers were imported. The company controlled sheriffs promptly commissioned the imported guards as deputy sheriffs. Mining properties were protected by barbed wire stockades. Machine guns were set up to command approaches to the mines. Armed and armored trucks were employed to transfer guards and strike breakers from place to place. The United Mine Workers in turn sent arms and ammunition to the strikers in their camps and the camps in turn were intrenched against surprise attacks.[22]

On October 29, 1913, the National Guard was called out. It at once took the attitude that it was there to deal with striking miners. The camp at Ludlow was entered and the tents searched for weapons. As the winter wore on there were numerous clashes between bands of strikers and the imported armed guards. Many of the latter were recruited directly into the National Guard so that the Guard became in effect a force controlled by the Mine Owners like their imported mine guards and no longer the independent arm of the state to maintain law and order. On April 20, 1914, the Guard units near Ludlow, one company of which was made up entirely of recruits from the armed guards, attacked the tent camp. It was ruthless bloody work. Unfortunately too many of the victims were women and children.

The affair was at once a national scandal. Congressional investigations were made. The National Guard was so discredited in public

---

[22] There was much testimony to this effect before the Industrial Commission. Sheriff Farr of Huerfano County submitted lists of his deputies appointed in 1913. He admitted he knew nothing of these men, that he did not pay them, that he appointed any one the mining companies requested, and he presumed the companies armed them. Lists show the names of 398 appointed between January 10 and September 1, 1913. Joseph H. Patterson, deputy clerk of Huerfano submitted a list of deputy sheriffs commissioned between September 1, and December 31, 1913, totaling 472. This makes a total of 870 such appointments in Huerfano county alone in 1913. Sheriff Farr also submitted a list of similar appointments for Las Animas county totaling 443 up to October 15, 1913. This makes a combined total army of deputies in these two counties alone of 913. *Report of Industrial Commission,* VIII, 7293-7311.

opinion that the governor had to withdraw it and call upon President Wilson for federal troops.[23]

The officers of the United States Army at once took the attitude that they were there to restore order and not to take sides in an industrial war. Both armed guards and strikers were promptly disarmed. Order was quickly restored and any further importations of men and arms into the state prevented.

Out of this bitter controversy came important reforms. John D. Rockefeller Jr. took serious steps to investigate and clean up conditions in the industrial empire of Colorado Fuel and Iron Company. Out of this came a form of worker and management organization that worked with reasonable fairness for over thirty years—at least there was no more open strife in that area. The provisions of Colorado's new mining law were enforced by the state and not left to be enforced by labor unions. After much investigation and discussion the state created an Industrial Commission with power to investigate and remedy improper or hazardous working conditions before their injustice could fester into open industrial strife.

The last of Colorado's tragic troubles was in 1927 at the Columbine Mine in Weld County. After the strikes of 1913-14 the Industrial Workers of the World gradually organized some of the Colorado coal mines. There had been numerous complaints about working conditions in some of the Rocky Mountain Fuel Company mines which were not corrected by the Industrial Commission. In addition the miners demanded that the scale of wages paid in the eastern mines, known as the Jacksonville scale, be extended to the Colorado and other western mines.

Instead of using the machinery of the Industrial Commission which provides for complaints, hearings, investigations, and a period of thirty days wait before either a strike or a lock-out, a strike was called. The Columbine mine was enclosed within a barbed wire fence. Heavy gates barred the only road leading to the mine shaft, which could be reached only by passing through the gate. The company placed armed guards at the gate to prevent striking miners from entering the mine enclosure. These were assisted by a force of State Police known as State Rangers that had been organized to maintain order in the mining districts after the strike of 1913-14. Too many of them had served as former mine guards and the miners distrusted them.

Early in the morning of November 21, 1927, a large party of miners assembled at the gate and insisted on their right to pass

---

[23] This episode is recorded in thousands of pages of testimony, much of it conflicting. Formal investigations and reports were made and are available in the following places: Report of Col. Edward Verderkberg, Camp Commander, and Minutes of the Court of Inquiry, manuscript reports, State Historical Society, and Denver Armory of National Guard, respectively; *Report of the Special Board of Officers Appointed by the Governor: Report of Committee to Investigate the Colorado Coal Strike,* House Document 1629, 63rd Congress. 3rd Session, U. S. Ser. No. 6889: *Report of the U. S. Industrial Commission,* U. S. Ser. Nos. 6935, 6936, 6937. The best study of this whole problem is in "The Use of Military Power in the Colorado Coal Strike, 1913-1914," by Oscar. R. Romine, unpublished master's thesis (1939), Library, Colorado State College of Education, Greeley.

through and go to the Post Office. They had been holding public meetings there early in the morning, about the time crews were shifted. It was rather obviously a form of mass picketing.[24]

The guards and the State Rangers denied them passage, fired upon them, killed six and wounded some 60 others. The National Guard was at once ordered to the scene, martial law was established and order maintained. Gradually the strike was broken and the I. W. W. ceased to be an important factor in labor organizations in the state.

Not long after the strike at the Columbine, majority control of the Rocky Mountain Fuel Company passed to Josephine Roche. The company had long been in financial difficulties. Its labor relations had been a source of public friction and very heavy expense. Miss Roche made a deal with the United Mine Workers by which John L. Lewis loaned the company $700,000 from U. M. W. funds and in turn was invited to organize the mines of the Rocky Mountain Fuel Company and was given a standard union agreement similar to those used in eastern districts. With this prestige, organization of the other coal mines in the state was achieved without difficulty and without interruption of work.

From the above account it is clear that serious labor difficulties in Colorado have been confined to its mining areas and in each case have been associated with attempts to organize the workers into strong national labor unions. They were not controversies based upon bargaining between labor and capital, but warfare preliminary to organization for bargaining. Many of the issues were of such a nature that they could not be remedied effectively by bargaining, but required state regulation and administration to correct.

QUIET DEVELOPMENT AND EXPANSION

Colorado's labor history has not been merely a record of strikes, riots, bloodshed and military suppression. There is also a history of quiet organization, of friendly collective effort to improve conditions, and cooperation with others to secure constructive legislation.

The oldest continuous labor organizations in the state are those affiliated with the American Federation of Labor, which was organized at Pueblo in 1896 by the Trades and Labor Assembly of that city. There were 85 delegates present and they adopted as their objectives: promotion of economic intelligence; opposition to harmful legislation; opposition to child labor; improvement of conditions in shops, mines and factories; and promotion of the eight-hour day for all workers. Otto Thum was the first president and Thomas C. Maloney the first Secretary-Treasurer. John McLennon was president from 1909 to

---

24 *Rocky Mountain News,* November 22-23-24-25, 1927. As in case of the Ludlow affair there was conflicting testimony. Miners insisted they were fired upon by a machine gun mounted on the tipple of the mine. This was denied by the Rangers. Reports in the *Rocky Mountain News* for November 22 show pictures of the machine gun so mounted. These were taken immediately after the shooting. The Rangers claimed they used only pistols. No evidence as to the kinds of bullets found in the bodies of the victims or in the area of the shooting was introduced at the inquests.

1917; Earl R. Hoage from 1922 to 1933; C. B. Noxon from 1933 to 1935; Frank Hefferly from 1935 to 1938; and George W. Brayfield from 1939 to the present time. Four men have served as secretary-treasurer since 1909: W. L. Hickey from 1909 to 1915; Ed Anderson from 1916 to 1922; John E. Gross from 1922 to 1937; and James A. Brownlow from 1938 to the present time.[25] Gross, Hefferly and Brownlow have been most frequently mentioned in the public press and have been active in legislation.

The separation of the C. I. O. from the A. F. L. in 1937 led to the separation of the miners unions in Colorado from the parent organization. It was this separation that caused Mr. Hefferly to terminate his services with the Federation to become head of the United Mine Workers in Colorado.

The affiliated organizations, such as the great railroad brotherhoods, the craft unions, and the typographical union have been active in Colorado almost from the start of the Federation. None of them have been involved in any major controversy. These organizations grew slowly and steadily and cultivated harmonious relations with their employers. The same can be said of most of the craft unions. With all of the vast amount of building needed in a new state there have been no serious controversies in the building trades nor have there been loose charges of labor racketeering in such trades as has been frequently reported from eastern cities.

Denver is the most fully unionized city in the state with 136 separate unions affiliated with the American Federation alone in 1945. Yet Denver has been very free from serious labor difficulties, with only two major strikes—that of the smelters and the more recent tramway strike. Both of these were of relatively short duration.

The older labor organizations in Colorado were formed along the line of craft unions. In recent years the horizontal union has come into common use by which entire factories and industries are organized into a single union. The leading advocate of this type of union is the Congress of Industrial Organizations, which had its beginnings in 1937 in Colorado with a drive to organize packing, rubber, steel, and metal mining industries. The packing house workers were the first to secure recognition; their membership rose from 250 to nearly 2,000 and they now hold a master contract with all the "Big Four" packers—Armour, Cudahy, Swift and Wilson. Similar success followed in the rubber industry, where the local union rose from 350 to about 2,000, and the great Pueblo steel mills were unionized with a membership of about 5,000. The C. I. O. now has an effective membership of about 15,000.[26]

The American Federation of Labor has also developed along similar lines. Its major groups of this kind are the bakeries, the postal workers, and recently the workers in the beet sugar refineries.

[25] *Official Colorado Year Book*, (A. F. L.) 1945.
[26] Letter from Thomas Long, Secretary, Colorado State Industrial Union Council, C. I. O., April 27, 1945.

Colorado now has three major labor organizations; the American Federation of Labor, the United Mine Workers of America, and the Congress of Industrial Unions. In some respects they are active competitors for members. So far, however, Colorado has been relatively free from jurisdictional strikes. While these organizations compete with each other for members and for a right to represent labor they are likely to show a common front of opposition to any legislation that they consider harmful.

There has been a considerable ebb and flow of labor union memberships. In periods of steady employment and high wages membership rises rapidly. In periods of depression there is a heavy decline in membership. The war with its regulations, together with the administration of the Wagner Labor Relations Act have promoted rapid growth of labor membership. Some of this is voluntary on the part of the workers and some has been forced upon them by contracts with management which required that all employees pay dues to a particular organization. This arrangement benefits the permanent membership of a union but seems to impose a burden upon those workers who are only employed for short periods, as has been the case with construction labor in erecting war plants and army camps. Much the same condition exists in the sugar refining plants, where hundreds of men are employed only for the few weeks when beets are being converted into sugar.

During all this period of labor organization and strife, employees in certain important industries have remained largely or wholly unorganized. Outstanding among these are the agriculture, stock-raising, fruit growing and truck raising industries. These are largely personally run businesses or small capital organizations. In general they do not employ very many laborers in a single venture. The truck and fruit industries have to employ large numbers of seasonal workers at times, but these have generally been recruited from groups that are willing to work for a short time and who depend upon other occupations for a living. There have been some attempts to organize such workers, but without much success. The union has little to offer workers who engage in an occupation for only a few days or weeks at the most. To them the union dues are just a fee paid to a labor organizer for the privilege of working. Producers have been definitely hostile to attempts to organize their workers because a stoppage of work for even a day could mean the loss of a crop and with it the efforts of an entire year. Beans, peas, fruits have to be picked within hours when they are at the right stage of maturity or the crop is worthless.

Sugar beets and potatoes require large amounts of hand labor at certain stages. This has involved recruitment and importation of labor for this special purpose. Practice has evolved a scheme of payment and employment not unlike the working agreements between labor unions and large corporations. Uniform wage scales are agreed to by the organized producers. Labor is contracted for the season. Its pay is made a part of the contract with the sugar company for the sale of beets. There is practically no hiring and firing during the growing season. Labor has all of the benefits of a yearly wage contract, although it has to finish its contract to receive its pay.

The contract system used in the beet industry involves family labor. A family takes a contract to thin and hoe a specified area at so much an acre. Sometimes only the man works; at other times all of the family, including the women and children, are in the fields. This has led to national investigations of Colorado beet fields, and demands from certain sources that child labor in Colorado be ended. In general, people of Colorado have not been sympathetic to this interference from the outside. In factory areas children are employed by the factory owner and are worked under factory conditions. In the Colorado beet fields the children work with and for their parents who are directly and personally interested in seeing that the health of their children is not injured.

There are many phases of the truck and fruit industries that require vast amounts of hand labor for short periods where children between the ages of ten and sixteen are very efficient help. There is no evidence that they suffer from such employment under proper conditions. Most of this employment of young people comes during the school vacation period of the year, but some schools have adopted special school schedules to free the older children at the special periods when their help with the crops is most needed.

LEGISLATION

From the beginning organized labor has sought legislation as one means of improving the conditions of employment. In general this has included hours of labor, decent living and working conditions, safety regulations, freedom of contract, right to organize and strike, prohibition of child labor, compensation for industrial accidents, regular payment of wages in money, good schools for their children, and pensions for those who were no longer able to work. In one way or another practically all of these have been written into law in Colorado.

Eight hours was made the legal day for all public work in Colorado in 1894.[27] Mining was declared a dangerous occupation in 1913 and labor limited to eight hours.[28] In the same year employment of women was similarly limited.[29] The same length of day was fixed for penal institutions in 1919.[30] Working in cement plants was declared a dangerous occupation in 1927 and hours of work limited to eight.[31] There has been no recent agitation to extend the scope of this kind of legislation. It is likely to be replaced by agitation for legal limitation of work to a shorter day.

[27] *Colorado Statutes Annotated.* (Denver, 1935) III, Ch. 97, Sec. 103.
[28] *Ibid.,* Sec. 100.
[29] *Ibid.,* Secs. 111, 112.
[30] *Ibid.,* Sec. 108.
[31] *Ibid.,* Secs. 114-115.

Labor organizations were made legal by legislation in 1889, supplemented by additional provisions in 1908.[32] Coercion of employees not to join a union was prohibited by laws of 1897 and 1908.[33] Contracts not to join a union were made void in 1931.[34] Agreements to leave an organization as a condition of employment, were made illegal in 1911.[35] Employment agencies have been subjected to a variety of regulations by a series of laws enacted in 1891, 1909, 1917, and 1935.[36] Child labor in practically all occupations other than agriculture and fruit raising was prohibited in 1911.[37] The system of paying workers by giving them orders for goods supplied by company stores was made illegal in 1899.[38] Requirements that workers for all private corporations must be paid in cash or by check every two weeks was passed in 1901,[39] supplemented by additional regulations in 1919.[40] Minimum wages for women and children were provided by legislation in 1917.[41] A workmen's compensation law was enacted in 1915 and made more effective in 1919.[42] Statewide old age pensions were established by constitutional amendment in 1936.

Most of Colorado's legislation designed to meet the needs of labor are embraced in three major codes: The State Industrial Commission, Inspection of Coal Mines; and Workmen's Compensation.

The Industrial Commission

The setting up of the Industrial Commission in 1915 was a long step forward in reducing industrial civil war in Colorado. Previous labor laws had been largely dead letters because they depended upon prosecution and fines for enforcement. The enforcing machinery was too often under the control of one or the other of the contending parties, consequently there was neither fairness nor evenness in the application of the laws. Under the new law there was set up a continuous machinery for investigation and correction of grievances as they arose, fitting the remedies to the ability of the employer to make them and the urgency needed to protect workers. In this way the endless problems of light, ventilation, sanitation, dust, general working conditions, hours, wages, etc., could be adjusted from time to time with fairness to all. With factory inspectors and mining inspectors constantly on the job there was little chance for complaints to fester until they flared into open resistance.[43]

---

32 *Ibid.*, Sec. 64.
33 *Ibid.*, Secs. 65-66.
34 *Ibid.*, Sec. 67.
35 *Ibid.*, Sec. 68.
36 *Ibid.*, Secs. 147-181.
37 *Ibid.*, Secs. 182-199.
38 *Ibid.*, Secs. 208-216.
39 Session Laws. 1901. Ch. 55.
40 Colorado Statutes Annotated, Secs. 200-207.
41 *Ibid.*, Secs. 236-256.
42 *Ibid.*, Secs. 280-429.
43 *Ibid.*, Secs. 1-63.

Both strikes and lockouts were prohibited until after 30 days notice had been given, within which time the Commission would seek to settle the strike by arbitration or other peaceful means. The Commission has vast powers to examine books and records, examine witnesses under oath, demand payrolls, and compel the production of evidence by both laborers and employers. Enforcement of factory, mine, and labor legislation was made a matter of investigation, proof and administrative order instead of prosecution in the courts by local officers. The practical enforcement of all labor legislation and factory laws has been transferred to the Industrial Commission.

The American Federation of Labor has consistently opposed the Industrial Commission, apparently because of the provisions against strikes. Even as late as 1945 President Brayfield wrote: "We still maintain today that it is a machine organized to fight labor's interests and should be repealed."[44] Every effort, however, to repeal the law has failed. The political power of labor at the polls stands as a safeguard against any administrative policy in the Commission that could be considered even remotely hostile to labor.

Workmen's Compensation

The Workmen's Compensation Law,[45] administered by the Industrial Commission, has operated to remove or minimize the hazard of accidents in mines and industrial operations. No small part of the bitterness back of the long years of strife in Colorado mines was the high toll taken by accidents. The law provided a theoretical remedy through damage suits against the employer. In actual practice these provisions were little real protection. Suits were expensive. Court costs and attorney's fees ate up much of any award that the courts might make. Awards when secured were in lump sums which were quickly dissipated. Employers resorted to insurance and attorneys to protect them against unfair and even deserving claims. There was little consistency to awards given by courts. Hazardous occupations literally forced the individual worker to carry his own risks when accepting employment. If he got crippled or killed it was just too bad.[46]

The Workmen's Compensation Act provides prompt, fair, and efficient settlement of all accident claims. Every employer of four or more workers must carry insurance unless specifically exempted

[44] "Brief History of 50 Years Progress of Colorado Labor," *Official Colorado Year Book,* A. F. of L. 50th Anniversary Edition, 1945, p. 40.

[45] Full text of this law is in *Colorado Statutes Annotated,* Chapter 97, Secs. 282-429.

[46] In Las Animas and Huerfano counties there apparently was direct company control of the local courts to prevent the prosecution of damage claims. In Huerfano County Sheriff Farr named all the Coroner's juries and in the ten years from 1905 to 1915 there were 90 inquests of 109 deaths. In only one case did the jury fix the responsibility on the company. All the others were recorded as due to unavoidable accidents or to the carelessness of the employee. The one case where the company was responsible was not filed in court. *Report of Commission on Industrial Relations,* VIII, 7265-7296; VII, 6786. J. C. Osgood, President of the Victor American Company, testified before the Commission that it was the practice of the coal companies to throw all of the burden of injuries upon the workers. *Ibid.,* VII, 6454.

by the commission. All workers must be covered. Schedules for payment for losses are established at fixed rates. Claims are settled promptly.[47] Payments are made out of the insurance fund. During the first 21 years of its operation the Industrial Commission passed upon 95,023 claims based upon 394,289 accidents; favorable awards were made by the Commission in 12,828 cases; and referees awarded claims in 30,258 cases; in addition there were voluntary compensation agreements which brought the total awards to 77,775. Among these were 1,768 cases where the accident resulted in the death of the worker and where there were persons wholly dependent upon the worker for support. In 87,309 cases there was temporary total disability. Amputations totaled 3,451 for the same years.[48]

Had the parties to all of these accidents been forced to seek remedies in the courts, there would have been fewer awards, and complaints of working conditions would have been more vocal. The fact that every accident has to be reported, investigated, responsibility fixed, and claims considered by the same responsible agency that checks on working conditions protects the workers from accumulative bad conditions. Inasmuch as industry as a whole has to carry the cost of accidents, it is directly to the interest of employers who maintain good conditions to have competitors who are less careful improve conditions.[49]

INSPECTION OF COAL MINES

There was a futile attempt to regulate coal mines by law in 1901, but the law was useless. In 1913 there was sweeping legislation intended to set up a workable code that would reduce the hazards to health and safety. The law includes detailed standards and regulations concerning ventilation, detection and walling off of explosive or noxious gasses, elimination or control of fires, dry mines to be kept wet down or otherwise treated to control dust along service tunnels and in the working areas, regulation of blasting, oils and greases to be stored and used outside the mines, safety lamps, protection of electric wires, prohibition of carrying matches or smoking materials into mines, safety zones, etc. Dangers from accidents caused by falling objects were reduced by elaborate regulations concerning cages, hoists, cables, safety locks, carrying of men and tools in the same cage, safety zones about the bottoms of shafts, etc.[50]

---

[47] Alva Kenneth Wolf, "Workmen's Compensation in Colorado," Unpublished Master's Thesis (1937), Library, Colorado State College of Education, Greeley.

[48] From August 1, 1915, to November 30, 1944, the Commission handled 138,225 claims, based upon 693,605 accidents. Claims were compensated by payment of a total of $32,500,790.02 during these years. Each year the payments now amount to nearly two million dollars. *Eighteenth Report.* Industrial Commission of Colorado (Denver, 1944), 43.

[49] The Colorado Coal Commission stated February 23, 1916, that in the first year of the operation of this law, fatal accidents had been reduced by seven per cent, that there was much more timbering than formerly and that in November, 1915, there was not a single fatal accident. House Document 859, 64th Cong., 1st Session, U. S. Ser. No. 7099, pp. 14-15.

[50] *Colorado Statutes, Annotated,* Ch. 110, Secs. 1-167.

Enforcement of these detailed regulations were placed in the hands of a State Coal Mine Inspector with a staff sufficient to examine every mine and enforce compliance. In addition miners were protected against frauds in weighing by the requirement that there be a check weighman appointed by the miners. All coal had to be weighed as it came from the mine and 2,000 pounds was defined as a ton. Eight hours was made the standard day for underground work. This did not include travel time in the mine nor time for lunch. All accidents are under the jurisdiction of the Industrial Commission and all fatal accidents in mines must have a coroner's investigation and report.

Such an elaborate set of regulations required time and large expenditures of capital to put into operation. Many small mines found the cost prohibitive and closed. Some mines complied slowly and reluctantly. One announced reason for the disastrous series of strikes in 1913-1914 was to force compliance with the new law. Complete compliance by all mines was an ideal. The state had announced and defined a policy. The Coal Mine Inspector has sought by administrative means to make that ideal real. Conditions in Colorado mines are not perfect but they are now far different from what they were in the days of Ludlow.

The cost of complying with safety regulations and the steady introduction of improved mining machinery has reduced the number of miners needed by about half those employed at the time of the strike of 1913-1914. In spite of improved conditions the accident rate is still relatively high. In 1944 there were only 22 fatal accidents, although the injuries still averaged 103.1 per 1,000 men or in excess of 10 per cent.[51] The report of the Industrial Commission shows that in 1943 workers in Colorado coal mines suffered 25.9 per cent of the fatal claims and 13 per cent of the non fatal accidents. This is a vast improvement over conditions between 1915-1920, when 43.46 per cent of the fatal claims were from the coal mines and 23.81 per cent of non fatal claims. Coal mining is still a dangerous industry, since 6,071 employees out of more than a hundred thousand in the state contribute more than one fourth of the total fatal accidents.

---

[51] *Report,* State Inspector of Coal Mines, 1944, p. 1.

CHAPTER XII

Social Legislation and the Welfare Program

Efay Nelson Grigg

*Director, Division of Research and Statistics, Colorado
State Department of Public Welfare*

Early History and Development of Public Welfare

THE history of the poor and neglected, the submerged of mankind, is as old as humanity itself. There have always been the aged, the mentally or physically ill, the handicapped, and persons unable to maintain self-dependency because of adverse conditions beyond their control. Furthermore, circumstances which affect the well-being of children and which make protection and care necessary are obviously not of recent origin.

The underlying principles on which modern social welfare programs in Colorado are based have evolved over a period of years. The change in the methods of helping persons with their individual problems has not been due altogether to the need for meeting the complexities of changing social and economic conditions. Changed or modified attitudes of the general public have played a very important role.

The influx of early pioneer population into the area which later became the state of Colorado brought persons who subsequently found themselves in dire need because of accidents, sickness, and numerous other misfortunes. In the absence of organized private or public facilities set up to meet these emergencies, benevolent individuals in the community and various church and fraternal organizations sought to fill the needs of those in distress.

Private charitable agencies and institutions had their beginning in Territorial days and apparently grew out of the necessity for meeting the requirements of the helpless for whom the lawmakers of the time made no provision. Health seekers were among the immigrants who came with little or no means for self-support, thereby creating serious charity and relief problems. Attention was focused relatively early on the destitute and oftentimes homeless child. In 1872, the Denver Orphans' Home was established to meet the need of these dependents. Two years later, a group of public spirited women in Denver organized the Ladies Relief Society to administer relief and charity to the distressed without regard for creed, nationality, or color. So far as known, the two foregoing organizations marked the beginning of private charitable agencies in the state. Sanatoria and hospitals under private auspices began to appear as early as 1879, the date of the founding of a hospital in Leadville by the Sisters of Leavenworth.

By 1887, the number of private agencies individually soliciting funds from the general public had grown sufficiently in Denver to cause criticism in the community. The Charity Organization Society of Denver, the first federation of charitable agencies in the United States, came into being in 1887. It put into effect a successful plan for financing, for preventing duplication, and for promoting cooperation among member agencies. This pioneer federation raised $21,700 in its first campaign and distributed the funds to ten agencies. In this early and progressive group, the community chest movement in Colorado had its inception.

Social legislation during Territorial days and two decades after Colorado became a state centered to a considerable degree on the care of paupers and on state institutions for various groups such as the insane, lawbreakers, the deaf and blind, delinquent youth, and dependent children.

The early poor laws, many of which yet remain with little or no change, were adoptions or adaptations of those enacted previously by colonial lawmakers. A law passed in 1865 placed the financial responsibility on the counties for maintenance of those dependents who were their residents.[1] In the same year, a law required the County Commissioners to give assistance deemed to be just and equitable to a nonresident falling sick within the county's borders. His county of residence was charged with any assistance given and could be told "to remove such pauper forthwith."[2] Bringing persons known to be paupers into a county carried a penalty of $200.[3] By the application of this provision the lawmakers apparently hoped to curb the immigration of dependent persons. An editorial in 1872, however, throws some light on its effectiveness:

> The immigration of paupers is getting to be a nuisance and an abuse. * * * Colorado never shrinks from the care of her indigent citizens, but she will hardly consent to forced contributions to foreign paupers. * * * They come hither by railway and doubtless as dead-heads in the character of paupers. The application of the law * * *, once or twice, would make railway companies, and their officers, very careful about passengers they carry. * * *[4]

By legislative action in 1865, the counties were authorized to establish a poorhouse whenever they deemed it proper to do so, to buy land for it, and to levy for its maintenance "should the labor of inmates be inadequate thereto."[5] Inasmuch as outdoor relief was practically unknown, almshouse or poor farm care was the prevalent form of aid given to those in need. The inmate population was a

---

1 *Colorado Statutes Annotated, 1935,* Chap. 124, Sec. 3.
2 *Ibid.,* Sec. 7.
3 *Ibid.,* Sec. 10.
4 *Rocky Mountain News,* June 8, 1872.
5 *Colorado Statutes Annotated, 1935,* Chap. 124, Secs. 11-13.

heterogeneous group; in some instances young children,[6] youths, the crippled, the feebleminded, the blind, and even the insane were included.[7]   The seriousness of the situation concerned many of the leading thinkers, one of whom stated in 1890 that nearly all of the county institutions were managed on the crudest plans and that he hoped public sentiment could be aroused in order to bring about more humane, wiser, and more economical methods.[8]   A few years later the State Board of Charities and Corrections in a report to the governor recommended revisions and improvement of poor laws which would bring about wise administration of the permanent care of paupers.[9] Even as late as the 1920s there were outstanding examples of frame poorhouses with fire hazards at a maximum and with no modern facilities.   The practice of permitting inmates with transmissible diseases to associate with others and to share toilet and bathroom facilities was almost universal throughout the state.[10]

County jails are also institutions of long standing.   The first Territorial General Assembly in 1861 provided for their establishment at county expense.[11]   This early law limited the diet of prisoners to bread, meat, and drink, but made no mention of quality and adequacy of the food.   This restriction was overcome by subsequent legislation and the statute now in effect states: "The sheriff of each county shall feed all the prisoners kept in confinement by him, with good and sufficient food; and the board of county commissioners of such county shall, at the expense of the county, furnish to such sheriff all the groceries, supplies, utensils, equipment, and assistants such sheriff may require to perform his duty of properly feeding such prisoners and shall also pay all the costs and expenses incurred therein."[12]   It was common practice to place the jail in the basement of the courthouse,[13] a practice not entirely obsolete at the present time.

The act of 1861 included provision for quarters for juvenile prisoners apart from those of experienced and hardened criminals, and humane treatment which would tend to promote reformation.[14] In the light of present-day thinking, the following act passed in 1868 appears extremely harsh.   "Infants under the age of 12 shall for all offenses the penalty whereof is imprisonment be punished by confinement in a county jail for a period not exceeding 2 years."[15]   For-

---

6 In the *Rocky Mountain News* of March 19, 1882, there is an account of an infant deserted by his mother.   The midwife in attendance at his birth asked the Commissioners to accept responsibility for him and he was placed in the poorhouse when 9 days old.

7 Bureau of the Census, 1890; Paupers in Almshouses, 1923; *Biennial Report, State Board of Charities and Corrections, 1894.*

8 *Proceedings of first State Convention, Charities and Corrections, 1890.*

9 *Sixth Biennial Report, State Board of Charities and Corrections, 1902.*

10 Harry C. Evans, *The American Poor Farm and its Inmates,* 1936.

11 *Colorado Statutes Annotated, 1935,* Chap. 91, Sec. 1.

12 *Ibid.,* Sec. 4.

13 *Biennial Reports,* State Board of Charities and Corrections.

14 *Colorado Statutes Annotated, 1935,* Chap. 91, Sec. 22.

15 *Territorial Laws of Colorado, 1868,* page 237.

tunately, later legislation such as the act with respect to setting up Juvenile Courts nullified laws of this type.[16]

The number and scope of legislative acts relative to children throughout Territorial years and those immediately following would indicate the existence of problems of the homeless, the neglected, and the dependent. A number of these early laws lacked provisions necessary to safeguard the interests of the child. The first Territorial General Assembly provided for the deeding of minor children by parents or guardians under certain conditions.[17] For 15 years, adoption proceedings were handled by the General Assembly, which took action on each individual case. In 1876 an adoption law was passed providing that any person or husband and wife desiring to adopt a child could do so by executed, acknowledged, and recorded deed, and with consent of parents or guardian.[18] There is little reason to doubt that questionable practices existed under this law; in 1882 for example, an infant was sold by her parents to a notorious prostitute.[19] Subsequent legislation revised or supplemented this early adoption law, the first of which appeared in 1885.[20] Indenture of children dependent on the county for support was provided by law in 1879. The County Commissioners, as guardians, were responsible for seeing that the contract with the person entitled to the child's services was fulfilled and that the child was given proper treatment.[21] There is record of a Board of County Commissioners adopting a resolution in 1882 which states:

> RESOLVED: That the superintendent of the poor of this county be and is hereby directed and required to find and procure, as far as is practicable, suitable homes for all pauper children chargeable to this county under the age of 18 years; and that in all cases, when any pauper child under the age of 18 years has been or shall have been chargeable to this county for six months, said superintendent of the poor is directed to bind out such pauper child to service in accordance with the statute in such case made and provided. The object of the resolution is to relieve the county by binding out children of families that are dependent on the county for support.[22]

Indenture by apprenticeship was authorized by legislative acts in the middle 1880s. The statutes provided that all minors might be bound to some appropriate industry, trade, art, or calling. There were some restrictions on the persons empowered to indenture; on

---

16 *Colorado Statutes Annotated, 1935,* Chap. 46, Secs. 199-220.

17 *Territorial Laws of Colorado, 1861,* pp. 348, 349.

18 *Ibid., 1876,* p. 38.

19 *Rocky Mountain News,* Denver, May 11, 1882.

20 *Session Laws of Colorado, 1885,* pp. 17, 18.

21 *Colorado Statutes Annotated, 1935,* Chap. 9, Sec. 28.

22 *Rocky Mountain News,* January 22, 1882.

the master with respect to return for services and to education of the minor; and the types of vocations or occupations to which an apprentice might be bound.   The provision relative to indigent children was:

> When any poor child is, or may be chargeable to the county, or shall beg for alms, or whose parents are or may be chargeable to the county, or shall beg for alms, or when the parents of such children are poor and the father an habitual drunkard, or if there be no father, when the mother is of bad character, or suffers her children to grow up in habits of idleness, without any visible means of obtaining an honest livelihood, it shall be lawful for the superintendent of the poor of the county wherein such child resides, who for this purpose shall be considered ex-officio guardian of such child, to bind such child under the order and direction of the county court of such county in like manner, and with like effect, as is provided in the preceding section of this chapter for the binding of orphan minors by their guardians.

Even before the turn of the century, there developed among advanced thinkers a general recognition of the need for state supervision or control of agencies and institutions dealing with social problems in Colorado. It was in 1891 that the State Board of Charities and Corrections was established, but it was delegated no definite control functions. It was given the power to investigate the whole system of public charities and correctional institutions; to examine the condition and management of all prisons, jails, reformatories, industrial schools, hospitals, infirmaries, orphanages, asylums, and all other institutions deriving their support wholly or in part from public funds.[24] The supervisory functions of this board were extended ten years later when it was given the power to investigate and license institutions supported through private donations.[25] Throughout the period of its existence, this board remained in advisory capacity only.   Conditions in the state were reported to the Governor each biennium together with recommendations for changes in existing laws and for new legislation.[26]

When the Twentieth General Assembly abolished the State Board of Charities and Corrections in 1923, it created a Department of Charities and Corrections with a secretary directly responsible to the Governor and appropriated funds for operation.[27] This department actually functioned for only two years, inasmuch as no appropriations were made thereafter for its continuance. By statute it remained a department for a decade but was inert for eight years of its existence. A part-time employee in the Governor's office carried on the

23 *Colorado Statutes Annotated, 1935,* Chap. 9, Sec. 6.
24 *Compiled Laws of Colorado, 1921,* Chap. 16, Sec. 525.
25 *Colorado Statutes Annotated, 1935,* Chap. 31, Sec. 7.
26 *Biennial Reports,* State Board of Charities and Corrections.
27 *Colorado Statutes Annotated, 1935,* Chap. 31, Sec. 1.

clerical work pertaining to the Penitentiary and the movement of population in other institutions during the eight-year period. The Department of Charities and Corrections was abolished in 1933 and all its rights, duties, and powers were transferred to the newly created Division of Public Welfare.[28]

Following the "crash" of 1929, distress was so widespread and the effect of drouth and crop failures, of loss in property values, homes, and jobs was so devastating that private charitable and county funds were entirely inadequate to meet the situation. It was in 1932 that the Official Colorado State Relief Committee was appointed by the Governor to administer Federal funds received from the Reconstruction Finance Corporation. This committee was recognized as a temporary state agency by a legislative act in 1933,[29] but it ceased to function in 1934, when the Federal Government assumed complete charge of the administration of work relief in the state. The General Assembly in 1935 declared the care and relief of the poor and destitute unemployed and unemployable to be a state as well as a county function. The Official Colorado State Relief Committee was created and charged with the responsibility of receiving, allocating, administering, and supervising funds provided by the state or the Federal Government and any of its agencies for relief of the destitute.[30]

The Welfare Organization Act of 1936, which established the State Department of Public Welfare and the county departments, designated the Official State Relief Committee as the State Board of Public Welfare.[31] The State Department of Public Welfare was charged with the administration or supervision of all welfare activities with respect to child welfare services, outdoor and indoor care of persons in need, assistance to the aged, aid to dependent children, aid to the blind, and such other public welfare activities or services as might be vested in it by law. This department is under the Division of Public Welfare in the Executive Department of state government.[32]

PUBLIC WELFARE PROGRAMS AND FACILITIES

BUREAU OF CHILD AND ANIMAL PROTECTION

The Colorado Humane Society, incorporated in 1881, was made the Bureau of Child and Animal Protection by legislative action in 1901. It was charged with the duty of securing enforcement of the laws for the prevention of wrongs to children and dumb animals.[33] A law in 1907 expanded its functions with respect to children by prohibiting any association, corporation, society or institution, other than a state, city, or county institution from receiving a dependent

28 *Ibid.,* Chap. 3, Sec. 10.
29 *Ibid.,* Chap. 141, Sec. 3.
30 *Ibid.,* Chap. 141, Sec. 7.
31 *Ibid.,* Chap. 141, Article 3.
32 *Ibid.,* Chap. 3, Sec. 9 (11), 1945 Supplement.
33 *Ibid.,* Chap. 151, Secs. 1-3.

child until approval had been secured from this bureau. In addition, any association, corporation, institution, or individual receiving the care, custody and guardianship of a dependent child was made subject to visitation or inspection by this bureau as well as the Board of Charities and Corrections and representatives of the court.[34] In conjunction with the State Board of Health, this bureau was given the power to license maternity homes and hospitals under a law passed in 1911.[35] This law also states:

> No child shall be given away or otherwise disposed of, except by legal adoption in a court of record, without first obtaining a permit for such disposition in each case from the state bureau of child and animal protection, which may issue such permit after due investigation into the fitness of the applicant for such child.[36]

Subsequent legislation with respect to protection and care of children, to licensure, and to investigation would appear to supersede provisions of earlier laws in some instances.

This bureau specializing in the enforcement of all state and local laws for the protection of children and animals has been among the institutions in the Division of Public Welfare under the Executive Department of state government since 1933.[37] From the standpoint of time involved in the performance of the work, the two phases of this program have been almost equally divided. Cases of cruelty to and neglect of children in 1945 totaled 676 with 1,955 children affected.[38]

DIVISION OF CHILD WELFARE

The Child Welfare Division within the State Department of Public Welfare was created by law in 1936. This department was charged with the administration or supervision of all child welfare activities. Furthermore, it was required to cooperate with the Children's Bureau of the United States Department of Labor in establishing, extending, and strengthening child welfare services.[39] (By Executive order in 1946, almost all functions of the Children's Bureau were transferred to the Federal Security Agency.)

This program launched almost ten years ago for the welfare of children in the state is operated by the state and county departments of public welfare in behalf of homeless, handicapped, neglected, and dependent children, and those in danger of becoming delinquent.[40]

---

34 *Ibid.,* Chap. 33, Sec. 12.

35 *Ibid.,* Chap. 78, Sec. 140.

36 *Ibid.,* Chap. 78, Sec. 142.

37 *Ibid.,* Chap. 3, Sec. 10.

38 Statements given to writer by Dr. Mary E. Bates, Secretary of Bureau of Child and Animal Protection.

39 *Colorado Statutes Annotated, 1935,* Chap. 141, Secs. 19-20.

40 Detailed information published in *Annual Reports* of the Colorado State Department of Public Welfare, 1937-1941.

The services under this program are varied in nature and broad in scope. Interest is focused on the welfare of all girls and boys irrespective of social or economic status. The program is not confined to any particular creed, race, or color; it is not limited to case work on the individual basis but extends into group work.

Foster home care is provided for the homeless and for other children whose interests can best be served by placement in carefully selected and supervised family homes. In some instances, parents or relatives contribute all or part of the cost in connection with care in these "substitute" homes. The public funds involved in the direct care phase of the program are County Support to the Poor or other available county funds and earmarked appropriations by the General Assembly. Children serviced in homes of parents or other relatives at all times exceed those living elsewhere. About three among every five of the 1,487 children under the program at the end of December, 1945, were living in family homes in which parents or other relatives were present. This would indicate the extent to which emphasis is placed on helping children to remain in their own homes whenever possible. At times this objective can be attained by making housekeeper service available to the home. Analysis of the December, 1945, case load revealed that the 1,487 children included wee infants and minors of all ages; however, the most representative age group was the 15 year-old youth.

The work of the Division of Child Welfare and the county departments of public welfare is closely interrelated with that of courts, churches, schools, the Bureau of Standards of Child Care, various private agencies and institutions dealing with children, the Division of Crippled Children, and state institutions for the dependent, handicapped, and delinquent.

Title V, part 3, of the Social Security Act of 1935 designated the Children's Bureau as the federal agency responsible for child welfare services. Eligibility for federal funds is based on compliance with a joint plan of operation approved by the Children's Bureau. Colorado receives $18,969 yearly, no part of which can be expended for the direct care of children. Federal funds are used primarily to meet the cost of personnel in the Division of Child Welfare serving as consultants in case and group work.

BOARD OF STANDARDS OF CHILD CARE

By legislative action in 1943, the Board of Standards of Child Care was established with broad duties with respect to the adoption of minimum standards for child care and the licensing of foster boarding homes and child placing agencies. In carrying out its functions the board was given the right to make use of the facilities and services of any existing state board or department such as the Department of Public Welfare and the State Board of Health. A foster boarding home was defined as any institution, residence, dwelling or home, including nursery schools or day nurseries, in which a home is maintained for a child or children under 16 with relationship to the operator beyond the second degree. Public, private, and parochial schools or colleges, and nursery schools operated under such auspices were excluded. A corporation, an individual other than a natural parent, or any association that places a child under 16 or arranges placement with persons not related within the second degree was defined as a child placement agency.[41]

The accomplishments of the Board of Standards of Child Care during its first year were in the preparation of a basis for operation. The members of the Board carried on research; formulated and published "Minimum Standards"; and established rules and regulations for issuing licenses, for hearings, and for the enforcement of standards. During the 12-month period ending June 30, 1945, foster boarding homes caring for 4,011 children were inspected and licensed. Other activities included formal hearings which resulted in the closing of 15 homes; inspection of 24 orphanages; and denial of licenses to homes below the required standards.

> The efforts of this Board are directed toward carrying out the intent of the Law, giving guidance to those who perform the noble work of providing substitute parental care, and advancing mutual understanding among all child caring agencies.[42]

AID TO THE BLIND

Soon after acquiring statehood, Colorado provided for the education of blind children in the institution previously known as the Colorado Institute for Deaf Mutes in Colorado Springs. Men and women, many of whom had been rendered blind by accident after reaching maturity, were first benefited through legislative action in 1907 when the Industrial Workshop for the Blind was established in Denver.[43] It was designed primarily for the purpose of training sightless adults and giving them safe, sheltered employment. Assistance to needy blind persons in the form of money payments and medical services began with the establishment of the Blind Benefit Commission in 1919.[44] The responsibility for all services to the blind and for assistance to those in need was subsequently placed with the State Commission for the Blind, an agency created in 1925. To it was transferred the custody, control, and operation of the Industrial Workshop for the Blind.[45]

With the establishment of the State Department of Public Welfare, effective April 1, 1936, all assistance to the needy blind became a responsibility of that agency under the Aid to the Blind Act. This

[41] *Colorado Statutes Annotated, 1935*, Chap. 33, Secs. 107-113, 1945 Supplement.

[42] *Biennial Report, Colorado Board of Standards of Child Care, 1943-1945.*

[43] *Colorado Statutes Annotated, 1935*, Chap. 22, Sec. 12.

[44] *Compiled Laws of Colorado, 1921*, Chap. 22, Secs. 720-736.

[45] *Colorado Statutes Annotated, 1935*, Chap. 22, Secs. 1, 5.

law not only provided for monthly payments to needy blind persons but for medical services required for the prevention of blindness or restoration of sight and for burial expenses.[46]

Financial aid and services to the visually handicapped have been materially strengthened by the removal of citizenship and age as eligibility requirements for assistance; liberalized methods of determining budgetary needs; the increase of the maximum monthly payment from $30 to $40; the appointment of a nationally known ophthalmologist to the staff of the State Department of Public Welfare; and the expansion of the definition of blindness.

The counties and the state each bear one-fourth of the cost of monthly payments and the Federal Government contributes the remainder.[47] The counties are reimbursed by the state for three-fourths of medical and burial expenditures and the remaining one-fourth is a local responsibility.

Although the Aid to the Blind program benefits a relatively small number of persons in comparison to the other public assistance programs, it is of great social significance. The number of these handicapped persons receiving monthly payments has never exceeded 651, and by December, 1945, there were only 442. Inasmuch as a considerable number of needy blind persons are in the upper age groups and are recipients of Old Age Pension, this figure in no way represents all the blind who lack self-dependency. Because of the liberal provisions of the Aid to the Blind Act with respect to medical treatment, many now lead full and active lives unrestricted by sight impairment. In 1945 alone, more than one hundred persons found there was no further need for assistance under this program because their sight had been restored or materially improved through successful surgery or other medical treatment.

Powers and duties formerly vested in the State Commission for the Blind with respect to teachers for the adult blind, welfare and social work, and home teaching were transferred to the State Department of Public Welfare in 1941.[48] Here a registry of the blind of Colorado is maintained as current and complete as possible. Persons regardless of economic status and extent of sight deficiency are serviced in their own homes by four teachers on the staff. Instruction in Braille or Moon type, in typewriting, and in handicrafts that can be learned without the use of sight are taught. Talking Book machines are at the disposal of the blind on a loan basis and they may be retained in the home, if in use, for any length of time. The Library of Congress assigned 255 of these machines to the State Department of Public Welfare for distribution. The Denver Public Library, the distributing center for Talking Book recordings in Colorado, sends these on request and at no expense. The program of services for the blind has outstanding phases such as helping persons to adjust to

46 *Ibid.*, Chap. 22, Secs. 38-68.

47 An amendment to the Social Security Act effective October 1, 1946, resulted in greater participation by the federal government.

48 *Ibid.*, Chap. 22, Sec. 11(12), 1945 Supplement.

blindness by various means, assisting them with activities which are conducive to normal living, and aiding them in the development of skills which, in many instances, form a basis for future employment.

The State Board of Industries for the Blind was created in 1941, when the State Commission for the Blind was abolished.[49] This new board of five members appointed by the Governor was given broad

Wildcat Point, Lookout Mountain

powers relating to economic education, vocational training, and employment of blind persons. Its functions therefore include the maintenance of a workshop, supervision of stands and concessions in Federal buildings; selection and licensing of blind operators in Federal, state, and other public or private buildings.[50] Services to persons with visual handicaps have been materially enhanced by the addition of a full-time industrial specialist to the staff. His functions include the supervision of vocational training; close supervision for an extended period when a person has been placed in private industry, and follow-up service thereafter to the end that satisfactory adjustment on the job is continued; and maintenance of a state-wide survey for the purpose of locating jobs in private industry that do not require the use of sight. The activities of the Industries for the

[49] *Colorado Statutes Annotated, 1935,* Chap. 22, Sec. 11(9) 1945 Supplement.
[50] *Ibid.,* Chap. 22, Sec. 11(7) 1945 Supplement.

Blind reached a high point in 1945 when 43 persons, following train-ing and placement, were employed in private industry; an additional 11 persons were operators of vending stands; and 30 others were receiving monthly remuneration or paid on the basis of piecework in the sheltered workshop located at 100 West 7th Avenue in Denver.[51]

AID TO DEPENDENT CHILDREN

The first Mothers' Compensation Law in Colorado was enacted in 1913. It provided that assistance could be given a child, "If the parent or parents of such dependent or neglected child are poor and unable to properly care for such child, but otherwise are proper guardians, and it is for the welfare of such child to remain at home, the court may enter an order finding such facts and fixing the amount of money necessary to enable the parent or parents to prop-erly care for such child, and thereupon it shall be the duty of the board of county commissioners, and in those cities operating under article XX of the constitution it shall be the duty of the department and authority performing that part of the functions of a board of county commissioners, or vested with power for the relief of the poor, to pay such parent or parents, or, if it seems for the best interest of the child, to some other person designated by the court for that purpose, at such times as said order may designate, the amount so specified, or when so ordered by the court, its equivalent in supplies and assistance, for the care of such dependent or neglected child until the further order of the court." It was administered in the counties by the County Judges, who determined the amount of awards to be paid by the County Commissioners. Participation in the pro-gram was optional on the part of the individual county until 1919.[52] As late as August, 1934, the law was functioning in only 33 of the 63 counties in the state.[53]

In 1936 the Aid to Dependent Children Act[54] supplanted the Mothers' Compensation Law in order to conform with the provisions of the Social Security Act, thus enabling the state to benefit from Federal participation in the cost of the program. The operation of the Aid to Dependent Children Act was made mandatory in all coun-ties and the responsibility for carrying out its provisions was placed on the State Department of Public Welfare effective April 1, 1936. All Mothers' Compensation cases, representing 2,346 children, were therefore transferred to that agency. The number of children increased almost consistently month by month until April 1, 1941, when 15,789 were benefited by cash payments. This group of depend-ents was materially affected by military allotments and allowances as well as increased employment opportunities during the war period. In December, 1945, there were slightly more than 9,000 child recipients

---

[51] Monthly reports (unpublished) Colorado Industries for the Blind.
[52] *Colorado Statutes Annotated, 1935,* Chap. 33, Secs. 7-11.
[53] Statewide Social Welfare Survey, 1934, D. S. Howard, Director of Research.
[54] *Colorado Statutes Annotated, 1935,* Chap. 33, Secs. 85-106.

under this program.   The Social Security Act limits Federal matching to one-half of the payments, which do not exceed $18 for one eligible child and $12 for each additional child in the family who meets eligibility requirements.   Prior to the passage of an amendment to the Aid to Dependent Children Law in 1945,[55] Colorado adhered to these restrictions.   The inadequacy of the Federal maximums was evidenced by the fact that it was necessary to supplement payments with General Assistance in a high proportion of the cases.   Under the provisions of the 1945 amendment, Aid to Dependent Children payments are made to care for all budgetary requirements.[56]   It follows therefore that General Assistance funds are used only to meet unforeseen emergencies, particularly those in connection with medical needs.   The state and counties share equally with respect to assistance payments in which the Federal Government participates, but they contribute three-fourths and one-fourth respectively in the amount above the maximums set by the Social Security Act for Aid to Dependent Children.[57]

Old Age Pension

Humanitarian methods of dealing with the problems of the needy aged in the state developed more slowly than those for the needy blind and dependent children.   Until 1933 the almshouse or poor farm remained the refuge for those in the upper age groups unable to maintain self-dependency.   It follows, therefore, that the vision of "going over the hill to the poorhouse" was no doubt vivid to many having reached the nonproductive span of life and those approaching this period.   The inauguration and growth of the pension program resulted in the rapid depopulation of county institutions operated primarily for the care of the aged.   By the end of 1945, only five were in operation, with a total population of less than 300.   These institutions are maintained chiefly as convalescent homes for needy persons who are too feeble or disabled to care for themselves and have no family members by whom the required attention can be provided.

The first Old Age Pension Law was enacted by the General Assembly in 1927,[58] more than a half century after Colorado acquired statehood.   No state funds were involved and the effectuation of the program was left to the discretion of the Boards of County Commissioners.   Payment could be made to persons with a minimum age of 70 who met specified "good behavior" requirements and 15 years of citizenship and county residence; the amount when added to the income could not exceed $1 per day.   If the estate of a deceased recipient was insufficient to meet the cost of a reasonable funeral,

---

55 *Ibid.*, Chap. 33, Sec. 89, 1945 Supplement.

56 The effect of removing "ceilings" on payments is discussed in *Public Welfare Statistics,* official publication of the Colorado State Department of Public Welfare, Vol. 3, No. 1, October, 1945.

57 An amendment to the Social Security Act effective October 1, 1946, resulted in greater participation by the federal government.

58 *Colorado Session Laws, 1927,* Chap. 143.

the County Judge could direct payment from Old Age Pension funds up to $100. Persons were ineligible for pensions if they had kin who were legally responsible for their support and were able to contribute such support. Ownership of property in excess of $3,000 was also a basis for ineligibility. The law required applicants to deed their property to the county in those instances in which the County Judge deemed it necessary. It further provided for the repayment of pensions with interest at 3 per cent if the estate of a deceased recipient could meet all or part of the amount. An amendment passed in 1931 reduced the minimum age to 65 and contained mandatory provisions with respect to the establishment of a system of Old Age Pension in each county.[59] Under this act, the Boards of County Commissioners were required to appropriate sufficient funds annually in order to carry out the provisions of the law. No payments were made to the needy aged under the original law nor under the amendment of 1931. Both acts were held unconstitutional because they conferred judicial duties on the County Commissioners.

When the General Assembly met in 1933, another Old Age Pension Law came into being.[60] Setting up the program in the counties was made mandatory and the County Judges were charged with the administration. State funds from specified sources were earmarked to meet the cost of payments and these funds were allocated to the counties on the basis of the last population census available. Although it was permissible under the law for the counties to levy a tax for additional funds, only one county raised revenue for this purpose. The maximum payments were $1 per day for subsistence and $100 for burial—identical provisions of the law passed six years before. Eligibility requirements were substantially the same as those stipulated in the law of 1927 with amendments in 1931. There were two points of definite liberalization, i. e., county residence was reduced to five years and the value of combined property of husband and wife was lowered to $2,000. Allocation of state funds on the basis of the relationship of total county population to that of the state resulted in inequitable distribution and worked hardships in many instances. Counties with a relatively high proportion of the population in the aged group were forced to keep the amount of pensions extremely low. On the other hand, counties in which the population tended toward the younger groups paid higher pensions to the needy aged and, at the same time, accumulated surpluses. March, 1936, was the last month in which payments were made under this law. There were 21,879 pensioners in the state receiving an average payment of $17.72 for that month. Average payments varied widely, from $5 in some counties to $27 in others.

At the second extraordinary session in 1936, the General Assembly enacted the Old Age Assistance Act and, in connection with its operation, specified the duties of the State Department of Public Welfare

[59] *Ibid., 1931,* Chap. 131.
[60] *Ibid., 1933,* Chap. 144.

and those of the county departments under its jurisdiction. It was necessary to include eligibility requirements less restrictive than those of the preceding law. Only by so doing could Colorado qualify for Federal participation in the cost of the program under the Social Security Act. Citizens of the United States who had reached the age of 65 and had resided in Colorado continuously for one year preceding the date of application and four additional years within the nine prior to this date met the citizenship, age, and residence requirements of the law. Such persons were not eligible for assistance if in need of continuing institutional care or if inmates of any municipal, state, national, or private institution. Furthermore, no payments could be made to the persons who, within five years prior to application, transferred or assigned property in order to make themselves eligible for this aid. Applicants were required to sign agreements to repay the fund for all assistance received and to give a lien on property holdings as collateral security.[61]

One of the main objectives of the program was the granting of assistance to aged persons who were without sufficient income or other resources to provide subsistence compatible with decency and health. The monthly payments, nevertheless, could not go beyond $30. If the estate of a deceased recipient was insufficient to meet the cost of a reasonable funeral and legally responsible relatives were unable to pay, Old Age Assistance funds could be used to a maximum of $100. Earmarked state funds and Federal funds financed this program, the latter restricted to one-half of the monthly payments to recipients. Assistance was granted under this law from April, 1936, through August, 1937, and during this period there was a monthly average of nearly 26,000 recipients. The average monthly payments remained close to $27.50 except in the first four months when the average ranged between $17.72 and $20.75.

It was at the general election in November, 1936, that Constitutional Amendment No. 4 appeared on the ballot by petition of the National Annuity League, an organization of Old Age Pensioners in Colorado. This amendment received 239,289 favorable and 134,377 unfavorable votes. Using the number of votes cast for gubernatorial candidates as a basis, it can be estimated that more than 108,000 persons failed to vote on this measure.

The significance of the amendment lay in the fact that many of the provisions of the Old Age Assistance Act were revolutionized. Monthly payments were set at $45 less net income. The age requirement was reduced to 60 years. A residence owned and occupied as a home and ownership of personal property exempt from execution or attachment were not disqualifying factors. Repayments for assistance to which recipients were entitled were made prohibitive. Specific state revenues including the sales tax, previously a temporary measure, could not be affected by repeal or amendment unless an equal amount or more were provided from some other source. The provision com-

61 *Colorado Statutes Annotated, 1935,* Chap. 119, Sec. 14.

monly known as the "Jack Pot" made the depletion of the balance in the Old Age Pension Fund as of December 31 of each year mandatory; such balances were to be distributed to qualified pensioners within ten days following the close of the calendar year.

January 1, 1937, was set as the date on which revenue would begin to accrue to the Old Age Pension Fund on the new basis. This was also the date specified for commencing payments as required by the amendment. In answer to the interrogatories of the Governor, the Supreme Court held that Constitutional Amendment No. 4 was self-executing with respect to revenues accruing to the fund on the specified date and the remaining provisions could become effective by enabling legislation only.

The $45 Old Age Pension Act came into being in May, 1937; however, it did not become effective until September 1, 1937.[62] Plans for its operation required approval of the Social Security Administration so that Federal aid for recipients aged 65 or more would not be jeopardized.

It was assumed by many persons that the statute was so clear that it would require little interpretation. When the law was put to a practical test, a host of problems presented themselves that could not be cleared except with the continuous help of the Attorney General's office. Even before January, 1938, when the first bonus payment was made, the National Annuity League applied to the Denver District Court for a declaratory judgment restraining the State Department of Public Welfare from paying the so-called "Jack Pot." The Court ruled that the funds must be distributed in conformity with the Constitutional Amendment; consequently, close to 35,000 pensioners each received $27.77 in addition to the regular payment in that month. In the five and one-half years thereafter, Old Age Pension funds were sufficient to pay the full amount of the authorized award in three months only. When there was a shortage of funds, all awards were reduced uniformly, the amounts ranging from $1 a month to $14. It was within this five and one-half year period that the number of recipients rose to almost 43,000. Authorized awards have been paid in full since August, 1943, and, in addition, the second bonus was paid in January, 1945. Each pensioner received the regular payment together with $48.12 from the "Jack Pot."

A reduction in the number of payments per month, averaging 40,491 in 1945, and a decided increase in revenues resulted in a surplus at the end of 1945 which provided for a bonus payment of $79.13 to each eligible pensioner in January, 1946. Thus for a third time, a new year began with the Old Age Pension Fund depleted.

An initiated act approved by the voters in Colorado at the general election in 1944 makes an annual appropriation from state funds available for Old Age Pension purposes when revenues are not sufficient to pay the awards of qualified recipients in full. The law provides

---

62 *Ibid.*, Chap. 119, Secs. 28(1)-28(27), 1945 Supplement.

for a maximum of $1,500,000 per year.[63] This resource has not been used thus far because of the adequacy of revenues accruing to the Old Age Pension Fund.

Based on the latest available census data, two out of every five persons in Colorado with an age of 65 years or more are recipients of Old Age Pension. Recipients in the 60 through 64-year group form a very small proportion of the case load. The peak was reached in June, 1941, when 3,631 received payments; only 1,903 of the 40,408 recipients in December, 1945, were in this age group.

It is an established fact that nearly one-half of all the pensioners on the rolls at any given time are without income in cash or kind and do not occupy homes which they own. These recipients are therefore those who are granted a monthly payment of $45, the maximum permitted under the law.

Old-Age and Survivors Insurance, administered directly by the Federal Government through regional offices of the Social Security Board, is the first line of defense against economic need and poverty in the latter years of life. Benefits are based on contributions of employers and employees in covered industries. Because this program was not in effect when many persons now in the aged group were working, it has had slight effect on the Old Age Pension program. There are approximately 1,000 pensioners whose awards are reduced by monthly payments received through this contributory insurance system. Because such payments are relatively small, they do not disqualify the recipients for Old Age Pension.

The federal government pays one-half of the Old Age Pension payment of $40 or less made to persons 65 years of age or more; the state meets the other half plus the entire amount paid to these recipients in excess of $40. In addition, all payments to the 60 through 64-year group and all burial expenses incurred for pensioners come from state funds exclusively.[64]

GENERAL ASSISTANCE

Pauper relief, or poor relief, carrying the demoralizing stigma of bygone days is outmoded in Colorado although those in need of this public relief are, in legal language, still known as "paupers." General Assistance has been generally accepted and used to designate this public welfare program, the cost of which was borne entirely by the counties until the early depression years. It was then that the county governments were caught between lowered revenues and increased relief loads. Failure of banks, low farm prices, drouth, and industrial unemployment contributed to the growing numbers of those thrown on the counties for support. The Federal Government recognized that economic insecurity and poverty were the greatest problems of modern society and stepped in with loans and relief before the state

---

[63] *Ibid.,* Chap. 119, Sec. 28(28), 1945 Supplement.

[64] An amendment to the Social Security Act effective October 1, 1946, resulted in greater participation by the federal government.

assumed a major role. The first direct allocation of state funds to the counties was made in July, 1935, through the Official State Relief Committee.

At each legislative session since 1935, appropriations have been made for the purpose of aiding the counties to meet relief needs. A high point was reached in 1937 when $5,000,000 was appropriated from the General Fund of the state for the biennium ending June 30, 1939.

Larimer County Court House, Fort Collins

The continued operation of the categorical programs with federal and state participation and the industrial absorption of persons with even limited employability during the war period relieved the county governments of much of their financial burden. The result was a reduction in state appropriations for this program; the General Assembly of 1945 made $1,250,000 available to the State Department of Public Welfare for the two-year period ending June 30, 1947. Authority was given for the transfer of funds from the Emergency and Contingent Account of the State Public Welfare Fund if the direct appropriation proves to be insufficient for the care and relief of destitute unemployed and unemployable citizens.

General Assistance is given to needy persons by the county departments of Public Welfare from two separate funds, *i. e.,* the County Support to the Poor raised by mill levy and the County Special State Relief Fund composed of allocations from state appropriation. Expenditures from the latter are restricted to persons who have resided in

Colorado continuously for three years with the intent to make it their home, and who have not received any aid from state or county funds during the three-year period. In case of dire need and destitution, however, a person with residence of one year may be given assistance from the County Special State Relief Fund if self-maintained during that period of time.[65]

Provisions with respect to expenditures from the Support of Poor Fund are less restrictive, inasmuch as the poor laws mentioned in the first part of this chapter are still in effect. In addition, under a law of 1933, any person acquires state residence for relief purposes at the end of one year of self-support or at the end of three years whether maintained at public expense for all or part of this period.[66]

Absence for one year constitutes loss of residence for General Assistance purposes and residence of six months in a county determines which county is liable for assistance under this program.

The General Assistance case load is chiefly composed of unemployable persons who fail to meet eligibility requirements for categorical assistance; of recipients of monthly payments under the categories unable to meet the cost of medical services; and of families normally self-dependent but incapable of remaining so when emergencies arise such as illness or disability of the breadwinner. In December, 1945, 3,214 cases received General Assistance payments with or without medical services and 801 cases received only hospitalization, medical care, and/or burial. The high incidence of chronic diseases and permanent disabilities among the needy unemployables has been confirmed by special studies made of this so-called "residual" group in Colorado.[67]

SURPLUS COMMODITIES

The Federal Surplus Relief Corporation, subsequently changed to the Federal Surplus Commodity Corporation, came into being in October, 1933. It was created as an instrument through which price-depressing surplus products might be removed from the open market and distributed to persons in need.

This program was under federal operation in the state until late in 1935 when the Colorado State Department of Public Welfare, then known as the Colorado Special State Relief Committee, was charged with the responsibility of distributing commodities to the needy. Commodities fell into two classifications; (1) those furnished by the federal government to the state for distribution and, (2) those produced or purchased in the state. The latter included fruits and vegetables canned on WPA projects, garments and mattresses made by employees of WPA, and mattresses manufactured by private firms under contract with the State Department of Public Welfare.

---

[65] *Ibid.,* Chap. 141, Sec. 33 (2a) (2b), 1945 Supplement.
[66] *Ibid.,* Chap. 124, Sec. 16.
[67] *Informational Report on General Assistance in Colorado,* Colorado County Welfare Directors Association and Colorado State Department of Public Welfare, January, 1943.
Public Welfare Statistics, State Department of Public Welfare, Vol. 2, No. 4, November, 1944.

Beneficiaries included recipients of public assistance and border-line cases certified by the county departments of public welfare, Rural Rehabilitation clients, public institutions, and private institutions rendering care and service to the needy and destitute. Foods were later made available to school children under the hot lunch program.

Commodities were shipped from the central warehouse in Denver to commissaries located throughout the state. The county departments of public welfare established the eligibility of recipients and distributed the items to individual cases.

With the inauguration of the Food Stamp Plan in 1939, the direct distribution of agricultural products to needy households terminated. The plan became operative in Denver County in November, 1939, and by the end of two years, there was state-wide coverage. Under this method, foodstuffs designated as surplus by the federal government passed through regular commercial channels. Certification by the county departments of public welfare on the basis of need made it possible for persons in low income groups and recipients of public assistance to avail themselves of the benefits under this program. The purchase of stamps which could be used for any food in markets or retail stores entitled the buyer to free stamps with one-half the value of those purchased. The stamps received without cost to the recipient could be given for surplus foods only. In the months just prior to the discontinuance of stamps in January, 1943, nearly 10,000 needy families and single persons participated in the plan, thereby securing highly nutritive foods at no cost to them.

Since the termination of the Food Stamp Plan, allocations of agricultural products have been restricted to institutions and schools. As of the close of 1945, the State Department of Public Welfare was making assignments to nine state and 59 charitable institutions having a total inmate population of almost 12,000 and to 216 schools serving hot lunches for the benefit of 27,249 children. Mattresses and articles of wearing apparel made in WPA sewing rooms continue to be distributed to needy persons by the county departments of public welfare.

Obviously, crop surpluses on a nation-wide basis ended with wartime demand. The lack of processing facilities through commercial channels, however, continued to make government price support action necessary in some instances. Conservation and utilization of produce of a perishable nature are essential not only to our national economy but to the program of alleviating world famine.

DEPRESSION YEARS[68]

The precipitous rise in unemployment after 1929 and the accompanying shrinkage in tax revenues laid a crushing burden on local

[68] Numerous other federal emergency programs were operative in the state in addition to those discussed here. These programs were confined chiefly to relieving agriculture, industry, business, and individual property holders. The Civil Works Administration, in existence for about four months only, functioned as a work relief measure and the Farm Security Administration made direct grants to farmers for a limited time. Valuable data relative to federal agencies are contained in the report of the Committee on Long Range Work and Relief Policies made to the National Resources Planning Board in 1942. (For sale by the Superintendent of Documents, Washington, D. C.)

communities for which they were totally unprepared. New sources of funds were urgently needed. Help from both state and federal governments was imperative in order to safeguard those affected by the consequences of the economic upheaval.

The gravity of the situation was first given recognition by the federal government in 1930 when the President's Emergency Committee for Employment was organized. No funds were made available to the states at that time nor in the following year, when this committee was superseded by the President's Organization on Unemployment Relief. Both committees merely urged industry to spread employment, advocated expansion of state and local public works, and suggested methods of meeting relief problems on state and local levels. The Federal Government did not authorize use of funds for the financing of unemployment relief until July, 1932, when the Emergency Relief and Construction Act was approved. Under its provisions, the Reconstruction Finance Corporation, created in January of that year, disbursed federal funds to the states on a repayment basis. Responsibility for the administration of funds thus obtained was vested in the governors.

The first federal funds, $250,000, reached Colorado in September, 1932, for relief in the drouth-stricken areas of the state. At that time there were 5,000 destitute families in 12 counties affected by crop failures.[69]

The Colorado lawmakers, meeting in regular session in January, 1933, made no direct appropriation to meet the ever increasing distress in the state. The duty of furnishing aid to those affected by the widespread unemployment was considered as primarily an obligation of counties and municipalities. They did, however, empower the governor to make application for federal funds and to disburse them through the Official Colorado State Relief Committee for the purpose of furnishing relief or work relief. At the same time, an appropriation was made to cover the actual operating expenses of the committee.[70]

Outright federal grants to states to aid in meeting the costs of furnishing relief and work relief and in relieving the hardship and suffering caused by unemployment were first authorized on May 12, 1933, upon approval of the Federal Emergency Relief Act of 1933. It was not the intention of the Congress to assume the entire burden but that the states contribute a proportionate share. On July 21, 1933, the Federal Emergency Relief Administrator requested the governor of Colorado to specify in an early answer the methods by which the state would arrange to meet its reasonable share of unemployment relief. In the letter it was stated that over 85 per cent of Colorado's relief funds since January 1, 1933, had been supplied by the Federal Government, less than 15 per cent by local communities, and nothing by the state. The administrator further stated that additional money

[69] *Rocky Mountain News,* September 18, 1932.
[70] *Colorado Session Laws, 1933,* Chap. 51.

would not be granted to Colorado unless provisions were made for greater participation in the relief load by the state and/or its local subdivisions.[71]

In August, 1933, Governor Johnson called a special session of the legislature to consider principally the manner of obtaining revenue for unemployment relief. At this session the Motor Vehicle Act was passed to provide funds by the imposition of additional fees upon the registration of motor vehicles during the remainder of 1933 and during 1934. The fees, based on valuation and ranging from $2 to $60, were to be collected and expended by the counties for relief purposes.[72]

The Supreme Court held that the "UR" tax imposed a property tax and was not a license fee; that its purpose was for revenue only; and that it violated the constitutional provision against the imposition by the legislature of any tax for a county purpose. Thus the state remained in the role of noncontributor while those dependent on relief or work relief grew to 225,000, approximating 25 per cent of the estimated population.[73]

The Twenty-ninth General Assembly convened in December in a second extraordinary session during 1933. Apparently there was some apprehension in Washington as to satisfactory action on legislative measures relative to relief. The Federal Emergency Relief Administrator notified the state of discontinuance of Federal funds awaiting action of the state to provide revenues for the relief of privation and destitution. Before the General Assembly adjourned January 22, 1934, it had appropriated $100,000 to the Official Colorado State Relief Committee with authorization to purchase cattle in Colorado and to distribute the beef in processed or cured form to the destitute unemployed. In addition, an excise tax of one cent per gallon on motor fuel had been imposed and 25 per cent of the funds accruing to the State Highway Fund from tax on such sales had been earmarked for relief purposes for a period of one year.[74]

In spite of the foregoing legislative provisions, 1934 was a turbulent year. The distress caused by drouths as well as continued unemployment in industrial areas made it necessary for the state to request more and more federal funds. There were times when allotments seemed meager and entirely inadequate to meet the crisis.[75]

Federal funds granted to Colorado in the early depression were used not only for direct grants to persons in their own homes and for work relief but for such other purposes as care of transients, continuation of rural schools, and aid to self-cooperatives. From September, 1933, until December, 1935, there was a Transient Division within the state relief setup for the relief of those individuals who, not content to stay at home and starve or stagnate for lack of employ-

[71] Edith Abbott, Public Assistance, Volume I, *American Principles and Policies,* pp. 786, 787, University of Chicago Press, 1940.

[72] *Colorado Session Laws, Extraordinary Session, 1933,* Chap. 14.

[73] *Rocky Mountain News,* May 14, 1933.

[74] *Colorado Session Laws, Second Extraordinary Session, 1933-1934,* Chap. 1, 16.

[75] *Denver Post,* April 5, 1934, and June 7, 1934.

ment, sought to better their condition by moving about the country in search of work. Oftentimes by so doing, they lost residence for relief purposes in their home community and state residence as well. The federal government met the entire cost of aid under this program and during its operation, sent more than two million dollars to Colorado.[76] In shelters maintained in the larger centers in Colorado, boys and single men were fed, clothed, and given medical attention. Later, work camps were established for able-bodied men. The physically unfit received care in sanatoria and infirmaries. Unattached women and families were provided for in living quarters such as rooming houses, apartments, or dwellings.

Financial difficulties of some rural communities in Colorado made it impossible for them to operate their public school systems. Had federal funds not been available for rural school districts adversely affected, thousands of children would have been deprived of educational opportunities. The cost of keeping 201 schools open during the 1933-1934 term was nearly $59,000. In the following year, 23 schools were able to continue because of federal funds totaling more than $11,000.[77]

Comparatively early in the depression years a limited number of self-help groups organized for the barter of goods and services. In order to benefit from federal aid, these self-help cooperatives were required to conform to certain general rules and policies established by the Federal Emergency Relief Administration with respect to membership; minimum rates of payment in scrip, credit, goods, or services; monthly reports of activities; and administrative procedures. Federal funds earmarked for this program in Colorado totaled nearly $195,000.[78]

By December, 1935, when the federal government discontinued relief grants to states, Colorado had received close to $48,500,000 for direct and work relief and for the special emergency programs operated. The peak month under FERA was reached in April, 1935, when 85,984 cases representing 276,762 persons were on the pay rolls.[79]

Several months prior to the cessation of grants under FERA, a new work program came into being. The Works Progress Administration, later known as Work Projects Administration, was created by executive order on May 6, 1935. Its primary function was to conduct a program of useful public work in cooperation with state and local governments. The work projects locally sponsored and approved by the Federal Agency were operated to provide work and wages for able-bodied unemployed persons who were currently certified as in need. Neither the size of a worker's family nor the number dependent upon him was a factor in determining the amount of wages. Compensation varied with the type or classification of the job only. As in

[76] Final Statistical Report of the Federal Emergency Relief Administration, 1942, p. 297.
[77] *Ibid.*, p. 112.
[78] *Ibid.*, p. 115.
[79] *Rocky Mountain News*, January 1, 1936.

the nation as a whole, Colorado attempted to operate projects in which the usual occupations of the workers could be followed. This was essential to the preservation of skills and morale as well as to the maintenance of efficient work standards.

As early as September, 1935, approximately 400 projects sponsored in Colorado had been submitted to the Federal Agency for approval.[80] The task of transferring employable persons from FERA rolls to WPA was nearly completed at the end of the year. The responsibility of caring for cases having no employable member remained with the state and local governments. At no time during the life of the program did the number on the pay roll exceed the 40,000 in February, 1936. The special assistance programs which began in April of that year absorbed a considerable number formerly dependent on WPA wages. From time to time WPA retrenchment was necessary for reasons such as dwindling federal appropriations and lack of adequate sponsored projects in certain local communities.

Despite the various merits of the WPA program, the earnings of the workers were insufficient to maintain a desirable living standard as a general rule. It was necessary for the county departments of public welfare to use General Assistance funds to meet the cost of hospitalization and other medical services for workers and their dependents. Furthermore, available surplus commodities were issued to WPA cases in an effort to raise health and living standards.

Changes in monthly average earnings occurred in Colorado not only from year to year but from month to month within the year, depending on the wage schedule in effect, the working time lost for various reasons, and other significant factors. That average monthly earnings did not remain static is indicated in a comparison of the averages earned in winter months. Based on earnings in December of the previous year and in the first two months of the year shown, the workers received a monthly average of $45.86 in 1936, $50.96 in 1938, $53.23 in 1940, and $67.14 in 1942.[81]

Colorado was the first state of its size to liquidate WPA. When the books were closed on March 31, 1943, it was shown that work had been provided for approximately 150,000 persons at a cost of 120 million dollars. Among the chief accomplishments of WPA throughout the state were 9,000 miles of highway built or improved; 500 public buildings constructed and 1,500 remodeled (estimated); storm and sanitary sewers, water mains, and other vital improvements installed; and innumerable facilities set up for recreation. Other outstanding and worthwhile enterprises included the operation of sewing rooms where garments and household articles were made for the needy; hot lunches prepared and served to school children; vegetables and fruits canned for distribution; and maintenance of nurseries for child care. Many needy persons in the so-called "white collar" class contributed to the success of art and theatrical projects,

80 *Ibid.,* September 3, 1935.

81 Donald S. Howard, *The WPA and Federal Relief Policy,* p. 183, New York. Russell Sage Foundation, 1943.

of the Colorado Guide Book, and of various clerical projects. Obviously, a large proportion of WPA work during the last three years of the program was in connection with national defense.[82]

Emergency conservation work for unemployed young men was originally authorized under the provisions of an Act of the 73rd Congress and approved March 31, 1933.[83] The name Civilian Conservation Corps was adopted by Executive order of April 5, 1933. The objectives were twofold: namely, the conservation of human values and the preservation or development of the country's natural resources. The first of these was attained through the employment of young men between the ages of 18 and 25, later changed to 17-28, thus upbuilding them in health, morale, confidence, and self-respect, in addition to bringing financial relief to distressed families. The second was realized in the conservation, restoration, and protection of forests; in soil erosion and flood control; in the development of public parks, recreational and historical areas; in wild life conservation; and in the performance of other useful public works.

Existing state-wide public agencies were asked to accept the responsibilities of administration of enrollee selection. Chronologically, the Colorado selecting authorities were State Relief Committee, Emergency Relief Administration, Works Progress Administration, State Department of Public Welfare. The latter functioned in this capacity from December 1, 1936, to June 30, 1942, when the Congress enacted legislation for the liquidation of the Civilian Conservation Corps.[84] During the time in which this program was operative, 32,501 Colorado youths were enrolled in the Civilian Conservation Corps.[85]

The second nation-wide step in the recognition of the youth problem was taken in the middle of 1935 with the establishment of the National Youth Administration.[86] The major objectives of the agency, formulated shortly after its creation, remained fundamentally the same throughout its life. The basic purpose was to provide constructive work at a wage for unemployed youths out of school and in need of a job, and for youths in school but who needed financial assistance in order to continue their education. The NYA operated successively within three federal administrative structures, namely, Works Progress Administration, Federal Security Agency, and the War Manpower Commission. Federal funds approximating six and one-half million dollars were expended in Colorado during the operation of the program, two-thirds of which represented expenditures for the out-of-school work programs and one-third for the student work phase.

82 *Rocky Mountain News,* March 28, 1943.

83 73rd Congress, 1st session, Public Act 5.

84 77th Congress, 2nd session, Public Act 647.

85 Detailed information in Colorado State Department of Public Welfare *Quarterly Bulletins,* Vol. 1, No. 1, through Vol. 6, No. 2.

86 For more details relative to the operation than given in this brief account, see *Annual Reports of National Youth Administration,* and *Final Report of the National Youth Administration,* (1936-1943), U. S. Government Printing Office, Washington, D. C.

The student program operated on the high school and elementary levels as well as college level. The work projects in the participating educational institutions offered basic work experience; helped students to develop good work habits and attitudes which would aid them in securing and holding a job; and made it possible for pupils to advance more rapidly in their chosen fields.[87]. In the state the average number of students employed monthly during the academic year 1939-1940 was 5,176. It dropped, however, to 1,143 in the last year of operation, 1942-1943.

Plans for work activities for out-of-school youths originated in the local communities and the types of projects were determined, in general, by the number in need of a job; their aptitudes and occupational interests; the needs of the community for particular goods and services; and the employment opportunities in the area. As co-sponsors, the local communities contributed a portion of the cost of materials and equipment which enabled a much larger percentage of Federal funds to go to the youth workers in the form of wages. The county departments of public welfare cooperated with the National Youth Administration by certifying young men and women who met eligibility requirements with respect to need. Relief status did not remain a requisite for employment, therefore NYA accepted direct applications from unemployed youths as well as referrals by the welfare agencies.

Throughout the state, work activities for the benefit of young people and their communities fell chiefly into the following classifications: land development and beautification; conservation and sanitation; sewing, arts and crafts; workshops of numerous types; clerical and semi-professional; carpentry and related work; and school, library, hospital, and home service.

The illustrations given are indicative of the operation and accomplishments in the state. (1) A project, in which 52 young people were employed in Fort Morgan, transformed a dump ground into a landscaped tract, swimming pool, and a recreational center. (2) Navajo Lodge located on the edge of Black Forest northeast of Colorado Springs was operated as a resident school and camp for unemployed girls. Accommodations were maintained for 80 girls, each of whom was enrolled for a period of three months. Here they received training in the various phases of homemaking and instruction in subjects such as home economics, social sciences, drama, music, art, and handicraft. In addition, a varied program of recreation and physical education was conducted. (3) Training classes for domestic service were given in the Emily Griffith Opportunity School located in Denver. Each girl received training for a period covering about three and one-half months. Emphasis was placed on cooking, serving, cleaning, and laundry work, supplemented with some instruction in marketing. Success of this project was evidenced by the fact that a large pro-

---

[87] Evaluation of the student work program in Colorado is given in "Efficiency of High School NYA Program in Colorado," by Robert A. Davis and Hazel Taylor, in *The School Review* (University of Chicago, May, 1943).

portion of the girls were placed in private employment following the completion of the courses. (4) An extensive library project was operated in Weld County. Girls and boys worked in every department of the Greeley Public Library and were trained to make and repair all types of library equipment. When the county established small branch units in other parts of the county, they were staffed entirely by NYA youths who had received their training in Greeley.

The rise of the defense emergency, bringing the impact of industrial, agricultural, and military demands, had far-reaching effects on the NYA program. There was a sharp drop in the number of projects and of youths employed, together with a change in work activities to meet anticipated defense needs. Beginning early in 1942, NYA projects which contributed the least to the war effort were discontinued in the state. In appropriating funds for the 1943-44 fiscal year, the Congress ordered the National Youth Administration to liquidate as rapidly as possible, but in any event not later than January 1, 1944. Liquidation of this agency marked the end of all federal emergency work programs instituted in the 1930s for persons who met economic catastrophe in the depression years.

EMPLOYMENT SECURITY

The state of Colorado and the Federal Government are partners in the program of compensation to unemployed workers. This partnership came into being in 1936 with the passage of the Colorado Unemployment Compensation Act, containing provisions in compliance with Title IX of the Social Security Act.[88] The gravity of the unemployment problem in Colorado was reflected in the declaration of policy in the state act: "* * * Economic insecurity due to unemployment is a serious menace to the health, morals, and welfare of the people of this state. Involuntary unemployment is therefore a subject of general interest and concern which requires appropriate action by the legislature to prevent its spread and to lighten its burden which now so often falls with crushing force upon the unemployed worker and his family. The achievement of social security requires protection against this greatest hazard of our economic life. This can be provided by encouraging employers to provide more stable employment and by the systematic accumulation of funds during periods of employment to provide benefits for periods of unemployment, thus maintaining purchasing power and limiting the serious social consequences of poor relief assistance. The legislature, therefore, declares that in its considered judgment the public good, and the general welfare of the citizens of this state require the enactment of this measure, under the police powers of the state, for the compulsory setting aside of unemployment reserves to be used for the benefit of persons unemployed through no fault of their own."[89]

[88] *Colorado Statutes Annotated, 1935,* Chap. 167A, Sec. 1, 1945 Supplement.
[89] *Ibid.,* Sec. 2.

The Division of Unemployment Compensation and the State Employment Service, established in 1933, were merged into a single division. This merger was affected in October, 1938, under provisions of a legislative act of the previous year.[90] The Division of Unemployment Compensation and Employment Service was set up in 1939 as one of the executive departments directly responsible to the governor and the name was changed to the Colorado Department of Employment Security two years later.[91] It has a liaison relationship with the State Industrial Commission which functions as a superior authority on appeals of employers and claimants desiring a review of departmental decisions affecting them. An additional function of the Industrial Commission is that of formulating regulations with respect to benefits and contributions not specifically covered by law.

The Division of Employment Service within the Department of Employment Security attempts to find the most suitable job attainable for all persons who request its service, and, furthermore, it endeavors to secure the best qualified available workers for employers. The Division of Unemployment Compensation handles all employer contributions and pays compensation to eligible persons who are unemployed through no fault of their own and for whom no suitable work can be found. The two divisions are jointly responsible for gathering and compiling statistics on employment and unemployment used as a basis for planning public works and other programs to supplement jobs in private industry when necessary.

Contributions from employers with eight or more employees and from employers voluntarily coming under the program began in January, 1936. Yearly contributions from covered industries reached a high point in 1943, when $6,119,462 represented the total placed in the Unemployment Compensation Fund. By the end of 1945, the balance in the fund had risen to $35,798,993, an amount which had not been reached previously. This peak was the result of relatively small withdrawals for benefits during the war years and the high level of employment in covered industries which increased payments into the fund. The first benefit payments were made in 1939 and by the end of 1945 a total of $11,172,954 had been paid to wholly or partially unemployed workers. The absorption of unemployed persons into war industries, expanded business activities, and the armed forces was reflected in the decline in unemployment compensation payments immediately following 1940. The termination of the war, however, brought a sharp increase in the number of claims filed for unemployment compensation. In 1945, benefit payments totaled $191,963, an increase of 41.6 per cent over the previous year.[92]

Under an agreement with the Veterans Administration in August, 1944, the Department of Employment Security accepts and pays claims to veterans under the Servicemen's Readjustment Act—commonly

---

[90] *Ibid.,* Sec. 10.

[91] *Ibid.,* Sec. 12.

[92] Source of data: Special report submitted to writer by Division of Unemployment Compensation.

known as the G. I. Bill of Rights. Established policies with respect to payment of state unemployment compensation are followed when they are not in conflict with this Federal Act. The veteran is required to register for work at the United States Employment Service. If no suitable job is available, he becomes eligible for a weekly benefit payment of $20. The act provides for a maximum of 52 weekly payments to veterans who were in active service after September 16, 1940, for a period not less than nine months and sixteen days. After the cessation of hostilities with Japan, there was a marked increase in claims and payments which until that time had not exceeded $8,000 in any month. Readjustment allowance payments to unemployed veterans reached $119,540 in December, 1945, a monthly peak for the period September, 1944, through 1945.

The Employment Service, which was placed under the federal government on January 1, 1942, at the request of the President, has gone through three major periods of development since its inception in 1933.

The first phase, 1933-1938, was a period of economic catastrophe, during which the Employment Service was used chiefly as a registration point for work under public auspices such as that of the Work Projects Administration. Although some private employers used the service regularly and many well-qualified workers registered, the concept that registrants included only the unemployable and persons with limited employability was nevertheless wide-spread.

The second phase of development followed the enactment of the Unemployment Compensation Act, which required all workers claiming benefits to register. Obviously, the Employment Service then dealt with a very good cross section of the labor resources of the state. The general reluctance of employers to place their job orders characterized this period as well as the one preceding it. Many employers, particularly the larger industrial establishments, had their own personnel departments. Others had no need for the service, inasmuch as sufficient workers made applications directly to them. As a rule, it was the employers with bad working conditions and low wage scales who found it necessary to recruit workers registered with the Employment Service.

With the launching of the National Defense program in the summer of 1940, the Employment Service entered the third period. It became necessary to place emphasis on service to employers engaged in war production and to offer little or no service to the so-called nonessential employers. During the war period, committees composed of equal representation of labor and management were established in each locality having a local office of the Employment Service. These labor-management committees participated in the development and operation of all manpower regulations. No regulatory programs were adopted by the public agency without approval of these local organizations. This procedure contributed greatly to community acceptance of the programs and to their success which resulted in enormous war production without the necessity of resorting to national service legislation.

In order to meet peacetime problems with respect to labor resources, the Employment Service is operating under a broad six-point program, *i. e.,* labor market analysis and information; employment counseling; personnel management services to employers; placement service; special employment services to veterans; cooperation with community organizations and government.[93]

Wartime Programs

A program put into operation in February, 1944, pertained to the giving of assistance and/or service to enemy aliens and other persons and their dependents affected by governmental action with respect to removal from restricted areas, detention, or internment. The county departments of public welfare administered the program under supervision of the State Department of Public Welfare. They worked closely at all times with the War Relocation Authority and the Immigration and Naturalization Service, and, in addition, they utilized all available resources in their respective communities in order to carry out the objectives of the plan. The federal government met the entire cost of assistance; reimbursements were made on the basis of claims sent by the county departments to the State Department of Public Welfare and submitted to the Social Security Board. Referrals to the county departments were made, in most instances, by authorities at the War Relocation Center from which the persons were released. The Granada Relocation Center, located in Prowers County, was Colorado's only center. This, as well as the vast majority of the others throughout the nation, was closed by the end of 1945.

American-born Japanese from the west coast were in predominance among the persons under the program in this state for aid to enemy aliens and other restricted persons. By July 1, 1946, when the program was terminated, 103 needy cases had been granted financial assistance, principally to meet maintenance and medical requirements. The services of the county departments of public welfare were also available to self-dependent persons restricted by governmental war measures. Helping to locate employment, assisting to find living quarters, and giving information or consultation were among the services rendered.

A welfare program known as Civilian War Assistance was designed for the purpose of providing aid to civilians in need as the result of enemy action. In April, 1945, the Social Security Board and the Colorado State Board of Public Welfare, with approval of the governor, entered into a contract whereby the counties would receive federal reimbursement for all expenditures made to or in behalf of such civilians. It has been necessary for this program to function only with respect to civilians returning from enemy internment camps.

[93] Source of data: Special report submitted to writer by Division of Employment Service.

Former residents of the state and other persons locating in Colorado who lack self-dependency because of enemy action receive the required financial assistance through the county departments of public welfare. By July 1, 1946, 22 cases with 52 persons had found it necessary to avail themselves of assistance under this program. All had been in camps under Japanese jurisdiction, and with few exceptions, Santo Tomas in the Philippines was the camp from which they were liberated. The major portion of the funds expended has been in connection with dental and other medical attention. At the present, there is no evidence of the discontinuance of this program on any specified date.

PRIVATE WELFARE PROGRAMS AND FACILITIES[94]

It is notable that facilities under private auspices have not relinquished their efforts with the rise of the public welfare programs. They have continued to stress efficiency; to foster a more humanitarian approach to social problems; and to extend the areas of service. The emphasis of private agencies, together with lay, fraternal, and religious organizations is on family and child welfare, health, recreation, and general community betterment. A high proportion of the private organizations are local in character, raising and expending funds within community limits. There are a number that function substantially if not fully state-wide. Examples of this group would include the American Red Cross, Boy and Girl Scouts, veterans' organizations, fraternal and church organizations, federated women's clubs, Colorado Tuberculosis Association, Parent-Teacher Associations, and business men's clubs.

The following account of the development and work of the Denver Community Chest is merely an example of what can be and is being done by federated private philanthropy.[95] Federations in other parts of the state such as Colorado Springs, Greeley, and Pueblo started at later dates and have developed successfully to meet the challenge of changing conditions in these communities.

The federation of charities known as the Denver Community Chest since 1922 had its inception in The Charity Organization Society established in 1887. The pioneer federation flourished until the panic of 1893, when the whole economic and social life of Denver was disrupted. For twenty years, the City Council made an annual appropriation of $10,000, making the existence of the federation possible. Its name was changed to The United Charities of Denver in 1911 and to The Denver Federation for Charity and Philanthropy

[94] Space does not permit giving a roster of organizations and institutions. Substantially complete coverage can be found in the membership files of the Colorado Conference of Social Welfare, the directories of the Councils of Social Agencies, membership lists of Community Chests, classified section of various city directories, and Colorado Social Service Directory compiled for U. S. Department of Justice Bureau of Prisons in 1938 (mimeographed).

[95] Source of data: Guy T. Justis, Executive Secretary, Denver Community Chest, *Twenty-five years of Social Welfare*, 1943, and verbal reports given the writer.

Flora Helen Ringle Hurlbut, Masters Thesis (unpublished) University of Denver. *History of the Federated Charities of Denver*, 1933.

two years later. A complete reorganization was consummated in 1922, when the present Community Chest originated. Emphasis was placed on more effective campaign methods, increased representation of private agencies operating in the city, and distribution of funds on the basis of carefully prepared budgets approved by the Chest. The original Chest affiliation of 25 agencies almost doubled in two years; however, the membership did not remain static. Subsequent years brought changes due to the formation of new agencies to fill unmet needs, the consolidation of agencies performing comparable services, and the withdrawal of agencies becoming self-supporting or privately endowed. Denver Orphans' Home, Ladies Relief Society, Mt. St. Vincent's Home for Boys, Social Service Bureau, and Visiting Nurse Association were members of the pioneer federation and have had almost sixty years of continuous membership.

Over a long period of time, it has been unnecessary for the members to devote time and effort to collecting funds individually. They have therefore been able not only to raise their standards of service but to assume additional responsibilities in connection with unemployment, war, and other emergencies.

The activities of the Community Chest with its 55 members as of 1945 extend into vast phases of social welfare such as child care and protection, care of or service to the helpless aged and the handicapped, youth protection and guidance, community health protection and welfare planning, recreation, and special services to families and single persons in misfortune or distress.

There have been some significant changes in the coverage of Chest campaigns in recent years. The American Red Cross, formerly a member of the Community Chest, began independent financing in 1941. In the years prior to this withdrawal, subscribers to the Chest averaged 50,000 and, exclusive of 1931, the annual donations ranged from $600,000 to $800,000. It was in 1931 that contributions reached $1,153,137, a portion of which was earmarked for unemployment relief. The War Chest for Denver County and the Community Chest campaigns were jointly conducted in 1942, whereas the War Chest for the four counties of the metropolitan area was combined with the Community Chest in fund-raising in the following three years. The most successful campaign within this three-year period was that in the fall of 1944 when the donations of 138,000 subscribers totaled $1,553,252. There is no reason to doubt that effective community planning has been progressive and that the unified financing method has had general community acceptance in depression as well as in periods of economic activity.

Throughout the state, local civic organizations have developed programs of various types for social betterment. There is no uniform pattern which these programs follow, inasmuch as local situations determine where the emphasis should be placed. In general, they are based on the principle that no group can remain in poverty, subjugation, insecurity, or social unrest without affecting the well-being of the entire community. The program of the Latin-American Service

Clubs,[96] characterizing unique community work, illustrates the important role that civic organizations play in Colorado's social progress.

The Latin-American Service Clubs are composed for the most part of leaders among the Spanish-speaking citizens in the community and of Anglo-Americans concerned with the problems of minority groups. Impetus given by the first club which was started in Rocky Ford early in 1945 led to the organization of similar groups in Alamosa, Greeley, Monte Vista, Montrose, Pueblo, Salida, San Luis, Trinidad, and Walsenburg. These self-financed clubs are making notable progress in carrying out their objectives—improving the social, economic, and cultural status of minority groups; integrating such groups into community life; and strengthening the entire social structure of the community.

Persons of Latin descent are encouraged to take advantage of educational opportunities available to them, to strive for higher education, and to assume positions of leadership as a service not only to members of the minority group but to the community as a whole. By rendering constructive service to schools, parents, and children, the club members are able to bring about more regular school attendance and higher scholastic standing. At times, students desiring to continue their education secure loans from club funds when unable to finance themselves. Other activities in the educational field include joint sponsorship with other organizations in the community of public forums, concerts, lectures, informational films, and distribution of literature on sanitation, nutrition, and other subjects.

Emphasis on the health phase of the program is no less pronounced than education. The clubs cooperate with local and state health personnel by making clinic facilities available to them. Although these civic organizations have operated for a very short time, persons in the minority group numbering well into the thousands have been immunized or vaccinated in these clinics.

Activities of the local clubs also extend into recreation, housing, employment, and other projects which will in the end help to solve many of the problems confronting communities as a whole.

Latin-Americans and Anglo-Americans working together on a coordinated program and merging their efforts toward a common goal of community improvement have taken a decisive, forward step in the democratic process.

Some Aspects of Social Welfare in Colorado[97]

One of the most effective tests of the efficiency and efficacy of any social welfare movement is its flexibility and responsiveness in

[96] Source of data: Special report submitted to writer by Miss Helen L. Peterson of Institute of Ethnic Affairs, Denver, Colorado. Minutes, constitution, and by-laws of Latin-American Service Club, Rocky Ford, Colorado, and special report submitted to writer by Don D. Sandoval, Secretary.

[97] Recognition should be given to the fact that social welfare in the state is by no means confined to the coverage in the chapter. Many of the laws which are encompassed in the broad definition of "Social Legislation" are given consideration in other chapters of this volume.

the face of changing social and economic conditions. Only by retrospection and by close scrutiny of present statutes and their operation can it be discerned to what extent and in which areas this state has succeeded or failed. In comparison with other progressive states, it would appear that Colorado has kept abreast or well in advance in some areas but has lagged behind in others. Social progress has encountered obstacles resulting in retardation at times and has even suffered setbacks. The trend nonetheless has been definitely upward in the motivation and development of concepts of common responsibility in organized society for the security of the individual.

Colorado has moved out of an era of voluntary and intermittent charity into organized, planned, and coordinated programs of public and private services. She has progressed from a period of almshouse care being the rule rather than the exception, through a stage of doles in the form of relief orders, to cash payments made regularly so long as the recipient remains eligible. Although there are a few county institutions now in the state which were established under the statutes pertaining to almshouses, poorhouses, or poor farms, they do not have the characteristics that these names would connote but rather those of convalescent homes. The institution which was used in the past as a repository for all types of dependency and maladjustment is nonexistent. The preference of care at home in normal environment as against institutional care is universally acknowledged. No less striking are the advantages of regular cash payments over so-called orders which designate the articles to be purchased and where such purchases must be made. Except under the Old Age Pension program in which the law provides for a flat grant less net income, budgetary requirements on a case-by-case basis establish the amount of the monthly cash payments. The individualized treatment and the regularity with respect to receipt of assistance promote a feeling of security. Cash payments help the recipient to maintain morale by allowing him responsibility as head of his family and by giving him a feeling of dignity which accompanies the privilege of using his own judgment in purchases and of paying for them in the same manner as others in the community.

That unemployment was unknown to Colorado until the "great depression" is refuted by evidence of panics or near panics at different times over the years. The local communities were poorly equipped to meet the emergencies as they arose. Persons out of work tended to migrate to urban centers, thereby intensifying the problems of these communities. Bread lines formed and missions were crowded. In various localities, soup kitchens, wood yards, commissaries, or similar devices were utilized to relieve the distress. These measures stand out in sharp contrast to some of the more recent programs designed to combat economic hazards such as planned public works, state-wide employment service, and unemployment compensation.

Children under 18 years of age in Colorado increased from 600 in 1860 when the first census was taken in the territory to an estimated 358,000 as of July 1, 1945. With changing social and economic conditions, obviously, at no time during the history of the state has she been free from problems affecting the well-being of children. Laws pertaining to adoption and to the indenture or binding out of children, together with the growth of institutions before and after the turn of the century are concrete evidence of the presence of dependent children in the early population. Viewed from a vantage point of many years later, the efficacy of some of the laws as they applied to the child's interests may be in question. Furthermore, there is some indication of deferred action in passing new legislation, in amending laws to provide further safeguards, and in abolishing laws detrimental to the welfare of children and those having outlived their usefulness. A great deal of legislation throughout the years pertained to the welfare of children with respect to education; hours and working conditions; rights of inheritance; institutional care if dependent, mentally handicapped, or delinquent; protection by juvenile court procedures; and numerous other phases related in nature. It was the White House Conference of 1909 which gave impetus to social movements crystallizing later in a program of assistance to dependent children in their own homes or in those of relatives and a program of foster care in licensed homes meeting specified standards. In the operation of public and private programs for the care of children, it can be seen that Colorado places emphasis on home life as the great molding force of mind and character, and is cognizant that children should not be deprived of it except for urgent and compelling reasons.

An example of Colorado's failure to adjust its public welfare machinery to meet the needs of the times is that with respect to the State Board of Charities and Corrections. Its establishment represented the first step toward state regulation of welfare but at no time during its life of 32 years was it given executive powers. Inasmuch as it functioned within supervisory limits, it was thwarted time and time again in effectuating some desired social improvements. After the abolishment of this board and, at the very time when many states were taking steps toward strengthening their welfare structures, Colorado had a state agency existing in name only. The dormant department was a grave concern to persons interested in the social problems of the state and attempts were made to rectify the situation a number of years before the present department came into being. The Colorado State Department of Public Welfare, created a decade ago with a broad functional scope, has comparable powers and duties of departments of like nature throughout the nation.

Recent years have witnessed the coalition of federal, state, and local governments in a concerted endeavor toward insuring the individual against the major hazards of life. Each unit of government has its own special responsibilities and authority in these welfare programs having as their immediate purpose and ultimate goal the protection and creation of human values. The role which each unit plays varies with the service involved in programs such as care and protection of children, assistance to the needy, health, rehabilitation, and employment security. Recognition of obligations and consolidation of efforts to meet the challenge of the ever-changing phases in modern society are not confined to governmental units. Councils of Social Agencies which are composed of public and private agencies attuned to local needs concentrate on community planning, higher standards of service, and problems affecting the welfare structure of the state as a whole. The Colorado Conference of Social Welfare, now in its 56th year, has played a dynamic part in the development of welfare in its broadest sense. The membership of more than 1,000 is composed of state and county officials, lawmakers, administrators and staffs of public and private agencies, and other interested persons and leaders from all walks of life. Here they pool their experiences, study commnity problems with a view to their solution, and participate in unified planning for social legislation. They are concerned with the betterment of social conditions, not for a segment of the population but for all Colorado's citizenry. The two meetings of the Colorado White House Conference are also significant; here again, there was state-wide participation. "Child Health and Protection" was the theme of the meeting in 1932, and "Children in a Democracy," in 1942. In each instance, recommendations for the extension and strengthening of fundamental services to children were based on extensive study and sound evaluation of existent facilities, programs, and statutes.

By social legislation and the development of sound principles of social welfare, many frontiers have been crossed since buffalo roamed the Colorado plains and the Indian knew no boundaries. Increasingly apparent is the recognition of society's fundamental responsibility for a firm welfare structure consonant with the well-being of all people. Today as in the past, Colorado is faced with a challenge to hold her gains and to advance in conformance with changing social and economic conditions.

CHAPTER XIII

The Growth of the Judicial System in Colorado

Wm. Hedges Robinson, Jr.

D URING the four centuries after Coronado's men reached the
borders of Colorado, Spain, France and the United States
wrote words of law into books for the territory stretching on
either side of the white breasts of the continental divide. But law has
never existed unless security, protection, and an orderly way of life
are wanted by the majority of the persons to whom the rules of
conduct are to apply. Systems of law may be set up, but if the people
to whom the system pertains have no desire for it, the law is merely
page after page of words in dusty books. In those centuries the
plains and the mountains were crossed by traders and trappers.
Bandits and outlaws hid in the canyons. Gold seekers pushed westward across this land to California. Most of these persons had no
desire for law, the less of it the better; and if the statutes written by
men many miles away did not suit their ends, they ignored statutes,
and made laws of their own.

It was not until permanent posts and towns became established
along trade routes and at the gold camps that law became a desired
thing.

On August 25, 1856, the legislature of the territory of Kansas
provided for a court system for the County of Arapahoe. This portion of Kansas territory extended from a line drawn from the northeast corner of New Mexico to the southern boundary of Nebraska
and westward to the Utah line. Judge Allen P. Tibbitts, the judge
appointed to this court, never came to Arapahoe County nor heard a
case from there. But with the gold rush of 1858-59, the increasing
number of inhabitants of the County of Arapahoe, Territory of
Kansas, began to demand security of life and property. They were
concerned with the need of protecting their mining claims, and of
conserving the precious water that nourished the towns, washed the
gold, and kept cattle and horses alive. They needed more than a
few futile statutes enacted by a territorial legislature six hundred
miles away.

The culmination of these needs and desires into a system of laws
in Colorado is one of the most interesting chapters in the legal system
of the United States. It stands as a recent example of the genesis
and evolution of self-government by a civilized people who transported themselves across an arid plain many miles from the futile
guidance of a territorial legislature.

The need for law was first recognized in the mining camps which
were scenes of violence, theft and chicanery of all sorts. To bring

some order and security into this chaos, the miners organized miners' courts which combined the executive, legislative and judicial functions of government in a "court"—in reality a town meeting of a truly democratic type. One of the first, if not the first, of these courts was organized in the Gold Hill Diggings in Boulder County. The district was known as "Mountain District No. 1, Nebraska Territory"[1] and later as "Gold Hill District, No. 1, N. T." Soon these courts sprang up at Idaho Springs, Black Hawk and Deadwood Diggings. At first they dealt with the problems of claim jumping, but soon extended their jurisdiction to try all classes of cases.

The form of all miners' courts (which began to appear in 1859) was similar. Its offices were a president, probate judge, sheriff or constable, surveyor and recorder, a secretary and treasurer, all of whom were elected by the male residents of the mining district at general meeting. Criminal and civil rules were enacted in plain simple language. The punishment for most offenses was death, banishment or whipping.

Defendants tried before these courts were permitted to be represented by a lawyer, except in the case of one district where there was a rule that no lawyer should be permitted to reside or to practice in the district. Cases before these courts were promptly heard and an appeal lay to the miners' meeting composed of all of the men in the district. The decision of the meeting was final.

In the more thickly populated plains region along the base of the foothills, another attempt for law and order manifested itself in a slightly advanced form of the vigilante committee. It was called the "People's Court." These "courts" were organized from time to time where serious crimes had been committed. There was not the permanency about these courts that there was with the miners' courts. The People's Courts generally had three judges, a jury of twelve, a bailiff and clerk. The form of court procedure was preserved, and the accused was given a fair trial and benefit of counsel, but there was no right of appeal. The usual punishment for most offenses was death, or banishment.

While these courts were beginning to function, the Kansas territorial legislature on February 8, 1859, divided Arapahoe County into the counties of Montana, Broderick, Fremont, El Paso and Oro. The county of Montana embraced the principally populated portion of the Pikes Peak country. But the act failed to meet any of the problems of the region and did not establish a needed court system. On March 28th the settlers in the Cherry Creek settlements organized their own court system based on the Kansas laws. A full complement of county officers was set up. S. W. Wagoner was elected as probate judge, and Marshall Cook as county attorney of the County of Arapahoe, Territory of Kansas, although the county had been abolished by the territory more than a month previously.

---

[1] Boulder was in Nebraska Territory at this time as the dividing line between the territory of Nebraska and Territory of Kansas was on the 40th parallel.

The jurisdiction of this court was immediately attacked. Some lawyers contended its jurisdiction extended over the entire County of Arapahoe created by the Act of 1855, and others contended it was limited to the new County of Montana. By autumn of 1859 the jurisdictional problem was increased by the establishment of the independent Territory of Jefferson. This new territory was created without the consent of the Territory of Kansas or of the Congress. But its sponsors argued that the Territory of Kansas did not include lands to which the Indian title had not been extinguished; and since title to the Pikes Peak country was still held nominally by Indians, Kansas was without jurisdiction in the region.

This view of the sponsors prevailed, and a constitution was adopted on October 24, 1859, for the Territory of Jefferson. A. J. Allison was elected Chief Justice; L. W. Borton and C. J. Johnson were chosen as associate justices of the newly created Supreme Court. O. B. Totten was elected Clerk of the Supreme Court, and Samuel McLean, Attorney General.

The salary of the judges was fixed at $2,500 per year. Each litigant who appealed a case paid a $10.00 docket fee which was divided equally among the three judges and deducted from the salary due them from the territorial government. Each judge was assigned to one of the three judicial districts of the territory. Upon subscribing to an oath to support the constitution of the United States, lawyers were admitted to the court upon proof of good moral character.

The legislature for the "territory" assembled at Denver on November 7, 1859. It established a judicial system and created a commission to codify the laws and to report to the next session of the assembly. At an extra session of the legislature held January 23-25, 1860, extensive codes of civil and criminal law were adopted. The criminal code, consisting of 487 sections, constituted a complete manual of substantive criminal law procedure. The civil code, consisting of 645 sections, covered the essential requirements of civil rights, corporate organization and management, and the administration of decedent's estates. These codes were copied in a large part from those of eastern states, but they were concise. The code of civil procedure was indeed far superior to the one which succeeded it under the laws of the territory of Colorado.

The judicial system established by the territory of Jefferson was popular among the lawyers. But difficulties soon beset the territorial government. The enforcement of its laws became increasingly difficult. There was a continual argument as to the jurisdictional basis for its courts. Some upheld its legality. Some declared that the territorial courts of Kansas were supreme. Some declared only the federal courts, of which there were none, had the authority to function in the territory.

Secessionists became vocal. The Mountain District at Gold Hill declared it was not a part of the Territory, as did the Upper Clear Creek mining districts. Denver, on October 1, 1860, established the "People's Government of the City of Denver," and separated from the Territory.   In the meantime the United Mining District at the headwaters of the South Platte, Arkansas and Blue Rivers, enacted a constitution and chose a circuit judge, marshal and recorder, and made provisions for a code of laws.   On October 24, 1860, a constitutional convention meeting at Idaho Springs adopted a judicial system under which ''Idaho Territory'' was to have three judicial districts, each to have a judge, a clerk and a sheriff.   These courts, acting as courts of appeal from the miners' courts, were bound to recognize the laws of the miners' courts.

In addition, claims clubs, which had come into existence to protect the rights of early settlers in agricultural lands against late comers and land speculators, began to assume the character and function of courts.   Actually protective associations which were designed to make it possible and practical for the settlers to acquire portions of public domain before it was offered for sale, these clubs soon began to adjudicate ''title'' to the lands.   However, since the white men were trespassers on Indian land without benefit of pre-emption, the clubs could adjudicate nothing with respect to the land. They were, however, attempting to prevent disputes from arising when the lands would become public domain by prejudging what person had the best right to make a claim for the land; and by providing a common repository for preserving written claims to specific lands.

Likewise, difficulties concerning the jurisdiction of Judge Wagoner's court soon arose.   Popular sentiment rapidly turned against Kansas, partly engendered by its attitude on the slavery questions, and partly because of its unconcern with the western counties.   Soon the Probate Court of the County of Arapahoe, Territory of Kansas, actually disintegrated.   Wagoner and the other officers either resigned or vacated their offices.

The Kansas crowd, largely the anti-slavery group, met this emergency by holding an election in November, 1859, and selecting a new set of officers including a probate judge for Arapahoe County, Kansas. By late 1860 there existed in Denver, the probate court of Arapahoe County, Territory of Kansas, a court of common pleas for each of the three districts of the city, and a court of appeals of the People's Government, a court of the Territory of Jefferson County, and the Arapahoe County Claim Club.   As a result, litigants sought the court most favorable to them and criminals took a change of venue until they found a court which would free them.

This chaotic condition continued until February, 1861, when the federal congress created the Territory of Colorado.   The organic act creating the new territory required the territorial legislature to divide the area into three districts, each to be presided over by a judge in residence.   These judges in sitting together constituted the Supreme Court.

R. W. Steele, the Governor of the Territory of Jefferson, resigned his office on June 6, 1861, and called upon all officers holding under the ''territorial government'' to ''submit to the laws of the United States and restrain themselves from deeds of violence.''   The transition to the Territory of Colorado was soon effected, and the old courts which had been created disappeared with the creation of the new judicial system.

The early appointments made to the Supreme Court of the territory were unfortunate. President Lincoln appointed Benjamin F. Hall of New York as chief justice on March 25, 1861. Judge Hall organized the Supreme Court and opened the first session with a long speech. Wm. R. Likin, I. N. Bassett, J. T. Coleman and J. Bright Smith were appointed a committee to examine the qualifications of those desiring admittance as attorneys. About 30 lawyers were admitted on the following day. Among them were Moses Hallett, H. M. Teller, Amos Steck, J. Bright Smith and Governor Gilpin. Judge Hall presided over the court for two years and acted as the judge for the Denver district. On July 10, 1863, he was succeeded by Stephen H. Harding, a former governor of Utah. Judge Harding was venal and generally unfit for the position. Lawyers refused to try cases before him. Harding resigned his judgeship in May, 1865, and returned to Indiana. His only contribution to

Judge Moses Hallett

Colorado was six cases, reported in Volume One of the Colorado Reports, dealing with common law pleading and practice.

The second of the original appointees, S. Newton Pettis, stated soon after arriving in Colorado that he was "clearly of the opinion he would never marry the territory." He confirmed this opinion by resigning the judgeship before holding a term of court. After his resignation, Allan A. Bradford was appointed to the court. Judge Bradford at the time of his appointment was a resident of the territory. He was assigned to the southern district, which ultimately had its headquarters at Pueblo.

Charles Lee Armour of Maryland was the third of the original appointees to the court. He was a talented, but cranky, inscrutable and many-sided tyrant. He was extremely unpopular, and within a year petitions for his removal were presented to congress. Failing to obtain relief from congress, the territorial legislature redistricted the state and transferred Armour from the Central City District to the counties of Conejos and Costilla. Armour ignored the legislative jerrymander, and remained in Central City where he sipped toddies, smoked imported cigars and drew his salary until the end of his term.

When Harding resigned his judgeship in 1865, and Armour's term was then ended, the rule of the carpetbaggers was over. Men of caliber, like Moses Hallett, William R. Gorsline, E. T. Wells, James R. Belford and Christian S. Eyster were appointed to the bench. From the organization of the territory until its admission as a state, there were only three chief justices—Hall, Harding and Hallett.

In 1872, Moses Hallett undertook to publish the reports of the Supreme Court of the territory. They were designated as the First Colorado, and reported decisions of the court—both as a territorial and state court—have continued uninterruptedly since that date.

The judges collectively constituting the Supreme Court were, nevertheless, trial judges in their circuits. When they rode the circuit, they were joined by court officials, lawyers, litigants, Spanish interpreters, and prisoners for trial. This motley caravan of wagons, buggies, horses and mules tracked over the dusty sage mesas and the snowy mountain ranges. Camps were made at night where wood, water and grass could be found. Food consisted of fish, an occasional antelope, or deer, jerky, or whatever might be in the grub sacks. At night the group gathered around camp fires where they smoked pipes, sang songs and told tall tales. At bed time they curled up in blankets spread upon the ground. Sometimes they came upon Mexican settlements where fandangoes were held in honor of the court. Lawyers and litigants and judges joined in the fun. Sometimes the towns provided some sort of hostelry. The accommodations ranged all the way from several hay mattresses spread in one room to the splendor of the Teller House.

In the hotels in the mining towns there was a prolonged bedlam until two or three o'clock in the morning. After an interval of an hour or so of quiet, the judge, lawyers and litigants were awakened by the poundings of the cooks getting breakfast in the kitchen, followed closely by the opening of the doors of the bar, a rush of cobbled boots across the threshold, and a persistent buzz of voices. Throughout the hotel at all times were the combined odors of tobacco smoke, unrectified whiskey, corned beef and cabbage, codfish, fried onions and burning bones.

Frequently sessions of court in the various districts were held in abandoned cabins, vacant stores, or other private places rented or seized for the occasion. On one occasion a saloon was used, and a rough scantling separated the lawyers and jury from the bystanders, and a few armed guards separated everyone from the liquor. Seats for the jury were planks set on blocks of wood. The judge's bench consisted of two packing cases, one piled on top of the other and covered with a wolf's skin. The chair provided for the judge was so low that when he sat in it, no part of his honor was visible except

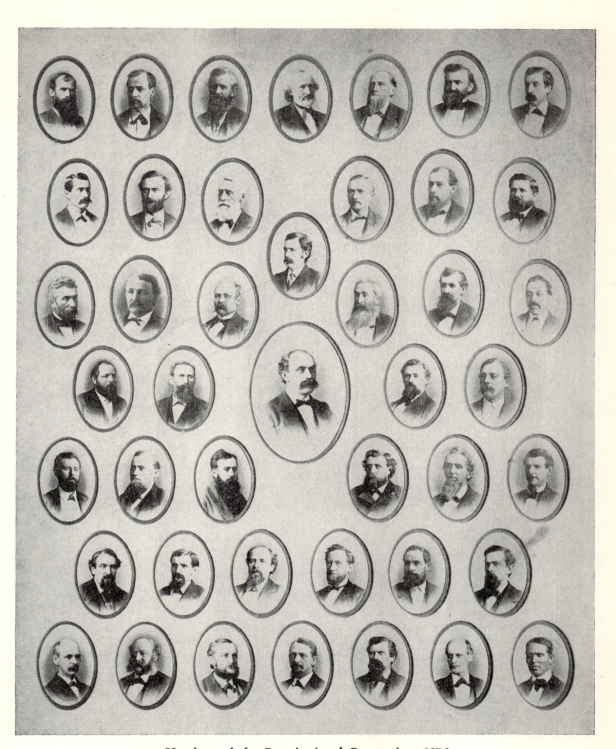

Members of the Constitutional Convention, 1876

the top of his head, which seemed to be a part of the wolf's skin. Withal the trial was orderly and the bystanders respectful.

The circuit riding days for the members of the Supreme Court were ended in 1876 when the territory became a state. The state constitution created four district courts, and left the Supreme Court to consist of three judges sitting at Denver. The first Supreme Court judges were Henry C. Thatcher, Samuel H. Elbert and Ebenezer T. Wells. Judge Wells resigned before his term expired and was succeeded by Wilbur F. Stone. The salary for the judges was set at $2,000.00 each year and $1,000.00 allocated yearly for the expenses of the court.

The bar of these days was largely centered in the mining towns of Leadville, Central City, Blackhawk and Georgetown. Driving through these towns today, one finds it difficult to reconstruct them as they existed in the last three decades of the nineteenth century. The streets were filled with an endless procession of wagon trains, horsemen and pedestrians. The precious metals that were being bored from the bowels of the earth attracted thousands of men and women to these camps. This easy pouring out of wealth brought about quarrels, litigation, and legal procedures. It produced a brilliant host of lawyers. There was, for example, Charles S. Thomas, who came to Leadville after serving a term as City Attorney of Denver. Thomas, who was counsel in some of the outstanding mining cases of the period, subsequently became governor of the state, a United States senator, a special assistant to the attorney general of the United States, and president of the Colorado Bar Association. Or there was James B. Belford, a member of the territorial court, the red-headed judge who tried cases while slouched down on the small of his back with his feet on the bench. It was Belford, who was one of the first senators from Colorado, who helped to launch the federal government on its program of reclamation, and who introduced the first bill for woman suffrage in the senate.

Another example was Henry M. Teller, later Secretary of the Interior. He always exhibited a mastery of the law and the facts of any litigation he handled. His well organized arguments were salted with sarcasm and in court he was a persistent and uncompromising adversary. As a national figure he pushed the western reclamation program, and was one of the leaders in the bitter battle to remonetize silver. His brother, Willard, was equally brilliant as a lawyer, but an aloofness, quick temper, and sharp tongue denied Willard of a reputation to which he was justly entitled. Willard was counsel in some of the most important railroad litigation in the West, and was generally recognized as a capable lawyer.

One might point also to Hugh Butler, prosecutor, politician, corporation lawyer, state senator and university professor—a man who appeared before the state Supreme Court more frequently than any other lawyer save two of his contemporaries. He was a partner of one of the firms having the largest corporate practice in Colorado— Sayre, Wright and Butler. Or Amos Steck, who in his lifetime was mayor of Denver, probate judge, president of the first street railway system in Denver, Receiver of Public Money for the Federal Land office, state representative and senator.   Or there was the man who has the distinction of the most "firsts" in Colorado—member of the first law firm in Colorado, first public prosecutor, senator in the first legislative assembly of the state, first president of the Colorado Pioneers Society, and numerous other "firsts"—Hiram Pits Bennet.

There were Robert S. Morrison, author of numerous volumes on mining law, and of Morrison's Code of Civil Procedure; and Bela M. Hughes, one of the great trial lawyers, and acknowledged leaders of the bar.   Or there were Charles E. Gast, Alfred Sayre, Mitchell Benedict, L. C. Rockwell, E. O. Wolcott, Thomas Patterson, Franklin C. Goudy, Sam E. Browne, Vincent D. Markham, Platt Rogers—the list is long and other names could well be added.

But by 1893, the spectacular opulence of these mining towns ended with the steady decline of silver and the financial panic.   The lawyers for the most part moved away to Denver, Colorado Springs or Pueblo.   The agricultural communities began to assume greater importance with the development of the irrigation systems; and the business of the courts began a steady increase which has never ceased.

It was apparent that the number of district courts provided for the state was inadequate.   Hence in 1881 the state legislature increased the number of districts and judges to seven and created a special criminal court.   The criminal court bill was subsequently declared unconstitutional; and in 1883 special criminal courts were created for Arapahoe, Pueblo, and Lake counties, and given jurisdiction on all criminal cases except capital offenses.   Furthermore a Superior Court was established in Arapahoe County and it had concurrent jurisdiction with the district court for the county.   The judges of the criminal court of Arapahoe County were Platt Rogers and Wilbur F. Stone.   In 1889 the Superior Court and the criminal courts were abolished by the legislature which in the previous session had increased the number of the district courts to nine and had provided for two district judges for Denver.   Gradually the number of district judges in Denver was increased until in 1891 there were five judges, and at this time the entire state was redistricted, and 13 judicial districts were established.   Pueblo secured a second district judge in 1893, El Paso in 1895; the eighth district in 1903, and the third district in 1915.   The fourth district received three judges in 1903, but this number was reduced in 1917 to two.   In 1921 the fourteenth judicial district was created and in 1945 a fifteenth district was established.   In 1925 two more judges were added to the Denver district making a total of seven.   At present the second district has seven judges; the first, third, fourth, seventh, eighth, tenth and thirteenth each have two judges and the rest of the districts have one each.   These courts have had general jurisdiction in civil and criminal matters.

The county courts exist in each of the sixty-three counties in accordance with the constitutional provisions.   They have original jurisdiction in probate matters, and certain juvenile matters, concurrent jurisdiction in some criminal cases and in civil cases up to $2,000 in controversy. In 1907 a juvenile court was provided for Denver County, due largely to the prodding of Judge Ben Lindsey, its first judge. Justices of peace have also existed in the state and their jurisdiction is limited to $300 in civil cases, is circumscribed in criminal cases, and denied in cases involving title to real property.

The appellate court system in Colorado has never been satisfactory. Congested dockets in the Supreme Court has been the rule rather than the exception. In 1887 a Supreme Court commission was

(Courtesy Pueblo Chamber of Commerce)

Pueblo County Court House

created to expedite the work of this court but it proved useless and was abolished after three years. On April 6, 1891, a Court of Appeals was created with George Q. Richmond as presiding judge and Gilbert B. Reed and Julius B. Bissell as associates. Subsequently Julius C. Gunter, later a governor of the state, became one of its judges. This court lasted for fourteen years but was abolished on April 4, 1905, when the number of judges in the Supreme Court was increased from three to seven.

In spite of the enlarged court, the docket of the Supreme Court again became congested and in 1911 a Court of Appeals consisting of five judges was created for a two year period. The judges of the court for this period were Tully Scott, presiding judge, Alfred R. King, Edwin W. Hurlbut, Stuart D. Walling, and Louis W. Cunningham. E. T. Wells, a judge of the territorial Supreme Court, was the reporter. When the existence of this court was terminated in 1915, it was the last fundamental change in the state court structure in Colorado to the present time.

The other group of courts in Colorado was the federal courts. The first session of the federal district court in the state was held in Fords Hotel at 1626 Larimer Street, Denver, on December 5, 1876. Judge Elmer S. Dundy, the federal district judge for Nebraska, opened the court. Judge Samuel H. Elbert of the Colorado Supreme Court moved the admission of seven lawyers to the bar of the federal district court. These men were Eugene P. Jacobson, Alfred Sayre, Hugh Butler, Westbrooke Decker, John W. Jenkins, Mitchell Benedict and Alfred T. Blake. These men then moved the admission of others. Judge John F. Dillion sat on the federal bench on the second and third days of the first term, and on January 23, 1877, Moses Hallett, first presided over the court as the newly appointed United States District Judge for Colorado. He was the judge of this court until May 1, 1906, when Robert E. Lewis, afterwards a federal circuit judge, was inducted into office. Colonel Edward F. Bishop was the first clerk of the federal district and circuit courts. A few years later his brother, Charles W. Bishop, who subsequently held the clerkship for many years, was made clerk of the district court. The federal court was moved to the Symes Block, 16th and Champa, on May 6, 1884, and continued in session there until November 29, 1889, when it was removed to Gettysburg building on Champa near 17th Street until February 3, 1893, from whence it moved to the Old Custom House and then to the present site in the post office building.

As the court system thus built itself into permanent structure, the legal profession, which by custom and law is a recognized part of the judicial branch of government, bonded itself into bar associations. While there was a bar organization existing in Denver as early as 1887, it was loosely organized and met infrequently. The founders of this pre-runner of the Denver Bar Association were Robert Bonynge, later congressman, Robert H. Latta, publisher of the *Colorado Graphic,* and F. T. Johnson, later a district judge. The present Denver Bar Association was organized on October 31, 1891, largely through the efforts of Judge Hallett and James M. Lomery, its first secretary and treasurer. One hundred fifty-nine members were subscribed at the organization meeting which was addressed by Judge Hallett. The first set of officers was Albert E. Patterson, later a Supreme Court Commissioner, president, W. E. Beck, vice-president, James M. Lomery, secretary-treasurer, and Elbry Stowell, sergeant at arms. The association remained unincorporated until August 19, 1903, when incorporation papers were filed. This association maintained a large law library which it subsequently donated to the Denver District Court. The Denver Bar Association has existed continuously since its organization, and now has over 600 dues paying members. It has published a law review since December, 1923, when the first volume of the Denver Bar Association *Record* came off the press. The *Record* was originated for the purpose of carrying notices to the members of the association but soon the magazine carried reviews and articles. In November, 1931, the *Record* became known as *Dicta. The Jealous Mistress,* official organ of the Colorado Bar Association, was first printed in 1925. Its issues were irregular. In 1938 the Denver and Colorado Bar Associations combined to publish *Dicta*.

On September 9, 1897, sixty-three lawyers gathered at the Brown Palace Hotel in Denver and laid the groundwork for the Colorado Bar Association. Caldwell Yeaman was the temporary chairman of the meeting which decided to perfect an organization and adopt by-laws. On October 4, 1897, the State Bar Association was organized with the following officers: Hugh Butler, President, Charles E. Gast, First Vice-President, Charles Cavender, Second Vice-President, and Lucius W. Hoyt as Secretary-Treasurer. The association was incorporated on January 8, 1898. The first annual meeting was held on July 6, 1898, at Colorado Springs and Justice David J. Brewer of the United States Supreme Court, then assigned to this territory as a Circuit Judge, was the chief speaker. Since that time the association has usually held its annual meetings at Colorado Springs, and has been addressed by a great number of the men who have served on the United States Supreme Court.

The Colorado Bar Association has been responsible for many of the reforms in judicial procedure in this state. It was awarded the American Bar Association Award of Distinction in 1943 for its work in establishing modern procedure rules in civil cases and was commended by the War Department for its part in establishing the legal aid plan for servicemen in World War II. This plan was originated at Lowry Field in Denver by members of the Lawyers War Emergency Committee. During World War I, the Colorado Bar Association took an active part in the Colorado State Council of Defense by giving legal aid to servicemen and throughout the years has filled an important place in the judicial system. The Colorado Bar Association, aside from various pamphlets and *The Jealous Mistress*, has published annual reports up to 1941, when they were discontinued. It now publishes a looseleaf service.

In addition to Denver, other local bar associations organized in the state. At present there are 17 local associations, having a membership of approximately 1,100 of the 1,628 lawyers in the state. Each member of the local associations is a member of the State Bar Association, and each local association is represented by a member on the Board of Governors of the Colorado Bar Association.

While these institutions were springing up in Colorado, changes were being made in the rules for admission. It was no longer possible for a person, after some exposure to the law, to take an oath of office and thereby become an attorney. Part of the responsibility for this change can be attributed to the growth of the law schools. In September, 1892, the regents of the University of Colorado organized a law school, and Judge Hallett was secured as dean. During the early days the faculty was chosen from practicing lawyers who devoted only a portion of their time to the school. Among these men was John D. Fleming, who subsequently became the dean of the school, John Denison, later a Justice of the State Supreme Court and an outstanding authority on pleading and practice, Judge John Campbell, then a member of the State Supreme Court, and Hugh Butler. Soon after the school was organized it switched from the lecture to the case method of instruction, and increased its course of study from two to three years. By 1899 the school had fifty students, and it has grown slowly until its enrollment is now over two hundred.

The University of Denver paralleled this development by offering courses on legal subjects by practicing lawyers as early as 1890. It was not until January 27, 1892, that the law school was established at the university, although classes at the school did not begin until the following October. Albert E. Pattison was named dean, and some of the early lecturers were Thomas M. Patterson, Lucius W. Hoyt, George C. Manley, subsequently appointed dean, Robert J. Pitkin, Joel F. Vaile, subsequently a congressman, Greeley W. Whitford, later a judge of the State Supreme Court, John F. Shafroth, Wilbur F. Stone and Charles E. Gast. The school shortly required a certificate of graduation from a high school for admittance and extended the course to a three year period. The school was housed in the Haish building at the corner of Arapahoe and Fourteenth Streets in Denver, and has been located in various places in Denver as well as on the University campus. It is now housed on the downtown campus of the University.

The third law school in the region was the Westminster Law School which was started in 1912. Its primary purpose was to provide a night law school where students, who were working during the day time, could secure a law degree.

This growth of the machinery of the law is one of the interesting developments in the legal system of this state. It demonstrates that once the desire for law makes itself felt, provisions will be made, either under an existing framework of government or apart from that frame-work, to provide a judicial system to administer and interpret the law. But there is another development in Colorado that was unique and that is the birth of a complete system of jurisprudence out of necessity. This development is shown from our present irrigation and mining laws.

When the first settlers came to Colorado they brought with them the legal theories of the Atlantic states. They also brought with them customs and living habits which were based on the industrial and agricultural conditions of the East.

But when they arrived in this western region they found that they were no longer in a well-watered country but rather in one where the water supply was generally insufficient to meet the wants of all. In addition, the civilization of the Pikes Peak country in the early years, was largely built around mining and not around agriculture and the requirements of the miners for water was vastly different from that of agriculture. Hence, some method had to be devised to apportion properly the scant water supply.

There was no possibility of developing the riparian right theory which had been used in the East, for it was totally inadequate to take care of many situations germane to the West, such as, for example, diversion of waters from one water shed to another or the use of water many miles from the bed of the stream. Nor was it possible to use the California system, founded upon the doctrine of implied grant, because that doctrine held that the United States as sole land owner was also the sole owner of the waters. Such a legal conception led to many unsatisfactory conclusions when the United States ceased to be the sole land owner. Since neither one of these legal theories was applicable in Colorado, the courts of this state

(Courtesy Boulder Chamber of Commerce)

Boulder County Court House, Boulder

created a substantive law coupled with an administrative development that today affects the lives of the citizens of nine states and of western Canada.

The Colorado system had no predecessors but was hewed out of necessity. Because an increasing number of people were demanding the right to use a limited quantity of available water, some method had to be evolved which would result in the maximum of benefit to the maximum of people and to the community as a whole. It was impossible at the beginning for any legislature to write laws which would solve the problems confronting this arid area. On the contrary the solution to the problems had to come by an application of principles to specific problems. The beginning in Colorado of the irrigation doctrine first appeared in *Yunker* vs. *Nichols,* 1 Colo. 551 (1872), in which case each justice of the court wrote an opinion. It was, however, the opinion of Judge Hallett, then chief justice, which profoundly influenced the course of water law in the West.

Instead of placing the use of water upon the theory of riparian rights or implied grant, Judge Hallett based it upon the broader and more fundamental ground of the necessities of climate; for as Judge Hallett said in his opinion: "In a dry and thirsty land it is necessary to divert the water of streams from their natural channel in order to obtain the fruits from the soil and this necessity is so universal and imperious that it claimed recognition of the law." In subsequent decisions and particularly in the cases of *Schilling* vs. *Rominger*, 4 Colo. 100; and *Coffin* vs. *The Left Hand Ditch Company*, 6 Colo. 443 (1882), the Supreme Court delivered the specific applications to the general principle laid down in *Yunker* vs. *Nichols*. From these early beginnings the irrigation law of arid areas of the West has been forged link after link by opinions from the court and with little aid from the legislature. From these decisions was developed not only the formula for determining the rights of the people and of the state in the waters of the streams but also was developed the formula for the procedure for determining these rights.

These decisions have pointed out on the one hand that the public policy of the state demanded that the widest possible use of the water be made and on the other hand have created a protection of individual property rights in water. Doubtless this latter concept was derived from the strong individual characteristics of the people, but nevertheless it submerges itself when there is a conflict between the two to the concept of the greatest good for the greatest number.

In addition to the development of the irrigation law there was a parallel development of mining law. The geology and climatic conditions of the West did not permit the wholesale adaptations of the mining system of the East or the mining system brought into the regions by the Spaniards and Mexicans. In the early days when eastern Colorado was a part of Kansas Territory the miners were forced to create their own laws. This law was based upon their experience in working their claims and in living with one another at the mining camps. These experiences were translated into decisions of the courts and as these decisions in the latter part of the nineteenth century began to be handed down it became apparent that a new form of law was being evolved. When the federal congress passed mining legislation, it was guided in a large measure by the local laws, rules, and customs which the miners in Colorado, Nevada, and California had adopted or followed and which the early courts had translated into decisions. As a matter of fact the mining statutes which were passed by the federal congress in most instances followed, and did not precede, the law which was announced by the courts.

The federal court in Colorado had a particularly important part in the development of the mining law. Judges of this court had to formulate decisions according to the necessities of the subject and the spirit of the law. These decisions from the federal courts and state supreme court played a large part in creating the present mining laws. While the courts were guided by legislation to a much greater extent in mining cases than in those involving irrigation, nevertheless they broke out new trails and explored fields uncharted by legislation.

The first act of Congress regulating and sanctioning the exploration of the public domain for mining purposes was passed in July, 1860. It was a very imperfect and crude statute, and in the next few years the legislation of the mining districts and of the territory was sketchy. A mining claim was recognized as a hundred feet in length along the vein and with fifty feet of surface. A certificate of claim was supposed to confer title, even though there was no act of possession. Likewise, it was contended that a locator could "swing his patent," that is, seize the vein wherever discovered even outside the limits of the patent. These conditions had to be corrected by the courts because of the failure of the various legislatures to act. Furthermore, there were problems which were inherent in the geographical conditions existing at the mining sites.

Instead of the hitherto familiar lode and pocket deposits, miners were confronted with blanket deposits and some of the most controverted questions on the subject of "lodes," "veins," "in place," "top," and "apex." The deposits were found on the surface or covered over only by a superficial mass of shale, debris, detritus, or movable stuff distinguishable from the general mass of the mountain, while in other cases the ore was found beneath a fixed overlying mass of rock and resting upon a similar underlying rock bed, a condition which was in sharp distinction to the usual situation in which a bed of ore descended into the earth so directly that no question could arise whether it was in the general mass of the mountain. It thus became essential to determine whether this was rock in place, for by the laws of the United States prescribing for the sale or occupation of ore-bearing lands, the lands were divided into those which contain lodes, veins, quartz or rock in place, and those which contained placers and forms of deposits other than those found "in place." Furthermore, it was essential to determine the meaning of "apex" and "top" as set forth in the statute. In blanket deposits it was difficult, if not impracticable, to fix upon any exposure as constituting the apex, and to add to the difficulty these terms were not to be found in the miner's vocabulary which supplied only the terms "vein" and "lode."

These questions, too, were answered by the courts in a series of cases, and these decisions became in many instances substantially embedded into the statutory law.

This development of both irrigation and mining law in Colorado is one of the amazing developments in modern jurisprudence unequalled, perhaps, since the birth of equity or the merchant law. Fortunately, there were judges and lawyers in the state who were intellectually capable of aiding in these processes.

The last important development which has brought about the jurisdictional pattern in Colorado originated in quite a different manner. It proceeded from a long voiced demand of the people for the elimination of delay in the trials of the courts. The Supreme Court of the United States heeding this clamor had created a committee in 1934 for the purpose of simplifying the rules of civil procedure. By 1937 this committee had submitted a final draft of proposed rules which the Supreme Court of the United States adopted. The character of these rules was so excellent that the Colorado Bar Association in September, 1939, unanimously adopted a resolution which provided that the then existing rules of procedure be amended to conform as nearly as possible to the recently adopted federal rules. A committee was appointed for this purpose, headed by Philip S. Van Cise. On January 6, 1941, the present rules of civil procedure as prepared by this committee except for some minor changes were adopted by the Supreme Court. These rules expedited and simplified procedure in the civil courts.

Colorado is one of the first states to adopt this modern procedure. These new rules of procedure have been hailed as one of the greatest developments of jurisprudence in the twentieth century. In the nine decades in which the judicial system has existed in Colorado there has developed a court system and two branches of the substantive law without benefit of substantial legislative enactments. In addition, the present procedure in the civil courts actually derives itself from the inherent power of the court to make rules governing the procedure within the court. These developments are an able and recent demonstration of the fact that civilized people can always effectuate self-government and self-control whenever they so desire to do.

CHAPTER XIV

Medicine, Public Health, and Hospitals

CHARLES S. ELDER
Professor of Surgery, Emeritus, University of Colorado

PRESIDENT JEFFERSON purchased the Louisiana Territory as school boys exchanged their pocket knives, "sight unseen." There was immediately great curiosity about the newly acquired territory. Lewis and Clark had started their explorations up the Missouri River. In 1806 Lieutenant Pike with twenty-five men in his command was following the Arkansas River toward its source. Among them was Dr. John Hamilton Robinson, the first physician, certainly the first American physician, to enter the present confines of the State of Colorado. Pike's superior officer, General Wilkinson, said in his directions to Pike: "Dr. Robinson will accompany you as volunteer. He will be furnished with medicine and for the accommodations which you give him he is bound to attend your sick."

"Accommodations" is a high sounding term. Even if Dr. Robinson's services were seldom required, the accommodations offered were poor and strange remuneration. He was furnished a horse to ride, the earth for a bed, thin clothes to protect him from the winter's cold and food insufficient except when supplemented by the hazard of the hunt. The phrase "furnished with medicine" starts one's curiosity. What medicines were in the saddle-bag across the back of Dr. Robinson's horse? Of a few, one need make no conjecture. The first to be thought of is opium, the most valuable drug man has ever discovered. True it has claimed as its victims men no less distinguished than Coleridge and De Quincy, but it has assuaged the anguish of millions. Not yet, but within ten years the active principle of opium, morphine, would be extracted. For the present Dr. Robinson must be content with the crude drug, the dried juice of the poppy. The next medicine in importance at that time and not less esteemed in our day, was Jesuit's bark, now known as cinchona, from which quinine was soon to be derived. It had been incontestably established that "bark" was curative in malaria. As other fevers were not then clearly distinguished from malaria it was given in many febrile diseases. Mercury in some form was a favorite drug of the great Benjamin Rush, signer of the Declaration of Independence and after the death of Franklin, first citizen of Philadelphia; his influence spread all over the United States. Hence, one must count calomel as one of Dr. Robinson's medicines and assume that it was given in unreasonably large doses. Within the memory of many living people, mercurial sore mouth, commonly called "salivation" is an unpleasant incident. Dr. Withering, in England had found the dried leaves of foxglove would relieve many people with dropsy. The nature of dropsy was not then understood but ever since then the leaves of digitalis have been in common use as the most valuable medicine in diseases of the heart. Besides such medicines one may not forget the ever ready lancet. Many people were bled who now would be given transfusions of borrowed blood. Only seven years before Dr. Robinson's adventure in the west, the father of his country had died after repeated bleedings, of streptococcic sore throat.

At the time of Pike's arrival at his camp in Pueblo he was twenty-seven years old. Dr. Robinson was only twenty-four. They were closely associated. As they traveled together or sat about their camp fire, they planned their future together. Pike wrote his superior asking for promotion. If a commission should be appointed to determine the southern boundary of Louisiana Territory he said truly that no one could be so well prepared to direct the work as himself. While advancing his own claim for promotion he did not forget the ambition of his young friend. "Dr. Robinson," he said in his lofty but not always rhetorical style, "has accompanied me the whole route, is still with me, and of whom I take pleasure in acknowledging I have received important services as my companion in danger and hardships, counsellor in difficulties and to whose chemical, botanical, and mineralogical knowledge, the expedition was greatly indebted. In short sir, he is a young gentleman of talents, honor, and perseverance, possessing, in my humble opinion, a military mind and would, I believe, in case of augmentation of the army, enter if he could obtain a rank above a subaltern." Pike's enthusiastic recommendation was without effect. But he was right. Dr. Robinson had a military mind, indeed, he was a soldier of fortune. Nine years later he joined the Mexican army in its fight for freedom from Spain. After four years he retired with rank of Brigadier General, settled in Natchez, Mississippi, and resumed the practice of medicine.

Dr. Edwin James was attached to the expedition of Major Long. He was supposed to act as botanist, geologist, and surgeon. To these duties the pressure of events added that of historian. About the end of June, 1820, Major Long and his men crossed the eastern boundary of Colorado. The plains at that time were parched by the midsummer sun. The historian's spirits were affected by the dreary and monotonous prospect. He could see no probability of this western land ever supporting a population. He noted the great number and varied species of wild animals—the bison, deer, badger, hare, wolves, eagle, ravens, and owls—but was unable to account for their presence and apparent prosperity in a region so lacking in fertility. Their course seemed to him to be, in the main, southward and he conjectured that they were on their way to more provident pastures. Varied as Dr. James' knowledge must have been of things that are, he lacked vision of things as they might be. He could not foresee that the valley where he was encamped would sometime be furrowed with the ditches carrying water over the lowlands which would arouse their latent fertility, and that the plateau about him would yield rich harvest to intelligent treatment.

Doctor James was the first person to ascend Pike's Peak, where Pike had failed. The later explorer had the advantage, however, of undertaking the ascent in midsummer. At the conclusion of his service with Major Long, Doctor James entered the army as a surgeon. He was a devout man, with an earnest solicitude for the welfare of the human soul, no matter in what body it made its temporary dwelling place. He translated the New Testament into the Chippewa dialect. After his retirement from the army in 1830, he undertook editorial work on the *Temperance Herald and Journal,* forgetting, or possibly repenting, that Fourth of July ten years earlier when, in camp near Brighton, he passed whiskey among the men of the expedition.

There was a strong revolutionary sentiment in Germany in 1833. Before the forces of insurrection were well organized, some students at the University of Jena seized the armory at Frankfort and called for a general uprising. In a few hours the rebels were overpowered. Many were arrested and imprisoned. One of the leaders, a young medical student, Adolph Wislizenus, escaped into Switzerland. He finished his medical studies in Zurich, and after spending some time at the hospitals of Paris, which was at that time the center of medical learning, he came to the United States in 1835.

St. Clair County, Illinois, just across the Mississippi River from St. Louis, was a haven for many German refugees. There Dr. Wislizenus joined his compatriots, followed his profession and the plow as a country doctor. St. Louis was the inland port from which all adventurers going westward departed, and to which they returned. Dr. Wislizenus need but look across the wide river and see it agitated with renewed life. Young, active, and curious he could not resist the temptation so frequently set before him to join some party and see what Europe did not possess, so large a territory untouched by civilization. He left St. Louis in 1839. With his party he followed the Platte to Ft. Laramie. There he decided to go on to the Columbia River. But when his party had gone as far as central Idaho some dissension arose, in which he was not concerned, and he decided to return by way of the Arkansas. He arrived at St. Louis six months after his departure. Not yet thoroughly familiar with the English language, he wrote an account of his trip in German,[1] six years before Parkman started his trip, reported in *The Oregon Trail.*

The autumn of 1858 found the gold prospectors led by the Russell brothers, still poor but hopeful. They had washed from the sand of the Platte enough gold to encourage them to continue their search for more. But that search must be interrupted while some provision was made for protection against the approaching winter. Dr. Levi J. Russell, one of the brothers, built a cabin on the west bank of Cherry Creek near its confluence with the Platte. Its floor was dirt. Its roof was covered with clay and grass. One half of the rude structure was occupied by John S. Smith, a fur trader, and his Indian wife.

---

[1] *Ein Ausflug nach den Felsen-Gebirgen.*

Reacting to the exaggerated reports of gold found in the Pike's Peak country, expectant immigrants began to arrive in great numbers. According to the social instincts of man, they established their camp near the solitary cabin. Such was the beginning of the City of Denver, and so it happened that a remote and lonesome doctor unwittingly attended the birth of Colorado's metropolis.

Doctor Russell continued to be a man of great influence in the young and growing community. When a municipal corporation was formed he was one of its officers. Though Doctor Russell made his bed at the foot of mountain grandeur, the odor of palmetto bloom and visions of plantations whitening with cotton found their way into his dreams. He named the new community "Auraria," after the little mining town in Georgia, he called his home. Doctor Russell was a delegate to a convention chosen to prepare a constitution for a new state and one of a committee to prepare an address to the people urging them to support the movement for statehood. He was one of a delegation of citizens of Auraria to bring about a union with Denver City, as the settlement on the east side of Cherry Creek was called. He had come into the West in search of wealth, and was now one of the owners of a site on which a great city was to rise. The knock of fortune at the rough-hewn door of his cabin might seem to have been distinct enough, but he was unmindful of it. His mind was still set on finding gold, and when a new prospect was uncovered he was ready to go to it.

Dr. W. A. Bell came to the United States from England in 1867. He was a graduate in Arts and Medicine from Cambridge and had served an apprenticeship at St. George's Hospital, London. He was happy to be appointed physician to a group of surveyors who were trying to find a southern route for a railway to the Pacific coast. The party was led by General William J. Palmer. A friendship and business association developed between Dr. Bell and his chief which divorced him from medicine entirely. He was interested in the founding of Colorado Fuel and Iron Co., the development of Colorado Springs, and the building of the Rio Grande railway. He was author of *New Tracks in North America*. His book is not a narration of experiences from day to day as are the books of Wislizenus and Parkman, but a scientific treatise of the whole territory his expedition explored, its physical geography, ethnology, fauna and flora. It was offered as a contribution to the Royal Geographical Society of England. What Dr. Wislizenus, in a happy vein did for German readers, Dr. Bell more seriously did for the English. He left Colorado after fifty years of residence among us and returned to England in 1920 where he died the following year. Dr. Bell's relinquishment of his profession was a distinct loss to Colorado Medicine but a great gain to western enterprise.

There were about twenty physicians in Colorado in the winter of 1860. A majority of these were located at the twin communities, Auraria and Denver City, at the junction of Cherry Creek and the Platte River. The remainder had followed the prospectors into the mountain ravines where some of them sustained the body by the practice of medicine and the spirit of hope by hunting gold. The economic conditions prevailing in the West were unlike those obtained in the East. The cost of living was high. It was, therefore, desirable that there should be some agreement among physicians concerning the fees which it would be proper for them, under the new circumstances, to demand. They had found themselves thrust together in a great popular movement. They were strangers practicing among strangers. Amicable competition demanded a new pledge of loyalty to those principles and ideals which are supposed to regulate the relations of physicians with one another. Accordingly, on June 2, 1860, a meeting was called for the purpose of forming a medical society.

Dr. W. M. Bell was made temporary chairman of the meeting. It was resolved that a society should be formed which should be known as the Jefferson Medical Society. This name was chosen because the people, without legal authority, had presumed to form a territory which they called "Jefferson Territory." Two committees were appointed, one to present a draft of a constitution, the other to draw up a code of ethics and a fee bill. A week later, the committees were ready to report. The doctors re-assembled, adopted the proposed constitution, and under its provisions, Doctor Belt was elected president of the society. The committee which was to write a code of ethics found nothing novel to present. It was advised that the society adopt the National Code of Ethics and pledge its members to abide by its provisions. The fees agreed upon did not differ materially from those which physicians and surgeons now expect to receive for their services.

While the Jefferson Medical Society was yet in the tender period of infancy, the whole nation began to stagger from the shock and weight of civil war. Physicians who had been active in the formation of the society entered the service of the army, and the new organization was left to languish without parent, guardian, or interested patron. The fees of the doctor were resigned to ruthless economic causes, as they must ever be in spite of fee bills, and resolutions. The conduct of the physician was guided by personal character rather than by measures of restraint and there, in any event, it would have found its compelling motive.

The war brought financial disaster upon both victor and vanquished. The new settlements of Colorado were not sustaining their early promises, certainly not the expectations of the settlers. The mountains gave up their treasure niggardly. The soil awaited more experienced treatment to arouse fertility. Times were hard. But the medical profession was gaining from time to time recruits who were not discouraged by hardships, men of determination, high character and sound judgment. Dr. R. G. Buckingham came to Colorado in 1863. He was destined to become the first president of the Denver Medical Association, and of the Colorado Territorial Medical Society. Dr. Frederick J. Bancroft, his duties as army surgeon ended, joined the Denver doctors in 1866. He was particularly qualified in the surgery of accidents, such as fractures of bones and dislocations of joints. He became the chief surgeon of the Denver and Rio Grande, and of the Colorado and Southern railroads. As his material fortunes grew, his once keen interest in medicine waned. The changes in surgical practice, after the nature of wound infections became known, were rapid, and Doctor Bancroft failed to keep up with them. He had a remarkable faculty of seeing the humor in events obviously grave. The stories told of him and his quaint remarks made under trying circumstances for many years, used to excite mirth at the meetings of medical men.

On the morning of April 9, 1869, a cloud of dust arising eastward along the Platte announced to the experienced the approach of the stage coach. On the top of the coach sat a tall gentleman of powerful frame. He had a handsome, kindly, but determined face. He was Dr. Arnold Stedman, physician of fine judgment, sound learning, and a citizen of strong social feeling. From his high seat he was anxious to get an early view of the place where he was to live, work, love, be loved, and die. Its ugly buildings, its ungraded streets, covered deeply with dust which almost suffocated the passengers as it was stirred by the feet of the four stage horses, its rude homes untouched by the hand of taste, its yards without grass or tree, were all in complete conflict with his cultured taste. He was not dissuaded from pursuing his venture, but his heart was heavy. How it would have cheered his drooping spirit if he could have foreseen the beautiful city which was to arise from such unpromising beginnings; that among its comfortable homes his was to be numbered; that in his profession and among his people he was to be a beneficent leader; that on the brown hill which stood against the eastern sky, a public school building would be given his name. These things time alone was to reveal; meanwhile, solace must be found in work and service.

Early in the year 1871, Doctor Stedman and Doctor Buckingham decided that the time had come for again getting the doctors of Denver into an organized body. They issued a call for a meeting to be held in Doctor Buckingham's office on April 4. Seven physicians responded and started the preliminary work. By the time a constitution was prepared, the number of prospective members had grown to twelve. They met, approved the new constitution, affixed their signatures to it, and became members of the Denver Medical Association. Meetings of the society were held in the offices of its members. At times the host of the evening entertained the members at dinner in his home in such generous spirit as to draw forth a eulogy directed to Mrs. Bancroft, Mrs. Whitehead, or another good wife who had borne the burden of the entertainment. These expressions of appreciation were incorporated in the minutes of the society.

In spite of pecuniary loss which their action entailed, the society took an active interest in the health of the new and growing city. The city officials were forcibly reminded that there was more to municipal management than furnishing sinecures to self-appointed patriots. In the spring of 1873 open meetings were held to discuss problems of public health. Physicians of the territory were zealous in advertising the advantages of Colorado's climate, but they seriously objected to the smell of the capital city. This seemed to be compounded of the odors arising from the sty, the stable, the cow-pen, and the slaughter-house. Doctor Bancroft declared that Denver was the dirtiest city in the United States. He asked for sewers, street sprinkling, more systematic alley cleaning, and restrictions on keeping domestic animals in the city. Typhoid fever was prevalent. The city water was suspected of being the source of infection. Dr. Charles Denison, in a way illustrative of his character as it was for years known to physicians of Denver, made drawings of the water supply and pointed out distinctly the probable source of contamination. The newspapers published the discussions of the physicians. The city officials and the management of the water company proved immune to the strongest criticism administered in the most heroic doses. They stood together. They had need of each other. Meanwhile, the doctors profited by the indifference of elected officials and public servants, but they never condoned such indifference. On the contrary, they exposed and condemned it.

Sometimes the physicians found it necessary to defend themselves against serious accusations. In the same year, 1873, an eloquent but irresponsible temperance advocate was holding meetings in Denver. He asserted in one of his addresses that physicians made many people intemperate by prescribing alcohol as a stimulant. Responding to this charge, the physicians assembled. The clergymen of the city and representatives of the press were invited to attend. Several members declared they had never known the desire for alcohol to be acquired from doctors' prescriptions. It was explained that many people would plead, in extenuation of their moral weakness, that they had been sick, whiskey was necessary to their recovery, and yielding to this necessity they had acquired a habit which had overmastered them. The experience of the doctors did not support the story. Dr. H. A. Lemen, a most patient student of medical writings, offered the statement of some of the most distinguished physicians of the day to the effect that they knew of no cases in which addiction to alcohol had been the result of prescribed medicinal doses. Dr. H. K. Steele changed the mode of battle from defense to aggression. He charged that ministers were more commonly the agents of alcoholic addiction than physicians; that all the so-called bitters were nothing more than cocktails glorified by claims of curative properties; that all of these bitters were sold to people largely on the recommendation of credulous clergymen who professed to have found them beneficial; that the manufacturers of these bitters designedly promoted self-drugging, and ministers of the gospel innocently contributed to it. Such self-drugging, the doctor argued, was far more dangerous than the supervised medication of the physician.

Bishop Spaulding, who sat in the audience, responded with good temper. The bishop hoped it would be found that alcohol was not necessary as a medicine. He conceded that physicians alone were the judges of its value and proper use. He knew that if anyone continued a doctor's prescription after leaving the doctor's care, the moral and physical consequences of such treatment should be charged to the patient alone. He disapproved of temperance revivals, as such periods of emotion were followed, in his experience, with periods of debauch. The hope of the bishop has at length been realized. Physicians rarely prescribe alcohol. The majority never do so.

Dr. H. K. Steele had come to Colorado in 1870. He lived in a modest frame house where the Gano-Downs store now stands. About its grass grown yard was a picket fence to guard against straying animals. Along the side of 16th St., in the summer, an irrigation ditch carried water to the thirsty grass and bubbled audibly on its way to the Platte River from which, indeed, it came.

In 1892 the citizens of Denver elected Platt Rogers mayor. He was one of the ablest lawyers in Denver, independent and progressive. He asked Dr. Steele to be health officer. The doctor had then retired from practice but he accepted the appointment and regularly turned his salary back into the funds of the department. He appointed Henry Sewall and W. P. Munn to do the needed work of the department fearlessly. There were no men in the profession more intelligent or eager to be of public service. They started the Steele hospital and at last people with communicable disease found a place to lie. They established a Health Department which no future health officer, no matter how disinterested, could greatly impair. Dr. Steele was the father of Justice Robert Steele of our Supreme Court.

At a meeting in Dr. McClelland's office it was decided to notify the physicians residing in the territory that a convention would be held in Denver, on the 19th of September, 1871, for the purpose of forming a Territorial medical organization. At a subsequent meeting, in preparation for this event, Dr. Buckingham was requested to prepare an address. Without much persuasion, the doctor consented. The brief report was made that "the address would be forthcoming." Mr. Ford was engaged to prepare a supper for the assembled physicians. Neither social nor intellectual desire was to be left ungratified.

At length the day arrived for the first meeting of the Colorado Territorial Society. It was held in the District Court room which, as Senator Thomas remembered, was on the second floor of a building at Fifteenth and Champs Streets. Dr. Bancroft's appearance excited the envy of the assembled physicians. He came to the meeting in a new buggy, its springs sagging under his great weight. He confided to Dr. Dodge, a pioneer of Boulder, the source of his apparent prosperity. He always had a strong propensity toward agriculture and had taken up a claim to a tract of land which is now Capitol Hill. He hoped to irrigate it from wells but the project failed and he had traded the land for the new buggy. His conscience was troubled about imposing that worthless land upon an innocent victim. Thereafter, when the original owner of the buggy was seen at a distance, he drove around the block rather than face him. On this day the doctor's horse with its shining appendage, was tethered to a post, and the stairway trembled and resounded to the tread of the foremost physician in Colorado.

Although travel in Colorado was difficult and time and space still maintained their primitive relations, physicians from Central City, Georgetown, Black Hawk, Laporte and Idaho Springs responded to the invitations. There were twenty-four, including the Denver men, in attendance. As soon as the preliminary organization was effected, Doctor Buckingham came forward with the promised address. It had a gloomy beginning and a glorious conclusion. The speaker's view of medicine as a profession was not a bright one, although he held his vocation in strong affection. Those who entered it, he thought, should be prepared to abandon all hope of wealth, fame or comfort, and hold to the single aspiration of being of service to others. No hour of the physician could be secure to his own indulgence, for the night's repose, the evening's entertainment, or for a period of solemn devotion. He was subject to call at any time regardless of financial recompense or just appreciation of his services. This frigid prospect was in strong thermal contrast with the exhortation which was to follow. He held out to his twenty-four listeners the advantages of being associated in a Territorial organization. There were men among them of accurate and extensive learning. With such, an exchange of opinion would prove profitable. Their association as friends would be agreeable, and soften the sting of envy which was apt to be felt too keenly by men working in close competition. With rare foresight, he urged them to be ready to act as one man in opposing any legislation threatening medical progress. Such cooperating energy was greatly needed when, fifty years later, an initiated measure was submitted to the people of Colorado proposing to prevent all forms of animal experimentation. It was defeated overwhelmingly through the efforts of those physicians who had inherited the spirit of Doctor Buckingham, aided as they were, most generously by men engaged in the live stock industry and by many other enlightened people who held truth above prejudice. Aiming a shaft of scorn at the most prominent medical cult of that day, the speaker drew his hearers together by his appeal to mutual interest and common antipathy. Finally he asked them not to falter now nor later, but to proceed with their purpose to form a society which might be as enduring as the mountains which rose in white and azure before them.

As time went on not a few of the men Doctor Buckingham addressed accumulated considerable wealth, in spite of his dark prediction. There have stood, or still there stand, in the business section of Denver, the Bancroft Block, the Steele Block, the McClelland Block, and the Stedman Building. The owners of these buildings, and many of their fellows, lived in well-appointed homes, which still show old-time comfort and elegance. They visited their patients in excellent carriages drawn by beautiful horses. Though they had no security against interruption, they had leisure, at times, to visit the theater, where they saw the dark Othello rant or the fair Ophelia rave.

But Dr. Buckingham was right. The wealth that came to these pioneer physicians did not come from the practice of medicine. Their homes were located in that part of Denver or other cities which became the business center. The growth of population made them the fortunate recipients of an "unearned increment." Dr. Jesse Hawes, President of the Colorado State Medical Society in 1884, lived in what is now the business part of Greeley. Dr. W. M. Strickler honored with the presidency of the society in 1891, lived in Colorado Springs. He came to Denver with an ample purse to pass his declining years with his brother, Montgomery Strickler. "Gom," he said, "buy us a home where we can live comfortably together." Then making a gesture toward the hazy outline of Pikes Peak he added, "but let it be in a place from which we can always see that mountain."

After the formation of the Territorial Society, meetings were held annually. Local societies were formed in all the populous counties which gave strength to the parent organization soon to become, in 1876, the Colorado State Medical Society. On March 24, 1882, Dr. Robert Koch, a German country doctor, announced that he had discovered the germ which caused tuberculosis. The essay in which Koch presented his work was one of the most positive and convincing papers ever written in all the annals of medicine. It even announced the principles with which proof of the relation of cause and effect between a germ and a disease must comply: The germ must in every case be found in the diseased body; it must be grown pure outside the body; inoculations of such a growth must produce the disease in susceptible animals; it must be obtained from such animals and again grown pure. No better illustration of applied logic can be found in the records of science and discovery.

In June the same year the Colorado State Medical Society met in Pueblo. At this meeting less than three months after Koch had announced his discovery, Dr. Charles Denison read a paper on the "Contagiousness of Phthisis." He showed that even Hippocrates, the father of medicine, who lived four hundred years before the Christian era, suspected that pulmonary diseases might be transmitted through the breath of affected people. Many wise physicians, in all the years since this early and acute observer expressed such suspicion, held well established opinions that tuberculosis was a contagious disease. Many experiments had been performed which gave firm ground to such opinions. Finally, seeing the importance of the work of Robert Koch, Doctor Denison presented the results of it in detail. This early consideration of one of the great discoveries in medicine shows how eagerly some members of the medical society stood on tip-toe to see the first ray of dawning light.

As the 19th century drew to a close, Denver had a new brownstone hotel at the upper end of 17th street. Never hesitant in the use of superlatives, the Denverites declared that it was the most magnificent hotel in the United States. The old Windsor Hotel was somewhat faded but still showed signs of former grandeur. There were 500 members in the Colorado State Medical Society. Its growing pains permitted no repose. Supported by ample hotel accommodations, an invitation was extended to the American Medical Association to hold its annual meeting in Denver, June, 1898. The invitation was accepted and provision for the entertainment of a large body of physicians was pressed forward. Dr. J. W. Graham, who owned a building at 16th and Curtis Streets, headed a subscription list with $500. He was followed by a long list of prosperous physicians who gave $250 each. The subscriptions then trailed off to a minimum of $1. The total was sufficient for any anticipated need. Fourteen hundred physicians attended the meeting. This number might seem small as compared with the 8,000 who attend meetings of the American Medical Association now, but that organization has grown greatly since then, and distance has diminished. There were then no stream-lined trains and even Chicago was two days and two nights away. Among the visitors, were distinguished men from every part of the country. They demonstrated their methods and skill in surgical operations. They examined patients and talked to the assembled physicians about them. They discussed among themselves all the medical problems of their brightening day.

A feature of the meeting in Denver was the address in surgery by John B. Murphy of Chicago. Murphy had lately attained considerable prominence by inventing a device for rapidly and securely uniting the ends of severed intestine. He yearned for wider and more enduring fame and had an irrepressible impulse to self advertisement. His wife was wealthy and beautiful. Dr. Murphy and his wife did not fail to occupy a prominent box at the opera nor did the papers fail to notice their presence. This persistent tendency to display estranged many physicians who did not doubt his very great ability. Murphy decided to make his entrance into the American hierarchy of surgeons in Denver by detailing some experiments he had made in treating tuberculosis by causing collapse of the diseased lung with nitrogen gas introduced into the pleural cavity. A similar procedure had been proposed by an Italian Floranini but as the suggestion attracted little attention no one has ever suspected Murphy of plagiarism. His paper was received with enthusiastic appreciation. The following morning the entire paper appeared in the Chicago Tribune, with his picture. Great headlines announced, ''Says he can cure consumption.'' Murphy denied responsibility for this breach of medical ethics. He and his wife retired in Colorado Springs until the storm of censure abated. Many physicians were inclined to accept his denial and suspected that his ambitious wife was responsible for the unfortunate publicity. When they returned to Chicago they found the doctor's office filled with patients with tuberculosis, which was not the kind of practice he sought. He referred them to his medical colleagues to be treated according to their judgment. It was a decade before Murphy's plan for giving rest to a diseased lung came into common use. Now it is frequently used, especially in all tuberculosis sanitoria. Murphy's oration in surgery in Denver has become a medical classic.

The success of the meeting of the American Medical Association in Denver was largely due to the direction and social talents of Dr. Walter A. Jayne. Dr. Jayne had come to Colorado with incipient tuberculosis. He rode the range as a cowboy at a time when life in Colorado's air and sunshine with moderate exercise was accepted as the most promising treatment for that disease. As his condition improved he resumed the practice of medicine for which he had been well trained in New York. He located in Georgetown. From the Central City region there was, later, a movement of people which brought both wealth and fine manners to Denver. In the nineties there was an exclusive social set in Denver called, perhaps by tongues of envy, "The sacred thirty-six," and Dr. Jayne was a member of that social group. He was honest, intelligent, and exacting in all his undertakings but never proud. His social engagements gave limit rather than extent to his practice. This was fortunate for the physicians of Denver and Colorado, for another enterprise was taking form over which Dr. Jayne was, some years later, to take control.

Dr. Henry Sewall was one of many physicians who came to Colorado in search of health. He had been educated in American and European schools as a physiologist and was professor of physiology in the University of Michigan when he was compelled to seek restoration of his failing health in Colorado. Here he found medical schools which could, indeed, confer upon him the title of professor but none which could afford to pay for the instruction to students he was so well prepared to give. He found employment as has been told in the newly vitalized health department of Denver but he yearned for those reference medical libraries he had known in the East. He talked to Mayor Platt Rogers. He had confidence in Rogers' judgment about any of the aspects of man's social relations. He learned how the lawyers had cooperated to form a law library. The plan was nursed and matured in Sewall's brilliant mind. Soon he had an organization called the Colorado Medical Library Association. He consulted with John Cotton Dana, librarian of the Denver Public Library. Dana promised to spend as much for medical books and journals as the Colorado Medical Library Association would spend. He built a gallery in the old East Denver High School room occupied by the Public Library where the medical books and journals found a temporary home. As soon as eastern libraries learned of the earnest purpose of the Colorado group, they donated duplicate books and journals and the medical library began to grow beyond the scanty fund provided for its support. Dr. Samuel A. Fisk and Dr. J. W. Graham relieved the financial tension as Sewall's energy found more books to be arranged and more journals to be bound. Dana was a vigorous advocate of the open shelf system of library control, if control it could be called. The students of the high school had as free access to the medical books as anyone. They found keen interest in the pictures of women in all stages of child birth, but nothing could shake Dana's faith in the open shelf system. He knew that book lovers liked to look into books, even hold them in their hands, and that knowledge sought, even by the vainest curiosity, was knowledge gained.

In 1898 the Colorado Medical Library Association found a voice as well as a hand. Dr. Charles D. Spivak became intensely interested in the library. He proposed that all medical books in Denver be opened to the use of all physicians. He canvassed the city and made an index of 6,000 volumes he found in doctors' offices which were not adequately used. He wrote articles for medical journals on the way to build a medical library even in rural regions. Not content with these exertions he started a small journal called "Medical Libraries," which contained accounts of the origin, growth, and size of the medical libraries. This publication continued for four years, always running at a financial loss but it gave an outlet to Dr. Spivak's emotional drive and carried his name into every library and every center of medical learning in the United States. When the Medical Society for the City and County of Denver became a strong organization the ownership of the medical library was transferred to that representative organization, and was under the capable direction of Dr. Jayne. It is now the proudest possession of the physicians of Colorado. Its shelves hold 35,000 volumes and journals from every quarter of the earth. Its assets consist of pledges, legacies, bonds, and cash of $156,500. The society hopes soon to build a home for its books and a meeting room for its members when its funds reach $250,000.

The development of antiseptic surgery since 1890 has made it almost imperative that a surgical operation should be a hospital procedure. Internal medicine since then has taken on complications of its own which cannot be brought to the patient's home. These the hospital is prepared to meet. Hospital management has been standardized and improved and the word "hospital" has acquired a new and happier meaning. One-half of the people of Denver and one-third of the people of the state have hospital insurance and expect hospital care in event of any serious illness. Ample as our hospital space seems to be it cannot now meet the demands that are made upon it. The belief that a hospital is a place for the homeless sick or a retreat for paupers has long since passed away. When any social institution reaches maturity it seems always to have been a part of communal life although its beginning still holds historic interest.

The need of hospital care was urgent in the early settlements of Colorado. Dr. J. F. Hamilton who seems to have been an important figure in the organization of "Denver City" was appointed city physician without pay in 1860. He opened a hospital in a house on 16th Street below Blake Street. In 1861 Dr. Hamilton was appointed surgeon to the First Regiment of Volunteer Infantry of Colorado. When he assumed the sword his hospital closed its doors. Thereafter, for a long time, the county officers found lodging for the sick poor in boarding houses.

In 1873 St. Joseph's Hospital was established at 22nd and Blake Streets. The equipment of this, the first private hospital in Colorado, was very simple. As Dr. Stedman remembered there was on the first floor a room about forty feet long and twenty-two feet wide. Along its walls were ten cots. Three Sisters of Charity were in attendance. St. Joseph's Hospital now stands at Eighteenth Avenue and Humboldt Street and is a large and well-conducted modern hospital. Since St. Joseph's Hospital made its timid and unpretentious start many other admirable hospitals have grown up in Colorado. They may be found in every important city. In this period of improved roads and easy transportation hospitals are accessible to nearly all of the most remote settlements. There is now in Colorado, one hospital bed for each two hundred people. This compares favorably with the ratio of one to two hundred and ninety-one which obtains for the whole Nation.

As the pioneer physician believed in the healing virtue of exercise in the open it would not have occurred to him that a hospital could ever be an appropriate place for one with consumption. The first sanatorium for tuberculosis patients to be established in America was a slow growth fostered by a man whom disease could not defeat, Edward Trudeau of New York. He had contracted tuberculosis as did John Keats the poet, from nursing a brother who died of the disease. His body worn and weak but with a resolute heart Trudeau decided to quit the city and retire to the Adirondack Mountains. There his health improved and he invited others afflicted as he was to join him. He provided cottages for them and guided them with his wise counsel. Trudeau's establishment grew in physical structure and fame. It became a Mecca for patients from every part of the world, some of them very famous, such as the late Robert Louis Stevenson.

In 1890, only six years after Dr. Trudeau had started his work at Saranac Lake, New York, the first sanatorium for tuberculosis was built in Colorado. The climate of the State had won a great reputation for its wholesome influence on tuberculous people. They came in large numbers. Some were homeless. Very few were properly housed. Many in need of rest and care were compelled to work at unwholesome occupations. The Jews were particularly pained at the condition of their people. They were easily persuaded by the eloquent importunities of Rabbi W. S. Friedman to build a hospital for consumptives which should be free and non-sectarian. Soon $42,000 was contributed, a building erected and the first free hospital in the world for tuberculosis invalids opened its doors. The project was greater and more burdensome than anyone had conjectured it would be and in a little while the panic of 1893 put an end to the great philanthropy. The building stood, as Dr. Friedman remarked, "like Rachel weeping for her children." In time the great order B'nai B'rith furnished the funds for reopening the hospital and promised a substantial contribution for its maintenance. Other notable gifts were made and the institution was assured a permanent existence. With a view to doing the greatest good to society as well as to the individual the National Jewish Hospital for Consumptives limited its admissions to those cases in which there was a strong probability of recovery. The principle rests solidly on ethical and economic ground but tuberculous Jews, learning that under a kindly sun a hospital had been established for their benefit, came to Denver in great numbers,

The National Jewish Hospital at Denver

some of them in the last stage of consumption. Still the appeal to the tender sympathy of the Jew found no abatement.

The same Dr. Charles D. Spivak who showed so much enthusiasm and energy in promotion of the medical library called his friends about him to arrange for the care of these unfortunate people. A little tent colony was formed and from this houseless and treasureless beginning a great hospital arose which was free to any needy person in any stage of tuberculosis. This "Jewish Consumptive Relief Society" now maintains three hundred beds. It operates a farm, a print shop, and a book bindery. These industries furnish appropriate employment for patients able to resume light work. Since the change in general opinion about the value of climate in the treatment of tuberculosis many of the sanitoria which were formerly prominent in Colorado hospital movement have closed their doors or have been converted to other uses.

During the war with Spain there were more deaths from typhoid fever than from the enemy's missiles. Before the country was to enter another war a protective inoculation against that disease had been discovered and typhoid fever was no longer a menace to the army. Tuberculosis, in spite of all progress, remained a camp follower, taking advantage of the exposure and privation incident to soldier life. When the United States entered World War I the Surgeon General of the United States Army began preparation for the proper care of a large number of tuberculous soldiers. A site for a hospital was selected about ten miles east of Denver. The tract of land chosen consisted of about one thousand acres. Construction of forty-eight buildings was started in April, 1918. The work proceeded with war-like haste and the hospital was ready for the reception of patients in October of the same year. It bears the name of Lieutenant William Thomas Fitzsimons, the first American medical officer to die of wounds after the entrance of the United States into the war. Fitzsimons Hospital has been enlarged even beyond the original extensive plans. It can now easily accommodate two thousand patients. It is a city in itself, having its own railroad, supply houses, amusements, educational institutions and all else that goes into the social structure of a modern well-organized community. It is the largest military hospital in the world.

When Doctor McClelland read his address as president of the Territorial Medical Society in 1873, he recommended that a committee be appointed to seek a donor of a block of ground to be used as a seat for a medical college. Additions to the City of Denver were becoming numerous. There were more building sites than prospective builders. It was probable that some one might be induced to set aside a square of ground with the prospect of a medical school being erected upon it. Doctor McClelland thought that Colorado was an ideal place for college life because of its wholesome climate. He professed to believe, moreover, that a student in Colorado could study twice as long as one in an eastern college before feeling mental weariness. Nothing seems to have come of Doctor McClelland's suggestion. The plan might have seemed, at the time, too ambitious, but subsequent experience in starting medical schools in Denver has proved that he was not unduly optimistic.

A medical school, such as several that appeared a few years later, required much less than a block of ground. A room for lectures, another for dissections, and strong influence with the county undertaker who was to furnish bodies for dissection, were the primary requirements. As potential professors were exactly as numerous as physicians in the state, it was not necessary to resort to military conscription in forming a faculty. Even chemistry was taught by lectures. The learned professor might bring before his class a glass tube containing a few particles of zinc immersed in dilute acid to permit the students to see the bubbles of hydrogen arising from the mixture. They saw quite certainly the effervescence. That it was hydrogen was a conclusion supplied by their own credulity—a quality they were required to have in great abundance, and to use freely. Too often the dissecting room, the only laboratory, was without its required material. The graves refused to give up their dead, and the conscience of the undertakers, designated to bury paupers, became more meticulous as the funds of the school were depleted.

In the fall of 1881, the medical department of the University of Denver opened its doors to students. The course extended over two years; a year in scholastic chronology consisted of six months. Dr. H. K. Steele was the dean. Although the faculty was made up of men of high character and considerable learning, they rarely weighed the responsibilities of their professorships. If it happened to be inconvenient to give a lecture at the appointed time, the professor was absent. The students felt no resentment at this neglect. They had their text-books, and would have relied on them for accurate information in any event. The professor regretted that some woman's ill-chosen hour of travail had deprived the students of their instruction. The students were not disappointed at having been spared a tedious hour. These opposing ways of viewing a teacher's delinquency maintained amicable relations and gave longevity to a school that might otherwise have perished before it matured.

For several years medical instruction was given in any available space in the old building of the Denver University at Fourteenth and Arapahoe Streets. When the room in use was needed for more important purposes, the medical school sought other quarters. For a time lectures were given in the old Chamber of Commerce building on Fourteenth and Lawrence Streets. After the completion of the Haish Building in 1889, the school was given permanent quarters, which it occupied until it became defunct.

After the University of Colorado had been giving collegiate instruction for six years, it was felt that the fulfillment of its legal designation, "university," demanded a medical department. Such a department was, accordingly, organized in 1883. It offered a four-year course of nine months in the school year. After a year's experience in teaching a class of two students, the length of the course was reduced to three years of nine months each. Life in the West had not become well tempered with patience. Students were anxious to get into practice, and in spite of the free tuition offered by the University of Colorado, they favored the school which would detain them the shortest time. Dr. W. R. Whitehead, of Denver, did the greater part of the teaching in the medical school during its first year; thereafter a gradually increasing number of Denver physicians made weekly trips to Boulder for the purpose of giving medical instruction.

For those branches of medicine properly taught in laboratories, Boulder was an ideal place for instruction. The laboratories and teachers were there. Economy might have demanded that these same teachers instruct medical students in the classrooms and work rooms already a part of the university, but there was in Boulder a scarcity of what doctors call "clinical material," in spite of the addition of a small hospital to the medical school. It was therefore decided in 1892 to give the last two years of the medical course in Denver, where hospitals were larger and the sick more numerous. As soon as this step was taken Dr. Samuel A. Fisk, a prominent member of the faculty of the medical department of the University of Denver, brought a legal action to prevent the alleged trespasser from continuing its medical instruction in Denver. After five years, the Supreme Court sustained the contention of Dr. Fisk, that the constitution of the state had designated Boulder as the seat of the University of Colorado and there, as a whole or as a part, it must remain. The school in Denver, after this decision, was necessarily abandoned, and the medical department of the University of Colorado went through a process of reorganization and renewed growth in Boulder.

The faculty of the medical department of the Denver University was composed of certain men who were prominent in the Denver Medical Association. The school was not able to satisfy the ambitions of all members of that society by offering professorships to them. The Denver Medical Association was not able to maintain amicable relations between its professors actual and its professors potential. A large body of its members withdrew, formed another society and another medical school. This new school was named, in honor of a distinguished Philadelphia surgeon, The Gross Medical College.

The homeopathic physicians were not to be outdone by their competitors of the "old school." They established the Homeopathic School and Hospital in 1894. There were at this time four medical schools operating in Denver. The keen appetite of Denver physicians for the title of professor was about to be, in some measure, allayed, when something happened that put an end to the almost insatiable lust.

The Journal of the American Medical Association began to collect statistics in regard to medical colleges, students and graduates. It desired to know what the equipment of each college really was. It refused to accept the eloquence of catalogues in lieu of facts. It dared to inquire about the preliminary preparation of students entering medical schools and about the standing of graduates before state examining boards. This investigation revealed that there were more medical schools in the United States than in all the rest of the world. Some of them were conducted for profit, some to satisfy the ambitions of those who would be known as professors, and a few for the serious purpose of giving thorough medical instruction and training.

As soon as an alien eye began to look into medical schools, pride prompted them to dress for inspection. Certain standards were being established for representation among worthy institutions. A general improvement in American medical schools rapidly took place. The Colorado schools strained every resource to meet the growing requirements but this effort entailed expense. The money derived from the tuition fees of students was not sufficient to meet the rising cost of the school. Men of pride, unwilling to be associated with a demonstrably inferior institution, contributed regularly to the school treasury. It was soon apparent that the honors derived from a professorship were only presumptive, while the cost of sustaining them was real. The envy which school connection formerly excited rapidly passed away and in 1902, The Denver School of Medicine, as it was then called, and The Gross Medical College were joined to form a larger and stronger institution.

The Homeopathic School was having a hard struggle. It gathered insufficient nutriment and gave forth insufficient energy. In 1909 it was closed. The Denver and Gross College now had the fertile field of Denver to itself. It enjoyed a period of prosperity but there were difficulties ahead of it still unseen. In 1910 the Carnegie Foundation for the Advancement of Teaching began a serious and searching investigation of colleges in the United States. It frowned upon all schools which were supported wholly from the fees of students, and gave hope of moral and financial assistance for those which were endowed or maintained by public funds. It promised to call the attention of philanthropists to the rising costs and needs of medical schools and to designate those which were worthy of support. The Denver and Gross College could see no possibility of raising an endowment sufficient to meet the new conditions imposed upon it. There was no obvious way of conducting the school that would keep it in good standing among medical colleges. Its prospects were dark. At this period of despair, it entered into negotiations with the University of Colorado for a fusion of the two schools, which negotiations were speedily successful.

The University of Colorado had tried many times, after the Supreme Court had decided that all its teaching must be given in Boulder, to have an amendment to the constitution submitted to the people permitting the last two years of medical instruction to be given in Denver. The University of Denver, or the faculty of its medical department, always was able to influence enough members of the legislature to prevent such a referendum. Now all opposition had passed away. The constitution was amended and in 1911 the teaching of the last two years in medicine was resumed in Denver after a suspension which lasted fifteen years. For ten years more the medical school was a great burden for the parent institution. The medical department needed more than it got. At length the long expected succor came in the form of substantial gifts from the Rockefeller Foundation, the Carnegie Foundation, Mrs. Verner Z. Reed, and appropriation from the legislature of Colorado, contributions from the people of the state, and from Mr. F. G. Bonfils, who gave an admirable site for a new school and hospital buildings, where they now stand complete at a cost of nearly two million dollars.

Hobbes, the great English philosopher of the 17th century, in his treatise entitled "Leviathan" said, "Man hath created that great Leviathan called the commonwealth or state which is but an artificial man; though of greater stature and strength than the natural for whose protection and defense it was intended." Since Hobbes' time philosophers have drawn even closer the analogy between man and

the state. One might guess that a course in medicine was preliminary
to one in statesmanship, but physicians have almost constantly
eschewed politics. No other profession has given so few of its members to legislative bodies or public administrative positions. The
physician has refused to take the hazardous step from physiology to
sociology no matter how closely related those sciences may be. Lately,
however, something has happened to make the physician feel more
keenly his part in the social organization. He sees the great and
powerful hand of the federal government reaching out to enfold his
profession into its gargantuan grasp.

On November 19, 1945, President Truman in a special message
to Congress asked for legislation for a national health program. He
declared that "millions of our citizens do not have a full measure of
opportunity to achieve and enjoy good health; that other millions do
not have protection or security against the economic effects of sickness." To meet this problem the President asked for the construction
of hospitals and related facilities, expansion of public health, maternal
and child welfare services, more medical education and research and
pre-payment of medical costs through compulsory social insurance
and protection against loss of wages from sickness and disability.
A bill called the "Wagner-Murray Bill" was introduced into the
Senate to comply with the request of the President.

Some physicians are favorable to the government plan. The
majority, one may say, are opposed to it. They call it "socialized
medicine," a term Senator Wagner repudiates for, he says, a physician may come into the plan or stay out as he wishes. To this the
reply is made that if as many as one hundred million are drawn into
compulsory insurance no doctor could afford to stay out and the
whole profession would pass into government control and be paid for
its services according to government prescription. Organized medicine opposes this regimentation of practice. It is willing to advise
and advocate any improvement in medical practice which leaves the
patient a free choice of his physician and the physician a free agent
in his practice. Whatever may be the result of this federal challenge
to present medical practice will make an interesting subject for the
historian of the future.

CHAPTER XV

*Dentistry in Colorado**

THE dentists of Colorado were early in arriving at the "shook" and mud-roofed log cabin community in the cottonwood grove where Cherry Creek straggles into the Platte River. In 1858 this town was called Auraria but soon expanded across the way to include a mushrooming rival, Denver City. But at that time dentistry was not recognized as a distinct profession, and now it is difficult to picture the actual personalities or dental conditions.

Although during the 1860s in Denver the directories carry certain names of men who listed themselves as dentists, and some biographical material yet remains about them, in general they drifted on in the wake of other western gold strikes. In fact, records of the earliest days do not reveal that there were any pioneers specializing in dentistry alone in the whole of what was then the western half of Kansas Territory who became permanent residents, the custom being at that time for physicians to pull teeth and to give what cursory dental care was thought important. Health standards were extremely primitive in the far West, where the primary interest was the latest gold strike. "Get rich quick and go back to the States" was everyone's ambition.

Dentistry in the world in general and in America's pioneer communities in particular had not yet been dignified as the profession it now is. Two outstanding leaders, Dr. Horace H. Hayden and Dr. Chapin A. Harris, had done much in the early nineteenth century to inaugurate this new calling. Dr. Hayden had opened offices in Baltimore about the year 1800, and in 1825 had become a teacher of dentistry at the University of Maryland. He had advocated a dental association as early as 1817, but his efforts were not crowned with success until 1840. Assisted by Dr. Harris, another outstanding dental leader at that time, he succeeded in calling a meeting in New York City where the American Society of Dental Surgeons was formed.

Dr. Harris was chosen first president, and held that office until his death in 1844. During his whole life, he was an ardent student of dental surgery and contributed many articles to medical and dental journals, his most notable publication being a book *The Dental Art, a Practical Treatise on Dental Surgery.* It was 358 pages and contained three lithographic plates. In 1845 he brought out a second

* Written by Caroline Bancroft. Information obtained from a typewritten history compiled in 1926 by a History Committee consisting of Dr. William T. Chambers, chairman, Dr. Wm. Smedley and Dr. Eugene R. Warner, supplemented with later facts gathered by the present History Committee of the State Dental Association, consisting of Dr. Charles F. Brown, chairman, Dr. Henry F. Hoffman, and Dr. Will P. Smedley, with legal information supplied by Dr. Ira C. Brownlie.

edition entitled *Principles and Practices of Dental Surgery,* a very much amplified volume. Except for these two men and their few pioneer followers, dentistry as a separate profession was at the time of the settlement of Colorado almost completely unrecognized.

The physicians carried on meanwhile, aided from time to time by dentists who might be residents a year or two, until the arrival of Dr. B. Wesley Rogers in 1867 and of Dr. William Smedley in 1870. Then dentistry gained two substantial representatives of the profession. These men formed a partnership, and the opening of their office may be called the real beginning of dental care in Colorado.

It was not until April, 1887, that there were enough dentists established in their profession and permanent residents of Denver to form a dental society. A preliminary meeting was held in the office of Dr. J. M. Norman, on 15th Street in Denver, for the purpose of organizing the Colorado State Dental Association. The following dentists were present: Drs. C. H. Bagley, J. H. Beals, Sylvanus Davis, George J. Hartung, H. P. Kelley, J. M. Norman, J. M. Porter, B. W. Rogers, P. T. Smith and F. H. Sutherland.

As a result of this preliminary meeting a permanent organization was effected June 18, 1887. The following dentists were present: Drs. C. H. Bagley, J. H. Beals, W. F. Bradner, James J. Burns, J. N. Chipley, Sylvanus Davis, John W. Gramis, George J. Hartung, H. P. Kelley, J. M. Norman, J. M. Porter, A. B. Robbins, B. W. Rogers, W. K. Sinton, William Smedley, P. T. Smith, Arthur C. Watson, W. H. Weems, and E. S. Williams.

These men constituted the original membership of the Colorado State Dental Society. A constitution and by-laws were adopted and the following officers elected: president, Dr. Wm. Smedley, Denver; vice-president, Dr. John W. Gramis, Colorado Springs; second vice-president, Dr. B. W. Rogers, Denver; corresponding secretary, Dr. J. N. Chipley, Pueblo; recording secretary and treasurer, Dr. H. P. Kelley, Denver. At this early meeting, four papers were read and discussion was held on a proposition submitted by Governor John Evans, planning the establishment of a Dental Department in conjunction with the Medical Department of Denver University.

The second annual meeting of the Colorado State Dental Association was held at the St. James Hotel, Denver, June 5 and 6, 1888, with Dr. William Smedley presiding and Dr. H. P. Kelley acting as secretary. Eight papers were read and fourteen more dentists were admitted to membership from Denver, Salida, Colorado Springs, Boulder, Central City, and Greeley.

A special meeting was called October 25, 1888, to consider a proposed dental bill which was later passed by the legislature in 1889 through the efforts of Dr. Reuben B. Weiser, state senator from Georgetown, and subsequently a resident of Denver, to whom the society gave formal credit when the bill was enacted. At this special meeting, the officers elected for the ensuing year were: president, Dr. John W. Gramis, Colorado Springs; first vice-president, Dr. Peirce T. Smith, Denver; second vice-president, Dr. Joseph H. Beals,

Denver; corresponding secretary, Dr. H. P. Kelley, Denver; and recording secretary and treasurer, Dr. J. N. Chipley, Pueblo.

After that, the Colorado State Dental Association was launched on its steady career and upward growth. Each year an increasing number of dentists were admitted to membership and a widening influence obtained throughout the state. In 1890 the membership

Fourteenth Annual Meeting of Colorado State Dental Association at Boulder, 1900

was 63; by 1902 at the 16th annual meeting, which was held at the Alta Vista Hotel in Colorado Springs, there were 83 members present, including three honorary members. The variety and scope of the papers presented at each meeting increased proportionately as the influence of the society mounted.

For a time, local organizations such as the Denver Dental Society were separate from the State organization, and it, in turn, from the National. But as the profession gained prestige and power, its organization also achieved integration. At the present time, there are nine components of the Colorado State Dental Association: The Colorado Springs, the Boulder County, the Denver, the Larimer County, the Northeastern Colorado, the San Luis, the Southeastern, the Weld County, and the Western Colorado Dental Societies, and the total membership is 600 dentists, the whole being automatically a component of the American Dental Association.

Formal dental education in Colorado began with the proposition submitted on June 8, 1887, to the State Dental Society by Governor John Evans, as mentioned above, the plan being to establish a Dental College in connection with the Medical Department of the University of Denver. On motion of Dr. J. M. Norman, nine members of the Colorado State Dental Association were appointed by the president to meet and confer with the committee from the university's Medical Department. Drs. P. T. Smith, J. M. Porter, J. M. Norman and A. B. Robbins were appointed to act with the officers of the society: Drs. William Smedley, John W. Gramis, B. W. Rogers, J. M. Chipley, and H. P. Kelley, as a Committee of Conference.

The Denver Dental School, acting as the Dental Department of Denver University, was organized shortly thereafter in 1887 and admitted to membership in the National Association of Dental Faculties in 1890. David H. Moore, A.M., D.D., Chancellor of the University, was president of the faculty. Dr. A. B. Robbins, M.D., D.D.S., was chosen as the first dean of the Dental School and also as professor of Principles and Practices of Dentistry. The faculty for the first session in 1888 consisted of:

J. M. Norman, D.D.S., Professor of Operative Dentistry.
M. A. Bartleson, D.D.S., Professor of Mechanical Dentistry.
J. T. Edson, M.D., Professor of Anatomy.
E. J. A. Rogers, M.D., Professor of Principles and Practices of Surgery.
J. C. Davis, M.D., L.L.D., Professor of Materia Medica.
J. A. Sewall, M.D., Professor of Chemistry.
W. E. Edmundson, M.D., Professor of Histology.
P. T. Smith, D.D.S., Professor of Clinical Dentistry.

Demonstrators

A. K. Worthington, M.D., Demonstrator of Anatomy.
George J. Hartung, D.D.S.
H. P. Kelley, D.D.S., Demonstrator of Operative Dentistry.
S. Davis, D.D.S., Demonstrator of Mechanical Dentistry.

Special Lecturers

J. M. Porter, D.D.S., Dental Pathology and Oral Surgery.

Clinical Instructors

William Smedley, D.D.S.
Charles H. Bagley, D.D.S.
J. H. Beals, D.D.S.
J. N. Chipley, D.D.S.

From that time forward an able faculty carried on with but few changes of personnel each year, the main body of men still serving. The graduates of the first class in 1889 numbered four, and were:

Anna D. Chamberlain, Leonard A. Sanderson, both of Colorado;
E. W. Varley of Ohio, and Wilbur R. Wilson of Michigan.

Dental education took another step forward in 1896 when president James H. Baker, the Board of Regents of the University of Colorado, and the officers of the Medical Department decided to establish a dental school in conjunction with their medical school at 18th and Stout Streets in Denver. The Medical Department was asked to arrange facilities for a Dental Department in the building it then occupied, and also to arrange for a dental faculty. Dr. W. T. Chambers was chosen to select a dental faculty, accepting the post with the provision that all medical subjects would be taught by members of the medical faculty. The following dentists were chosen to complete the dental faculty: Drs. Hiram A. Fynn, Manfred S. Fraser, J. Stewart Jackson, and A. LeRoy Whitney. This organization was accomplished during the spring and summer months and by fall, the following students matriculated, composing the school's first class: M. F. Bauchert, Mary R. Bradner, W. F. Brierly, Belle R. Hendricks, H. F. Hoffman, E. D. Linton, J. L. Murray, Adam Turnbull, and George R. Warner.

As a result of court action instituted by the University of Denver restraining the University of Colorado from conducting departments in Denver, the dental department was reorganized in 1897 and was conducted until 1901 under the name of the Colorado College of Dental Surgery, the equipment being purchased by Drs. W. T. Chambers, H. A. Fynn, M. S. Fraser, J. S. Jackson, and A. L. Whitney.

Application had been made for membership in the National Association of Dental Faculties in the fall of 1896, but because of its reorganization and legal difficulties, the school was not admitted to membership in the N.A.D.F. until July, 1899. During 1901 pacific efforts were made which resulted in the consolidation of the Denver Dental College and the Colorado College of Dental Surgery, the consolidated school being affiliated and acting as a Dental Department of Denver University. The school continued to be known as the Colorado College of Dental Surgery, Dental Department of the Denver University.

Upon consolidation of the two schools, Dr. L. S. Gilbert was chosen as dean, but resigned one month later, at which time Dr. W. T. Chambers was elected and served the school as dean until 1914. Dr. H. A. Fynn served until 1918, and Dr. M. S. Fraser until 1923, at which time Dr. A. T. Newman from the University of Minnesota assumed the position. The school continued to flourish for a number of years after that, but in 1932 Denver University discontinued this department.

Legislation in dental history has followed similar lines to the growth of dental organization and dental education in the state. As previously mentioned, it was through the efforts of the newly formed association that the first dental law was passed March 15, 1889. This original law created a Dental Board to examine and license all dentists; it provided penalties for illegal practice, and it gave the Board power to make rules of procedure. The license fee for dentists was set at $10.00, with further provisions for penalties in case of violations. Since each Board of Dental Examiners serves two years, 58 boards have now served. On April 1, 1891, an amendment was approved requiring a dentist to have a diploma from a dental college approved by the Board as a prerequisite for examination.

On April 17, 1897, the 1891 bill was repealed and a new law enacted, largely due to the efforts of a committee headed by Dr. W. T. Chambers and sponsored in the legislature by Dr. W. F. Graves, a practising dentist then serving in the state senate. This law required the governor to select three of the five members of the Board from a list of five submitted by the Colorado State Dental Association. It prohibited the issuance of temporary certificates and incorporated in the new law the 1891 amendment of the old law, requiring each applicant to have graduated from an approved dental college. On April 10, 1905, an amendment was approved which enacted more severe penalties for illegal practice by making a second offense punishable by six to twelve months in jail. On May 28, 1911, still another amendment was approved raising the license fee from $10.00 to $25.00.

On March 5, 1919, a law governing dental hygienists was passed, again through the efforts of a Dental Society committee, this time headed by Dr. Henry F. Hoffman. This law made it possible for a dental hygienist, under the direction of a licensed dentist, to perform certain defined services in the mouth. It also provided for the licensing of such hygienists after examination by the Board of Dental Examiners, graduation from an approved school being a prerequisite to applying for the license and taking the examination. The license fee for dental hygienists was set at $10.00.

In 1921 all state laws were compiled and clarified and all existing dental legislation was included. On March 30, 1929, an amendment to the clarified dental law was approved providing for an annual registration fee of $2.00, and penalties for failure to register. It also required publication of the list of licentiates.

On March 8, 1935, the present Dental Practicing Act of Colorado was passed by the legislature through the efforts of a committee headed by Dr. Ira C. Brownlie. This is a comprehensive law with many new provisions, particularly those designed to regulate advertising and professional conduct and placing such control within the profession itself. The new law gives additional powers to the Board while retaining those granted by the old; it also provides a method of state-wide balloting by the licensed dentists, a majority vote on professional conduct being binding on the members of the profession throughout the state. It also clarifies all legal procedure.

This law owes its impetus to the activities throughout the preceding decade of William Randolph Parker, a New York dentist. For advertising purposes, Parker had assumed the name of Painless Parker. His publicity was so objectionable that the New York law requiring a dentist to practice under his own name, was enforced against him. He moved to California and by a legal process, changed his name to Painless Parker in order to begin again his blatant advertising. A pulpit-like entrance was established at his offices and barkers harangued the passersby with his virtues, at the same time insulting and condemning other dentists. Parker expanded and established offices in many western coast-state cities with assistants who used his name.

In 1915 he incorporated the California Dental Supply Company to own, equip, furnish and lease offices and furnish dental supplies. The stock was owned by Frances E. Parker, his wife. Another company, the Painless Parker Dentists, was formed to lease and operate dental offices. Three stockholders owned one share each. An annual report, filed March 2, 1926, at the Colorado State House, recited that the capital stock was $5,000, of which $30.00 was paid up and $1.16 was employed within the state borders. The company had debits of $2,914.22 and property and cash of $2,944.22, of which $113.49 was located in Colorado. This setup made Parker himself judgment proof against any creditors. Malpractice suits for thousands of dollars were already on file in the various states where he operated, three of these suits being in Colorado. Thus Parker could skim all the profits and assume no liability.

His unique chain-store method of dental practice was so successful that he attempted to change the laws of Colorado, California, and Oregon by initiated amendments in order to permit free exchange of dentists without examination. In the 1926 state election, the Dental Association's efforts, aided by the active support of practically all business and professional organizations, overwhelmingly defeated the Parker-initiated amendment. In California and Oregon he lost by only small majorities.

In 1927, ouster proceedings were brought in Colorado against the operating company, The Painless Parker Dentists, Incorporated. The District Court, presided over by Judge Charles C. Sackman, held that a corporation could lawfully practice dentistry. On appeal, the Colorado Supreme Court in a unanimous decision reversed Judge Sackman's decision and ordered the District Court to enter an order of ouster. Parker's appeal to the United States Supreme Court was denied, as they refused to take jurisdiction.

Faced with a Colorado ouster, the company which had previously been incorporated in Delaware planned to sell stock to the public and establish chain-store dental offices in the United States and Canada. California denied Parker the right to sell stock on account of the Colorado decision. Evidence was introduced to show that Parker, a corporation, was conducting the Denver offices by subterfuge and charges of unprofessional conduct were brought by the Colorado State Dental Association against the locally employed dentists.

Further evidence showed that the lessee was required to deposit all receipts to the account of the California Supply Company and all payments were made by checks sent from San Francisco. The lessee-dentist was required to buy all supplies from the lessor company and charged in monthly installments an annual rental of $18,000.00 and $4,200.00 for use of the company system.

The Dental Board revoked the licenses of Colorado dentists working in the Parker office. The District Court in a lengthy hearing reversed the Board and ordered the licenses restored. On appeal, the Colorado Supreme Court in a caustic opinion by Chief Justice John T. Adams, unanimously reversed the District Court decision of Judge E. V. Holland and the licenses remained revoked. Parker's appeal to the U. S. Supreme Court was denied.

The dental profession, recognizing what dangers lurked in a repetition of such unethical operations as Parker's, and of such expensive litigation as he had provoked, obtained the passage of the present Dental Practice Act, now recognized as an outstanding example of professional legislation designed for the protection of the public.

As education and knowledge grew, more and more need was felt by the profession for ready access to a growing volume of information. Plans for a dental library were inaugurated. The idea was promoted by the Denver Dental Association and its committee of Dr. Ralph N. Pullen, Dr. J. Terrance Williams, and Dr. V. C. Smedley. A second committee composed of Drs. G. E. Kuhl, Louis Adelman, and Henry F. Hoffman took over the purchase and assembly of books and arranged an agreement with the Medical Society of the City and County of Denver for the housing and care of the Library with that of the Medical Society.

The Denver Dental Library was opened in 1914. It is operated in conjunction with the Medical Library of the County Medical Society on the first floor of the Metropolitan Building in Denver. By arrangement, all resources of the two libraries are available to all members of both State Societies in Colorado. The Dental Library now contains about 1,600 volumes, besides a number of museum pieces.

In 1932 a committee composed of Drs. A. G. Kelly, Howard H. Reed, E. Pearl Bishop with F. A. Peterson, president of the Denver Dental Association, and Henry F. Hoffman as advisors, arranged a new contract with the Medical Society whereby the Dental Association furnished financial assistance for enlarging and furnishing the library rooms while the Medical Society continued to furnish secretarial care for the Dental Library.

Another factor, besides the library for the dissemination of information was the starting of a monthly *Bulletin of the Colorado State Dental Association,* the name of which was later changed to *The Journal of the Colorado State Dental Association.* This publication started in September, 1915, under the editorship of Dr. Earl W. Spencer and a staff composed of Drs. V. C. Smedley, E. I. Backus and O. L. Whitson. It still appears regularly and is invaluable to those dentists in outlying districts who find it difficult to attend meetings. Through the Journal's pages even the remote members of the profession can keep abreast of the newest developments in specialized fields.

During the years of growth of our state with its several substantial educational communities, the standard of requirements for a dental degree was keeping pace. Today two years' academic college work and four years' dental education are required for a degree, thus making the standard nearly similar to that for a medical degree except for the period of internship. Such requirements have brought a fine caliber of men into the dental profession. These men have been civic-minded and contributed to their communities in many ways.

One of the finest of the civic contributions made by the Denver Dental Association has been to the work of the Dental Clinic in the Denver Public schools. The Association opened a free clinic in the West Side Neighborhood House in January, 1912, under the sponsorship of the Denver Oral Hygiene Committee, composed of Drs. R. A. Adams, W. A. Brierley, A. C. Hamm, Henry F. Hoffman, and Will P. Smedley. Soon the clinic was moved to Longfellow School for the remainder of the 1912-1913 school year, and then to the Opportunity School.

In the autumn of 1913, the School Board undertook to bear the expense of the clinic, while the Denver Dental Association continued to be in charge of the actual management. This arrangement worked very well, Dr. L. T. Walsh being in charge until 1916, and Dr. Paul E. Barker until 1924 when Dr. Wm. J. McMenamy, the present head of the clinic, took charge. The general health condition of underprivileged children began to improve immediately following concerted attention to their teeth.

But in January, 1920, the *Denver Post* procured an injunction restraining the Denver Board of Education from continuing its health work. The Denver Dental Association jumped to the rescue. They launched a campaign to finance the dental clinic until such time as proper legislation might be secured to allow the Board of Education to continue paying for the work. About $1,800 was raised. The clinic reopened in February, still in charge of Dr. Barker. In May of the same year the Supreme Court rendered a decision making it legal for the Board of Education to continue its health work, and the children's clinic returned to its former financial basis.

A second dentist, Dr. W. A. Brierley, and two dental hygienists were added to the staff during the school year of 1921-1922 and in 1923, with certain changes in personnel, the clinic was moved to the Administration Building of the Denver Public Schools.

In 1926, Dr. E. E. Bailey, president of the Denver Dental Association, instituted a plan for making a study of McKinley School children to demonstrate the benefits in health and school-grades to be derived from improved dental health conditions. A Mouth Hygiene Committee, composed of Dr. Louis Adelman, Dr. H. F. Hoffman, and Dr. W. O. Brubaker, worked with Dr. William J. McMenamy, head of the school clinic, to carry out the plan. Over 135 of the Denver dentists contributed their time under the supervision of Dr. McMenamy and the Association expended some $3,000 in the three years of this study.

When depression gripped the city in the summer of 1933, the Board of Education announced they would have to close the clinic during June and July because of lack of funds, despite the fact that 3,000 children had not been cared for during the school year. The Denver Dental Association through its Mouth Hygiene Committee, composed this time of Drs. Henry F. Hoffman, Louis Adelman, W. O. Brubaker, G. E. Mallett and S. F. Brannan, again came to the rescue. They made arrangements whereby 198 Denver dentists during the remainder of the summer gave their services without cost for 2,245 appointments to 1,696 public school children.

Two of the clinic's dentists, Dr. Benjamin Kletsky and Dr. Henry C. Gage, served in the U. S. Navy during World War II. Dr. Gage returned to the clinic in February, 1946, and is now a full-time dentist. The clinic operates the year round, excepting for the month of August, and is a permanent memorial to the vision and civic-mindedness of our dentists.

In still another field they have shown enterprise. In June, 1937, Governor Teller Ammons was persuaded to appoint a dentist to the State Board of Health. Dr. H. C. Dolph was the first dentist to serve. In January, 1939, Governor Ralph Carr appointed Dr. Charles G. Grover to the Board and he is now completing his eighth year. In 1941, due to his influence, the State Dental Health program was created as a separate entity, making it on a par with the other divisions in the Health Department. Dr. Grover has also had the unusual distinction of serving two and a half years, from July, 1943, through December, 1945, as President of the State Board of Health.

The Division of Public Health Dentistry under the directorship of Dr. Robert A. Downs, works with local health departments and the dental profession in promoting dental health. Briefly, the dental program primarily provides dental examinations, consultations, education both for lay and professional groups, refresher courses for the dental profession, liaison activities, program planning, studies on dental problems and arranges for the needed dental care of patients of other divisions of the Colorado State Division of Public Health.

In the six years' existence of the department, Dr. Downs has supervised ever-broadening activities. Refresher courses for dentists were sponsored in Steamboat Springs, Grand Junction, Durango, Monte Vista, La Junta and Sterling. Dental care was incorporated as an integral part of a Maternity Demonstration program in Otero County. A survey was made as to dental health conditions in all eleven state institutions. Fluorine studies were conducted. Colorful and educational exhibits were prepared for a variety of public meetings. Dental care supervision was inaugurated for hospitalized patients of the Division of Crippled Children as well as a general program for providing orthodontic care to indigent children.

The dentists have shown themselves patriotic as well as civic-minded. During World War I, 35 Colorado dentists enlisted for service and Dr. R. O. Smith received the Distinguished Service Cross for action in France. During World War II, 234 served in the Armed Forces and two lost their lives. In June, 1946, there were still 78 from Colorado in service and 128 had received Congressional Selective Service Medals and certificates for their services in making examinations during the war emergency, while Dr. William P. Carlin was the possessor of a Purple Heart. However, complete figures and awards on World War II have not yet been tabulated.

The Colorado State Dental Association has kept up its standing outside the state as well as within. The local men have not only been alive to a growing mass of research throughout the nation, but have made friends with many of its most prominent scientists. As an organization it has twice been host to the American Dental Association, the first time in 1910 when they entertained over a thousand dentists from all parts of the United States, and the second in 1930 when they were hosts to over four thousand.

Three Colorado dentists achieved the honor of offices in the National Dental Association, Drs. W. T. Chambers, Eugene R. Warner, and Max Giesecke, each of whom was elected to the vice-presidency. In addition, Dr. Warner was elected trustee of that association in 1911 and at the time of his death in 1936, was a member of the research commission and research institute of the national association. Dr. Chambers is further remembered for his fine work as an organizing member of the national dental relief fund, his twelve years' membership on the Dental Educational Council of America, his fellowship in the American College of Dentists with his presidency of the Colorado branch of that organization and, finally, his industrious research for the *History of Dentistry in Colorado,* a volume which, while written with other collaborating dentists, was largely Dr. Chambers' work.

A review of the history of dentistry in Colorado, from whatever viewpoint, shows that though the dentists were slow in achieving independent identity in the pioneer state, they have since made up for their slow beginnings by the vigor of their contribution to Colorado. Much credit is due to this active and wide-awake body of men, the dentists.

CHAPTER XVI

Art, Drama, and Music

Edgar C. McMechen

Art

WHEN Lewis and Clark returned from their trek into the vast unknown, curiosity swept the nation like a prairie fire. A new world had opened. What lay beyond the ranges? What manner of beasts and men roamed mountain and plain?

The printed word alone could not satisfy this hunger for knowledge. When gold was discovered in 1858 the demand was greatly intensified. Magazines, periodicals and newspapers wanted pictures. Since photography was then in its incipient stages, illustrators and artists were dispatched to record graphically the story of the new frontier. They accompanied the military explorers, and rode with the wagon trains to Santa Fe, California and Oregon. They penetrated the mysterious mountains with the Pikes Peak gold seekers. They fought the Indian warrior and sat in the council lodge. They hunted the buffalo and followed the great trail herds.

Thousands of illustrations were printed by such periodicals as *Harper's* and *Leslie's Weeklies, Scribner's* and *Century,* sketched by young men, many of whom were destined to become notable artists of their day; some of whom already had arrived as painters of power and conviction.

Thus begins the story of Colorado art. To these adventurous wielders of pen and brush must go credit for recording ethnological and historical detail of imponderable value that otherwise would have been lost forever. Their influence in stimulating the western migration can hardly be over-estimated.

The first artist to sketch upon Colorado soil was S. Seymour, who accompanied the Major Stephen H. Long expedition in 1820. Lieutenant J. W. Abert of the U. S. Topographical Engineers was with Kearny's expeditions of 1845 and 1846 and gave us many fine scenic sketches, as well as the best representation of Bent's Old Fort on the Arkansas. With John C. Fremont, the Pathfinder, came Benjamin Creutzfeldt, Richard and Edward Kern. Dr. Benjamin J. Kern, while returning to the San Luis Valley with Parson Bill Williams to recover equipment abandoned by Fremont after his disastrous attempt to cross the San Juan Mountain during the winter of 1848-49, was killed by the Ute Indians.[1]

These early artists devoted their attention mainly to scenic views, reproduced by the lithographic process in black and white, or colored

---

[1] Reproductions of these early sketches may be found in the official journals of their expeditions.

prints. There is a certain ethereal quality in this work which challenges the imagination today, as it must have intrigued the pioneer spirit of America at the time.

With the Pikes Peak Gold Rush came a horde of artist-correspondents who have left an invaluable heritage of intimate detail. There were so many of these illustrators that it is difficult to determine just who was the first to dispatch sketches to the States. One of the earliest was John D. (Captain Jack) Howland of the First Colorado Volunteers, who had come to the mountains before discovery of gold on Cherry Creek. There is little doubt that he was the first resident artist. More will be said of this noted painter of wild life as we proceed.

Possibly the first attempt to represent pioneer Denver was made by J. Y. Glendenen, who sketched the town of Auraria in 1859.[2] This curious character is chiefly interesting today because of his copy of Stuart's Richmond painting of George Washington, which hangs in the Masonic Temple at Central City. Since Glendenen could secure nothing but house paint, since he had to work entirely by candlelight in the windowless room, and since he was a disciple of Bacchus, he succeeded remarkably well. The Central City lodge has refused high offers for this work.

Two important resident artists of the 1860s were J. E. Dillingham and A. E. Mathews,[3] lithographers, whose work is historically valuable because they left the best pictorial records of the pioneer towns, buildings and mining scenes. Mathews published two books of views in colors, which now are rare collectors' items. He worked in Denver during the late sixties and died on his Big Thompson ranch November 6, 1874. Dillingham's views of early Denver are, perhaps, the rarest of all Colorado prints. Both of these men were capable artists.

The great art event of the sixties was the arrival of the celebrated German artist, Albert Bierstadt, a painter of landscape and *genre,* after whom Mt. Bierstadt, Colorado, is named. His landscapes of Rocky Mountain and California scenery brought him world renown. Bierstadt was a frequent visitor during the sixties and seventies, and he did more than any other man to bring Colorado scenery to the attention of the world. His famous "A Storm in the Rocky Mountains," now in the Metropolitan, was painted near Chicago Lakes in 1865, and was exhibited in Europe. He was decorated with the French Legion of Honor, Order of St. Stanislaus (Russia), and Imperial Order of Midyi (Turkey).

Ralph Albert Blakelock, the noted landscape painter, came to Colorado in 1865 by wagon train, and remained in Denver and its vicinity for about one year.[4] Still a boy in his teens, he filled many sketch books with line drawings, most of them made around Golden and the Clear Creek Valley. These later appeared in Harper's.

[2] *Rocky Mountain Herald,* June 23, 1860, p. 1.

[3] Mathews published *Gems of Rocky Mountain Scenery* and *Pencil Sketches of Colorado.* The State Historical Society of Colorado has two of Dillingham's prints.

[4] *Artists' Club Scrap Book* in Denver Public Libary.

The most colorful artist in Colorado's history was Charles Stewart Stobie,[5] "Mountain Charlie," who crossed the plains in 1865 and became a friend of Jim Beckwourth, mulatto war chief of the Crow Indians, of Kit Carson and Mariana Modena, famous Mountain Men of the fur days. Stobie had a mission. He yearned to follow the footsteps of Catlin, and record on canvas the story of the mountain and plains Indians. He learned the secrets of the fur trappers, became an army scout during the Indian wars, joined the buffalo hunters and otherwise lived the life that he depicted. Stobie dressed in fringed buckskins. He numbered among his close friends, Charlie Utter, greatest of the Rocky Mountain Nimrods and the closest companion of Wild Bill Hickok, Major Powell, and Jack Sumner, who was Powell's guide through the Canyon of the Colorado. He made an exacting study of the Ute Indians, having been coached by U. M. Curtis, Ute interpreter. Stobie painted prolifically and, whatever may be said of him as an artist, he painted truthfully. His work, therefore, has considerable ethnological value. He maintained a studio in Denver, but was seldom there. Frederic Remington learned of Stobie's remarkable fund of information and was a frequent visitor, securing much of his information of the early West from Mountain Charlie. One of Remington's drawings has the scout in it. Stobie died in Chicago in 1929. His collections and some thirty of his paintings came to the State Historical Society of Colorado.

Frederic Huet[6] is a name almost unknown in the annals of Colorado, yet he might have ranked among the great. This man was a pawn of fate. Born of rich and influential French parents, educated in the Gobelau (the French government school of arts), a school mate of Gustave Doré, he seemed to have destiny in his hands. He died a pauper on the county poor farm of Clear Creek County. Huet, always a non-conformist, left Paris when twenty years old, and landed in Boston in 1848. He soon won recognition from able contemporaries, and was employed by *Leslie's Weekly* to make sketches of Civil War battles. His outrageous sense of humor led him to send in a sketch of the Battle of Bull Run, depicting a cloud of blue-clad figures scampering before a herd of bulls. He was summarily discharged, drifted to Old Mexico and finally ended at Georgetown. For twenty years he did not touch a brush, but took a delight in making pencil caricatures of fellow townsmen. Several of his rare landscapes which reveal the well-trained professional touch, are owned by residents of Georgetown or Empire. Huet's addiction to the convivial glass proved his utter undoing. He died in 1913.

A notable visitor of 1861 was Emanuel Leutze, best known as painter of "Washington Crossing the Delaware." He spent several weeks in the mountains securing sketches later used in decoration of the National Capitol.[7]

[5] *Rocky Mountain News,* July 26, 1869; May 25, 1877.
[6] *Rocky Mountain News,* March 31, 1912.
[7] *Ibid.,* September 11, 1861. *Dictionary of American Biography,* XI, 195-196.

The period of the seventies opened in a dull and listless way insofar as the art movement was concerned, yet the first indications of art colonies began during this decade in Denver and Colorado Springs. These were feeble and sporadic because this was still the era of chromos which sold by the thousands. William D. Edmonston of Edinburgh, graduate of the Royal School of Arts, settled at Larkspur, in 1871, painted until 1893, and then became an agriculturist.[8] A Mr. Whittridge of New York spent the summers of 1870 and 1871 painting in the neighborhood of Greeley and elicited from the *Greeley Tribune* a panegyric.[9] One of his canvases won the dubious verdict "a picture which annihilated space." Seemingly it annihilated Mr. Whittridge also, as we hear no more of him. Miss Jennie Bartlett won a premium at the Boulder County Fair in 1871 for the best portrait in oil.[10] In Colorado Springs, the same year, Walter Paris took up permanent residence. His forte was water color, and his style has been described as "delicate and true to nature."[11] His meticulous fidelity won high praise from Professor Hayden.

The advent of the great western landscape painter, Thomas Moran, with the Powell surveys, however, gave the needed impetus to the art movement. From the Powell expeditions Moran drew the inspiration of his famous paintings of Yellowstone Canyon and the Grand Canyon of the Colorado, both of which were purchased by Congress. Moran was in Denver in 1874, having just returned from a trip to the Mount of the Holy Cross.[12] This year also marked a sketching trip by J. Tarvernier and Paul Frenzeny, top illustrators for *Harper's Weekly*. The former was then a noted painter of Western life.[13]

A prominent figure in Denver's embryonic art world during the seventies was "Professor" H. A. Streight.[14] The Professor was a man of parts. He came to Colorado in 1870 from California and made his home in Denver for some twelve years, then he went to Chicago. A friend of Josiah Gregg Holland, the erudite editor of *Harper's Magazine,* he also sold a painting to Henry Wadsworth Longfellow. While in Denver he indulged in spiritualistic seances. Presumably, he painted landscapes in the dark, under spiritualistic guidance. During these seances the soft strokes of a brush could be heard. When the lights went on the charming landscape, still wet and glistening, received the proper "ohs and ahs," and was promptly

8 Wilbur F. Stone, *History of Colorado,* III, 693.

9 *Greeley Tribune,* July 19, 1871.

10 *Boulder News,* October 13, 1871.

11 Manly D. and Eleanor R. Ormes, *The Book of Colorado Springs* (1933), 337.

12 *Rocky Mountain News, Weekly,* September 9, 1874.

13 *Rocky Mountain News,* February 17, 1874. Robert Taft, *The Pictorial Record of the West, I. Frenzeny and Tavernier.*

14 *Transcript* (Golden, Colo.), May 2, 1877; *Colorado Graphic,* May 5, 1888, p. 8; and January 14, 1888, p. 8, cites *The Indicator* (Chicago, Ill.), *Rocky Mountain News,* September 17, 1882.

sold. A wet painting had been substituted for a blank canvas while the lights were out.

During the eighties Professor Streight worked in Chicago, painting large six-by-eight landscapes for the Kansas Pacific Railroad, which "portrayed upon canvas the grandeur of the everlasting hills." With a flair for the dramatic, he painted the Mount of the Holy Cross with adoring pilgrim in the foreground, and labelled it "Nearer My God to Thee."

The Professor's most prodigious stunt, however, was his famous "Cyclorama of the Battle of Gettysburg." Having exhibited it in the New Orleans Exposition of 1883, he sent it to Denver and promoted a special building for its display. This was a round building on Champa, where the Chamber of Commerce now stands. One entered and passed through a sort of Plutonian subway, coming up in the center. There, encircling him, he gazed in awe upon the story of carnage. The building afterwards became known as the Colosseum, and, appropriately enough, later housed the carnage of Reddy Gallagher's prize fights and numerous hectic political conventions.

The noted painter Hamilton Hamilton, N. A., was for a long time a resident of Denver. He came to Denver in 1873 and made a hasty sketching trip through the mountains, bringing back forty-seven canvases. The *Rocky Mountain News* criticized him severely for careless work.[15] He remained in Denver for almost two decades. His studio was a frame shack on Cherry Creek just south of the Broadway bridge.

About the middle seventies art activities took a turn for the better. In 1877, W. F. Porter, a landscape painter, opened a class.[16] At this time, J. Harrison Mills, Professor Streight and J. M. Bagley, a pen and ink artist, were working in the city with, of course, John D. Howland. Bagley was Denver's first engraver and a very capable craftsman.[17] Mills, one of Colorado's better early day painters, and a potent influence in raising art standards, was a New Yorker, who had come to Colorado in 1869 and built a cabin near Long's Peak, where his wife taught a country school.[18] He was a skilled penman and engraver, and his work had considerable vogue. With his brother he controlled the calotype process and established an engraving company. But he also was a portrait and landscape painter in the academic tradition. He wrote poetry well enough to win a national award from the *New York Herald*.

This group was followed, about 1877, by Mrs. J. A. Chain,[19] whose husband was a partner in the Chain & Hardy Bookstore. She, there-

15 *Rocky Mountain News,* August 17, 1873.

16 *Colorado Miner,* No. 52, p. 2; May 5, 1887; also see *Denver Tribune,* December 22, 1875.

17 *Denver Inter-Ocean,* June 6, 1880, p. 286.

18 *The Tabor Grand Opera Company* (Dove and Temple, printers, 1883), 37-38; *Denver Daily Tribune,* April 19, 1879; February 16, 1879; *Rocky Mountain News,* September 17, 1882.

19 *Rocky Mountain News,* April 20, 1877, and *Denver Daily Tribune,* same date.

fore, had a better outlet than the California-Colorado landscape artist, Edwin Deakin, whose "elegant" oil painting "Lake Tallac" was put up for raffle in March, 1877, at $1,000.[20] Like the pioneer actor, who took "benefits" whenever he could get them, the pioneer painter was forced to take measures to fill the larder. Mrs. Chain was a pupil of Innes. Two of her landscapes are in the State Museum. She opened a class in painting in 1877.

Diploma Awarded to John D. Howland for an Oil Painting, 1877

It was in this momentous year, 1877, that John D. Howland won the award for an oil painting at the Colorado Industrial Association's exhibition, the first diploma awarded for art in Colorado that has thus far come to light. The elaborately decorated certificate is in the possession of Howland's daughter, Kate Howland Charles of Denver.

In 1881, the business leaders of Colorado determined to hold a Denver Exposition.[21] The Mining and Industrial Exposition was projected by the Denver Mining Association, headed by H. A. W. Tabor and, on Colorado Day, August 1, 1882, the great fair opened in its own building, a mammoth structure 500 feet long, situated at Broadway and Exposition Street.[22] Though the basic purpose was to

---

[20] *Denver Daily Tribune,* March 18, 1877; also see *Tabor Grand Opera House,* p. 39.

[21] *Denver Daily Tribune,* January 9, 1881; *Colorado Condensed,* S. H. S. Pam 917.88-R484.

[22] *Ibid.,* August 1, 1882.

tell the world of Colorado's mineral wealth, industrial, agricultural, and art exhibits were included.

The *Tribune* article describing the exhibit records many revealing observations from the audience, one man having been heard to exclaim: "Seems to me that marble gal orter have some clo's on."[23]

Winner of the gold medal was the now well known landscape painter Charles Partridge Adams. He was a pupil of Mrs. Chain, and it is said that she never spoke to him again.

At this time, the artists were organized as the Academy of Fine Arts Association of Colorado. The origin of this Academy dated back to the Centennial Year, 1876, when J. Harrison Mills interested leading clergymen, doctors, lawyers, artists, architects and other professional people in a project to meet regularly for the study and discussion of art and its history, and of literature.[24]

Mills supplemented the work of this informal group by formation of the Denver Sketch Club, organized in 1880. This club was revamped in 1881 under the title Kit Kat Club, or the Colorado Art Association.[25] The club took rooms in the Symes building, with Governor F. W. Pitkin as president; Julius Knapp, secretary; Mr. Sturgis as treasurer and Mills as Principal. Membership in the Kit Cat totaled about twenty, equally divided between men and women. By solicitation enough money was raised to bring a set of plaster casts from New York. The movement developed rapidly and on February 7, 1882, the Academy of Fine Arts Association of Colorado was incorporated with J. Harrison Mills as first president. Directors included: Governor Pitkin, W. H. M. Coxe, William G. Evans, T. J. O'Donnell, A. T. Mills, M. C. Rovira and E. L. Shorb. The School of Design opened with twenty-seven pupils.[26]

The following year, Mills arranged with Senator Tabor and his associates to take over the fifth floor of the Tabor Grand Opera House as the Studio Flat. This was Denver's first Bohemian center. Doors were opened at 4 P. M. for visitors, and Saturday afternoon receptions were held.[27]

---

[23] This was the first major art exhibit held in Colorado. Those who exhibited included: Mrs. J. A. Chain, six landscapes; J. Harrison Mills, three landscapes and "The Academy Owl"; W. Winter, two classical subjects and several landscapes; I. M. Broadway, portraits; Mrs. D. L. Shorb, "The National Game" (poker); Mrs. Frank McClure, panel and flower pictures; Charles Partridge Adams, two landscapes; Mrs. Emma Wild, a painting of Pikes Peak, which elicited the nostalgic comment from the *Tribune* art critic, "Sometimes we wish there never had been a Pike"; Mrs. A. W. Bailey, "Yucca"; Alexis Comparet, landscape and "Prairie Schooner"; Mrs. Wheeler, landscape; Ida Miller, still life; Miss C. C. Dixon, wood carving; Miss Jessie Converse, china painting; Ida V. Vieta, plaques and painted tambourines; J. M. Bagley, "Susan of the Utes"; W. H. Coxe, landscape; Charles Craig, landscape; the latter two were Colorado Springs artists.

[24] *Tabor Grand Opera House*, p. 34.

[25] *Ibid., Denver Tribune*, January 27, 1882.

[26] *Denver Daily Tribune*, February 12, 1882; August 13, 1882.

[27] *Ibid.*, August 13, 1882.

Mills was the "master" and head of the Academy.[28]   Tutoring with him were Jack Howland, Alexis Comperet, Edwin Deakin, and Charles Partridge Adams.[29]   Studios on the frontier in the eighties were as full of plaster casts as a graveyard bristling with tombstones. Modelling from life just was not nice in the eyes of Denver matrons whose daughters studied art.   The Misses De Milo and De Medici Venus, Mr. Apollo Belvedere and similar white spirits stood at every hand.   One of the famous models was a stuffed owl, called by the students "The Academy Owl."   They struggled helplessly with the recalcitrant bird until Mills finally painted it to see what was the matter.[30]   His was the "master's" owl shown in the exhibition.

An interesting character in the school was Fanny Tarbell, the girl who "painted 'em by the yard."[31]   Prang of Boston took her entire output of roses and pansies.   She later studied portrait under William Chase and gained an international fame.   Her "Last Rose of Summer" was suggested to her while in London by the Shakespearian actor, Frank Mayor, who wanted a soul in the rose.   So she introduced very delicately among the petals "the exquisite face of a woman with tears like dew drops falling athwart across a rose."

The Kit Kat got lost somewhere in the jungle, so the Denver Artist's Club was organized in 1886 with John D. Howland as president.[32]   Howland lived in Denver longer than any other artist.   He began as an illustrator for *Harper's* and *Leslie's* weeklies and grew in stature.   He came West in 1857 and lived for a time with the Sioux Indians; served as clerk for the Indian Peace Commission at the Treaty of Medicine Lodge; was a captain in the First Colorado Volunteers, Civil War.   After the war he studied in Paris under Armand Dumaresque.   His paintings of western animals had a wide vogue and are in some well-known collections.[33]   No man could tell a better yarn of Indians and soldiers, of buffalo hunts and adventures on the frontier.

[28] *Tabor Grand Opera House*, pp. 33-40.   Artists having studios in the Tabor were: Miss Carrie E. Swan, drawing and painting in oil and water color, and painting upon china and velvet; J. M. Bagley, designer and wood engraver; Mrs. E. S. Wild, oil landscapes; E. Lansdale Fox, portraits, landscapes, and historical paintings; George H. Johnson, portraits in crayon, ink, and colors; Mrs. S. Shedd, teacher of landscape; Curtis Chamberlain, designer and letterer; Mrs. Clara Zimdars, decorative art, oil and water color painting, and Kensington embroidery; William Winter, who painted boxcar-size paintings and paintings after the Daguerre style; Edwin Deakin, landscapes, architectural paintings, and fruit; Fanny V. Tarbell, teacher of oil, water color, and china painting; Florence Boyd, teacher of wood carving, drawing, and painting.   In Chamberlain's studio was A. Phimister Proctor, then studying painting; now one of the foremost animal sculptors in America.   He was a Denver boy.   A pupil of Mills was Albert Wilbur Steele, the famous cartoonist of the *Denver Post*.

[29] *Rocky Mountain News*, June 31, 1923.

[30] *Ibid.*

[31] *Ibid.*

[32] State Historical Society Library; p. 706, H384d and P. B. H384.   Associated with Howland as officers of the New Denver Art Club were: Curtis Chamberlain, Vice-President; Charles Partridge Adams, Treasurer; and Alexis Comparet, Secretary.   The Board of Trustees included: Charles Partridge Adams, Mrs. C. G. Richardson, Mrs. John Elitch, J. M. Bagley, R. H. Tallant, Curtis Chamberlain, Alexis Comparet, Helen De Lange, James Byrne, D. Mackenzie and H. C. J. Moore.

[33] *Denver Post*, September 11, 1914, *Rocky Mountain News*, December 21, 1900.

The club lasted only a year. Their room was taken away from them because of violent disagreements among some of the members. Before the schism occurred, however, Howland was appointed, as President of the Art Club, Superintendent of the Art Department at the River Front Park, September 13 to October 22, 1887.[34] He was appointed in 1885 one of the judges to award the "Marguerite Evans" prizes at the University of Denver Art School.[35]

Frequent mention has been made of Alexis Comparet, or Compera, as he was later known.[36] This strange genius is almost a legend today. Born of French parentage in Indiana in 1850, he ran away from a good home and came west by wagon train. Arriving at Colorado City, as the story goes, when only twelve or thirteen years old, he asked a bartender for a job. Asked what he could do Alexis said: "play the guitar, paint pictures and sing." He is said to have spent several years painting Pikes Peak and the Garden of the Gods on a back bar. Later, he came to Denver and made friends with John Elitch and his wife. Several large landscapes and figure paintings by Comparet still adorn the old theater at the Gardens.

In 1890 some of Comparet's admirers sent him East to study. He exhibited in some of the better galleries in New York and Chicago. He was reported also as in Paris. Returning to Denver he married Stella Kent, naming one of his two sons Harvey Young Compera after his friend. His style of painting changed materially, as did his name. He dropped the "et" ending and added "a" because he grew tired of having his name mispronounced. Comparet became a painter of vagrant moods, adopting simplified compositions, delicately handled in the French manner. Domestic troubles and creeping paralysis brought him low and he died in his studio at Coronado Beach May 14, 1906, a rather tragic figure of dreams unfulfilled.

The German Baron, W. B. von Richthofen, who built the castle in Montclair near Denver and wrote engagingly of the open range cattle industry, proposed a grandiloquent scheme in 1890 for the establishment in Denver of an International Art Gallery, which he offered to back liberally.[37] The Chamber of Commerce did nothing about this, but the proposal excited again the ambitions of local artists to establish a museum.

The University of Denver in 1880, had instituted an art course, which, at first, was little more than a drawing class, taught by Ida De Steiguer.[38] This was still functioning, but the Academy of Fine Arts of Colorado had petered out with the departure of Mills, who had developed a market for his work in New York. Governor John

---

34 Letter from Denver Chamber of Commerce and Board of Trade to John D. Howland, August 4, 1887, in collection of Kate Howland Charles.

35 Letter to J. D. Howland from Ida de Steiguer, Principal of Art Department, University of Denver, September 22, 1885, in Denver Public Library.

36 Joseph H. Morris, p. 8—0738, State Historical Society of Colorado. *The Artists Club Scrap Book* in the Denver Public Library also contains much about Comparet.

37 *Events,* III, No. 7, p. 10.

38 *The Coloradan,* V. 1, No. 7, p. 10.

Evans had offered, in the late eighties, to donate one-fourth of a block at the corner of Colfax Avenue and South 13th Street on condition that money be raised to build an art gallery and academy building.[39] This plan could not be made to work. The suggestion of Baron Richthofen, and the approach of the Knights-Templar Conclave, held in 1892 furnished the needed sparks.

Mrs. Harriet Hayden, a successful Chicago art teacher, had arrived in January, 1891, to open an art school in Denver. She called a meeting at her studio and organized the Le Brun Art Club, composed entirely of women artists, both professional and amateur. The name was derived from the celebrated French portrait painter, Madame Vigee Le Brun.[40] She specialized in Royal Families.

The *Coloradan,* a semi-cultural magazine of the period, in supporting the new movement, indignantly stated: "There has been sold in Denver and the State enough bad canvas to make a covered way from the grand opera house to the City Park. Thousands of dollars have been spent for the poorest and gaudiest of chromos, lithographs, etchings."[41] The article might well have included steel engravings of the Roman Colosseum, Trajan's Arch, et al.

There followed, almost immediately, an organization called the Denver Art League, consisting of seventy-nine incorporators. The list included the leading bankers, business and professional men of Denver, such as David H. Moffat, Col. D. C. Dodge, C. B. Kountze, J. A. Thatcher, Walter S. Cheesman, Governor J. B. Grant, Charles S. Thomas, Joel F. Vaile, Willard Teller, Senator N. P. Hill, Henry R. Wolcott, and Roger W. Woodbury. Anyone familiar with Colorado history will realize the power behind the Denver Art League. The president was William Shaw Ward, Leadville mining man and promotor extraordinary. United States District Judge Moses Hallett was vice-president; William Hayden, secretary; and John L. McNeil, treasurer. The purpose as set forth in the articles of incorporation, filed June 14, 1892, was to establish a School of Design, and a Museum of Art.[42]

Secretary Hayden called the Le Brun Club "the mother of the League."[43] Events moved swiftly. With the Knights-Templar Con-

---

39 *Ibid.,* V. 1, No. 9, p. 10.

40 *The Coloradan,* V. 1, No. 1, p. 12. Officers were: Mrs. Hayden, President; Mrs. Emma Richardson Cherry, Vice-President; Helen De Lange, Secretary; and Mrs. Alice Wheeler Wrisley, Treasurer. The first exhibition was held in the post office in May, 1892, with the following member exhibitors: Miss Nettie (Henrietta) Bromwell, Mrs. Cherry, Miss Janette Conine, Miss Annie Dailey, Miss Helen De Lange, Miss Ida C. Failing, Mrs. Hayden, Mrs. Irene Jerome Hood, Mrs. Egbert Johnson, Miss Helen Power, Miss Katherine Smalley, Mrs. Ida M. Stair, Mrs. Wrisley. Non-member exhibitors included Ida De Steiguer, Mrs. Mary Hallack Foote, the authoress whose Leadville stories were published in the leading magazines of the country; Miss Emily Miles, Miss N. Munson, Miss Christin Nielsen, Miss Cora Sanborn, Miss Elyria B. Shoemaker and Miss Constance Van Diest. The names are important because this group shook Denver business and social leaders from their apathy toward art.

41 *Ibid.,* I, No. 4, p. 10.

42 *Ibid.,* V. 1, No. 2, p. 4.

43 *Ibid.,* V. 1, No. 13.

clave in view a loan exhibit was arranged in the Equitable Building, featuring notable European and American painters.[44]

The Denver Art League opened its School of Fine Arts in the California Building September 26, 1892.[45] Samuel Richards, trained under German teachers, had long maintained a studio in Munich. He had arrived in Denver a few months previous, a victim of tuberculosis. It was stated at the time that the Boston School of Fine Arts had offered him its directorship.[46] Hence, he was the logical man to head the new school, and became its director and instructor in painting.[47]

The first exhibition of the Denver Art League was an exhibition of the paintings of Walter McEwen,[48] who had exhibited in the Paris Salon and had been chosen by the American art colony in Paris to represent them at the Chicago World's Fair. The most outstanding exhibition of the League was a one-man, Thomas Moran, show displaying 260 of his paintings, held in January, 1893.[49]

This gave Denver two strong art schools, because the Denver School of Fine Arts, University of Denver, at the opening of its fall term in 1892, had been placed upon a comparable basis under the direct patronage and direction of Mrs. Margaret Gray Evans, wife of Governor John Evans.[50] It occupied a building at 1330 Arapahoe.

The faculty was headed by Preston Powers,[51] sculptor son of Hiram Powers, whose "Greek Slave" had created a national interest.

"The Closing Era" group on the State Capitol grounds, Denver's first monumental outdoor statuary, is the work of Preston Powers. However, he was not the first sculptor to work in Colorado, as this distinction goes to Byron M. Pickett, who maintained a studio in Denver in 1878.[52] The State Museum has one of the rare examples of his work, a bas-relief of John Q. Charles, who built the Charles Block. George W. Platt, trained in the Royal Academy of Munich and the Academy of Fine Arts, Venice, at this time instituted at the

44 *Ibid.*, V. 1, No. 6, pp. 11-12.

45 *Ibid.*, V. 1, No. 7, p. 8. The staff included: Frank H. Collins, drawing, life, and mechanical; Charles Partridge Adams, landscape painting; Frederic Hart Wilson, cast, antique, and drawing for illustration; Harriet W. Hayden, water color, and Ida C. Failing, china painting and decorating. With the exception of Adams and Miss Failing, the faculty had all studied under the leading French or German art teachers of the period.

46 *Ibid.*, V. 1, No. 6, pp. 11-12.

47 *Ibid.*, V. 1, No. 6, pp. 11-12. The exhibit represented Corot, Daubigny, G. Pelouse, A. Schramm, Munier, Charles Jacque, Guilleminet, F. S. Church, Thomas Moran, Jean Francois Millet, Albert Bierstadt, Edward and Percy Moran, De Haas, William Hart, Cropsey, H. Bolton Jones, T. Welch, Hamilton Hamilton, J. Harrison Mills, Samuel Richards, and the then leaders of the Denver group—J. D. Howland, Charles Partridge Adams, Harvey Young, Henry Read, Richard H. Tallant and Mrs. J. A. Chain. It was only a few months after this exhibit that Denver art circles were shocked by the news that Mr. and Mrs. Chain had been lost at sea when the *SS Bokhara* sank during a typhoon in the China Sea, October 10, 1892.

48 *The Coloradan,* V. 1, No. 10, p. 11, October 15, 1892.

49 *Ibid.,* V. 1, No. 15, p. 11.

50 *Ibid.,* V. 1, No. 6, p. 13.

51 *Ibid.* Others of the staff were: Ida De Steiguer, drawing, life, and casts, the first art teacher of the University of Denver; George W. Platt, painting, painter of game and scenery; John R. Henderson, design and wood carving; Howell T. Pershing, M.D., lecturer on anatomy; and Harriet McCreery Shaw, assistant teacher of drawing.

52 *Denver Directory,* 1878, p. 199.

Denver School of Fine Arts the first class in the nude of which we have record.

Wolfe Hall, a finishing school for girls, also had its art department during this period, headed by Henry Read.[53] This preceded the establishment of Mr. Read's studio in 1895, known as the Student's School of Art.[54] Denver should never forget the debt it owes to this modest and sincere, English-born artist. He was a product of the English school of painting, a devotee of the highly finished 18th century style. He was one of the organizers of the Artists Club, formed in 1893, from which emerged the Denver Art Museum; father of the Denver Municipal Art Commission, regent of the National Academy of Design, and director of the American Federation of Art. It was he who induced Mayor Robert W. Speer to inaugurate the Civic Center in Denver. That he was a sound teacher is demonstrated by such pupils as Waldo Love, whose backgrounds in the Colorado Museum of Natural History have won national fame for that institution; Will Foster, Hanson Puthuff, Wilbur Steele, the cartoonist, and Albert Byron Olson, than whom no finer master of color harmony ever left a legacy to Denver.

At this period the perennial fission in schools of thought, always and necessarily present in creative art, took the formal names: "Detailists" and "Impressionists." Continual wrangling resulted, almost simultaneously, in the resignations of Directors Richards and Platt in June, 1893.

The Le Brun Club did not hold up as well as expected either, fading in little more than a year, but the spark it kindled bore permanent fruit.

On December 4, 1893, Mrs. Emma Richardson Cherry called a meeting in her studio on the top floor of the McPhee Building to form a new art club.[55] This resulted in the formation of the Artists' Club of Denver, which in turn, became the Denver Art Association and then the Denver Art Museum.[56] The constitution was revised December 7th and adopted December 16th. The organizers profited through previous experiences by providing that the club be governed by an executive committee, and that no officers be chosen because "as such offices are considered honors they could cause dissatisfaction and therefore should not be created." Harvey Young, Charles M. Carter and Emma Richardson Cherry were elected by ballot, and in turn appointed the other two members of the committee, Charles Partridge Adams and Henrietta Bromwell. Mrs. Cherry was made chairman and Miss Bromwell, secretary. Hamilton Hamilton was made an honorary member by acclamation. Later, on January 27, 1894, Ida C. Failing, Blanche Dougan, Ida De Steiguer, Thomas Sloan

[53] Edgar Carlisle McMechen, in Baker and Hafen, *History of Colorado*, VIII, p. 1269.

[54] *Directory of Cultural Organizations in Denver,* Pam. 7, City Club, p. 17.

[55] Present at this meeting were: Mrs. Cherry, Charles M. Carter, Henry Read, J. R. Henderson, Alice M. Howes, Ida C. Failing, Henrietta Bromwell, Helen Munson, Charles Partridge Adams and Marion J. Johnson.

[56] This brief account of the organization of the Artists' Club of Denver is drawn from the unpaged *Artists' Club Minute Book,* State Historical Society Library.

Bell and Alexis Comparet were made active members. A large group of associates were chosen, consisting of the most influential women of the city.

In this group, the name of Annie Evans appears for the first time. She was the Miss Anne Evans, daughter of Governor Evans, who later played such a commanding part in the formation of the Denver Art Museum, and the Central City Opera House Association.

Through the good offices of Mrs. Margaret Gray Evans, her mother, the group was provided a club room in the University arts building at 1330 Arapahoe Street, and held its first exhibition there in April, 1894.[57]

The Artists' Club functioned courageously throughout the Panic period, holding exhibitions regularly, due to the devoted work of Miss Anne Evans, Miss Marion Hendrie and Miss Elisabeth Spalding. After erection of the Denver Public Library, exhibitions were hung on the top floor of this building for many years. The Artists' Club had become by this time the "Denver Art Association" and was incorporated under that name February 5, 1917.[58]

In 1921, George William Eggers, then Director of the Chicago Art Institute, came to Denver as director of an infant museum without a building. He was intrigued by the spirit of creative art that he found in the Colorado capital and took this amazing step because of the opportunity to build a new type of museum. With the arrival of this inspirational leader the art museum, at long last, became a reality. Eggers had the rare gift of drawing about him in warm companionship unusual people; of stimulating creative powers in the talented; and of activating latent impulses in those who, heretofore, had made no use of their creative ability.

There followed an efflorescence in the creative arts such as is seldom experienced in any city. Architects began to specify murals and sculptured ornament in their business and residential designs. School buildings, business blocks and homes were enriched. The Atelier of the Beaux Arts became a joyous and bubbling font of ideas. A staid tile manufacturer caught the fire, went to Italy and brought back color and texture studies of beautiful Renaissance roofing tiles, and reproduced them with brilliant commercial success. Under the leadership of Mrs. George E. Cranmer an Allied Arts group was formed to foster creative art, and provide training for talented young artists and musicians.[59] Pictorial photography was stimulated by a Denver Camera Club, and a Business Men's Art Club drew together those interested in art as an avocation.

[57] *Ibid.*

[58] *Directory of Cultural Organizations in Denver,* Pam. 7, City Club, p. 12. The officers were: Edward C. Stimson, President; Elisabeth Spalding, Vice-President; Edward Ring, Secretary-Treasurer, and Horace G. Wetherill, William B. Berger, S. Nelson Hicks, Frank M. Taylor, George Elbert Burr, Walter C. Mead, Marion G. Hendrie and Mary E. Worthington, directors. The first director was Reginald Poland, now director of the San Diego Museum.

[59] *Ibid.,* p. 13.

In 1922, Mrs. Cranmer and her brother, Delos Chappell, gave the large red sandstone Chappell home at 1300 Logan Street to the Art Association as a memorial to their parents "for the use of creative artists." This became the first permanent home of the Association, which incorporated April 17, 1923, as the Denver Art Museum.[60] Upon completion of the Municipal Building facing Civic Center, in 1932, the Art Museum was given one wing on the top floor, which now houses its permanent collections. Plans are now under way for erection of an art museum facing Civic Center.

Within the last twenty years gifts of money, painting, sculpture and other objects have totaled well over $1,000,000. Among the important contributors have been Rachel Schlier, Miss Helen Dill, Walter C. Mead, who presented his valuable collection of furniture and Japenese bronzes, Miss Florence Martin, who endowed the Cooke-Daniels lectures, and Mrs. J. Brown, who donated the Brown collection, the largest private collection in the city.

No account of Denver's art development would be complete without mention of Brinton Terrace, sometimes described as "Denver's Greenwich Village." This historic building on East 18th Avenue between Trinity Church and Lincoln Street, flourished as a Bohemian center for twenty years, beginning in 1906 when Mrs. E. Dismukes, a painter of that day, opened a studio.[61] Most of the leading artists of the succeeding generation had studios there at one time or another. During this period many musicians had their studios in the Terrace.

A protege of Miss Anne Evans, Margaret S. Van Wagenen, who later married Dudley Carpenter, the mural painter, was the one who originated the idea of creating in Brinton Terrace an artists' retreat, where like spirits might derive inspiration from one another.

During the winter of 1906-07 R. L. and Cyrus Boutwell opened their first commercial art gallery in studio No. 23. The first well-organized art exhibitions in Denver were introduced in this building by the brothers. They gave George Elbert Burr, nationally famous etcher and water colorist, a one-man show, induced him to make his home in Denver, and made their studio headquarters for an informal Arts and Crafts Club, embracing both artists and patrons.

The Burrs occupied part of the Boutwell apartment for several years, until the etcher built his own studio at 1325 Logan Street, now the home of the Denver Women's Press Club. Burrs' beautiful and ethereal Desert Set is almost a requisite of every important art museum today. This was executed in Arizona after ill health had compelled him to move to Phoenix. The Boutwells remained in Brinton Terrace for five years, when Cyrus opened a gallery in his own building, and R. L. moved to Colorado Springs, where he later became first director of the Broadmoor Art Academy.

In 1915, Abigail Holman opened her Fine Arts Academy of Denver in Studio No. 35. This was a school of fine ideals, staffed by

---

60 Records of the Secretary of State.
61 Edgar C. McMechen, *Brinton Terrace, Colorado Magazine,* XXIV, 3, pp. 97-114.

capable teachers. Among these latter were: Albert Olson, Lawrence Murphy, and Mrs. Walpole. Students of this Academy won the highest honors in the Art Students' League competitions in New York.

Some years later a second private school, the Denver Academy of Fine and Applied Arts, opened in the same studio. The owner and dean was John G. Cory, a prominent New York cartoonist, who had come to Denver for his health. He also had some notable teachers. Among these were John Thompson, teacher of drawing and painting; Robert Garrison, teacher of sculpture; Henry McCarter of Philadelphia, painting; David Spivak, painting, and Margaret Tee, interior decoration. H. A. W. Manard bought the Cory school in 1924 and transferred it to Chappell House as the Chappell School of Art. This was later taken over by the University of Denver, which retained the name and continued the location at Chappell House.

In the current article the author has given much attention to the incipient stages of art development in Colorado because the pioneer era in any cultural movement is important to the student and historian. The result has been the mention of many people who contributed little or nothing from the creative standpoint, yet they helped lay the foundation for the development that was to be.

The real achievement has come within the last twenty-five years. In the space allotted, however, it is impossible to comment in detail upon all the artists active during this later period. That must be left to some future historian, treating the subject in a more exhaustive way. Comment will, therefore, be limited to art works of a monumental or decorative character, easily accessible to the public, and in connection with public works or business structures.

The greatest individual contributor has been Allen Tupper True, a native of Colorado Springs, who has spent his life in Colorado. True began as a magazine illustrator. He later studied under Howard Pyle and Brangwyn, the famous English mural painter, with whom he collaborated. His work is found in the Colorado State Capitol, the Colonnade of Civic Benefactors, and the Voorhies Memorial on the Denver Civic Center, the Denver Public Library, Colorado National Bank, Continental Oil Building, Cosmopolitan Hotel, in the Missouri and Montana State Capitols. He was color consultant of the U. S. Bureau of Reclamation for the Boulder, Shasta and Grand Coulee dams.

True is primarily a painter of the West. The Indian and trapper motifs, which he has mastered with great success, prevail in much of his work. Until recent years he followed the Brangwyn style, using delicate tones. His "Indian Memories" series in the Colorado National Bank is one of his most successful murals, not only in execution but in his approach to the subject. True's murals interpret the Indian with dignity and understanding. The mysticism and beauty of Indian mythology is treated with the respect that it deserves.

Of late years, True has changed his method materially. The best example of this is found in the murals interpreting Thomas Hornsby

Ferril's poem on Water, in the central rotunda of the Colorado Capitol Building. These paintings are solidly executed, the color strong and definite. The two styles indicate an interesting intellectual achievement by the artist. The Indian lived in a divided world of reality and dreams, and True interprets this in his ethereal treatment of the subject. But to the pioneer, reality was bare and stark and strongly defined; and so True records it in the Capitol's compelling mural.

Albert Byron Olson, born in Montrose, Colorado, was equally facile with mural or easel painting. His Don Quixote murals in the Elyria Branch Library are not well known to Denver people or to her visitors, because they are located in a section of the city not on beaten paths. This is a great pity because they are among the best murals ever produced in Colorado. Olson's triptych, "The Ascension of the Angels," in St. Marks Church, East 14th Avenue and Lincoln, also is a masterpiece. These works reflect the artist's highly imaginative mind and mastery of color harmony. Olson's death, at the height of his powers was a distinct loss. He was not a prolific producer.

John E. Thompson, a pupil of Tudor-Hart, was a nationally known mural painter, whose forte was conventionalized design. However, he was a painter of versatility, and one of the ablest teachers Colorado has had. In easel painting he followed the modern school of thought, either in oil or water color. Highly intellectual, he always had something definite to say in his painting.

Another able muralist was Dudley Carpenter, who worked in Denver during the 1920s. The best examples of his work are found in the Dexter Branch Library, where he executed "The Pied Piper of Hamelin," and "The Lady of the Lake and Sword Excalibur;" and the Mary Louise White Memorial in West Side High School, interpretative of Milton's *L'Allegro* and *Il Penseroso*.

Nationally known and admired are Waldo Love's backgrounds in the habitat cases in the Colorado Museum of Natural History. Love is the staff artist at this institution, mentioned before as a pupil of Henry Read. One familiar with Read's precise, meticulous and academic style, could hardly believe that the freedom and sweep of the Love backgrounds and their bold assertion of color, could come from a pupil of the old English teacher. He is one of the few excellent miniature painters left in America today. His Historical Map of Colorado in the Colorado State Museum is a beautiful exemplification of this talent.

Among the more notable public monuments in sculpture[62] is "The Closing Era" by Preston Powers, standing on the Capitol Grounds, depicting an Indian standing with one foot upon a slain buffalo. The bronze smacks of the J. Fenimore Cooper tradition and is chiefly interesting because it is the first bit of monumental sculpture produced in Colorado. It was shown in the World's Columbian

[62] *The Lookout,* Denver Public Library, *Art in Denver,* April, 1928, p. 17. For further information on notable works of art in Denver see this publication.

Exposition in Chicago, 1893. Powers was never paid for it and died guiding tourists in Rome.

The bronze "Grizzly Bear Group" in front of the Colorado Museum of Natural History, is by Louis Paul Jonas, once a Denver taxidermist, now a recognized master of wild life sculpture. In the Civic Center stand "The Buckaroo"—which irritates artists because it never comes to rest—and "The Indian Warrior," both by A. Phimister Proctor, Denver born, who started in 1882 by sketching in pencil in the old Studio Flat. Proctor is internationally known as an animal sculptor.

Elsie Ward Herring, a Denver-born girl, has left an exquisite angel in the Oakes Home Chapel and other works in Denver private collections. She submerged her identity when she married her sculptor husband.

Arnold Ronnebeck, a German sculptor, who came to Denver in the twenties, has contributed many works of art. A brilliantly balanced modernistic design is the reredos in The Chapel of St. Martin, "Madonna and Attending Angels." The wood carving was done by John Henderson, one of the founders of the art museum.

Robert Garrison, a pupil of Gutzon Borglum, was a prolific producer during the 1920s and '30s. Garrison's mental attitude was largely responsible for the style he employed so frequently, the Romanesque. Evidences of his labors are scattered well over Denver, in the Civic Center, at the State Office Building, Polo Club, South Denver High, and elsewhere. His best known achievement in Denver is his "Covered Wagon" frieze on the Midland Savings Building, in which he preserved the spirit of the pioneers, yet treated the subject humorously through the Romanesque technique. He did an interesting panel for the Rockefeller Center, New York, shortly before his death.

Enrico Licari, a Sicilian-born sculptor and winner of the Prix di Rome, also was a Denver resident for some ten years. He is well represented. Among his characteristic works are the "Reed Memorial" at the University of Denver, and the "Angels" of St. Thomas Seminary, both executed in the best tradition of the Italian classical school.

Non-resident sculptors of national reputation represented in Denver include: Lorado Taft, "Fountain of the State," City Park; Frederic Macmonnies, "Pioneer Monument," Civic Center; Leo Lentelli, "Agriculture" and "Mining" groups on the Sullivan Memorial Gate, City Park Esplanade; and the exquisite McPhee Memorial, "Memory," in Mt. Olivet Cemetery, by Mario Korbel, the Hungarian sculptor. No more delightful group exists in the city than "Wynken, Blynken and Nod," illustrating in marble the three little girls in the wooden shoe, after Eugene Field's poem. This is the work of Mabel Landrum Torrey, a native of Sterling, Colorado. It is located in Washington Park.

An arresting base relief of huge proportions on the fourth floor of the Municipal Building, at the entrance to the Art Museum Galleries, was carved by Mrs. Gladys Caldwell Fisher, one of the brilliant young sculptors selected by the Allied Arts for advanced education in Paris. The work is entitled "Manitou and His Children." and depicts the Indian deity surrounded by animals of the chase. Mrs. Fisher's forte is animal sculpture in stone, and the monumental mountain sheep on the 18th Street entrance of the Post Office Building are among her works.

From the earliest days the contribution of Colorado Springs to art development in the state has been extremely important. Walter Paris, who established his home there in 1871, was its earliest resident painter and etcher.[63] He worked in both water color and oils, as well as with the pen.

Thomas and Anne Parrish followed within a year or two.[64]

Thomas was a brother to Stephen Parrish and uncle to Maxfield Parrish. Both opened studios and conducted classes. Thomas, an etcher and portrait painter, illustrated Ernest Whitney's *Myths and Legends*. Anne was the better portrait painter of the two. F. T. Lent worked with them, and these three combined with Louis R. Erich to give loan exhibits, which they considered "desirable for the cultural uplift of the community."[65]

Erich was one of the finest influences in the town in the development of music and art. He was a man of considerable wealth, who had in his beautiful home on North Cascade Avenue the largest and finest private gallery west of the Mississippi River. With aid from the private galleries of Mrs. E. C. Goddard, Verner Z. Reed, J. J. Hagerman, W. A. Otis, J. C. Connor, Godfrey Kissel, the Parrishes, Erich managed to give a number of excellent exhibitions without leaving the precincts of the town.[66]

When Erich left the Springs his collection of old world paintings was placed in the Erich Galleries of New York. He often was consulted as an expert to determine the authenticity of old masters.

Eliza Greatorex came to Colorado Springs in 1873 with her friend Grace Greenwood (Mrs. Lippincott), who wrote copiously of early Colorado. Miss Greatorex even then was something of a national celebrity, because she had been admitted to the National Academy in 1868, the first woman so honored. She published a booklet of ink sketches while in the Springs, with foreword by Grace Greenwood.[67]

Literature and art again teamed when Alice Stewart Hill, the painter of Colorado wild flowers, illustrated Helen Hunt's *Procession of the Flowers of Colorado*. Her original water color illustrations still are in the Springs.[68]

63 *Colorado Springs Gazette,* June 7, 1924.

64 Ormes, *The Book of Colorado Springs,* 337, *Colorado Springs Gazette,* September 10, 1924.

65 Ormes, *op. cit.,* 337-338.

66 *Ibid.,* 343.

67 *Ibid.,* 338.

68 *Ibid.,* 334.

The great event of the eighties in the history of Colorado Springs art was the arrival of Harvey Young.[69] He established his home in a hillcrest cottage in Manitou in 1879 and remained for six years. The life of this noted western landscape painter reads like a romance. Personal friend of Robert Louis Stevenson, John Singer Sargent, and Bret Harte, he was equally at home on a Parisian Boulevard or in a pioneer mining camp. Throughout an adventurous life, he roamed both sides of the Atlantic, and explored the gold fields of California as a prospector, traveling with burro and gold pan, paint box and palette. He was an inveterate miner and, as a partner in the Star group of mines at Aspen, amassed a large fortune. He spent many years in Denver painting; lived in the bridal suite at the Windsor Hotel, or at the Brown Palace, and kept a studio in the Kittredge Building. His famous painting of Mt. Hood brought a staggering sum from Leland Stanford.

Young had taken steamer to Panama and crossed the Isthmus on foot, to participate in the California gold rush, alternately wielding the prospector's pick or dashing off a sketch of mountain scenery. In 1870, he went to Paris, where he remained for nearly ten years. He studied under such teachers as Carolus Duran. He met Stevenson at Grez when the great Scotch stylist was writing *Inland Voyages*.

The studio door and the kindly criticism of this handsome and debonair wanderer was always open to young students. Adams, Comperet, and Tallant, owe to him some measure of their success. Young was a friend and protege of General William J. Palmer, builder of the Denver & Rio Grande Railroad, who fitted up a studio car for him. This he was privileged to hitch to a train or to have it sidetracked at his whim.

Harvey Young's paintings reflect his deep love of nature. All his paintings have atmosphere, and his burros were exceptional, because he painted them as friends.

Charles Craig, who established a studio in Colorado Springs, was an accurate and capable painter of Indians. In 1885 he made a trip to the Southern Ute Reservation with the artist Charles Sauerwen.[70] It was at this time that Buckskin Charley, who succeeded the great Ouray as head chief of the Utes, gave Craig his name "Pinkface Charley," by which he was afterward known to the Utes. Craig's portrait of Buckskin Charley as a young man, hangs in the Colorado State Museum. Craig later settled in Taos.

Also in 1881, William Bancroft took up residence in the Springs. He was noted for his Colorado landscapes and his devotion to public service.[71] Bancroft learned much from Moran, for whom he carried the latter's equipment. For a number of years he earned his living as a house painter while he studied art.

W. H. M. Coxe was an important Colorado Springs painter of the '80s. He was one of the exhibitors in Denver's Mining and

[69] *Denver Times,* September 14, 1889; February 7, 1891, *Denver Post,* May 14, 1901.

[70] Ormes, *op. cit.,* 343.

[71] *Ibid.,* 344.

Industrial Exposition of 1883. Another early portrait and miniature painter was William Martin Shettle,[72] who later made an enviable record in New York by doing portraits of such notables as Ada Rehan, Commodore Vanderbilt, Edith Kingdon and Mrs. Howard Gould. Rose Kingsley, sister of Charles Kingsley, the poet, and Katherine Smalley were in the early group.

The first organized art exhibit in Colorado Springs was held in 1888 in the old Presbyterian Church for the benefit of the Bellvue Sanitorium. Two hundred fifty-two numbers were shown.

In the succeeding decade Leslie J. Skelton began his untiring efforts to bring the best in art to Colorado Springs. A conservative landscape painter himself, he became an early director of the Colorado Springs Art Society. With the completion of Perkins Hall at Colorado College Skelton launched an artists' show in 1900 to inaugurate a new era.[73]

The leading artists at this time included Louis Soutter, who opened studios at Perkins Hall the same year; Paul Lotave, a pupil of Zorn and an excellent portrait painter, whose ashes were afterward scattered from the summit of Pikes Peak in accordance with the wishes of the suicide; John McClymont, a product of Scotland's schools, who painted several of Colorado's governors, and Artus Van Briggle.

Miss Ella Warren had previously opened a studio in Hagerman Hall at the College, adjoining the dining hall. Mr. William Greenbury later had that studio, which developed into the art department of Colorado College.

After Soutter's departure for Paris, the studio in Perkins was taken over by Artus Van Briggle, and he was succeeded by Dell Heizer.

Van Briggle's contribution was of major importance.[74] He came to the Springs in the late '90s, via Paris and the Rookwood Potteries in Cincinnati. He began to experiment with clays with the intention of reproducing the dull, velvety finish found on old Chinese vases. Professor William Strieby of the College lent his encouragement by providing a spot in his laboratory for Van Briggle's work. In 1898, Van Briggle produced his first successful vase with the desired matte finish. This pottery took honors at the Paris exposition and won awards wherever shown. A pottery kiln was built, and General Palmer lent encouragement. Within a few years a $100,000 pottery was erected, but Van Briggle's death in 1904 sounded the knell for the enterprise. The capable landscape, portrait and still life painter, Anne Gregory, married Van Briggle and greatly assisted him through her designs. After her husband's death she continued to operate the pottery but it proved too much for her strength. It went into bankruptcy in 1915, and was revised as a commercial enterprise.

---

[72] *Ibid., Denver Times,* April 13, 1901.

[73] Ormes, *op. cit.,* 342. In addition to Skelton, others who exhibited at this time were: William Bancroft, John McClymont, Artus Van Briggle, Anne Gregory, Charles Craig, Paul Lotave, and Mrs. Eleanor Ormes.

[74] *Ibid.,* 345-346.

Mrs. Van Briggle later married Etienne Ritter, a mining engineer, and went to Denver. She organized the first classes under Robert Reid and John Carlson when the Broadmoor Art Academy was founded.

The Misses Leaming opened the Colorado Academy of Fine Arts in 1912. Four years later they took charge of the art department of Colorado College at Perkins Hall, Miss Susan Leaming succeeding Miss Marie Sahm as lecturer on the history of art.

The first art society of Colorado Springs was instituted just prior to the first World War by Reverend Arthur N. Taft, former rector of St. Stephens Church, and by Mrs. Clarence P. Dodge. Exhibitions were held in the post office, and later at Perkins Hall. Colorado Springs artists held exhibitions of their work in 1914 and 1915 in the de Graf Building. At the close of the second exhibition, at the suggestion of the Misses Leaming, the Colorado Springs Art Club was founded. Henry Russell Wray was president, Mrs. Anne Gregory Ritter, vice-president, and J. I. McClymont, secretary-treasurer. The two groups merged within a few years, thus combining patrons and professional artists.

This Society was successful in interesting Mr. and Mrs. Spencer Penrose, who offered their residence at 30 West Dale to the Society in October, 1919, together with an annual gift of $1,000 for five years. Acceptance brought a change of name to the Broadmoor Art Society and on October 5, 1919, the Broadmoor Art Academy was incorporated. Officers of the Broadmoor Society were: Mrs. Spencer Penrose, president; D. V. Donaldson, Vice-President. Anne Gregory Ritter, Francis Drexel Smith, and C. L. Tutt served with the two mentioned as the Board of Directors. The same Board administered the Academy. Drexel Smith, whose fine landscapes have been exhibited in many leading galleries of the country, started to paint when 40 years of age.

Donaldson was first president of the Academy, and R. L. Boutwell, the first director. Robert Reid was given the first show, and became the first teacher of figure painting. Reid, with his flowing white mane and smart Van Dyke, looked like a senior diplomat. Winner of awards in America and Europe, one of the "Ten" of the National Academy, Reid is most widely known by his murals in the Library of Congress, Washington, D. C. Teaming with Reid on the initial staff of the Broadmoor Academy was John Carlson, lecturer and teacher of landscape.[75]

The Academy received a Carnegie Foundation Grant of $25,000 in 1926, at the time when Colorado College agreed to collaborate with the Broadmoor Academy and discontinue classes at Perkins Hall.[76]

In the latter '20s, Mrs. F. M. P. Taylor, a wealthy resident of Colorado Springs, became interested in collecting specimens of Indian

[75] Since 1919, some of the nationally known artists who have taught at the Academy are: Robert Reid, John Carlson, Lloyd Moylan, Everett Warner, Birger Sandzen, Randall Davey, William Potter, Ernest Lawson, Boardman Robinson, Willard Nash, Charles Farrar, Ward Lockman, Ernest Fiene, George Biddle, Henry Varnum Poor, Frank Mechau.

[76] For information about the Broadmoor Art Academy and the Fine Arts Center the author is much indebted to Mr. Percy Hagerman, President of the Center.

Art and Spanish southwest material. In 1930, she offered to erect a Fine Arts Center on the site of the old Penrose home and transfer her collections to the new institution. This offer was accepted. Construction of the new museum was started in 1934 under the direction of the Colorado Springs architect, John Meems, now of Santa Fe. Members of the Broadmoor Art Academy authorized a charter amend-

Fine Arts Center, Colorado Springs

ment, January 4, 1935, changing the name of the institution to the Colorado Springs Fine Arts Center. However, the Broadmoor Art Academy still retains its identity, although the entire set-up is under a general director.[77]

Mrs. Taylor contributed $400,000 to the building fund and later established an endowment of some $50,000. The El Pomar Foundation (Penrose Foundation) has given $47,000 during the last ten years for operations, and $5,000 for the permanent collection. Mrs. Penrose has been a heavy contributor.

[77] At the present time this is Mitchell A. Wilder. Boardman Robinson, who took charge of the Broadmoor Art Academy in 1930, still is serving in this capacity. The lithographic department is especially strong under the direction of Lawrence Barrett, whose work is found in all major collections. Directors of the Academy have been: R. L. Boutwell, Stanley Stoner, Stanley Lathrop, Paul Parker, Mitchell A. Wilder. Percy Hagerman, current president of the center, has achieved success as an etcher, starting at the age of seventy.

The Colorado Springs Fine Arts Center has become what its name implies. Associated with the Center are the Drama school, Symphony, Colorado College. Classes are conducted for high school students, college students and those with the serious objective of becoming professional artists. The children's program is one of the major activities. Pupils from thirty states attend.

During the last generation this city of 40,000 at the foot of Pikes Peak has established a plant, and developed a creative art center that many cities of two to three hundred thousand people cannot equal.

DRAMA

The story of the stage in Colorado divides readily into two eras, each approximately forty years in duration. The first was the pioneer, or territorial period, in which the key figures were the actor-managers John S. (Jack) Langrishe, George B. Waldron and Nate C. Forrester. This was the period of growing pains; of ups and downs; of triumphs and failures, common to all struggling stock companies of the frontier West.

The key figure of the second period was not an actor; nevertheless, the man who gave Colorado its dramatic cake—the uncouth, but warm-hearted and generous Leadville silver king, H. A. W. Tabor. The impact of the Tabor Opera House upon drama and the arts in this state was terrific. It brought to Denver the flower of the American stage at the apex of its greatness; it stimulated an already discriminating taste in music, and even animated to some extent the feeble and dispirited art movement.

With the coming of the movies, the legitimate stage in Colorado ceased to exist. Like a wax pear, the color was there but the essence was gone.

The first theatrical performance given on Colorado soil was presented October 3, 1859, in Apollo Hall by Thorne's Star Company.[80] The building was a two-story frame, covered with siding and painted white. A small balcony extended over the side-walk. The lower floor was occupied by Harry Gunnell's billiard parlor and saloon. Twelve candles served as footlights for the temporary stage.[81] The rough board benches would hold 350 people. The clink of glasses and click of billiard balls, together with raucous laughter, floated up the stairway.

The opening bill presented *Cross of Gold,* or *The Maid of Croisay,* and a farce, *The Two Gregories.* Actors appearing that night included: Col. C. R. Thorne, M'lle Haydee, Miss Louise Wakely, S. Hunter, William Thorne and Thomas Thorne. Miss Flora Wakely sang the sentimental ballad, "Maggie's By My Side," and M'lle Haydee danced. The performance was highly praised by the *Rocky Mountain News.* At the end of a week Col. Thorne and his son William boarded the stage for Leavenworth and never returned.

[80] *Rocky Mountain News,* October 6, 1859.
[81] Albert D. Richardson, *Beyond the Mississippi,* 306.

Col. Thorne was an experienced manager and an accomplished actor. He had successfully headed his own companies and managed his own theaters in New York City, and is credited with having pioneered the stage in Australia and California. The Denver of 1859 could have held little attraction for him.

Sam Hunter, scene painter and actor, was engaged by Col. Thorne after his arrival in Denver. He later played an important part in development of the early Colorado stage. According to General William Larimer, who knew Thorne in Leavenworth, the Haydee Sisters were in Denver when the Colonel arrived.[82] Harman Brown, their brother, stated that the family came west with Thorne.[83]

These girls deserve attention as they were the real pioneers of Colorado theatrical history. Three girls, Rose (M'lle Haydee), Flora and Louise Brown comprised the group, although they went under the name of Wakely in Colorado. All were step-children of George Wakely, Denver's first photographer, who had an ambrotype gallery across the street from the Apollo Theater.[84] Rose, an accomplished dancer and the leading lady, was accounted the most beautiful woman in Denver during her stay. Flora's specialty was ballad singing, while Louise took secondary parts in the plays. They had had some professional experience in Missouri River towns before coming to Denver. All the build-up was centered upon M'lle Haydee, the nominal head of the company, although Frank Hall, the historian, who knew the family well, credited "Madame" Wakely with the management. Rose eloped with Thomas Evans, a gambler, while her parents were in Central City, and married him November 24, 1860.[85] She died in Kansas City in 1865.

Col. Thorne's strategic retreat left his company stranded in Denver. The Haydee Sisters took over management as the Haydee Star Company and, with a little help from several of Denver's enterprising young amateurs and the fortunate appearance of M. J. (Mike) Dougherty, went forward without a hitch.

An outcome of this "help" was the first native drama written in Colorado, a play in stilted, mid-Victorian verse by A. B. Steinberger, hinged upon the formation of the extra-legal Territory of Jefferson, the legislature of which was then in session. The play was entitled, *Skatara, The Mountain Chieftain.* It was given at the Apollo by a company of amateurs as a benefit to Louise Wakely. Steinberger took the leading role of Skatara; E. W. Wyncoop, who later played an important part in the Civil War and the Indian Wars of early Colorado history, played Hardicamp, a mountaineer; George Wyncoop was Governor Whitcomb of the State of Jefferson, and John C. Moore, that Southern Beau Brummell and master of the *code duello*, who shortly thereafter became Denver's first mayor, appeared as Ralph Delaney, leader of the punitive expedition.[86]

82 Herman S. Davis, Ed., *Reminiscences of General William Larimer,* 143.
83 *Kansas City Journal,* January 14, 1923.
84 *Ibid.*
85 *Rocky Mountain News,* November 28, 1860.
86 Melvin Schoberlin, *From Candles to Footlights* (1941), 26.

Mike Dougherty joined the Haydee company for an engagement of six nights only on November 6. This was a great stroke of luck, for the "inimitable Mike" was a successful low comedian who had won his spurs in Philadelphia and Cincinnati before coming to Denver in quest of gold. He later joined the Jack Langrishe Company as actor, and became Langrishe's partner. No man who ever trod the stage in Colorado history was better loved than this genial portrayer of Irish character parts.

The Haydee Company soon had serious rivalry when James Reid opened with the Cibola minstrels in his log billiard hall on Ferry street, Auraria. To advertise his show he employed the Earle Brothers Band from Chicago to parade the streets daily in a wagon drawn by six yoke oxen, all placarded with handbills. C. H. Mortimer, dramatic director of this company, long was an important figure in pioneer theatricals; Charles Marion, a blackface comedian, was reported by Langrishe after his Mexican tour, to have become Governor of Sonora. A. O. McGrew, who trundled his belongings toward Denver in a wheelbarrow, presented a skit in Reid's Theater called The Wheel Barrow Man. In after years he was city editor of the *New York Evening News*. As correspondent of an Omaha paper, he published that famous menu of Denver's first Christmas dinner, which featured mountain rats.

M'lle Haydee took the first troup to Golden on New Year's Day, 1860, and both the Haydee Company and the Cibola Minstrels played in Mountain City, now Central City, during January of this year. M'lle Haydee opened Central's first theater, a two-story log building belonging to Major Hadley.[87] In October, 1860, she opened in the upper story of the Veranda Hotel there, with Mike Dougherty. This became the Olympic, and was Jack Langrishe's first theater in Central City.

The summer of 1860 also marked the conversion of the Criterion Saloon to theatrical use as the home of Converse and Petrie's minstrels.[88]

The outstanding theatrical event of 1860 was the arrival in September of the Langrishe Dramatic Company, which opened at Apollo Hall, September 28, 1860.[89] As one reads the fulsome praise of the Langrishe players by Editor Byers of the *Rocky Mountain News,* he is impressed with Byers' determination to have a theater in Denver, willy nilly. Nevertheless, Jack Langrishe was an excellent actor and his stock companies maintained a high average. He is rightfully called the "Father of the Colorado stage." For nearly twenty years, with certain lapses while his company was on tour, he entertained the people of Denver and Central City. In California, in New England, and elsewhere in the country, while on tour, he and his troopers drew well and won commendatory notice from critics.

---

87 *Daily Central City Register,* February 8, 1876.
88 *Rocky Mountain News,* August 22, 1860.
89 *Ibid.,* September 29, 1860.

Langrishe's most serious opposition came in 1861, when the Pioneer Company, organized by Sam Hunter and A. L. Gooding, an actor brought to Denver by M'lle Haydee, took the field in the gold camps, more particularly in Georgia Gulch and at Delaware Flats on the upper Blue River.

This company was formed of the remnants of the Haydee Star Company, and played during the late summer of 1861 in a huge tent in Georgia Gulch. M'lle Haydee, then with the Colorado Minstrels, played nightly in Gayosa Hall in the same Gulch,[90] while Prof. Gordon, the wizard and magician of the day, added to the competition.

Langrishe moved in and built a frame theater on the main street of Georgia Gulch, crossed the range and gave the first and probably the last theatrical performance in California Gulch, the forerunner of Leadville, and then opened in rapid succession in his own buildings in Delaware Flats and French Gulch at the head of Blue River; and in Buckskin Gulch and Montgomery across the Range in South Park.

On September 11, 1861, George W. Harrison opened the National Theater in Central with the Criterion Minstrels. He was followed by the Pioneer Company with a three weeks season, but Langrishe then opened a six weeks season in Central at the old Veranda Theater, changing the name to the Olympic.

Both Langrishe and the Pioneers then returned to Denver. H. B. Murphy, together with several mechanics, in the meantime, had been constructing the Platte Valley Theater, at the Northeast corner of Sixteenth and Lawrence Street. Sam Hunter leased the building, then the finest theater in the town, and opened with Richard III on October 26, 1861. Included in his company were M'lle Haydee and M'lle Marietta.

Sensing the danger of this movement, Langrishe took over the entire building of Apollo Hall, extended it and renamed it the Peoples' Theater. The interior was decorated in white and gold by DeWitt Waugh, artist and musician.[91] Within a few weeks the Pioneer Company was forced to close, and this ended all opposition from that quarter.

Langrishe's season this winter was highly successful. The dress circle of the Peoples was filled nightly with officers of the First Colorado Volunteers and their well-dressed ladies, while the enlisted men crowded the balconies.

Langrishe's only serious opposition in Central City came from George Harrison, who owned the National Theater in September, 1861, and later built the historic Montana.[92] Harrison, however, shot and killed a rival manager, Charley Swits. Swits had a character of doubtful value and Harrison was acquitted. Some previous quarrel generally has been ascribed as the cause of this tragedy, but Frank Fossett, author of *Colorado*, who knew both men, wrote that the trouble originated over M'lle Marietta, the same who helped open

[90] *Rocky Mountain News,* August 21, 1861.
[91] *Ibid.,* November 30, 1861.
[92] Melvin Schoberlin, *op. cit*

the Platte Valley Theater.[93]   Harrison disappeared from the scene entirely about a year later.

Langrishe bought both the Platte Valley Theater in Denver and the Montana in Central City and, for the next ten or twelve years, had no rival in legitimate theatricals.   Until 1865, when Dougherty died, the team offered too much competition.   Intemperance ended the life of the "inimitable Mike."   In 1866, Langrishe brought to Denver in a starring role George B. Waldron, a noted California actor.[94]   He later became Langrishe's partner.   Waldron was not known to eastern audiences for he was entirely a product of the Far West, but he ranked next to Langrishe as guiding genius of the drama during territorial history.

The Panic of 1873 ruined the drama in Colorado for several years. Added to this was the calamity suffered when the Montana and the Denver Theaters were burned, the former in 1874, the latter in 1877.[95]

During his tenure Jack Langrishe furnished to Denver and Central City stock companies highly consistent.   He brought many stars of national reputation, among the number James Stark, C. W. Couldrock and daughter, McKee Rankin, Kitty Blanchard, Madame Scheller, Annette Ince and others of equal ability.

The plays presented were the standard of the day, varying from Shakespearean drama to light farce.   Melodrama was especially popular.   Langrishe himself excelled in comedy roles, never failing to bring down the house, never for a moment losing the respect and admiration of his audiences. His "great role" was that of O'Callaghan in *His Last Legs*.   His outstanding "heavies" were Harry Richmond, a member of his original troupe, and George B. Waldron.   It is noteworthy that when H. A. W. Tabor opened the Tabor Opera House in Leadville in 1879 he sent for Jack Langrishe and company to dedicate the structure.   Langrishe was the first manager of this theater. He died in Wardner, Idaho, December 6, 1895, editor of the *Wardner News*.

The old Denver was in its day the finest theater in the Colorado region.   Judged by later standards, it was a cold and dismal barn; but its history would fill a volume.   At various times it was known as the Denver Lyceum, the Denver Opera House, and the Wigwam. George Francis Train delivered the speech here before the Denver Chamber of Commerce and Board of Trade in 1867 that ignited the spark that brought Colorado the Denver Pacific Railroad.   Artemus Ward, P. T. Barnum, Cassius M. Clay, Vice-President (then Speaker of the House) Schuyler Colfax, and other national political leaders addressed Denver audiences from its stage.[96]

The only serious rival to the Denver Theater during the seventies was Governor's Guard Hall, on the northwest corner of Fifteenth

93 Frank Fossett, *Colorado* (1876 ed.), 67.

94 *Rocky Mountain News,* May 2, 1866.

95 The Montana Theater was destroyed May 21, 1874.   The historic Concert Hall was burned at the same time.   The Denver Theater was burned March 19, 1877, presumably in a fire of incendiary origin.

96 *Rocky Mountain News,* March 20, 1877.

and Curtis streets. This building was erected by a stock company of Denver business men as an armory and hall for the Governor's Guard. It was dedicated by a musical program, and address by General Sam E. Brown on February 21, 1873. A fountain played before the stage. Tents were pitched to right and left, and every window had its cage of singing canaries. It was the intention of the builders that the structure should be an opera house, but its impossible construction made it useless for that purpose. George B. Waldron remodeled the stage but failed to make the venture pay. John J. Mortimer took over with a little better success in a season of sensational melodrama, but the panic of 1873 struck and the stage suffered a dreary succession of years. In February, 1876, Langrishe returned to Denver with a new company and reopened the Denver. He attempted at this time to establish a new circuit, taking in Denver, Boulder, Central City and some Southern Colorado towns, but in a few months gave up and left for the Dakota mining camps.

The most important result of this Colorado venture was the introduction, in Langrishe's Company, of Nate Forrester and Mrs. Forrester. Both were fine actors of national reputation. Forrester leased Guard's Hall and conducted it with great success until overshadowed by the magnificence of the Tabor Grand. He it was who first definitely placed Denver upon the big time. Among the great attractions he brought to the city were Joe Jefferson in Rip Van Winkle, the elder Southern, Janauschek, De Mursko, John T. Raymond, Lawrence Barrett, Mrs. D. P. Bowers, Tom Keene, Mrs. Scott Siddons, W. E. Sheridan, the Rignold Opera Company, and Charlotte Thompson.

Paralleling the rise of the legitimate drama, and overshadowing it from the commercial standpoint, was the variety house. This institution was merely the glorified saloon and gambling hall, with strong emphasis upon the entertainment lure. The more pretentious establishments were equipped with enormous carved mahogany bars, the costliest of cut and imported glassware, luxurious hangings, oil paintings and mural decorations. They presented variety acts of dancing, singing, minstrelsy, magic, and farce, often offering fifteen or twenty numbers in an evening. Whatever scale the theater held, however, flashily-gowned and pretty girls continually mingled with the men patrons, who bought them beer at $1.00 per bottle, wine and champagne at $3.00 to $5.00 per bottle. Each girl received a check from the waiter, which she deposited in her purse by the simple expedient of slipping it down her stocking. By the end of the evening it looked as though she wore gold bangles around her lower legs.

The variety house is an important link in the history of frontier drama. From it arose the legitimate vaudeville stage. Many of the acts were extremely clever. Not all of the girls sang in whiskey baritones by any means. There were beautiful, well-trained voices in some instances, and clever comedians to stimulate mirth and gaiety in the hall. The famous Eddie Foy, for illustration, made his start in the notorious Palace Theater. Usually the bars and the dance hall occupied the first floor, while the second story, carpeted with expensive rugs, hummed with the incessant click of the roulette wheel and the muted shuffle of cards. Stakes were high, running into the thousands. The successful mining magnate wanted action for his money.

The most notorious variety house in the early sixties was Criterion Hall, which stood upon the site now occupied by the graystone Railroad Building at 1515 Larimer Street. The structure was opened by Ed Jumps, but later was bought by Charley Harrison, notorious gambler and desperado, whose henchmen kidnapped Editor William N. Byers and took him to the hall for judgment. Harrison had not anticipated, nor ordered this abduction and promptly released Byers. The most noted entertainer was M'lle Carolista, or Carlista, ballet dancer and tight-rope walker, who gained fame by walking and dancing a wire stretched between the Criterion and the New York store across the street. This stunt was performed July 23, 1861, and a number of "sporting gentlemen" gave her a purse of $165.75. This she acknowledged by the following ingenuous note:[97]

> The gentlemen presenting the purse stated that they were anxious to show their appreciation of my talents in a substantial manner. Gentlemen, your discrimination is only equalled by your kindness of heart. I shall endeavor in future to work with renewed energy, and faithfully promise to do all in my power to merit a continuation of the public favor and good will.
>   Yours truly,
>   Carlista.

The most startling entertainment in early Denver history was a ball given at the notorious Cricket in honor of the Demi Monde by Charley Ward, who "organized a ball in special honor of the Nymphs due pave."[98] The *Denver Daily Tribune* commented:

> From shortly after dark till far in the morning, bevies of the frail sisterhood were making the Cricket their object point. In fact, it was after 1 o'clock this morning when the festivities fairly commenced.
> An initiative "drink all around" furnished the necessary stimulus for a start and, from that hour till long after sunrise, there was a continuous dance—waltz, schottische, polka or quadrille—the intermission being occupied by fortifying the "inner man", or woman.

Laura, Winnie, Gertie, Cora, Dutch Nellie, and Mormon Ann; Frankie, Annie and a host of others were there, but the ball was con-

---

[97] *Ibid.,* July 25, 1861.
[98] *Denver Daily Tribune,* February 28, 1874.

spicuous by the absence of the "Madames." The Cricket, located on Blake street, west of Fifteenth, was opened the winter of 1869-70 by Ed Chase.[99]

There was a vast difference in the variety halls. At the bottom in iniquity was the Central Theater, formerly highly respectable East Turner Hall, on Market Street, between Twentieth and Twenty-first streets.[100] In 1885, the building fell into control of Laura Le Claire, a burlesque queen, who had stood even wild Leadville upon its toes by her high voltage personality. Besides a regular variety show and dances, the Central staged chicken fights, dog fights, and prize fights every week. The most notorious soubrette was beautiful Birdie Estelle, whose mad career ended on the beach at Oakland, California, with her throat cut from ear to ear.

The "key game" was worked to perfection at the Central, women workers in the boxes selling ten or twelve keys to their rooms every night at $3.00 to $5.00 per key. Few of the dupes ever had courage to return and complain of "no such number," because guests and habitues of the place would greet them with ribald laughter.

By far the most famous of the variety houses was the Palace Theater of gambler Ed Chase. This building, which underwent a face-lifting operation, still stands on Blake Street between Fourteenth and Fifteenth, and covers part of the site of the Elephant Corral. The Palace was run under rigid discipline and disorder was not allowed. Shows put on there featured the best variety acts in the country at the time. One noted performer, who appeared at the Palace in 1876, was Thomas L. Connors, who rose to prominence under tutelage of Ben De Bar, the great American Falstaff, at De Bar's Opera House in St. Louis.[101] Forrester brought him to Denver and he died two years later at Georgetown.

Among the many amateur groups that contributed to the hilarity of the fun-loving pioneers two had the element of novelty. The strong German segment, through sponsorship of the Vorwarts Turnverein, opened a German Theater in Sigi's Hall in 1877, headed by Herr Stoessiger.[102] These German comedians attained considerable popularity with the Teutonic population. Sigi's Hall became known to modern Denverites when the Town Hall shows were conducted there.

The same year the African M. E. Church sponsored an all-negro company of amateurs at Turner Hall. They presented *Honeymoon* with a novelty that won a hilarious welcome.[103] Magicians were frequent visitors throughout the pioneer era, starting with Signor Franco,[104] who swallowed stones and swords without visible impairment to his digestion, at the old Diana Theater (1864), and culminating with Herman, the Great.

99 Melvin Schoberlin, *op. cit.,* 195.
100 *Denver Post,* July 28, 1901.
101 Randall Clippings, State Historical Society, V 2, p. 169; July 28, 1878.
102 *Denver Tribune,* January 24, 1877.
103 *Ibid.*
104 *Rocky Mountain News Weekly,* August 31, 1864.

In 1879, Walhalla Hall was opened by Joseph Proctor in Macbeth.[105] This was a two-story brick structure on the northeast corner of Sixteenth and Curtis, and paralleled the Tabor Grand when that theater was built. Here Langrishe, in 1880, made his last attempt to recoup his waning fortunes in Denver. The building later became known as 16th Street Theater and was not razed until 1916.

The interesting history of Walhalla Hall began when Charles E. and Edward Leichsenring converted the first floor into a glittering saloon and beer garden where concerts and theatrical performances occasionally were interlarded. On the second floor, during the early eighties, Bill Cate, former Pony Express rider, soldier of fortune and prospector, conducted an ornate "palace of fortune," patronized by the wealthy mining magnates and political leaders of Denver, Leadville, and Central City.[106] Tabor was among the high-stake players here. Cate was known as a square gambler, hence his place was popular with the captains of industry.

The most important dramatic production ever staged in Walhalla Hall was Charles W. Couldock's subtle presentation of *Hazel Kirke*, with Effie Ellsler in the title role. There seemed to be a hex attached to this building, perhaps because it profaned the site upon which once stood the "Baptist Dugout," a queer growth, like a mushroom over a hole in the ground.

Throughout the state in these early days the dramatic menu was slim except in a few large centers. In most instances the performances featured a minstrel show, a hilarious farce, or wild melodrama with, of course, the ever present individual acts while the girls worked the boxes and received commissions of ten to twenty-five cents on each bottle of beer or wine sold.

In only a few locations were stands of one week possible. Phil Kirby, agent for the Edouin Sparks Company, took a troupe from Cheyenne through Colorado, New Mexico, Arizona, and California in 1882, playing Colorado on the following schedule: Fort Collins, one night; Boulder City, one night; Denver, three nights; Leadville, three nights; Colorado Springs, one night; Pueblo, one night; Trinidad, one night.[107]

Aside from Denver, Leadville, Central City, and Georgetown were the important towns in the early eighties. Aspen in its heyday had several theaters, including the Wheeler Opera House, but could not attract the top flight shows because of the terrors of the great range between it and Leadville. In 1885, C. J. Coles and John Eitel built the Aspen Theater and engaged Charlie Boyd as manager.[108] He was an experienced and widely traveled trouper in variety who came first to Denver with Haverly's Minstrels. He returned to fill an engagement at the Palace Theater, managed the old Globe Theater in Leadville and then turned his attention to Aspen where, for

105 *Denver Daily Tribune,* May 25, 1879.
106 *Denver Post,* July 9, 1916.
107 *Denver Inter-Ocean,* January 28, 1882.
108 *Aspen Weekly Times,* January 1, 1887.

several years, he conducted a profitable varieties theater. After the
first season he changed the name to the Comique, and the *Aspen
Weekly Times* made this appraisal of his theater: "Outside of the
box-work, which in western variety shows is a necessity, there is not
a feature of Charlie Boyd's Comique which would offend the most
fastidious pleasure seekers."[109] The Rink Opera House also opened
in 1885, using local talent in such plays as *Led Astray, Sweeheart*
and Augustin Daly's *Under the Gas Light*. In 1889 a new opera house
was built.[110]

Several variety halls operated in Golden, in the early seventies,
the most pretentious, perhaps, being Ford Street Varieties.[111] Jack
Langrishe's Company also played in Golden, a notable occasion being
the appearance of McKee Rankin and Kitty Blanchard in April,
1871.[112]

At Georgetown an entirely different situation existed. Erskine
McClellan, who built many of the ore mills in Gilpin and Clear Creek
counties, erected there a pretentious and well-designed stone theater[113]
in which Forrester presented his best attractions. One of the most
memorable productions was that of the celebrated Mrs. Scott-Siddons
in 1878.[114] The old McClellan Opera House, long since destroyed
by fire, adjoined the famous Hotel de Paris of Louie Dupuy. There
were many cultured and wealthy people in Georgetown who could
appreciate the best.

There also was a second-story theater in Silver Plume that did
not rate the better attractions.

Colorado Springs was fortunate in being on Tabor's Silver Circuit[115] and received many of the great shows from the Tabor Grand.
The theaters, however, were nothing of which the community could be
proud until erection of the Burns. A ramshackle opera house was
built in 1876 and operated under the management of S. N. Nye.
This was succeded by another Opera House, more pretentious, also
under the management of Mr. Nye. It could hardly have been entitled
to the description of Eleanor Ormes as "very grand in that day,
the best of its kind west of the Mississippi, except the Tabor Grand

109 *Ibid.*

110 *Colorado Topics,* IV, No. 5, p. 2.

111 *Colorado Transcript,* May 7, 1873.

112 *Ibid.*

113 Randall Clippings, S.H.S., V. 2, p. 224.

114 *Georgetown Courier,* December 7, 1878.

115 Under the management of Peter McCourt Tabor's Silver Circuit included: the Tabor
Grand, Denver, capacity 1,500; Colorado Springs Opera House, 1,100; Pueblo Grand Opera
House, 1,300; Jaffa Opera House, Trinidad, 800; Salida Opera House, 800; Tabor Opera
House, Leadville, 1,000; Wheeler Opera House, Aspen, 1,100; Provo City Opera House,
800; Salt Lake Theater, 1,800; Grand Opera House, Ogden, 1,700; Park City Opera House,
800; Grand Junction Opera House, 700; and Glenwood Springs Opera House, 600. The
insignia used on the letterhead was a dollar printed in silver, with the words printed across
its surface "Silver Circuit Peter McCourt Manager." The reverse of the letterhead contained the name printed above, the upper half of the sheet having a map of the Silver Circuit,
which indicated that Cheyenne, Rawlins and Rock Springs, Wyoming, and Canon City, Colorado, also were on the circuit. Originals of this letterhead are in the Tabor Collection, State
Historical Society.

in Denver."[116]   On a wild April night in 1888, with Kate Castleton starring in *Crazy Patch*, a sudden gust of wind tore the tin off the roof and left the audience in a state of panic.[117]   This was the old Opera House built in 1880 by B. F. Crowell, Irving Howbert, and J. F. Humphrey with the money they had made in the Robert E. Lee Mine at Leadville.   It was said to have cost $100,000.[118]

The finest theater constructed at the Springs was the Burns Opera House, erected by James F. Burns, the Cripple Creek mining magnate.   This handsome white marble structure was opened May 8, 1912, with the Russian Symphony Orchestra as the attraction.   However, as theaters go, its life as home of legitimate drama was brief.[119]   In 1928 it was converted into a moving-picture house.

Pueblo's first theater was Conley Hall on Seventh Street, erected by Lewis Conley in 1869.[120]   It was an amusement hall, which later became the Thespian, and then Montgomery's Opera House.   In 1889 it was relegated to disuse by the De Remer Opera House.[121]

The town of Gunnison, in the early eighties, then in the flush of lusty youth, had serious intentions to take the capital from Denver. It built a splendid and later famous hotel—The La Veta—and took its drama seriously.   A very popular soubrette, Miss Jennie Engle, a favorite at Dillon's Varieties, Gunnison's first playhouse, was presented a magnificent solid silver horseshoe upon terminating an engagement.[122]   A very pretentious opera house was built in 1882 by S. E. Dawson, George L. Smith and E. H. Taylor, and given the name Smith's Opera House.[123]   This was opened by a presentation of the Gunnison Dramatic Club, composed of local amateurs, January 3, 1883.[124]   The production was *The Turn of the Tide*.   However, some stellar attractions later played this theater.   The most noted of Gunnison's variety houses was the Globe, operated for a time in 1882 by James Le Clair and his dazzling wife.[125]

Montrose also had an opera house where appeared in 1888 the talented Effie Ellsler in *Hazel Kirke*.   Delegations came from Ouray, Grand Junction and other neighboring towns.[126]

However, Ouray pioneered the drama in this section by a presentation of *The Charcoal Burner*, attended by a "large crowd." Admission must have been very low as the total receipts were $11.25.[127]   Ouray also had a local Thespian Society at this time.

116 Manly D. and Eleanor R. Ormes, *The Book of Colorado Springs* (1933), 346-348.
117 *Colorado Topics*, III, No. 1, p. 2; April 6, 1888.
118 Ormes, *op. cit.*, 346-348. Also, *Denver Inter-Ocean*, July 3, 1880.
119 Ormes, *op. cit.*
120 Frank Hall, *History of Colorado*, III, 461.
121 *Colorado Topics*, III, No. 40, p. 2; January 4, 1889.
122 *Gunnison Daily Review*, October 20, 1882.
123 *Ibid.*, September 1, 1882.
124 *Gunnison Daily Review-Press*, December 27, 1882.
125 *Ibid.*, September 1, 1882.
126 *Colorado Topics*, II, No. 48, p. 2; March 3, 1888.
127 *Ouray Times*, October 22, 1881.

Durango, in the far southwest, hemmed in by the high Continental Divide, was not to be outdone. A popular local theatrical organization was formed in 1882, under the name of *The Rustlers*.[128] The usual variety hall also existed in the Clipper Theater. An odd feature was a box on the wall near the Faro bank, which bore this legend: "Don't Forget Parson Hoge."[129] This remarkable Durango character was equally well liked by cattle rustlers, bank robbers

(Courtesy of the State Historical Society of Colorado)

Tabor Grand Opera House, Denver

and bankers, a tribute, certainly, to his large and charitable heart. Everyone contributed to his church.

These random notes on the stage in the smaller cities of Colorado could be extended further, but they are intended to be merely indicative of the times. We must pass now to the golden age of the Colorado stage, beginning with erection of the famous Tabor Grand Opera House in Denver.

This theater has been so thoroughly described in newspapers, magazines, books and scholarly dissertations that to describe it again would be repetitious. Suffice to say that it summarized in its interior the ultimate in the opulent, but somewhat somber, red plush era of America. The red cherry woodwork, the red plush opera chairs, red hangings and prevailing red tone of the carpets; the heavy and costly

[128] *Denver Inter-Ocean,* February 11, 1882.
[129] Mrs. Eliza G. La Court. A. L. Soens, interviewer, S.H.S. Pam. 362.

tapestries, and the famous Hopkin's curtain,[130] richly painted but macabre of subject, were slightly depressing, but very impressive. We may never again see in America so perfect a monument to a period in our history devoted to ostentatious display; prophetic shadow of a man who tried too hard to dramatize himself.

The Emma Abbott Opera Company opened the Tabor September 5, 1881, in *Maritana*. All Denver was a little drunk with excitement over the occasion. The boxes and the parquet glittered with Parisian toilets and gems. And so, for the next twenty years a procession of all that was great in drama during the period, a procession never equalled filed across its stage—Edwin Booth, Lawrence Barrett, Madame Janauschek, Charlotte Thompson, Madame Christine Nilsson, Minnie Maddern, Modjeska, Dion Boucicault, Nat Goodwin, the Bostonians, Clara Morris, Madame Patti, Madame Nordica, Effie Ellsler, Maggie Mitchell, James O'Neill, Madame Ristori, W. E. Sheridan, Frederick Warde, W. J. Florence, Viola Allen, Alexandro and Tomasso Salvini, Mary Anderson, Joe Jefferson, McKee Rankin, Lotta Crabtree, Louis James and Marie Wainwright, Sara Bernhardt, E. H. Sothern, Robert Mantell, Rose Coghlan and Thomas Keene, to mention but a few.

It must have brought a thrill to old Denver theater goers to see Mrs. Nate Forrester playing with the Dion Boucicault Company in *Colleen Bawn* in September, 1883, and the following week to attend performances of the Eastern Drama Company, starring the old favorite John S. Langrishe. But think what a thrill he must have received when he harked back in his mind to the old Apollo on Larimer Street in 1861.

Elmer S. Crowley, in his thesis on the Tabor Grand Opera House, has compiled an interesting tabulation which shows the types of dramatic presentations during the first ten years.[131] During this period approximately 345 weeks were devoted to plays, 54 weeks to opera, 21 weeks to minstrels, and over 40 weeks to specialties, extravaganzas, magicians and similar forms of entertainment. Shakespeare's works were repeated most to Denver audiences, with the exception of Sheridan Knowles' *Virginius*, which occupied the bill 18 times. *Othello*, with seventeen repetitions was second, with *Hamlet, Camille, Twelfth Night, Julius Caesar, As You Like It, Richelieu, Richard Third, Ingomar, The Merchant of Venice, Lady of Lyons, Romeo and Juliet, Adrienne Lecouvreur, Frou-Frou, East Lynne, Fanchon, School for Scandal, Francesca da Rimini* and *Pygmalion* and *Galatea* following.

This intellectual feast culminated in the early nineties in a rash of cultural activities that broke forth like an epidemic of measles. It is doubtful whether Denver ever had in its history more musical

---

130 Charles S. Hathaway of Detroit, lifelong friend of Robert Hopkin, who painted the famous Tabor curtain, has stated that Hopkin used the Kingsley verse beginning "So fleet the works of men," on the Detroit Opera House Curtain, as well as on a large painting "The Baptism of Christ" before he painted the Tabor Curtain, thus indicating that Tabor did not make the choice of this verse. Mss. XIII, 4c, State Historical Society Library.

131 Elmer S. Crowley, *The History of the Tabor Grand Opera House, Denver Colo.,* 1881-1891 (Thesis, University of Denver).

organizations, choruses, orchestras, string and vocal quartettes, amateur dramatic organizations, elocution schools and art clubs at one time.

In Mrs. Scott Saxon's College of Oratory and Dramatic Art[132] and Josephine Beemer's elocution class at Wolfe Hall[133] every prospective debutante was declaiming with passion, or weaving her arms about weirdly in the sweetly sick postures of Delsarte. In Mrs. Scott Saxon's School students took Swedish Gymnastics under the Swedish Professor Lof, swung Indian Clubs under direction of Miss Pike, or snaked their way through the Delsartian manual under the critical eye of Miss Holmes.

Maud Durbin, leading lady and wife of Otis Skinner, was a product of the Wolfe Hall School. Douglas Fairbanks, Walker Whiteside, Edward Ellsner,[134] and Maude Fealy were among the notable Denver contributions to the stage.

An important social and dramatic feature of the time was the Denver Dramatic Club, composed of the more talented products of the various elocution schools. This group had a small theater at Thirteenth and Broadway, but frequently staged plays at the leading theaters, usually in the interest of some worthy charitable movement. The Club's repertoire was extensive and it managed to present plays regularly each week for a period of about two years. Emmett Shackelford was director. Joe Newman, Denver's most popular entertainer of the period, was a member and frequently took part in the productions. A farewell benefit was given him at the Tabor Grand, June 23, 1893, just before he left to join the Patti Rosa Company.

The most important theatrical event of the Gay Nineties was the erection of the Broadway Theater, which opened August 18, 1890, with the Emma Juch Grand English Opera Company in *Carmen*. It was constructed by Bush and Morse, and we can well believe that William H. Bush hoped to gain revenge for the bitter legal battle with Tabor in the mid-eighties which resulted in his ouster as Tabor's manager. His place had been taken by Peter McCourt whose inborn talents made him the dominant theatrical manager in Denver until the movies ended the reign of the legitimate stage. He was the brother of the fabulous Baby Doe Tabor who, had she fallen into the hands of a Frohman or Belasco at the right period, would have become one of the greatest actresses the American stage has produced.

However, the influence of the Tabor Grand was still too potent to be seriously threatened, and the Broadway soon was acquired by Tabor, with McCourt as manager. The Broadway was, and is, a very handsome theater. As opposed to the ''heavy'' effect of the old

---

132 *Events,* III, No. 6, p. 11, adv.; also No. 5, p. 11, adv.

133 *Ibid.,* III, No. 9, p. 11.

134 Edward Ellsner was the adopted son of Dr. John Ellsner of Denver, noted pioneer and art collector. He made his first appearance with Janauschek, as "Poor Joe" in *Bleak House,* played with W. S. Sheridan, Lawrence Barrett, Louis James and Marie Wainwright, as well as being a successful playwright himself.

Tabor, it is light and airy. The gilded arabesques and bulbous domes of the boxes convey the oriental atmosphere that seems built around the curtain—"A Glimpse of India."

In December, 1890, Tabor bought the Peoples' Theater at the northeast corner of Fifteenth and Cleveland Place,[135] now part of the University of Denver's downtown university. He secured a bargain, paying $33,000 for the $105,000 structure. This building was supposedly modelled on the lines of a Spanish castle, built of gray lava-stone by Charles Fagenbush. The latter was decidedly eccentric. It seemed to be his idea that he could combine a sort of Roman Forum and Roman bath. The people of Denver called the structure Fagenbush's Folly. The building had a jinx upon it and was never very successful. It was leased for the fall season of 1891 to Clay Clement,[136] a prominent actor-manager of the day and some excellent dramatic productions were staged, but shortly thereafter fire gutted it. For many years its gaunt gray walls cluttered the landscape.

During the early nineties Elitch's Gardens and Manhattan Beach opened in stock. Since a history of the Gardens has been published it seems unnecessary to go into the story of this resort to great extent. It has the honor of having played Bernhardt. David Warfield brought his *Music Master* there. Tyrone Power, the elder, appeared in his great role of *Svengali*. Many great stars played the boards of the old theater, and stock companies of high caliber performed. It is now the oldest continuous stock theater in America. Perhaps its greatest charm lies in its cool orchards and shady walks. The Lady of the Gardens—Mrs. Elitch-Long,—is gone and with her went a wonderful heritage.

Manhattan was a worthy rival of Elitch's. Situated on the shore of Sloan's Lake, where the present yacht harbor is located, it also had a handsome, round theater, a dancing pavilion, boating, and the little side-wheel steamer, "City of Denver" that chugged patiently around the lake. Heading its stock companies were such stars as the dynamic Henrietta Crosman, Amelia Bingham, Blanche Bates, Edwin Arden and many others who will be remembered by the old theater-goers at Elitch's, as they played both gardens. Manhattan Beach theater burned to the ground one winter night some thirty-five years ago and was never rebuilt.

The New Lyceum Theater was an outgrowth of the Denver Dramatic Company. It was opened January 29, 1894, with a double bill of light comedy, *My Awful Dad* and *Art and Nature*. The theater was located next to the Cooper Building on Curtis Street. Ferdinand Stark's Austro-Hungarian Orchestra, formerly at the Tabor, was engaged.[137]

---

[135] *Rocky Mountain News,* December 3, 1890.

[136] *Denver Music and Drama,* I, No. 4, p. 5.

[137] This orchestra was patterned after Rosner's Austro-Hungarian Orchestra of Vienna, which introduced electrical effects to create realism. The effect was sensational, but like all fads the custom did not last.

Harry Evans and F. E. Carstarphen, among the founders of the
Denver Dramatic Club, were General Manager and Secretary, respectively. For a time amateurs were used, but apparently this did not
prove profitable, because the theater switched to travelling stock companies and, about 1900, went to vaudeville. This probably was the
first theater to use that term in Denver. A separate treatise could
be written about the Curtis Street theaters, but space will permit
mention of a few only. The Denver Theater, concurrent with the
New Lyceum, was a Hayman, Klaw & Erlanger affiliate, managed by
D. A. Barton. The Empress was a member of the Pantages Circuit,
and featured amateur nights. The old Curtis and Isis represented
the hist-hist-histrionics. The snarling Villain in full dress, with
waxed moustache; the Sweet Young Thing; the two-fisted Hero who
arrived just as the Sweet Young Thing swooned, all were there,
stereotyped types of melodrama in the raw from time immemorial.

The Curtis, however, had one immortal night. Harry Lauder once
came to town—so unexpectedly that he could secure a booking nowhere
except at the Curtis. The piano was too large to bring in through
the wings, so the movers came up from the orchestra. An insignificant little man with a horse's profile, dressed in a brown business
suit and derby hat, had his shoulder to the lower corner of the concert
grand and shoved with considerable vigor. Few in the audience
recognized him as the mover when he came out a few minutes later
in tartans, tapping his crooked blackthorn cane on the board and
rolling forth his rollicking Scotch songs.

The Tabor Grand continued to dominate the theatrical scene until
about the turn of the century, but after that the Broadway, featuring
great stars such as Richard Mansfield, Robert Mantell, Minnie Maddern
Fiske, George Arliss, Otis Skinner, De Wolf Hopper, Eva Tanguay—
Shakespearean tragedy, drama, comedy, extravaganza—drew away.

For many years the Denham presented excellent stock, starring
Gladys George, Eva Long, George Barnes and other good actors. On
this stage, E. H. Sothern, the younger, made his last appearance.
He foretold the death of the legitimate stage and advocated the formation of little theaters by amateurs as the sole means of preserving
dramatic art. Then, in the midst of a Shakespearean reading, he
staggered, placed his hand upon his forehead, and would have fallen
had not attendants rushed from the wings and carried him away.
He never rose from his bed again.

Among vaudeville houses the Orpheum on Welton Street, erected
in 1903, was undisputed king. It brought the best in vaudeville to
Denver for many years, and it is of interest to note that Sarah Bernhardt made her last appearance in Denver on the Orpheum circuit.
She gave a reading from L'Aiglon. This was after she had lost one
of her legs. She was an old woman. The golden voice had lost some
of its lustre, but the talking hands were there, and the heart was
youthful still.

There will always be those who desire to see or to participate
in dramatic production for the intellectual pleasure that it can give.

Upon this principle the little theater movement is based. In Denver, this desire has been expressed in the University Civic Theater which, for seventeen years, has functioned successfully in the Margery Reed Memorial Hall at the University of Denver.

This theater is sponsored by but has no working connection with the University. Its membership, now numbering some 3,000 people, come from all walks of life. About 500 participate in some way in the actual production of plays. Since its inception it has been under the able direction of Walter Sinclair. The range of production is wide—classic drama, farce, melodrama, comedy and tragedy—but a glance at the list of playwrights represented reveals that each had some message to convey. The Civic Theater is essentially a cultural institution, and provides good entertainment at all times. The problems of staging, lighting, and costuming require people of many skills. Such titles as *Twelfth Night, Rain, The Emperor Jones, Abraham Lincoln, Arms and the Man, Washington Jitters, East Lynne, Murder on the Second Floor* indicate that this is a dramatic laboratory, unfettered and free.

The most significant development in the preservation of the legitimate stage is the successful establishment of the Central City Opera House Association.

This movement took form in 1931, when the heirs of Peter McFarlane, one of the original builders of the stone opera house erected in that city in 1878, deeded the property to the University of Denver.[138]

Fortunately, two extraordinary women became interested in this movement and, to them, is due success. Mrs. Ida Kruse McFarlane, born in Central City and then a member of the University of Denver faculty, was instrumental in securing this gift. Cultivated, magnetic and imaginative, she contributed her talents unstintingly to the enterprise. Miss Anne Evans, daughter of the Second Territorial Governor, teamed with Mrs. McFarlane. Miss Evans, whose great work in development of the Denver Art Museum and the Denver Public Library has been very largely responsible for their present advanced stage, must go down in history as a great Colorado builder. She too was highly educated, endowed with faultless taste and, what is more important in such movements, had an unquenchable enthusiasm that she was able to convey to others. It was her exceptional ability as an organizer and planner, however, that turned the corner for the Central City Opera House Association. She laid down the dictum at the start that whatever was done must be the ultimate in performance.

The old Central City Opera House, therefore, was inaugurated as a monument to the pioneer mining men of the State. Nothing that was not superlatively done could be presented.

The first play festival was held from July 16 to 23, 1932. The sponsors went directly to Robert Edmund Jones, an international figure in the theater. He came to Central City, was thrilled with the

---

[138] Undated Brochure, *The Central City Opera House Association* (Bradford-Robinson Ptg. Co., Denver), S.H.S. Library.

dignity, the simplicity and the permanence of the structure, and agreed to join in the work. The first production starred Lillian Gish in *Camille.* Restoration work on the theater was placed under direction of Mr. and Mrs. Burnham Hoyt. The great chandeliers were rehung and the frescoes were recleaned and retouched by the noted muralist, Allen True.

From 1932 to and including 1941 annual play festivals were held, attracting dramatic critics and notable personages from all parts of

(Courtesy State Historical Society of Colorado)

Central City Opera House

America. Notable directors who have supervised productions have included: Robert Edmund Jones, Frank St. Leger, Felix Brentano, Jed Harris; Richard Aldrich, Donald Oenslager and Herbert Graf of the Metropolitan Opera Company. Choruses and dancers have been drilled by Mrs. Florence Lamont Hinman and Lillian Cushing of Denver.

Productions have included: Lillian Gish in *Camille,* 1932; an All-Star New York cast in the *Merry Widow,* 1933; Walter Houston in *Othello,* 1934; an All-Star New York cast in *Central City Nights,* 1935; an All-Star cast in *The Gondoliers,* 1936; Richard Aldrich in *A Doll's House,* 1937; Helen Chandler and Bramwell Fletcher in *Ruy Blas,* 1938; All-Star cast in *The Yeoman of the Guard,* 1939; All-Star cast in *The Bartered Bride,* 1940 and an All-Star cast in the double bill *The Barber of Seville* and *Orpheus,* 1941. World War II then intervened, but guides were maintained to show visitors through the theater and the Teller House, the historic hotel presented to the University of Denver through the Mayor and Council of Central City. The next few seasons were financially profitable although the theater was dark, an indication of the hold that the enterprise had taken upon the public mind.

In 1946, the Festival was revived with an All-Star cast in the double bill, *The Abduction from the Seraglio* and *La Traviata.*[139] Thousands were unable to secure tickets.

The famous Teller House, where President U. S. Grant walked across silver bricks to become a guest, has been filled with historic suites of furniture typical of the period when the Opera House was built.

The enterprise is, in fact, a highly successful historic house museum or to be exact, two historic house museums. It bids fair to become a lasting tradition in the theatrical world. It also serves to keep alive the noble traditions of the legitimate stage. The old hickory chairs of the theater have been dedicated, one by one, to pioneers who helped build the West, or to those who helped establish the great traditions of the American stage. The development also has served, undoubtedly, to save historic Central City from becoming a ghost town. The unpainted houses, rapidly falling to ruin, have been purchased by wealthy Coloradans for occupancy during the Festival, which now operates for three weeks each summer. But this is characteristic of any well-established and worthwhile historic house museum.

It seems appropriate to close this dissertation upon the history of the Colorado stage with this triumphant note. The Central City Opera House Association will do much to preserve those outstanding contributions of the legitimate stage; its intellectual force, its contribution to cultivated taste and creative thought, and its preservation of traditions tending to stabilize our American way of life.

Music

Music was the first cultural art to make an impression upon the Western Frontier. Around the flickering campfires of Santa Fe traders, Argonauts and Pikes Peakers, rousing songs brought courage to flagging spirits. The fiddle was almost as necessary as the rifle in the march of pioneers. In many instances these first musical instruments were home made, holding rattlesnake rattles to give sound effects.[140]

Next in order, came the impromptu dance orchestras of the variety houses, the brass bands and the pianos and melodeons of the housewives. As early as July 4, 1859, the Council Bluffs band

---

[139] Broadside, *Central City Victory Festival,* undated, but issued in 1946.
[140] *Missouri Historical Review,* V. 24, p. 137.

was brought across 600 miles of prairie to help the pioneers celebrate Independence Day.[141]

The first concert in Denver was given December 11, 1860; its
purpose, to purchase a melodeon for the "Choir."[142] Though there
was a large attendance, net receipts were only $43.85. The violinist
and violoncellist, hired for the occasion, took a large cut of the proceeds, even as now. Editor Byers of the *Rocky Mountain News*, looking as usual through Tidbottom's spectacles, declared the entertainment "the most brilliant affair in the history of Denver." The
assemblage "reminded us of fashionable concert occasions in eastern
cities," while "The Misses Sopris won golden opinions by their
chaste and elegant execution of the most difficult passages." At this
concert also, "Mr. St. Vrain handles his violin with the skill of a
master," and his numbers were "most rapturously applauded."[143]

Such were the natal cries of the prairie Euterpe in Colorado.

Aside from the sketchy orchestras of the variety halls, Denver
had little to choose from the musical menu until 1864, when Alex
Sutherland, the bugler who sounded the charge of the Light Brigade
at Balaklava, took up his residence in the town.[144]. In that year,
chance stranded Mr. and Mrs. Gruenwald of Thomas Maguire's San
Francisco Opera Company in Denver. On December 8th the pioneers
had their first taste of grand opera.[145] The "cultured minority" praised
the performance, but the proletariat threw verbal stink bombs. The
Gruenwalds went to Central City and appeared at the Montana
Theater—with Editor Byers' anxious blessing—but no comment was
printed in this home of choral-loving Welsh and Cornish miners.

The first musical organization in Denver, the Denver Musical
Union, was organized September 17, 1868, with T. G. Cooke, first
music teacher at Wolfe Hall, as director.[146] The Union gave concerts
for the next eight months in the Denver Theater with indifferent
success. The President of this organization was General Bela M.
Hughes.

In the spring of 1872 the Denver Choral Union was formed, with
B. M. Woodward as President and C. W. Sanborn as Director.[147] This
organization gave its first concert May 21, 1872, and produced the
first cantata ever sung in the mountain region. The Choral Union
held a musical convention in Denver under direction of Prof. H. S.
Perkins of Chicago and presented choruses from Mozart's *Twelfth
Mass* and Mendelssohn's *Elijah*. This event opened November 19,
1872, and its programs lasted for a week. Mrs. Belle Cole, later the
star contralto of the Theodore Thomas orchestra, made her first public

---

[141] *Rocky Mountain News,* July 9, 1859.

[142] *Ibid.,* December 19, 1860.

[143] *Ibid.,* December 12, 1860.

[144] Paul Porchea, *Musical History of Colorado,* p. 20. Paul Porchea was the pseudonym
of Mme. Baber-Pathrone.

[145] *Rocky Mountain News Weekly,* December 7, 1864; also *Daily,* December 14, 1864.

[146] *Colorado Tribune,* October 28, 1868; *Rocky Mountain News Weekly,* April 28, 1869;
Paul Porchea, *op. cit.,* pp. 26-27.

[147] Paul Porchea, *op. cit.,* pp. 28-29.

appearance under Choral Union auspices. Other notable singers of the period were Lilla Bearce, Emma Zern, Mrs. H. L. Thayer, who later sang with success in New York; Mrs. J. Q. Charles, leading soprano of the First Presbyterian Church, and C. Y. McClure, first tenor of the Denver Quartette, which made history as campaign singers during the political campaigns of 1876-80. The members were: McClure, W. W. Knight, C. W. Sanborn and C. Morrison.

In 1874, the Choral Union changed its name to the Haydn and Handel Association, directed by Frank Rose, organizer and director of the Rose Band, the best band in Colorado's early history. On February 18, 1875, the Association gave a notable presentation of *Creation,* featuring Belle Cole, Mrs. Banta, Frank Kratzer, Porter Warner, and B. F. Woodward. There were seventy voices. Soon after this Mrs. Cole left for further study and appeared with success in many European capitals.[148]

A barren period of four years in presentation of public concerts followed, but a revival occurred in 1878, when the Haydn and Handel Association and the Abt Society united to form the New Choral Union. Sullivan's *Pinafore* and the opera *Don Munio* were produced without pronounced success and the organization thereafter confined itself to concert work.[149]

The coming of the railroad in 1870 really gave a great impetus to musical advancement in Denver, and brought the first artist of importance in 1873, Wieniawski, who brought with him the piano virtuoso, Carl Wolfssohn.[150] During the decade Carl Beck, De Murska, Adelina Patti and Camillo Urso made their appearances.

One of the great influences for fine music was the Denver Maennerchor, the most powerful and successful German singing society in the city's history, organized December 17, 1870.[151] Prof. L. Schormeyer was the first director. The first concert was given April 10, 1871, in Sigi's Hall. The Maennerchor was a joyous group, which interlarded concerts with picnics, mask balls, excursions and other entertainment. Several concerts were given in Manitou House in Manitou and in Colorado Springs. Among the Maennerchor stars were Belle Cole, Lilla Bearce, A. Friese, Fritz Thies (the best amateur violinist in early Colorado history), and Madame Ilma De Murska.

The first band of any consequence in Denver was organized by William Earle Reid, who had been leader of the 11th Zouaves under General Lew Wallace. He found one embryonic band struggling against the insurmountable odds of an empty treasury and a dearth of musical instruments. Reid's band started under auspices of the G.A.R., but later was rechristened the City Band.

However, an excellent orchestra functioned during the seventies under direction of Frank Rose. This was known as the Rose Band, but played the most difficult of classical music, and was the only

148 *Ibid.,* p. 29.
149 *Denver Tribune,* November 19, 1872.
150 Paul Porchea, *op. cit.,* p. 49.
151 *Ibid.,* pp. 105-111.

instrumental rival of P. Gottesleben's Mozart Quintette, of which Fritz Thies and E. Gehrung were soloists.[152]

Beginning about 1881, the custom of giving private musicals in the home was instituted by Mrs. Charles Denison, and soon attained wide popularity.[153] Such well known pioneer leaders as Judge and Mrs. Owen Le Fevre, Judge and Mrs. Luther M. Goddard, Dr. and Mrs. John Ellsner, Mr. and Mrs. Fritz Thies, the Misses Wanda and Hilda Gottesleben, Emil Zietz, Governor and Mrs. John Evans, and Mrs. William Iliff followed the lead of Mrs. Denison, and the influence was far reaching in maintaining a high standard of musical taste.

Among the most important influences musically were the Episcopal and Methodist churches, more particularly St. John's and the Lawrence Street, afterward Trinity Methodist. Their demands upon the services of singers, however, were quite exacting, and this led the best singers to turn to the Denver Choral Union.

The period of the seventies closed in a whirl of activity, with the Choral Union doing the best work in its history. The Union presented in the stone opera house at Central City the first opera given in Colorado by an amateur company—an excellent production of *The Bohemian Girl* with Miss Hattie Schroeter in the leading role. Frank Rose was director.[154]

This same opera house has the credit of having sponsored the first appearance, on February 17, 1879, of one of Colorado's greatest native born singers, a Central City girl, Miss Hattie Louise Sims, of whom more will be told later. [155]

An amusing incident of this period was the first exhibition in Colorado of the Edison phonograph, brought to Denver in 1878 by the firm of Silver and Laws. Although the primitive instrument squeaked and screeched, it did repeat ''Mary had a little lamb,'' and sang *Yankee Doodle.*

''It is rather a scrawny looking instrument,'' said the *Tribune,*[156] ''larger and by no means as intricate as the machinery of a sewing machine.'' Said a rancher, ''The darned thing talks; it just talks and that's all of it; but it is mighty blamed strange.''

Two men, the cultural and intellectual antithesis of one another, induced a resurgence of musical activity as Time ushered in the ''Elegant Eighties.'' One worked through the professional stage; the other through the church.

H. A. W. Tabor, who adored the stage because of its glitter and gayety, rather than for its intellectual force, unloosed a flood of light and grand opera through the gateway of the Tabor Grand. During the next two decades Denverites were privileged to hear many leading operatic companies of America and Europe. Through Tabor's Silver Circuit some of these companies traveled to nearby Colorado towns.

152 *Ibid.,* pp. 111-115.
153 *Ibid.,* p. 68.
154 *Ibid.,* p. 47.
155 *Ibid.,* p. 48.
156 *Denver Tribune,* September 26, 1878.

The Emma Abbott Company, the Melville Opera Company, Conreid's Opera Company, the Bostonians, the Duff Opera Company (starring Lillian Russell), the Milan Grand Opera Company, Her Majesty's Opera Company (starring the prima donnas Gerster, Patti and Nordica), and the Templeton Opera Company, were among those that thrilled and inspired Tabor audiences. It was inevitable that the ease and finished performances of the great professionals should have a profound effect upon local musicians.

Dean Hart's activity, however, was of greater consequence to local singers because it touched directly local music lovers and amateur singers through the church choir and the choral society. The Tabor tended to discourage amateur efforts to produce opera. Since Dean Hart was and always remained English to the core, it was natural that he should turn to the mother country for his precentors and organists. Hence, the English influence dominated Denver musical circles for many years.

The first notable organist brought to St. John's from England was Arthur U. Marchant, organist and director of philharmonics.[157] He, in turn, brought to Denver Prof. E. G. Passmore of Union College, Wisconsin, as one of the teachers in Marchant's new college of music. With A. Kaufman, first director of the Tabor Grand orchestra, Passmore formed the Denver Opera Club. This started with great prominence and enthusiasm.

A newspaper critic had the temerity to question one of Marchant's productions.[158] The latter derided American musicians and the battle was on with Marchant, the Dean and the newspaper critics matching one another's caustic comment.

On October 4, 1880, Marchant organized a Philharmonic Society, but most of the prominent Denver singers and musicians did not respond, resentful of the Englishman's criticism. The Association presented *The Lay of the Bell* and the *Dettingen Te Deum* in 1881, but met with no enthusiasm. Marchant soon returned to England in a huff.[159]

The Denver Opera Club had become involved in the Marchant incident with the result that a rival group, the Colorado Opera Company, was organized December 7, 1881. The following spring the Denver Opera Club produced with notable success at the Tabor Grand *The Pirates of Penzance, Pinafore,* and *Mascotte.*[160] About this time the ministers of the city began to preach against opera, and did much to kill the budding interest.

The Colorado Opera Company, on January 23, 1882, produced at the Tabor the first native Colorado opera, *Brittle Silver,* the libretto written by Stanley Wood, a newspaper man who had gained

---

157 Paul Porchea, *op. cit.,* p. 91.

158 *Ibid.,* p. 54.

159 *Ibid.,* pp. 52-53.

160 *Ibid.*

local fame as a poet, and the musical score by H. H. Hunt of Lead-ville. This was distinctly local color as evidenced by the cast:[161]

The Hon. Ezekial Bogus, who owns the Brittle Silver Mine.................	M. Harrison
Clorinda, daughter of Bogus, Beautiful and dutiful	Mrs. A. Slaght
Broncho Kate, friend of Clorinda, a mountain maid with a mind of her own	Miss Annie Wiegle
Jack Drillsby, who "hasn't struck the contact," but loves Clorinda........	W. S. Ingersoll
Keno Bill, a gambler but honest.......	D. J. Kelly
Sumende Potowatomic, chief of the Uncompahgre Utes	F. J. Stevenson
Professor Polycarp P. Phillicamps, scientific and sentimental...........	Wm. H. Kohnle
Captain Bomb, a modern mining guards-man	J. O. Rogers
Jessie	Flora Collins
Bob Whim	N. McLeans
A. Kaufman	Director

It takes a Bret Harte to handle successfully the narrowly restricted vernacular of the mining camps, and the play was fore-doomed to failure for this reason alone. The performance was greeted with mixed emotions. Some newspaper writers praised it, but the *Inter-Ocean* critic viewed it with jaundiced eye. He described Mrs. Slaght, a Denver music teacher in private life, as "entirely innocent of any attempt at acting," and seemed personally irritated because Will Kohnle made faces at the audience. He concluded with this little pleasantry: "There should be uniformity of costume. It is very hard to place the season of the year, when one member of the chorus wears a white lawn dress, and another bundles herself in an ulster and wraps."[162]

The company took the road for Colorado Springs and Pueblo, but the whole incident soon was forgotten save as an historical item.

Dr. Frank Damrosch, son of the great Leopold, arrived in Denver July 1, 1879, to serve as organist at the First Congregational Church. Later he served in this capacity at the Unitarian Church and the Synagogue. In 1882, he organized the Denver Chorus Club and revived interest in choral work.[163] Before he left Denver for New York in 1885, his chorus had performed Handel's *Messiah*, Mendelssohn's *Elijah,* and Gounod's *Redemption*. In 1884, Damrosch was appointed first Director of Music in the Denver Public Schools, District No. 1. He attributed much of his later success as music director

---

[161] *Denver Inter-Ocean,* January 21, 1882, p. 40.
[162] *Ibid.,* January 28, 1882, p. 58.
[163] Denver Public Library: *The Lookout; Music in Denver, and Colorado,* p. 13.

of the New York public school system, with its 11,000 teachers and 600,000 children, to his varied experience in Denver.

Professor William Mason Broad took over direction of the Denver Chorus Club after Damrosch's departure, and continued in this capacity until it disbanded and sold its property to the Church Oratorio Club. During this period Professor Broad organized the Broad Opera Club and gave many performances of the Gilbert and Sullivan operas in Denver and other points in the state. Among the operas he produced were: *The Mikado, Patience, Pirates of Penzance* and *Fatinitza*.[164] Damrosch's position in the schools was filled by Professor Herbert Griggs, organist at the First Congregational, who retained this position until he left Denver in 1894. He was first director of the Apollo Club of Denver, and organized a Teachers' Club Chorus.[165]

The University of Denver played a conspicuous part in contributing to musical development during the eighties and nineties. Dr. Otto Pfefferkorn was imported from the New England Conservatory of Music in 1885 to head its department of music.[166] Other early directors of this school were: Dr. Saurien Blanpied, Dean Blakeslee, Frederick W. Schweiker, Horace E. Tureman and Anthony Carlson. Dr. Pfefferkorn was one of the critics of *Denver Music and Drama*, the well-edited, cultural periodical published by the Denver Music Company, of which I. E. Blake was head. This paper and its successor *Events* were superior to any critical journals of the arts published in Denver since that time.

During the eighties Dean Hart brought to Denver an extraordinary succession of talented English musicians. W. E. Hall succeeded Marchant as organist at St. John's, with Frederick Stevenson as precentor. The latter became organist at St. Mark's Episcopal Church and at the Synagogue, Director of the Denver Conservatory of Music and leader of the Concert Choir. Dr. Hall was succeeded by Dr. John H. Gower, who remained only a short time, recommending another English organist, Henry Houseley.[167]

Dr. Gower was an organist of international fame when he came to Denver,[168] having received the degree of Doctor of Music at Oxford at an earlier age than any aspirant within the previous century. He had been appointed organist at the Princess Royal Chapel, Windsor, at the age of 11. Dr. Gower also was a distinguished composer. His home in Brinton Terrace was, for many years, a center for gatherings of cultured people interested in music, literature, poetry, and spiritualism. He was an intimate friend of the noted English spiritualists Sir Oliver Lodge, Conan Doyle, the Balfours and others of this stripe. Dr. Gower amassed a fortune in mining, but lost it in the Panic of

164 *Ibid.,* p. 15.
165 *The Coloradan,* V. I, No. 1, p. 11.
166 Paul Porchea, *op. cit.,* pp. 115-117.
167 *Ibid.,* pp. 133-134.
168 The Lookout: *Music in Denver and Colorado,* pp. 129-132.

1893 and returned to professional work, serving as organist at the Unitarian Church.

Henry Houseley, who came to Denver in 1888, remained as organist of St. John's until his death thirty-seven years later.[169] He served as organist at the Temple Emanuel for thirty years, and as Musical Director of the Ancient and Accepted Scottish Rite Body of Masons for twenty-five years. Houseley was a rare musical genius, an internationally known composer of sacred music, orchestral pieces and opera. His Denver Choral Society won three firsts in national Eisteddfods and took first prize at the World's Fair at St. Louis. He succeeded Herbert Griggs as Director of the Apollo Club, the most famous of Denver's male choral clubs. No musician in Denver's history has exercised a better influence upon musical development than this gentle, lovable musician. His most popular opera was *Pygmalion and Galatea;* his greatest composition *Omar Khayyam,* a dramatic cantata for quartette, chorus and orchestra, performed in New England, Pennsylvania, Chicago, and other places. Among his famous anthems were *Crossing The Bar, Lead Kindly Light, Nearer My God to Thee, Abide With Me.* He composed many songs, including *Rock of Ages,* and produced notable piano and organ works.

The contribution of Trinity Methodist Church also has been consistently important. Upon the departure of Frank Damrosch, his Denver Choral Union united with the Trinity Choir under the direction of Isaac E. Blake, donor of the fine Trinity organ. About this time, 1887, Wilberforce J. Whiteman came to Denver as Supervisor of Music for the West Denver Schools, and remained with the Denver School System until 1919. Coincident with this work was his direction of Trinity Choir, where he presided for twenty years. The Choir usually was kept at a hundred or more voices, and such notable soloists as Mrs. Smith Hunsiker, Mrs. Whiteman, and Allan Jackson, later of the Chicago Opera Company, were featured. Mrs. Whiteman had a magnificent contralto.

Professor Whiteman was a stern mentor who often fretted over a seeming lack of ambition in his since famous son, Paul Whiteman. It was largely because of this that Paul decided to branch out for himself and, in San Francisco, conceived the idea that jazz might be played as good music. The Professor always remained Paul's severest critic and was chary of praise when Paul was about; but he was immensely proud of his famous son, while Paul's unswerving devotion to his parents was a beautiful thing.

Another fine musical influence during the period under discussion was the Glenarm Reading Club, organized in 1884 by the Rev. Myron Winslow Reed,[170] ranked as a pulpit orator with Henry Ward Beecher. This club made music one of its important activities and paid leading musicians of the city to direct its musical programs. Among those who served thus were Prof. Emil Zietz, Frederick Stevenson, Herbert Griggs, and Henry Houseley. Not only did the Club do much to

169 *Ibid.,* pp. 133-134.
170 Paul Porchea, *op. cit.,* pp. 115-117.

encourage promising local talent, but it engaged such visiting artists as Camillo Urso, the Boston Stars and Mme. Albani, and her London Concert Orchestra.

The Brinker Institute, which built the structure made famous by the Navarre Cafe, had a brief but meteoric career during the eighties, teaching debutantes social graces and cultural avocations. Prof. Isaac Brinker had a talented musical family and they cut a decided swath for a time. His daughter Callie was one of Denver's better sopranos of the day.[171]

With the opening of the nineties many quartettes were active. Some of these were of exceptional quality. Among these were the Denver Quartette, mentioned previously; the Concert Quartette; the St. Cecelia Quartette, featuring Callie Brinker; the Mendelssohn Male Quartette; the Apollo Quartette; the Euterpe Quartette; and the Lotus Quartette, organized by Hattie Louise Sims in 1891 and composed of Mrs. H. W. Carter, Mrs. John Mignolet, Mrs. Wilberforce J. Whiteman and Mrs. Perry Gardner.[172] The Mendelssohn, perhaps the most successful of all, necessarily underwent changes during its long life, but its most successful combination included Henry Martin, Robert Brown, Kale Schmidlap and the bell-like tenor of Robert Slack, the well-known Denver impresario.

The outstanding choral groups were the Denver Glee Club, Prof. Houseley, Director; the Select Choir, Dr. Gower, Director; the Concert Choir, Prof. Stevenson, Director; and the Church Oratorio Club, I. E. Blake, Director.

Among the more notable chamber music groups were: the Baker String Quartette, founded by Horace Tureman; Mansfeldt Quartette; Bezman Quartette; Dawkins Violin Quartette; Symphony Club, founded by Florence Taussig; Cavallo Symphony Orchestra; and the Saslavsky Chamber Music Orchestra. Lizzie Dawkins came to Denver in 1882 and was then a popular concert violinist.[173] She played first violin at Trinity and was the teacher of Genevra Waters Baker, who later made a name in San Francisco.

Two very distinguished choral societies started in this period were the Tuesday Musical Club, of which Hattie Louise Sims was first director; and the Apollo Club for male voices. Both are still functioning.

Hattie Louise Sims was one of Denver's most distinguished teachers of voice. After her debut in Central City she went to Europe and studied under Lamperti. After three seasons of opera and concert in Italy she appeared with the Boston Symphony, the New York Symphony, and the Worcester Massachusetts Festivals. Frederika Le Fevre Bellamy was one of her brilliant pupils who appeared successfully in Europe.

[171] *Brinker's Collegiate Institute;* Rocky Mountain News Printing Co., Denver, 1879. Course of Study and Annual Announcement.
[172] *The Coloradan,* V. I, No. 1, p. 5.
[173] *Ibid.,* V. I, No. 9, p. 8.

Red Rocks Amphitheater Near Denver

In addition to the musical entertainment furnished at the Tabor Grand and Broadway Theaters, both Elitch's Gardens and Manhattan Beach provided some excellent music. John Philip Sousa's Concert Band appeared at Manhattan Beach as early as 1896.[174] Later the Stewart Opera Company gave a series of ten operas there with Rafaello Cavallo directing the orchestra and Paul Whiteman playing the viola.

Cavallo rendered a great service during his long career, his symphony orchestra playing several seasons at Elitch's, Manhattan Beach, Lakeside Park, the Broadway, and in Pueblo. Lillian Nordica appeared with his orchestra shortly before her death.

Dr. James M. Tracy, a pupil of Liszt, came to Denver in 1908 to head the piano department of the Denver Conservatory of Music,[175] which had its start in 1887 as the music department of the University of Denver, when Mr. and Mrs. Oliver B. Howells came to Denver and organized a school of music in cooperation with the University. Dr. Tracy, an accomplished pianist who had engaged in concert work in Europe, was an important factor in the musical life of the city. In 1907 he founded the Liszt School of Music, and later delivered a course of forty lectures for ten seasons in connection with his Liszt Music Study Club.

Also in 1898 John C. Wilcox came to the city from New York. He was the first to illustrate Charles Wakefield Cadman's songs. Partly as a result Cadman lived in Colorado for several years and composed several of his operas here. Wilcox prepared the Indian mezzo-soprano, Princess Tsianina Redfeather, for the part she played as vocal illustrator of Cadman's works.

About 1912 Robert Slack began his career as an impresario. Over the years since then he has brought many great artists to the city, forming a partnership with Arthur Oberfelder. Modern Denverites are well acquainted with the history of the Oberfelder-Slack Series.

The part played by the city government of Denver is interesting and unique. The late Mayor Robert W. Speer took great interest in this type of development. His basic idea was to give to the people of the city ordinarily not able to attend high-priced musical attractions an opportunity to hear the best. As early as 1890, however, Denver had a city band under the direction of Givens. Since that time the municipal band has been directed by such leaders as Oswald H. Richter, Satriano, Rungle, Foreman, Garguilo, Herman Bellstadt, Frederick W. Innes, Rafaello Cavallo, and Henry Sachs.

With completion of the Municipal Auditorium in 1908, Mayor Speer arranged with the Schuberts for a popular priced theater. A long run of musical extravaganzas and light opera followed. In 1918, the great municipal organ was completed and dedicated by Margaret Wilson, daughter of President Woodrow Wilson, and Evan Williams,

174 *Manhattan Beach Amusement Programme,* June 20, 1886; p. 3.
175 *The Lookout: Music in Denver and Colorado,* pp. 19-37.

the Welsh tenor.[176]   Clarence Reynolds, nationally known organist, was engaged as municipal organist and conducted daily noon-day recitals in the Auditorium during the summer, which were free to the public. Reynolds was a great organist and the concerts were always heavily attended by people from all walks of life.

Mrs. Blanche Dingley Mathews, who had a studio in Brinton Terrace, was the one who suggested a Municipal Music Commission. The idea met with favor and, in 1918, Mayor W. F. R. Mills appointed the first such commission in the world. Its members were: Frank Shepard, chairman; Charles Wells, Fred R. Wright and Mrs. Dingley-Mathews. Under the commission's stimulus a Music Week Association was formed and a Municipal Chorus built up under direction of John C. Wilcox. At times, this reached a membership of four to five hundred singers, drawn from church choirs throughout the city. The first Music Week was celebrated in 1920. Denver and New York City were the first cities in America to launch such a movement and, while New York's festival antedated that of Denver by about two months, no city in the country ever equalled in the variety of activities and wide participation of elements these Denver Music Weeks. During a decade the Music Week Association presented such operas as *Martha, Robin Hood, The Bohemian Girl, The Geisha Girl, I Pagliacci, Cavalleria Rusticana, Rob Roy, Shanewis,* and the premiere of Cadman's *Sunset Trail.*

State High School contests for choruses and orchestras were inaugurated in 1924, culminating in 1926 with eighty-three entries. The attendance averaged 70,000 persons annually, with 6,000 performers. Christmas carols, involving between 4,000 and 5,000 church singers were featured every winter as a side issue.[177]

The active directors of this organization were John C. Wilcox, Freeman H. Talbot, and several of the heads of the large music stores in Denver. As the leaders moved to other cities, or other occupations, and several deaths occurred, interest waned and the tremendous organization collapsed like a bubble. Denver always has been a city prolific in creative ideas culturally, but even its most ardent workers in such causes must admit that it is a fickle city, strangely lacking in tenacity of purpose, or in appreciation of traditional values.

The history of the Civic Symphony Orchestra, organized in 1921, is more cheerful. Mr. and Mrs. Richard Hart and Horace Tureman, its conductor during many years of bitter struggle for its place in the sun, were the enthusiasts who started this movement. The city furnishes the Auditorium and the Musical Protective Association, the union, has always taken a very advanced and intelligent attitude toward the movement. During the formative years about one-half of the members were union musicians who played with amateurs. In 1934, the professional members of the orchestra organized the Denver Symphony Orchestra. The Civic Symphony, comprised of amateurs, with professionals in a few key spots, now constitutes the training

[176] Denver *Municipal Facts,* March, 1918.
[177] *The Lookout,* pp. 48-50.

school. During the year 1946, under direction of Saul Caston, ten Professional and six Civic concerts were given. The Denver Symphony Orchestra now has 85 members, the Civic Symphony 95. The orchestra has reached a high standard of perfection, and now ranks with some of the better symphonic groups of America.

Among the important schools of music that have contributed largely to musical development during the last generation may be mentioned the Denver College of Music, an outgrowth of the music department of the Wolcott School; the Denver Conservatory of Music, which had its origin in the University of Denver; the Lamont School of Music, now the music school of the University of Denver; the Blanche Dingley-Mathews School of Music. There has been considerable fluctuation in these schools, but those mentioned above performed notable services.

The Tuesday Musical Club, the Apollo Club, the Orpheus Male Chorus, Mrs. Hinman's Treble Clef Club, and Pro Musica, Inc., also have outstanding records.

The Colorado State Music Teachers' Association, now a large and active group, was an outgrowth of the Musicians' Society, which appointed a committee to form such an organization.[178] The first conference was held in Denver October 19, 20, and 21, 1920, at the Wolcott School Auditorium.

The first musical organization in Pueblo was the Pueblo Musical Union, which gave a concert October 29, 1881, with Mrs. E. K. Alden as leading soprano.[179] This was followed by the Arion Club, which presented the cantata *Belshazzar* in Montgomery's Opera House early in 1882, with Thornton Chase as Musical Director. It was not successful and the Arion Club died suddenly. Later that year the Pueblo Musical and Dramatic Club was organized and gave a concert featuring scenes from *The Bohemian Girl* and *Il Trovatore*. In 1883, a volunteer group presented *Patience* at the Pueblo Opera House with great success for three nights, moving then to Colorado Springs for a one night performance. The leading roles were taken by Mrs. Alden and Lizzie Frost, later a successful singer in Chicago. Prof. Mason Broad went to Pueblo in 1886 to stage and direct *The Mikado,* which he put on at the DeRemer Opera House March 21-23 before crowded houses. After the establishment of the Silver Circuit, Pueblo was one of the cities to benefit most from the Tabor attractions.

Leadville had its first attempt musically in 1880 when William H. Nash organized and directed presentation of the cantata *Esther*.[180] It was sufficiently successful to result in the organization of the Apollo Club, with Nash as director, and this organization presented a number of concerts, including presentations of *Belshazzar* and the *Haymakers*. The club sent Minnie Huff to Germany to study. She later was a success in San Francisco. D. P. Flinn was first president of this club. It was hampered, however, by the constantly shifting

178 *Ibid.,* pp. 114-120.
179 Paul Porchea, *op. cit.,* pp. 127-134.
180 *Ibid.,* pp. 135-137.

population of a mining camp and it was not until the Tabor Opera House was opened in Leadville that anything like stability was reached.

One of the most advanced musical programs among Colorado's smaller towns in the early days was accomplished at Del Norte, where O. L. Sloat, teacher of music, organized an excellently trained chorus in the late eighties. Sloat had previously taught in Alamosa, where he and Mrs. Charles Hayt staged a very successful presentation of Gounod's mass of *St. Cecelia* in the early eighties.[181] The backbone of the chorus was the choir of the Episcopal church, already so well drilled that visitors were surprised to hear antiphonal singing.

Durango had its Choral Union, as early as Denver, that presented opera in 1886.[182]. When Prof. Broad went to Durango in 1887 to give the opera *Mikado*, he found the chorus and soloists so well trained that only one rehearsal was needed before it was presented to the public.

Other early musical organizations in the smaller Colorado towns included Georgetown's Brass Band in 1871;[183] Golden's Choral Union of 1870;[184] Gunnison's string band of 1882[185] and the Welsh Eisteddfod chorus of 80 voices that came to the Eisteddfod in Denver in 1888 from this little coal mining community and captured first place.[186]

Colorado Springs and Boulder have fared well musically, due largely to the activities of the Universities in those towns. The University of Colorado appointed Charles H. Farnsworth as instructor of music in 1893. The work was theatrical until 1920, when the College of Music was created, leading to the degree of Bachelor of Music. The Boulder Friday Musical Club, the Boulder Choral Union and Orchestra, men's and women's glee clubs followed. The Friday Musical Club, of which Mrs. Farnsworth was first president, brought such noted artists as Edward MacDowell, Herbert Witherspoon, Johanna Gadski, Ernestine Schumann-Heink, and the Flonzaley Stringed Quartette to Boulder. Henry Houseley, John C. Wilcox and Hattie Louise Sims were among the directors of the chorus.[187]

The Colorado College Conservatory was extraordinarily fortunate in having as its director Rubin Goldmark from 1895 to 1901. With Mr. and Mrs. Leslie Skelton, he formed the Musical Club, which brought to Colorado Springs artists of the highest quality. About 1910, the American Music Society was formed.[188] The erection of the new Fine Arts Center provided an excellent auditorium for the presentation of musical programs, and the Colorado Springs symphony orchestra now gives its concerts there.

[181] *Ibid.,* pp. 137-138.

[182] *Ibid.,* pp. 138-139.

[183] *Daily Central City Register,* May 19, 1871 and July 13, 1871.

[184] *Golden Transcript,* June 4, 1873.

[185] *Gunnison Daily Review-Press,* September 23, 1882.

[186] State Historical Society Pam. $\frac{366.}{5}$

[187] *The Lookout,* pp. 81-83-136.

[188] *Ibid.,* p. 128; also Ormes, *op. cit.,* pp. 333-337.

In an article of this length many items of interest and many fine musicians must be omitted of necessity. However, certain notable composers who did much of their work in Colorado should be mentioned. These include: Frederic Ayres, who lived in Colorado Springs from 1902 until his death in 1926; Rubin Goldmark; John H. Gower; Edward Danforth Hale, appointed Dean of Music at Colorado College in 1895; Francis Hendriks, whose compositions have been played by leading symphony orchestras of America and Europe; Henry Houseley; Frederick Neil Innes; Albert G. Pearson of Colorado College; Edward J. Stringham; Charles Wakefield Cadman; and Paul Whiteman.

CHAPTER XVII

History of Higher Education in Colorado

GEORGE WILLARD FRASIER, *President*

and

WILLIAM HARTMAN
*Assistant Director of Public Relations
Colorado State College of Education*

THE history of higher education in Colorado is the history of people with vision and indomitable courage who realized that the region would some day become one of the most important states in the union and one of the most desirable places in which to live.

The pioneers also realized that in the new country there must be provisions for education. Consequently several state and private institutions were organized and have subsequently more than fulfilled the expectations of their founders.

Today the schools of higher learning in Colorado rank well among the leaders in the United States and are continuing to grow and develop. The history of the institutions is summarized in the following section.

ADAMS STATE COLLEGE

The Adams State College was authorized by the legislature of 1921 as the State Normal School of Alamosa. Appropriations for a building and provision for its erection were made by the legislature of 1923, which also changed the name to Adams State Normal School.

In the fall of 1924 the property was placed under the control and management of "The Trustees of the State Normal School." The General Assembly of 1927 provided a millage tax (.05 of 1 mill) on all property of the state for general support and maintenance. In 1929 the legislature changed the name to The Adams State Teachers College of Southern Colorado and made appropriations for an enlarged heating plant and for the erection of the auditorium and the south wing of the Administration Building. Succeeding legislatures have made appropriations for building maintenance and operating costs.

The legislature of 1935 provided a tax levy for a ten-year building program from which, with federal grants-in-aid and a revenue bond issue, two residence halls for students, the gymnasium, and the north wing of the Administration Building were constructed.

In 1945 the General Assembly changed the name from The Adams State Teachers College of Southern Colorado to Adams State College of Colorado.

During the college year of 1944-45 a fifth year of work, leading to the Master of Arts Degree, was added. Provision was also made for the organization of a two year, or lower division, program leading to the Associate in Arts Degree.

Colorado A. & M. College

The history of the college goes back to 1870, when the Council and House of Representatives of Colorado Territory passed an act

Adams State Normal School, Alamosa

establishing an "Agricultural College of Colorado." With the adoption of the state constitution by Colorado in 1876, the college became a state institution. Students were first registered on September 1, 1879, and first graduated in 1884.

In 1879 the Colorado General Assembly accepted the terms and grants of the federal Morrill Act of 1862 and the institution became one of the Land-Grant Colleges, with part of its support provided by the federal government. Other acts of both the state and federal governments up to the present time have increased the income and enlarged the facilities of the college, including provision for the Agricultural Experiment Station and the Extension Service.

The State Board of Agriculture, controlling body of the institution, created by the general assembly in 1877, consists of eight members appointed by the governor of the state, the governor, and the president of the Colorado Agricultural and Mechanical College, who are members *ex-officio*. From time to time the duties of the board have been increased. It now acts as the board of control of the Colorado Agricultural and Mechanical College, the Agricultural Experiment Station, and the Extension Service. The Eighteenth General Assembly in 1911 made the Fort Lewis School at Hesperus, near Durango, a part of the Colorado Agricultural and Mechanical College system.

Colorado College

Colorado College received its charter from the Territorial legislature of Colorado and was open for instruction in 1874. The college was founded by Congregational churches and established in Colorado Springs. There has been no interruption in the work of the college since its founding.

The early presidents were clergymen; Reverend Jonathan Edwards, Reverend James Dougherty, and Reverend E. P. Tenney served as presidents in the order indicated from 1874 to 1885. There was no one designated as president from 1885 to 1888. William Frederick Slocum was elected president in 1888 and served until 1917. Clyde A. Duniway was president from 1917 to 1923, Charles Christopher Mierow from 1923 to 1934, and Thurston J. Davies from 1934 to the present time.

The oldest building on the campus, Cutler Hall, bears the date 1878. The total number of buildings, including residences for students, now numbers twenty-seven.

Schools of engineering and forestry were established early in the century, but were discontinued as separate units in 1931. Colorado College has always maintained its distinctive character as a liberal arts college. In addition to the generally accepted fields of instruction in languages and literature, the sciences and mathematics, and the social sciences, the college has developed a strong department of music and the fine arts, the latter in cooperation with the Colorado Springs Fine Arts Center.

Colorado School of Mines

The Colorado School of Mines is the oldest institution in the United States devoting itself entirely to the training of mineral engineers. In 1868 Bishop George M. Randall made provision for a school of mines when he established his Episcopal University one mile east of Golden. The territorial legislature made its first appropriation in 1870 for a building for the Randall school. This building was completed in 1871, and instruction in assaying and chemical tests was begun at that time.

The Colorado School of Mines was legally established by an act of the territorial assembly, approved February 9, 1874. At this time Bishop Randall transferred his department of mines, consisting of one building and five acres of land to the territorial authorities.

The general management of the school is vested by statute in a Board of Trustees, consisting of five members appointed by the Governor of the State. The financial support of the School of Mines is derived from annual mill levies and special appropriations.

Students of the Colorado School of Mines have opportunities to study the occurrence of minerals and the processes of recovering and refining them. Within a short distance of Golden are mines, mills, smelters, oil fields, and petroleum refineries to which the students take inspection trips to observe practical producing and refining methods.

COLORADO STATE COLLEGE OF EDUCATION

The history of Colorado State College of Education can be traced back to the early days of the Greeley Colony, which was established on the banks of the Poudre River in 1870.

In his first circular calling for volunteers to join his colony, Nathan C. Meeker said that there should be "* * * a church, a town hall, a schoolhouse, and the establishment of a library. * * *" When the colony was only eighteen years old, a movement was started to establish a state school for the education of teachers. As a result there was created by the legislature the State Normal School. On April 1, 1889, Job A. Cooper, governor of the state, signed the bill.

With continued growth, a constantly widening field of activity, and increased authority in the granting of advanced degrees, the name was changed first, from the State Normal School to Colorado State Teachers College, then in 1931 to Colorado State College of Education.

The college is under the management of a Board of Trustees of seven members, six of whom are appointed by the governor of the state. The state superintendent of public instruction serves *ex-officio*.

Colorado State College of Education offers curricula leading to the degree of Associate in Arts, Bachelor of Arts, Bachelor of Music, Master of Arts, and Doctor of Education.

REGIS COLLEGE

Regis College is conducted by the Jesuit Fathers. Its foundation was laid as far back as 1877, when Las Vegas College was opened in New Mexico. In 1884 Most Reverend Joseph P. Machebeuf, Bishop of Colorado, asked the Jesuits to open a college at Morrison, Colorado. Sacred Heart College there had Father Dominic Pantanella as President of the institution. By 1887 it was evident that Las Vegas and Morrison were not suitable locations for institutions of higher learning, so with the encouragement of Bishop Machebeuf ground was broken for the new Sacred Heart College in North Denver and the college was opened on September 5 of that year.

The college was authorized to confer degrees by Section 1 of an Act of March 28, 1889. In 1890 the first graduates received degrees. The college was incorporated on November 27, 1893. On April 19, 1921, the Articles of Incorporation were amended so as to change the name from "College of the Sacred Heart" to "Regis College."

Modern developments began in 1922 when a new wing was added to the Administration Building and continued in 1923 with the erection of Carroll Hall for use as a dormitory building and class room building.   In the fall of 1945 a Downtown Division was opened and evening classes were made available to men and women in the fields of business and general education.   The Golden Jubilee of the college was celebrated in October, 1938.

Men's Dormitory, University of Colorado, Boulder

UNIVERSITY OF COLORADO

The University of Colorado was incorporated by an act of the First Territorial Legislature of Colorado in 1861, and the location fixed at Boulder.   In 1872, three public-spirited citizens of Boulder gave the university fifty-two acres of land adjoining the city.   Two years later, the legislature appropriated $15,000 to the university, and with the contribution of an equal amount by the trustees, plans for the erection of a building were made.

In 1875, Congress "set apart and reserved for the use and support of a state university" seventy-two sections of public lands.   The constitution of Colorado, adopted in 1876, made the "University at Boulder" an institution of the state, thus entitling it to the land appropriated by Congress, and provided for its management and control.

The institution was opened September 5, 1877, with two departments, Preparatory and Normal.   The former had an enrollment of 36 men and 16 women, and 3 men and 11 women composed the student body of the Normal division.   The faculty numbered four.

In 1891, the Normal department was dropped, and in 1907, the Preparatory department was discontinued.

At present, the university offers courses in the following fields: arts and sciences, medicine, law, engineering, nursing, business, education, pharmacy, home economics, journalism, physical education, and fine arts. There are more than 11,000 students taking courses offered by the University of Colorado. Of this number, 5,687 are on the campus, 1,200 are in evening classes, and over 5,000 are correspondence students. There are 300 faculty members.

University of Denver

The University of Denver is a privately endowed institution, with campuses at Denver's Civic Center, and in University Park on the city's southern edge.

Located in a compact area adjoining the Civic Center, are the Colleges of Business Administration, Law, and Librarianship; the Schools of Art, Public Administration, and Hotel and Restaurant Management; the Denver Junior College; the Department of Government Management; the Air Center; and the Bureau of Business and Social Research. The School of Music is housed in its own building a short distance away.

Situated on the spacious University Park Campus are the Colleges of Arts and Sciences, Engineering, and Graduate Study; the Schools of Education, Speech, Social Work, and Theatre; the Social Science Foundation; the National Opinion Research Center; the Hill-Young Speech Clinic; the University Civic Theatre; and the Chamberlin Observatory.

Faculty members number nearly 600, and students approximately 6,000.

Under the leadership of John Evans—the Territory's second governor, a physician, inventor, and founder of Northwestern University—Colorado Seminary was opened November 14, 1864, by a small group of Methodist ministers. The University of Denver was incorporated in 1880 as the degree-granting body of the institution, and charged with academic training. Colorado Seminary continued as the property-holding and managerial unit of the University's affairs. Trustees of the two corporations are identical.

Removal to a campus in University Park from the Seminary's original site at 14th and Arapahoe Streets was effected in 1892. In 1945, professional education in law, business administration, and public administration was centralized on the Civic Center Campus, thus assuring close relationships between the University and the commercial, legal and governmental interests of the city.

Western State College

Western State College was established in April, 1901, by the Colorado General Assembly as the State Normal School at Gunnison, but the actual beginning of the first school year was not until September 12, 1911.

As the school grew and the demand for a broader program increased, its functions as a "teacher training" institution were not sufficient. The General Assembly on March 30, 1923, changed its name to Western State College of Colorado.

Western State College began as an institution offering two years of college work in teacher training, but in 1920 its program was extended to four years and the Board of Trustees authorized it to grant the Bachelor of Arts degree. In 1921 the Board authorized

Western State College, Gunnison

the extension of the curriculum to five years and the college to award the Master of Arts degree and the life certificate. The pre-professional curricula have been added since the late '30s because of increased demands for this type of college program from prospective students.

In April, 1915, the college was admitted to full membership in the North Central Association of Colleges and Secondary Schools as an "institution primarily for the training of teachers." In March, 1929, it was given full membership in the "College and University" class of this association. This rating was further defined in 1939 as a "liberal arts college with a professional school of education."

BACA-PROWERS JUNIOR COLLEGE

The Junior College of Southeastern Colorado was organized in the spring of 1937. The first registration was held in September of that year. The college is located in Lamar, a city of about 5,000 people. Lamar is in the center of a large and fertile farming area in the Arkansas River Valley and is the trade center of southeastern Colorado.

On May 6, 1946, the electors of Baca and Prowers Counties voted to form a junior college district of the two counties. With the opening of the fall term of 1946-47 the junior college was known as Baca-Prowers Junior College.

Colorado Woman's College

In 1886 Dr. Robert Cameron, pastor of the First Baptist Church of Denver, and several Baptist laymen, took the initial steps to found Colorado Woman's College.

The first Board of Trustees' meeting was held November 15, 1888. At that time Governor Job A. Cooper set aside twenty acres of land for the campus. The State of Colorado granted a charter on November 14, 1888.

The cornerstone of the first building was laid March 25, 1890. John Evans, first territorial governor of Colorado and founder of Northwestern and Denver Universities, gave the address.

The building was completed and opened as a senior college under the presidency of Mr. Jay Porter Treat in 1909. The large north section of Treat Hall was added in 1916. The president's residence, a $20,000 edifice, was completed in 1922. The college became a junior college in 1920.

Foote Hall, a quarter-million dollar dormitory, was erected in 1930. Re-landscaping of the campus was completed in 1931. Poplars, a fourteen capacity dormitory, was acquired in 1928. Ground breaking for Porter Hall was held December 9, 1937. The building was completed in 1938. Quince Hall, housing twenty students, was purchased and remodeled for use in 1945.

The cornerstones were laid on April 25, 1946, for the Mason Activities Building, a $240,000 structure, and the Pulliam Dormitory, to cost $200,000.

La Junta Junior College

In 1939 the voters of La Junta School District No. 11 voted $30,000 in bonds to be used to partially finance a junior college building and equipment. The PWA granted $50,000 to finance a $75,000 building. The cornerstone was laid in April, 1940. The Junior College plant consisted of an administrational-classroom building and a vocational industrial shop. In 1940 the National Youth Administration authorized the construction of a $10,000 industrial arts shop.

The college opened in September, 1941, with fifty-eight students enrolled for regular college work, and, in addition, an adult program was started with fifty-one men and women participating.

After a period of reduced enrollments during the war, the college enrolled a total of 286 students during the year of 1945-46. The college. will benefit from a bond issue in excess of $400,000 passed early in 1946. An addition is now under construction to the main building. Enrollment for the summer term of 1946 exceeded the regular terms.

A Class "B" Veterans' Guidance Center has been approved and contracts under Public Laws 16 and 346 are in operation.

Mesa Junior College

Mesa Junior College was started in September, 1925, when the governor of the state approved the Junior College Bill that had been passed by the legislature, "Providing instruction in the arts and sciences and in such branches of knowledge as may be designated by the board of trustees of said institution."

Classes were started in September, 1925. Dr. L. L. Hyde was the first dean of the college.

Financial support of the college until 1937 was from civic organizations and private individuals. In 1938 the college first received county and state aid.

Before the war a $300,000 administration-classroom building was completed to accommodate an increased enrollment.

Pueblo Junior College

Pueblo Junior College is a vital part of the educational system of Pueblo County and the State of Colorado. The college was organized in the summer of 1933 as the San Isabel Junior College, later known as the Southern Colorado Junior College. Classes were first held in September, 1933, in the county court house with sixty students attending. Seventeen of these students were graduated in 1935.

In 1937 an act of the General Assembly made the college a part of the public school system supported by county-wide taxes. The name was changed to the Pueblo Junior College.

In September, 1937, the college occupied a new $50,000 building constructed by popular subscription and federal aid on a ten-acre campus.

In 1938 the taxpayers authorized a $120,000 bond issue to be added to a $90,000 PWA grant for additional facilities including a library, classrooms, laboratories, and a gymnasium. Since its beginning the college has had a continued growth in enrollment and educational facilities. All bonds have been retired.

Sterling Junior College

The Sterling Junior College, originally a private institution, became tax-supported in accordance with the state Junior College law in January, 1945, at which time the name was changed from the Junior College of Northeastern Colorado.

The Sterling Junior College occupied its new home, a completely remodeled three-story brick building, for the opening of the fall quarter 1946. Since its organization in 1941 the Junior College has operated in conjunction with the Sterling High School. When fully equipped, the college will have all necessary facilities except a gymnasium and vocational shops. These the high school will provide until other buildings can be added by the college.

Trinidad State Junior College

The Trinidad State Junior College was established by the State Legislature in 1925, and, in September of the following year, enrolled its first students in one year of regular college work. Two-year curricula of regular college were first offered in 1932; the first annual commencement occurred in May, 1933.

With the establishment of Las Animas County as a junior college district in 1937, a levy of .75 of a mill was approved for the support of the college. The same year witnessed the establishment of the Department of Vocational Education, and, in 1938, the college for the first time operated with a separate full-time faculty. A regular two-year course in commercial education was set up in 1940.

In September, 1941, the college occupied its new administration-classroom building, and the following year the new gymnasium was completed. At present construction is under way on a mechanic arts building.

Loretto Heights College

Loretto Heights College was incorporated under the Loretto Literary and Benevolent Institution of Colorado in 1918 and empowered by the State of Colorado to confer degrees.

The institution owes its inception to the pioneer spirit of a small band of noble Sisters of Loretto at the Foot of the Cross, from Kentucky, who crossed the plains in 1864 and settled in Denver when it was only a small town and where not even a railroad gave promise of future progress. There they opened the historic St. Mary's Academy, still a flourishing academy for girls. To those Sisters, who endured all the hardships of the early makers of Western civilization, is due the credit of bringing Catholic education for girls to the territory and later the state of Colorado. During the intervening years their successors conducted primary, intermediate and secondary schools in Denver and elsewhere throughout the state, founding in 1890 Loretto Heights Academy, which was closed in 1940 because of the expanding needs of the College. Loretto Heights College is the only senior woman's college in Colorado. More than 85 courses are offered in art, home economics, journalism, languages, literature, mathematics, music, philosophy, religion, science, social studies, secretarial studies and speech. More than 300 students from 22 states are enrolled at the College.

CHAPTER XVIII

Mining in Colorado

PERCY S. FRITZ

Assistant Professor of History, University of Colorado

THE history of Colorado is most intimately connected with the discovery and development of its mineral wealth. The first white men to visit this region were seeking its rumored riches. The gold rush established its first permanent English settlements. For over half a century mining has been its leading industry. Even today Colorado ranks as one of the leading mineral producing states.

THE BEGINNINGS OF MINING

Neither the Indians nor the Spanish had done any extensive mining in the region which is now Colorado. The reports of Indians who used gold and silver utensils and emerald tipped arrows lured the ill-fated Coronado expedition in the sixteenth century. About the time George III of England was forbidding the British colonists to cross the Allegheny Mountains, a mining expedition led by Juan Maria de Rivera was prospecting and mining in the San Juan Mountains and along the Gunnison. With what success we do not know.

Rumors, however, persisted. Pike on his exploratory trip did not find any gold mines, but did report meeting a trader at Santa Fe who had found some gold as he passed through in 1805.[1] It is interesting to note that just as Indian reports had caused the Coronado expedition to set out, so Indian reports were responsible for the Pike's Peak gold rush. Strangely, these Indians were not members of the Western tribes which roamed the region. A group of Cherokee Indians who had mining experience in Georgia found evidence of gold on the South Platte river while on their way to California in 1850. This find led to the organization of the Russell party which found the first paying placer in Colorado in 1858. A Delaware Indian, Fall Leaf, was responsible for the organizing of another of the first three parties to arrive in the gold rush of 1858.[2]

The beginnings of mining as an industry in Colorado began with the Pike's Peak gold rush. In January of 1859 three discoveries were made. From these three discoveries eventually sprang the three counties of Gilpin, Clear Creek, and Boulder which were the dominant mining regions before Colorado became a state. The first discovery was made on January 7, 1859, at Idaho Springs. George Jackson, who had started out to hunt elk, had no mining equipment along.

---

[1] Z. M. Pike, *Exploratory Travels Through the Western Territories of North America,* 347.

[2] Luke Tierney, et al, *Pike's Peak Gold Rush Guidebooks of 1859,* 59.

To mine his first nugget and half ounce of gold, the frozen gravel had to be thawed by building a fire on it. He dug the gravel with his belt knife and washed it in his treaty tincup with melted snow.[3] About the middle of that month John H. Gregory found a gravel deposit at Black Hawk.[4] The third discovery was made by a group of six men at Gold Hill about eight miles northwest of their camp at the mouth of Boulder Canyon on January 16, 1859.[5]

The objective in the gold rush was gold and little attention was given to other minerals. That silver as well as gold was present in quantity was known as early as 1859. The United States Assay Office in New York assayed some samples of ore furnished by Cronise and Company from the Gregory lode. The specimen assayed at the rate of 10½ ounces of gold and 16¾ ounces of silver to the ton.[6] In September, 1860, a silver lode was recorded at the Ida mine near Empire.[7]

The coal measures along Coal Creek and the banks at Marshall, Colorado, were known in 1859. Individual settlers collected it from the outcrops just as they collected wood for fuel. In 1860 the editor of the *Mountaineer* at Golden called attention to the availability of coal and its advantages as a fuel. The beginning of coal mining as a business existed as early as 1861. Weir and Middaugh were advertising in the *Rocky Mountain News* in 1861 that they were ready to supply coal in any amount on short notice.[8] In 1862 E. L. Berthoud had discovered the outcrop along Clear Creek at Golden.[9] By 1864 Joseph M. Marshall used the coal from his mine in his iron ore furnace at Marshall, Colorado. Here was the first smelting of native iron ore in Colorado.[10] In the same year Anson Rudd of Canon City began to make use of coal in his blacksmith's forge.[11]

Oil springs were discovered about six miles from Canon City by Gabriel Bowen in 1862. From these springs A. M. Cassidy manufactured and sold 300,000 gallons of illuminating and lubricating oil between 1862 and 1865.[12] This was the beginning of the Florence oil field which is said to be the second oil field commercially developed in the United States.

But oil, coal, and even silver, were not what the Pike's Peakers sought. It was gold, and gold alone, which interested them. And thousands turned back because they could not pick up a fortune off the sandy creek beds. The first phase of Colorado mining was dominated by gold.

3 Geo. A. Jackson Diary, January 6-8, in *Colorado Magazine*, XII, 205.

4 Jerome Smiley, *Semi-Centennial History of the State of Colorado*, I, 251.

5 Frank Hall, *History of Colorado*, III, 289-290.

6 *The Rocky Mountain News*, August 20, 1859, 4.

7 *The Works of Hubert Howe Bancroft*, XXV, 493.

8 *The Rocky Mountain News*, November 19, 1861, 2.

9 O. L. Baskin, *The History of Clear Creek and Boulder Valleys, Colorado*, 367.

10 Albert B. Sanford, "The First Iron Manufactory in Colorado," *Colorado Magazine*, VIII, 144.

11 Wilbur Fisk Stone, *History of Colorado*, I, 450.

12 *The Works of Hubert Howe Bancroft*, XXV, 392.

Early in May, 1859, the first gold bearing veins were discovered. Scott's lode at Gold Hill and Gregory lode at Black Hawk being the first. Mr. J. M. Fox of the Leavenworth and Pike's Peak Express Company in a letter dated May 8, 1859, wrote that "I heard this evening that rich quartz discoveries had been made near Boulder Town some thirty miles up in the mountains * * *."[13] William

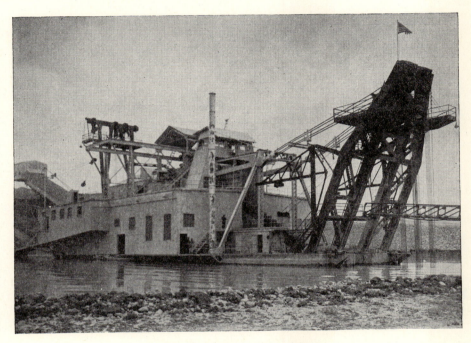

Gold Dredge Near Fairplay

Byers in the May 28th issue of the *Rocky Mountain News* stated that Gregory had discovered his lode on May 6th.[14] These veins of gold bearing quartz were the beginning of deep gold mining in the Rockies.

MINING DISTRICTS AND THE EMERGENCE OF MINING LAW

The most significant achievement of the Pike's Peak Argonauts, next to their discovery of the gold, was their effort to establish law and order by setting up mining districts. For three years between the discovery of gold and the establishment of a territorial government for Colorado, the miners in the region set up their own governments, elected their own officers and established a system of mining

13 Letter of J. M. Fox to John S. Jones, Esq., dated Office of Leavenworth and Pike's Peak Express Co., Denver City, K. T., May 8, 1859, published in the Daily *Missouri Republican,* May 25, 1859.

14 Caroline Bancroft, "The Elusive Figure of John H. Gregory," *Colorado Magazine,* XX (July, 1943), 122.

law. These early districts are especially significant because the rules and regulations which they adopted became the basis of our state and national mining laws. These districts were necessary because the gold regions were in the extreme western parts of Kansas and Nebraska Territories which under the Kansas-Nebraska Act of 1854 were reserved to the Indians. The miners were on United States land on which they had no right to be. There were no sheriffs or law enforcement officers within four hundred miles. If a man discovered a gold mine, how could he protect himself against being jumped by another individual or group? The answer was to do as Gregory and Jackson did.

Jackson very carefully destroyed the evidence of his mining, and covered the spot where his fire had been, then marked a tree so he could later relocate it. When the spring thaws came, he organized a company of friends, promising to lead them to something good. This group agreed to fair and simple rules by which Jackson (according to Spanish custom) was to have two claims on his discovery and each of the others one claim each. The strength of the group was increased as those who came later were permitted to file on an adjoining claim until all promising locations had been taken up.

Although Mountain District No. 1, Nebraska Territory, appears to be the first mining district organized in Colorado,[15] the first documentary evidence we have is the reference in the *Rocky Mountain News* to a meeting of miners at Jackson Diggings on May 9, 1859.[16] As soon as the meeting was organized, three by-laws were adopted: First, that the size of claims should be 50 by 200 feet, second, that they should be staked with at least two stakes and improved within ten days and, third, that the discoverer should be entitled to one extra claim. A permanent secretary was chosen and a committee appointed to draft a permanent constitution by the next meeting a week hence.

Over at Gregory Diggings the miners held a meeting on June 8th and organized Gregory District. This meeting created a typical mining district. They elected a president and secretary to call meetings and record their claims. They adopted eleven resolutions which (1) defined the boundaries of the district, (2) prescribed rules for the acquisition and holding of claims, and (3) provided methods for the settlement of disputes.[17]

Scores of such districts were organized and some of their constitutions were quite long. The Sugar Loaf constitution and by-laws adopted October 31, 1860, had forty-three sections covering fifty-one pages. The Russell District laws and regulations as adopted July 28, 1860, contained seventy-five sections.

The mining districts varied in size from sixteen to thirty-five square miles. Some were rectangular in shape.

15 *Colorado Magazine,* XV, 81-89.
16 *The Rocky Mountain News,* May 14, 1859, 2.
17 *The Rocky Mountain News,* June 11, 1859, 2.

Resolved that this District be called Mountain District No. 1 and that it shall extend two Miles in each Direction from Capt. Scott's Discovery Claim * * *.[18]

Others were bounded by ridges. Gregory District commenced

at the mouth of the North Fork of Clear creek following the divide between said stream and Rallston Creek running seven miles up the last named stream to a point known as Miners Camp. Thence South West to the Divide between the North Fork of Clear Creek and the South Branch of the Same to place of beginning.[19]

The officers of the districts were elected and paid on a fee basis. Most districts had a president, recorder, and constable or sheriff. Some districts felt the need for a surveyor or a vice-president or a vigilance committee.

Rules for the holding of claims were a major part of every constitution. Among the most typical were:

1. "Each person comming in to the District shal be entitled to one clame on each Lead and one Clame for each Lead he may Discover"[20]
2. "Gulch claims [shall be] 100 feet in length and from bank to bank, Lead claims [shall be] 100 feet along the lead and 25 feet on each side."[21]
3. "Any man holding a claim in this Mining District shall work at Least one Day in every ten upon the same untill he shall have Done ten full Days work upon it"[22]

Thus they limited the size and number of claims a single individual might hold, and offered the incentive of an additional claim, which could be held without working, to a discoverer of a new lode. Such simple rules helped to prevent disputes. However, they recognized that disputes would occur and that crimes would be committed.

Several methods for settlement of disputes were usually available. Disputants could plead their case before the president or a board of arbitrators and agree to accept their decision. Jury trial procedure was also provided, the number of jurors varying in the different districts from a 3-man jury to a 12-man jury. In most of the districts appeal from the verdict of a judge or a jury could be made to a miners' court consisting of a general assembly of the miners.

A strong prejudice existed in the early districts against lawyers. Many of the districts prohibited lawyers altogether, except in cases

---

[18] *Gold Hill District Laws of 1859,* revised constitution of July 30, 1859.

[19] Thomas Maitland Marshall, *Early Records of Gilpin County, Colorado, 1859-1861,* 11.

[20] *Constitution and By-Laws of Sugar Loaf Mining District,* October 31, 1860, 7.

[21] *Downieville District Laws,* Book A, July 25, 1859, Art. 5.

[22] *Gold Hill minutes,* July 30, 1859, res. 3, sec. 2.

where the defendant or plaintiff happened to be a lawyer, in which case his opponent was permitted to hire an attorney.[23] Their feeling was concisely expressed in the Ward law "Common Law and Substantial Justice shall be the rule of practice in all cases. No technicalities will be allowed to defeat the ends of justice."

Their punishment of criminals was equally forthright and effective. Murder was punished by hanging. Those found guilty of perjury, removing stakes, jumping claims, or salting mines were fined, whipped and banished from the district. For example, Coral District in Clear Creek County declared that

> Any person found guilty of grand larceny [theft of over $10] shall be fined in a sum double the amount stolen and receive not less [than] fifty nor more than one hundred lashes on his bare back and [be] banished from the District and such other punishment as a jury of six men may Direct.[24]

When the Territory of Colorado was established in 1861 the titles and rights established under the laws of these mining districts were given full validity. The Territorial judges were ordered to adjudicate disputes in accordance therewith.[25]

It was not until 1866 that the United States Congress adopted a national mining law. This first mining law is known as the Patent Law of 1866. It declared the mineral lands of the public domain to be free and open to occupation by all citizens, subject "to the local customs or rules of miners in the mining districts, so far as the same may not be in conflict with the laws of the United States." The influence of the local mining districts can be seen also in the provisions of this Act relating to the size of claims and the method of location.[26]

The law regarding tunnels and tunnel rights illustrates the evolution of these district laws into the law of the United States. In the Gregory District laws of July 16, 1859, is the following provision relative to tunnels.

> When any Company is formed for the purpose of Tunneling for discovery the parties engaged may Stake off record and place Notices on ground two hundred and fifty feet Each way from the Tunnel and running as the Tunnel is intended to run. After that all new leads discovered in Tunneling belong to the Company to that Extent. Claims already taken are to be respected, but New Claims Cannot be within the limits Staked off if work be progressing on the Tunnel. If work on the Tunnel be Stoped for one week at any time the

[23] *Sugar Loaf District Constitution,* May 4, 1861, sec. 15. *Ward District By-Laws,* April 4, 1861, Art. 10. *Hawkeye District Laws,* April 27, 1861. *Independent District Laws,* February 15, 1861, sec. 15.

[24] *Coral District Revised Laws,* July 1, 1861, chap. 6, sec. 5.

[25] *General Laws * * * First Session of the Legislative Assembly of the Territory of Colorado * * *,* 166-168.

[26] 14 *U. S. Statutes at Large,* 251-2 (July 26, 1866).

original Claim shall be forfeited and Shall be again open to Claimants.[27]

Three principles were embodied in this resolution.

(1) That a company engaged in the more expensive task of running a tunnel might claim 500 feet along a lode which they discover instead of the usual 200 feet.
(2) New Claims could not be staked within the limits claimed so long as work was progressing on the tunnel.
(3) Cessation of the work meant forfeiture of the tunnel rights.

The United States in its first mining law in 1866 made no reference to tunnels, but in the amended Act of 1872 it was provided that

> Where a tunnel is run for the development of a vein or lode, or for the discovery of mines, the owners of such tunnel shall have the right of possession of all veins or lodes within three thousand feet from the face of such tunnel on the line thereof, not previously known to exist, discovered in such tunnel, to the same extent as if discovered from the surface; and locations on the line of such tunnel of veins or lodes not appearing on the surface, made by other parties after the commencement of the tunnel, and while the same is being prosecuted with reasonable diligence, shall be invalid; but failure to prosecute the work on the tunnel for six months shall be considered as an abandonment of the right to all undiscovered veins on the line of such tunnel.[28]

The aims of the district law were embodied herein. The tunnel right was twice as long as the length of a claim on the surface allowed by the law of 1872 (3,000 feet instead of 1,500 feet). New locations on the line of the tunnel were declared invalid. And cessation of work for six months meant forfeiture of its rights to undiscovered veins. The amount of the vein which belonged to the tunnel owners was not specifically stated in the Federal law. The Department of Interior ruled that the line of the tunnel meant only the actual width thereof. The Colorado Territorial law specified that those working the tunnel were entitled to 250 feet each way from said tunnel on each lode discovered. Some tunnel builders claimed 1,500 feet on each newly discovered lode. Obviously it was a matter which the courts would have to decide. And it is interesting to note that the Supreme Court reasoned along similar lines and upheld the same principles as the miners of Gregory District.

The first case occurred in connection with the Corning tunnel at Gold Hill.[29] The case in non-legal language was as follows. The law[30] permitted a tunnel company to project a tunnel 3,000 feet long

27 Thomas Maitland Marshall, *Early Records of Gilpin County, Colorado, 1859-1861*, 15.
28 Section 4 of Patent Law of 1872 (May 10, 1872).
29 18 Colorado 510-524, Ellet *v.* Campbell.
30 Sec. 2323 *U. S. Revised Statutes.*

into the side of a mountain for the purpose of searching for ore. Any vein which they thus discovered in driving their tunnel belonged to them for 750 feet on each side of the tunnel. On September 18, 1872, George C. Corning located a tunnel claim, posting a stake every 200 feet along the course of the proposed tunnel and ran lines of stakes parallel therewith 750 feet on each side, and marked all four corners with monuments as required by law.[31] On February 3, 1875, the Corning Tunnel Company cut a rich vein 594 feet from the mouth of the tunnel. They immediately posted a notice at the mouth of the tunnel claiming 750 feet each way of this lode which they called the Bonanza lode. They recorded this discovery with the county recorder.

Eleven years later Cyrus Taylor and David F. Campbell discovered on July 10, 1886, a lode on the surface east of the line of the tunnel bore. They named this the J. L. Sanderson lode, sank their discovery shaft and recorded their claim in accordance with the law. Then they applied for a patent and Ellet, owner of the Corning tunnel, adversed. The question at issue was: Must a discovery in a tunnel also be located on the surface by means of a discovery shaft and valid surface location? The case was tried in the district court at Boulder which held it must. On appeal to the Colorado Supreme Court this decision was reversed. The court held that the purpose of the tunnel law would be destroyed if, after spending thousands of dollars to discover veins not visible on the surface, their rights to 1,500 feet on such veins were not protected as against later locations made on the same vein on the surface.

Ten years later the case was appealed to the Supreme Court of the United States which upheld the decision of the Colorado Supreme Court. The court said that "the discovery of the vein in the tunnel, worked according to the provisions of the statute, gives a right to the possession of the vein to the same length as if discovered from the surface, and that a location on the surface is not essential to a continuance of that right."[32]

In Enterprising Mining Company *v.* Rico-Aspen Mining Company the Supreme Court of the United States (1897) held that all lodes, undiscovered at the time the tunnel location was made, belonged to the owners of the tunnel. Thus were upheld the essential principles of the Gregory District law on tunnels.

EARLY MINING METHODS

The development of a great industry can be traced through the evolution of its tools. Mining is an ancient occupation. Yet in Colorado the methods used advanced from the most primitive to the most

---

[31] This tunnel law caused considerable resentment among the miners and prospectors. Although surface prospectors might seek lodes on this tunnel location, except directly above the bore, the practical effect was to withdraw from exploration a very large block of land (1,500 by 3,000 feet) on which no one would wish to search for mineral as long as the tunnel company did $100 worth of work annually.

[32] 167 *U. S. Reports,* 116-120, Campbell *v.* Ellet.

scientific and complex, all within the memory of men still living. Colorado miners and metallurgists have shown great inventiveness and ingenuity in adapting their tools to the conditions which confronted them.

The man who rushed across the plains to acquire a gold mine had only the most simple equipment. A pick and a shovel to loosen the gravel and a pan to wash the gold-bearing sands was the usual outfit. The pan is the most primitive method for the recovery of gold. A placer

Underground Mining by Hand Methods. Two Miners at Left are Drilling with Double Jack, while the Third from Left is Drilling with Single Jack

miner's pan is made of sheet iron. It is circular in shape about 10″ to 18″ in diameter at the top and about 2″ to 2⅜″ deep. The sides slope about 35 to 40 degrees from the horizontal.[33] The pan is significant because it illustrates the basic principle underlying most of the later methods for the recovery of placer gold and free gold found in veins. The whole theory of operation of the pan is based on the principle that gold being the heaviest material will settle to the bottom. Gold is nearly twice as heavy as lead and nearly eight times as heavy as the quartz and rock where it is usually found. A shovelful of gravel is placed in the pan. Water is added or, more generally, the pan is partially submerged in the water of a creek. As the pan is agitated the mud and sand can be washed over the edge of the pan while any particles of gold, if present, will sink to the bottom.

---

[33] C. F. Jackson and J. B. Knaebel, *Small Scale Placer Mining Methods.*

A placer miner can pan about one half a cubic yard of gravel a day. That is slow, hard work, so means were devised to increase the per man per day output. The rocker, the long tom, and the sluice-box all served the purpose. The rocker is somewhat like a child's cradle with a metal sieve inside. While one man shovels in the debris, another adds water and rocks the cradle back and forth. The long tom is an inclined trough or chute with a screen in the bottom. It is wider at the bottom than at the top and has a small stream of water flowing over it. The sluice-box is a long trough from eight to twelve inches wide and from six to ten inches deep, and often one hundred feet or more in length. On the bottom are removable riffles or cleats to catch the gold particles as a strong stream of water washes the gravel along. Each of these methods depend on the fact that the heavy particles of gold will gravitate to the bottom as the water loosens them from the mud, dirt, and rocks. These methods were applicable to placer mines—where the pure grains of gold were loosely mixed with mud and sand.

When veins were discovered, another problem arose. The gold-bearing quartz had first to be crushed before the gold could be washed out by panning or sluicing. An ingenious crusher was devised at Gold Hill. It was simply a huge granite boulder with a depression hollowed out with a pick. In this hollow they crushed their ore to a fine powder and then took it to a stream and washed it in a gold pan. This first Colorado quartz mill now serves as a pioneer monument near the public library in Longmont.

Miners who had had experience in Mexico and California introduced the arrastre. This consisted of a circular trough or basin about ten feet in diameter and made of stone, or wood with a stone floor. A horse or water-wheel was used to turn a cross-arm to which were attached huge boulders. The grinding action of the two stone surfaces would pulverize the disintegrated quartz just as the ancients used to grind their grain. The first arrastre in Colorado was started in July, 1859, by Lehmer, Laughlin and Peck at the mouth of Gregory Gulch.[34]

By the fall of 1859 stamp mills had already begun to be freighted across the plains. The stamp mill crushed the ore by means of series of stamps weighing four hundred to nine hundred pounds each. The stamps were raised by means of a cam-shaft and fell of their own weight. The crushed ore then flowed over a trough or table covered with a blanket or over a copper plate coated with mercury to trap the precious metal. Some of the early stamp mills were of wood and were run by water power. The first steam stamp mill was started by Prosser, Conklin and Co. in Gregory District on September 17, 1859.[35] A large fifty stamp mill was imported from Grinnell, Iowa, by the Niwot Mining Company at Ward in 1865. It was on the road for four months.[36]

[34] O. J. Hollister, *The Mines of Colorado*, 103.
[35] O. J. Hollister, *The Mines of Colorado*, 103.
[36] O. J. Hollister, *The Mines of Colorado*, 268.

In the rich placers and in the veins near the surface these methods worked satisfactorily. But as the mines became deeper, more complex ores were encountered. These defied recovery by means of crushing in arrastres, stamp mills and the process of amalgamating with mercury. James W. Taylor in his report on gold and silver mining east of the Rockies said that less than twenty per cent of the assay value of the pyritic ores was being recovered by 1866.[37]

Mining in Colorado Territory

The Pike's Peak gold rush had brought enough people to the region to warrant a government of their own. In 1861 Colorado Territory was created by Act of Congress. Counties were organized. An assembly was elected. A mining code based on the laws of the mining districts was adopted. The titles acquired under the local district laws were validated.

But this alone could not stop the slump in the mining industry. The refractory ore, the hostile Indians, and the Civil War in the States made the first years of the Territory poor indeed. Immediately after the Civil War three things occurred to bring about a great mining revival.

The first stimulus to a mining revival was the passage of the Patent Law of 1866. By this law the mineral lands of the United States were thrown open to all citizens for exploration. Still more important, if one was successful in finding a valuable mine he could obtain clear title thereto by developing the mine to the extent of one thousand dollars, which was later reduced to five hundred dollars. Renewed incentive was thereby given to the prospector. Capital too could now be interested. And mining had reached the stage where more expensive machinery and chemists and metallurgists were needed. Capital was willing to take the risks once the United States assured them title to the hidden riches they might find.

The second stimulus to a mining revival was the solving of the problem of the refractory ores. Foremost in this development was the Boston and Colorado Smelting Company. Nathaniel P. Hill, a professor of chemistry at Brown University, was engaged to apply his scientific knowledge to the ores in Gilpin County. He visited Colorado and then took samples to the best metallurgists in England and at the School of Mines in Freiburg, Germany. In 1867 he built the experimental plant at Black Hawk which was commercially successful on those ores which could stand the high costs. The ores were crushed, roasted, and finally fused in a reverberatory furnace until "about ten tons of mixed ores produced about one ton of matte." Wood was the fuel used in all operations.[38]

Eventually the cost of fuel was a major factor in the company's building the new and larger smelter in 1873 at Argo, Colorado. The

[37] J. Ross Browne and James W. Taylor, *Reports Upon the Mineral Resources of the United States* (1867), 345.
[38] T. Egleston, "Boston and Colorado Smelting Works"; A. I. M. E. *Transactions*, IV, 284.

Boston and Colorado Smelting Company was a leader in the concentration of gold, silver and copper ores until it closed its doors in March, 1910. One of the major causes for its demise was the scarcity of copper ores in Colorado's production which placed the smelters using lead as a base in a better competitive position.[39] The Boston and Colorado Smelting Company employed, besides Hill, other pioneers who contributed much to the early development of the smelting industry. Professor Herman Beeger, one of their metallurgists, has been called "the father of smelting in the West."[40] Professor Richard Pearce, who came to Colorado from the School of Mines in Truro, England, built and developed many new principles at the Argo plant.

The adaptation of the smelter to the rich, but refractory, ores of Colorado was a necessary preliminary to advancement. The achievement occurred simultaneously with the discovery of the rich silver lodes. This combination ushered in the second great phase of Colorado mining, which was the silver phase.

The third stimulus to a mining revival was the discovery of very rich silver lodes. On September 14, 1864, the first paying silver mine in Colorado was discovered about eight miles above Georgetown.[41] This precipitated a rush to the Argentine district. Then two days before Christmas in 1869 the Caribou lode was discovered about five miles west of Nederland. It was from the ores of this mine concentrated at the mill at Nederland that the silver bullion bricks which paved Grant's pathway into the Teller House were made. On May 1, 1872, the second deposit of tellurium found in the United States was discovered near Sunshine, Colorado, in the Gold Hill district. This discovery was named the Red Cloud. The discoverers, unable to afford an assay, took their samples to the assayer at the Denver Mint. He was so impressed that he showed it to the Territorial geologist, Professor J. F. L. Schirmer, who identified the mineral as tellurium. The surface ore assayed $19,652 of gold and $2,282 of silver per ton.[42] After the rich gold placers of California Gulch had played out, the advent of the smelter caused a few to persist in trying their luck. This led to the discovery of the rich lead carbonates in 1874. And when Colorado became a State, few of its citizens were aware that it was on the threshold of the greatest rush in its history. A few log cabins suddenly became a city of 15,000 population. In 1879 Leadville was the smelting center of Colorado with sixteen smelters with thirty-four furnaces in operation.[43]

The discovery of the Leadville deposits brought new problems of mining law. The first federal mining law in 1866, based upon the laws of the mining districts, limited the miner to the vein he had discovered. But as mining became more expensive, the demand arose

39 *Biennial Report of State Bureau of Mines for the Years 1909-10,* 10.

40 Richard Pearce, "Progress of Metallurgical Science in the West." A. I. M. E. *Transactions,* XVIII, 56.

41 Charles W. Henderson, *Mining in Colorado,* 32.

42 A. Eilers, "A New Occurrence of the Tellurides of Gold and Silver," A. I. M. E. *Transactions,* I, 317.

43 *The Works of Hubert Howe Bancroft,* XXV, 546.

to give all the minerals which might be found within the boundary lines to the owner of the claim. The Territorial Assembly of Colorado on February 9, 1866, gave to the owner of a claim all valuable minerals found within twenty-five feet on either side of his discovery lode. Influenced by this principle the United States Patent Law of 1872 granted the apex right. It permitted on a priority basis a claim to be staked on a lode not over 1,500 feet long and from 50 to 600 feet wide along the lode. The locator had exclusive right to the surface and to all veins throughout their entire depth "the top or apex of which lies inside of such surface lines extended downward vertically," even though such veins in their downward course left the side lines of the claim. In common law a grant of lands would convey the surface and whatever minerals underlie the surface within the planes projected downward toward the center of the earth through the boundary lines. The apex right departs from this principle in that it gives to the claimant all lodes, the top or apex of which lies inside these planes. And in addition the privileges of following such veins laterally wherever they go, even if they undercut an adjoining claim or claims. The interpretation of this right has caused the greatest amount of litigation and controversy. The Leadville and Rico areas contain many veins which lie nearly horizontal, which cross each other at many angles, or which are hard to distinguish from beds of ore. Here the question of defining what constituted the "top or apex" was especially prolific of different situations which required judicial interpretation.[44] Only great corporations could bear the expenses of this extensive litigation. Law suits were one of the costs of mining, as well as machinery and equipment.

But some further clarification of the mineral law of the United States resulted. And Colorado judges and attorneys played the leading role.

It was Judge Moses Hallet who in Iron Silver Mining Company v. Murphy defined the apex as "the end or edge or terminal point of the lode nearest the surface of the earth. It is not required that it shall be on or near or within any given distance of the surface."[45]

The case of Iron Silver Mining Company v. Elgin Mining and Smelting Company was one of the most important judicial decisions defining end lines of a claim. This was the horseshoe case in Lake County which in 1885 went to the Supreme Court. The Stone claim owned by the Iron Silver Mining Company was laid in the shape of a horseshoe and by claiming apex rights had undercut the Giltedge claim. The court held that the owners of the Stone mine had exceeded their rights.[46]

One of the greatest apex cases was Del Monte Mining and Milling Co. v. Last Chance Mining and Milling Co. And leading Colorado lawyers, Charles S. Thomas, Wm. H. Bryant, Harry H. Lee, Joel F.

44 Curtis H. Lindley, *A Treatise on American Law Relating to Mines and Mineral Lands,* I, 701-718.

45 Wilson Snyder, *Mines and Mining,* I, 688.

46 118 *U. S. Reports,* 196-209.

Vaile and Edward O. Wolcott, argued the case before the United States Supreme Court. Henry Hershey has called the case "the greatest mining case in all the history of mining litigation."[47] This case originating in Mineral County was decided in 1898.

Some insisted that in view of the judicial interpretation the law should be rewritten to eliminate extra-lateral rights.[48] The advantages and disadvantages were so closely balanced that Congress would take no action.

The original principle still is the general rule, except in two types of cases. All minerals found within the boundary lines of a claim belong to the owner of the claim. One exception is in the tunnel claims discussed earlier. The other is in the case of veins, whose apex lies in some other claim.[49]

Progress Due to Metallurgical Science and Mechanical Invention

In the early days of Colorado mining many mining promoters spoke long and loudly about the great and glorious future of Colorado's mines because "the deeper you go, the richer the vein." Now it sometimes was true that a vein was wider and richer below the surface than at the surface. As a general statement it was not true and the fallacy was pointed out by those interested in the progressive growth of the mining industry.[50] On the other hand, it was a fact that the deeper the mines became the more costly became mining operations. What hope or future then was there to Colorado mining with the rich deposits of ore being exhausted and the expenses of mining tending to increase? The answer was in the development of better and cheaper methods. Metallurgical practices were improved. New processes were invented. Hosts of patents and inventions vied with each other and the best survived and the mining industry continued to grow.

Some notion of the vast progress made can be obtained by comparing the average recovery of gold per ton of ore. A careful estimate by Hollister in the 1860s gave the average yield in Colorado by means of the stamp mills as twenty-five dollars per ton. That was in the days when stamp mills were losing more than half the gold in the ore.[51] In 1925, when recovery was nearly 100 per cent, the Bureau of Mines estimated that the average recovery per ton of ore was 0.330 ounce of gold. That was approximately $6.82 per ton.[52] In other words modern metallurgy has made it possible to mine at a profit much leaner veins and even rework many of the old mine dumps. Improvements in placer mining were equally impressive. The miner with his gold pan in 1859 washed about a half cubic yard of gravel a

47 Baker and Hafen, *History of Colorado*, III, 1030.
48 C. W. Purington, "Do the Geological Relations of Ore Deposits Justify the Retention of the Law of the Apex," *Economic Geology*, I, 572.
49 Charles H. Shamel, *Mining, Mineral and Geological Law*, 247.
50 *Mining Review*, December 13, 1875, 105.
51 Ovando J. Hollister, *The Mines of Colorado*, 348.
52 *Mineral Resources, 1925*, I, 702.

day. In 1941 the South Platte Dredging Company built a dredge at Fairplay which was rated as being able to wash 17,000 cubic yards per day.[53]

Gold is found in two forms. Some is free gold or gold in a pure state which can be recovered simply by separating it from the sand or quartz in which it is found. Gold also occurs in physical or chemical combination with other elements. It is this latter form which attracted all sorts of patented and unpatented processes for the concentration and recovery of the gold. As early as 1862 the Keith desulfurizing process[54] was patented. It was a process whereby the finely crushed ore was roasted in a furnace until all the volatile substances were driven off and the gold melted into fine globules which amalgamated readily with mercury. The right to use the process was sold for $5,000. It was used by several mills, including the Mammoth Mill at Black Hawk. This process together with many others was described as a "miserable and expensive failure" in 1871.[55]

There are four fundamental chemical methods employed in metal extraction: (1) amalgamation, (2) roasting, (3) chlorination, and (4) cyanidation.

Amalgamation was known to the early gold seekers and is based upon the chemical affinity of mercury for the precious metals. Whether in the gold pan, in the sluice boxes, or on the copper plates in a stamp mill, the mercury would readily combine with any free gold or silver present. The amalgam, heated in a retort, would readily give off the more highly volatile mercury which could be condensed and re-used.

The presence of sulphur hinders the action of the mercury. And it was the fact that many of the Colorado ores contained sulphur that caused great losses in the stamp mills. Sulphur, however, burns readily. Thus *roasting* was the next method adopted. Many processes, like the Keith, were developed for the more efficient roasting of the ores until all the objectionable sulphur was removed.

The *chlorination* process is based upon the fact that if, after crushing and roasting, the gold ore was subjected to the action of chlorine, it would form a soluble gold chloride. The gold could then easily be precipitated from this solution in the presence of iron. The source of the chlorine was at first common salt. The Caribou Mill at Nederland used about 100 pounds of salt to a ton of ore. In 1875 they used 1,374 barrels of salt.[56] Far from a railroad, transportation of the salt alone was an important item of expense.

Another process based on the affinity of chemicals for each other is the *cyanide* process. If the crushed ore is mixed with a solution of potassium cyanide a soluble potassium gold cyanide is formed. The gold can be readily extracted from this solution with zinc or by electrolysis. The first real reference to the use of cyanide in mining

[53] H. W. C. Promell, "Colorado Attracts Another Large Bucket-Line Dredge," *Engineering and Mining Journal,* CXLII (October, 1941), 35.

[54] O. J. Hollister, *The Mines of Colorado,* 350-351.

[55] *Rocky Mountain Directory and Colorado Gazeteer* (1871), 231.

[56] Frank Fossett, *Colorado* (1876 ed.), 383.

which I have found is that made by Fossett in 1879.[57] Colorado was the first state to introduce a patented cyanide process. The Gold and Silver Extraction Mining and Milling Company, owners of the McArthur-Forrest patents of 1889-90, were active until 1893 when they were purchased by a Scotch corporation. In 1894 the American Cyanide Gold and Silver Recovery Company was incorporated in Denver for the advancement of the American dioxide-cyanide process.[58]

A battle royal was staged between the chlorination and cyanidation processes in the newly discovered Cripple Creek district.[59] Cripple Creek ushered in the third phase of Colorado mining which like the first was dominated by gold. The progress of metallurgy, however, kept the production of other metals high. More of the by-products of gold mining were recoverable at a profit. The cyanide process was especially good for the treatment of the lower grade ores of the Cripple Creek district. The richer ores went to the smelters. And it was generally used in the treatment of tailings. The use of cyanide is more dangerous and, if the ores must be roasted, may not be more economical. The cost of transportation of the chemicals (even when sulphuric acid and bleaching powder were used instead of salt) in the chlorination process was exceedingly high. Chlorination required 35 pounds of chemicals per ton of ore in 1895, while the cyanide process required only 2½ pounds.[60]

Many mechanical improvements also were developed in Colorado. James Douglass had Colorado in mind when he said that "the West has been the most fertile field of inventions by miners and metallurgists, by reason of its great and varied mineral wealth," locked securely in lean ores, located far from fuel and building materials, and extracted under wages much higher than in Europe.[61]

In 1878 Henry Bolthoff patented the Bolthoff-Boss Pulverizer. This was actually a ball mill claimed to be able to do the work of an eighteen stamp mill. It was a revolving cylinder about five feet in diameter containing about 1,000 pounds of balls. It was fed ore and water from a hopper running through the center.[62]

Colorado's development of the stamp mills was so distinctive that they were referred to as the Colorado mill. Mills preferred in Colorado had a deep mortar, and a long slow drop. The stamps dropped 30 to 40 times per minute as compared to the 90 per minute

[57] Frank Fossett, *Colorado* (1879 ed.), 228.

[58] Robert B. Turner, "Cyanide and Chlorination in Colorado," *Colorado Bureau of Mines Report for 1897,* 127.

[59] Compare William E. Greenwalt, "Chlorination in Colorado," *Engineering and Mining Journal,* LXXVIII, 668-670 and 821 and Philip Henry Argall, "Metallurgical Progress in Colorado", *Mining and Scientific Press,* vol. 100, 35-40.

[60] George A. Packard, "The Cyanide Process in the United States", A. I. M. E. *Transactions,* XXVI, 710.

[61] James Douglass, "Summary of American Improvements and Inventions in Ore-Crushing and Concentration and in the Metallurgy of Copper, Lead, Gold, Silver, Nickel, Aluminum, Zinc, Mercury, Antimony and Tin," A. I. M. E. *Transactions,* XXII (1893), 321.

[62] Frank Fossett, *Colorado* (1876 ed), 168, describes the invention which led to this patent.

stroke in California.   A finer screen was used.   The Bobtail mill crushed the rock to a fineness of 200,000 particles to the solid inch, about double the fineness of the California mills.[66]

The first use of a power drill in mining in the United States was in the Burleigh tunnel at Silver Plume in 1869.   Charles Burleigh invented this rock drill.   He first used steam, but soon developed a compressed air machine for power.[67]

One of the great inventions in the history of mining was the water drill.   Since its invention in 1903 the use of the water drill has become standard practice throughout the world. John George Leyner,

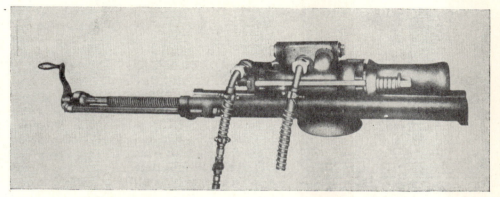

(Photo Courtesy Ingersoll-Rand, Denver)

Leyner's Drill

the first boy born in Boulder County, was its inventor.[68]   He had already developed the hammer drill when he conceived the idea of the water drill.   Through a hollow steel drill he passed a jet of water and air under pressure.   Three practical advantages resulted.   First, the water cooled the steel and prolonged its life.   Second, the compressed water and air kept the hole clean, enabling faster drilling. Third, and most important of all, was allaying of the great scourge of mining—rock dust.   That dread occupational disease variously called phthisis, silicosis, or miner's consumption was largely caused by inhalation of rock dust in the mines.   The water drill has contributed much to the saving of human life.

In 1903 Arthur R. Wilfley of Denver patented[69] his concentrating table which he had invented at Kokomo in Summit County in 1895. As the finely crushed ores from the stamp mills flowed across the Wilfley table the metals of varying specific gravity flowed in distinct

---

[66] A. N. Rogers, "The Mines and Mills of Gilpin County, Colorado," A. I. M. E. *Transactions*, XI, 34.

[67] Frank Fossett, *Colorado* (1879 ed), 396.

[68] U. S. Patent No. 739551 (September 22, 1903), and U. S. Patent No. 756972 (April 12, 1904).   According to Albert M. Leyner, his brother John George was born one mile from the mouth of Left Hand canyon on August 20, 1860.

[69] U. S. Patent Nos. 719,401 and 719,402 (January 27, 1903).

streaks and could be collected separately. The Wilfley table has practically supplanted the Frue-Vanner concentrating table which had been used since 1877.

Another outstanding advancement in the history of mining in Colorado began in the 1880s. That was the adoption of electricity. In 1885 Eugene Alfred Cowles patented an electric furnace for the reduction of zinc ores.[70] The first application of electricity in the mines of Colorado was in July, 1888. The Aspen Mining and Smelting Company built the first electrical hoist in America at their Ventura mine.[71] Manager Fred G. Buckley adapted a 7½ H.P. street car motor geared to the hoist which was used to draw back up the tunnel incline the ore cars, which when loaded came out by gravity. Their electric power was generated 6,000 feet from the mouth of the tunnel by a 50 H.P. 500-volt Edison dynamo operated by a Pelton jet-propelled water wheel. Ingenuity and adaptability is characteristic of a successful mine operator. To lessen the noise, and to reduce leakage of current and liability to shock, the iron pinions in the armature shaft were replaced by rawhide pinions. The advantages they noted were the fact that electricity could be carried longer distances with less loss than either steam or compressed air. It required less space and it did not vitiate the air in the mine. This same firm in July used the first electric diamond prospecting drill in the State.

The Wilfley Concentrating Table

In 1890 the Caroline Mining Company near Ouray used electricity to operate their pumps in their Virginius mine at an altitude of 12,700 feet. They built their Revenue tunnel and mill to operate by electricity even down to an electric locomotive.[72]

In 1891 the San Miguel Consolidated Mining Company of Telluride supplied power to the mills in the district. They changed from direct current to alternating current because it was somewhat cheaper at long distances. They also furnished light for the town of Telluride. By 1897 the Telluride Power Transmission Company had

---

[70] Charles W. Henderson, *Mining in Colorado*, 144.

[71] M. B. Holt, "Electricity in Mining, as applied by the Aspen Mining and Smelting Company, Aspen, Colorado," A. I. M. E. *Transactions*, XX, 316.

[72] Irving Hale, "Electric Mining in the Rocky Mountain Regions," A. I. M. E. *Transactions*, XXVI, 410.

established a record for the United States by transmitting power seventeen miles to the Camp Bird mine.[73]

In 1894 the Silver Lakes mines at Silverton had a thoroughly electrified mine.

By 1896 thirty-five mines and mills in Colorado were using electricity for hoisting and ore reduction. This was only the beginning. The perfection of the electrical furnace was soon to develop an entirely new metallurgy, which ushered in the era of the rare metals and powder metallurgy.

In coal mining, electricity was more slowly introduced because of the more explosive gases found in coal mines and the danger of sparking. The dangers of electricity were gradually overcome so that electricity could be used for ventilating systems, coal cutting machines, and for haulage. The Victor lamp, an electric lamp for use in coal mines, was designed by the employees at the Hasting mine of Victor-American Fuel Company.[74]

Mechanization of the coal mines in the twentieth century is one of the most significant developments. Colorado, which is the largest coal producing

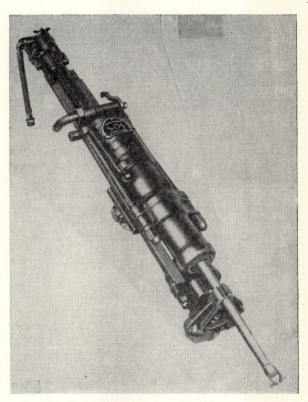

Ingersoll-Rand's Current Successor to the Leyner Drill

state west of the Mississippi River,[75] has kept pace with the mechanical improvements in the industry. In 1913 only 25% of the coal in Colorado was cut by machines. In 1922 one-half and by 1941 over 70% of the coal was cut by machine.[76] Prejudice against mechanization still exists in some quarters. There were 3,000 mules being used in Colorado coal mines as late as 1937 because many miners believed them to be safer in a gaseous mine than electrically driven equip-

73 Charles W. Henderson, *Mining in Colorado*, 12.

74 *15th Biennial Report of the State Inspector of Coal Mines* (1911-12), 7.

75 *Mineral Resources, 1921*, II, 566.

76 *Mineral Resources, 1923*, II, 582, and *Minerals Yearbook, 1942*, 870.

ment.[77] Hay stored underground for the mules was a fire hazard. The fire in the Fremont mine in 1910 was thus caused.

One of the outstanding improvements in modern oil drilling practice was the Zero Hour Electric Bomb. This is a detonator bomb used in shooting oil wells. William J. Cheley and Warren F. Bleecker invented and patented their first bomb in 1925. It was a small torpedo type shell including an electrical timer unit.[78] After a charge of explosive had been placed in the well, the zero bomb was lowered in the well, set to fire the charge at a given time. An improved timing mechanism enabled the operator to delay the blast for a whole day or more if he wished. This gave time to seal the blast in a specific part of the well.

Colorado's Mines at War

The opening of the twentieth century marks a new phase in the history of Colorado mining. It is a period dominated by the so-called rare metals. It is the age of tungsten, molybdenum, and uranium. This new phase had to wait the perfection of the electrical furnace. By means of the electrical furnace, forms of these elements could be obtained which began to have practical applications. Filaments for electric light bulbs, cathodes for X-ray machines, alloys for high-speed tool steel, and coloring matters for the ceramics industry began to create a market. An entirely new metallurgy—a powder-metallurgy—developed.

Many miners in Boulder County had found that "damned black iron" and abandoned mines because of it for a long time, before any one suspected it was tungsten. The first person to recognize this as tungsten was John H. Knight of Ward. That was in 1899.[79] From that time on Colorado produced nearly all of the tungsten in the United States until 1918, when the competition of Chinese tungsten caused the industry to collapse. Since 1940 Colorado has lost its leadership in tungsten to California, Idaho, and Nevada.[80]

In the 1930s tungsten carbide was produced and marks the beginning of a new metallurgy.[81] William Loach of the Wolf Tongue Mining Company at Nederland successfully introduced the use of a tungsten carbide drill instead of a diamond drill for mining.[82] Warren F. Bleecker patented an electric furnace which he assigned to the Tungsten Products Company.[83]

[77] *The Rocky Mountain News,* October 5, 1937.

[78] U. S. Patent No. 1,832,924 (November 24, 1931) ; U. S. Patent No. 1,541,790 (June 16, 1925).

[79] P. S. Fritz, "Tungsten and the Road to War," *University of Colorado Studies,* Series C, Vol. I, No. 2 (1941), 197.

[80] *Minerals Yearbook, 1943,* 673-4.

[81] Gregory Comstock, "Tungsten Carbide, the First Product of a New Metallurgy," *Iron Age,* CXXVI, 1381.

[82] *Mineral Resources, 1931,* I, 183.

[83] U. S. Patent No. 1,469,033 (September 25, 1923).

Molybdenum was another orphan element which was catapulted into fame by a warring world. In *Mineral Resources* for 1903 reference was made to Mr. Hugh Leal of Cresco, Nebraska, developing a molybdenum deposit on Bartlett Mountain, one mile east of Climax, Colorado. Twenty-five years later this became the world's greatest molybdenum mine.[84] In the interim progress was slow. Sixty tons of ore shipped to Denver in 1911 from Summit County did not pay for treatment.[85] During World War I Climax mine produced and

The Primos Tungsten Mill at Lakewood in 1917

the Urad mine near Empire shipped concentrates. Then until 1924 even the Climax mine was idle. In 1939 the Climax Molybdenum Company was producing two-thirds of the world's supply of molybdenum. The molybdenite is mined in the usual way of hard rock mining, with electric locomotive haulage. But caving is also practiced to a large extent, causing whole areas of the mountainside to sink. This is done by blasting out the supporting pillars in undercut areas. This can be done by blasting out a few pillars at a time. Huge areas are sometimes blasted by a big blast. In 1941 over nine tons of dynamite were used in one blast and resulted in caving one and a quarter million tons of ore.[86]

The existence of uranium in Colorado has been known for a long time, but interest in it has been sporadic. Uranium appears mainly

[84] John W. Vanderwilt, "The Occurrence and Production of Molybdenum," *Colorado School of Mines Quarterly*, XXXVII (October, 1942), 38.

[85] *Mineral Resources, 1911,* I, 955.

[86] Claude L. Barker, "The World's Largest Molybdenum Mine," *Mines Magazine*, XXXI, 563.

in two types of Colorado ores — pitchblende, the ore from which radium was first extracted, and carnotite, which is a mixture of uranium and vanadium salts. Carnotite is a characteristically yellow powder found abundantly in the sandstones of Western Colorado. The presence of uraninite in the pitchblende ores of Colorado was noted by Richard Pearce as early as 1871 in the Wood mine in Gilpin County.[87] In 1873 Nathaniel P. Hill of Black Hawk reported: "A discovery was made sometime since, about a mile from Central City of pitchblende. It is now found in large quantities, several tons of ore containing fifty per cent of uranium oxide having been shipped to England. The ore has commanded a price of $1 per pound thus far."[88] In 1900 the Commissioner of Mines reported 306,655 pounds of uranium ore mined in Gilpin and Montrose counties.[89] The interest in the newly discovered element of radium was reflected in this activity. Dr. J. Ohly working with the Mine and Smelter Supply Company of Denver developed a process for recovering these metals in 1901.[90] Mr. A. B. Frenzel of Denver perfected a process in 1902 for the extraction of vanadium oxide.[91] The Haynes process for the extraction of vanadium and uranium was invented and patented by Justin H. Haynes and Wilbur D. Engle of Denver in 1906. The uranium was precipitated with sodium hydroxide.[92] The vanadium process required boiling the crushed ore with alkaline carbonates, drawing off and precipitating with slaked lime.[93] The first production of vanadium in Colorado was made in 1906.

World War I caused a great falling off in mining for radium, the carnotite ores being much more in demand for their vanadium content. But research in radium continued despite the war. A radium reduction plant was established in Denver in 1914 by Dr. W. A. Schlesinger. The National Radium Institute in Denver in cooperation with the Bureau of Mines obtained two tons of uranium oxide from the low grade material in the dumps of the Crucible Steel Mining Company in Long Park, Montrose County. In 1915 the Institute produced three grams of radium at a cost of $37,599 per gram. This new process greatly reduced the cost of radium.[94] In 1916 the Colorado-Gilpin Uranium Company sold 1,018 tons of ore mined from the German-Belcher and the Wood mines near Central City for their radium content.[95] Colorado furnished the largest part of the world's radium from 1913 to 1923. Since then the world's chief source has been the Katanga mines in the Belgian Congo. Colorado ranked

[87] *Colorado Scientific Society Proceedings,* V (1895), 156.
[88] N. P. Hill, "Pitchblende and Tellurium Gold Ores in Colorado," *Am. Journal of Science,* 3rd series, V, 386.
[89] *Mineral Resources, 1900,* 265.
[90] *Mining and Metallurgy,* October 1, 1901, 562.
[91] *Mineral Resources, 1903,* 309.
[92] U. S. Patent No. 808,839 (January 2, 1906).
[93] U. S. Patent No. 828,850 (August 14, 1906).
[94] *Mineral Resources, 1915,* I, 831-2.
[95] *Mineral Resources, 1916,* I, 805.

first among the states of the Union in the value of uranium and
vanadium ores recovered in 1939. In 1943 Colorado produced about
three-fourths of the vanadium in the United States, a total of
7,428,267 pounds valued at $2,610,207. Not until the atomic bomb
helped end the war did our people guess that the vanadium was a
by-product of the frantic race for Uranium 235.[96]

Mill of the Fifty Gold Mines Corporation at Black Hawk

HISTORY REVEALED BY PRODUCTION RECORDS

The history of mining in Colorado is a story of gold rushes and
ghost towns. It is a continuous series of booms and depressions
followed by new booms and the inevitable decline thereafter. These
booms and depressions are clearly observable in the production records. And when the figures are placed in parallel columns on the
same chart the overall growth and progress of mining in Colorado
can be seen. On the statistical chart[97], I have so arranged not only
the figures for gold and silver, with the industrial metals lead,
copper, and zinc, but have included also coal, oil, and the so-called
rare metals which are a substantial part of the wealth mined in
Colorado.

---

96 *Minerals Yearbook, 1943,* 664.
97 Appendix.

These records reveal a number of interesting things about the progress of mining in Colorado. The rising and falling curve of production is influenced by many complex factors such as the discovery of a great new ore body, like Leadville or Cripple Creek, improved metallurgical practices, like the smelter or the electrical furnace, passage of a law like a tariff bill, the patent law of 1866, or the order closing the gold mines in World War II, and a host of others.

The Gold Rush of 1858-9 marked the birth of mining in Colorado. This first boom lasted only a few years. The exhaustion of the easily worked placer gold, the problem of the refractory ore, the Civil War, and Indian attacks caused the first great depression in Colorado in the early 1860s. The population of the region actually declined.

About 1870 the first great revival of mining occurred. This was due to a number of factors. General conditions were better. The Civil War was over. The Arapahoe and Cheyenne Indians were no longer a threat. The success of the Hill smelter at Black Hawk opened the way for the handling of the refractory ores. The advent of the smelter and the beneficial effect of the Patent Law of 1866 caused a steady rise in production from 1868 to 1871. A decline in lode gold and silver production in 1872 was checked by the discovery of the rich tellurides at Sunshine. The first railroads reached Denver in the summer of 1870. Although many locomotives were wood-burners, they as well as the smelters began to use coal and coke. Branches in a few years were built to the coal fields of Erie, Golden, Marshall, and Trinidad. And beginning in 1871, a phenomenal expansion in the production of coal began.

Then in 1877 the second great boom period in Colorado mining occurred. The Leadville rush was on. The production figures beginning in 1877, attest to the richness of these silver lead carbonate ores. Although the price of lead declined ten per cent, the value of the lead output nearly tripled. In 1879 lead became a million dollar industry and from 1880 to 1892 the value of the lead mined exceeded that of the gold mined. The Leadville boom boosted silver production above $16,000,000 in 1880. About that time the boom aspects began to vanish. Over-speculation, labor troubles, problems of fuel and the declining price of silver brought the inevitable depression. In spite of these depressing factors the State's output in ounces of silver remained rather consistent, staying over 10 million ounces annually.

In 1881 the value of coal produced in the State reached the million dollar mark, by 1882 the two million and by 1885 the three million dollar mark. The railroads pushing into the mountain mining camps, the increased demand for iron and steel, and the impetus given to the smelting industry by the Leadville discoveries were factors in creating this increased demand. In 1885 Colorado became the greatest coke producing area west of the Appalachian basin.[98]

[98] *Mineral Resources*, 1883-4, 157.

In 1885 metallurgists discovered economical ways for recovering
the zinc from the ores. In the first year production of 100,000 pounds
worth about $4,000 was recorded. The output increased steadily. By
1901 zinc joined the millionaire group of metals.

In 1887 an oil boom struck Florence and the production increased
until in 1892 it was valued at $692,160. This Florence field including
Canon City was the sole producer until 1902.

The third great boom in Colorado mining began in 1890. In that
year Congress passed the Sherman Silver Purchase Act. And for
three years silver production climbed and had an annual value exceeding $20,000,000. The disastrous effect of the repeal of that act in
1893 is reflected in the decline in the new mineral wealth produced
in the United States in the following year. The rich new silver mines
discovered at Creede were cut off in their infancy. The value of
silver produced dropped in one year from twenty million dollars to

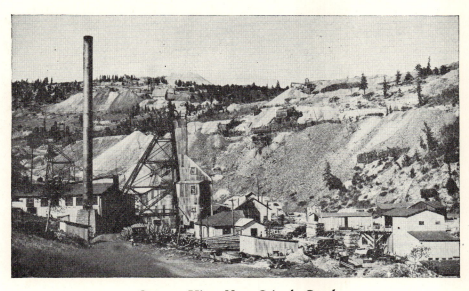

Cresson Mine, Near Cripple Creek

fourteen million dollars. There was a decline in the output of all
the metals except gold. The nation was saved by the discovery at
Cripple Creek. Cripple Creek became the greatest gold camp in
the world. For a few years every one abandoned the old camps
and rushed to Cripple Creek. The fame of Cripple Creek had made
it easier to get capital to invest in Colorado mining. The stimulus of
Cripple Creek was felt in every branch of mining. In 1897 the annual
production of copper passed the million dollar mark. In 1900-1902
gold production exceeded $28,000,000. The annual gold production
alone from 1898 to 1910 consistently remained above twenty million
dollars.

A peak in Colorado mining production was reached in 1900. The total product of Colorado's mines was that year in excess of $56,000,000. Mining is an extractive industry. Eventually the mines will become exhausted. A gradual decline is evidenced in the figures after 1900 until World War I. An important fact which is not revealed by this chart is that Colorado has been steadily growing as an iron and steel center. In 1905 Colorado ranked twelfth among the states in the production of iron ores. Production amounted to 133,471 long tons worth $398,700.[99]

In 1901 an oil boom developed near Boulder.[100] Excitement ran high and many wells were sunk. Colorado's second oil field had been developed. The Florence field still continued to hold the lead down to 1923. But Boulder's production increased until it reached $129,812 in 1909.[101] It held second place until 1923 when the Rangely field, discovered in 1910 in Rio Blanco County, jumped to second place.

A fourth mining boom came to Colorado as a result of the four years of war. In 1915 gold production once again jumped to $22,000,000. England's need to purchase much silver from the United States boosted silver production by 1918 to seven million dollars. The war boosted the production of zinc to seventeen million dollars, lead to five million dollars and copper to two million dollars. The boom and depression above mentioned were most evident in the production of tungsten. The demand for high speed tool steel to manufacture the implements of war caused the price of tungsten to jump from $7.32 a unit in 1914 to $33.98 a unit in 1916. During the war years Colorado produced over two million dollars worth of tungsten annually. The bubble burst in 1919. In 1921-2 production was nil. The reasons for this collapse was the discovery of huge surface deposits in China, the higher wages and increased expenses of mining in this country, and the cessation of the war demand. In spite of a protective tariff the coolie-picked tungsten of China could be shipped here as ballast more cheaply than it could be mined and transported by the United States.

In 1926 oil production hit an all time high of five million dollars. The cause was a trio of outstanding oil discoveries.[102] In 1923 at Wellington, ten miles north of Fort Collins, the Union Oil Company of California brought in at 4,285 feet a gas well which spouted eighty million cubic feet in twenty-four hours. For several days it spouted uncontrolled. Then the oil began to flow. In 1923 the town of Craig began to boom with the discovery of the Moffat dome at 3,805 feet by the Texas and Transcontinental companies. And just west of Moffat the Iles dome was discovered, which was the leading producer from 1938 to 1942. The depression of 1933 reduced oil production to

[99] *Mineral Resources, 1906,* 70.
[100] N. M. Fenneman, "The Boulder, Colo., Oil Field," U. S. *Geol. Survey Bulletin,* No. 213 (1902), 322.
[101] Baker and Hafen, *History of Colorado,* II, 552.
[102] *Mineral Resources, 1924,* II, 396.

$540,000. But it soon recovered. In 1937 the first Tertiary (Eocene) oil in the Rocky Mountain area was found in Moffat County.[103] In 1938 the discovery wells in the Wilson Creek field 45 miles from Craig were completed.[104] By 1940 there were about 190 producing wells in Colorado.[105]

The great depression in the 1930s is clearly reflected in the production statistics of the mining industry. Coal production dropped in 1933 to eleven million dollars, the lowest it had been since 1906. Some of the decline in the coal industry which reached a peak of 42 millions in 1920 is attributable to the growth and competition of the oil and gas industry. Nevertheless the production of petroleum in 1931-33 fell below the million dollar mark which it attained in 1925. Zinc showed the most phenomenal drop. Zinc produced in 1928 was worth $4,359,182 while the product in 1932 was worth $6,540. This slump was only temporary and mining resumed operation that was normal. It is to be noted that the value of gold production since 1934 has been almost doubled with only a moderate increase in the ounces of new gold mined. Before 1934 the mint value of one ounce of gold was $20.67. In 1934 the legal number of grains in a gold dollar was reduced so that an ounce of gold is now legally equivalent to $35.00.

The fifth and most recent boom in Colorado mining occurred in the early 1940s. World War II would undoubtedly have had the same stimulating effect on all kinds of mining as happened in World War I. But the war brought strict governmental control of mining. Price fixing policies, allocation of tools, machinery and manpower, and the determination of so-called strategic materials affected the mining industry profoundly. Gold and silver were not strategic metals and their production was almost entirely stopped. Production of strategic metals, like lead and zinc, were encouraged by price increases and priorities for machinery and labor. Consequently lead in 1943 rose to $2,704,800 and zinc to $9,524,304. To the end of 1941 Colorado produced more silver than any other State. As a result of its decreased output in 1942 and 1943 Colorado, the Silver State, yielded first place to Montana.[106]

The boom was greatest in the field of the rare metals. Colorado produced most of the world's supply of molybdenum and most of the vanadium produced in the United States. Official statistics are still incomplete and shrouded with elements of secrecy. But the production figures already published show that the mining products of Colorado in 1942 reached an all time high. The following is a conservative estimate of those products whose value exceeded one million dollars for 1942.

---

103 *Minerals Yearbook, 1937,* 1011.
104 H. B. Gernert, H. A. True, Jr., and T. O. H. Matteson, "Problems Created by the Mountainous Terrain in Deep Colorado Field," *Oil and Gas Journal,* XL (June 5, 1941), 56.
105 *Minerals Yearbook, 1941,* 1051.
106 *Minerals Yearbook, 1943,* 315.

Molybdenum produced in Colorado			....	$29,000,000[107]
Coal	"	"	"	$23,163,270[108]
Gold	"	"	"	$9,401,945[109]
Zinc	"	"	"	$5,991,990[110]
Sand & Gravel produced in Colorado			....	$3,220,706[111]
Lead	"	"	"	$2,034,254[112]
Vanadium	"	"	" ......(1943)......	$2,610,207[113]
Petroleum	"	"	"	$2,440,000[114]
Silver	"	"	"	$2,201,750[115]
Clay & Clay Products	"	"	....	$1,640,824[116]
Natural Gas	"	"	"	$1,066,000[117]

The official estimate for the total mineral product of Colorado for the year 1942 was $95,278,822.[118]

The history of mining in Colorado affords the best evidence of a still great future. It is an extractive industry and necessarily must yield first place to agriculture and manufacturing. But mining will continue to flourish until the already known reserves of coal and oil are exhausted. How long will it take to extract the last drop of oil from the vast beds of oil shale? Who dare say that Colorado has had its last mining boom? Colorado's uranium and vanadium ores could not find a market in the early 1920s. Hugh Leal was glad to sell his molybdenum claims on Bartlett Mountain for any reasonable price.[119] Phosphate! Titanium! Which reminds me of a statement made by Professor Regis Chauvenet of the Colorado School of Mines in 1890. In discussing the iron resources of the State of Colorado, he referred to the wide diffusion of titanic acid in Colorado. He noted that there were some fine ore bodies which were worthless as iron ore, "owing to the presence in large quantities of this pestiferous enemy of the iron smelter."[120] Who can tell which elements the atomic age will find most valuable?

---

[107] *Minerals Yearbook, 1942,* 658-9 and *1943,* 652. Estimate based on the Climax production alone which mined 73% of U. S. total.

[108] *Minerals Yearbook, 1943,* 51. Based on a tonnage of 8,085,680. The carefully checked records of the State Coal Mine Inspector gives 8,372,683 tons as the final figure.

[109] *Minerals Yearbook, 1943,* 315.

[110] *Minerals Yearbook, 1943,* 315.

[111] *Minerals Yearbook, 1943,* 52.

[112] *Minerals Yearbook, 1943,* 315.

[113] *Minerals Yearbook, 1943,* 664.

[114] *Minerals Yearbook, 1943,* 51.

[115] *Minerals Yearbook, 1943,* 315.

[116] *Minerals Yearbook, 1943,* 51.

[117] *Minerals Yearbook, 1943,* 51.

[118] *Minerals Yearbook, 1943,* 52.

[119] *Fortune,* "Element Number Forty-two" (October, 1936), 107.

[120] Regis Chauvenet, "The Iron Resources of Colorado". A. I. M. E. *Transactions,* XVIII, 267.

Footnotes, 121-126 inclusive, cover a "Comparative Chart of Mineral Production in Colorado from 1858 to 1943," to be found in the Appendix.

---

[121] The production and value of gold, silver, copper, lead, and zinc for the years 1858 to 1923 are by Charles W. Henderson, *Mining in Colorado* (U. S. Geological Survey Professional Paper, No. 138), 69. Since 1923 the *Reports of the Commissioner of Mines of the State of Colorado Bureau of Mines* were generally used. Also from 1923 to 1931 the *Mineral Resources of the United States* were used. From 1932-1943 the *Minerals Yearbooks* of the U. S. Bureau of Mines were used.

[122] Figures for 1900-1906 are from R. D. George, *Colorado Geological Survey,* First Report, 1908, 86. Values are calculated on the basis of the average price per unit reported by the U. S. Bureau of Mines and Geological Survey. For other years the reports in *Mineral Resources of the United States* and *Minerals Yearbook* were used. From 1910 to 1938 a summary is given in *Minerals Yearbook, 1939,* 621. Unit prices 1900 to 1919 are given in *Mineral Resources, 1919,* I, 724. Values after 1923 begin in *Mineral Resources, 1924,* I, 87A. The value for the year 1912 is my estimate based on a unit price of $6.27.

[123] Before 1932 the figures for molybdenum are from *Mineral Resources of the United States.* Since 1932 the reports in the *Minerals Yearbook* were used. Figures from 1924-1930 are the figures for Climax molybdenum—no other production being recorded *Minerals Yearbook, 1941,* 630.

[124] Few official figures on value have been released, because publication would reveal individual corporation returns. From 1925 to 1941 a fair average estimate would be seventy-five cents per pound.

[125] For coal the tonnage and values used were mostly based on the United States Bureau of Mines figures as reported in *Mineral Resources* and *Minerals Yearbook.* Although checked against the annual and biennial reports especial acknowledgment should be made to the following summary statements: U. S. Geological Survey, *Mineral Resources of the United States,* 1921, II, contains chart showing coal produced in the United States from 1807 to 1921 by States. Tonnages for Colorado in short tons, 1864-1913, are in *Minerals Resources, 1913,* II, 824. Tonnage, value, and unit price from 1889-1902 are in *Mineral Resources, 1902,* II, 361. Values for 1864 to 1881 are the estimates given in Baker and Hafen, *History of Colorado,* II, 548-549. These estimates of $2.00 to $2.25 per ton are extremely undervalued. F. V. Hayden reported that the lignite coal from the Marshall mine in 1868 sold for $4.00 per ton at the mine and for $12 to $15 per ton in Denver. It should be noted that the tonnage reported by Thomas Allen, State Inspector of Coal Mines, *Twenty-eighth Annual Report,* 1940, is somewhat higher. This is due mainly to the inclusion of the output of the small wagon mines. Revised tonnage figures for 1935 to 1943 are 1935—5,953,601; 1936—6,868,801; 1937—7,222,092; 1938—5,730,291; 1939—6,002,125; 1940—6,673,359; 1941—7,008,037; 1942—8,131,764; 1943—8,372,683.

[126] Figures for petroleum for 1887-1925 are from *Mineral Resources, 1925,* II, 319; *Minerals Yearbook, 1937,* 1008-09; values are taken from *Mineral Resources.* The figures given in Baker and Hafen, *History of Colorado,* II, 552-3 are more accurate, but vary so slightly that for uniformity the figures from *Mineral Resources* and *Minerals Yearbook* were used in the chart.

CHAPTER XIX

Engineering

Arthur Ridgway
*Formerly Chief Engineer of the Denver and Rio Grande
Western Railroad*

THERE is a thread woven into the social fabric of civilization that is often obscured in the entangling meshes of modern life. For want of a better name, years ago it was called "Engineering," a term nowadays attached so loosely as to need clarification. Engineering in present day parlance is applied science, an implication of the close relation of scientist and engineer. The line of demarcation between is difficult to describe. A scientist may be said to search out and record the laws of the physical world, while an engineer fashions the resources of nature and directs the forces thereof to the use of the people. Since both must be well grounded in the accumulated knowledge of all the physical and associated sciences it often occurs that the fences between their respective fields of endeavor are obliterated.

In the period when life was simply a matter of mere existence, purchased at the expense of the utmost hardship, the efforts of the engineer were confined to conserving the strength and easing the severe physical burdens of the people through the substitution of mechanical for animate energy.

The matter of economics grew more and more important in the scheme of things as time went on and civilization developed, lest there be a consumption of the materials and potential energy of the earth inconsistent with the benefits to be derived therefrom. This resulted in the primary principle of engineering, which serves more than any other in distinguishing the engineer's place among men, namely, whatever is done must be accomplished with the least possible expenditure of material and energy, either human or mechanical. Knowledge of the physical characteristics and behavior of materials under every conceivable condition of use, and the effects of diverse forces potential and actual is his stock in trade. The accumulation of this sort of wisdom has been going on for many years and is being continually augmented by the discoveries of the scientist and the experience of the engineer.

Necessity has always been the prime mover in the growth and development of civilization and many theories have lain dormant until some crying need forces their practical application. With the increase in population and the attendant complexities of life, the problems of the engineer multiply in number and intricacy. The worth of his accomplishments must be appraised in the light of contemporary conditions.

The Place

The story of the birth of the Commonwealth of Colorado is no less fantastic than the age-old myth of the pot of gold at the end of a rainbow, this one arching from the Missouri River on the eastern boundary of Kansas to the fabulous Pikes Peak region of the Rocky Mountains. The bow string was approximately 600 miles or more in length, stretching over a dreary waste of prairies the treasure seekers had to traverse in much the same fashion as slow crawling things of the earth. The lure of a pot of gold for everyone and the feverish anticipation of its possession sustained the plodders in their long trek across treeless plains infested with hostile Indians. The disappointment in finding none was so overwhelming that many braved the dangers of the long return and straggled and struggled back whence they had come. But some stayed and were joined in the succeeding months by thousands of others coming to seek easily acquired fortunes. Thus the Pikes Peak gold rush in 1858, 1859 and 1860 was responsible for the beginning of Colorado.

Once here and here to stay, the general quandary among the determined people was, "Just where are we?" About the extent of their knowledge as to whereabouts was that they were somewhere between Overland Trail on the north and the much older Santa Fe Trail on the south, with a sea of prairies to the east and a formidable barrier of high rugged and mysterious mountains of unknown extent to the west. Their isolation was complete. Undaunted by the lack of exact knowledge of the extent and natural physical features of the terrain over which they felt compelled to set up a provisional government of some kind they descried the boundaries of their Jefferson Territory astronomically, that is by meridians of longitude and parallels of latitude, the most precise of all definitions of large spherical areas. The dimensions were later reduced by 1° (about 53 miles) on the west and 2° (about 138 miles) on the north, and the name was changed to Colorado in the official creation of the territory by Congress. It should be noted this was the first state in the Union to be defined wholly by meridians and parallels and one of the only two among the 48, quadrangular in shape, Wyoming being the other. Even at the date of official creation of the territory the boundaries had not been astronomically determined except at the southeast corner where they had been fixed in the survey of Kansas Territory in 1858. Survey of the boundary on the south was completed in 1868, on the east in 1872, on the north in 1879 and on the west in 1879.[1] It was therefore nearly twenty years before the confines were marked on the ground.

By Act of Congress approved February 28, 1861, Colorado Territory was defined as all that area of the United States between the 37th and 41st parallels of north latitude from the 25th to the 32nd meridian. The same limitations were retained in the admission as a state on

---

[1] U. S. Geological Survey, *Bulletin,* No. 689.

August 1, 1876.[2] The nearest corresponding meridians in full degrees west from Greenwich are the 102nd and 109th respectively, popularly though incorrectly assumed to be the east and west boundaries.

Beginning officially on February 28, 1861, the people of Colorado had for development a piece of the earth approximately 375 miles long and 277 miles wide, or 103,948 square miles in area, practically all of which was public land of the United States. The magnitude was vaguely realized through the laborious means of travel, but no one had the faintest conception of vast and varied resources of the land they had journeyed so far to occupy. Nor had they any idea of the ruggedness and severely surface shattered character of the portion to the west, consisting of some 59,000 square miles as we know now. This place then for the commonwealth can be considered as divided into 43% plains and 57% mountains.

THE FACILITIES

Only those articles necessary to a bare existence could be hauled across the plains with the gold seekers. Evidence of the eagerly sought treasure was found in the sands of the creeks but in such minute and widely scattered quantities as to discourage all except the most persistent. The discovery of lode gold found the people without means for its recovery though the revelation served as the magnetic attraction for the second Pikes Peak Rush which made the first pale into insignificance. These newcomers penetrated the nearby mountains from which Longs Peak, Pikes Peak, and the twin Spanish Peaks stood out like sentinels on the Rampart Range. Their search generally followed the water courses where placer gold could be recovered by simply washing the sand and gravel in pans or crudely constructed sluice boxes.

Steam was the only known mechanical power that could be artifically produced and the overland ox team transportation of boilers and engines for its generation and application was impractical if not absolutely prohibitive. Nor was any fuel available except wood from the forests. Means of crushing and grinding the gold quartz dug by hand from the lodes or veins consisted of arrastres and wooden stamp mills run by home made paddle water wheels of very low power. However, Henderson is authority for the statement that a small steam-powered stamp mill was installed at Gregory Gulch as early as 1859.[3]

The absence of adequate mechanical power at first prohibited the installation of lumber saw mills, and timber for cabins had to be hewn and framed with hand tools from logs skidded or dragged down rough steep slopes.

[2] The longitude of the U. S. Naval Observatory was 77° 03' 02.3" west from Greenwich and therefore the east and west boundaries of the state are respectively 102° 03' 02.3" and 109° 03' 02.3" west longitude.

[3] Unless by other specific citation, authority for statements pertaining to mining and metallurgy will be found in the comprehensive work on the growth and chronology of mining and associated activities entitled, *Mining in Colorado, a History of Discovery, Development and Production,* by Charles W. Henderson, published 1926.

There were no means of intercommunication nor with the outside world except by pedestrian courier or by ridden or driven beasts of burden. The first telegraph line was a single wire running from Denver to Julesburg, installed late in 1863 and connecting at the latter place with the transcontinental line which had been built two years previously. No artificial lighting was available except by candles, oil lamps and firebrands.

Lest an erroneous impression has heretofore conveyed to the effect steam was then the only known mechanical power, let it be said that the age-old force of flowing streams was applied in a primitive way at an early date. A very simple water powered grist mill was built in 1856 near Antonito by early settlers from New Mexico, and possibly a few more crudely constructed mills of the same type were then in the lower part of the San Luis Valley. An American mill was built at San Luis in the fall of 1859 and possibly another about the same time on the Huerfano River. Still another was reported in use on the Fontaine qui Bouille in 1860.[4] These were probably driven by wooden paddle water wheels installed in a flowing ditch or stream, the current thereof being the source of energy. It is obvious however they could be of little use to the people generally because of remoteness and prevailing modes of trade and travel.

The one great encumbrance in utilizing the natural resources was isolation. This situation rapidly improved until the War of the Rebellion necessitated a heavy withdrawal of men and animals from the plains traffic. The crippling effect of the draft, together with a drought shortage of feed and water for animals, the sole source of energy for animate power, resulted in a heavy curtailment of the overland traffic in 1862 and 1863. The severe winter of 1863-1864 and the following spring floods prolonged the depression which, with a further disruption of attempted resumption by plains Indians on the warpath, really lasted until 1865.

In the meantime wagon roads and pack trails were extended into the mountains. These roads were roughly built by individuals or partnerships with little regard for gradients or alinement or anything else constituting an easily traveled way. Notwithstanding tolls were charged for their use by vehicles, ridden animals, pack animals and animals driven loose, they often were impossible of negotiation in bad weather. Little or no work was done to keep them in passable condition.[5]

THE NATURAL RESOURCES

The first and fundamental resource of nature is land—space on which to dwell. Here was a spacious area free for occupancy regardless of whether it provided subsistence from its surface or treasure from its depths. The detailed measurement of the surface began early and strange to say is not yet completed.

[4] Chapter on "Agriculture," in *History of Colorado,* prepared by the State Historical and Natural History Society, 1927.

[5] "The Mission of Colorado Toll Roads," in the *Colorado Magazine,* IX, 161-169.

Immediately on the establishment of the Territory in 1861 a Surveyor General's office was set up in Denver. There had been previously surveyed as early as 1858 a few townships in the southern part of the Territory before the south boundary had been defined. In the first five years of activity public land surveys resulted in the fixing of a number of townships and their subdivision into sections from Pueblo north along the base of the mountains. Seven districts for mineral surveys were instituted and the first official mineral survey was made in Gilpin County in 1867. The incessant demand for the surveying of mining claims necessitated large numbers of U. S. Deputy Mineral Surveyors. Each mining district, localized in a small area or at some particular gulch or mountain, made its own rules governing the size, shape, and position of claims as well as the method of staking them.

It was not until 1872 that the General Land Office issued comprehensive regulations providing for uniformity in size of claims and all other matters pertaining to mineral lands and procedure in cases of disputes and conflict of rights. It is estimated about 75,000 or 80,000 claims have been surveyed in 27,914 separate surveys to date. Of these claims surveyed about 50,000 have been patented.

Township and sectionizing surveys were made when and where there was an urgent appeal for the establishment of authoritative land lines. These surveys are still in progress, yet nearly 2,250,000 acres remain unsurveyed, or 3.37% of the total of 66,538,880 acres within the state boundaries.

Preliminary to the determination of the physical characteristics of a land it is necessary to first ascertain its surface features or in other words "how the land lies." The early explorers sought only information of the surface character contiguous to their routes of travel. Much later the prospectors for gold searched almost every nook and corner of the mountain region. Their reports of the ruggedness were startling enough but they were not correlated with each other and so were valueless to depict what was later discovered to be one of the most deeply scarred areas of like extent in the world.

Eleven years passed after the establishment of the Territory before the Congress of the United States authorized and appropriated funds for the Geological and Geographical Survey of the Territories, under the direction of F. V. Hayden. The field work was undertaken in Colorado in 1873 and completed after six years of the intensive though hurried activity of a substantial force of engineers and scientific experts. Even so, the mountainous portion only was covered and the results were not published until 1881. A map of the triangulation system used to determine the position of surface features and elevations (topography) is illuminating even to the uninitiated. Fifty peaks were selected as corners and the position and elevation of the thousand others obtained from these. Altitudes were generally computed by triangulation from barometric bases but their near approximation to later and more precisely determined figures has been a source of wonder to this day. Thus was located and measured the formidable array of everlasting natural monuments which relegate into insignificance the mightiest and most enduring engineering works of man.

These topographical data were augmented by numerous individual and private enterprise surveys incident to railroad, mining, and irrigation projects. The U. S. Geological Survey, organized in 1879

The Red Cliff Bridge, Rails and Highways Meet at the Junction of the Homestake and Eagle Rivers near Red Cliff

has continued the accurate mapping of selected areas through financial cooperation of the State. Many square miles remain to be covered, only about 30% having been resurveyed in detail.

The position of State Geologist was created in 1872 by act of the territorial legislature, but the first incumbent of that office was not appointed until 1874. It was more than twenty years later or in 1907 that the Colorado Geological Survey was organized with an appropriation to defray the expense thereof, and a year later the first topographical map of the whole State was issued as a compilation of data previously collected by Hayden, King and the U. S. Geological Survey.

The discovery of placer gold in the streams indicated gold bearing lodes in the surrounding mountains. Placer mining rapidly waned and was soon supplanted by lode mining which immediately disclosed that other metals such as silver, copper, lead and zinc were often associated with gold or with each other. As time went on still other metals and non-metallic elements, the usefulness of which was then unknown, were found in chemical combinations throughout the mountain region. Coal seemed to abound everywhere and geologists now tell us there may be as much as 500,000,000,000 tons within state boundaries. Colorado was the second state in the Union to produce petroleum, discovered here in 1860.

Of no less value than the subterranean treasures were the surface resources of nature. The broad expanse of the treeless plains surely should be of great value for grazing or the growing of some sort of food crops for man and animals. True the moisture precipitation in the growing season was insufficient to mature the then commonly cultivated grain and forage vegetation but there were visions of developing strains of drought resisting stands. The valleys of the South Platte and Arkansas were fertile and embraced many thousand acres. Back of the foothills and front range were the great parks, North, Middle, and South where natural hay grew luxuriantly, and the agricultural possibilities of the phenomenal San Luis Valley in the very heart of the Rockies were then as they are today apparently unlimited. On the Pacific slope were the rich valleys of the Colorado and Gunnison and their tributaries. Perhaps the most obviously extensive and valuable surface resource were the native forests of coniferous or needle leaved trees that covered the mountains from the foothills upwards to a fairly well defined tree growth margin along the high peaks and ranges. Many of the innumerable forest products later proved essential to the development of the economic, social, and cultural life of the people.

Most precious of all nature's gifts and vital to human existence is flowing water. It was conspicuous here on the arrival of the earliest settlers but only the passage of years, even decades, could disclose its true value or measure its manifold benefits to a people otherwise richly endowed by nature.

ENGINEERING WORKS

From a mid twentieth century eminence Colorado in retrospect with its varied and unique natural resources is a veritable engineering training school. Here has been developed a high order of technical skill and experience in the application of both fundamental and natural sciences to the betterment of society, and much has been added to the ever accumulating store of technical knowledge. The subterranean resources were predominately attractive, hence the earliest demand for geologists followed closely by mining engineers. Then scarcely separable in point of time came the metallurgists and chemists. The reduction of complex ores and their segregation into precious and various useful metals required equipment and power-driven machinery that could be designed only by mechanical engineers from material which had somewhere, sometime, been dug out of the earth and processed into metal. Contemporaneously over all came the civil engineer, the builder of works and all sorts of structures needed for the activity of the others.

Most of the works of the mining and geological engineers lie underground, and therefore are hidden from view. They consist of tunnels and shafts from which drift tunnels lead. The only visible indication of their magnitude is the size of the waste dump built up of excavated material so low in mineral content as not to warrant processing. However, the dump is not always a criterion, nor are surface structures a reliable measure of the underground works.

It is impossible to collect into a total the varied lengths of tunnels or depths of shafts in the mine workings of the state, scattered as they are over the mountainous area. Some, however, owing to to their length, difficulty of driving, or accomplished purpose merit special mention. The earliest of these notable projects is the Yak Tunnel at Leadville, originally started as the Silver Cord Tunnel in 1886. With its portal in California Gulch at an elevation of 10,330 feet and designed for both drainage and haulage of ore from deep shafts it attained a final length of 4.5 miles in 1910.

Chronologically, the next of the larger mine tunnel projects was started in 1893 as the Newhouse Tunnel and driven to a final length of 4.17 miles in 1910. A noteworthy feature of the Newhouse Tunnel, now known as the Argo Tunnel, is that from a portal in Clear Creek County it extends under the mines in Gilpin County to afford subterranean transportation to the oldest mining district in the state. Over in Gunnison County the Carter Tunnel at Ohio City was started in 1897 and attained a final length of 1.5 miles.

The "Silver San Juan" with its many famous mines in the Silverton-Ouray-Telluride triangle has a tunnel that must be included with outstanding mine workings. The Treasury Tunnel was opened at its portal in 1899 at Red Mountain and driven to a length of more than a mile by 1916. To provide transportation of ore from the lower workings of the Black Bear Mine in the San Miguel district the tunnel was extended in 1943 and a branch 0.75 miles long was driven to serve the Barstow Mine, making a grand total of 3.35 miles of ore transportation tunneling all above an elevation of 10,625 feet. Mention too should be made of the Cowenhoven Tunnel, 2.5 miles long at Aspen, where several other adits of substantial length have been constructed. The longest and most recently constructed mine tunnel is the Carlton, 6.25 miles in length, driven for the purpose of draining a group of deep mines at Cripple Creek.

Time was when the mining regions were dotted with mills and smelters, but with adequate rail transportation for ore, coal, coke and fluxing materials, smelting and reduction works were clustered round transportation centers to which the different kinds of ore and fuel would gravitate, as for example Denver and Pueblo, where at each place several large smelters were grouped. When the Denver and Rio Grande reached Leadville in 1880 there were a dozen smelters operating in the district and eight more just over the continental divide in Summit County. All these and all others but one of the smelters strewn around the mountains drew heavily upon nearby forests for furnace charcoal before coal and coke were available by rail, the exception being at Durango, where coking coal was mined at the smelter site. The Durango, with the Greene Smelter moved from Silverton as a nucleus in 1881, was the most successful of the remotely situated smelters and continued in operation until 1931.

The mining and metallurgical engineers were confronted with unprecedented problems in the saving of values of precious metals in the complex ores. With the lapse of time and continued chemical and metallurgical research new uses were found for old elements, either in the metallic state or in chemical combination, as for example, manganese, tungsten, vanadium, uranium and molybdenum, all produced in the mountains of Colorado. It was not until 1918 that production of molybdenum was begun at Climax (formerly Fremont Pass) literally on the roof ridge of the continent. The mine and mill has an output of 80% of the world's production of molybdenum.

Concentration works and mills were erected for the larger mines and the products shipped by rail for smelting or use direct. Some of these works required aerial tramways from mine to mill or mill to railroad and in some cases both. One of the recently installed and modern reduction mills merits more than passing mention as an engineering work. It is located at the Belden Mine in Eagle River Canon just below Red Cliff. Here a complete concentrating mill with all its associated facilities occupies inter-connected rooms or caverns hewn in the solid rock wall of the canon which is so congested with a main line double track railroad and side tracks as to leave no space in the open for the milling of ore. Many of the concentrating mills were replaced as better or more successful processes were developed or like the smelters were merged into larger plants along with the growth of improved transportation and collection facilities.

In the heyday of mining, say the activities of the '80s and '90s, mining engineers, geologists, metallurgists, chemists, assayers, mineralogists, and associated professionals formed an important section of the population and once being rooted in Colorado soil established the still prevalent fame of the state as a national center for those branches of science and engineering. Many technical processes of concentration, reduction and separation of crude ores originated here.

Prior to the advent of the railroads into Denver in 1870, the mechanical engineers were handicapped in meeting the demands for power machinery and tools because of the difficulty of transporting overland across the plains the ponderous steam generation equipment and heavy mechanism for its application to useful work. Subsequently steam boilers and engines were available for operating ore crushers and grinders, mine hoists, and lumber saw mills. Though not readily at hand, pig, bar, and plate iron could also be obtained at considerable cost. In order to meet the inordinate pressure there rapidly arose iron foundries, and forge and machine shops for making crushing, milling, pumping, smelting and hoisting machinery.[6] Equipping the mines with all such was slow and difficult until rail transportation could be had for at least most of the distance to place of installation.

Before the use of power drills, all tunnel driving, shaft sinking, and rock excavation was performed by striking hammer and hand held drills. Dynamite for blasting was not available until after 1880. The process of drilling and blasting rock to any kind of a pattern was slow and laborious. During the '80s machine drills of the piston type actuated by steam and later by compressed air were used and it was not until the late '90s that the hammer type hollow steel compressed air rock drill was perfected here by Colorado engineers. Air compressors were thus added to power generating machinery. The modest iron foundries and machine shops grew into flourishing engineering works of widespread fame. In late years the production has included the design and fabrication of machinery and equipment for sugar factories and oil refineries. The results of their work and technical skill in making available resources of nature and conserving animate energy constitute an enduring monument to the mechanical engineer.

Brief mention has been made heretofore of the greatest and most vital of all resources of nature—water. Early explorers had reported the dearth of anything like luxuriant vegetation on the areas of the great plains except along the two threads of water courses, the Platte and the Arkansas, and ventured many conjectures as to the utilization of these areas for agricultural purposes. Were there not copious flows of these streams and their tributaries issuing from the mountains? Who knows but at the particular time visited the rivers were abnormally high by reason of unusual accumulation of snow on the peaks and ranges or were swollen by flash floods known now to be of common occurrence. The first settlers learned very definitely after two or three summers had come and gone that there was not enough rainfall during the short growing season to mature familiar agricultural crops.[7] The only alternative in raising food for man and beast was artificial watering of plant life, but there was little previous experience to guide.

Very early in the settlement period small ditches were dug leading from flowing streams to individual tracts of low lying flat land contiguous to the channels. Little or no engineering was required for their construction. The ditches served to demonstrate that a regular and systematic watering as plant growth progressed produced unprecedented yields at harvest. This induced an influx to the already increasing population and hastened an expansion of irrigation on higher lands farther back from the streams. Obviously with different ownership of adjacent tracts of land lying at various elevations above the stream banks no single owner could have his individual ditch, nor

[6] Chapter on "Industrial Development in Colorado," in the *History of Colorado,* prepared by the State Historical and Natural History Society, 1927.

[7] The U. S. Weather Bureau was not established at Denver until 1872.

could irrigation be practicable without partnership, community or group participation in any such project the feasibility of which dictated a main canal flowing above the highest tracts to be watered with branches leading to the lower, much like the reverse of a river system of tributaries. Works of this kind to accomplish the desired purpose could not be constructed except through engineering design, planning, and execution. Here the engineer was confronted with a multitude of technical problems new and foreign to his previous experience. Quantity of water necessary per acre of cultivation, limiting velocities to avoid erosion or silting of channel through various characters of soil, carrying capacity of channels at limiting velocities, alinement and gradients coordinate with the velocities, losses by seepage and evaporation, and flooding and stability of channels in times of storm were only a few of the fundamental and generally common factors that had to be determined for each project.

The oldest of the larger canals was constructed by the Greeley Colony in 1872. This was rapidly followed by others not only on the Platte and its tributaries but on the Arkansas as well. One of the two largest of these is the High Line Canal, constructed in 1879, diverting water from the South Platte near Platte Canon, and carrying it to lands just east of Denver. The other is the Bessemer Ditch, built in 1888, and carrying 400 cubic feet a second from a diversion point on the Arkansas ten miles west of Pueblo to mesa lands lying easterly therefrom.

The Rio Grande del Norte and its tributaries supply water for the San Luis Valley, Colorado's greatest mountain park. Large irrigation canals were built there in the '80s, but because of the almost level floor of the valley few unusual engineering problems were involved in their construction. Indeed irrigation in most parts of the valley requires also drainage ditches.

No large irrigation works were constructed on the Western Slope until the U. S. Reclamation Service undertook the Uncompahgre Project which replaced most of the small irrigation structures previously installed in the Uncompahgre Valley.

A second U. S. Reclamation Service project of large magnitude was constructed in the 1912-1915 period and is known as the Grand Valley project. The main canal is 55 miles long and takes water by direct flow from the Colorado River 20 miles northeast of Grand Junction, where a roller crest diversion dam across the stream stands a prominent feature of the project. A third and very recent project completed in 1941 by the Reclamation Bureau occurs in La Plata County, not far from the Colorado-New Mexico border. The principal feature is a reservoir of 126,000 acre feet capacity formed by an earth and rock fill dam 152 feet high constructed across Vallecito Creek, a tributary of Pine River, which in turn is tributary to the San Juan.

Two general schemes of storage reservoirs for irrigation are common, one involving what might be termed a flood or high water canal leading from natural stream to reservoir and the other a dam

high up in the drainage basin using the natural channel of the stream
for augmenting its flow to supply a needed draft lower down during
the irrigation season.   There are outstanding examples of both
schemes in Colorado. The valley of the Platte from foothills to state
boundary and the Arkansas valley in somewhat lesser degree from
Pueblo to the Colorado-Kansas border are strewn with off stream

*Pine River Project Dam Across Vallecito Creek, U. S. Bureau of Reclamation
in Southwestern Colorado*

reservoirs. The Fort Lyon Canal on the Arkansas, with its system
of reservoirs and distributing canals is the largest of its type in
the state.

Owing to their magnitude and length of natural channels utilized,
reservoirs on the upper reaches of streams warrant particular mention. The South Platte drainage basin has only one of large size, the
Antero on the margin of South Park at an elevation of 8,934 feet,
utilizing 70 miles of natural stream channel. It was built to supplement the supply of the High Line Canal. The following are in the
Arkansas Basin: Sugar Loaf (Turquoise Lake), constructed in 1902,
elevation 9,700 feet, for Colorado Fuel and Iron Corporation's Minnequa Works water supply, using 125 miles of natural channel; Twin
Lakes, constructed in 1896, elevation 9,000 feet, using 175 miles of

natural channel; and Clear Creek, constructed in 1902, elevation 8,600 feet, using 180 miles of natural channel. On the Rio Grande del Norte for irrigation in the San Luis Valley three occur as follows: Santa Maria, elevation 9,500 feet, utilizing 35 miles of natural channel; Rio Grande, elevation 9,500 feet, using 50 miles of the Rio Grande Channel; and Continental, elevation 10,000 feet, using 80 miles of the Rio Grande and tributary. The Western Slope has an outstanding and recent example in the Taylor Park Reservoir constructed by the U. S. Reclamation Bureau, 1937-1939, to provide supplemental water for the Uncompahgre Project. It is situated on the Taylor River in Gunnison County at an elevation of 8,500 feet, and uses the natural channels of the Taylor and Gunnison Rivers for a distance of about 70 miles to the diversion into the Gunnison Tunnel. The dam is of the earth fill type, 204 feet high and impounds 106,230 acre feet of water.

There are about 20,000 miles of irrigation main canals and laterals in the state with an aggregate flow capacity of 140,000 cubic feet a second. The 1,071 reservoirs have a total storage capacity of more than 2,000,000 acre feet.

Seriously involved with the irrigation overdraft from the normal flow of the South Platte is Denver's water supply. Cheesman dam and reservoir, on the South Fork of the South Platte, was completed in 1905 for storage. The dam is notable as an engineering work because of its magnitude and the conditions prevailing at the early date of construction. Built of masonry to a height of 232 feet and impounding 79,000 acre feet of water, it stands as one of the state's monuments to engineering achievement. Another dam forming the Eleven Mile Canon Reservoir, was constructed of concrete masonry farther up the stream for the same purpose in 1932, and with a height of 122 feet impounds 81,900 acre feet of water.

Two striking instances of diversion by tunnel between streams tributary to the same river occur, one on the eastern slope and another on the western. The Laramie-Poudre Tunnel was started in 1902 but not completed until 1911. It is 9.5 feet by 7.5 feet in section, 2.14 miles long and carries irrigation water from the Laramie River to the Cache la Poudre. The Gunnison Tunnel near Montrose is a prominent feature of the Uncompahgre Project, one of the earliest undertakings of the U. S. Reclamation Service. With a section of 12.5 feet by 13.0 feet and a length of 5.79 miles, the tunnel under a maximum depth of cover of 2,157 feet diverts water from the famous Black Canon of the Gunnison into the Uncompahgre Valley canal system. Construction of the tunnel was started early in 1905 and on September 23, 1909, the initial flow of water passed through.

The storage of water from streams on the eastern slope together with the heavy over appropriation of normal flow during the irrigating season makes a complicated procedure of the administration of water decrees and the just distribution among appropriators in accordance with the well established principle of priority of user. The administration of water rights in all the streams of the state is vested in the office of State Engineer, the first incumbent being appointed in 1881. Seven division engineers, one for each of the seven divisions into which the state is divided, constitute his administrative staff. The seven divisions are subdivided into 70 districts, with a water commissioner in charge of each district.

It has long been known through the accumulation of data in measuring the flow of streams[8] that if all the storage practicable were

Cheesman Dam

effected there still would not be enough water on the eastern slope to adequately supply the cultivable lands. Cumulative records have also shown greater annual precipitation on the western slope of the mountains than on the eastern. The flows of western slope rivers, Yampa, Colorado, Gunnison and San Juan are larger than those of the Arkansas, South Platte, Purgatoire and Rio Grande while the areas of cultivable land west of the continental divide is less. The subject of "trans-mountain diversion" has for years been given intensive engineering study and investigation. Indeed the only obstruction in the way of carrying out such projects was one of economics. It was not until 1933 that the first trans-mountain diversion was undertaken. In that year construction of a 3.85 mile tunnel under Independence Pass was started in order to bring water from the Roaring Fork

---

[8] The first station for the gaging of Colorado streams was established by the State Engineer on the Cache la Poudre in 1883.

catchment basin on the western slope to replenish irrigation drafts on Twin Lakes reservoir previously mentioned. The tunnel is at an elevation of 10,500 feet, has a section 8.2 feet in diameter, and was completed in 1935. Before its completion the actual work of effecting another and much more extensive trans-mountain diversion was started. This incorporated in the plan the pioneer tunnel utilized in driving the Moffat railroad tunnel which it paralleled in both gradient and alinement. The railroad tunnel, and of course its pioneer bore, 6.21 miles long was completed in 1928, but seven years passed before the work of adapting the pioneer tunnel to the carriage of water was started early in 1935. This work required the enlarging and lining with concrete to an inside diameter of 10.6 feet the westerly 3.6 miles as a pressure tunnel (maximum static pressure 65 pounds per square inch) to force the water over the "hump" or apex in the gradient on which it was originally constructed. The many other interesting and technical features of the project as well as its magnitude make it one of the outstanding engineering works of the state. Planned and constructed by the City of Denver as an adjunct to its water supply, the tunnel and a part of water collection structures on the west and conduits, channels and other works on the east were completed in 1936. The remaining facilities, including the Ralston dam, an earth fill structure 200 feet high, were completed by the end of 1937. A third water tunnel under the continental divide was completed in 1939 by the City of Denver at Jones Pass to carry water from the Williams Fork drainage area on the western slope to the headwaters of Clear Creek to augment the supply for the city sewage disposal works. The Jones Pass, or Williams Fork Tunnel as it is sometimes called, is 7 feet in diameter and three miles long.

Mention must here be made of the most extensive trans-mountain diversion of water thus far undertaken and now under construction by the U. S. Reclamation Bureau. The dominant feature already completed is the Alva B. Adams Tunnel, 13 miles long and 9.75 feet finished diameter under the continental divide for carrying 550 cubic feet per second of water from Grand Lake in the drainage basin of the Colorado to the Big Thompson, a tributary of the South Platte River. The purpose of the project is to supply additional water for the irrigation of northern Colorado farm lands not now adequately watered and to generate electric power. The Colorado River compact between States having territory in the drainage basin exacts replacement by flood storage of any water diverted out of the basin tending to reduce the normal flow rights of users farther down the stream. The Colorado-Big Thompson project incorporates structures and works to accomplish this purpose. One such structure in the form of the Green Mountain Reservoir and hydro-electric power plant has been constructed on the Blue River 16 miles southerly from its confluence with the Colorado at Kremling in Grand County. The dam is earth and rock fill type 274 feet high and was completed in 1943.

No mention has been nor can be individually made of the innumerable engineering structures that must be incorporated in any large reservoir or canal system for successful and continued operation. The 20,000 miles of main canals and laterals of various flow capacities and the 1,071 reservoirs great and small have involved an incredible amount of engineering planning and execution. Diverson dams, reservoir outlet works, headgates, bridges, culverts, inverted syphons, wasteways, flood protection, are structures common to almost all irrigation systems and each requires particular study and design depending on conditions peculiar to its site and its function in the system.

Irrigation is only one of several benefits accruing to a people from water resources. Still more vital is the domestic water supply for communities. For town and cities in or close to the mountains where gradients of streams are abnormally steep as universally they are in the Colorado Rockies, simple gravity supplies with relatively short aqueducts and a house to house pipe distributing system constitute the entire engineering works. On the eastern slope in some cases mountain storage of substantial proportions is necessary, notably at Denver, with a third of the state's population concentrated in the metropolitan area and where even storage of water brought from the western slope must needs be resorted to. The varied engineering works involved in Denver's water supply and sewage disposal have grown from a small steam pumping plant on the south margin of the Platte near the mouth of Cherry Creek to a coordinated system of many structures of great distinction. Farther eastward out on the plains where watercourses have flatter slopes, pumping from wells or from channel underflows is the usual means of obtaining community water supplies. The Arkansas River furnishes the supply for Pueblo, Colorado's second most populous city, by a direct diversion into settling reservoirs from which pumping plants distribute the water to the people through mains and pipe line systems. Grand Junction, the largest city on the western slope, is supplied by a conduit 20 miles long leading from upper Kahnah Creek to the city distributing reservoir.

Reference has heretofore been made to the primitive means of obtaining mechanical power from the energy of flowing streams. This power had to be applied at the site where it was produced. Generation and transmission of electric power was unknown for decades after the settlement of the territory. It is proper to first record some of the developments in producing electrical energy before continuing the account of engineering as it pertains to water resources.

The Brush system of electric arc lighting was introduced in 1878. Three years later, or in 1881, Denver streets were lighted by 64 arc lights supported on eight steel towers situated at street intersections in the several parts of town. The current was of course generated by steam engine power. Commercial lighting of stores and business houses was effected with arc lights that same year, replacing to some extent lighting by artificially produced illuminating gas which had been available after 1870. The Denver generation for arc lighting in 1881, said to be the first dynamo-electric plant west of the Missouri River, was followed in 1883 by one at Leadville, likewise steam driven.

Incandescent lamps energized by a central electric generation plant were first used in New York City in 1882. By 1887 there were 4,000 or 5,000 incandescent lamps in service in Denver, and as a matter of passing interest it may be added that in 1900 there were in service in the state 48 central lighting stations of 22,180 aggregate horse power and 3,695 arc and 150,255 incandescent lights.

The practicability of transmitting electrical energy to points removed from the place of its generation having been so commonly demonstrated, the mountain streams were vested with a new resource value. The small volume of flow for power purposes was in large measure compensated for by precipitous gradients. High heads could be easily and cheaply attained with the steep gradients, and impulse wheels of the Pelton type were definitely indicated. All of the early installations were of this kind.

The first water power plant for the generation of electricity in the state was installed at Aspen in 1885 for electric lighting, and two years later the capacity was increased to provide power for mine hoists. So far as known this was the first application of electric power for hoisting purposes. Many of the hydro-electric installations in the mountains were small and almost universally employed for public utility lighting, the private and industrial generation being produced by steam plants. However, the outstanding accomplishments in electrical engineering were in connection with water power.

The first known transmission of high voltage alternating current was accomplished near Telluride where a 3,000 volt current was generated at Ames by a Pelton water wheel and transmitted 3 miles to the King mine in 1890. Later the voltage was increased to 11,000 and the transmission distance to over 17 miles. This Telluride plant and its pioneer transmission lines in the rugged and lofty (13,000 foot altitude) mountainous district infested with severe thunder storms in summer and snowslides in winter became a sort of research laboratory and school for high voltage power transmission. The severity of the storms was such that as many as 100 distinct discharges were counted in a single hour.

The most distinguished achievement in water power generation of electricity in the state occurs at Shoshone in Colorado River canon, about ten miles northeast of Glenwood Springs. Water is taken direct from the Colorado River by a diversion dam and carried in a 2.34 mile tunnel driven through the granite wall of the canon and lined with concrete to a minimum section of 10.3 feet by 16.8 feet. The carrying capacity of the tunnel is 1,250 second feet which provides 18,000 horse power for electric generation. The energy produced is transmitted 154 miles to Denver over what is said to be the world's first 100,000 volt line and the longest transmission line of so high a voltage in the United States. Crossing the continental divide at Argentine Pass, with an altitude of 13,628 feet, the conductors are carried on 1,096 steel towers averaging 50 feet in height. The project is not only notable because of its magnitude at so early a date of construction, 1907-1909, but also because of the successful operation and maintenance of the extreme pressure transmission line in very high altitudes for most of its length.

Another remarkable hydro-electric plant of the Public Service Company of Colorado is the Boulder project, also completed in 1909. This consists of the storage of 115,000 acre feet of water in a reservoir formed by a reinforced concrete dam 177 feet high across Middle Boulder Creek at Nederland, a concrete pipe aqueduct 11.7 miles long

High Tension Line Crossing the Continental Divide

from the dam to a small regulating reservoir, and 1.76 miles of steel pressure pipe of 50 inches average diameter from regulating reservoir to the power house where water under 1,820 feet head drives two Pelton water wheels with a combined output of 21,000 horse power. The electric energy generated is transmitted at 100,000 volts pressure 28 miles to Denver. The great height of head under which this plant operates makes it nationally famous.

Altogether there were 72 hydro-electric plants of 100 or more horse power operating in the state on January 1, 1944, with an aggregate capacity of approximately 142,000 horse power and producing 29% of all the electric energy for public use.[9] The very much larger

9 Federal Power Commission.

proportion, 71% was generated by steam power and internal combustion engines. Considering the great amount of electrical energy produced whether by water power or fuels and its widespread distribution and application to the many labor saving devices it is evident electrical engineering has had a large share in bringing the benefits of our natural resources to the people.

The one great and ever present encumbrance in the progress of civilization is the difficulty of moving things, and untold benefit to humans has come through devices employed in the carriage of objects from one point to another. Beasts of burden, draft animals, and wheeled vehicles propelled by animate power have been for ages the common means of transportation.[10] When Colorado became a Territory, steam railroad transportation was only about 35 years old but its phenomenally rapid growth and development in that time had made it essential in advancing the frontiers westward. The dire need for railroads across the plains was only exceeded by the crying necessity and keen urgency of their construction into the mountains. Rails, locomotives and cars were available at the base of the mountains when the plains railroads reached Denver in 1870 and could haul them from eastern points of production. By that time too coal for fuel, forests for timber cutting and stone for building were known to exist in abundance almost everywhere in the mountains. But railroad construction in the Colorado Rockies was a far different engineering work than any previously undertaken. Limitation of gradients and curvature were inconsistent with the ruggedness and abrupt sinuosity of the canons, the excessively steep grades of the watercourses, the precipitous slopes of the mountains, and the very great elevations to be overcome in attaining defiles between peaks and passes over ranges. A thorough consideration of these physical difficulties together with the necessity for limiting investment funds to an absolute minimum led to the adoption of three feet gage of track for mountain railroads. The gage of most American railroads and all trackless vehicles was at that time and still is 4 feet 8½ inches.

The economic theory of railway location had scarcely been heard of and the first engineering achievement to be attained consisted simply in locating routes of practical operation that would result in lowest cost of construction. Compliance with even this elementary principle was not easy. Indeed it was due to the necessity of obtaining a vast amount of advance engineering data that revealed the astounding ruggedness of the Colorado mountains. Young men out of the engineering schools of the East were lured to the state by new and unique problems to be solved and the highest order of engineering talent was attracted by the unprecedented experience. The coordination in design of rolling stock with narrow gage track of heavy curvature and steep gradients was a challenge to the mechanical engineers. And over all, time was the essence of the matter. Sub-

---

10 For the origin, use, and development of all forms of land transportation from the earliest times, see Chapter XV, "Transportation," in the *History of Colorado* prepared by the State Historical and Natural History Society. Familiarity therewith is necessary to appreciate the significance of engineering accomplishments in Colorado.

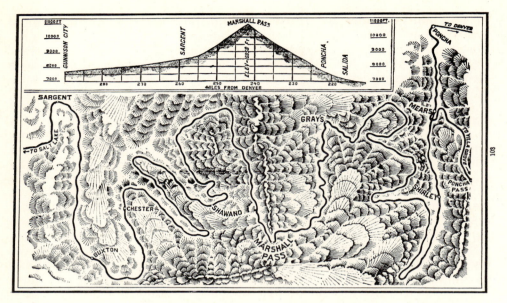

Surmounting the Continental Divide with Rail Transportation at Marshall Pass. Elevation 10,858 Ft. Constructed, 1881

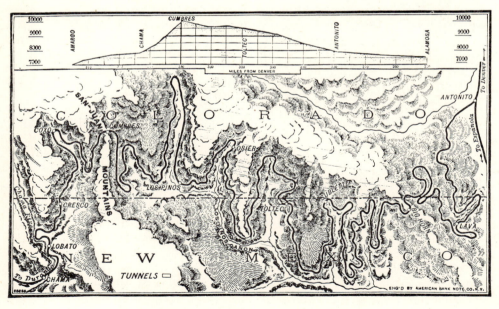

Alignment of Toltec Gorge District
Alamosa-Durango Rail Line Constructed in 1880

stantial utilization of the natural resources could only accrue through rail transportation even though it might be crude.

The existing lines of railroads with their appurtenant fixed structures and rolling stock constitute engineering works, but a mere enumeration of miles of track, quantities of materials moved in the formation of the roadbed, bridges, buildings, service structures, locomotives, cars and other equipment could not convey even the remotest idea of the incredible amount of engineering that has been devoted to their design, construction, maintenance, and improvements through the years.

There are however some distinctive though obscure features that warrant more than passing notice and of which a permanent record should be made. As an entity The Denver and Rio Grande Western Railroad, constituting with its associate The Denver and Salt Lake Railway almost the entire railroad mileage in the mountainous part of the state, is perhaps the most outstanding engineering work in Colorado. The Royal Gorge, Marshall Pass, and Toltec Gorge were early proclaimed as places where notable engineering feats were accomplished. The Royal Gorge is doubtless the most widely known of any of Colorado's natural monuments. The long tortuous ascent necessary in surmounting the continental divide at Marshall Pass, elevation 10,858 feet, even with the maximum permissible gradients has always been a wonder in railway location. The Toltec Gorge section of the Alamosa-Durango line crosses the Colorado-New Mexico border eleven times in its meandering towards Cumbres Pass and the Gorge proper is in New Mexico. This section also incorporates two short tunnels at an elevation of 9,400 feet, constructed in 1880, the first to be driven in the Colorado Rockies. A year later the Alpine Tunnel, 1,780 feet long, was constructed by the Denver South Park and Pacific Railroad through the College Range at an elevation of 11,608 feet. Incidentally it may be mentioned the slow progress in driving this tunnel permitted the Rio Grande to antedate its contemporary rival, the South Park, in reaching Gunnison.

The 1880-1890 decade was the period of greatest activity in railroad construction, an increment of 3,100 miles occurring in those years. No small part of the increase was in mileage of the plains railroads but by far the greater portion was in the mountains. In anticipation of the imminent standard gaging of the Rio Grande, necessitating new construction of the difficult Tennessee Pass-Red Cliff section, or the seriously considered alternative of an entirely new route over the ranges directly west of Denver, coupled with the urgent appeal for rail transportation from Aspen, Lake City, and Ouray, the mountains were literally swarming with engineers of all kinds in the latter part of the decade. The ill fated Colorado Midland was then under construction from Colorado Springs via the historic Ute Pass and South Park to Leadville and on to Aspen, Glenwood Springs and New Castle, an activity that also drew heavily on the available engineering talent. The standard gaging was completed via the Royal Gorge in 1890, leaving the newly constructed Tennessee Pass-Red Cliff section as a notable and enduring engineering work.

One of the most difficult feats in railway engineering was the location and construction of the Denver and Salt Lake Railway (Moffat Road) from Denver west across the Main Range. The many tunnels of varying length (30 in a distance of 20 miles) on the easterly approach to the continental divide are mute witnesses of one of the roughest and most severely gashed regions that could be traversed by a railroad. The most outstanding single engineering structure of the state is the Moffat Tunnel used jointly by the Rio Grande and the Moffat railroads. It was driven through the Main Range at an elevation of 9,239 feet under a maximum cover of about 4,000 feet with a length of 6.21 miles. Construction was effected at public expense through the agency of the Moffat Tunnel District authorized by act of the state legislature in 1922. The first train passed through the tunnel in 1928.

Inseparably associated with the Moffat Road and the Moffat Tunnel is the "Dotsero Cutoff" constructed by the Rio Grande through the incorporated Denver and Salt Lake Western Railroad Company. The Dotsero Cutoff, started in the fall of 1932 and completed June 15, 1934, is the latest example of modern railway construction and incorporates in its route the practicable minimum of physical characteristics adverse to economic operation. Efforts to obtain the shortest distance between the termini, Orestod on the Moffat Road and Dotsero on the Rio Grande, resulted in a line 38 miles long with two tunnels, and nine bridges across the Colorado River. This connecting link between the two older railroads shortened the rail distance via the Royal Gorge and Tennessee Pass 175 miles from Denver to Glenwood Springs and points beyond.

During the 25-year period, 1890-1915, the rail mileage in Colorado increased to a total of 5,700 and then declined through abandonment of little used branches and duplicated routes to somewhat less than 4,500, where it stands today.

Prior to action by the State Legislature in 1913 all public roads were under the authority of the County Commissioners and were built and maintained by property taxation. The engineering such as was required was furnished by the County Engineers. Few roads outside city and town streets were surfaced with other than the natural wayside material. In 1914 there were 1,200 miles of improved roads and 38,600 miles of unimproved in the state. By this time the number of automobiles in use had so increased that the demand for surfaced and improved alignment highways suitable for pneumatic tires and speedier vehicles could be met only by state wide engineering design and construction of new roads or reconstruction of the old. The rapid growth of traffic both in number and weight of high speed vehicles was accompanied by a constantly increasing need for engineering skill and technique. Notwithstanding the power and flexibility of the automobile to negotiate heavy gradients and severe curvature there were of necessity limitations of these route characteristic beyond which the highways would be unsafe and impracticable for public use. The location and construction of highways in the mountains under such limitations is difficult and requires a high order of engineering skill and experience. Outstanding heavy traffic routes are too numerous to mention individually and the whole network of state highways and national park and national forests roads constitute one of the great engineering works in Colorado. There are now 12,400 miles of highways in the state system and 62,600 of county and local roads, or a total of 75,000 miles of roads of all kinds.

The sources of most great western rivers lie in the Colorado mountains and the resultant streams are not of unusual magnitude at the state boundaries. No long bridges are therefore necessary to carry highways or railroads over the streams, but the incredible number and intricacy of structures over rivers and their tributaries, dry gulches, and waterways of intermittent flow form engineering works of eminent proportions. The numerous and fine viaducts of Denver and Pueblo are also permanent monuments to engineering skill.

The airplane came into use as a form of transportation early in the current century and closely following the application of the internal combustion engine to wheeled vehicles. Here at last was a carrying device that needed no land built path for its operation over distances far or near. But it did need take off and landing fields for the start and finish of its flight. Size, weight, and speed of planes increased enormously and it wasn't very many years until runways of great length and stability were required. These, together with signals, illumination, and other facilities and equipment for dispatching and landing of planes form fixed engineering works of great distinction. All of the larger cities in Colorado now have airports, notably Denver, Pueblo and Grand Junction.

Communication wire lines, telephone or telegraph, usually parallel highways and railroads in close proximity but not always. In the mountains a practicable minimum length of line often necessitates a departure from channels of travel. These departures especially in the higher altitudes involve sturdy and difficult construction. The first telephones appeared in Denver in 1878, and in 1889 the famous long distance line was built over Mosquito Pass to Leadville. Today there are 774,000 miles of telephone wires and 29,500 miles of telegraph in the state and even the remotest portions thereof are adequately served.

The growth of mountain rail transportation made possible the production of "home grown" engineering materials of all kinds by the use of native minerals. Outstanding historically and now nationally is the Minnequa Works (established 1880) of the Colorado Fuel and Iron Corporation which produces among the many other ferrous construction materials, steel rails and fastenings, structural shapes, reinforcing bars, merchant bars, plates, bolts, wire and cast iron pipe. The most widely used of all engineering material is cement. It is produced of native Colorado rocks by the Ideal Cement Company with works at Portland, completed in 1902, and at La Porte near Ft. Collins, established in 1929. The aggregate annual capacity of the two plants is 2,500,000 barrels.

Engineering Societies, Institutions, and Education

In conformity with an ancient tenet of scientists providing for full and free interchange of newly acquired knowledge and discoveries, the Colorado Scientific Society was organized in 1882 for the "promotion of scientific observation, record, and intercourse." The charter membership consisted of three geologists, seven chemists and metallurgists, and one clergyman, the late Rev. H. Martyn Hart. Subsequent membership never exceeded 250 and is now about 40, made up principally of geologists, engineers and physical scientists. Thus far the Society has published 14 octavo volumes made up of 340 technical papers, of which many are accompanied by topographical and geologic maps of great value. The publications of the Society are a distinct contribution to scientific literature and through exchange with other scientific associations have found their way to various parts of the world. The Denver Society of Civil Engineers was organized in 1890 and in 1891 published one small volume of technical papers. Subjects treated in this one and only volume pertained to irrigation, railway engineering and the building stones of Colorado. Records of this society have been lost, but apparently it was dissolved after a year or two of activity.

In 1908 the Colorado Section of the American Society of Civil Engineers, instituted in 1852 and earliest of the founder societies, was formed and has continued to grow in influence and professional recognition. The 348th regular meeting was held June 11, 1946. The local membership is 300. The Colorado Section of the American Institute of Mining and Metallurgical Engineers, founded in 1871, was organized in 1913 and now numbers 280 Colorado members.

The American Institute of Electrical Engineers, the last of the four great national engineering societies to be incorporated, was formed in 1884, the third being the American Society of Mechanical Engineers, organized in 1880. However, the Denver Section of the Institute of Electrical Engineers with a present membership in Colorado of 225 was formed in 1915 while the Colorado Section of the American Society of Mechanical Engineers was not organized until 1919 and now has 100 members.

In 1916 the Colorado Society of Engineers, a Colorado incorporated institution, was formed, and because it receives into membership engineers of all branches, its growth and popularity has been remarkable, members now numbering 1,300.

In the last twenty years local sections or chapters of several national engineering societies and allied associations have been formed, the most recent as late as 1944, notwithstanding some of the parent institutions date from many years ago. Notably among these older societies having local chapters here are the American Chemical Society, 1876; American Water Works Association, 1881; American Society of Heating and Ventilating Engineers, 1894; and Society of American Foresters, 1905.

For want of a better and less objectionable form, resort is had to a simple tabular statement showing the number of members in engineering and allied scientific societies in Colorado as of this date thus:

American Society of Civil Engineers	300
American Society of Mechanical Engineers	100
American Institute of Mining and Metallurgical Engineers	280
American Institute of Electrical Engineers	225
American Society of Heating and Ventilating Engineers	65
Rocky Mountain Chapter of the Illuminating Engineering Society	75
Colorado Group of the Society of Automotive Engineers	150
American Society for Metals	225
Rocky Mountain Association of Petroleum Geologists	150
American Water Works Association	55
American Chemical Society	110
Society of American Foresters	250
Colorado Scientific Society	40
Fort Collins Engineers Club	60
Pueblo Engineers Society	110
Colorado Society of Engineers	1,300
All Colorado groups	3,495

There are many duplications in the enumeration of members in these local groups. Not a few engineers are members of two or more associations, and the Colorado Society of Engineers draws from all the others as well as from non-members of any group. Eliminating all such duplications the total number of individuals would not exceed 3,000. It is to be observed that all these Colorado associations include in their membership engineers and geologists attached to the several U. S. Agencies maintaining state or regional headquarters in Denver, namely U. S. Geological Survey, U. S. Bureau of Mines, U. S. National Forests, U. S. Bureau of Reclamation, and U. S. Public Roads Administration.

The quality of engineering practice and public recognition of engineering as a profession was sought to be enhanced through the passage by the state legislature in 1919 of an act designed to regulate the practice of professional engineering. Amended in 1921 and again in 1927, the statute provides for the registration of professional engineers and land surveyors. Eligibility for registration is granted by a State Board after an examination as to fitness and qualifications. The current number of registrants is 600 professional engineers and 50 land surveyors. There are eighteen classes certified by the Board for practicing, almost all stemming from the five main branches of engineering, Civil, Mining, Mechanical, Electrical, and Chemical. Among all the 46 States of the Union that have laws governing the practice of engineering, Colorado's is unique in that all monies derived from initial and annual registration fees in excess of the expense of administration of the act are used for the purchase of technical books and literature. About $60,000 has been spent for this purpose since the law went into effect, which with a nucleus of 2,500 volumes loaned by the Colorado Scientific Society and substantial City appropriations has resulted in a total of 40,000 volumes in the Engineering and Science Division of the Denver Public Library.

Colorado has four institutions of higher learning where engineering degrees can be obtained, The Colorado School of Mines at Golden, The University of Colorado, The Colorado State College at Fort Collins, and The University of Denver.[11]

The Colorado School of Mines was legally established by the Territorial Legislature in 1874. The first engineering degrees were conferred in 1883. Since 1926 only degrees in Mining, Metallurgy, Geology, and Petroleum have been granted. Engineering degrees in other than the mineral industries were conferred prior to that date. A total of 3,129 engineering degrees have been granted by the Colorado School of Mines at the beginning of 1946. A student chapter of the American Institute of Mining and Metallurgical Engineers is maintained at the school.

The Colorado State College at Ft. Collins was authorized by legislative act in 1870 but was not really open to students until 1879. Civil engineering and mechanical engineering students were first graduated in 1890, and in that year curricula were expanded to provide for degrees embracing Irrigation Engineering. Degrees are now granted in Civil Engineering, Mechanical Engineering and Electrical Engineering. Up to 1946 the College had graduated 1,052 students in engineering. The American Society of Civil Engineers maintains a student chapter at the Ft. Collins school.

Incorporated in 1871 by territorial legislature and made a state institution in 1876, the University of Colorado started the School of Engineering in 1893 and conferred the first engineering (Civil) degree in 1897. A total of 3,528 engineering degrees have been conferred since that year. Degrees are now given in Civil, Mechanical, Architectural, Electrical, Aeronautical, and Chemical Engineering and in Engineering Physics. Student chapters are maintained at the University by each of the Civil, Electrical, Mechanical, Chemical and Automotive national engineering societies.

The University of Denver, originally chartered as Colorado Seminary in 1864, first organized engineering curricula in 1918 and

---

11 For the history of these institutions see the chapter on "Higher Education" in this work.

granted degrees in Chemical and Electrical Engineering in 1920. Thus far, 1946, a total of 371 degrees in these two branches of engineering have been conferred by Denver University. World War II has drawn heavily on faculty and student personnel in all these institutions, and in the war years the number of engineering degrees granted declined substantially from the normal. This year, however, will see a full scale resumption of engineering education.

Finally, observing Colorado is well prepared for the education and training of engineers to cope with the unknown future, it seems fitting to close this sketchy review of the first 85 years of its organized existence with the suggestion that much relief from drudgery has accrued to the people, urban and rural, on the farm and in the factory, in the home and abroad, through engineering.

CHAPTER XX

Colorado Libraries

MALCOLM G. WYER
Librarian of the Denver Public Library

OFFICIAL LIBRARIES OF THE STATE

THE official libraries or library services which a state provides to meet its official needs or to carry on library activities that seem important to be under state supervision should receive first attention. In Colorado these include the State Library, Supreme Court Library, State Historical Society Library, the Legislative Reference Bureau, and the Library Extension agencies: namely, (1) Board of Library Commissioners, (2) the Traveling Library Commission, and (3) the Colorado Library Commission which resulted from the merger of the two preceding agencies.

The State Library. A state library in some form was provided for by most states in their territorial and state organization either under constitutional provision or in the first legislature by appropriate legislation. There was not uniformity in the way the library was fitted into the state organization and in each case the arrangement seemed to have been made in accordance with the ideas which influential members of the organizing body possessed concerning a library for the state. In some cases the Secretary of State was made state librarian. In others the library was attached to the educational department. Some times the library was made a separate department but more often it was related in some way to a law library for the use of the Supreme Court. In fact, the early conception of the purpose of a state library was usually to collect state documents for the use of state officials and law books and reports for the needs of the Supreme Court. In Colorado the territorial library was established in 1862 under legislation which named the territorial treasurer as *ex officio* librarian for the territory. The principal duties as outlined were for the librarian to have control of the sale of reports of the Supreme Court and statutes and to arrange for exchange of publications with other states. The early librarians were W. S. Walker, Alexander W. Atkins, A. C. Hunt, John Wanless, Columbus Nicholls, and George T. Clark. Mr. Clark seems to have been the most active in carrying out responsibilities of territorial librarian including the location of quarters for the library, funds to secure books, and preparation of a catalog. The first catalog, issued in 1870, lists about 2,500 volumes in the library. It is interesting to note that Mr. E. L. Berthoud was deputy librarian for a time and helped secure scientific and mining publications. When Colorado became a state in 1876 the state constitution recognized the educational value of the library by naming the State Superintendent of Public Instruction as *ex officio* state librarian. In 1877 the law department of the state library was transferred to the supervision of the State Supreme Court.

The provision which placed the state library under the control of the State Superintendent of Public Instruction was not a very happy choice, probably because the State Superintendents have not had the vision and imagination to realize the importance of library service to educational development in the state. This was not surprising in the early days, but after the educational value of library extension had been demonstrated in other states it was strange that its importance was not grasped by our own *ex officio* state librarians.

In 1876 the librarian's salary was $500. In 1883 it was increased to $1,000, and in 1919, to $1,500, where it remained until 1933 when the Colorado Library Commission was transferred to the state library. The appropriation for books and equipment was also meager until 1933. Furthermore, under the unfortunate system of classifying state expenditures the small funds appropriated for the state library often became unavailable because the state appropriation did not cover the classification in which the library was placed.

Under the statutes the library hours were from 10:00 A. M. to 12:00 noon and from 2:00 P. M. until 4:00 P. M. and these were observed until 1933. It was also the duty of the state librarian to establish and to maintain a state cabinet containing specimens in geology, mineralogy and fossils, with such specimens clearly classified and labeled.

The administration of this library due to the small appropriation, the meagerness of book collections, and the short hours caused considerable dissatisfaction and complaint. This reached the point where Governor Johnson offered to dispose of the state library entirely because of its failure to meet any real need in the state organization and to render a satisfactory library service to the state departments and officials.

This was the situation until 1933 when the Code Bill proposed by Governor Johnson was adopted and transferred the property, the duties, and the responsibilities of the Colorado Library Commission to the State Library. The appropriation was thus increased and library extension with the circulation of traveling libraries became the most important feature of the work of the library. From this time on the State Superintendent was impressed with the importance of the extension library service and she has given her support to these activities of the State Library and to increasing the appropriation. She has also recognized the need of professional supervision of the State Library and has insisted on the importance of library training among the qualifications of the appointment of the deputy librarian. Consequently the appropriations for the library have increased and have reached the amount of $29,208 for the biennium ending July 1, 1947.

Through the united support of the State Superintendent, the Colorado Library Association, the various women's clubs and other organizations, and library supporters generally a comprehensive library bill was adopted by the Legislature in the spring of 1947. This bill will completely change the functions and future development of the State Library since it emphasizes the development of a reference library service for the state officials and the leadership and stimulation of libraries throughout the state on the appropriate unit best adapted to meet local needs.

Supreme Court Library. From 1877, when the law books in the State Library were transferred to the supervision and responsibility of the Supreme Court this collection has steadily grown. The Supreme Court and the several librarians have carried out a constructive policy for building up a comprehensive collection of reports, text books, digests, and the most important publications covering foreign legislation. It is now recognized as one of the strong law libraries in the Rocky Mountain region.

State Historical Society. The State Historical and Natural History Society was established by the Legislature of 1879. One of the functions outlined was the collection of documents, books and other material relating to history and archeology of Colorado. Later the natural history features of the Society were eliminated and whatever scientific materials were considered unnecessary were transferred to other institutions.

The Society has gathered important collections of books, pamphlets, newspapers, magazines, documents, letters, family papers, etc., relating to the early history and development of the state. Much important material is constantly received by the Society as gifts from individuals. The library is now of great value for historical research relating to the state.

In 1943 the Legislature designated the State Historical Society as the official custodian and trustee of all documents, papers, manuscripts, newspapers, books, letters, maps, plans, pictures, photographs, recordings, and other public records and archives and created a department of state archives and public records. This was a most progressive step and it placed the Society and the State in an advanced position concerning the preservation of state archives. Provision also was made for reproducing all official archives and records by microfilm for permanent preservation and microfilm copies were made legal records. Under this authority the Society has appointed a state archivist and is proceeding to microfilm the state records in a systematic program. It has established a modern and up-to-date microfilm laboratory for this purpose.

The Legislative Reference Bureau. The state of Wisconsin demonstrated the value of providing official guidance and assistance to the Legislature in the study of legislation and in the formulating of laws. The Legislative Reference Bureau attached to the Wisconsin Library Commission attracted wide interest and the idea was adopted in one state after another. In Colorado the Legislature of 1927 established the Legislative Reference Bureau which was attached to the office of the Attorney General and which was intended primarily as a bill drafting service with library reference as a secondary function. This agency has been of great value to the legislators and it has contributed greatly to a uniform type of legislation. The staff of the Bureau has secured for its own use and for that of members of the Legislature laws from other states on subjects under consideration and study by the Legislature in Colorado. A weakness of its status is that it is subject to the political changes of the state organization.

Colorado Board of Library Commissioners. This agency was established by an act of the Legislature in 1899 and was composed of five members appointed by the Governor. The function of this Board was to give assistance, advice, and counsel to all free libraries of the state and to give advice and suggestions to communities wishing to establish a free public library. The Board also was directed to secure from each public library an annual report and to publish the important statistics contained in these reports. An appropriation of $500 for the biennium was provided. This agency was established at the request of the librarians of the state but the appropriation was never large enough to carry on any program of library extension. Members of the Board did receive many requests for counsel and advice and this was freely given through the years by those who served the state through their membership. The small appropriation was used for publishing library statistics, traveling expenses, and incidental items. From time to time members of the Board did travel around the state to meet with librarians, library boards, and to discuss difficulties and problems with them, and thus much valuable information concerning libraries and library development in the state was accumulated.

Colorado Traveling Library Commission. At the end of the last century the development of traveling libraries in such states as New York and Wisconsin was publicized with great dramatic effect because these libraries brought books to rural families in remote locations making reading possible where no other facilities had been available. The members of the State Federation of Women's Clubs of Colorado were greatly impressed with the value of these traveling libraries and under the leadership particularly of Mrs. Julia von der Leith Welles, built up a group of traveling libraries and distributed them around the state as a state service of the clubs. The books were gathered, the boxes prepared at the expense of the State Federation and all of the work connected with their distribution and circulation was done as voluntary service by club members. To stimulate the interest of groups in different parts of the state and to add a touch of human interest, traveling library collections were given the name of the club which contributed the books and shipping box. The work attracted so much attention throughout the state and the service was so greatly needed that the Legislature of 1903 established the Colorado Traveling Library Commission to begin work officially on July 1, 1903. The work of the Commission was supervised by a board of five members appointed by the Governor from a list submitted by the State Federation of Women's Clubs.

Since the Traveling Library Commission was the outgrowth of the work of the clubs and since the State Federation was influential in securing the legislation for this agency a feeling of club ownership of the traveling library work grew up.

Small appropriations were secured from legislatures but the demand for traveling libraries was always in excess of the supply and club women devoted themselves faithfully to supplementing the meager funds with gifts and donations and with furnishing personal help for the office work.

In the fourth biennial report the statement was made that the Traveling Library Commission would sponsor an effort to amend the state constitution so that a state library department might be provided in charge of all official library activities of the state. However, nothing seems to have been done in this direction and in later years this suggestion did not seem to interest the Commission.

The traveling libraries were circulated throughout the state, most of them going to small schools, although libraries and small groups were also provided with collections. Thousands of people throughout the state, especially in the rural districts, were able to secure good books through this system of traveling libraries. It was difficult to secure appropriations adequate for the demand in spite of the human interest and personal appeal which indicated the value of this book service. By 1927 the appropriation had only reached the sum of $6,000 for the biennium.

Colorado Library Commission. After many years of unsuccessful efforts, in 1928 representatives of the State Federation of Women's Clubs and of the Colorado Library Association held several conferences and agreed on a plan to merge the Board of Library Commissioners and the Traveling Library Commission in a Colorado Library Commission which would have broader functions than either of the other two agencies. As a result of this agreement the bill creating the Colorado Library Commission was passed in 1929 and the Legislature expressed its approval of this sensible merger by providing a larger appropriation than the two agencies had ever received. In 1933 Governor Johnson proposed his Code Bill which was approved by the Legislature and which abolished many of the separate state boards and commissions. Among these was the Colorado Library Commission which thus passed out of existence and all of its property, duties and responsibilities were transferred to the State Library. While this arrangement increased the activities and services of the

State Library it did not develop the leadership in encouragement and stimulation of library organization throughout the state on the appropriate local unit.

Library Legislation

The library laws of the state are of two kinds, those that relate to the state library, and those that apply to local municipal and county libraries. Both types of legislation have been extremely out of date and unsatisfactory until the Library Bill of 1947 was adopted by the Legislature.

In the states which have achieved the greatest success in developing a system of library service throughout the entire state, the various library agencies have been consolidated in one strong state library organization. In such states the state library usually includes the general library collection, the law library, the legislative reference service, the state historical department and the library extension service. The trend in state library organization is to adopt this centralization of library services and thus form a strong state library organization which can assume leadership and influence in the development of library service for the entire state on the appropriate unit. In Colorado the State Library Association has made many efforts to follow this trend. Several proposals towards this end based on advice from the American Library Association and specialists in public administration, for example the late Don C. Sowers of the University of Colorado, were formulated in bills introduced in the Legislature but these all failed largely because of the constitutional provision making the State Superintendent of Public Instruction *ex officio* state librarian. The opposition was largely from the State Superintendent who maintained that such a program would interfere with her constitutional responsibilities and from the local representatives of the State Federation of Women's Clubs who evidently feared that the strengthening of the state library would lessen their influence in the traveling library work.

Accordingly, the Colorado Library Association prepared a library bill with less far reaching changes for the state library but which defines its objectives and activities clearly in line with the greatest need at the present time. After several defeats this bill was finally passed by the Legislature in April, 1947. This law outlines the duties of the state library as an agency to promote the organization and improvement of local libraries throughout the state and to supply reference service and information to state officials.

If the state library shapes its activities in accordance with this bill, it will become a field agency and a reference library.

The statutes providing for the organization of local libraries whether municipal or county have not been satisfactory. The library Bill of 1947 broadens the provisions for local libraries on the appropriate unit. It states that any tax-levying body may set up a library, or any group of tax-levying authorities may do so, or any tax-levying body may obtain library service by contract. In Colorado many towns are too small to support a library and this law allows a county to operate a library for all the people in its borders and even allows two or more counties to combine in building a library service. Or one county might contract with a public library to extend library service to residents of the county. It offers many possibilities fitted to the needs of the state, and the state library should give the leadership required to inform citizens how simple and easy it is to have effective local libraries.

COLORADO LIBRARIES

Colorado, like most states with few large cities and with a scattered rural population, does not provide adequate library service to its residents. It is estimated that at least 350,000 people in the state are without any library service. There are twelve counties with no free public libraries within their boundaries and as many counties with only one library within the county area. In addition to this most of the libraries in the smaller towns are so restricted in their appropriations that they cannot build up a book stock sufficient for the needs of their own residents to say nothing of offering service to the people outside the boundaries of the town or city.

States such as California and Oregon have found that the only practicable method to provide library service to residents of rural areas is through the county library where a county tax is levied to support a free public library furnishing books to all sections of the county. In sparsely settled cities such as those in Colorado, the town is too small a unit to support active library service and therefore, a larger unit such as a county or group of counties is necessary to secure an appropriation sufficient to maintain active library service.

While there are supposedly thirteen libraries organized on the county unit in the state, only two of these are operated under the county library law and receive regularly tax income in accordance with the provisions of the county law. These two libraries are in Weld and Larimer counties and they have demonstrated the success of library service under county law in Colorado. Without doubt the other libraries will gradually advance to complete support from county tax funds.

The new library bill which is elsewhere described outlines as a major function of the state library, leadership in the promotion and organization of libraries on the county or group of counties unit and it may be expected that county libraries will come into existence during the near future.

It is not possible to give a history here of all of the libraries in the state for that would require a book in itself. These libraries include public libraries ranging from a village of 500 or 600 to the public library in Denver, a city of more than 400,000 people and of course the organization and type of service differs in the various localities between these two extremes. There are also libraries operated by groups for the benefit of the community but without tax support, school libraries, junior college libraries, private college libraries, and libraries in the various state educational institutions. All of these have an important part in the library picture of Colorado and each does its best with the means available to make books accessible in its immediate neighborhood.

The greatest credit must be given to the women's clubs of the state for their part in realizing the need for books and libraries and for organizing libraries to meet this need. Nearly all of the public libraries of the state owe their beginning to a group of women or to a library association formed under the leadership of women. At the present time many of the libraries of the state are being operated by women's clubs, members taking turns in supervising the library and gradually building up the community interest to the point where the administration takes over the support and makes an annual appropriation. And so tribute should be paid to the women's clubs for their part in the development of local public library service as well as in establishing the traveling library collections which furnished books to many places in the state where no others have been available.

During the years of the WPA one of its important fields of operation was in connection with the libraries. While in my judgment the policy of the WPA in relation to these libraries was entirely wrong from an administrative point of view, nevertheless it must be conceded that WPA enabled libraries to accomplish many things which otherwise would have been impossible and also provided library service in areas which had never known the meaning of libraries. It thus enabled libraries to improve their own services and built up an understanding of what books can mean to a community. Furthermore, the book-mobile service loaned to Larimer and Weld counties contributed greatly to the effort of securing the support of the county Commissioners for this new educational agency. In the larger libraries of the colleges and universities many important projects were undertaken and completed with the help of WPA. The Bibliographical Center would not have been able without WPA aid to enter the regional library holdings in its union catalog.

Carnegie Library Buildings. Perhaps the most effective influence for the establishment of free public libraries during the early years of this century was the policy adopted by the Andrew Carnegie Corporation for grants for public library buildings. Mr. Carnegie's conception of a public library was for an institution supported by taxation and free to all the citizens. One of the conditions for receiving a library building grant was that the local governing body agree to a tax support for the library equal to one-tenth the cost of the building. The communities of Colorado shared in the Carnegie Library Building program and thirty-five buildings for public library purposes were erected in this state with the aid of Carnegie funds. These included buildings for the following communities:

Alamosa	Denver	Lamar	Pueblo
$ 6,000	Main Building	$12,000	$70,000
	$200,000		
	8 branches		
	$160,000		
Boulder	Durango	Leadville	Rocky Ford
$15,000	$15,000	$20,000	$10,000
Brush	Florence	Littleton	Salida
$ 6,000	$10,000	$ 8,000	$ 9,000
Canon City	Fort Collins	Longmont	Silverton
$13,000	$12,500	$12,500	$12,000
Colorado City	Fort Morgan	Loveland	Sterling
(now Colorado Springs			
$10,000 branch)	$10,000	$10,000	$12,500
Colorado Springs	Grand Junction	Manitou	Trinidad
$60,000	$ 8,000	$ 6,500	$15,000
Delta	Idaho Springs	Monte Vista	
$ 6,500	$10,443	$10,000	

Among other gifts for library buildings should be mentioned the Mary Reed Library, University of Denver, erected at a cost of $400,000 donated by Mrs. Verner Z. Reed.

The Coburn Library of Colorado College is a gift of Nathaniel P. Coburn who erected the building at a cost of $45,000 and added $5,000 for the purchase of books.

At La Junta the Woodruff Memorial Library was constructed with funds donated by Thomas T. Woodruff, who also left an endowment fund.

School Libraries. The Public Schools have long recognized the importance of an organized school library and of course they have responded to the emphasis of school library standards by the national education agencies. The progressive and highly professional system of school libraries established many years ago by the Denver Public Schools has had its effect through the state and many schools have endeavored to follow the example set in Denver.

College Libraries. The largest library of this group is the University of Colorado collection which is most satisfactorily housed in the fine Norlin Library. It led the way in university libraries for adapting building plans to functional services fitted to the educational pattern of the institution.

Library Cooperation. Colorado is a state which is separated from large library centers and there is little opportunity for contact with other libraries and interchange of library policies. The College and University libraries and the Denver Public Library realized that the total library resources in the state and in the region were far below those in other sections of the country. Many suggestions were made for these libraries to cooperate closely in dividing the field of specialization so that duplication of purchases would be kept at a minimum and the total library facilities of the state increased. Definite plans

Air View of Library, University of Colorado, Boulder

in this direction met with many difficulties but in 1931 representatives of these libraries agreed on a program of cooperation in developing the field of bibliography at a place in Denver which would be accessible to all the libraries. This plan developed into the Bibliographical Center for Research, Rocky Mountain Region, which was subsidized by the Carnegie Corporation as a new form of library cooperation. The most important series of national bibliographies were secured, subject bibliographies and catalogs of special collections added and a depository catalog of the Library of Congress secured, since none existed in the region. The next step was to dexigraph the author cards of the leading college libraries in the state and in Wyoming and to transfer this information to the Library of Congress catalog making this serve as a union regional author catalog. The Bibliographical Center has thus become the agency to receive requests for

interlibrary loans and to fill these requests from the libraries of the
region where possible and to locate them in outside libraries when not
available in the region. In this way the total resources of the regional
libraries are available for any one library or any one individual
through interlibrary loan. The Center is also the best agency to
supply reference information concerning bibliographical matters and
books and printed material available on various subjects. This
agency is now supported by contributions from the libraries in the
Rocky Mountain Region and receives annual amounts from libraries
in Montana, Utah, Wyoming, Kansas, Oklahoma, New Mexico and
Arizona. The idea for the Bibliographical Center which originated
here now has been adopted in other parts of the country.

COLORADO LIBRARY ASSOCIATION

The professional association of librarians was organized in 1892
and Mr. John Cotton Dana was the first President, Charles R. Dudley,
first Secretary. The Association held regular meetings, issued a
number of publications helpful for improving library work and was
instrumental in bringing to Denver the American Library Association
conference in 1895.

One of the most important projects of the Association was the
publication of *The Occasional Leaflet,* a periodical giving news items
concerning the libraries of the state and professional papers relating
to various subjects in library service. The name was later changed to
Colorado Libraries. In times of financial stress this publication was
carried on through individual subscription by Charlotte A. Baker,
C. Henry Smith, Chalmers Hadley, Helen F. Ingersoll, Albert F.
Carter, Rena Reese, Lucretia Vaile, and others. Also the Denver
Public Library carried the responsibility of publication for short
periods from time to time. The Colorado Library Association supported many campaigns for securing more satisfactory library legislation, some of which, such as the passage of a county library law,
were successful and others providing for the reorganization of the
state library did not meet with success.

LIBRARY EDUCATION

One of the most eminent librarians of the country, John Cotton
Dana, began his library career in Denver as Librarian of the Denver
Public Library. Here he conducted a training class and through his
strong individuality and personal enthusiasm for library service introduced many young people to the library profession. As an outgrowth
of this training class Mr. Dana prepared and published one of the
important early handbooks on library administration. This was called
The Public Library Handbook, which served as a text book for training classes in libraries all over the country. It is now recognized as
one of the landmarks in library economy.

Soon after Chalmers Hadley became Librarian in 1911, a training class was established with Miss Rena Reese in charge. This training class continued until 1930, when it was given up because the School of Librarianship was established by the University of Denver. The last three classes were directed by May Wood Wigginton following the resignation of Miss Reese. The policy of the training class was one of careful selection of a limited number of students based on personal qualifications and a competitive examination. The plan for the training class was to devote half the time to instruction and the other half to practical work in the various departments of the Public Library. A very high standard was set both for the selection of students and for the type of training given and full recognition should be given to Miss Reese and her successor for developing a trained staff in the Denver Public Library with an unusual interest in their work and a high ideal of service to the community. Librarians all over the country were familiar with the high character of the training given and many of its graduates found their way to important positions in other libraries. Credit was allowed by the University of Denver for the training class course.

Joseph F. Daniels was librarian at the Colorado State Teachers College from 1896-1901 and at the Colorado Agricultural College from 1901-1911. Later he went to Riverside, California, where he founded the library school at the public library there. He did some apprentice class training at both of the colleges in Colorado but on an elementary scale.

Nearly all of the colleges have carried on some form of library training, especially at the State Teachers College at Greeley and the University of Colorado at Boulder. However, these were not a systematic library training course but classes covering elementary classification and cataloging, use of reference books, organization of school libraries, etc.

After Charlotte A. Baker became librarian of the College of Agriculture at Fort Collins she became very active in the library activities of the state. As a member of the Board of Library Commissioners she visited libraries throughout the state and received much correspondence from libraries, library trustees, and individuals in regard to library problems. She felt keenly the need of some training for librarians in the Rocky Mountain region and in 1918, she established at the College of Agriculture a summer library school. She did this without any financial assistance from the College and assumed full financial responsibility for the school expenses including instructors, supplies, etc. This school was continued for fifteen years and was not given up until the School of Librarianship was established at the University of Denver. Miss Baker rendered an unusual service to the libraries of Colorado and the region by providing this summer course of instruction in library organization, ideals and service. Miss

Baker had secured her training in the apprentice class of John Cotton Dana and she was imbued with the high ideals and enthusiasm for making books useful to individuals and communities through organized libraries. Her influence upon the students who took the work during the summer sessions was very strong and was carried out to libraries in many states.

College of Librarianship, University of Denver. In the late 1920s many requests were made for a comprehensive library training course for young people who wished to enter library work as a career in the Rocky Mountain region. This was reported to the Board of Librarianship of the American Library Association and a committee was sent to learn the possibilities and needs for a library school in Denver. This committee recommended that a definite need existed for a library school and that Denver was a strategic place for its location because a close association would be possible with the Denver Public Library. The American Library Association recommended to the Carnegie Corporation that a grant be made to establish a library school in Denver. The Librarian of the Denver Public Library received a communication from the Carnegie Corporation stating that the Corporation would be glad to make a grant of $35,000 payable over a period of three years to establish a library school of high standard if the University of Denver would be willing to sponsor such a school. The University authorities agreed not only to establish a school under these conditions but to maintain the school on the high standards which would be established and it would meet the accrediting conditions of the American Library Association. Under an agreement between the University of Denver, the Library Commission, and the Mayor of the City and County of Denver, the Librarian of the Public Library was named Dean of the proposed school and a faculty was secured consisting of Harriet E. Howe, Director; Helen L. Butler, Professor of Book Arts; and Agnes Camilla Hansen as Professor of Cataloging and Classification. The school began its first year in September, 1931. An original plan for the curriculum was developed radically different from the typical library school courses and the Denver school led the way to a new approach to a library training program. The school was accredited by the American Library Association after its experimental years and it is now recognized as one of the outstanding library schools in the country. Students come from all parts of the country especially for the summer quarter and many students have enrolled from foreign countries. The School was organized to offer the full year's course during the senior year and students carrying the work on that basis receive the A.B. or B.S. degree with a major in Library Science. Students taking the course with a baccalaureate degree receive the degrees of B.S. in L.S. In 1946 the name of the school was changed to College of Librarianship to conform to the University of Denver policy. In 1947 a radical change in the policy of the College was adopted to meet the changing conditions in the library profession and new demands from libraries of all types. This change involved the offering of introductory library courses in one quarter of the senior college curriculum, and placing the library course on a graduate basis with two quarters of library offerings and one quarter of subject specialization, leading to the Master's degree.

The Carnegie Corporation has given this College an endowment fund of $50,000.

CHAPTER XXI

Women

EUDOCHIA BELL SMITH

Former State Senator, Journalist, and a Leader in Civic, Cultural, and Religious Activities

THE very earliest times in Colorado had the twain: the man and woman, as in the beginning of human life. Indeed, so far, Colorado holds the visible record of prehistoric communal life, going back 3,000 years and more, say archeologists; and before that the nomadic domestic scene is revealed by excavation of stone arrow and spear heads as evidences of fires. Imprints of women's fingers on pottery found in pithouses prove they fashioned and fired cooking utensils; and by the same sign it is certain they helped make and lay the adobe bricks used in the construction of America's first apartment buildings, the cliff dwellings at Mesa Verde and elsewhere in southwestern Colorado.

The first permanent settlement of New Mexico by colonists under Don Juan de Onate in the closing years of the sixteenth century brought Spanish blood, some of it gentle blood of illustrious name, into Colorado in the years that followed. The very first church to be built in the state was at the Spanish settlement of Guadalupe, now Conejos, in 1858. That was the year the Green Russell party of gold seekers from Georgia reached Cherry Creek at its confluence with the Platte River. Here was built a wickiup, surrounded by a picket fence, occupied by John Simpson Smith from Kentucky, trader and trapper, his Indian squaw, and their small son, Jack. Other cabins, built in line with the wickiup, formed the first street of what was to become Denver.

On "Indian Row," as it was named, were the first homes. S. M. Rooker with his wife, daughter, and son, arrived from Salt Lake August 30, 1858. Mrs. Rooker and her daughter were the first white women to press the soil of Denver. Rooker finished his cabin October 27. Two days later, in a blinding snowstorm, Charles H. Blake and A. J. Williams came with an ox-train of loaded wagons, and opened the first store. In November, the couple that figure in many stories the pioneers were never tired of telling, Henri Murat and his wife, Katrina, arrived. Richings L. Wooten, "Uncle Dick," and his wife drove in with groceries, dry goods, and flour, from Fort Union, New Mexico, Christmas eve. At the beginning of 1859, only four white women were in this then "cheerless locality of privation and pioneers."

Murat, who claimed to be a count, and the nephew of Napoleon's king of Naples, was accepted as a titled Frenchman. With David Smoke he built a log hotel, the "Eldorado," which was opened February 1,

1859. The countess, blue eyed, rosy cheeked, golden haired, was the cook and chambermaid. In May, when news came that an express line had been established between Leavenworth, Kansas, and Denver, she made the first flag to fly over the "towns" of Auraria and Denver City, the newcomers having forgotten to bring one. From her trunk she took a red merino skirt purchased in Paris and other garments to make the stars and stripes. It flew proudly from a pole fashioned from a tall pine tree cut by Murat in the "pineries" on Cherry Creek, and which stood in front of the first hotel. When the first stage coach arrived, this flag was the only one to celebrate the coming of rapid transportation, which meant the influx of wives and sweethearts in greater number than by "prairie schooners"—the covered wagons drawn by yokes of oxen or spans of mules.

Because of the first flag and the fact that she was the only one of the four white women to remain, Mrs. Murat is known as "the Mother of Colorado," and was so honored by the Pioneer Society which made her its ward the last years of her long life.

Mrs. Mary M. Hall, who came in 1859 and was a close follower of Mrs. Augusta Tabor in the California Gulch rush of that year, was another flag maker, and thought hers was the first. She used some strips of white muslin, a blue sunbonnet, and a little red petti-coat. Patriotism was a characteristic of the pioneer women.

A third flag maker was Mrs. Joseph Wolff, who came to Auraria with her husband and baby in 1859. As the story runs, a famous Indian chief visiting the little group of pale faces en route from Ohio to Colorado, picked out Mrs. Wolff and handing her a pumpkin, ordered her to take it to his tepee and cook it. She showed true pioneer spirit by promptly boxing his ears, an act that made her extremely unpopular with her associates who were afraid the Indians would retaliate. Great was the relief of everybody when the old squaw came calling and, in high good humor, asked to be shown the "squaw" who had the nerve to defy Spotty. She then invited Mrs. Wolff and her husband to a grand pow-wow the following day. Of course, Mrs. Wolff would not go without a flag. All night long her fingers flew in tearful stitching as she appliqued the stars and made the flag, all devised from the only material at hand, one of her most prized possessions, a gorgeous quilt which her mother had given her for the baby crib as they pulled out of the East for the rough and woolly West.

Two wives of newspaper men became firm friends in 1859 and did much to help each other through the early day trials and tribula-tions. They were Mrs. William N. Byers, whose husband established the *Rocky Mountain News* in April, 1859, and Mrs. Wolff. Mr. Wolff had been driven out of Wheeling, West Virginia, for running an anti-slavery newspaper. Mr. Wolff could set type, and arriving in Denver at about the same time as Byers, went to work on the *News*. The Wolffs went first to the Denver House, the new hotel, a large, frame building with very few conveniences. They slept on the floor, their own blankets serving as beds. After six weeks, they moved into their own new log cabin which had no floor but plenty of grass shoots cropping up. Later they moved into the back of the printing office, which was hard on the Wolff children. So, in the winter of '59-'60 they made another move, this time into a canvas-lined frame house on the west side of Cherry Creek. All the houses had dirt roofs, and Mrs. Wolff recorded with great pride that she refused to have her better things sent out from Omaha until she really had "a roof (shingle) over her head."

Pioneer women of this period had other worries besides housing and physical hardships to combat. For instance, both the Wolffs and the Byers were stricken by fire and water; their belongings were washed away in the great flood of May 21, 1864, within a year after they had suffered from the conflagration that devastated a large part of the town. There is true inspiration in Mrs. Byers' words of solace to her husband, "We will try again, William. Never fear but that we will make good at what we have started. Denver must have a paper!"

All the while, children were being born. The first saw the light of day March 3, 1859. William McGaa, one of the first operators of the ferry across the Platte, and his Indian wife, christened their son, William Denver. He, Denver's first born, died in May, 1925, at Ogalala, South Dakota, after an active life, first as a cowpuncher, and then as instructor in farming to the Indians on the Pine Ridge reservation. The first white child born in Auraria was a girl, in the fall of 1859, to Mr. and Mrs. Henry Hubbell, who conducted a bakery in the former Hotel Eldorado on Tenth Street near the corner of Larimer Street. She was named Auraria and mother and child were donated several corner lots by the Town Company for their enterprise in helping to populate Auraria. October 16, 1859, saw the first wedding, between Lydia Allen, daughter of the first postmaster, and John B. Atkins, assistant auditor of Jefferson Territory when it was brought into being by the election October 24, 1859.

Auraria, the larger settlement, boasted a far greater number of residences. General William Larimer, head of the party from Kansas which, in November, 1858, laid out and named Denver City on the east bank of Cherry Creek, called upon Count and Countess Murat, offering them building lots as a gift at what is now Curtis and Sixteenth Streets if they would move over to Denver, arguing that the many women who would shortly be coming with their men would be far more willing to settle where there was another woman, especially one as hospitable and as excellent a housewife and cook as the countess. The Murats moved.

The now legendary Tabors left their farm in Kansas in the autumn of 1859 and with their little son, Maxcy, struck out across the plains for "the Pikes Peak country." It was the cattle and not the woman that slowed the journey. The wife, Augusta, rested for three weeks in Golden for the sake of the footsore cattle while her husband, eager to begin prospecting, went into the mountains. Augusta kept guard over stock and provisions and the baby until Tabor's return.

They went to Idaho Springs, their progress three miles a day. Tabor earned his first money in Colorado by hard manual labor at mining there, but the hardships of the mountain winter drove them back to the plains, and in Auraria Mrs. Tabor opened a boarding house. In the spring of 1860, they went to Colorado City "where they made me a present of some building lots, too," she wrote in her reminiscences.

Augusta, so far as is known, was the first woman to conduct her own placer mining operations, sifting in the pan the black sand to disclose the specks of gold; frequently she devoted the day to picking the yellow metal out with a little magnet, so tedious the job that there was not a pennyweight when evening fell and she had to return to the family cares and her boarding house.

At Colorado City was Mother Maggart's Hotel, known for its superior table. The first Legislature of the Territory of Colorado, which met in Denver in 1861, named Colorado City the capital. The Assembly members of the second session boarded at Mother Maggart's. When the Legislature met in the log cabin which served as the capitol building, the country members fought the proposition to make Denver the capital, giving as reasons, among others, that Denver was "trying to hog all the governing" and "there is a woman running Maggart's Hotel, and she knows how to cook." But Denver won out, after nine stormy days, to the extent of getting the session. Judge W. F. Stone, a member of the Assembly, relates, "the members were finally brought together in Mother Maggart's Hotel under pretense of compromising the matter, locked in, and when the vote was finished we adjourned to Denver," where the body resumed its labors July 16, 1862. Before final adjournment, Golden City was designated as the seat of Territorial government.

From all accounts, the first traveling saleswoman in Colorado was Mrs. L. E. Miller from Wisconsin, who in 1860 drove a covered wagon introducing the sewing machine to the West. By way of demonstration, she exhibited her own fine work and sold a goodly number at $160 each! The sewing machine having made inroads, it was natural that the piano and home organ should follow. The first piano to come over the plains to this region was owned by Mrs. George Clark, nee Kate Goss. It was small, square, and inlaid with ivory. Rico's oldsters like to tell of its first piano, prized possession of the family of Helen M. Wixson, and how the natives gathered round to hear "the gal who could paw hell out of the ivories at the same time she sang like an angel." Mrs. Thomas Macon's piano was the first in Canon City.

Mrs. Eli M. Ashley, whose husband was in the surveyor general's office in Governor Gilpin's administration, gives a vivid account of early Denver social life. Like other wives, she followed her husband, and arrived by stage in November, 1861. From Omaha to Denver it took eight days and nights by the Central Overland California and Pikes Peak Express. The Concord coach traveled night and day, stopping only long enough for three meals in each twenty-four hours, and took fresh horses every fifteen or twenty miles. The bill of fare at the meal stations usually consisted of jack rabbit, buffalo or antelope steak, soda biscuit without butter, coffee without milk, and dried apple pie for dessert; price $1.50.

"Nearly every coach from the East at this period brought wife or sweetheart who on arrival became wife, and social entertainments for them were always planned," she wrote. "If the entertainment was to be larger than a dinner, the hostess invited her most intimate friends to help her in the preparation of salads, cakes and ices, for few private houses in Denver knew the luxury of hired help before 1864. Not until 1871 did we know the freedom from responsibility furnished by a caterer."

At what is now Lawrence and Seventeenth Streets, where Judge Vincent D. Markham was afterwards to build his hotel, still standing, Oscar and Joe Cass, bankers, lived in a story and a half double cottage. The brothers were among the most lavish of the many entertainers of this, even then, most hospitable town, and there, just one week after her arrival, Mrs. Ashley attended a social function. On this first Thanksgiving in Denver, Mr. and Mrs. Ashley also dined with Dr. and Mrs. Oscar Cass "who had paid $12 for a moderate size turkey."

Josephine Antoine

Nearly every lady in the city's socially elect—fifteen or possibly twenty in all—called on her during her first week in this town of log, frame and adobe buildings with an occasional brick structure, all mostly unplastered and unpainted, and housing the population of 3,000. Indians of the Cheyenne and Arapaho tribes were seen in numbers on the streets almost every day. They peered through windows and entered, begging, if doors were unlocked. Apparently they were friendly, but the fear of trouble to come "made it advisable in these earlier years for all women living on this frontier to know how to load and use both revolver and rifle. Target practice was one of the amusements in which both men and women participated in the early sixties, and many women became very expert marksmen.

"At a ball at the Tremont House," Mrs. Ashley continues, "there were present not only those whom I had met at the bankers' house, but also many men whose wives and sweethearts were back in 'the states.' When quadrilles were danced they were mostly formed by two women and six men, two of the men with handkerchiefs tied on the left arm personating ladies in order that they might in 'the swing at the corner' and the 'grand right and left' at least touch the hands of women and, if possible, secure one as partner for a later dance. All women were belles.

"Miss Ring, the school teacher, the Misses Irene and Indiana Sopris, Lida Scudder, Deme Adams, Mary Voorhies, and Mary Carpenter were the much sought young ladies of Denver then and, with the exception of Miss Ring, very soon were persuaded to join the ranks of the married, becoming the Mesdames J. Sidney Brown, Samuel Cushman, John C. Anderson, Billy Bailey, Frank Hall and Web Anthony, and taking their places among 'Denver's first families.'

"Governor Gilpin, then a bachelor, held his first levee in the theater in the fall of 1861, and to attend this function people came from far and near. It was a crush! The *Rocky Mountain News* described it as a 'most elegant and recherche affair.' To this, as to all evening parties, guests were taken in covered mountain wagons dignified by the name of 'hacks.' Even our bankers had not set up carriages in 1861. But those early parties were none the less enjoyable; all were young and vigorous. Colorado was a land of youth. Mr. and Mrs. John W. Smith, Mr. and Mrs. Richard Sopris, Dr. and Mrs. Steinberger and Rev. J. H. Kehler are the only families I recall who had reached even middle life."

It was this year, 1861, that Denver saw its first military wedding, that of Miss Fannie Walthall and Lieutenant George H. Hardin, a brilliant ceremony with Rev. Mr. Kehler, first rector of St. John's in the Wilderness Episcopal Church, officiating. It was at Camp Weld, where now stand the Burnham shops of the Denver & Rio Grande Western Railroad, and it drew an enormous crowd.

The first women's organization was a soldier's aid society with Mrs. William N. Byers president. Fifteen ladies met regularly in the Broadwell House, Sixteenth and Larimer Streets, where genial Mr. Broadwell, the proprietor, gave them free of charge the use of his largest room and supplied chairs and tables for cutting the underwear, bed garments, bandages and lint for Colorado's first regiment.

At Lawrence and Sixteenth Streets stood the large unpainted frame theater where Jack Langrishe, Mrs. Langrishe, and handsome Harry Richmond were the stars of a stock company presenting the popular comedies and dramas of the day to packed houses.

Mrs. Ashley notes that at the first reception given at the residence of Governor John Evans, who in 1862 had succeeded Governor Gilpin, the mantels were banked with flowers "and all the appointments equalled those of an Eastern city home." By 1863 milliners and dressmakers had arrived and entertainments were on a more elaborate scale. The city had home-grown vegetables, chickens and eggs in limited supply. Chickens cost $2 each, eggs $1 a dozen, and roasting ears by the dozen, 75 cents. Everything was high, especially freight charges from the Missouri River. Mrs. Ashley paid $200 freightage to bring her Steinway piano to Denver. By 1864 many trees had been planted. These were watered by means of ditches along each side of the streets, and at much expense and care lawns became possible.

Excitement was rampant when a huge overland freight shipment was disclosed as nothing other than the mansion of General and Mrs. John Pierce, brought piecemeal, lumber, glass, and all, from the Missouri River. Society took on new life with the gracious entertaining that began when the mansion was reconstructed. The first guest was General Pierce's former teacher, Louis Agassiz. Then came Vice-President Schuyler Colfax's distinguished party, accompanied by several charming young ladies, the special stage drawn by six dapple gray horses, and a solid line of young men double-breasting the sidewalk. One might well believe lovely Sue Hall when she said, "It was no trouble to be a belle in Denver in those days. Seven young men called on each girl that first night."

During a camping trip in the mountains, Miss Nellie Wade promised to become Mrs. Colfax; and two other maidens lost their hearts, Miss Carrie Matthews later becoming Mrs. O. J. Hollister, and Miss Sue M. Matthews marrying Secretary of the Territory Frank Hall, newspaper man and author of a history of Colorado, which is especially valuable because of the large amount of first hand knowledge of men and deeds from the earliest arrivals of gold seekers until the nineties. In the Colfax party were William Bross, lieutenant governor of Illinois and a founder of the Chicago Tribune; Samuel Bowles, editor of the Springfield, Massachusetts, *Republican,* and daughter Sallie; Mr. and Mrs. G. W. Matthews, daughter and niece; Miss Nellie Wade, and William D. Todd, who remained to become a Denver banker.

Of interest is the fact that in this summer of 1868, the Republican party candidates for the two highest offices in the gift of the nation visited Colorado. General U. S. Grant, successfully seeking the Presidency, arrived over the Smoky Hill route by stage in Denver July 21, accompanied by Generals Sherman, Sheridan, and Frederick T. Dent. The following day they took the stage to Central City and Georgetown. Colfax, candidate for the vice-presidency, with his party drove in from Cheyenne, August 8. Mrs. Daniel Witter of Denver was his half sister, and during the visit of several weeks the guests were extensively entertained.

President Grant's second visit to the Territory of Colorado, in 1873, had as an outstanding incident in his honor the laying of a twenty-foot pavement of solid silver bricks from the coach stop into the Teller House, his hotel in Central City.

And what of Central City and its county, "the golden kingdom of Gilpin," considered by many the cradle of Colorado culture? There, in the earlier days they established a library, organized churches, among the very first, taught Sunday School, hired Bayard Taylor, Grace Greenwood, and other celebrities to lecture, and offered visiting Charles Dickens $500 to mount their platform. As early as 1867 Central sent a commissioner to the Paris Exposition to spread the word about Colorado. After the Territory's admission as a State, Central furnished the nation three United States senators, a Cabinet officer, and a representative in Congress. Senator Clark of Montana did his first mining there and at Central Pullman dreamed of his "palace sleeping cars." General Irving Hale, Colorado's most distinguished military figure in the Spanish-American War, came from a Central City home: his parents were among the finely educated folk who contributed generously to the culture of the times.

Take an early social roster of Central. You follow through with names that still hold sway in the social and industrial life of the State: the N. P. Hills, the Tellers, Thatchers, Belfords, Sayres, Youngs, George Randolphs, Richard Pearces, Henry and Edward Wolcott. Mrs. James B. Belford well typified the part played by the helpmates of the pioneer men who laid the foundations of the rich heritages we of today enjoy in a great commonwealth. While her husband busied himself in his lawbooks so recently brought out from Indiana, she reared the children with one hand and taught Dante with the other, an achievement nationally recognized by the Dante Society of America. When Mr. Belford was appointed one of the three Territorial Supreme Court judges, the other two being Moses Hallett and E. T. Wells, Mrs. Belford matched her husband's increasing civic responsibilities by organizing study clubs and W.C.T.U. groups to combat the corner saloons which outnumbered churches, schools, and libraries added together. She was the first woman to be appointed to the State Board of Charities and Corrections. She and the judge, later Congressman, were stars of first magnitude in every endeavor of the literary West, and their work still carries on in the person of their daughter, Mrs. Frances Wayne.

Oldtimers who grew up in the glory days of Gilpin like to tell of Aunt Clara Brown, the first Negro woman to cross the plains, and in whose humble home were held early meetings of groups that led to the organization of Central City's first churches. She was born in 1800, a slave, in Virginia. When she was nine, her master moved to Kentucky where, when eighteen, she was married. At his death in 1835, she and her husband and four children, three daughters and a son, were sold to different purchasers. Aunt Clara was taken to Russellville, Kentucky. When her second master died, she was again sold; in 1859 she was manumitted by her new owner and that year for her services in cooking and washing, was given transportation to Denver by a company of men with a large wagon train which brought her stove, tubs, and wash boilers.

Starting a laundry in Central City she had accumulated by 1866 about $10,000. Her one ambition had been to free from bondage her family; now she went to Virginia and Kentucky, pursuing an uninterrupted search until she had located thirty-four relatives, including her daughters. These she brought to Colorado. There never was a wedding, a large entertainment, or celebration in which some of Aunt Clara's kith and kin did not have a hand. Respected and beloved, the kindly old woman was cared for by the Pioneers Society, of which she was a member, in her last years, after she had given to charity what remained of her worldly possessions. Hundreds of mourners attended her funeral.

Illustrative of the heroism of women in the perilous days, is the story of Mrs. Elizabeth Lewis Entriken, sister of Rev. John Lewis Dyer, the famous "snowshoe itinerant," first Methodist circuit rider in the Rocky Mountains, and whose portrait hangs in the dome of the capitol among the sixteen pioneer builders of Colorado. For years she lived alone in her log cabin in Platte canyon where now stands the village of Bailey. It was on the road from Denver to South Park and California Gulch, highway in the sixties and seventies for freighters and travelers afoot and horseback to Fairplay, Tarryall, Buckskin Joe and other camps. Desperate men, criminals with a price on their heads, men lost to all decency, were among those traveling that road. Mrs. Entriken conquered fear in her isolation, with no neighbor in many miles, by putting a lighted lamp in her window and leaving her door unbolted at night.

Regardless of the hour when some one entered, she prepared a hot meal; in the attic upstairs were two rooms with clean beds and plenty of blankets. Furtive and filthy men crept to that beacon of friendliness in the night; rough and insolent men burst in to become gentle, abashed before the cheery welcome of a motherly little woman. She was never mistreated, nor was her hospitality abused, except once when the huge Ute chief, Colorow, and twelve of his braves, coming from South Park on their way to Denver to receive quarterly rations from the Indian agent, demanded biscuits of which all Indians were inordinately fond.

They crowded into her living room that sunny afternoon in October, 1875. She baked pan after pan of soda biscuits, which disappeared immediately her back was turned. Their demand, "more biscuit," was insistent. Suddenly came the realization that, with the long winter ahead, her flour barrel was becoming empty. She rebelled with words that cracked whippingly, and waving her apron as though shooing her chickens from her carefully tended flower garden, she ordered them out instanter. Her too-greedy guests were slow in rising, so she seized the broom and began sweeping them off the floor.

In the doorway she watched them carefully mount their ponies. Colorow, who weighed more than 300 pounds, was wearing what was perhaps the largest "biled" white dress shirt ever manufactured. It had been ordered in the East by storekeeper Sam Cohen of Fairplay as a jocular gift to Colorow and resembled a tent rather than a garment. The chief wore it with satisfaction on state occasions and always when the tribe went to Denver.

The chief had difficulty in getting an enormous leg over the back of his patient steed. The tail of the bulging shirt came out of the buckskin trousers and biscuits by the dozens cascaded to the ground. Colorow sat immovable during the shower, then motioned to the woman who, with growing anger, noted that the shirt of each Indian was stuffed knobbily tight. Her eyes met the haughty stare of the chief; she smothered a sudden impulse to laughter, knowing that would mean an ugly enmity. She nodded to the commanding finger. With a dignity matching his, she said, "I will pick them up." Using her apron as a basket, she gathered the biscuits and, as the impassive braves watched, handed them, one by one, to Colorow who securely stuffed the deflated shirt tail in his waist band and then the biscuits in the bagging shirt, shaking them down with movements of his immense torso from side to side. After that, again and again, the Utes stopped in for biscuits, but they consumed in comparative moderation. No more tricks. Colorow and Mrs. Entriken both possessed dignity.

Dr. Florence Sabin

The coming of the first railroad, the Denver Pacific, in 1870, was followed by gas lighting, the Holly water works system, horse-drawn street cars, and a steam heating plant. Denver's population rapidly increased, new additions were platted, the residence district went eastward and the new residences were of brick and stone, many of pretentious architecture. Soon the newspapers were to inaugurate regular "society columns."

Royalty first put foot in Denver when the Grand Duke Alexis, youngest son of Emperor Alexander of Russia, arrived with a glittering retinue, January 23, 1872. Alexis, a young blonde giant several inches over six feet, had been on a buffalo hunt with "Buffalo Bill"— William F. Cody—and Generals Sheridan and Custer, representing the United States government. In his party were Admiral Possuet, his tutor, and Count Olsenfieff, Consul General Bodisco, Count Starlingoff, Lieutenant Tudur of the Imperial Navy, and several servants. General Sheridan's staff comprised General George A. Forsythe and Colonel M. V. Sheridan, aides-de-camp; General George A. Custer and General Sweitzer.

The day following their arrival the visitors were driven about the city in carriages and in the evening "a grand ducal ball" was given in the dining room of the American House, the largest and newest hotel. The "first lady of the Territory," wife of Governor Edward M. McCook, was confined to her room at the American House, seriously ill, but disobeying the firm orders of her physician not to leave her bed, had her maid dress her, support her in the dizzying descent of the stairs, and led the grand march with the duke. At its conclusion, as the orchestra with a flourish played the last bars, Mrs. McCook quietly slipped from the duke's arm to his feet in a faint.

No history of Colorado Springs, "Little Lunnon," so called from the many English who came to reside there in the seventies and eighties, would be complete without the names of Mrs. William J. Palmer, wife of the builder of the Denver & Rio Grande railroad and founder of the city, Mrs. William A. Bell, whose husband developed Manitou into a world famed resort, and Helen Hunt Jackson, author of *Ramona*. Among the earliest residents were Maurice Kingsley, civil engineer, and his sister, Rose, for whom Mont Rosa is named, she being the first woman to ascend it. They were visited in the summer of 1874 by their father, Canon Charles Kingsley, one of the notables of the time, poet, naturalist, author of *Westward Ho!* and numerous other works, one time chaplain to Queen Victoria and canon of Westminster Abbey, London. Canon Kingsley preached the first sermon in Grace Episcopal Church, just completed, and was induced to deliver a fascinating lecture on Westminster Abbey, in the town hall.

Central City and Colorado Springs were not the only towns where brains and beauty mingled with pioneering. There was Leadville, "amazing mother of millionaires," where the beautiful Goodell sisters reigned in the early eighties, with another sister, Mrs. Whittemore, coming frequently from Denver to visit in the home that was the center of social distinction in a camp that was purging itself of desperadoes by vigilante lynchings! Mary Goodell became the wife of James B. Grant, who shortly was to be Governor of the State; Clara married John C. Mitchell, banker; Olive, Mrs. Zeph T. Hill, died early. Jennie, the wife of A. A. Blow, celebrated mining engineer, became a world traveler. Mrs. Grant and Mrs. Whittemore combined brilliant social careers with leadership in women's club activities.

Mrs. J. D. Ward had four lovely daughters, and the Daly, the Campion, and C. S. Thomas families brought the wealth of Leadville mines to Denver to build homes of beauty, centers of the society that interested even the "effete East" in the golden days when Denver boasted of more millionaires than any city of comparable, or, for that matter, twice its size, in the country.

At the same time, Pueblo was making her contribution to culture with leaders including Mrs. Alva Adams, Mrs. M. D. Thatcher, Mrs. J. B. Orman. They founded in 1882 a club that is recognized as one of the first and foremost cultural influences in the West.

Women's wider opportunity for usefulness to society in general came with the successful termination of their long struggle for equal rights. In this they were aided by men whose names are outstanding in Colorado's list of leaders in political, professional and business life. The first comers appreciated to the full the stamina in the courage of the women who, through the hardship and poverty years, with strengthening love and faith stuck to their men, working shoulder to shoulder and making a home in tent or shack. The written code of the miners' courts recognized no difference in citizenship rights between the sexes; the word "male" was absent.

Former Governor John Evans and D. M. Richards of Denver in 1868 unsuccessfully attempted to bring a test vote in the legislature on equal suffrage. January 3, 1870, Governor E. M. McCook in his annual message to the legislature, said: "It rests with you to say whether Colorado will accept this reform in its first stage, as our sister Territory of Wyoming has done, or in the last; whether she will be a leader in the movement or a follower; for the logic of a progressive civilization leads to the inevitable result of a universal suffrage."

The measure introduced, advocated by Judge Amos Steck, Judge M. DeFrance, D. M. Richards, and Willard Teller, was defeated in the House by a two-thirds vote against it.

When it became certain that Colorado would soon be admitted to statehood, at a crowded meeting in Unity Church, Denver, January 10, 1876, the Woman's Suffrage Society was organized with these officers: President, Alida C. Avery, M.D.; vice-presidents, D. M. Richards and Rev. Mr. Hosford of Denver; J. E. Washburn of Big Thompson; Mrs. H. M. Lee of Longmont; Mrs. M. M. Sheetz and Rev. William Shepard of Canon City; Mrs. L. S. Ruhn of Del Norte; Mrs. Nathan C. Meeker of Greeley; Willard Teller of Central City; J. B. Harrington of Littleton; A. E. Lee of Boulder; recording secretary, Mrs. Eunice D. Sewall of Denver; corresponding secretary, Mrs. A. L. Washburn of Big Thompson; treasurer, Mrs. Ione T. Hanna of Denver; executive committee, J. K. Hanna and M. E. Hale of Denver; Mrs. W. F. Shields and Mrs. W. A. Wilkes of Colorado Springs; A. L. Ellis of Boulder; Mrs. S. C. Wilber of Greeley; Rev. Dr. B. F. Crary of Pueblo.

The society presented a petition signed by 1,000 citizens to the Constitutional Convention, which also was memorialized by the Suffrage Association of Missouri and by other state organizations. Judge H. P. Bromwell and Agapito Vigil were the only members of the convention to sign a report granting women the voting privilege.

The members felt that the matter should be referred to the voters, but a concession was made in granting women the right to vote for school district officers. Though equal suffrage lost in the convention by 24 to 8, a resolution nevertheless was adopted instructing the First General Assembly of the state, which was to meet in 1877, to pass a law whereby the question of woman suffrage should be submitted to a vote of the electors.

Miss Emily Griffith

Following the suffrage association's annual convention, February 18, 1877, an active campaign was waged. Former Governor John Evans, Birks Cornforth and his wife, N. C. Meeker, Mrs. T. M. Patterson, General R. A. Cameron, Benjamin H. Eaton, W. B. Felton, Mrs. H. S. Mendenhall, Henry C. Dillon, Colonel Henry Logan, Dr. R. G. Buckingham, Captain Richard Sopris, and others enlisted in the fight. August 15, a mass meeting in Denver was addressed by Judge Bromwell, H. C. Dillon, and John Evans. A second and overflow mass meeting, October 1, at the Lawrence Street Methodist Church, was addressed by Lucy Stone and Matilda Hindman, noted suffrage workers from the East, and by Doctor Avery and Mrs. W. W. Campbell. Susan B. Anthony also came to the aid of the Colorado women.

Election day saw a vote of 10,000 for and 20,000 against. It was a stunning blow and the women discontinued their organization. In April, 1890, Miss Hindman again visited Colorado, this time to lecture and raise funds for the equal rights campaign in South Dakota, which that year was to be admitted into the Union. The women wanted the word "male" eliminated from the new State Constitution. A public meeting in Denver resulted in a generous subscription list headed by Mrs. T. M. Patterson, and interest was revived. Miss

Georgiana E. Watson, Mrs. Mary P. Nichols, Mrs. Sherman, Jennie P. Root, Amy K. Cornwall, and Mrs. Laverna C. Dwelle organized the Colorado Equal Suffrage Association which steadily grew in membership and influence.

J. Warner Mills drew for the women a bill providing that the question of woman suffrage be submitted to a vote of the people at the next general election. The measure was presented in the House of the Ninth General Assembly by Representative J. P. Heath. It passed both houses and was promptly signed by Governor Davis H. Waite.

Mrs. Carrie Lane Chapman came to assist in the campaign, touring the state and making convincing speeches; the state headquarters were opened in the Tabor Grand Opera House building, Mrs. Elizabeth Tabor donating rooms for three months; more than 100 representative women organized the City League of Denver with Mrs. John L. Routt as president; Misses Mary E. Patterson, Margaret Patterson and Isabel Hill organized the Young Women's League, and similar associations spread throughout the state. This time, press, pulpit, and political parties endorsed the movement. Mrs. Laura Ormiston Chant of London came and gave two lectures in Denver to standing-room-only audiences. Colorado's own Patience Stapleton, noted writer, Minnie J. Reynolds, newspaper woman and talented speaker, and Mrs. H. S. Stansbury, labored unceasingly in the cause. The state was flooded with literature.

Complete returns of the 1892 election were: 35,698 votes for, 29,461 against.

Mrs. John L. Routt was the first woman registered as a voter in the state. The first woman seeking office was Miss Carrie West in the spring of 1894. She was a candidate for town clerk of Highlands, then a suburb of Denver, but was defeated. At the state election, 1894, Mrs. Clara Cressingham and Mrs. Frances S. Klock, Denver, and Mrs. Carrie Clyde Holly, Pueblo, Republican nominees, were elected to the House of the Tenth General Assembly. Two women nominated by the National Silver Republican Party, Mrs. Martha B. Conine and Mrs. Olive Butler, and one by the Populist Party, Mrs. Evangeline Heartz, all from Denver, were elected to the Eleventh General Assembly. Thus started the long procession through the years of women legislators who invariably have introduced bills and worked for laws to improve social conditions. Among the first of these, obtained by the women in 1895, were the law raising the age of protection from sixteen to eighteen years, the law giving the mother an equal right to her children, and the law creating a home for friendless and incorrigible girls.

Women as lawmakers have proved their worth; they have been responsible for many of the reforms that for long have been accepted as indispensable to good government, to health, and to the well being of humanity.[1]

---

[1] Mrs. Smith is herself the most notable and successful woman legislator who has served Colorado.—Ed.

CHAPTER XXII

*Manufacturing History of Colorado**

ElRoy Nelson

THE history of mining in Colorado and, in fact, that of agriculture with attendant irrigation, have been so dramatic that the story of manufacturing has more or less been relegated to the background. However, manufacturing in the state followed closely that of mining and agriculture and in some instances preceded those industries. This is best shown with the growth in mining following the development of various types of milling and mining machinery, without which part of the early mining history would not have been told. To the same extent, this is also true in agriculture. The refrigerated car for meat packing products, the sugar beet factory machinery, and the canning factory equipment are all closely associated with and even preceded the development of agriculture industries, including feed lots, as well as sugar beet and vegetable production.

Food Industries

Meat packing, sugar beet refining, flour milling, and canning industries are the four largest food manufacturing industries in the state. All four of these became important about the turn of the century, and followed closely the development of the refrigerated car, sugar-beet factory machinery, the inexpensive tin can, and flour milling equipment. Before 1900, food processing was confined largely to local processing for local demand.

Meat Packing

From the standpoint of size of the industry, meat packing has developed into the most important of the food processing industries in Colorado. Prior to the turn of the century, meat packing was a localized industry serving only the people of the surrounding area. One of the first of the meat packing firms to extend its market beyond its area was the Nuckolls Packing Company, established in Leadville.

---

* This is by no means a complete history of manufacturing in the state. Processing including milling, smelting, and refining of non-ferrous minerals is included under mining. A number of other segments of manufacturing history are likewise omitted. These include paper and cotton mills and apparel. Assistance in preparing this report was given by the following: Ellsworth T. Mitick, who wrote "Manufacture of Mining Machinery in Colorado," unpublished master's thesis at Denver University; Leonard O. Anderson, Edgar W. Brazelton, Marvin E. Coulter, Arnet E. Craven, Carl E. Davis, N. C. Delli Quadri, J. F. Fishburne, Harold E. Handsel, John C. Hauser, David F. Kerr, N. E. LaSelle, Joe M. Robertson, David L. Svalberg, John F. Van Natter, Jr., Kenneth E. Worl, students at Denver University; also L. H. Kittel, Secretary-Manager Manufacturing Association of Colorado, and the manufacturers themselves.

Market for the products from this firm were distributed beyond the mountain counties. The firm had to find a new location, however, and Pueblo was chosen. The company was one of the first locally owned meat packing plants to qualify for federal inspection under the various pure food and drug laws. The company itself was sold in the early 1940s by the Nuckolls family to the American Packing and Provision Company. Establishment of the larger companies began in 1912 with the purchase of the National Packing Company's Denver plant by Swift and Company. Armour and Cudahy later opened their plants in Denver. Growth of the industry became significant after 1910, more than tripling in size from that date to 1920. Growth was slower from then to the early 1940s. It is significant that the industry developed coextensively with sugar-beet processing and the attendant feed lots for cattle and sheep. In fact, this three phase industry of livestock feeding, sugar-beet raising, and meat packing are closely interrelated. Development of Denver as a marketing center for livestock was a natural transportation growth.

Beet Sugar Production

Beet sugar production in Colorado had its beginning in Grand Junction in 1899. The first commercial production of beets in the state had been near that city in 1893, and the beets had been shipped to the Lehi, Utah, sugar factory for processing. It was but natural from the light of experience in the Grand Junction area that the first sugar factory constructed and operated in Colorado should be at that location. However, the next two factories built in the State were at Rocky Ford and Sugar City in the Arkansas Valley. Within four years, factories had also been constructed at five locations in Northern Colorado at Eaton, Greeley, Fort Collins, Longmont, and Windsor. From the standpoint of company ownership and operation, the National Sugar Manufacturing Company, organized in Colorado in 1899, is the oldest company in the state and constructed the second sugar factory, that at Sugar City. American Crystal Sugar Company formed in 1899, acquired the factories built at Rocky Ford and Las Animas. The Holly Sugar Company, incorporated in 1905 in Colorado, and named after the town of Holly, now operates at Swink and Delta. The largest of the companies, the Great Western Sugar Company, was organized in 1905 to consolidate the factories that had been constructed as separate organizations in the Platte Valley in the previous five years. The total number of factories owned and operated by this company in Colorado was later expanded to thirteen, all located in the Platte River Valley.

This industry ranks second only to meat packing in value of production, and is closely related to that industry.

Canning Industry

From the settlement of the state until the turn of the century, the canning industry of Colorado was confined largely to the making of pickles, preserves, and ketchup, as well as in the drying of fruits and vegetables. At the turn of the century and the development of the inexpensive tin can, the canning industry had its real beginning and growth. A number of companies have been organized and have operated in the major irrigated sections of the state, including the Platte, Arkansas, and San Luis Valleys, as well as on the Western Slope. The largest and oldest company is Kuner-Empson.

Kuner-Empson. The beginning of food processing in Colorado and continuation to date, is best described in the history of Kuner-Empson. In 1872, J. C. Kuner and son formed a pickle manufacturing company, and Kuner's nephew, Max, became at an early date associated with the company. It was he who led in incorporation of the business in 1884 as the Kuner Pickle Company. Vinegar and ketchup, then tomatoes, were added to the line of products.

In 1900, with expansion beyond Colorado borders, the two Mayer brothers, K. K. and E. R., joined the firm. Expansion that followed was part of the national trend toward the use of cans, following improvements in can-making processes. In 1917, the factory was moved from Denver to Brighton, to be located nearer the sources of supply of most of the vegetables. This had followed a considerable amount of community action on the part of the citizens of Brighton.

J. H. Empson, a candy maker in Cincinnati, moved to Denver in 1883 and entered the business of jobbing candy. The market, however, was not extensive, so he returned to Cincinnati. He came to Longmont in 1886, and with backing from the citizens of that town, he and his daughter formed the J. H. Empson and Daughter Company, in the following year. Empson took part in the company's growth until his retirement in 1920. The major products of the Empson Company after the turn of the century were peas and table beets.

In 1926, expansion of both Kuner and Empson was marked in the construction of canning plants in various areas of the state. It was in 1927 that the two companies combined to form the Kuner-Empson Company. At that time, the Empson Company had plants in Longmont, Loveland, and Greeley, and the Kuner Company had plants in Brighton and Fort Lupton, and a leased plant at Fort Collins. At a later date, the company cancelled its lease at Fort Collins and acquired a factory at Grand Junction. This factory had been started by the Currie Canning Company. Another plant at Appleton, near Grand Junction, was later acquired.

The Company has expanded its marketing area throughout the Mountain States and Western Plains area.

Fort Lupton Canning Company. The Fort Lupton Canning Company developed indirectly from the creamery business. O. P. Frink had moved from New York near the turn of the century and entered the produce market at 1640 Market Street, Denver. He soon opened a number of creameries and milk-receiving stations to serve an area within a radius of 125 miles of Denver. Together with his son, E. P.

Frink, he organized the Silver State Creamery and Produce Company in 1904 at Fort Lupton. At the death of the senior Frink in 1916, the canning properties were leased to W. N. Blayney, and one year later the Fort Lupton Canning Factory was organized to take over the properties. The company processes vegetables from the Weld and Adams County areas for marketing in Colorado and neighboring states.

Stokes Canning Company. The Stokes Canning Company had its beginning as a restaurant in 1902, in Colorado Springs. Within ten years, home-made chili became the most important and best adver-

Delta Canning Factory

tised food sold. In 1912, F. E. Stokes, the owner, gave up the restaurant in order to devote full time to production of chili-con-carne.

Most of the product was marketed in Denver and, for this reason more than for the source of supply of raw materials, the factory was moved to 20th and Blake Streets in Denver in 1912. In 1918, the factory was moved to larger quarters at 194 West Dakota Avenue. F. E. Stokes' son entered the business in 1928 and assumed full control in 1932. In 1937, the corporation charter was given up in favor of a proprietorship.

A number of products had been added to the line, but in 1931 the company reverted to specialization in chili-con-carne only. Since that date, the only exception to the single line product was in the "relief" years when the Canning Company, beginning in 1934, was chosen for experimental canning of beef to be distributed through relief agencies.

Restrictions, in 1942, on canning of products that could be processed in the home, caused a shutdown at the Stokes factory, but in 1944, tin again became available and the line of chili-con-carne was resumed.

Among important developments was the production and patenting, in 1938, of a bean picking machine that separated foreign matter such as pebbles and leaves from the beans; consequently, as a side line today the production and marketing of these machines is an important adjunct of the business.

Morey Mercantile Company. The Morey Mercantile Company began processing food in 1900. John Morey, like many other founders of manufacturing establishments in the state, came to Colorado to recover his health. This was in 1872. He formed a partnership with W. L. Beardsley in the cattle business. One year later, however, he re-entered employment with Sprague-Warner and Company, a Chicago mercantile house for whom he had worked from 1868 to 1871. His new assignment was that of developing the company's trade west of the Mississippi. He became a partner in the firm in 1881 and was made manager of the company's Denver office. In 1884, the C. S. Morey Mercantile Company was incorporated under Illinois laws and took over the assets of the Sprague-Warner partnership. The company was re-incorporated in Colorado in 1887. It was in 1910 that charter was amended by changing the name to the Morey Mercantile Company.

About 1900, demands for certain spices and other products in the region was such that the company began its own packing of goods, and since that time, has been a prominent manufacturer, processor, and packager of coffee, honey, tea, jams, jellies, and preserves. Also included is a line of extracts, drink flavors, gelatine dessert, mayonnaise, and other salad dressings, peanut butter, salted nuts, household ammonia, and bluing. Almost all of the spices imported and produced domestically are processed or packaged by the company. One of the most important parts of the business is that of jellies, jams, and preserves. These are processed the year round from fruit kept in cold storage from the time of harvesting. The company's sales are an important key to the eating habits of the people of the state and of the neighboring states.

Tasty Foods. Historically, one of the "new" companies and products in Colorado manufacturing is the Tasty Food Company and its dehydrated and canned shoestring potatoes, French-fried onions, as well as packaged potato chips. The company, a partnership, was organized in 1934; the partners, Leon and Silam M. Kobey. In addition to providing an additional market for two of Colorado's most important vegetables, the potato and the onion, the company has developed and patented an automatic machine that peels, cooks, and slices potatoes. This machine is marketed throughout the country.

Flour Milling and Bakeries

Flour milling is almost as old as the state itself. Although Colorado history is usually dated from 1859, flour milling was noted that year in the San Luis Valley among the settlers from New Mexico.

At least one other mill was established before 1859. The first American mill was established in San Luis about this time. Other mills were soon started and by 1862, dotted the settled areas of the state. In 1876, twenty-six mills were listed in Colorado Territory.

Colorado Milling and Elevator Company. In 1879, however, extensive milling operation began with the arrival of J. K. Mullen and his purchase of the Excelsior Mills. Mullen built the business in Denver, and then reached out to acquire other mills, and modern equipment (modern at that time) replacing the old burr mills. Mullen's organization was known as the "combination". He incorporated his holdings in the formation of the Colorado Mill and Elevator Company on August 26, 1885. The expansion since that date has been in terms of acquisition of flour mills, elevators, country elevators, bean elevators, and in the production of food and feed. Expansion beyond the state border was natural. Although the company is not the only milling concern in the state, it far outshadows both in size and history, the remainder of grain milling. Of the various flour mills, there is only one operated today that was constructed before the formation of the company in 1885, and that is the largest of the three Denver flour mills owned by the company.

In the process of expansion, mills were acquired or built in Fort Collins, Grand Junction, Greeley, Lamar, Monte Vista, and Pueblo. Less than 50 per cent of the company's flour milling capacity is in Colorado; the rest is in Idaho, Kansas, Missouri, Utah, and Nebraska. Through subsidiaries, other property is managed in California and Nebraska.

One of the important parts of history is the development by this company of country elevators and the location of many of these elevators on ground leased from the railroads.

Merchant's Biscuit Company. Although only one of 150 odd bakeries in the state, the Merchant's Biscuit Company, historically, is one of the most prominent. The company was founded in Denver by Clinton A. Bowman on April 6, 1906. The forty-year growth has been supervised by the founder and his son of the same name. The original site of the company at 9th and Walnut has been retained. The first building, 50 feet by 100 feet, was a reconstructed soap factory. Fourteen varieties of cookies and crackers were originally marketed.

One of the first orders received by the company was for a carload of cookies and crackers to be sent to California for victims of the "fire". Filling this order in twenty-four hours established at once a reputation for the new company. The original building was "added to" in 1910, 1914, 1922, and 1943. In 1912, the basement was floodproofed following the flood of the Platte in that year.

The Merchant's Biscuit Company was merged with United Biscuit Company in 1927, and the former's trade-mark, the four-leaf clover identified with the word "supreme", was adopted.

Merchant's Biscuit expanded beyond Colorado to Abilene, San Antonio, Amarillo, Fort Worth, Wichita Falls, and El Paso, Texas, in the late 20s and early 30s. The original line of fourteen types of cookies and crackers has expanded to 258.

Much of the machinery used in the business was developed by the company. One was a cellophane packaging machine. The company was one of the first bakeries in the country to adopt this type of packaging, and additional machinery was necessary. Production of this machinery is an important sideline of the company. Another development by the company was Merchant's Park, Denver's Baseball Park, originally operated by the company.

Dairy Products

Processing of dairy products into butter, cheese, condensed and evaporated milk, and malted milk has grown over the years into an industry rivaling in size and economic significance that of meat packing and beet sugar production. As early as 1870, one firm was producing butter; by 1880, two firms. A peak was reached in 1929, which was again equaled only after the close of World War II. The industry has been characterized by the growth since 1924 of relatively large companies.

In condensed and evaporated milk, six establishments have become important, largely in the Platte Valley area.

In 1916, Coors of Golden began production of malted milk, largely as a means of providing employment for those who were no longer needed to produce beer; and, secondly, as a market for milk produced over a wide area in northeastern and northwestern parts of the state.

Candy

Candy production in the state began in answer to the sweet tooth demand of the early settlers and when transportation of sugar by ox team and wagon was necessary. However, none of the early small companies continued in business to the present date. The O. P. Baur Confectionery Company is the oldest candy manufacturing company in Colorado, having been in continuous existence since 1871. In that year, Otto P. Baur had organized his business, and located his refreshment parlor at 16th and Lawrence "to satisfy the wants of higher income or 'society' groups for ice cream, bakery goods, and fine candy". Otto Baur had come to Denver from Pottsville, Pennsylvania, in 1867, but had gone on to Elizabethtown, New Mexico, where he had opened a bakery. He soon returned to Pennsylvania and again came west in 1869 and opened a bakery at Evans, where he remained for three years before coming to Denver.

Baur's grew with the city and the area. In 1871, Otto Baur alone could handle all his own business, including custom production of bakery products. By 1891, the firm employed 25; by 1906, 50; by 1920, 150; and doubled after that date.

Baur's first partner from 1878 was Theodore L. Meier, and later, Joe J. Jacobs joined the firm in 1882, becoming president in 1904. The firm remained a partnership from 1878 until 1906, when incorporation took place.

HARD AND SOFT DRINKS

The story of Colorado must include the production of hard, as well as soft, drinks. The former began as an industry soon after the settlement of early communities in the state. In fact, overland stage charges for hauling liquid refreshments to the territory were too high for the early settlers.

Within ten years after the first settlements were established at Denver and Central City and other points, ten breweries were operating in the state. There was also some production of whiskey.

Beer

The number of companies engaged in brewing reached a peak around 1880, when twenty-three companies, scattered in various parts of the state, were producing beer. The number of companies and plants decreased in number until 1920, when but four companies were listed. These were Adolph Coors at Golden, Tivoli Brewing Company of Denver, Philip Schneider of Trinidad, and Walters of Pueblo. These same four companies ceased production of beer with the advent of prohibition and reopened with subsequent repeal. In that interval of no brewing, three of the plants carried on very little activity, but Coors of Golden developed an important business of malted milk. (See Dairy Industries.) The Brewing Industry is somewhat smaller today than it was in 1910—when eleven companies were producing. In the early 1940s Walters acquired the Schneider properties.

For the most part, the brewing industry was originally developed by men with German background.

Distilleries

Two important distilleries at Johnstown and Arvada were constructed near the turn of the century. The Johnstown plant closed before prohibition. The Arvada plant remained primarily as a warehouse after 1920 with some production of alcohol for industrial purposes. Production of whiskey was resumed at Arvada only on a small scale after the repeal of prohibition.

Soft Drinks

Non-alcoholic beverage production and bottling works became important with adoption of prohibition. The growth in total size of the industry, rather than individual companies, is noticeable. By 1940 the industry was approximately double the size of the brewing industry so far as value of product was concerned. The industry, which to some extent has a background in production of mineral waters, was in 1940 seven times as large as the mineral waters industry which had reached a peak around 1910.

Wine

The wine industry of Colorado is almost synonymous with the name of Jay Ambrose. Ambrose founded his winery in Pueblo after repeal of prohibition in 1933; but in 1935, moved his company to Denver partly to be near the market and, secondly, because of the freight rate pattern on barreled wine from California. At the Ambrose plant wines are bottled and labeled "Richeleau". A second operation is the distillery where brandies, champagnes, and other by-products of grapes are produced. A third operation, born in World War II, is the production of jams and jellies. One of the new products of the company for distribution in the states that prohibit sale of products containing over 3.2 per cent alcohol, is a carbonated wine.

FEEDS

Dehydration of alfalfa and production of alfalfa meal began on a large scale with the organization of Denver Alfalfa Milling and Products Company in 1908. The original founder was Floyd M. Wilson. The first plant was built at Hartman, Prowers County. For ten years after the founding of the dehydrating and feed plant, the headquarters were advertised as the Alfalfa Center of the Universe.

Expansion of the company largely in the Arkansas Valley, then in the Platte Valley, led to establishment of dehydrating and milling plants in Bristol, Wilson Junction, Wiley, McClave, Cheraw, Ordway, King Center, Johnstown, Fowler, Fort Lyon, North Lamar, and Holly in Colorado, and Deerfield and Garden City, across the border in Kansas. Expansion elsewhere in Michigan, Missouri, Nebraska, Texas, Arizona, and California is but a recent development. Main offices and headquarters have been maintained at Lamar. The name was changed recently from Denver Alfalfa Milling and Products Company to National Alfalfa Dehydrating Company, and Fred H. Udell replaced the original founder, Wilson, as president.

Market and expansion of the industry is due primarily to changes in feeding of poultry and livestock in eastern as well as western parts of the country.

SERUMS

Development at the Kansas State Agricultural College of a serum to control blackleg and the outbreak of the disease in a herd of Colorado cattle on pasture in Kansas led to the formation of the Franklin Serum Company of Denver.

In 1917, Dr. O. M. Franklin and T. P. Haslam completed a research project at Kansas State Agricultural College in Manhattan. The result of this research was a blackleg aggressin as an effective vaccine; and was to replace spore vaccine administered in pill or powdered form with but little success. Immunity from spore vaccine was usually three to six months at most.

Shortly after completing the research, Franklin, together with F. S. Schoenleber and R. V. Christian, who had been associated with the project, formed a partnership — The Kansas Blackleg Serum Company—to manufacture the serum. Headquarters were established in Wichita. At about this time, Charles E. Collins shipped, as was his usual custom, some of his cattle into Kansas for winter pasture on wheat stubble. Blackleg soon developed; the 1890 remedy of spore vaccine in pill form was administered but with little result. Collins, in the meantime, heard of the new aggressin type of vaccine. Some was obtained, and immediately upon inoculation of the herd, spread of blackleg was halted.

The outcome of this group of events was an agreement whereby Mr. Collins and a Mr. J. B. Case agreed to finance a new company to be formed for the manufacture and sale of the serum. Incorporation papers were filed in Denver in May, 1917, for the Kansas Blackleg Serum Company. Mr. Collins was president of the new corporation until his death in 1944. Equipment was moved from Wichita to Amarillo, Texas, and branch storage and sales offices were established in leading cities in the cattle country of the west and middle west.

A major project of the new corporation was production of a surer, less expensive vaccine. By 1923, vaccine was produced from a culture of sterilized hog liver, brains, and lean meat, inoculated with black-leg culture. The dose was reduced from 5cc to 1cc and a price of ten cents per inoculation was established. From 700,000 inoculations marketed seasonally in 1917, the amount of serum marketed has advanced beyond 5.5 million annually.

A number of other animal vaccines have been developed. Following 1940, and a meeting of various vaccine producing companies, practices were standardized. Today, the company produces 15-16 vaccines, and distributes some additional ones such as anti-hog cholera serum.

In 1927, the company name was changed to the O. M. Franklin Blackleg Serum Company, and in 1937, the word ''blackleg'' was dropped from the company name.

In 1933, the company began major manufacturing in Denver, and has expanded since that time into production in Denver of branding irons, dehorners, tattoo instruments, horn weights, ear notching pliers, combs, and other instruments, including the electrified prod poles. The total metal products now manufactured is in excess of fifty. Local Denver foundries supply castings for most of these instruments. An important foreign market for these products has been developed.

IRON AND STEEL AND THEIR PRODUCTS

Development of iron and steel production and the fabricating plants for these products, together with the manufacture of machinery, especially mining machinery, has been far ahead of the purely local demand. In no other field in manufacturing in Colorado, except-ing only that of the Gates Rubber Company, is the market for prod-ucts so worldwide as it is in iron and steel products and machinery.

Colorado Fuel and Iron Corporation

Until 1942 and the construction of the Geneva Steel Plant in Utah, and the Fontana Steel Plant of the Kaiser Company in California, the Colorado Fuel and Iron Corporation was the only integrated steel company west of the Mississippi River, producing finished steel and operating mines, blast furnaces, open hearth furnaces, rolling

Colorado Fuel and Iron Company Steel Plant at Pueblo

mills, and fabrication plants. The company's history antedates that of the Centennial state by five years. Its earliest predecessor company was organized in November, 1871, and incorporated in January, 1872, as the Central Colorado Improvement Company. The original purpose was the development of land along the Arkansas River and for South Pueblo, primarily as part of the development of the railroads. The moving power back of the organization of the company was General William Jackson Palmer. In 1870, he had led in the organization of the Denver and Rio Grande Railroad with dreams of extension south from Denver to the Rio Grande and on into Mexico. Pueblo had been chosen as a center for mines, smelters, and iron works. Within a few years, coal mines had been developed in Fremont County. A second company, the Southern Colorado Coal and Iron Company, was formed to develop coal lands in Las Animas and

Huerfano Counties. In addition, the company began production of coke at El Moro in 1878. In 1879, the Colorado Coal and Iron Company was organized by the same men who had founded the two predecessor companies, by consolidation of the Improvement and Coal Companies. The new company began construction in 1880 of its blast furnaces, a Bessemer converter, and a rolling mill, and in the first year produced 284 tons of pig iron. A small amount of coke and of pig iron had been produced in Boulder County and in Denver in the early 1870s by John Marshall, after he had left the Colorado Iron Works. By 1881, the Colorado Coal and Iron Company's production had increased to 1392 tons, and by April, 1882, the first rails were rolled. These were 30-foot iron rails for the Denver and Rio Grande Railroad. Until that time all rails were shipped in from Chicago and points east at very high costs. General Palmer, who had organized the predecessor companies, remained president until 1884.

The year 1892 marked the beginning of a new era for the iron and steel industry. In that year, three companies, the Colorado Coal and Iron Company, the Colorado Fuel Company, and the Grand River Coal and Coke Company, consolidated to form a new corporation— the Colorado Fuel and Iron Company. The total assets of the three companies were listed at $18,642,000. The products of the new company were increased to answer the needs of the growing market.

From the standpoint of ownership, the Rockefeller interests became apparent about 1901 and continued in control until 1944, having supplied in the expansion program a major portion of the capital. In 1944, the Rockefeller interests in the company were sold to Charles Allen, Jr., investment banker.

The company had entered receivership in August, 1933, and emerged from the Federal Courts on April 25, 1936, as the Colorado Fuel and Iron Corporation. In 1937, the corporation expanded production facilities beyond Colorado by acquiring the California Wire Cloth Company and its subsidiary, the Pacific Steel and Wire Company of Oakland and South San Francisco. In 1945, the Wickwire Spencer Steel Company was acquired with blast furnaces, rolling mills, and fabricating plants in New York, Massachusetts, and Pennsylvania.

From the standpoint of iron and steel production, the company, since the 1890s, has produced quantitatively an amount of rails and rail products in excess of that used in the eleven western states, as well as a substantial amount of other steel products. The rated steel ingot capacity is 1,272,000 tons per year, approximately 1.4 per cent of the nation's capacity, although during World War II this capacity was exceeded by actual production. Rolling mill capacity in rails and rail products is approximately 12 per cent of the nation's total. The company is also one of the leading producers of chemicals in the West, not only with its by-product coke ovens, but with the newly acquired plant at the Rocky Mountain Arsenal for the production of chlorine and caustic soda.

The company is the largest manufacturing and mining employer in the Mountain States Region, with iron mines in Wyoming and Utah, coal and other raw materials, mines and quarries in Colorado and other states. During World War II the company also produced large calibre shells for the army.

MACHINERY MANUFACTURE

The manufacture of machinery to service the mining industry of the state antedated the state's history, and, to some extent, preceded the Colorado Fuel and Iron Corporation. Lack of transportation from centers of production, either for new machinery or for repairs, actual absence of types of machinery to service the needs of the new mining industry, were the most significant factors. However, the inventive genius of many of the founders was of equal importance as a factor in the establishment of this type of industry in Denver and the mining areas. Despite the relative importance of other industries as compared with mining, the volume of manufacture of mining machinery has predominated in the state over production of other types of machinery.

From the standpoint of beginning, the machinery manufacturers might almost be classified as the Central City Group, the Leadville Group, or the Denver Group.

General Iron Works Group

The group comprising ownership of General Iron Works is by far the largest engaged in manufacturing of machinery in the state in 1947. In 1921, the group of companies headed by Stearns-Roger Manufacturing Company (whose shops had been destroyed by the Pueblo flood in 1921), the Colorado Iron Works, Vulcan Iron Works, Queen City Foundry, and Denver Engineering Works, formed the General Iron Works as the manufacturing company to serve all of their interests. Of the five companies, only the first three named were ready to occupy and use the services of General Iron when it was completed in 1924. In the meantime, the Queen City Foundry had been sold to American Manganese Company, and the Denver Engineering Works had ceased to exist.

Colorado Iron Works. The pioneer establishment in the manufacture of mining, milling, and smelting machinery is the Colorado Iron Works, founded in 1860, just one year after the Gregory, Jackson and contemporary gold discoveries. Machinery from the east was often not suited for the mining, milling, and smelting demands for the Colorado ores, and this, together with the expense and time of transportation by wagon was costly and annoying.

In 1860, two men, Fraser and Scoville, established a foundry and machine shop on half a block of ground on the west side of Larimer Street, just south of Cherry Creek, to do custom work for any of the nearby mines and newly developed mills. In December, 1860, the shops were sold to Joseph M. Marshall, but two years later, as Marshall's interests shifted to coal fields near Erie, Colorado, the shops were sold to A. G. Langford, William L. Lee, and Milo Lee. These men found that the demand for mining equipment and machinery was not in Denver but near the mines and mills, so the plant was moved to Blackhawk. The name was changed to the Blackhawk Foundry and Machine Shop, but was locally known as the Lanford and Company's Foundry. John Wellington Nesmith of Central City was selected as the foundry manager. In 1875, the Blackhawk Foundry was sold to Silas Bertenshaw who continued operations there, but Langford returned to Denver. Here he interested F. J. Ebert, Samuel S. Davidson, and William R. Havens, and this group formed on December 17, 1875, the Colorado Iron Works with a capitalization of $25,000. Shops were located at 471 Larimer Street. Incorporation actually took place on February 26, 1876, five months before Colorado became a state. The four organizers became the officers of the corporation. In 1879, Elbert Headley and John W. Nesmith, who left the foundry at Central City, joined the company following three years of financial difficulties.

The plant specialized in the manufacture of hoisting and milling machinery such as stamp mills, crushers, cornish rolls, as well as lead and blast furnaces.

A fire in Denver in August, 1881, brought attention to the Colorado Iron Works with the destruction of their property. A fireproof building was soon constructed at 33rd and Wynkoop Streets. The total floor space of the new plant of 24,000 square feet was at that time the largest plant of a single works between St. Louis and San Francisco. New machinery had been purchased and employment increased from 100 to 275.

Nesmith assumed leadership of the company in 1886, and ten years later the company was reorganized with a Maine Charter.

Among the new innovations in milling introduced by the company, were steel cyanide tanks to replace concrete and wooden tanks. Ore gates, and irons, ore feeders, hydraulic classifiers, concentration mills, impact screens, dumping cars, and complete ore reduction plants were listed in the 1905 catalogue. T. A. Dickson, who had joined the company in 1903, became manager of the company in 1917, and his family controls the company to 1947.

During World War I the company manufactured ship winches for merchant ships of the U. S. Fleet. This was simply an adaptation of the old mine hoists. During World War II the company was concerned largely with the production of mine equipment used throughout the world for the production of metals. This included equipment not only for mines in the United States, but also for lend-lease. Today the equipment is marketed throughout the world.

The company since 1924 has operated no separate manufacturing establishment, but uses the facilities of the General Iron Works.

Stearns-Roger. The small town of Leadville, Colorado, has been the birthplace, like Central City and Blackhawk, of many Colorado manufacturing industries, but none is more important in the development of the state than that of the Stearns-Roger Manufacturing Company. This company traces its beginning to 1883; the first shop was acquired in 1888. Thomas B. Stearns was the founder, and proved to be one of Colorado's industrial giants. Stearns had received his technical training in the School of Mines of the Brooklyn Polytechnic Institute. He began work in the mining areas of Utah, Colorado, and Montana in 1880. After considerable work with Nelson Hallock of the Colorado Iron Works, he opened the company's office in New York City and headed this office for two years from 1882 to 1883. He returned to Colorado in 1883, and began installation of water works in Colorado Springs and Durango. His major interest, however, was in mining and he opened mine machinery repair shops at Idaho Springs and Georgetown. In 1885, he organized the T. B. Stearns Company, and later that year was joined by his friend, John Roger, in forming the partnership.

While the manufacturing was in Leadville, the office was in Denver, which by this time had assumed a position of leadership among the towns and cities in the state.

Incorporation of the company as the Stearns-Roger Manufacturing Company was completed on May 23, 1891, and the shops were moved to an area along the Fountain River four miles north of the center of the city of Pueblo, which by this time had become a center for smelting non-ferrous as well as ferrous ores. A small plant had been in operation in that city for two years. One of the major reasons for selecting Pueblo was the proximity of the Colorado Fuel and Iron Corporation. The Pueblo shops were almost completely destroyed in the flood of 1921, which carried away patterns, machinery, and other items. Most of the machinery was buried in the sand of the Arkansas River and the wooden patterns floated downstream into eastern Colorado and into Kansas.

At this point, the five companies (mentioned under General Iron Works) were organized, and the company moved to Denver, and Stearns-Roger, the largest of the five firms, assumed leadership of the formation and operation of the General Iron Works.

Business in the early history of the company consisted of general machinery manufacture, together with the design and erection of metallurgical mills, dredges, and power plants, but additional activities have expanded the company's operations into many fields.

In 1889, the company contracted to build the Holden (Globeville) smelter in north Denver. Furnaces and various other items including large quantities of castings were furnished from the company's general manufacturing plant at Pueblo. Additional types of mining machinery were manufactured for smelters at Leadville, Pueblo, and Durango, for the treatment of mixed ores: gold, silver, lead, zinc, and copper.

Since 1917, the company's activities have fallen into five classifications: mining machinery, sugar machinery, power machinery, and gas equipment and general manufacturing.

In sugar beets, the company designed and built the Delta, Utah, 1000-ton daily capacity factory in 1917. In 1937, a plant was designed, and construction supervised for a Canadian sugar beet factory and for another Canadian factory, Stearns-Roger acting as consulting engineers. Specialized factory equipment is also produced, including

Stearns-Roger Manufacturing Plant, Denver

vacuum pans and juice extractors, high pressure evaporators, circular diffusion batteries, crystallizers, granulator pulp presses, ballou beet feeders, and pineapple driers. Specialized equipment is adapted and installed in canning factories and in dehydrating plants.

For the mining industry are included amalgamation flotation plants, cyanide plants for gold and silver ores, dry grinding plants, selective flotation plants and wetherill magnetic separation plants. Part of this work is directly from the company's design and a great deal of it is custom manufacturing for other Denver firms producing mining, sugar factory, and other equipment.

In power and utility plants, production includes municipal water and sewage plants, industrial and power plants for hospitals. One of the most interesting plants is the Kirk Power Station of the Homestate Mining Company of South Dakota. This plant was especially designed and constructed to meet fluctuation loads with 8000 B.T.U. lignite. A number of electrical plants have been built.

In oil and gas equipment Stearns-Roger has specialized in design and construction of absorption plants to extract gasoline from natural gas. The company has also designed and constructed natural gas pipeline dehydration plants to eliminate problems of freezing.

General activities include coal handling equipment, beet loaders, as well as additional equipment for many other industries. During World War II Stearns-Roger entered the field of machine tools including turret lathes. Part of these lathes were designed and built for the machining of 105 mm. and 155 mm. shells; many were used for universal work in the aircraft industries.

Vulcan Iron Works. The third member of the General Iron Works group, the Vulcan Iron Works located in Denver, was organized in 1894 from a small machinery company operated by Gilbert Denton for three years preceding that date. With Mr. Denton in the organization were D. C. West and J. W. Latham. The office and shops were located at 1709 Blake and a few years later property on Wazee was added. In 1898, West's ownership was purchased by Denton and Latham. Denton interests continue, although Latham died in 1921.

With the formation of General Iron Works, the company shops operated from 1910 until 1923 were dismantled.

The company since its founding has been associated with mining and general machinery manufacture. The market which at one time was confined to Colorado, New Mexico, and Wyoming, has since expanded to the entire United States.

During World War I, Vulcan manufactured various kinds of ship machinery, but conversion of the shops and tools for such manufacture was not necessary. Today, Vulcan engineering staff develops mining and sugar beet factory and miscellaneous machinery, as well as winches and steering tubes, and various types of mining equipment for world-wide markets, with manufacturing at the General Iron Works.

OTHER MACHINERY MANUFACTURE

Mine and Smelter Supply Company. The Mine and Smelter Supply Company dates its founding to 1879 with the formation of a partnership of H. N. Kennedy, C. E. Kennedy, and M. A. Dolan, and was located at 307 Fifteenth Street. It was a sales organization, distributing rock drills, compressors, hoists, wire rope, and other mining supplies. In 1881, the partnership was dissolved and E. E. Kennedy continued as a proprietorship until Charles B. Pierce, a banker in Colorado for twenty years, joined him to form the partnership of Kennedy-Pierce. In order to supply needs for the Leadville district, new quarters were purchased at 17th and Blake. From 1890 to 1893, the company rented space at Seventeenth and Wynkoop (now Hendrie and Bolthoff), but moved back to 17th and Blake at the latter date. Exodus from Leadville following the panic of 1893 brought Robert J. Cary and his brother, John Cary, from their supply store in Leadville to Denver. For one year, John Cary became sales manager of Kennedy-Pierce when he left to join Fairbanks-Morse. However, by 1895 Cary left Fairbanks-Morse and its sale of scales, windmills, and mining machinery, to purchase Kennedy's interest in the partnership. (Kennedy moved to California to operate an orange grove.)

On April 23, 1895, Cary organized Mine and Smelter Supply Company. As partners, he had his brother, Robert, Eben Smith, Frank L. Smith, and John Y. Oliver.

For two years the company acted as a wholesale supply house, primarily for the Leadville district, but in 1897, became interested in manufacturing mining machinery. The new men who had become part of the firm had a long background history in mining operation. Eb. Smith had participated in the California Gold Rush of 1849, and with Jerome Chaffee, had brought a stamp mill from St. Joseph, Missouri, in 1860. The Smith and Chaffee Stamp Mill operated at Lake Gulch in Gilpin County. Smith and Chaffee, in the meantime, purchased interests in H. A. W. Tabor's Little Pittsburgh Mine at Leadville and the Tam-O-Shanter Mine in Pitkin County, as well as others in Red Cliff and Leadville. Smith was one of the builders of the Florence and Cripple Creek Railway and, with David Moffatt, constructed the largest and most completely equipped cyanide mill at Cyanide, Colorado. Together with Moffat, Smith and Chaffee were instrumental in founding the First National Bank of Denver.

Smith was president of Mine and Smelter Supply Company from 1895 to 1901. Under his leadership the Mexico Mine and Smelter Supply Company was formed, with a store and warehouse in Mexico City. This was terminated in 1914, and the Mexican business has been handled from El Paso since that date. A branch was opened in Salt Lake City in 1900.

Joseph Seep, a Standard Oil Company buyer from Pennsylvania, became interested in the company in 1900, and from 1901 to 1904, purchased the Smith-Cary interests. From 1904 to date, the company has been closely associated with the Seep family.

Names attached to specialized milling machinery from Mine and Smelter Supply Company are Wilfley and Marcy. By 1905, Mine and Smelter acquired manufacturing rights for the Wilfley Concentrating Table, and A. R. Wilfley, the inventor, had become associated with the company as consulting engineer and director, which positions he held until his death in 1927. The trend toward the use of low grade ores, especially in copper, corresponded to the development and use of this famous concentrating table. Over 24,000 of these tables, weighing in excess of 60 million pounds, have been shipped to all parts of the world where low-grade ores have been handled.

A second inventor, Frank E. Marcy, who had been manager of the Mine and Smelter Salt Lake Office, developed the famous Marcy Ball mill to improve the coarse crushing and grinding equipment, particularly the stamp mills. Modifications of the ball mill were developed in 1917, with production of the Marcy Rod Mill substituting the use of rods for balls in the crushing process. These mills, while produced primarily for copper, have become important in the pulp and paper industry, and promise to become more important in the iron ore industry as lower grade ores require beneficiation.

From the standpoint of manufacturing, the Wilfley shops at 13th and Huron proved inadequate; consequently, since 1921, first through Queen City Foundry and later through Vulcan Iron Works, the jobbing contracts have been done by the General Iron Works.

Besides the standbys, the Wilfley tables and Marcy ball and rod mills, hot milling machines, rock bit grinders, density controllers, rubber push valves, belt feeders, laboratory crushers, pulverizers, circuitrons, placer equipment, amalgamators and the Massco-Fahren-wald flotation machines are produced.

In World War II, the company's activity was accelerated in furnishing vital machinery to copper, nickel, lead, zinc, vanadium, and other metallics industries. A second activity was that of furnishing as supplier a number of articles needed on an emergency basis.

Many of the employees have been with the company in its machinery development for many years. Among these, in addition to Albert Seep, are Oscar Johnson, Herman F. Seep, J. D. Nicholson, and H. J. Gundlach.

Hendrie and Bolthoff Manufacturing and Supply Company. Second only to the Colorado Iron Works in age as a machinery manufacturing plant in the state is the Hendrie and Bolthoff Manufacturing and Supply Company. Today the company is one of the largest distributors of machinery equipment and hardware in the Mountain States, and until World War I, was one of the leading manufacturers of mining machinery. As an additional item, it is a company organized in Colorado within two years after the Gregory Gulch gold discoveries.

The Hendrie Iron Works was a going concern in Burlington, Iowa, in the 1850s, and the discovery of gold in Colorado led Charles Hendrie, Sr., to come to Colorado to investigate the machinery needs of the infant mining industry. He traveled to California in 1860, and secured a number of prints of mining machinery from that state. At Burlington, he began work manufacturing mining machinery for use in Colorado. The machinery produced was shipped via Hendrie's own ox-train service to Central City and other mining camps.

In 1861, Charles Hendrie, together with a John Butler, organized the Eureka Foundry at Central City, and within a few years, the new plant completely overshadowed the one at Burlington, Iowa, and Charles F. and William C. Hendrie, sons of one of the founders, came to Colorado to manage the plant established by their father.

Within a few years, Henry Bolthoff joined the Hendries in Central City. He had been with the Hendrie Iron Works since the early fifties, and was superintendent at the Burlington, Iowa, plant at the time they had decided to move to Colorado. Bolthoff was known for his remarkable skill as a mechanic, and was known to the river boat industry along the Mississippi. With equal facility he could design a drawing, build a pattern, mould, or perform machine shop work. A co-partnership was formed in 1874 as Hendrie Brothers and Bolthoff. Bolthoff's mechanical genius was soon known, and orders came from Mexico, Alaska, and many other countries. Especially successful were the Bolthoff steam hoist and the Bolthoff sample grinder. The latter is still in use in 1947, although patented in 1876. A number of complete mills were constructed, including an old overshot water sheet which supplied power for a mill near Blackhawk. Bolthoff had personally moulded the segmented driving gear bolted to the arms of the wheel.

The Hendrie and Bolthoff firm was the first important user of coke in the state, but had to bring the coke from east of the Mississippi and the anthracite from Pennsylvania, using the famous ox teams for the transportation projects until the opening of coke plants some years later by the Colorado Fuel and Iron Company.

In 1876, a branch office was opened in Denver, just east of the present Great Western Sugar Building.

In addition to manufacturing and repair work, the firm had specialized in giving service beyond that of installation of machinery, and the distribution part of the business developed as a natural sequence. This included shipments to Mexico of products far outside the field of machinery and mining goods.

Among the important problems was that of hauling heavy equipment to the mining areas. H. and B. designers met problems with such items as the sectionalized mine hoist, cast in small units so that it might be packed on mule backs. The cable problem was solved by tying several loops of the cable upon a mule, extending the cable to the next mule, repeating the coil process, and thus continuing until all the cable had been loaded. If one mule went over a cliff, he could go only a few feet. The Hendrie and Bolthoff teams became rather famous in the state.

The company moved to Denver in 1879, and in 1898, reincorporated under the name of Hendrie and Bolthoff Manufacturing and Supply Company. In addition to the two founders, other names prominent in the history of the company, include the Watermans— Henry P., who joined the company in 1881, his brother, Herbert, who joined in 1885, and Herbert's son of the same name, Robert W. Harrington, Everett Brown, James S. Smith, and Walter G. Tripp.

Among the early customers whose names are shown on the books are: Charles Boettcher, Eben Smith (Mine and Smelter Supply Company), H. A. W. Tabor, J. K. Mullen, founder of the Colorado milling industry, Chester S. Morey, Senator Nathaniel P. Hill, founder of the smelting industry of the state, Hallack and Howard, Roebling Sons, National Tube Works, Gardner-Governor Company (Gardner-Denver), Governor James B. Grant, and others.

Silver Engineering Company. In 1902, William A. Box and Frank A. Dillon bought an interest in a tooling and repair shop at 19th and Blake. This company was dissolved in 1910 and became the William

A. Box Iron Works Company. The shops of the W. O. McFarlane Company at 33rd and Blake were purchased.

The original purchase in the partnership had been financed by Box from sales of a patent on a rock drill. After 1910, the Box Company manufactured lathes, boring mills, and gear cutting equipment, and a world-wide market was developed. Of the machinery and equipment, including sugar factory equipment, the best known was the Leadville hoist. During World War I, Box served as president of the Denver Ordnance Company, formed to promote the production of equipment needed by the government in conduct of the war. (Other companies participating were Shaw Iron Works, Vulcan Iron Works, Queen City Foundry.) The Box Company engines for warships were produced by this organization.

At the death of Box in 1931, the factory and equipment were sold to Fred H. Roberts, and in 1934, Roberts joined Harold Silver in forming the Roberts-Silver Engineering Company. In 1935, Silver purchased Roberts' interests to form the Silver Engineering Company. The Silver Engineering Company, although relatively young in Colorado Manufacturing History, has achieved, since 1934, a prominent position, especially in the newer sugar beet factory equipment, complementing types of equipment produced by the other companies in the Denver area and by the Silver Iron Works of Ogden, Utah. This organization has developed its market for such machinery throughout sugar beet producing areas of the United States and Canada. The old McFarlane, and later, Box Iron Works, were completely revamped and re-tooled for the new types of production for sugar beet factory equipment as well as many other types of industrial machinery. The company has also established the largest steel warehouse between the Missouri River and the Pacific Coast.

The Dorr Company. The Dorr Company history begins with the invention of the Dorr Classifier in 1904, although the company was not incorporated until 1916. The original form of the classifier, the Model A, used a crank and rollers traveling on a track equipped with a switch to get a raking motion, and was developed by the Lundberg, Dorr, and Wilson Mill at Terry, South Dakota. The classifier made the difference between success and failure in many of the metal mills. Two machines for use in New Mexico and one in Wyoming were built on a royalty basis. A Chicago firm (Skillin and Richards Manufacturing Company) for a number of years manufactured the metal parts, but the wood box was built in the plant.

The Dorr thickener developed in 1906, for the 300-ton mill of the Mogul Mining Company of New Mexico, proved its value from the start. This was somewhat unusual, inasmuch as no test work was done on any small operation. A Mr. Eames of Stearns-Roger Manufacturing Company assisted John Van Nostrand Dorr in designing the thickener, and Stearns-Roger began manufacturing Model B and Model C, which proved to be the standards.

Dorr had moved to Denver in 1906, and the company became the Dorr Cyanide Machinery Company in 1909. Dorr retained control of mills in South Dakota. In 1910, expansion in use of Dorr equipment became world wide. In 1912, the Dorr agitator was developed for use in the cyanide process. This had been designed for an Ontario Mill, but was installed in the Ophir mills in Ophir, Colorado.

The Dorr thickener was tried in the slime plants of the Anaconda Copper Company in Montana, and this experiment led to the first Tray Thickener or the anaconda or superimposed type, and from that came the first closed type installed at the Homestake mines. Model D was then forthcoming.

In 1914, the Dorr equipment, with but slight changes, was adapted for sanitary engineering, and within the same year, added to the paint industry. Other names and firms assisting in this development of machinery included Reybold from Hendrie and Bolthoff, Blomfield from Golden Cycle, and W. A. Neill from Allis-Chalmers.

By 1919, the Dorr equipment was serving the sugar beet industry, and was also introduced in 1919 as thickeners in cane sugar factories in Cuba. In 1920, work with sanitary engineering was expanded, and with the tanning industry. In June, 1931, union of Dorr Company and Oliver Company of Canada was brought about. New fields entered into include mercury, titanium, oil, nickel, insecticides, phosphates, bauxite, paper, rayon, diamonds, asphalt, alcohol, fertilizer, molybdenum, cadmium, sulphur, distilling starch, vegetable oil, and acetic acid, in which the Dorr Company equipment is used.

Morse Brothers Machinery Company. The S. and H. Supply Company was formed in 1896 as a sales agency for a number of Denver firms manufacturing mining equipment. In 1898, this company was reorganized as the Morse Brothers Machinery and Supply Company (George and Bradbury Morse), and manufacturing was added to the sales and distribution phases. To date, the repair and reconditioning of mining machinery and equipment remains the most important part of the business. After the turn of the century, the company began the manufacture of machines for concentration and treatment of all ores, metallic as well as non-metallic. Old smelters throughout the state were purchased and the machinery therein reconditioned. In 1936, the name of the company was changed to the Morse Brothers Machinery Company (the name "Supply" was dropped), and a new phase of business was added, that of design and manufacture of entirely new machinery. The market is world-wide. The reorganized company was headed by Max Grimes.

Rock Drills and Special Mining Equipment

Perhaps no problem in mining in Colorado, as well as in other areas, has been more serious than that of producing rock drills that were both efficient, and at the same time, avoided dread rock or mine dust. Development of efficient drilling machinery is actually later than that of the development of other types of milling, rock crushing, and smelting machinery. Colorado manufacturers have played a prominent part in development of this type of machinery.

Rock drill machines were produced in England and Germany as early as 1844 and 1853, and application made in the driving of the Mount Genis tunnel in Switzerland in 1861. A drill had been invented in Boston as early as 1860, and was improved and used in drilling the Hoosac Tunnel in Massachusetts in 1866. Later improvements are associated with Colorado from the early mining days, primarily by J. B. Ingersoll, A. Sargeant, and J. George Leyner, and by 1897, a protoype of the present rock drill was developed.

The first organization in Colorado to develop this type of drill was the Storey Electric and Power Company, headed by Joule Storey of Boulder in 1889. This company was apparently quite unsuccessful, partly because the compressed air drill has become the most important type in this field, replacing the electric drill.

J. George Leyner, the first white child born in Boulder (1860), had worked with the Burleigh steam-operated rock drill which had replaced the single jacking and double jacking drilling methods in the larger mines. Leyner invented a hammer drill operated by compressed air, which actuated a hammer striking the end of the drill steel, while the steel was rotated in the hole, thus greatly reducing the required time for drilling as well as increasing the work done. He pioneered another important improvement in making drill steel with a hole through the axis so that a stream of water could be introduced at the bottom of the hole, thus preventing dust and washing out the rock particles resulting from drilling operations. Leyner's supposedly basic patents as related to commingling of air and water through hollow drill steel, proved valueless, but his contributions had been made.

The J. George Lehner Engineering Works, near Littleton, were established in 1893. Development of this company was rapid and basic patents were purchased by Ingersoll-Rand and later the Leyner Engineering Works was purchased by Ingersoll-Rand in 1920.

By 1905, two other drills had become important in Colorado. These were the Murphy drill, manufactured by the C. T. Carnahan Manufacturing Company, and the Shaw drill, made by the C. S. Shaw Manufacturing Company. Shaw was the first to use the expanding air feed principle today in universal use.

The name, Waugh, is most closely associated with rock drill manufacture. Daniel S. Waugh, in 1905, recognized the inadequacies of the Shaw and Murphy drills. In that year a company had been formed to develop the Iler Rock Drill designed by F. M. Iler, and was known as the Iron Rock Drill Manufacturing Company. This drill was somewhat crude, but was used with some success in the Cripple Creek District. This drill, partly because of its weight (20 pounds), was too cumbersome for a man to support and drill holes above the horizontal. The company's plant was one room on Blake Street west of Cherry Creek. In the manufacture of this drill, first at the Blake Street address and later at 1415-1419 Eighteenth Street, the gauges were actually hand made. There were no standarized gauges, micrometers, or calipers used. Waugh joined the company in 1906 and designed the drill, which became world famous as the Waugh drill. Another member of the combination was William H. Leonard, from Cripple Creek. He had come to Colorado at the age of eighteen, and had been associated with Spencer Penrose, Charles MacNeill, and Charles L. Tutt in Cripple Creek in starting the first chlorination mill. Leonard served as president of the Denver Rock Drill Manufacturing Company from its creation until 1927, when he became chairman of the Board of Directors of the successor company. (He died June 29, 1947.)

Iler Rock Drill Manufacturing Company was reorganized on January 12, 1907, by incorporation of the Denver Rock Drill Manufacturing Company as successor. The most successful drill produced by this company was the old 8c. and the first big order came from Cananea Consolidated Copper Company at Cananea, Sonora, Mexico. It was Hendrie and Bolthoff that installed the machine tools.

The Denver Rock Drill did not win a coveted 1000-pound contest in South Africa in 1907, but, as a result of that experience, the company developed drills that met the mining demand of the Rand Area. The first big orders, however, came from the Kimberley diamond mines.

Numerous other drills were developed, but certain ones proved unpopular or unsuccessful. However, Dreadnaught and Clipper drills were built. The No. 60 (Dreadnaught) was used in construction of the Rogers Pass Tunnel for the Canadian Pacific Railroad. By 1912, the business was well established in both the Rand and Kimberley districts in Africa. The Clipper drill proved popular in Utah. On June 30, 1927, the Denver Rock Drill Company was consolidated with the Gardner Governor Company of Quincy, Illinois, to form the new company, Gardner-Denver Company. The plants have continued to be operated separately, each complementing the other in the types of drills and other machinery produced. Manufacture of rock drills, drill steel sharpeners, air motors, mine car loaders, and other mining equipment, remained in Denver. Other company ownership is in LaGrange, Missouri, for the production of iron castings, and another factory at Johannesburg, South Africa, which serves part of the needs of the gold, diamond, and copper fields in that country.

A. R. Wilfley and Sons Company. A. R. Wilfley came to Colorado from Missouri at the age of 18, and with some experience in operation of a grist mill. At Kokomo, Colorado, he operated as engineer, assayer, and deputy U. S. assayer, then took a lease on some of the inactive properties around Kokomo. In 1886, he drove a tunnel to reach the ore-bearing veins from the low part of the ridge on the Searle Gulch side. Mines developed there, such as "Aftermath", "White Quail," and others proved bonanzas largely because of Wilfley's first great invention, the Wilfley's Concentrating Table The first patent granted on the table was in April, 1897.

The Wilfley table incorporated the best ideas of all other concentrating tables, and handled the finest slimes or the coarsest sands with excellent results. Action of the old jig was preserved with the upward and downward movements of water flowing across the riffles of the table. After the ore had been ground in the ball mill and screened, the discharge was ready for the Wilfley table and its removal of the free gold before flotation.

Exclusive sales rights to the table were purchased by the Mine and Smelter Supply Company of Denver, and the Wilfley Ore Concentrator Syndicate of Moorgate Street, London, in 1905.

Wilfley had, in the meantime, moved his operations from Kokomo to Denver. (See Mine and Smelter Supply Company.)

In 1913, Wilfley and his two sons, George and Elmer, began work on a sand pump, and following 1920, on an acid pump. One of the principles was design and construction of new machinery and equipment in Denver during the winter, and testing out during the summer at Kokomo and Silverton. Not until after the death of the father in 1927 did incorporation take place as A. R. Wilfley and Sons. Since that time, the company had devoted efforts to the design and manufacture of sand, acid, and slurry centrifugal pumps. The sand and acid pumps are sold through the McFarlane-Eggers Company.

C. S. Card Iron Works and Mine Cars. The Card Iron Works had its origin in the formation of a partnership founded in Denver by two machinists, C. S. Card and George W. Weber, in 1882. The original location was 1437 Blake Street, and repair and custom work on mining machinery occupied most of the shop facilities. Within ten years, the company began specializing in mining machinery and mine haulage equipment.

On January 17, 1900, George Weber retired, and a corporation, The Card and Weber Machine Company, was organized; on February 4, 1907, the name was changed to C. S. Card Iron Works Company. The company moved to 2501 West 16th Avenue in 1911. Mine cars for coal, metal, and quarry work, as well as industrial cars, small wheels, track work, frogs and switches, hoisting cages and skips rope haulage supplies are included in the equipment produced. The company became the largest manufacturer of mine cars and small wheels west of the Mississippi.

Stroehle Machinery and Supply Company. Actually, there is only one machinery manufacturing company in Colorado today whose span of single family ownership outdates the state. This is the Stroehle Machinery and Supply Company. George Stroehle, a Civil War Veteran, came to Blackhawk in 1865, and established his business in that year. He had begun by traveling among mining camps repairing boilers, hoists, pumps, and other mining equipment. The demand for new boilers was high in Gilpin County, so Stroehle began manufacture and repair work there.

Stroehle helped build the first boiler used in Gilpin County, and expanded his business from that point. He died in 1912 and, since that date, two of his sons have directed the activity of the company from Idaho Springs and Blackhawk. The greatest production of the company was before electricity and air pressure had taken the place formerly held by steam. The company's business, today largely that of repair work, is found almost entirely in Gilpin, Clear Creek, and Boulder Counties.

McFarlane-Eggers. Peter McFarlane, together with his brother, William O. McFarlane, organized the W. O. McFarlane Company in 1869 in Central City. At this time, Peter was but twenty years of age, but had been in Colorado at various mining camps for four years. The foundry and machine shop manufactured crushing, hoisting, and milling machinery. It was Peter McFarlane's genius that developed the Gilpin County Bumping Table following the stamp mill and amalgam plate operations. The McFarlane shops also built the Blake type of ore crushers which were driven by power and thus greatly increased the capacity of the mills. The McFarlane shops also manufactured steam engines for driving the crushing and auxiliary machinery of the mills as well as steam hoists.

In 1892, the W. O. McFarlane Company moved to Denver, purchasing the machine shops of James W. Jackson at 1734 Fifteenth Street. This was the oldest and best known of the Denver foundry shops, having been in continuous business since 1870. McFarlane continued Jackson's business, turning out Blake and Dodge crushers, stamp mills, automatic ore feeders, ore cars, as well as boiler engines, hoists, mine pumps, and the only Finlayson Reverse Hoist in the region.

Shops were too small and in 1898, McFarlane built a group of buildings at 33rd and Blake (later the William A. Box Iron Works, Roberts Engineering, and, later, Silver Engineering). However, Peter McFarlane and his two sons continued business in Central City as Peter McFarlane and Sons, until 1912, when they established shops at 2763 Blake as a partnership with Frank Eggers. The McFarlane-Eggers Company was incorporated in 1916. Fred McFarlane, one of the two sons of Peter McFarlane, heads the company. The biggest business is manufacture of the Wilfley pump for A. R. Wilfley and Sons.

Other companies

Four companies now generally forgotten, that at one time played an important part in the manufacture of machinery, are Hendey and Meyer Engineering Company, Denver Engineering Works, the Queen City Foundry, and F. M. Davis Iron Works.

Arthur Hendey and H. H. Meyer organized the Excelsior Foundry and Machine Shops on April 1, 1878, on a site at 16th Street, just below the Colorado Central Railroad Depot. Meyer had come from Germany as a child, and had received his apprentice training in St. Louis. He worked at various foundries in Colorado for eleven years before forming the partnership with Hendey. Meyer invented a valve for steam engines, and Hendey specialized in ore concentrators preceding the Wilfrey table. Incorporation was accomplished on May 1, 1884. H. R. Wolcott was president; Meyer and Hendey were the other officers. In 1895, the company was acquired by the Denver Engineering Works, which had been in existence since 1876, and had occupied a large plant at 13th and Blake since 1882.

In the year of acquisition of the Meyer and Hendey plant by the Denver Engineering Works, Frank E. Shepherd became associated with the company. He brought with him a background of training from M. I. T. and machinist experience in locomotive shops of the Boston and Albany Railroad. He had come to Colorado in 1889. At Leadville, he had designed and constructed the ore roasting plant for the union smelter and Citizens Electric Power Company. In Denver, he had designed the Flue Dust Settling Chambers for the Omaha and Grant Smelting Company. Shepherd had become president of the Denver Engineering Company in 1906. The company manufactured the first ball and rod mills made in Colorado. Other products included the Brunton and Snyder ore samplers, crushers and crushing equipment, Richards pulsator jigs and classifiers. Other equipment was manufactured for metal and coal mines in Utah, Colorado, and Montana, as well as for mines in Japan, British Columbia, and Mexico. The company also designed and furnished mill machinery and equipment for the Globe Smelter, the Arkansas Valley Smelter at Leadville, and the Mercur Smelter near Salt Lake. The company also designed and furnished mill machinery and equipment for various ore treatment plants at Boulder, Clear Creek, and Summit Counties in Colorado, for the slime plant of the Gold King Mill at Gladstone, Colorado, and the Gold Prince Mill at Animas Fork, and the Liberty Bell Mill at Telluride.

The Denver Engineering Company was one of the original companies of the General Iron Works group, but did not continue, and the work of the company was taken over largely by Stearns-Roger in 1924.

The Queen City Foundry was founded in 1891, although incorporation was not completed until February 18, 1895. Five Cordingly brothers owned and operated the business of manufacturing crushers, flanges, fittings, machinery castings, and mining car wheels. They hoped to supervise the foundry work at General Iron Works, but sold to American Manganese in 1924. Harvey Cordingly, last of the five brothers, died in 1946.

Francis M. Davis, junior partner with M. Ensminger in the firm of Ensminger and Davis, who operated after 1876 at 8th and Larimer, was from Jamestown, New York. He came to Denver in 1874.

Ensminger retired from partnership March 12, 1881, and John Smith became junior partner to Davis. The company operated under the name of Denver Foundry and Machine Company until June 29, 1891, when the company was incorporated as F. M. Davis Iron Works. On December 11, 1888, Davis received a patent on his favorite invention, the Horse Power Hoisting Whim, which received praise wherever it was used. Also produced were ore cars and buckets, smelting furnaces, and quarry machinery.

Davis died in December, 1912, and his iron works passed into control of the shortlived Plaines Iron Works.

Iron and Steel Fabrication

Exclusive of machinery manufacture, iron and steel fabrication have played a prominent part in Colorado Manufacturing History. Some of these companies began as forge shops or foundries, as did the machinery manufacturers, and their history goes back at least to 1870. The major steel fabricators became highly publicized during World War II, with the construction of pre-fabricated escort vessels, and other nautical items.

As early as 1940, leaders of a number of the important fabricators visualized the dangers involved in impending war, and began planning accordingly. Gairald Garrett, vice-president of Thompson Pipe and Steel, assumed the leadership. Through co-operation with leaders of other "flat" and "structural" steel producers, he presented the picture of capacity for steel fabrication to army, navy, and maritime officials on both coasts. A number of reports were made to procurement officials, and after thorough investigation, Mare Island Navy Yard officials granted a contract for thirty-nine destroyer escorts to Denver fabricators. The price was approximately three million dollars each. Before the order was completed, the cost was reduced to approximately one million dollars each. Many additional orders were placed for such items as navy bulkheads, decks, deck houses, gun platforms, engine mounts, bits, and clocks, parts of baby flat tops. Also included were buoys for torpedoes and anti-submarine nets, pontoons, heaters. For the army there were floating piers and rocket heads.

The first dry land launching of goods produced for the navy took place at 32nd and Walnut—when the first "Shipyard of the Rockies" was christened on October 24, 1943. The major fabricators were Thompson Pipe and Steel, Eaton Metal Products Company, Denver Steel and Iron, Midwest Steel and Iron, and E. Burkhardt and Sons Steel and Iron Works. Also included as partial fabricators, or forge or machinery contractors, were American Forge Company, and Silver Engineering.

Thompson Pipe and Steel. The Thompson Pipe and Steel Company, known for its tremendous contributions to war work, had its beginning in the 1870s in a small shop at 15th and Larimer Streets. The name at that time was the John Young Sheet Metal Works. It was in 1878 that this shop produced a strong, light wall riveted steel pipe. This was the real beginning of pipe fabrication, or for that matter, important flat steel fabrication in Colorado.

In 1881, Young moved to Blake Street between 16th and 17th Streets, and again in 1888, to 23rd and Blake. In 1892, William A. Weigele opened a shop at 3206 Blake, and soon thereafter, bought the "Young" Shop and moved the Consolidated Company to 2949 Larimer. The new company was Weigele Riveted Steel Pipe Works.

In 1921, Lloyd E. Thompson and Associates purchased the Weigele Plant and organized the Thompson Manufacturing Company, and moved the plant to its Larimer and 30th Streets location. In 1941, the name was changed to Thompson Pipe and Steel.

The original steel riveted pipe was demanded originally by the gold mining industry to carry water for sluice box operations and other needs. The next fabricated flat steel products were high pressure steel pipe and smokestacks. The former was needed in the gold mining districts to carry a stream of water under high pressure—nozzled down until the force became strong enough to cut through hard rock. This process antedated hard rock electric drills. The smokestack was needed for the "Globe" smelter.

After the early demand in mining and smelting industries, came the need for agricultural, construction and manufacturing industries, and a line of welded steel pipe, long span steel pipe, riveted steel pipe, and standard steel pipe was developed. Also included are well casings, culverts, guard railings and reflector signs, storage tanks, and pressure tanks.

As leaders of the company, John Young and William Weigele are listed first, then Lloyd Thompson. Gairald Garrett, vice-president of the company, in addition to his war activity, is credited with introducing steel head gates, metal flumes, and irrigation equipment. James L. Brown, president since 1930, is credited with a number of innovations in steel fabrication.

Eaton Metal Products Company. The Eaton Metal Products Company is one of the newer steel fabricators. It was established at 1841 Wazee Street on June 25, 1919, but moved within three years to 33rd and Walnut. In 1924, the company purchased acreage at 4800 York Street—and built a modern plant at this site. In its short history, it became the largest fabricator of flat steel products in Colorado.

During the war period, its activities were confined to production of War Goods (outlined above). The company's history is closely allied with the petroleum industry as well as chemicals, mining and agriculture. The first line is tank trucks, then filling station and gas and gasoline equipment, pumps, compressor hose, and other tippers for coal mines. The men who first organized the company in Denver, as a subsidiary of the Eaton Metal Products Corporation of Omaha, include J. R. Travis, Earl Liston, and R. H. Preston.

Other Fabricators

Midwest Steel and Iron, Burkhardt and Sons, and Denver Steel and Iron Company, all prominent in shipbuilding during World War II and in production of fabricated structural steel products, trace their history to the 1900s, and to some extent beyond that time. All three companies have been prominent in fabricating structural steel for buildings, bridges, and other items. A fourth company, the Hardesty Division of American Rolling Mills, dates its history to the 1880s when production of a cocoa grinder became necessary to sell part of the food products being distributed. From the original patent was developed one of the foremost flat steel fabricators in Denver and the Rocky Mountain area.

PRECISION INSTRUMENTS

Heiland Research Corporation. Heiland Research Corporation was formed in 1934 by C. A. Heiland and J. C. Hallister, to explore for oil. Lack of adequate seismic instruments led the firm into development of equipment sufficiently sensitive to record accurately geological formations. The company began manufacturing instruments for other companies as demand developed, and manufacturing rather than exploration for oil became the major purpose of the firm. Exploration for oil in the United States, Canada, and Mexico was discontinued in 1941.

The seismic equipment has found extensive use by the Bureau of Reclamation and Army engineers in locating bed rock for dam foundations.

A second field is that of photographic equipment, and flash synchronizers. This development is because an employer of the firm was an amateur photographer.

The plant, originally located at 1731 Arapahoe, moved to 130 East Fifth Avenue.

Hathaway Instrument Company. The Hathaway Instrument Company was organized and developed by Claude M. Hathaway, his two brothers, Paul and Edward, a sister, Olive, and wives of Claude and Edward.

Claude Hathaway entered employment of General Electric soon after his graduation from Colorado University in 1928. Some few years later his wife's health required the family's return to Colorado. Claude Hathaway set out to establish his own business to (*a*) engage in research in technical instruments, (*b*) render a development and engineering service, and (*c*) to manufacture special instruments and apparatus for industry. The first plant was established in the basement of Hathaway's home at 517 University Boulevard. After the plant had overrun the upstairs, time to move was recognized and, at the same time, the old Ellis Canning Factory at Bucklel Boulevard and South Clarkston became available. At this address, Hathaway entered the development stage. The first instruments developed were seismic oscillographs. This was for use in the oil drilling industry. This type construction of instrument aided in determining rock, sand, and shale strata below the earth's surface.

A second type of instrument developed was the "strain gauge." This instrument determines the amount of strain to which structural parts are subjected.

In wartime, production was geared to the airplane industry—in precision instruments to measure strain and in the machining of airplane parts. These included the flight analyzer, landing analyzer, parachute drop recorder, velocity gain recorder, and the general purpose oscillograph.

Gauges, oscillographs, have a world-wide peacetime market.

Dental Specialty Manufacturing Company. Four companies, all developing after 1920, are prominent in the production of special tools and equipment used in dental offices. Manufacture of dental equipment, especially that of hand tools, began in 1910, with William O. Mussey, Sr. He had been a retailer of such equipment for twelve years. The original manufacturing was carried on in the home as a proprietorship. Incorporation took place in 1939. W. O. Mussey, Jr., and R. W. Brown have developed a business which has no relationship to Colorado from the standpoint of major marketing area or as a source of raw materials. Like a number of other manufacturing establishments, Dental Specialty Manufacturing Company has a world-wide market. Other companies have become prominent in manufacturing dental equipment, following somewhat the leadership of the Dental Specialty Manufacturing Company, and producing equipment that complements that of Dental Specialty.

William Ainsworth and Sons. William Ainsworth arrived in Denver in 1874 to begin the watchmaking trade which he had learned in the factory of the Elgin Watch Company. After one year in Denver, he moved to the more thriving Central City. His talent in repairing precision equipment and machinery soon came into general use. At that time, Colorado assayers were purchasing assay balances and repair services from Oertling Manufacturers in England. The time consumed in shipping to and from England would require from three months to more than a year. Ainsworth, from his Central City jewelry and watch repair shop, offered his services to local assayers in the repair of their balances, and soon convinced them that shipment overseas for repair was unnecessary. His jewelry shop soon became the center for repair of balances used in weighing the precious metals mined from various areas in Colorado.

Ainsworth then set to work to build assay balances and to make improvements on those in use. He completed his first new equipment in 1878. This was the first balance made in America in which the short beam was used.

Ainsworth moved to Denver in 1880, to be in a better geographical location to serve mining areas of the entire state. He located his shop in the "Good Block", and later at 18th and Larimer, and began making his "Button Balance." During 1886, he began construction of a building on what is the present site of the company, at 2151 Lawrence Street.

The majority of tools used in the factory were of his own design and construction, because they had to conform to special requirements for fine workmanship. Lathes and milling machines were made with the help of a hand plane which Ainsworth had shipped in to shape up the bed of his lathe. In 1894, was begun the manufacture of the Brunton Pocket Transit. This remains a major production item to date. It was adapted for use by the U. S. Army in both World Wars.

Large transits and levels for use in surveying in the mining districts were at one time a major item of production, but were discontinued before the turn of the century. Since 1925, production of the analytical balance has been a prominent part of manufacturing activities. Market for the products is world-wide.

The company was one of the first users of aluminum. This was imported as early as 1885 at $14.00 an ounce, and was used in the balance beam. Also adapted was the all-aluminum case for balances to replace the wood case of European and eastern United States manufacture.

Edges and bearings of clear hard agate are made entirely within the Ainsworth factory. Most of the agates are imported.

The company was not incorporated until 1923. It had been at first a proprietorship, and then in 1900, a partnership, when William Ainsworth had added his two sons, Robert G. and Alfred W., as partners. William Ainsworth died in 1917. Robert Ainsworth withdrew his interests in 1937. In company history to 1947, the name of Gordon S. Clayson must be added to that of the Ainsworths.

SPORTING GOODS

One of the smallest, but, nevertheless, important Departments of Dave Cook's Sporting Goods Company in Denver is the manufacture of fishing tackle. This enjoys a world-wide market. Many nationally known flies have been "invented" by this company. A number of companies engaged in manufacture have developed in Colorado in the past few years.

Fineline Tackle Company. The Fineline Tackle Company traces its beginning in late 1890s with the organization of a partnership— Gorstine-Finch Sporting Goods Company. For many years it was strictly a retail and jobbing company. It was in answer to demands of the retail trade that manufacturing was begun.

Products include snelled hooks, spinners, split short sinkers, and flies. An important part is the patterns for trout flies. One of its important products is the patterned Pott's hair trout fly. The company is significant in that hand methods are used. Except for an office staff, the employees work in their own homes manufacturing "tying" flies. Included in the employees are a number of handi-capped—even one who is deaf, dumb and blind.

Wright and McGill. Wright and McGill Fishing Equipment Com-pany had its inception in the demand of two intrepid fishermen for flies that would catch Colorado trout. Two cousins, Stan M. Wright, a bank examiner, and his cousin, A. D. McGill, a sporting goods sales-man, were both Izaak Walton devotees. Following their World War I army experience, they decided not to return to their former occupa-tions, but to enjoy full time their fishing and its offshoot production of lure to entice the wisest trout. In 1921, the business was organized and established in Clayton Building at 17th and Lawrence. Success with dry flies led to expansion into snelled hooks and loose hooks. They later moved to 1463 York, from there to Colfax and Lincoln, and to 431 Grant. One of the early developments was the "Eagle Claw."

The company entered in 1946 the production of fishing rods by purchasing the former Granger Rod Factory at the Grant Street address. The company now produces all the equipment needed by the "compleat angler."

Outbreak of the Spanish Civil War closed the line of supply of silk thread—and Wright and McGill asked Dupont to supply a sub-stitute for the Spanish silkworm gut. The synthetic Dupont supplied was a new product, mono-filament nylon. It was in the 1940s that the Wright-McGill catalogue contained this statement, "Nylon material—in addition to the manufacture of fishing tackle, will find a ready market in other industries such as sewing thread, women's hosiery, brush bristles * * *."

The production of flies is still a hand process, but development of machinery immediately preceding and during World War II was significant in production of the "Eagle Claw," and types of loose hooks. Production of sixty million fishhooks for export to Iceland was one of the war activities of this firm, largely for the Icelandic fisherman to supply England with fish. Sporting tackle business was, therefore, "out" at Wright-McGill during the war, and commercial tackle took its place. Other orders include thirty-five tons of fish-hooks for South Africa. Emergency kits of Navy and Air Forces contained Wright-McGill fishing tackle, designed especially for salmon and cod. Renewal of sporting tackle products followed cessation of hostilities. Largest exclusive fishing tackle manufacturing in world.

LEATHER AND RUBBER INDUSTRIES

The manufacture of leather products of Colorado, including har-ness, saddles and a miscellaneous array of products, began almost immediately following the arrival of the first gold seekers, and reached its peak near the turn of the century. Although but remotely related to the leather industry, the development of rubber manufac-turing by the Gates Rubber Company began just as the demand for Colorado-made leather products was on the decline.

In the saddlery and harness business there were four firms in the state in 1870, and a peak was reached before 1900, when 89 organizations were making saddles or harnesses, or both. This corresponded to the growth of wagon and carriage shops, which also reached a peak in 1890 when 40 odd firms were producing wagons, surreys and other similar conveyances.

The making of saddles antedates the cattle raising industry as the making of harness preceded agriculture. Both saddles and harnesses were needed in the mining industry, or in prospecting.

Saddlery and Harnesses

From the standpoint of continuous growth, the Heiser saddlery is representative of the industry. Technically, the company began on January 1, 1866, when Herman Hugo Heiser and partner arrived in Denver from Plattville, Wisconsin, disposed of the load of freight, the wagon, 4 oxen and all other equipment, excepting only that needed in a harness shop. Heiser was 34 years of age, but had as background an apprenticeship in bookmaking and leather craft in Germany, years on his uncle's farm in Wisconsin, and 8 years in his own harness shop in Plattville, Wisconsin. The demand for harnesses and saddles was too small in Denver, so he moved his equipment to Central City, and opened shops in that mining town, as well as in Blackhawk. The next year he visited Wisconsin, but returned to discover that all the equipment in his Blackhawk and Central City harness shops had been sold by his partner, who had left for California with the funds. With credit obtained from mining groups, Heiser purchased equipment to begin again making harnesses and saddles. He moved his shop to 1528 Blake Street, Denver, in 1873. His sons assumed responsibility for the shop and other business interests after the father's death in 1904, but divided the business in 1914, when harness making and saddlery were becoming relatively less important. The brothers bought out most of the competitors, including Names and Company, the Denver Harness Company, Leonard and Scheck, and the Colorado Saddlery before 1916. By 1920, Heiser was the only prominent saddle and harness manufacturer in Colorado. The Denver Dry Goods harness and saddle production developed later.

The original products included hand-sewn saddles and harnesses—the latter principally for four-horse ore teams. Most of the harness making was replaced after 1914 by the production of various other types of leather products. In addition to saddles, holsters became an important product. Orders were received from marshals and gunsmiths for custom-made holsters. Hand-made jobs became a specialty. The advertising in 1910 provided for "quick draw and body fit." The holsters were made from prime leather, instead of strap leather. This part of the industry required samples and models of important revolvers and automatics, especially Smith and Wesson and Colt.

The raw materials for the saddles have come principally from California, the rawhide covered trees from Denver, and the saddle trees from Denver, oak-treated leather from Ohio, Pennsylvania and Virginia. The harness business was always for the local market; the saddles and holsters for national and international markets. Old Chief Colorado made the shop his headquarters. Saddles were trimmed for frontier days celebrations. Highest priced saddles ranged up to $500.00, depending upon the amount of hand-tooled leather and silver. In 1945, the Heiser Company was sold to the Denver Dry Goods, but is operated separately from that company's own harness and saddle shop, and the products are distributed to different markets.

Other Leather Products

The H. H. Tammen Company was founded in the 1890s by one of the two organizers of the Denver Post. The company occupies the Tammen Building. Original products of this company included various types of novelties for the tourist trade of Colorado. The market for goods soon extended to other tourist centers from Alaska to Atlantic City. Metal novelties are produced along with the leather products.

The Western Art Leather Manufacturing Company was organized in Denver in 1941 to produce various souvenir articles, principally pillows and pennants, and has also found its market far beyond Colorado borders. It was originally organized by Max Fischer, and has grown into an important manufacturing concern in Colorado, under the direction of Harry Rosebaum.

Gates Rubber Company. The Gates Rubber Company, which has grown to be the second largest manufacturing employer in Colorado in 1947, had its beginning in leather goods soon after the turn of the century. Charles and John Gates began the manufacture of leather half-soles for rubber tires. The market was by mail order. It was Charles Gates's inventive idea that involved the use of cement to get uniform thickness for the manufacture of halters. These were advertised as "never break" halters. They were of blue leather, sewed with yellow thread, and became familiar on farms and ranches beginning about 1910.

Gates soon ran into the problem of inadequate supply of leather, so began making half-soles for tires out of rubber, and developed a national market for these. Around 1920, Gates developed the V-Belt, prepared primarily as fan belts for various types of automobiles. It was this V-Belt made of leather that became the forerunner of the famous internationally known Gates Rubber V-Belts of today. The Gates Rubber Company, with real beginnings in 1921, developed a national and international market for its growing line of rubber products. Raw materials used by the company are assembled from international sources. The products sold by the company have an international market.

Building Materials

The clay products industries of Colorado represent perhaps the oldest manufacturing in the state, antedating even flour milling. The industry today has but remote relationships to original production of pottery and of adobe building materials. The demand outside of the San Luis Valley after 1860 was coextensive with the population growth in the state. One reason for the growth of brickmaking industries was the excellent building clays located in or near most of the cities and towns. The companies organized to produce brick were local so far as raw materials and markets for products were concerned. Six plants were established in the state as early as 1870, and by 1890, the peak in number of companies—83—was reached. From that date to World War I, there was a decrease in number, but an increase in relative size of companies. A decline in number became more rapid after World War I. Of interest is the fact that by 1946, except in Denver, there was but one single company in any leading city or town—but in many instances, the single company was larger than the total of its predecessors. Throughout the state, the best known company was the Robinson Brick Company, with its 7-odd plants in Denver and vicinity. Production of firebrick became important at an early date in Denver, Golden, Canon City and Pueblo, with construction of furnaces, forges, foundries and machine shops.

Denver Sewer Pipe and Clay. The Denver Sewer Pipe and Clay Company is representative of the industry, and was organized on October 29, 1889. The founders were William C. Miller, George Steinmitz, and James Green. Sewer pipe for Denver was the first product. The company was sold in 1892 to William Geddes, David Seerie, and Ed R. Ball. They expanded the plant to include the manufacture of brick, refractories and locomotives arch tile. Construction of a plant for the manufacture of hollow building tile was completed in 1917. The manufacture of face brick was begun in 1924.

Geddes and Seerie had been partners in a stone masonry construction firm. They had built the State Capitol, Brown Palace Hotel, Trinity Church, and the Cheesman Dam. The company they headed supplied brick for many buildings, including East and South High Schools, Daniels and Fisher, The Albany and Cosmopolitan Hotel, as well as all the permanent buildings at Lowry Field, Rocky Mountain Arsenal, and Denver Ordnance. The company developed 5 major types of products—sewer pipe, firebrick, building brick, hollow tile and cable tile. Officials who have expanded the company into the largest clay products company in the mountain states included: R. W. Osenbaugh, C. J. Treush, Oscar Temple and George O. Ogier.

Corrs Pottery. The Corrs Pottery was founded at Golden, primarily as a source of employment for people in the vicinity. The fact that refractory clays were available in the vicinity was significant, but Adolph Corrs, who was successful in the brewing industry near the turn of the century, was equally interested in Golden's future.

He acquired an old glass factory, and from this was developed the famous scientific ceramics produced by the company. Among the early products was that of spark plugs, but this part of the industry was abandoned in the middle 20s in favor of expansion into scientific ceramics, and to a minor extent into pottery, especially hotel china.

Wood Products

The wood products industry of the state includes the processing of various types of lumber, the history of which is discussed elsewhere. From a manufacturing standpoint, Schwayder Brothers and The Koppers Company represent significant processors.

Schwayder Brothers. Jesse Schwayder began the manufacture of luggage as an individual enterprise in 1910, but incorporated in 1912 as Schwayder Brothers, with expansion of his business. The plant was originally located at 1051 Santa Fe Drive, but moved from that address to 1551 Platte Street in 1916, and to the 1050 South Broadway location in 1924. Originally the company manufactured trunks for a local market only, and followed styles and patterns of the day. However, new styles, designs and processes have been developed, and the company has been prominent in establishing luggage styles since 1924. The trade mark—5 men standing on a suit case—has been publicized for an international market. Beginning in 1932, the company developed the folding card table, and began research work in folding chairs. These products were manufactured beginning in 1936. The company's manufacturing has expanded to Detroit, and the products from both the Denver and Detroit establishments are sold under the trade mark "Samsonite". Jesse Schwayder and his family have developed this company into one of the leading luggage producers in the country, and one of the leading manufacturing employers in Colorado.

Koppers Company. A National Lumber and Creosoting Plant was established in Salida in 1925. The offices were moved from Texas to Salida in the following year. In 1931, construction began on a wood processing plant near Denver. In that same year, property was purchased near Fraser, Colorado, and the company was sold to Koppers Coke. The company processes pressure-treated timber to resist decay, steam, termites, fire and acid. The products include cross ties, piling, and timber. The manager of the original company, R. C. Johnson, has remained over a period of 20-odd years, as the head of the company.

CHAPTER XXIII

Penal, Correctional and Eleemosynary Institutions in Colorado

Virgil V. Peterson

Introduction

WITH the opening of the Colorado gold fields in 1859 the lure of the Rocky Mountains attracted thousands of fortune seekers from every part of the nation as well as hundreds from Europe. Where for decades the area had been merely part of the highway to the west, as an Indian hunting ground or a trapper's refuge, it now became the scene of intense mining activity. Men from practically every walk of life, driven restlessly onward by an insatiable "gold fever", streamed into the mountain valleys and gulches which emptied into the plain.

With the mass movement westward came in intermingling of "wanted characters"—men who felt that the West offered them not only protection from debt or a single-minded sheriff but also an opportunity to remold their lives or make a fortune. Claim-jumping, theft and murder were not uncommon.

The control of crime early became a paramount issue. With the establishment of towns and mining districts, the new settlers frequently banded together and formulated regulations to protect property rights and to curb crime. Judgment was speedy and usually effective. Since there were few jails or full-time peace officers, punishment was by hanging, ostracism or whipping, depending on the nature of the offense.

When, in 1861, the Territory of Colorado was created out of portions of New Mexico, Kansas and Nebraska, a new source of protection came to the unorganized mining camps at the foot of the Rockies. Federal officials assumed the responsibility of maintaining and operating the government and thereby shared the task of protecting the citizenry. It was, however, not until the late 'sixties that authorization was given to establish a penitentiary in the territory, consequently offenders sentenced to imprisonment were either taken care of in local jails or sent to other territorial or state penitentiaries.

Framers of the constitution of Colorado in 1876 visualized the future needs of the state and provided that "educational, reformatory and penal institutions and those for the benefit of the insane, blind, deaf and mute, and such other institutions as the public good may require, shall be established and supported by the state, in such a manner as may be prescribed by law."[1] As the need arose these educational, penal, correctional and eleemosynary institutions were formally created by the legislative assembly.

A law creating the State Board of Charities and Corrections was passed on March 19, 1891. Consisting of six members appointed by the governor this board was empowered . . .

> to investigate the whole system of public charitable and correctional institutions, to examine into the condition and management of all prisons, jails, reformatories, reform and industrial schools, hospitals, infirmaries, orphanages, public and private retreats and asylums for the insane, and any, or all other institutions which derive their support, wholly or in part from state, county or municipal appropriations.[2]

In 1915 the State Board of Corrections was created. A law passed in 1921 gave the board full control of the management and supervision of the penitentiary, the reformatory and the state hospital.[3] This board as well as the Department of Charities and Corrections, which had earlier replaced the Board of Charities and Corrections, was abolished under the provisions of the 1933 Administrative Code.[4] Provision was also made in the new code for the establishment of the State Division of Public Welfare to be headed by the governor. All the authority and duties imposed by law upon the Board of Corrections and the Department of Charities and Corrections were transferred to this new division and a Board of Visitors appointed whose duties are to inspect all state penal, correctional, and eleemosynary institutions and to make recommendations to the governor.[5]

In the past three-quarters of a century millions of dollars have been expended by the State of Colorado in the housing and care of criminals, mental incompetents, and wayward and indigent persons. Biennial appropriations made by the 1947 legislature for the maintenance and operation of the institutions considered in this chapter totaled more than nine million dollars.[6] In addition, millions more will be used in the construction of additional buildings. Yet with all these expenditures, seldom, if ever, has there been a time when the heads of these institutions have not reported an urgent need for additional facilities, staff, and research.

COLORADO STATE PENITENTIARY

The Colorado State Penitentiary had its inception in January 1868 when the Territorial Legislature declared that such an institution should be established for Colorado at Canon City for the protection of society against offenders of the law.[7] In comparison to present prison facilities and methods of reform, those of eighty years ago were crude and out of date. Progress over the years has come only through the concerted effort of far-seeing administrators such as Thomas J. Tynan (1909 to 1927) and Roy Best (1932 to the present). Mr. Best is one of the youngest men in the nation to hold such a position, having been appointed when in his early thirties.

The first cell house was built by federal authorities and opened for occupancy in June 1871 with accommodations for forty-two prisoners. Mark A. Schaffenberg, United States Marshal for Colorado, was given active charge of the prison for a three-year period after which it was turned over to territorial officers. Ben F. Allen then became the first state warden.[8] In 1875 Congress provided through the Enabling Act, fifty sections of land which could be leased or sold to derive funds for penitentiary buildings.[9] The first General Assembly of the newly-created state of Colorado officially adopted the penitentiary as a state institution in 1877 and made its first appropriation of badly-needed funds for buildings and maintenance. Prisoners were at that time received at an average rate of fifty per year.[10]

Before the turn of the century little was done to rehabilitate prisoners. Drastic measures of punishment were frequent and accepted. The traditional picture of men in stripes, under heavy guard, on the proverbial rock pile was not an exaggeration. The ball and chain, bread and water diets and solitary dungeon treatment, though seldom effective, were in common use. Idleness and overcrowding were doubtlessly the greatest barrier to prisoner rehabilitation. At best, the prisoners were employed in farm and garden work, in cutting and dressing stones, in making lime and brick, and in the construction and repair of walls and buildings.

In 1897 a law was enacted providing that every able-bodied convict should be given work suitable, as nearly as possible, to his skills and capacities. Money earned for such labors, after deducting a satisfactory amount for maintenance, was to be sent to the family or dependents of the prisoner, or be paid to him on discharge if he had no dependents.[11] The next General Assembly passed the indeterminate sentence and parole law which provides for the commutation of unjust sentences and the release of prisoners to parole.[12] Under the 1935 revision of the law, a man, for example, with a ten-year sentence may secure his release in six and one half years. Additional "good time" may also be accorded him if during that period he acted as a trusty and performed his work in a creditable manner.[13] The principles laid down in these two laws are basic and have been used in most of the reform measures at the penitentiary in the past half century.

Prison labor on an organized basis for highway construction was inaugurated in 1900 when it was given official legislative sanction. Several highways were built and improved with convict help in the next decade. It was not, however, until March 1909 when Thomas J. Tynan was appointed to the office of warden that the program took on signficance. Tynan was by nature a reformer. He made it possible for every man who would work to have employment. Road camps were set up and prisoners working unguarded were away from prison walls days at a time. He reports that "instead of sending broken revengeful men back into the world—in no wise reformed but simply trained to greater cunning—there are being restored mended men eager and willing to be made as such use as society will permit. By removing the continual threat of arms, by eliminating oppression and brutalities, by establishing a system of graded rewards for cheerfulness and industry, the penitentiary has been given a wholesome, helpful atmosphere.''[14] Tynan went on the assumption that putting men in stripes for ninety days, the usual practice on entering the prison, was the wrong psychology. Beginning early in 1911 he put all new arrivals in blue and made them ''convicts of the first class.''[15] If they made good and followed prison routines, they were never subjected to the wearing of striped clothing.

The road building program with convict help lost some of its forcefulness after World War I, but was replaced in a measure by small scale manufacturing ventures. A factory for making license plates, highway signs, road markers and booster plates was installed in 1925. In addition to the work done for the state a number of contracts were filled for the federal government and the state of New Mexico during the first year of operation.[16] The factory was destroyed by fire in 1929[17] but was later rebuilt. Work is still being done for the highway and revenue departments of the state. In 1925 the penitentiary purchased a canning factory valued at $125,000 for $40,000, and ninety acres of full-bearing fruit trees, berries, vineyard and truck garden for $30,000. Its appraised value was $90,000.[18] The canning venture proved highly remunerative. Not only were all the other state institutions requiring canned food stuffs well supplied, but also there was a large surplus which could be disposed of to outside markets at a good profit. Many fruit farmers in Canon City area marketed their produce to the state at prices in excess of what they could have otherwise obtained.[19] Other small scale manufacturing was also instituted. Additional ranches were purchased and stocked with cattle, sheep, hogs and poultry. A saw mill was operated on one of the ranches.[20]

The period between the Tynan and Best administrations was one of comparative inactivity. Idleness became common and disciplinary measures were of necessity based on force. Political issues stripped the warden of many of his powers making his position vulnerable from sources inside and outside the prison. Under these decadent conditions there occurred in 1929 what was perhaps one of the worst prison breaks and riots ever experienced by the institution, resulting in the death of thirteen men. The warden in charge at this time was subsequently discharged for incompetency by the State Civil Service Commissioner through charges preferred by the State Board of Corrections.[21]

The task of rehabilitation was not an easy one when Best assumed the responsibility in 1932. Having served for a short time as deputy warden he had already advocated vocational training and was promoting recreation such as baseball, football, handball, horseshoe pitching and boxing. His plans for full-scale employment, however, were hampered partially when the General Assembly in 1933 made it ''unlawful for persons or corporations to use, consume, sell or store, in this state, goods, wares, or merchandise manufactured, produced or mined, wholly or in part, by convicts or prisoners in the state penitentiary or reformatory.[22] Coupled with this was an Interstate Commerce Act which placed a ban on interstate trade of prison made goods. The state legislature did, however make it amendatory that all state institutions purchase from the penitentiary any required goods which they may produce so long as they are available within ten percent of outside prices, the quality being considered.[23] In 1934 a sock-knitting machine was installed at a cost of $29,000, capable of producing one thousand pairs of sox per day at cost of four cents each. Prior to this time the state institutions had been paying $.075 per pair. Underwear is manufactured in large quantities, and all clothing worn by the prisoners is made in the institution. Soaps of all kinds, scouring powder, cold cream, vanishing cream, skin softener, lotion, shampoo, hairoil, insect powder, stock and poultry sprays, fly spray, disinfectants, sheep dip, sal soda, furniture polish, sweeping compound, bluing, ink, and flavorings, are manufactured in quantities sufficient to supply all state institutions. Likewise the penitentiary maintains a slaughter house and packing plant with facilities of sufficient capacity to meet the cured and fresh meat needs of these institutions.[24] In 1937 a coining press was installed to make state tax tokens.[25] During the war, shirts for military and lend-lease programs were turned out at the rate of seven hundred per day. These and many other phases of a program of rehabilitation demonstrate Best's statement that "a progressive industrial program has been my paramount objective."[26] In 1946 Best was brought under severe criticism for allowing prisoners to make leather goods on their own time and dispose of them to outside sources. The value of such activity is perhaps best illustrated in the case of a man paroled on March 5, 1948 who, in twenty-three years spent in the penitentiary, had saved $10,000 payable to him on release.[27] Contrast this with $5.00, a suit of clothes and a railroad ticket as provided by law.[28]

During the period of 1870 to 1940 the penitentiary received 21,888 prisoners. [29] Out of the 1940 population of 1378 [30] seventeen were women.[31] Prisoners are coming in at the present time at the rate of five hundred to six hundred per year. Seventy-five percent of the men received since VJ day are ex-GI's and now seventeen percent of the prison population is ex-servicemen.[32] It is estimated that the one hundred thirty-three lifers now incarcerated will serve an average of seventeen years.[33] The average age of all prisoners in the Canon City institution is between twenty-eight and twenty-nine years. One hundred sixty are less than twenty years, two of whom are fourteen year old boys serving sentences for murder. One of the most recent arrivals at the penitentiary is a twelve year old murderer sentenced for twelve years to life.[34] Setting what is perhaps a precedent among prison officials Warden Best has taken the boy into his home outside the prison walls to raise him as one of his own, advocating that he be allowed to attend the public schools and receive a normal education.

Colorado State Reformatory

The State Reformatory at Buena Vista is a creation of the Constitution of Colorado.[35] Established by an act of the General Assembly on April 19, 1889, it is maintained by legislative appropriation for the sustenance, correction and education of young men convicted of felonious offenses—those who have started a criminal career. The original law concerning these convictions, which has undergone but minor changes over the years, states that:

> Courts having criminal jurisdiction in Colorado shall sentence to the state reformatory all male persons, and none other, duly convicted before them of felony for the first time, who shall at the time of sentence be of the full age of sixteen years and not more than twenty-one years of age; and those over twenty-one and not more than twenty-five shall be sentenced either to the state reformatory or the state penitentiary at the discretion of the trial judge; and also all male persons between said ages, duly convicted before them of a misdemeanor, where the imprisonment for the offenses charged shall not be more than ninety days; provided that they shall sentence to the state penitentiary at Canon City any male person between the ages of sixteen and thirty who shall be convicted of crimes involving the penalty of imprisonment for life, or the crime of murder in the first or second degree or voluntary manslaughter.[36]

At the time the reformatory was established, harsh punitory methods were in common use in most penal and reform institutions in this country and were adopted in Colorado as a mode of correctional punishment. Records show that the ball and chain method was used by the reformatory on captured escapees[37] in the early days, but the idea was abandoned before the turn of the century. Warden C. P. Hoyt, in 1898 reported that:

> Upon taking charge here, I abolished the dungeons and bread and water treatment as a mode of punishment, as I believe it to be a cruel and ancient idea. Instead, as I am a believer in corporal punishment, we spank them, using a paddle two feet, two inches long, three inches wide, and three-quarters of an inch thick, made of pine, weighing fifteen ounces. We do not strip the patient, but punish him as he is in ordinary attire. Our prison physician is always present, as is required by law. I have found by several years experience, that this is the most humane and decent method of punishment. [38]

Paddling, as a mode of punishment, prevailed for many years at the institution, but has been replaced by whipping. This latter practice has been intermittently ruled out by pressure from outside groups, but restored as many times at the discretion of the warden in charge. "Hanging"[39] also was resorted to on some occasions but was abolished through the efforts of the State Board of Charities and Corrections.[40]

Depriving individuals of privileges held by the group in common while on good behavior, such as letter writing, has proved a most humane and satisfactory method of correction. Honor systems and educational training to a great degree have supplanted many of the early practices of corporal punishment. To emphasize the idea of detention for reformation through effective training, Warden Arthur C. Dutcher in 1903 abandoned the use of customary prison garb and substituted a neatly-designed gray cadet suit.[41] Semi-military routines were also instituted.

The reformatory is located in a mountainous area near the town of Buena Visita in Chaffee County on a tract of land consisting of three thousand two hundred eighty acres acquired by purchase and lease. At this high altitude (seven thousand eight hundred feet) the growing season is short but root crops, grains and hay are grown successfully and often in amounts in excess of the needs of the institution. A herd of purebred Holsteins is maintained to supply dairy products. Other livestock is also raised on the prison farm for local consumption.

The first temporary buildings on the Buena Vista site were constructed by trusty prison labor from the state penitentiary. On completion in 1891, a number of the younger prisoners were transferred from the Canon City institution. As subsequent building and improvement appropriations were made available, construction of cellhouses, barns and other buildings proceeded under the direction of competent supervisors, most of the work being done by the reformatory inmates. Today the physical plant is composed of fifteen buildings. The inventory value, as of June 30, 1942, of all land, buildings and equipment owned was $604,120.00.[42] The 1947 biennial appropriation for maintenance and operation was $352,500.00 plus a deficiency measure in the amount of $27,650.00 covering an over-expenditure of the preceding biennium.[43]

Youths committed to the reformatory, some of who are illiterate on entering, are required to attend school until they reach eighteen years of age. Those who have attained majority are also encouraged in their educational pursuits and are given an opportunity to learn a trade. Work is required of all inmates and ranges from domestic duties to farm work, tailoring and a number of other trades.

Releases as a rule come as a recommendation of the warden and the commissioners upon proof of reform on the part of the individual. There have been times in the history of the institution, however, when terms of commitment have been shortened because of inadequate housing facilities. During the 1917-1918 biennium four hundred twenty-five men were accounted for at the institution, yet there was but an average daily population of one hundred thirty.[44] Released inmates are usually placed on parole, and may be returned to the institution if they break parole, provide the crime committed in the breach is not more felonious in nature. Prospective parolees often are granted permits to work on adjacent farms. Money earned in such instances is retained by the workers or may be sent to their families.

In the early years of the institution difficulties were often experienced when hardened criminals were among those committed to the reformatory. This situation was finally alleviated when arrangements were made to send the more notorious characters to the penitentiary in exchange for less offensive individuals.

Larceny and burglary are the principal offenses committed by the reformatory inmates. The range is from petty thievery to grand larceny and from house burglary to large scale jobs. Occupations represented are predominantly laborer and farmer. If we consider statistics over the years, teamsters, truck drivers, waiters and clerks are also quite common among the prisoners and there is a fair sprinkling of miners, painters, firemen, mechanics and cooks.[45]

In 1944 a study of the needs of the institution was requested by the governor. The investigating committee recommended that a well-planned program of education be instituted, which would include instruction in high school subjects; that a competent director of vocational education be employed to coordinate and direct vocational training; that trained recreational and musical instructors be employed; that an adequate library be provided; that parole officers be employed to check parolees and assist them while they are on probation; that a system to upgrade inmates from individual cells to modern dormitories and then to rooms housing three boys each be instituted; that mental tests be given to all prisoners; and that a staff adequate to meet the needs of the institution be maintained at all times.[46] These recommendations have been put into effect as appropriations have been received.

STATE INDUSTRIAL SCHOOL FOR BOYS

Situated near Golden at the foot of historic Lookout Mountain the State Industrial School for Boys has served as a home and training center for more than eight thousand boys since it was formally opened in July 1881. In that year, the site and buildings of the old Colorado School of Mines were abandoned and were taken over by the Industrial School as the first center of operation. Many of the structures were in a bad state of repair and additional buildings and equipment were needed. The state legislature had failed to provide the necessary monies for these improvements in 1882; consequently, Governor Frederick W. Pitkin, in conjunction with fifty-two other interested citizens signed notes providing sufficient funds to take care of the emergency.

In 1883 the institution was still in financial straits, the legislature having appropriated only sufficient money to operate the school until November of that year. "In this dilemma His Excellency, Governor James B. Grant, was applied to for aid, who after thoroughly examining into its affairs, and assuring himself that its business had been well and economically conducted, gave his personal note as collateral security for the sum of twenty thousand dollars, the amount needed to carry the school until January, 1885."[47]

During the next decade improvements in the school failed to keep pace with the population increase. In 1892 the superintendent declared that the majority of the releases from the institution were "simply and solely to make room for new commitments."[48] In the same report he complained of the inadequacies of the law and of the inefficiency of the training programs saying,

> I would also strongly urge upon the Board the crying need of radical changes in our law. We are twenty years behind; we have a time sentence; we teach trades only incidentally; we do not look after the released inmates. I am ashamed of my State when I give the above information to the people of States which have kept up with the times in such matters. It seems time that this Board should *demand* something better.[49]

Under the law at that time any man or woman could "take a boy before a justice and have him committed to this School for three years, without witness, without trial, without council, without advice."[50] Superintendent Dorus R. Hatch goes on to say, "This is done in a large proportion of the cases. Boys who are expensive or troublesome or diseased are thus easily disposed of. It is an injury to the Institution. It is an imposition on the State. It is an injustice to the boy."[51] As a result of the recommendations of Superintendent Hatch the law was altered in 1893 to provide that all commitments be made by district and county courts and for the period of minority.[52]

The school organization is semi-military and the boys are grouped into companies each of which is under the direction of a cottage counselor. Military drill is held frequently, not for the training value, but to improve the carriage of the boys and to facilitate their handling. Khaki uniforms are the standard dress at the school. Boys between the ages of ten and sixteen who have committed offenses drawing fines or imprisonment, life imprisonment excepted, are accepted at the school.[53] Larceny and burglary are the most common offenses. The majority of the boys come from broken homes where the opportunity for good training is nil. Based on a merit system of behavior the school's training is designed to rehabilitate them and return them to normal life. They remain under the jurisdiction of the school until eighteen years of age. Conduct determines the length of the commitment. When a boy has earned his way out and has a job and a home to go to he is released. While on parole he keeps contact with the school by a monthly letter and is visited by a parole officer who assists him in making the new adjustment. If parole is broken the offender is returned to the school and must again earn his way out. Boys committing no infractions of the rules for a period of two months are allowed to visit their homes for three days. This privilege is granted each month, as long as the boys have a clear record.

Standard educational training is given to every boy who enters the school. In addition each one has an opportunity to learn a trade, such as carpentry, baking, farming, dairying, barbering, shoe repairing and manufacturing, tailoring, drafting, plumbing, painting and decorating, steamfitting, boiler making, blacksmithing, sheet metal work, weaving, electrical work and printing.[54] Nearly half of the eight hundred acres owned by the school is under cultivation. Provision is also made for the boys to be employed in the cultivation of lands held by the Home and Training School for Mental Defectives at Ridge under which arrangement the two institutions share alike the crops produced. Ten pure-bred dairy cattle and other livestock are maintained as a part of the training program of the school and as a means of keeping the school in part self-sustaining.

Three periodicals have for years been published by the school: the *Yearbook;* the *Industrial School Record,* an eight-page news sheet issued semi-monthly; and a monthly, the *Industrial School Magazine*. These publications reflect the talents and training of the boys, for all work, including make-up, editing and printing is done at the institution.

During the sixty-six years the school has been in operation it has been headed by twenty-three different superintendents.[55] Only one has served for a prolonged period, namely, Fred L. Paddleford, who held the position from August 1902 to November 1924. He succeeded in establishing a sound administrative policy and was responsible for many improvements to the physical plant of the school. During the year following his retirement three superintendents served with varying success.

In general the institution has experienced something of a stormy career. Political battles and legal controversies have upset normal operations and resulted in several investigations. Personnel changes have been multiple and in 1939 a petition to close the school was circulated. By legislative intervention a new board of control was appointed in 1941 and the school was made an immediate ward of the governor. Numerous administrative changes were also affected. More competent instructors at increased salaries were employed to give the school an improved educational standing, and a dietician was employed to supervise the preparation of menus.

Six different superintendents were in office during the five years following the legislative reorganization. In 1945 the State Civil Service Commission set up stringent requirements for the position in an attempt to obtain a person whose training and competence would qualify him for the responsibilities of the position. Qualifying examinations resulted in the appointment of Gunnar Soelberg formerly affiliated with the State Department of Education, to the position.

STATE INDUSTRIAL SCHOOL FOR GIRLS

Situated in Bear Creek Valley about ten miles southwest of Denver the State Industrial School for Girls is the only institution in Colorado maintained for the detention and education of juvenile delinquent girls. Although the school today rates among the best in the United States there is behind these years of outstanding achievement a story of struggle and sacrifice, beginning in 1887 when legislation was first enacted providing for such an institution.[56]

The first girls committed were housed at the Boys Industrial School at Golden, but in 1895 a separate board of control was appointed and housing provided for the girls at the St. Cloud Hotel in Denver. Funds for its operation were provided through the various women's groups in the state. Although conditions were very unsatisfactory in this three-story structure, they remained here until March 1898 when under the direction of a new board the school was moved to Aurora, a suburb of Denver. Renting five cottages the expenses were greater than usual. Indebtedness was soon incurred resulting in the resignation of the second board in July 1898, and the appointment of a third board.[57] Under their direction operations were considerably improved yet the superintendent described the work as being "greatly hampered by the lack of a building adequate to the needs of such a school."[58]

Expiration of a second-year lease on the Aurora property compelled the board to make new arrangements. The 1899 General Assembly had appropriated $25,000.00 for the purchase of lands and erection of building, but these funds never became available. Consequently when the board finally contracted to purchase a forty-acre tract near Morrison on which was located a twelve-room home, for $8,000.00, the $1,000.00 down payment was taken from a $5,000.00 maintenance and operation fund which had been appropriated but never used by the school.[59] The move to the new quarters was made in August 1900, but the space provided was still inadequate. More than sixty girls and seven officers were crowded into a twelve-room house.[60] It was May 1902 before the critical housing shortage was alleviated, a new cottage accommodating forty girls having been built at a cost to the state of $16,572.00.[61] In subsequent years four more cottages, an executive cottage, a chapel and grade school, and a high school building have been added to the campus. The capacity of the school is now one hundred fifty, each girl being provided with an individual room.

That the school struggled for sufficient funds for operational purposes is evidenced by the fact that up to 1906 their sole support was from the counties at the rate of fifty cents per girl per day. During these first eleven years the state failed to provide maintenance funds in any degree, and because of this lack of support, the school had two different boards and three different superintendents during the fiscal year November 30, 1905 to November 30, 1906.[62] In some instances, the counties not wishing to assume the responsibility, sent diseased and pregnant girls to the school thus imposing an added burden to the already over-taxed institution.[63] During the biennium 1900-1902, $22,799.50 was expended in the maintenance and operation of the school, all of which was furnished by the counties.[64] In the 1943-45 biennium $148,828.30 were spent for this purpose, approximately $55,000.00 of which was county funds.[65] Total salaries for the biennium forty-five years ago amount to $9,120.01 as against $98,387.65 for the two years ending June 30, 1945. The superintendent's salary in 1902 was $100.00 per month, while her assistant received $50.00. Two matrons received $40.00 each and two others $35.00 each. A farmer was paid $40.00 and an investigator $10.00, making up a total monthly payroll of $390.00.[66]

All commitments to the school came through the various county courts and the juvenile court of Denver. Girls ranging in age from six to eighteen years may be accepted and kept until age twenty-one if not paroled earlier. On being received at the school, each girl is kept in strict isolation for ten days during which time she receives a series of physical and mental tests. There is no segregation of new and old enrollees. Smoking, gum chewing and vulgar and abusive language is prohibited. Girls are graded on cleanliness of person, room and speech, courtesy and respectfulness, cottage and school deportment, cheerfulness, cooperation, promptness, responsibility, truthfulness, and group work. All girls are required to complete a full course in domestic science and to participate in making their own clothes, in the preparation of meals and in the general maintenance of their cottage. Many of the girls come to the school from one to six years retarded in their school work.[67] In each case an attempt is made to bring them up to average. Preparatory courses, equal to those in the public schools are offered on all grade levels. Business courses, including training in the use of duplicating machines, dictaphones, dictagraphs and electric posting machines are available. A number of girls graduating in business courses have been placed in responsible positions with business concerns and in the government civil service. Special musical training in voice, piano, mandolin and violin is available to all who wish to study.[68] An educational fund supported by the friends and employees of the school is maintained to enable girls to continue their educational pursuits after being paroled or released. Under this arrangement some have completed their college training while many have become graduate nurses. The majority of the girls marry while comparatively young and usually while on parole.[69]

One of the major problems of the school today is the adjacency of a federal reformatory for male prisoners located within a distance of one-half mile. Lands owned by the two institutions are contiguous and on a number of occasions federal inmates have been apprehended on Industrial School property. Location of the prison in this particular spot is clearly one of political design and unless some change is made it will always constitute a menace to a smoothly-operated girls' school program.

In 1906 the board of control, for the first time in the history of the institution obtained the services of a competent and well-trained superintendent. Miss Marion B. Rudgers, a woman of considerable ability and experience in New York institutions reorganized the complete plan of operation. On her death in January 1912 Elizabeth Purcell assumed the responsibility of leadership and continued until 1923, at which time Anna L. Cooley, the present superintendent was placed in charge. Her accomplishments in her past thirty-five years of service are perhaps best summed up in a citation given her by the Denver Kiwanis Club in 1946 and read by the late Dr. Frederick J. Cox, for many years a loyal friend and supporter of the school. It is given in part as follows:

> . . . Today we pay our tribute of grateful appreciation to the superb contribution of Anna L. Cooley as Superintendent of the Colorado State Industrial School for Girls at Morrison. For a score of years and more every report on Colorado State institutions has given highest praise to this school, and throughout the nation this school is looked upon as an ideal example in the field.
>
> Anna Cooley is a native of New York City . . . She came to our State Industrial School for Girls in October 1912, first as teacher of the Arts and Crafts, then became Assistant Superintendent, and in 1923 she was elected Superintendent. Our own Kiwanian Judge Philip Gilliam of the Juvenile Court calls the school a "miracle," referring to the almost incredible quality of its results. Judge Gilliam makes his statement on the basis of comparison with other such schools throughout the country. The academic standard is high enough to permit its students to maintain their grade when they transfer to other public schools or to college. The training in vocation and home-making is such as to bring real success to the girls after they leave school. But above everything else the school is a home where through the years thousands of girls have found care, understanding and affection. The great majority of the girls remember the school with thanksgiving the rest of their lives, and come back to visit there with sincere pride and happiness. There are many persons, of course, who have shared in the labors and fruits of the school, teachers, administrative officers, directors, and students, but these all yield the crown of achievement to Anna Cooley, as a teacher of rare skill, as an administrator of unusual ability, but above all as a person of great power of spirit. Her spirit is the cement which holds together the whole enterprise, teachers, pupils and all, and makes it like one family, living together in a real unity of mutual concern and purpose. Her spirit is the discipline and the strength. Through the years her faith has kept the school advancing toward a high ideal, her love has made the institution a home of understanding and affection. Denver Kiwanis Club gratefully makes this humble recognition of Anna Cooley's unique success in our State School, and of her superb qualities as a citizen in our community.

COLORADO STATE HOSPITAL

Established as an asylum for the care and treatment of the insane February 8, 1879,[70] the Colorado State Hospital at Pueblo has under its supervision continuously one out of every two hundred twenty people who reside in Colorado. With more than five thousand inmates it exceeds in population numbers all but nineteen or twenty of Colorado's two hundred thirty-one cities and towns. The institution was officially opened October 23, 1879,[71] housing twelve people who had been boarded by the state in an Illinois hospital. The original site for the asylum was a plot of forty acres located west of Pueblo and acquired at the cost of $22,308.00. Included in the purchase was the former residence of United States Senator George M. Chilcott which was used as the first housing unit. At the end of the first fiscal year, December 1, 1880, the superintendent of the asylum reported seventy-seven patients admitted and twenty-five discharged, twenty-three of whom were completely recovered. During the period two escaped and twelve died. Two deaths were due to phthisis (tuberculosis), two from epilepsy, four from paralysis, one from typhoid and three from maniacal exhaustion.[72] Total assets of the institution at this time including land, buildings, furniture, fixtures, stock and implements were $24,276.38.[73] Its capacity is reported to have been thirty inmates.[74]

An "insane tax" of one-fifth mill was levied and assessed upon all real and personal property in the state for the creation and support of the asylum by the 1879 legislature.[75] Monies derived from this tax were in turn appropriated to the institution by succeeding legislative bodies. It was 1917 before an additional levy was made. Known up to this date as the Colorado Insane Asylum the name was changed to the Colorado State Hospital and an additional one-fifth mill assessment was made. The law specifically states that "the entire fund derived from such levy is to be appropriated for the support and maintenance of the hospital."[76] In 1937 a new and supplemental levy of .30972 mills was made for the years 1937-1941 inclusive, and one of the .20528 mills for the 1941-1946 period.[77] This later levy was cut by amendment to .10973 mills in 1941.[78] The 1947 legislature provided in addition to all other levies an assessment of .03876 mills for 1947 and 1948 and for the years of 1949-1956 a .38768 mill levy on every dollar of assessed valuation. The funds derived from this most recent assessment will be used principally for the construction and equipping of new buildings and the remodeling and rehabilitating of existing structures.[79] Appropriations to the hospital made by the 1947 General Assembly for the 1947-49 biennium amount to $5,500,000.00. This is in addition to two deficiency appropriations made by the same body, totaling $1,354,919.62, for the purpose of completing the operations of the institution in the 1946-47 fiscal year.[80]

The June 30, 1945 inventory value of all property of the Colorado State Hospital was $4,972,285.00. This includes lands, buildings, machinery, tools, furniture, bedding, linens, libraries, automobiles, livestock, water rights, and supplies such as food, drugs, feed and coal.[81] The per capita cost of all inmates supported by the hospital in the 1943-45 biennium was $1.0792 per day of $391.42105 per year.[82] However, the true cost to the taxpayer is not reflected in these figures, inasmuch as there was during this period profits in the amount of $30,661.98 realized from the operation of the dairy, $14,985.00 from the piggery, $23,914.44 from the chicken ranch and $3,299.59 from the turkey farm.[83] There was also a saving of over $45,000.00 in the fruit and vegetable canning projects for the same period. Apples, apricots, cherries, peaches, pears, peas, plums, string beans and tomatoes are the products usually canned.[84] The greatest benefit of these projects, in which many of the inmates participate, is not reflected in the dollar value returned. Occupational therapy has been used to restore hundreds of the mental ill to health and has kept many others occupied who in idleness would be greater burdens to the institution.

Prior to the establishment of an asylum for the insane in Colorado, lunatics and other mental incompetents were housed either in jails, hospitals, or homes and a few in mental institutions of other states. This blacklog of potential occupants for the newly-created state asylum soon resulted in an overcrowding of facilities causing the State Board of Lunacy Commissioners to limit the quota of inmates from each county.[85] This discrepancy called for corrective legislation. In 1917 a law was passed making it illegal to deny an insane person state care which was afforded another insane person. Any individual adjudged insane was made a ward of the state. All limitations were waived even to the number of insane persons that may be kept in any one building at the insane asylum.[86] As a result the institution has been severely taxed beyond its facilities for space. In 1946 the superintendent reported the buildings used for the care of the aged and infirm were more than fifty percent overcrowded and in general the hospital was taking care of twenty-five percent in excess of its stipulated capacity. Most of the overcrowding has resulted from the larger number of commitments of the aged. In 1941 seventeen percent of the people entering the hospital were over seventy years of age. By 1945 this number had increased to thirty percent,[87] and to thirty-five percent by the end of June 30, 1947 fiscal year. Most of these elderly people are literally worn out not only mentally but physically, imposing a heavy responsibility on the psychiatric, medical, nursing and dietetic staffs. Paroles are few among the aged thus the average age of all inmates gradually becomes greater.

Most commitments to the hospital are made through the various counties, each of which has a local board of lunacy consisting of two licensed physicians of reputable character appointed by the county judge.[88] Persons exhibiting signs of insanity or mental incompetency may on complaint or writ of petition be taken before a court and held until judgment is rendered by the lunacy commission. The county judge then has the prerogative of issuing a certificate of insanity. Guided by the facts of the case he may place the person in the State Hospital, the State Home for Mental Defectives or any other hospital or home where care is given for the feeble-minded or insane.[89] Monies used by counties for the support of lunatic paupers is reimbursable from state funds.[90] Persons who are mentally ill but whose condition does not warrant their being issued a certificate of insanity may be admitted to the State Hospital for care and treatment. However, the state does not bear the cost of the care and treatment of these sane but mentally ill patients. The rate paid is the daily per capita cost for all inmates. In the two year period of 1943-45 one hundred ten such cases received treatment at the Pueblo institution.[92]

There were in this same biennium a total of 1524 admissions. Psychoses of some of those committed are as follows: psychoses with syphilitic memingo-encephalitis, ninety-one; psychoses due to alcohol, thirty; psychoses with cerebral arteriosclerosis, two hundred fifty-seven; senile psychoses, three hundred fourteen; involutional psychoses, twenty-eight; psychoses due to convulsive disorder, forty-two; manic-depressive psychoses, fifty-two; dementia praecox, three hundred forty-three; psychoses with mental deficiency, forty-three; psychoneurosis, twenty-one; and without mental disorder, two hundred thirteen.[93]

The original legislation creating the insane asylum provided for a superintendent and a board of three commissioners.[94] In 1899 this commission became the Board of Lunacy Commissioners. The Lunacy Board was abolished in 1917 and its duties assumed by the Board of Corrections.[95] With the demise of the State Board of Corrections in 1933, operations of the hospital continued under the guidance of the State Board of Visitors.[96] Since its beginning sixty-eight years ago, the institution has functioned with a good administrator at its head. Each of the four superintendents has served on an average of thirteen years in this position. All of them have visualized the complicated problems and needs of the hospital. Dr. P. R. Thombs, the first superintendent, emphasized in his first annual report that "this is not a prison but a hospital, designed for the cure of disabled minds, and every measure tending to that end should receive the first attention."[97] Thombs resigned in 1899 and was replaced by Dr. A. P. Busey who served until 1913 when he became head of the Home and Training School for Mental Defectives at Ridge, Colorado.[98] The post was then filled by Dr. H. A. La Moure who served until 1928 and subsequently became superintendent of the Ridge institution, which position he now holds. Dr. F. H. Zimmerman, the present head of the Pueblo hospital, has successfully administered its affairs since 1928. He has brought to the patients a high type of service by establishing residency training for doctors specializing in neuro-psychiatry, pathology and medicine. In conjunction with the University of Colorado School of Nursing, student nurses are trained at the hospital in psychiatric nursing. Five hundred sixteen nurses received training there in the 1943-45 biennium. One year dietetic internships are also offered. The Pueblo hospital is the only institution in the Rocky Mountain area and the only mental hospital in the world approved by the American Dietetic Association for such training.[99]

Colorado State Home And Training School For Mental Defectives

Located at Ridge in Jefferson County twelve miles west of Denver on three hundred ten acres of state school land, the Colorado State Home and Training School for Mental Defectives was created by legislative enactment and approved by Governor John F. Shafroth on May 5, 1909.[100] Experience at the Colorado Insane Asylum at Pueblo, which was by this time in its thirtieth year of operation, had long indicated the need for a special institution to care for and train mental defectives, particularly the younger individuals. As early as 1892 the need for such training center was urged by the State Board of Charities and Corrections. Each report of this board over a period of sixteen years mentioned the desirability of such an institution. Papers read at medical society meetings stressed that action be taken. Pressure from various sources finally resulted in presentation of bills for the creation of such a school to the 1905 and again to the 1907 General Assemblies. In each case the bills failed to pass the final reading. Credit for bringing the problem before the law makers is due to Mrs. James Williams of Denver. Undeterred in her efforts, she personally visited every state legislator immediately prior to the gathering of the 1909 assembly, and laid before each one conclusive proofs of the dire need of such an institution.[101]

The primary function and objective of the school and home is the mental, moral and physical education and training of feeble-minded children incapable of receiving instruction in the public schools; and the treatment and care of persons so mentally defective as to be incompetent to care for themselves or their property. Applicants or their legal guardians must have been bonafide residents of the state one year prior to application in order to qualify for admittance to the home. If the parents or guardians of a child who is admitted are financially able to pay any part or all of the cost of maintenance, they are required to contribute towards the upkeep of the child.[102]

The school is operated under the direction of a superintendent who is responsible only to the governor. Originally a board of commissioners functioned as an intervening body. They were appointed by the governor and in conjunction with the superintendent rendered annually reports of the activities of the home. They served without compensation other than actual out-of-pocket expense. Under the Administrative Code of 1933 these appointments were discontinued. In the original bill creating the home, provision was made to secure a competent and experienced physician capable of directing the administrative, medical and industrial interests of the institution. He was to receive a salary of $3000.00 per annum plus living expenses and was required to have residency at the school.[103] To date there have been three superintendents who have served at Ridge.

The home was officially opened July 1, 1912.[104] Soon thereafter the same interests who were responsible for getting the original bill through the legislature began agitation to enlarge the school. The need was evident, but it was not until 1919 that an expansion program was approved. Instead of making further additions and improvements at Ridge, the legislature created a branch school at Grand Junction. Buildings, formerly a part of the Indian School, located two miles east of the city, were taken over as a plant nucleus of the new addition.[105] The division of the school brought resentment from some quarters on the grounds that the land included in the new location was so alkaline as to be unproductive. This condition, however, was satisfactorily overcome through scientifically applied methods of draining and leaching the land, resulting subsequently in profitable farming operations. In the fiscal year ending June 30, 1947 an income of $44,987.26 was reported from the operation of the farm, dairy and livestock projects. Nearly $7,000.00 of this amount was profit, in addition to produce valued at more than $39,000.00 which had been furnished to the school.[106] Today the Grand Junction branch with twenty-two Buildings and an inventory value of $985,585.41 has outgrown its parent institution in size and accommodations.[107] Under the ten-year building program approved by the 1947 legislature both branches will receive extensive additions and improvements. The Grand Junction School will receive the benefit of a 1947-1948 levy of .00297 mills and .02971 mills of every dollar of assessed valuation in the state for the years 1949-1956. In comparison the Ridge section will receive for the same respective periods .00362 mills and .03623 mills.[108] The two homes operate virtually as two seperate and distinct units and each superintendent renders separate reports. The purpose and mode of operation, however, is essentially identical.

It is estimated that there are approximately 2500 feeble-minded and mentally defective people in Colorado in need of institutional care.[109] There are, at the present time, about four hundred sixty at the Grand Junction school, three hundred at Ridge and two hundred fifty at the State Hospital in Pueblo. Intelligence ratings of the inmates ranges from idiots to morons. In 1947 the Grand Junction home had one hundred thirty-eight idiots, one hundred eighty-nine imbeciles and one hundred thirty-two morons many of which are spastic and epileptic.[110] Hydrotherapy treatment has been used at both institutions with some degree of success.[111]

Upon entrance to the home each child capable of comprehension is given a series of performance, achievement and intelligence tests. This affords a scientific knowledge of the child's needs and serves as a guide to the type of training program used.[112] Experience has shown that many of the children placed in the home respond to training very well and often become adept in the manual arts. Provision is made to keep as many occupied as possible. The girls are training in sewing and in various household chores while the boys participate in farming activities, the care of livestock and other vocational pursuits. There are in the homes, however, many children who require constant attention and constitute nothing more than a burden to the attendants. For these there is no hope of improvement.

COLORADO STATE HOME FOR DEPENDENT AND NEGLECTED CHILDREN

With more than fifty years of active participation in the child welfare program in Colorado, the State Home for Dependent and Neglected Children is annually aiding in the social and economic adjustment of hundreds of the state's future citizens. Though humble and ill-equipped at its inception it has expanded with its ever-growing needs. Through wise supervision the superintendents of the institution have maintained a home-like atmosphere and have attempted to give each child coming under their charge experiences which are considered normal and conducive to a good life.

Most of the children committed to the Home at the present time are subsequently placed in private homes for adoption. Approximately seventy-five per cent of the placements are children two months of age or less, most of whom are adopted within the first year following placement.[113] Despite the fact the placements and adoptions have nearly doubled during the past five years, the Board of Control still has a waiting list of seven hundred couples who have petitioned to adopt children.[114]

In the *Third Biennial Report* published in 1900 a statement of "facts concerning the State Home for Children" was made. Some of these facts are basic to the successful operation of the institution. They have been reprinted in each succeeding report and are considered worthy of repetition here:

> This is the only State Institution for the care of the dependent, neglected and maltreated children of Colorado.
>
> No church collections or individual contributions are solicited. It is supported by State appropriations.
>
> The children are all committed by the Juvenile or County Courts of the various counties of the state.
>
> Parents are never encouraged to part with their children.
>
> According to Chapter 26, Session Laws of 1895, all children free from chronic or contagious disease, of sound mind and body, placeable in family homes, who are dependent upon the public for support, and who are neglected, maltreated, or in evil environment, are eligible as inmates of the State Home.
>
> No remuneration for placing a child is permitted by the counties, or individuals who are charitably disposed.
>
> The county pays the court cost and expense of transportation for the children to the Home.
>
> There are desirable children now in the Home, to be placed in good families upon adoption or special contract.
> The court and other expenses for adoption papers are paid by the individuals securing them.
>
> The State Agents receive no commission on the children received, or on those placed in private homes.
>
> The members of the Board of Control serve with compensation. This Board is required by law to meet four times a year, however, in this two-year period forty-one regular meetings were recorded. This does not include any special meetings.

"The said Board are hereby made the legal guardians of the persons and estates of all children admitted to said Home, pursuant to law, which guardianship shall continue during the minority of such children, except in cases where, under this act, the guardianship may be cancelled by resolution adopted by said Board." (From Section 5 of Chapter 26, Session Laws, 1895).[115]

In territorial Colorado, neglected children were usually cared for through the goodness of friends. Laws based on the common laws of England provided for the deeding of children to their adoptive parents.[116] Later adoptions were made directly through the Legislature.[117] In 1879 indentures were permitted through the county and district courts.[118] The Board of Charities and Corrections and the Board of County Visitors were created about this time and empowered to assist in regulating both adoptions and indentures.

In 1895 the General Assembly enacted a law creating a State Home for Dependent and Neglected Children and appropriated $10,000.00 for operational expenses for the biennium. Only a part of the first year allowance was made available, however. This was used to repair and furnish a rented building located in North Denver at Bert Street on West Thirty-second Avenue. Sixty children were committed to the home during the ensuing year, of which seventeen were adopted, nine indentured and a number placed on trial.[119] Dr. Rose Kidd Beere, superintendent, and the board of control consisting of Dora E. Reynolds, president, Louisa Arkins, Sarah L. Curtis, Anna Marshall Cockran and Tyson S. Dines, secretary, recommended that the home be granted $25,000.00 for the next two years.[120] The sum of $20,000.00 was appropriated but according to H. W. Cowan, who succeeded Dr. Beere as superintendent, this amount was not sufficient to provide even the necessities.[121]

In 1899 the legislature appropriated $30,000.00 for the purchase of a home. These funds, however, did not become available until April 1902, at which time forty acres of land and a large stone dwelling at South Clarkson and Iliff Avenue were purchased.[122] Subsequent expansion has added another eighteen acres of land and an additional thirteen buildings. Erection of an eighty-bed nursery, a machine shop and a barn is being planned for the near future.

It has been the object of the administration to encourage the young people who remain in the home to participate in providing food and clothing which they use. The girls are taught sewing and given an opportunity to participate in other domestic responsibilities, while the boys do most of the gardening and dairying. Five acres of land are at present devoted to gardening from which most of the vegetables in season are provided for consumption at the home. Some root crops are also stored for winter use. During the 1943-1945 biennium the dairy which is managed by the home produced 209,088 quarts of milk, all of which was consumed at the home.[123]

Operational and maintenance costs of the home were $266,946.11 in the fiscal biennium July 1, 1943 to July 1, 1945[124] as compared with

$40,000.00 for the 1902-1904 biennium.[125] These costs have risen approximately in direct proportion to the added responsibilities assumed.

Annual admissions to the home have shown consistent growth since its opening. Up to December 1904, five hundred fifty-five had been admitted,[126] an average of about sixty-two per year. At that time indentures[127] far outnumbered adoptions in some years as much as four to one. By 1918 this ratio had exactly reversed itself and in the 1921-1922 biennium there were eighty adoptions and but one indenture.[128] By this time the home had received 2,718 children as compared with 10,810 admittances up to January 31, 1947.[129] The recent war and post-war periods have brought mounting responsibilities to the home. The number of children admitted under six months of age has tripled in the period from 1941 to 1946. There were four hundred seventy of this age group admitted in the fiscal year July 1, 1945 to July 1, 1946,[130] while during the period July 1, 1940 to July 1, 1941 there were but one hundred fifty-seven.[131] Total admissions for the same periods were five hundred eighty-one and two hundred seventy-four, respectively. Out of the eight hundred thirty-three admitted in the 1943-1945 biennium six hundred fifty, or more than seventy-eight percent, were children born of illegitimate parental relations.[132]

The 10,710 children admitted to the home in the past fifty-one years are accounted for in the following manner:[133]

In homes on trial	483
In homes adopted	5,780
In free and vocational homes	304
Formally returned to parents	676
Married, attained majority, self supporting	1,988
Died	459
Returned to counties	714
Returned to counties (temporary commitments)	47
Returned to guardians	3
Present in home, January 31, 1947	256
	10,710

COLORADO SOLDIERS' AND SAILORS' HOME

Located at Homelake, adjacent to the town of Monte Vista in the San Luis Valley the Colorado State Soldiers' and Sailors' Home was established by legislative enactment March 15, 1889. It was formally opened and its first members admitted April 1, 1892. Prior to this time the state had made no provision for the care of indigent service men. The General Assembly in 1887, however, had provided burial expenses in the amount of $50.00 for any soldier, sailor or marine who died a pauper.[134]

The original one hundred twenty acres on which the home was located was donated by public-spirited citizens of Monte Vista and the surrounding area. One thousand two hundred perches of building stone, sufficient to construct the first two buildings on the premises were also contributed. Monies, to be matched by appropriated funds, were raised along with essential funds for the drilling of two artesian wells. One thousand cottonwood trees measuring eight to ten feet in height were also furnished and planted through the efforts of the citizens sponsoring committee.[135]

The home is operated under the direction of a commander and a four-member commission appointed by the governor. Three of the members must be honorably discharged soldiers, sailors or marines and the fourth member may be a woman. Each one is bonded in the amount of $5,000.00 to insure the faithful discharge of duties.[136] They serve four-year concurrent terms and their only remuneration is actual expenditures. If the commander of the Grand Army of the Republic for Colorado and Wyoming is a resident citizen of the state he becomes an ex-officio member of the commission as does also the Colorado department commander of the United Spanish War Veterans. The commission is empowered to appoint the principal officers of the home, such as the commander, the adjutant, the bookkeeper, the quarter-master and the commissary and to prescribe the duties and salaries of all officers and employees. Selection of all employees is made by the commander, subject to the ratification of the commission. Each year, on or before the fifteenth day of December, the commission through its president and secretary, is required to submit to the governor a full report of the activities of the home.[137]

The commission is authorized to accept monies, lands and other valuables as donations to the home.[138] The principal source of revenue, however, for the operation, maintenance and improvement of the home is legislative appropriations. The first appropriation consisting of $40,000.00 was made in 1893. That the state may have had difficulties in meeting its commitments is evidenced in the fact that the commissioners of the home were obliged to take up court proceedings in order to obtain the full stipulated amount.[139] Appropriations for the home during the 1947-48 biennium total $85,000.00 for maintenance and operation and $75,000.00 for additional buildings.[140] More than sixty buildings are now in use in the operation of the home. Supplementing the appropriations are: any overage of funds from the State Boxing Commission, net proceeds from the sale of produce from the home farms which are now composed of more than six hundred acres, and federal aid amounting to $10.00 per month per man.

Revisions of the original provisions for eligibility to membership in the home have been enacted several times in the past half century; the most recent one being made by the 1947 legislature. According to the 1947 law the home is

maintained for the care and treatment of not dishonorably discharged soldiers, sailors and marines who served in the Union or Confederate Armies between the twelfth day of April, 1861, and the ninth day of April, 1865; or who served in the Spanish-American War, or the Philippine Insurrection, or the China Relief Expedition, between the twenty-first day of April, 1898, and the fourth day of July, 1902; or who served in the regular or volunteer army or navy in any foreign war or Indian war in which the United States has been engaged; or who serve in any war in which the United States in the future may engage; and who have been bona fide residents of this State for at least seven years next preceding their application for admission to said home . . . . Any veteran who is now or may hereafter become a member of said Home in accordance with the provisions of this Law having a wife so dependent upon him for support, shall be entitled to have said wife so dependent upon him at said Home as a member thereof; provided, however, that such dependent wife has been married to said veteran for a period of seven years and is of more than fifty years of age; and, provided further, that if the husband is a confirmed invalid, and as such requires the constant attention of said wife, any such wife of such member may remain in said Home during her natural life if she was in said Home at the time of the death of said member.[141]

Most men and women who enter the home are either indigent or ill, the basis of admission being the need of care or treatment.[142] All who are able to work are assigned to care for lawns, gardens and grounds on the basis of two days work per week. These duties are performed without compensation. Wherever possible veteran members who are able to carry full-time responsibilities are employed in regular remunerative jobs at the home, such as firemen, farmhands, cooks, bakers, etc.[143] Minor hospitalization facilities are available. In the event of illnesses requiring prolonged hospital care, the patient is removed to one of the veterans' medical centers for further treatment. Cottages are provided for couples, affording them considerable privacy. However, to facilitate operations and to keep the group intergrated no cooking is allowed in cottages or rooms. All eating is done from a central dining room.

During the fifty-five years of operation there have been approximately three thousand two hundred men and women who have received benefits from the home. Statistics show that out of two hundred seven men who were in the home in 1898, there were one hundred sixty privates, eight corporals, nineteen sergeants, five second lieutenants, two first lieutenants, two captains, two seamen, two landsmen and seven in miscellaneous categories.[144]

References, Chapter XXIII

INTRODUCTION

[1] *Colorado Constitution*, Article VIII, Sec. 1.
[2] *Biennial Report of the State Board of Charities and Corrections, 1892*, p. 7
[3] *Session Laws, 1921*, p. 216.
[4] *Ibid, 1933*, pp. 242-243.
[5] *Ibid*, pp. 213-214.
[6] *Ibid, 1947*, passim.

STATE PENITENTIARY

[7] *Revised Statutes of Colorado, 1868*, pp. 475-76.
[8] *Annual Report of the Colorado State Penitentiary, 1876*, pp. 10-14.
[9] *Ibid.*, pp. 10-14.
[10] *Annual Report of the Colorado State Penitentiary, 1876*, pp. 20-25.
[11] *Session Laws, 1897*, p. 32.
[12] *Ibid, 1899*, pp. 233-35.
[13] *Ibid, 1935*, p. 342.

[14] *Biennial Report of the State Penitentiary, 1910*, p. 12.
[15] *Ibid*, p. 13.
[16] *Ibid, 1926*, pp. 11-12.
[17] *Ibid, 1930*, p. 9.
[18] *Ibid, 1926*, pp. 12-13.
[19] *Ibid*, p. 13.
[20] *Ibid, 1928*, pp. 8-9.
[21] F. E. Crawford who served from December 1, 1927 to October 9, 1931.
[22] *Session Laws, 1933*, pp. 391, 781.
[23] *Ibid*, p. 783.
[24] *Biennial Report of the Colorado State Penitentiary, 1940*, pp. 5-6
[25] *Ibid, 1938*, p. 5.
[26] *Ibid, 1940*, p. 5.
[27] *Denver Post, March 5, 1948*, p. 26.
[28] *Session Laws, 1909*, p. 329.
[29] *Biennial Report of the Colorado State Penitentiary, 1940*, p. 28.
[30] *Ibid*, p. 18.
[31] *Ibid*, p. 33.
[32] Statement made in a speech to the Denver Rotary Club, January 22, 1948.
[33] *Rocky Mountain Life, February 1948*, p. 15.
[34] Jimmy Melton sentenced February 26, 1948 for the murder of his sixteen-year-old sister.

STATE REFORMATORY

[35] *Colorado Constitution*, Art. VIII, Sec. 1.
[36] *Colorado Statutes Annotated, 1935*, vol. 2, ch. 48, pp. 1152-3.
[37] *Annual Report of the Colorado State Reformatory, 1902*, p. 8.
[38] *Biennial Report of the Colorado State Reformatory, 1898*, p. 12.
[39] Punishment by "hanging" was effected by placing hand cuffs on a man's wrists, attaching a rope or the hook of a block and tackle thereto and suspending the man for a period of from five to twenty minutes.
[40] *Report of the Investigation of the State Reformatory by the State Board Charities and Corrections, 1895*, pp. 6-9.
[41] *Biennial Report of the Colorado State Reformatory, 1904*, p. 16.
[42] *Ibid, 1942*, p. 14.
[43] *Session Laws, 1947*, p. 199.
[44] *Biennial Report of the Colorado State Reformatory, 1918*, p. 6.
[45] *Ibid, 1898*, p. 35; *1908*, pp. 89-91; *1931*, p. 13.
[46] *A Study of the Educational Needs of the . . . Colorado State Reformatory . . . made by the Committee for the State Association of University and College Presidents . . . at the Request of Honorable John C. Vivian*, Governor of the State of Colorado, November 15, 1944.

STATE INDUSTRIAL SCHOOL FOR BOYS

[47] *Biennial Report of the State Industrial School for Boys, 1883-1884*, p. 6.
[48] *Ibid, 1891-1892*, p. 9.
[49] *Ibid.*
[50] *Ibid*, p. 10.
[51] *Ibid.*
[52] *Ibid, 1893-1894*, p. 9.
[53] *Session Laws, 1925*, p. 305.
[54] *Biennial Report, 1943-1944*, p. 5.
[55] *Ibid*, p. 27.

STATE INDUSTRIAL SCHOOL FOR GIRLS

[56] *Revised Statutes of Colorado, 1908*, Sec. 3046.
[57] *Biennial Report of the State Industrial School for Girls, 1898*, pp. 7-9.
[58] *Ibid, 1896*, p. 10.
[59] *Ibid, 1901*, pp. 5-7.
[60] *Ibid, 1902*, p. 7.
[61] *Ibid*, p. 8.
[62] *Ibid, 1906*, p. 3.
[63] *Ibid, 1904*, pp. 4-5.
[64] *Ibid, 1902*, p. 22.
[65] *Ibid, 1945*, pp. 16-17.
[66] *Ibid, 1902*, p. 38.
[67] *Ibid, 1945*, p. 5.
[68] *Ibid*, p. 6.
[69] *Ibid*, p. 5.

STATE HOSPITAL

[70] *Session Laws, 1879*, p. 87.
[71] *First Annual Report of the Colorado Insane Asylum, 1880*, p. 9.
[72] *Ibid.*
[73] *Ibid*, p. 4.
[74] *Ibid*, p. 5.
[75] *Session Laws, 1879*, p. 89.
[76] *Ibid, 1917*, p. 146.
[77] *Ibid, 1937*, p. 466.
[78] *Ibid, 1941*, p. 337.
[79] *Ibid, 1947*, p. 346.
[80] *Ibid*, pp. 59-61.
[81] *Biennial Report of the Colorado State Hospital, 1945*, p. 26.
[82] *Ibid*, p. 30.
[83] *Ibid*, pp. 37-40.
[84] *Ibid*, p. 36.
[85] *Colorado Statutes Annotated, 1935*, vol. 4, pp. 23-24.
[86] *Session Laws, 1917*, p. 273.
[87] *Biennial Report of the Colorado State Hospital, 1945*, p. 8.
[88] *Session Laws, 1915*, p. 336.
[89] *Ibid*, p. 340.
[90] *Ibid, 1879*, p. 80.
[91] *Ibid, 1893*, p. 336.
[92] *Biennial Report of the Colorado State Hospital, 1945*, p. 8.
[93] *Ibid*, p. 18.
[94] *Session Laws, 1879*, p. 87.
[95] *Biennial Report of the Colorado Insane Asylum, 1900*, p. 5.
[96] *Biennial Report of the Colorado State Hospital, 1934*, p. 2.
[97] *Biennial Report of the Colorado Insane Asylum, 1880*, p. 12.
[98] *Ibid, 1914*, p. 8.
[99] *Biennial Report of the Colorado State Hospital, 1945*, pp. 9-10.

State Home And Training School For Mental Defectives

[100] *Biennial Report of the Colorado State Home and Training School for Mental Defectives,* Ridge, 1912, p. 4.

[101] *Ibid,* pp. 3-4.

[102] *Session Laws, 1909,* pp. 180, 182.

[103] *Ibid,* pp. 180-181.

[104] *Biennial Report,* Ridge, 1912, p. 3.

[105] *Session Laws, 1919,* p. 267.

[106] *Biennial Report,* Grand Junction, 1947, p. 11.

[107] *Ibid,* p. 12.

[108] *Session Laws, 1947,* pp. 826-31.

[109] *Biennial Report,* Ridge, 1940, p. 4; 1943, p. 4.

[110] *Biennial Report,* Grand Junction, 1947, p. 3.

[111] *Ibid, 1931,* p. 13.

[112] *Ibid,* pp. 17-19.

State Home For Dependent And Neglected Children

[113] *Biennial Report of the Colorado State Home for Dependent and Neglected Children, 1945,* p. 15.

[114] According to a statement made to the author by the superintendent, John C. Stoddard.

[115] *Biennial Report, 1945,* p. 3.

[116] *Territorial Laws of Colorado, 1861,* pp. 348-349.

[117] *Ibid, 1867,* p. 142; 1872, p. 223; 1874, p. 319; 1876, pp. 194-201.

[118] *Ibid, 1879,* pp. 28-29.

[119] *Biennial Report, 1896,* pp. 7-8.

[120] *Ibid,* p. 16.

[121] *Biennial Report, 1898,* p. 15.

[122] *Ibid, 1902,* p. 12.

[123] *Ibid, 1945,* p. 8.

[124] *Ibid.*

[125] *Ibid, 1904,* p. 14.

[126] *Ibid,* p. 16.

[127] Indenture is obsolete—no longer in use.

[128] *Biennial Report, 1923,* p. 13.

[129] From a statement rendered the author February 14, 1947 by Miss Emma Cassady, Coordinator of the Home.

[130] *Ibid.*

[131] *Biennial Report, 1941,* p. 11.

[132] *Ibid, 1945,* p. 13.

[133] Cassady, *op. cit.*

Soldiers' And Sailors' Home

[134] *Colorado Statutes Annotated,* Ch. 150, p. 1094.

[135] *Report of the Soldiers' and Sailors Home, 1894,* pp. 6-9.

[136] *Session Laws, 1895,* p. 105.

[137] *Ibid,* p. 108.

[138] *Ibid,* p. 107.

[139] *Report of the Soldiers' and Sailors' Home, 1894,* p. 19.

[140] *Session Laws, 1947,* pp. 143-144.

[141] *Ibid,* pp. 797-798.

[142] *Report of the Soldiers' and Sailors' Home, 1892,* p. 3.

[143] *Quarterly Bulletin,* Colorado State Department of Public Welfare, vol. 2, no. 3, 1938, p. 1.

[144] *Report of the Colorado Soldiers' and Sailors' Home, 1898,* pp. 14-24.

CHAPTER XXIV

History of Colorado Railroads

HERBERT O. BRAYER

GOLD AND RAILS 1858-1870

WITH the confirmation of the discovery of gold in the Pike's Peak region in 1858, men ceased to use the area as just part of the highways to the Pacific—to California and Oregon—and began the unceasing search for new and richer "mother lodes" in the Rockies. The excitement caused by the early successes of the Argonauts in the rocky canyons and stream beds of the eastern frontal range was mirrored in the press throughout the nation and repeated—and exaggerated—by the depression-weary inhabitants of farm and industrial areas who hungrily envisioned a recurrence of the hectic though profitable period following the California gold rush of 1849.

From the outset the miners and their supporters recognized the difficulties of their geographical position. Unlike their earlier counterparts in California, supplies and equipment could not be cheaply brought in by sea from the East, but had to be shipped over the tortuous and expensive overland trails from the Missouri and Mississippi valleys. So long as mining activities were largely confined to panning and elementary placer operations the problem, though vexatious, was not acute. It was not long, however, before the stream beds began to peter out, forcing the anxious Argonauts to work the more difficult ore bodies on the rugged mountain slopes. This was an entirely different type of operation requiring heavy and expensive mining, milling, and smelting equipment. To make matters even more difficult it was discovered that the refractory ores required a special refining process available only at Swansea in Wales. Until plants were erected and the Welsh process developed in the Rockies, heavy wagon loads of matte were hauled overland to be transhipped from an eastern port to Europe for refinement.

Wagon trains of wheat and preserved foods from Kansas, Iowa and Missouri, and produce from New Mexico and Utah, brought in the necessities of life for the miners, but the perils of such long and irregular trips only added further to the high costs of the goods in the mountain settlements, thereby further depreciating the income of the miners and their families. As Colorado's mining industry grew, the demand for adequate and improved transportation facilities increased. Within a few months after the opening of the first large diggings on Clear Creek, leaders among the gold-seekers and energetic land speculators were discussing the possibilities of securing a rail connection with their supply and market centers to the East.

Simultaneous with the Pike's Peak discoveries the agitation for a railroad to link the eastern portion of the United States with California and the Pacific Northwest rapidly approached a climax. Up to 1859 members of Congress and many of the principal protagonists of the Pacific Railroad were still irreconcilably divided over the route such a railway should follow. The transcontinental surveys had demonstrated the feasibility of a number of routes including one investigated by Captain John W. Gunnison through the Rockies in 1853. Gunnison projected a railroad west of Kansas City which reached the mountains by following the Arkansas, crossed the mountains through the Sangre de Cristo Pass to the San Luis Valley and struck northwesterly to Cochetopa Pass where it would have followed the valleys of the Gunnison and Grand rivers to Utah and then westerward to California.[1] The inability of the advocates to unite upon this or any of the other routes surveyed by the Army engineers repeatedly blocked favorable Congressional action upon the Pacific railroad.

It was at this point that the "Pike's Peak fever" became a vital factor in the ultimate decision. Freight and passenger traffic with the newly opened region—which was heralded as a "New California" with a long and prosperous future—would provide the revenues necessary to the success of the transcontinental line. Henry Villard, special correspondent for the *Cincinnati Daily Commercial*, after visiting the newly discovered Gregory Diggings in 1859 reported:

. . . But the most important consequence of last year's [1859] labor in the Rocky Mountains remains to be told. It is the influence it will exercise upon the realization of the favorite national idea of a connection of the Atlantic and Pacific States and Territories by a railroad and telegraph line. The result of the mining season of 1860 in the Pike's Peak gold regions, will definitely settle the long-mooted question of their location and construction. In less than twelve months, no sane mind will doubt the certainty that the first chain of iron and wire, that will render the circulation of the life-blood of our great Republic through the agricultural, industrial, and commercial systems of all its parts, possible and perfect, will be strung across that portion of the Rocky Mountains that has lately been found to abound in mineral wealth.[2]

With the secession of the southern states the principal Congressional opposition to a central route for the Pacific Railroad was removed. A combination of western interests united with representatives of the "Old West"—in whose states active railroad construction and extension had been widespread—brought about the enactment of

[1] Gunnison, however, reported this route to be far inferior to the middle central route by way of the Medicine Bow River and Laramie Plains. *House Exec. Docs.,* 33 Cong., 2nd sess., no. 91, II, 70.

[2] Henry Villard, *The Past and Present of the Pike's Peak Gold Regions . . .* (Sunderland & McEvoy, St. Louis, Mo., 1860), 147. For similar expressions in Congress during the debates on the Pacific Railroad measure see *Congressional Globe,* 1861-1862; Allen M. Kline, "The Attitude of Congress Toward the Pacific Railway, 1856-1862," American Historical Association, *Annual Report,* 1910, 199 *et. seq.*

the Pacific Railroad Act in 1862 and its vital revision in 1864. In the meanwhile local promoters were hastening to capitalize upon the nationwide interest in the mountain gold regions by announcing plans to extend their proposed roads to the Rockies. Their publicity was chiefly designed to attract the attention of investors and speculators who for some time had viewed with obvious reluctance the securities offered by such lines. Among such companies were: the Missouri River & Pike's Peak Railroad from St. Joseph; the St. Joseph and Denver City Railroad; the Atchison and Pike's Peak Railroad; the Leavenworth, Fort Riley and Western Railroad; the St. Louis, Lawrence and Denver Railroad; the Pacific Railroad of Missouri from St. Louis and Kansas City; the Cedar Rapids and Missouri River Railroad from Chicago to Denver with a line to South Pass.[3]

Citizens of the new mining settlements anxiously watched the battle for passage of the Pacific Railroad Act. Meetings were held in Denver as early as February 1859 to consider ways and means of assisting the venture.[4] The "legislature" of the "Territory of Jefferson" memorialized Congress on behalf of the project urging federal support for a railroad from the Missouri River to the base of the Rockies.[5] As new gold and silver lodes were discovered the settlements grew and the demand for supplies and equipment far exceeded the supply. Governor Gilpin officially recommended to Secretary of State Seward that the Pacific Railroad be constructed through central Colorado.[6] His successor, Governor John Evans actively lobbied for the transcontinental route and, in 1862, became one of its commissioners.[7] The Colorado press, youthfully optimistic and frequently over zealous, carried detailed accounts of the progress of the Congressional debate over the Pacific Railroad measure and glowingly hailed its passage in 1862.

The national preoccupation with the war, high costs, the shortage of labor, and the inability of the newly organized Union Pacific Railway to market its securities prevented any immediate or material construction by the company, a disappointing circumstance to the impatient Argonauts. From the passage of the act, however, the Colorado promoters sought to insure the construction of the line to central Colorado.

A struggle over the location of the future rail center of Colorado, destined to have far-reaching consequences, now developed between the citizens of Denver and Golden. Each group was anxious to secure the mountain terminus of the Pacific Railway, and with it the commercial domination of the Territory. Headed by the enthusiastic

[3] Microfilm copies of various reports, articles of incorporation, and promotional publications issued by these companies are part of the valuable collection of economic documents assembled by the State Historical Society of Colorado. The author also acknowledges the generosity of Mr. Thomas Streeter who permitted the filming and use of a number of rare documents issued by the companies cited.

[4] *Nebraska Advertiser,* February 10, 1859.

[5] *House Misc. Docs.,* 36th Cong., 1 sess., no. 10.

[6] *House Ex. Docs.,* 37th Cong., 2 sess., no. 56.

[7] Edgar McMechan, *Life of Governor Evans* (Wahlgreen Publishing Co., Denver, 1924), 145.

promoter William A. H. Loveland and the capable Central City attorney Henry M. Teller, the Golden clique secured the initiative. Early in 1865 Loveland and Teller headed a group of eight Coloradans and fourteen Easteners (including a number of Union Pacific promoters and officials) who secured legislative incorporation for Clear Creek and Colorado Railway Company. According to its charter this line was to start at Golden and extend up Clear Creek to Central City, and from Golden to Boulder with a third division from Golden to Denver and south to Bijou.[8] It is apparent that this action by the Golden promoters was in anticipation of the construction of the Union Pacific to Colorado.

Vice President Durant of the Pacific Railroad had definitely expressed his desire for the extension of his road to the mining settlements and Loveland confidently indicated that his road would link up with the Union Pacific. Negotiations with the transcontinental company officials had led to a definite understanding between the Golden organization and the Union Pacific directors previous to January 1866 when Loveland secured an amended charter and changed the name of his company to the Colorado Central and Pacific Railroad. Five Union Pacific directors were among the incorporators of the reorganized company which now was authorized to lay its rails from Golden to the Utah border on the west, to the southeastern border of the Territory, and to the northeastern boundary where it would join the Union Pacific.[9] Durant, undoubtedly sincere in his desire to have the transcontinental line pass through central Colorado, ordered a reconnaissance of the area with the view of locating a practical pass through the mountains to the West. During 1866 a surveying party made an extensive examination of ten mountain passes: (1) via the South Platte and Hoosier Pass; (2) via the South Platte and Tarryall Pass; (3) via the North Fork of the South Platte; (4) via Berthoud Pass; (5) via Boulder Pass; (6) via Cache le Poudre and Antelope Pass; (7) via Evans Pass; (8) via Lodge Pole Creek, Cow Creek and Evans Pass; (9) via Lodge Pole Creek and Cheyenne Pass; (10) via Lodge Pole Creek and South Pass. The result was disappointing to the Colorado promoters. Not one of the routes through central Colorado met with favor.[10] A second circumstance now developed which further weakened the chances of the Union Pacific building to the Cherry Creek or Clear Creek settlements. A new revision of the Pacific Railroad Act permitted the Central Pacific to extend its construction eastward until its rails linked with those of the westbound Union Pacific. This amendment served to promote a construction race in which each company was interested in constructing as much line as possible in the shortest period in order to get as large a share of the government subsidies (lands and securities) as possible. Such a costly race practically doomed the Colorado route of the Union Pacific, as the directors demanded that

8 *House Journal* [Colorado], 4th sess., 54, 107-108, 138. The incorporation act was signed by the Governor on February 9, 1865.
9 *Teller Papers*, University of Colorado; see also the revised charter in the *Berthoud Papers* in the collection of the State Historical Society of Colorado.
10 Ralph Budd, "Railroad Routes Across the Rockies", *Civil Engineering*, February, 1940, 97; March, 1940, 161; April, 1940, 222.

the line be constructed as rapidly as possible. This meant that the heavy mountain construction required by the suggested Colorado routes would necessarily be eliminated in favor of the shorter and less rigorous route through Cheyenne Pass and Bridger's Pass. In November 1866 the announcement was made: the central Colorado settlements were not to be on the main line![11]

While naturally disappointed, Loveland and his Golden colleagues were quick to alter their plans to suit the new situation. Since they obviously could not be a part of the main line it was determined to construct a branch line which would link Colorado's mineral empire ("and its capital at Golden") with the Union Pacific to the north. During the Spring of 1867 an agreement was negotiated between the Colorado Central and the Union Pacific whereby the former would construct the roadbed from Golden to the Pacific company's tracks. The latter agreed to iron the roadbed, furnish the rolling stock and to secure itself for this outlay by taking the first mortgage bonds of the Colorado company. In return the Colorado Central was to receive thirty percent of the profits from all business over its line for the first five years, and twenty-five percent for the succeeding five years. Clearly, the Union Pacific officials and directors who also served on the board of the Colorado road directed the policy of the local company. To activate the contract Captain Berthoud was directed to survey the projected routes, one north and one south of the Platte from Golden to the Union Pacific main line. The first completely avoided Denver, while the latter was surveyed down Clear Creek to South Platte, then north along the river and Lone Tree Creek to a junction with the Pacific road. A seven-mile branch was designed to link Denver and Golden.

Denver leaders were energetically seeking methods to circumvent the plans of the Golden promoters. Governor John Evans valiantly sought to promote Denver as the terminal point. During the summer of 1867, however, it appeared that the Golden-Union Pacific alliance would eventually win. Early in July Thomas J. Carter, a director of the transcontinental road, made an official visit to the territory for the expressed purpose of securing aid for the construction of a local branch line to connect with the transcontinental road. He publicly espoused the cause of the Colorado Central suggesting that the road be constructed so as to link both Golden and Denver with the Union Pacific. He proposed that the counties through which the Colorado Central would run should share the estimated six hundred thousand dollar expense of constructing the roadbed from Golden through Denver and Boulder to the transcontinental tracks. Arapahoe County (Denver) was apportioned one-third, or $200,000 of the expense which the county was expected to bear through the issuance of twenty-year eight per cent county bonds. Jefferson County's (Golden) share was set at $100,000, with Gilpin County (Central City) to provide $200,000, Boulder $50,000, Weld $25,000, and Larimer $25,000. The Union

---

[11] *Rocky Mountain News*, December 4, 1866, 2: 1-2.

Pacific, according to Director Carter, would provide and lay the track, supply the rolling stock, and operate the completed line. In exchange for the bonds voted by the counties, the railroad agreed to give the counties equivalent amounts of Union Pacific stock.[12] All but Boulder County ultimately approved the bond issue requested, but such limitations and stipulations were added as to preclude their acceptance by the company.[13] Loveland tried desperately to save the program but found the differences between the various counties and local interests irreconcilable. The plan was a failure, and a costly one for Golden. Oliver Ames, one of the leading Union Pacific officials, let it be known in Denver that he considered the agreement between the Colorado Central and his road abrogated. The way was now open for the Denver promoters to gain the initiative.

Sparking the Denver drive for a railroad link with the East were Governor John Evans, General John Pierce, Jerome Chaffee, General Bela M. Hughes, and David A. Moffat. The apparent alliance between the Golden entrepreneurs and the Union Pacific forced this Denver group to seek an alliance with the Union Pacific Eastern Division. Despite the similarity in names the Union Pacific Eastern Division was an independent company authorized by the the Pacific Railroad Act of 1864 to construct a railroad from St. Louis along a central route ultimately to link up with the Union Pacific near Fort Kearney, Nebraska. The latter provision was amended in 1864 to permit the road to make its connection west of the one hundredth meridian, but no additional subsidy (land or securities) was granted for this projected extension. A further revision in 1866 authorized the Eastern Division to join the Union Pacific main line at or near the Denver parallel.[14] The elation of the Denver promoters soon abated, however, as the St. Louis road made little progress in extending its roadbed toward the "Queen City of the Prairies." Rumors of a plan to extend the road south to the Arkansas and then on to the Pacific via New Mexico worried the Coloradans. When, the following year, an Eastern Division survey party under General William J. Palmer undertook a survey of possible routes to the Pacific along the thirty-second and thirty-fifth parallels this worry became outright alarm.[15]

It was at this juncture that the real blow fell upon Denver. Just after the failure of the Colorado Central proposition in November 1867, Colonel James Archer of the Eastern Division appeared in Denver, explained the critical financial position of his company, and then proposed an advance to the Eastern Division of two million dollars by Denver. The request contained the thinly veiled threat that if it were not met the railroad would not be built to Denver at all![16]

[12] *Colorado Tribune,* July 12, 1867; Frank Hall, *History of Colorado,* (Blakeley Printing Co., Chicago, 1890), I, 413.
[13] S. D. Mock, "The Financing of Early Colorado Railroads," *Colorado Magazine,* vol. XVIII, no. 6, November 1941, 201-209.
[14] 14 U. S. Stat., 79-80; For Denver reaction to the change see *Rocky Mountain News,* March 28, 1866.
[15] William J. Palmer, *Report of Surveys Across the Continent in 1867-'68, on the Thirty-fifth and Thirty-second Parallels, for a Route extending the Kansas Pacific Railway to the Pacific Ocean at San Francisco and San Diego.* Philadelphia, 1869.
[16] *Daily Colorado Tribune,* January 15, 1868.

In mid-November, while the astounded Denverites were considering this unexpected turn, the ubiquitous George Francis Train, premier agent for the Union Pacific, visited Denver and, after ridiculing the Eastern Division's pretensions, proposed the organization of a local company to construct a line from Denver to the Union Pacific. Under the influence of Train's colorful discourse the idea met with enthusiastic favor. With John Evans, Bela Hughes, and John Pierce actively promoting the plan—supported by the newly organized Board of Trade whose members greatly feared the eclipse of their city by Cheyenne—the Denver Pacific Railroad and Telegraph Company was organized at a public meeting on November 18, 1867, and formally incorporated the next day. By personal solicitation among the members of the Board of Trade, Evans succeeded in obtaining two-hundred thousand dollars in subscriptions to the two million dollar capital stock of the company.[17] In a special election on January 20, 1868, the citizens of Denver and Arapahoe County approved a special half million dollar bond issue to aid the enterprise.[18]

A wave of unbridled optimism swept Denver. Branches of the Denver Pacific were "created" daily. One serious plan actually adopted by the railroad was aimed directly at the Loveland clique in Golden; in January 1868 a line was projected from Denver to Central City and Georgetown—the route preempted on paper by the Colorado Central.

While Chief Engineer F. M. Case, on loan from the Union Pacific, surveyed a line from Denver to the Union Pacific right-of-way at Pine Bluffs a serious effort was made to consolidate the Colorado Central and the Denver Pacific, or to at least compose their differences and draft a non-competing operations agreement. Apparently these negotiations failed, for renewed activity by the Golden group led to the sale of $273,000 worth of its securities and the ratification of its earlier agreement with the Union Pacific. On New Year's Day 1868, amid enthusiastic celebration, ground was broken at Golden for the Colorado Central. Simultaneously Union Pacific Eastern Division officials, fearing that the success of the Union Pacific might freeze them out of the Chicago-Colorado business they hoped to obtain, did an about face and sought to recapture the favor of the Denver promotors. The latter, however, now convinced that a "bird in the hand was worth two in the bush" were not to be deterred and went ahead with plans to link Denver with the main line of the transcontinental route.

Despite their failure to market the securities of the Denver Pacific or the bonds of Arapahoe County, the promoters continued to place their faith in the promises of the Union Pacific and to work for a Congressional land grant subsidy. In April 1868, following a preliminary agreement with the Union Pacific, a supplementary contract was signed whereby the transcontinental company undertook to construct the entire line while the Denver company subcontracted the

[17] *Daily Colorado Tribune,* November 19-21, 1867. Certificate of Incorporation, Office of the Secretary of State, Denver. Original statement by Governor Evans in the files of the Denver Chamber of Commerce, successor of the Board of Trade.

[18] *Daily Colorado Tribune,* December 28, 1867, January 17, 21, 1868.

grading and tieing. The Pacific road agreed to lease and operate the Denver to Cheyenne line and guaranteed an eight percent annual interest on the stock of the local company. All securities, except the Arapahoe County bonds, and any subsequent land grant voted by Congress were to be turned over to the Union Pacific. On May 20, 1868, ground was broken for the Denver Pacific and all Denver cele-brated—unmindful of the difficulties still to be faced.

Congress twice refused to approve the land grant subsidy to the Denver Pacific. After the second failure Evans and his colleagues conferred with officials of the Eastern Division who had an approved land subsidy for their projected line to link up with the Union Pacific and succeeded in securing Congressional support for the transfer of a portion of that subsidy to the Denver Pacific. The measure was approved on February 2, 1869.[19] In return for its cooperation the Colorado line granted the Eastern Division a perpetual right-of-way over its road. Grading on the road linking Denver with the Union Pacific began from both ends in 1868 and this phase of the work was completed in May 1869. At this point the work slowed and then came to a full halt. Governor Evans called upon the Union Pacific to fulfill its contract to iron and equip the line, only to be informed that the Pacific road was financially unable to do so. Consternation reigned in Denver when Evans reported the facts to his supporters. The Denver Pacific was heavily in debt, its securities could find no market, it had a graded roadbed with no rails or rolling stock, and no money with which to purchase these essentials. Evans was prevailed upon to take over the personal direction of the company's tangled affairs.[20] In a series of rapid and brilliant moves the former governor contracted for the purchase of rails, cars and locomotives. He founded a construction company made up of himself, Walter S. Cheesman, and President Robert Carr of the newly named Kansas Pacific Railroad (formerly the Union Pacific Eastern Division). By this arrangement and sub-sequent security purchases the Kansas Pacific group obtained a large interest in the Denver road. Evans and Carr formed a profitable partnership which engaged in the development of townsites along the right-of-way of the Denver Pacific. Track laying made slow progress and it was not until June 22, 1870 that the first train entered Denver over the completed line.[21]

In the meanwhile the Kansas Pacific, having dropped its original name in order to avoid erroneous and frequently embarrassing identi-fication with the Union Pacific, had again been refused Congressional aid for its contemplated extension to the Arkansas, New Mexico and on to the Pacific. In order to secure the Colorado trade—the one remaining source of substantial income readily available [part of the Santa Fe' Trail traffic was already reaching its terminus at the

[19] *Congressional Globe*, 40th Cong., 3rd sess., 781, 1082, 1240, 1809.
[20] See Evans' own account in the *Denver Daily Times*, May 3, 1877; *Daily Colorado Tribune*, June 22, 1870; McMechen, *Life of Governor Evans*, 166-167.
[21] *Daily Colorado Tribune*, June 22, 1870. Additional stories published on succeeding days gave a good account of the celebration in which all Denver, and the mountain mining settlements, readily joined.

Kansas-Colorado border]—it was decided to push the extension to Denver as rapidly as possible. In spite of this decision it was not until April 1870 that the rails reached the prairie town site of Kit Carson. Early in the year the construction of the rest of the line to Denver had been assured when representatives succeeded in disposing of $850,000 of the company's bonds in Germany.[22] Headed by General William J. Palmer, youthful Pennsylvania war hero, the construction crews rushed work at both ends of the line. Amid wild demonstrations and celebrations the first train over the Kansas Pacific arrived in Denver at the resplendent new depot located at the foot of Twenty-second Street on August 15, 1870.[23]

An anti-climax occurred some five weeks later when, on September 23, the long comatose Colorado Central completed its rails linking Golden and Denver. Curiously, the road continued its earlier antipathy and refused to build directly into Denver. It joined its tracks with those of the Denver Pacific at a junction six miles north of Denver, and operated its trains over the rails of the latter company through a rental agreement. Behind the Colorado Central activity was the Union Pacific. Belatedly Ames, Durant, and their associates realized that their rival, the Kansas Pacific, had gained the favored position in Colorado, and through operations and traffic agreements with the Denver Pacific could control a large share of the trade with the booming mining communities. Oliver Ames and other Union Pacific leaders renewed the interest in the Golden company which they had permitted to lapse when the agreement with the Denver Pacific had seemed the more promising.[24]

By the end of 1870 Colorado had two major rail links with eastern markets and one with those on the Pacific. Both the Union Pacific and Kansas Pacific were able to tap the mineral wealth of the mountain communities by their connections at or near Denver with the Colorado Central and over the Denver Pacific trackage. Projected lines radiating in all directions from Denver were announced with such frequency that even the press was unable to keep up with the "paper network". The 'sixties had witnessed the successful completion of the first steps in the development of Colorado's railroad system. The 'seventies were to see the extension of the system and the first of many battles for strategic passes and lucrative markets in the mountain areas.

EXTENSION, DEPRESSION AND WAR 1871-1880

Completion of the Denver Pacific and Kansas Pacific railroads foreshadowed the end of the large wagon freighting organizations. In place of the high and fluctuating rates charged by the freighters,[25]

---

[22] The Kansas Pacific representatives at the same time marketed $1,500,000 worth of Denver Pacific first mortgage bonds in London, England. *Daily Colorado Tribune,* February 2, 1870.

[23] *Daily Colorado Tribune,* August 15, 1870.

[24] *Daily Colorado Tribune,* April 17, 1870; *Daily Central City Register,* April 19, 1870; *Golden Transcript,* April 27, 1870.

[25] During the 'sixties rates from the Missouri frequently ran as high as $25.00 per 100 pounds of freight, but a study of prices on the Denver market would indicate that on large commodity shipments the rate was considerably less. Rates were, of course, much higher during the winter months than in summer and autumn.

the rail tariff on first class freight averaged about twenty cents per ton mile, and seven cents per ton mile on ores and matte as compared with the old freight wagon rate of approximately twenty cents. The passenger rate varied between eleven and eleven and one-half cents per passenger mile. While not low by present standards,[26] such rates were a marked improvement over the stage-coach and bull-wagon charges. Except for Denver and the surrounding settlements, however, the cost of transportation was still high. It was necessary to reload and haul by wagon the vast quantities of merchandise and equipment needed by the many communities located at considerable distances from the new railroad terminals. It was to alleviate this condition that most of the railroad ventures were undertaken in Colorado during the 'seventies.

The period from 1871 to 1880 in Colorado's railroad history was characterized by two forces: first, the rapid advance of new transcontinental lines from the Missouri Valley to the Rockies; and, second, the projection of scores of local lines within the territory with the actual construction of several of real significance. An unbridled and disastrous rivalry for both traffic and rights-of-way, intensified by a prolonged world-wide economic depression, were factors destined to affect the Colorado carriers throughout the ensuing quarter century. Despite these adverse factors the period from 1871 to 1880 was one in which the foundation of Colorado's modern transportation network was laid. It was a decade of visible progress, yet it contained within it the invisible seeds of financial catastrophe—seeds which germinated from undisciplined competition, insatiable greed, and a lack of public responsibility. Such traits were not confined to the railroad industry during that era, but were a part of a lusty, immature, and expanding economy in America; they were the "trademark of the era."

Jubliant Coloradans wasted little time in capitalizing upon the completion of the iron rail highways to the base of the Rockies. Optimism radiated throughout the Territorial press, from the rostrum and pulpit, and among the more calculating entrepreneurs who recognized the speculative opportunities afforded by the construction of short lines to link the rugged mining camps with the newly completed transcontinental outlets. Expressive of this feeling had been the remarks of one territorial leader, W. R. Thomas, who, even before the completion of the Denver Pacific and the Kansas Pacific, ecstatically effervesced:

> The pioneers work is almost accomplished, and in a land of peace and plenty, with pride and with joy, he bids today the coming railways hail! Hail to the iron horse! Hail to the multitudes which follow his rapid course! Hail to the increase of production, the impetus to industry, the new days of prosperity which he

[26] The average rate per passenger mile in the West during 1947 was two and one-tenth cents. Early in 1862 the fare from Denver to Central City by stage was $4.00, but in the same year was reduced to $2.00; on October 26, 1871, the fare from Pueblo to Trinidad was $19.00 but was soon changed to $15.00; in 1880 the stage fare from Lake City to Gunnison was $8.50, and to Pitkin $12.50; during the 'Sixties and early 'Seventies the tariff from Atchison, Kansas, to Denver was $70.00 per person.

brings! Hail to the progress of which he is a harbinger! Hail, all hail, to the hopes inspired by his coming, whose full fruition will realize our brightest anticipations, and cast new rays of light above the horizon of our western civilization.[27]

The completion of the Kansas Pacific to Denver and its operating alliance with the Denver Pacific served as a catalyst for both the Union Pacific and the Colorado Central. Both the latter quickly sensed the danger of being shut out of the rich trade with the mining region through an exclusive and discriminatory traffic and rate agreement between the Denver Pacific and the Kansas Pacific.[28] Because of her own financial structure, as well as her hard won position in the Chicago market, the Union Pacific had no alternative but to challenge the position of the competing coalition. An immediate alliance with the Colorado Central (which had earlier been deserted to support the founding of the rival Denver Pacific) offered the solution desired by the transcontinental operators. The board of directors of the Colorado company was reorganized so as to embrace five prominent Union Pacific officials including Oliver Ames. Grading up Clear Creek canyon toward the gold camps of the "Kingdom of Gilpin" began in the Spring of 1871, and the first locomotive over the narrow gauge mountain division linking Golden with Black Hawk steamed noisily into the latter boom town in December 1872. In succeeding months the road was extended to Floyd Hill.

Simultaneously the combined engineering and surveying staffs of the Colorado Central and Union Pacific surveyed during 1871 a standard gauge road down the South Platte from Golden across the broad unfenced pastures of "Cattle King" John W. Iliff to a connection with the transcontinental line at Julesburg. The projected line completely by-passed Denver, and was laid so as to link Golden with the Marshall coal fields, Boulder, Longmont and Greeley. The purpose of this stratagem was to tap the traffic of the "gold fields" with a direct line to the Union Pacific thereby eliminating any need for a Denver connection and thus starve the Denver Pacific-Kansas Pacific combine. Aided by a $200,000 county bond issue from Boulder County and an additional $150,000 issue from Weld County, construction began in September 1872 and by April 1873 the line was in operation to Longmont.

A third phase of the campaign to isolate Denver—this time from the southern Colorado traffic—was attempted in 1872. The Golden company negotiated a contract with the newly developed Denver & Rio Grande Railway for a connection with that north-south line at Littleton. This ambitious and thoroughly practical program of isolating Denver was interrupted by the depression of 1873 which forced the Union Pacific to curtail its support of the Colorado Central construction program.

---

[27] *Proceedings of the Third and Fourth Annual Exhibitions of the Colorado Agricultural Society* . . . (Central City, 1870), 85.

[28] Henry M. Teller, in Teller papers, University of Colorado: The Union Pacific promoters also recognized that the Colorado traffic was the most important then existing between Omaha and California, and that it could well mean the difference between an operating loss or a profit until other traffic was developed along the line.

All major construction by the Colorado company was suspended until the Spring of 1877 when the improved economic situation warranted the resumption of such activity. Abandoning the plan to build from Longmont to Julesburg, they hastily constructed a line northward through Fort Collins to a point on the Union Pacific four miles west of Cheyenne.[29] In August of 1877 Loveland and his transcontinental company directors completed the line to Georgetown and in May of the following year reached Central City, the heart of the Gilpin County mining activity. With the completion of these extensions Colorado had two connections with the Union Pacific, one by way of the Denver Pacific from Denver, the other from Golden over the Colorado Central— and the latter road could pick up ore and matte at the most productive mines and mills and deliver them to Chicago without the delay occasioned by the transfer of equipment at Denver!

The struggle for the control of the Colorado railroads and their traffic was now in full swing, and the centers of such activity were in Omaha, St. Louis, and New York. Jay Gould, who had secured control of the Union Pacific system in 1873, attempted in 1875 to consolidate a number of companies in Colorado including the Colorado Central, but failed because of the opposition of local stockholders of the Golden road, especially the county commissioners who controlled the railroad's stock given in exchange for county bonds. Following an undercover campaign early in 1879 Gould secured Loveland's resignation as head of the company, and, in the autumn, obtained a lease of the entire Colorado Central properties for the Union Pacific.

Faced with the Union Pacific's concerted campaign to eliminate the threat of the Denver Pacific and Kansas Pacific, Governor John Evans resigned as head of the Denver company in March 1872 and President Robert E. Carr of the Kansas Pacific succeeded to the presidency.[30] The St. Louis corporation took full control of the Colorado line and its properties, operating both lines as a single system.[31] The panic of 1873, and the resulting depression, plus an already precarious financial situation aggravated by the costly rivalry with the Union Pacific forced the Kansas Pacific and its subsidiary into receivership in 1874. Following a disastrous rate war and after considerable negotiation Gould succeeded, in 1879, in obtaining control of the Kansas Pacific. In January 1880 the Kansas Pacific and Denver Pacific were consolidated into one system with the Union Pacific and its leased line, the Colorado Central, thereby forming a unified system which lasted until 1890.

---

[29] Laramie County, Wyoming, had earlier voted a special bond issue to assist in this extension to the Union Pacific main line.

[30] A branch line—constructed under the name of the Boulder Valley Railroad—was opened January 24, 1871 from Hughes Station (Brighton) to the Erie coal fields. The company owned large interests in the field and used the Erie coal as fuel for the Denver Pacific locomotives. On September 3, 1873 the line was completed to Boulder.

[31] The Kansas Pacific, still with ambitions to build south to New Mexico and on to the Pacific, extended its roadbed in 1872 from Kit Carson to Las Animas on the Arkansas River where it obtained a profitable trade in hides and wool. Until the construction of the Atkinson, Topeka and Santa Fé Railroad west from Granada, the Kansas Pacific enjoyed a good share of the New Mexico trade. The line from Kit Carson to Animas was abandoned by the Kansas Pacific in 1877, the first such abandonment in Colorado rail history.

While Gould was engaged in forming the augmented Union Pacific system, and, incidentally, obtaining control of the financially wavering Missouri Pacific then slowly building westward toward the Rockies, the enthusiasm for local railroad building in Colorado had reached major proportions. Scores of railroad companies were organized and incorporated with ambitious plans for construction throughout the Territory.[32] Some companies made serious though vain efforts to carry out their announced projects, others turned out to be merely another method of gouging thousands of dollars from citizens gullible enough to buy securities on non-existent railroads, while a few were successful and contributed to the rapidly increasing rail mileage of the territory. By far the most successful and important of the latter organizations was the Denver & Rio Grande Railway.

Snowplows of the Denver and Rio Grande Railroad, circa 1885

Organized by General William J. Palmer on October 27, 1870, the Denver & Rio Grande Railway was an unique experiment and a decided innovation in a number of ways. Undoubtedly influenced by his personal and detailed observations of New Mexico during his direction of the Kansas Pacific survey to the Pacific in 1867-68,[33] Palmer determined to build a north and south railroad—the first of its kind west of the Mississippi—which would link Denver with Mexico City

---

[32] *See Incorporation Record,* volumes 1-10, Office of the Secretary of State, Denver, Colorado.

[33] Palmer, *loc. cit.*

and would have branch lines to various mineral and agricultural areas adjacent to this main trunk.[34] In addition to a branch to South Park via the South Platte, Palmer planned an extension up the Arkansas and across the divide to the valley of the Grand, and thence westward to the prosperous and expanding "Mormon" communities in the Valley of the Great Salt Lake. Some evidence exists, though inconclusive, that the line was eventually to be extended to the Pacific.

The main line of the projected narrow gauge railway was designed primarily to capture the Santa Fe' Trail trade and to divert its valuable traffic northward to Denver where it would have ready outlets to the East (over the Kansas Pacific and Union Pacific railroads) and West (over the Union Pacific). In addition to the Chihuahua traffic, Palmer anticipated a lucrative business in carrying much needed agricultural products from the New Mexico settlements to the expanding mountain mining communities of Colorado.[35] The latter, of course, were counted upon to provide a sizable revenue through the transport of mining equipment and supplies as well as ores and metal. Upon completion of the Kansas Pacific to Denver, Palmer had resigned from its staff and set about organizing his own company. The nucleus of his field corps came from his associates in the construction of the Kansas Pacific, while the executive and a goodly number of the promotional positions (and later a considerable number of operational jobs) were filled with old friends from Pennsylvania and former comrades-in-arms from his Civil War command, the Fifteenth Pennsylvania Volunteers.[36] In collaboration with one of Colorado's pioneer promoters and developers, former Governor Alexander C. Hunt, lands were purchased along the proposed right of way with a view to the location of future colony settlements and the development of mineral and timber resources. Such foresight ultimately led to the founding and development of Colorado Springs, El Moro, Cucharas, La Veta, Alamosa and a score of other southern Colorado communities by the Denver & Rio Grande Railway and its numerous subsidiary land companies.

---

[34] Palmer's north-south line was not the first of its type projected in Colorado. In January 1868, the Denver and Santa Fé Railroad and Telegraph Company was incorporated. The following autumn the United States and Mexican Railway Company was organized in Denver. *See* original articles of incorporation in Office of the Secretary of State, Denver, Colorado.

[35] Throughout the 'sixties and 'seventies large quantities of foodstuffs were brought into the territory from New Mexico and Kansas for the mining camps. Despite local agricultural developments the demand for grains and other foods far exceeded the local supply during the two decades. Food prices were high, and even exorbitant, and the profit to the carriers was substantial.

[36] These included Colonel Greenwood, William S. Jackson, Charles and Robert Lamborn, W. F. Colton, William Wagner, Robert F. Weitbrec, W. W. Borst, Howard Schuyler, and Captain Henry McAllister, Jr. Palmer's personal friend and participant in the Kansas Pacific survey, Dr. William A. Bell, English physician, became the "number two" man in the D. & R. G. organization. President J. Edgar Thompson and Vice President Tom Scott of the Pennsylvania Railroad—both personal friends of General Palmer and heavily involved financially in the Kansas Pacific Company—became trustees for the bondholders of the new Colorado company founded by Palmer and his associates.

Unlike most contemporary railroad promoters in the West, Palmer determined from the outset to finance his road without a federal land grant or bond subsidy. With the assistance of William Blackmore, English financier, and of Dr. Bell and Charles Lamborn, both of whom had aided in the marketing of the Kansas Pacific securities in Europe in 1869, Palmer succeeded in marketing his first mortgage bonds in England and Holland.[37] An effort was also made by Palmer and Hunt to secure financial aid from the counties and cities through which the line was projected, but in spite of favorable bond elections in both Pueblo County and in Canon City only slight assistance was secured in the latter instance. The local subsidy plan largely failed because of the promoters' policy of building their line to company owned townsites usually located but a few hundred yards from the outraged older communities. This was especially true in the cases of Trinidad, Canon City and Pueblo. While the policy did bring additional profits to the railroad promoters it was a costly program in the long run, bringing emnity which the narrow gauge line could ill afford during its later struggles with its larger and more powerful competitors.[38]

Grading operations were begun on the narrow gauge roadbed south from Denver in March 1871, and following the receipt of English-rolled thirty-pound rails the first iron was ceremoniously laid on July 27. Ostensibly built by the first of a number of especially incorporated construction companies headed by Palmer and his various associates, the road was completed to the company controlled townsite of Colorado Springs, at the base of Pike's Peak, on October 21 and officially opened for business on January 1, 1872. With Engineers John McMurtrie and J. R. DeReemer energetically directing the field crews the line was completed to Pueblo on June 15, 1872 and up the Arkansas Valley to the company's townsite of Labran (Florence) on November 1, 1872. From 1871 to 1873 the "Baby Road of America" enjoyed a healthy popularity and received worldwide advertising in general as well as technical publications. Palmer was not satisfied, however, as the heavy traffic anticipated from the mines and New Mexico had failed to materialize. Only the extension of the line southward to Trinidad and westward over the Sangre de Cristo Mountains to the San Luis Valley, he believed, would accomplish these ends. A second factor entered into Palmer's desire to continue construction without delay; the threat posed by the westward extension of the Kansas-founded Atchison, Topeka & Santa Fe' Railroad and the much heralded road to be built by Governor Evans and his colleagues from Denver to South

[37] According to records in the archives of the Denver & Rio Grande Western Railroad Company, the sources of money for construction of the road from 1870 to 1886 were: 50 percent Dutch; 40 percent English; 10 percent United States of America and miscellaneous. Through the active efforts of William Blackmore, Oewel & Co. [Wertheim & Gompertz] of Amsterdam, who two years before had purchased the Costilla Estate of the Sangre de Cristo Grant in the San Luis Valley, purchased and marketed the bulk of the first mortgage bonds issued by the Colorado Company. Herbert O. Brayer, "Early Financing of the Denver & Rio Grande Railway, 1870-1878," *William Blackmore, English Entrepreneur in America* (Bradford Robinson Printing Co., Denver, 1948), II, *passim.*

[38] Brayer, *loc. cit.*

Park and southwestward.[39] The onslaught of the panic of 1873 and the prolonged depression which followed quickly dried up the Rio Grande's European and American sources of money. Work on the new extensions halted.

Freight Train at the Crest of Raton Pass

Throughout the depression period in Colorado, 1873-1877, Palmer managed to pay the interest on his mortgage bonds. Local traffic supported the road but failed to provide sufficient revenue for dividends or additions to the main line. After placing the railroad on a "pay as you go" basis, the promoters concentrated on developing the townsites at Colorado Springs (Colorado Springs Company, and Mountain Base Investment Company), South Pueblo (Southern Colorado Development Company), and on opening the coal fields near Labran. During these critical years the energetic Palmer endeavored to secure further funds from France and England, as well as in this country, but without success. The seven percent mortgage bonds sold at discounts as high as fifty percent when it was possible to find a buyer. Canon City voted a small subsidy and the few miles of rail between Labran and the strategically located Canon City at the mouth of the Royal Gorge were completed in 1874. Revenues continued to decline but Palmer remained confident of the ultimate soundness of his enterprise.

[39] *D. & R. G. W. Archives.*

The discovery of excellent coking coal near Trinidad in 1874 led to the formation of the Southern Colorado Coal and Town Company by the railway associates who acquired a large interest in the new field. A program utilizing the securities of the new company as an inducement (actually a bonus) to investors in the bonds of the railroad was devised. Despite the adverse discount at which the Rio Grande securities had to be sold, Palmer went ahead with the extension of the road to El Moro, five miles north of Trinidad. Construction began in January 1876, and on April 6 the rails reached the company's El Moro townsite, in plain view of the enraged citizens of Trindad. Palmer was now confident that he would obtain a large share of the New Mexico trade (Santa Fe' Trail traffic) which, during the last few years, had been freighted through Trinidad to the end of the Atchison, Topeka and Santa Fe' line at Granada, where the Kansas road had developed a profitable trading center after 1872. Several freighting companies did build warehouses and loading docks at El Moro, but the bulk of the traffic continued to go to the Atchison company which surreptitiously offered the freighting organizations enticing rate reductions in order to keep the trade. The failure of the narrow gauge line to extend its rails into Trinidad was a disastrous error which deeply offended the residents of that community; they not only actively cooperated in diverting the trade from the Rio Grande but ultimately engaged on the side of the Atchison company in the "Battle of the Passes."

Palmer simultaneously undertook to construct his westward extension from Cucharas over the Sangre de Cristo range to the San Luis Valley where he hoped to capture a large part of the trade of the newly opened San Juan mining district. After 1874 a large freight wagon trade had developed between the mining area and the Granada terminus of the Santa Fe' railroad. Palmer determined to turn this traffic to the advantage of his own road. In spite of declining revenues and the inability to market his securities except at the most disadvantageous discounts, the general stubbornly pushed the road forward. On July 1 1876, the narrow gauge line reached the rapidly expanding town of La Veta. Much to the promoter's chagrin, adverse freight rates, the need of reloading, plus the lack of return loads for the freighters at La Veta prevented the diversion of much of the San Juan traffic to the Denver & Rio Grande Railway. The only solution, as Palmer analyzed the situation, was to build over the mountains. Engineer McMurtrie, after a series of surveys over other passes, selected the La Veta Pass and projected a four percent grade for the new line to the San Luis Valley. The road was completed to Fort Garland in August 1877, and to the company townsite (secured by Governor Hunt) at Alamosa, on July 10, 1878. The Denver & Rio Grande had reached the Rio Grande!

Financial difficulties beset the narrow gauge line in 1877 as a result of Palmer's expansionist policy in the face of an already overburdened financial structure. Unable to pay his construction crews for almost four months and confronted with the threat of a strike, he resorted to the use of current income to pay the costs of the new extension. This dubious practice left the road's treasury without funds to pay the interest due on the first mortgage bonds. The subsequent default not only affected the securities and credit of the railroad, but reverberated throughout the pyramid of land and development companies organized by the railroad promoters. So acute had become the financial position of the company that Dr. Bell had been forced to pledge the bonds of the company at twenty-eight percent of their face value in order to secure a small loan in Great Britain.

To complicate matters further, the much feared westward expansion of the Atchison, Topeka and Santa Fe' Railroad (known as the "Santa Fe'") became a reality in 1877. The Kansas road had reached Granada, almost eleven miles west of the Colorado-Kansas border in July 1873, but despite its enterprise and the rapid growth of that terminus as the receiving and forwarding point for the New Mexico-Southern Colorado trade, the panic and subsequent depression put an abrupt end to plans to build on to Pueblo. For almost three years the Santa Fe' had to be content at this point, while Palmer threatened to capture both the Santa Fe' and San Juan traffic with his southern and westward extensions from that Arkansas Valley community. Palmer, however, was unable to take full advantage of his position. His own financial problems precluded his extending into New Mexico while at the same time pushing his San Juan division over the mountains to the San Luis Valley. Secondly, the land policy adopted by the narrow gauge line, whereby new towns were founded and developed in place of promoting the older and established communities, had so antagonized the citizens of Pueblo that they undertook to undermine the Rio Grande position and to secure the extension of rival roads.

When the Kansas Pacific failed to construct its road from Las Animas to Pueblo after that community, and the surrounding county, had voted bonds in support of the project, the local committee offered similar inducements to the Santa Fe' company. A new corporation, the Pueblo and Arkansas Valley Railway Company, was organized by the Santa Fe' promoters early in 1875, and, aided by $150,000 in bonds voted by Bent County and $350,000 worth of Pueblo County securities, the road was completed to Pueblo on March 1, 1876. Though both companies were still deterred from major extensions by financial stringencies, the scene was now set for a major clash between the Denver & Rio Grande and the Atchison, Topeka and Santa Fe' railways. Both desired to secure and dominate the same traffic areas to the South and West and the entire transportation system of Colorado was to be affected by the impending struggle.

Depression had wreaked havoc among the nation's railroads; many failed outright while others were so severely crippled through over-expansion, floating debts, over-capitalization and ruinous operational practices that reorganization was inevitable. Construction of new lines and the extension of old ones quickly stopped. The securities of all roads in the West went begging at any price in the money markets of New York, London, Paris, and Amsterdam. Colorado's newly constructed railroads suffered heavily. Of all the major lines Palmer's Denver & Rio Grande seemed in the best condition financially to weather the storm. A favorable tripartite agreement for dividing the transcontinental traffic originating in Colorado and New Mexico with the Union Pacific and Kansas Pacific was replaced in 1877 by a new contract which included the Santa Fe'. By this arrangement, plus the prolonged effects of the depression, Palmer sought to gain time to extend his own lines into New Mexico, to the San Juan, and latterly up the Arkansas. He hoped thereby to stave off the impending competition by Gould and the Union Pacific group aligned with Dr. Evans and the recently activated Denver, South Park and Pacific as well as the imminent threat posed by projected Santa Fe' extensions to New Mexico and the San Juan country.[40] Each party to the traffic agreement, however, secretly sought to secure more than the allotted share of the traffic, the Union Pacific and South Park group offering special inducements to shippers in the mountain mining communities, while the Santa Fe' granted lavish rebates to New Mexico and San Juan freighters if they agreed to haul their loads directly to or from the platforms of that line.

The Kansas Pacific representatives, aided by contracts with the freighting companies, added to the unhappy situation by cutting rates and talking openly of construction southward from Denver to Pueblo and westward into the mining area from which the bulk of the heavy traffic was then obtained. Palmer was well aware of the danger to his own position but sought to steer a middle course between his larger and more powerful competitors, a stratagem which in reality only accentuated the problem, for each line feared a possible "secret pact" between Palmer and one or more of the competing eastern lines to the exclusion of the others. Such was the unhealthy position in November 1877 when William Barstow Strong left the Chicago, Burlington & Quincy Railroad and became general manager of the Santa Fé.

In Strong and Chief Engineer Albert A. Robinson the Atchison company had in the field two energetic and able railroaders comparable to Palmer and his associates—except that the general was also directly concerned with securing financial support whereas the former were not. This made a singular difference. Palmer, knowing the financial position of his rival, thought the latter would be unable to move out of Pueblo before he could complete his extension to the San Luis Valley and undertake the line southwards from El Moro. He reckoned without Strong and Robinson who, while fully cognizant

[40] Evans and his local Denver Pacific associates had organized the Denver & South Park Railway on September 30, 1872 during the rush to the Fairplay and South Park gold fields. It was planned that the projected Kansas Pacific's mountain extension, the Denver, Georgetown & Utah would use part of the South Park line. In June 1873 the company was reorganized as the Denver, South Park & Pacific Railway Company without regard for any plans to link up with the Kansas Pacific. A narrow gauge line was completed to Morrison on June 1, 1874 when the acute depression caused the cessation of all further construction. The exciting news of the Leadville "strike" spurred the Denver promoters to renewed efforts and in the summer of 1878 the tracks were completed to Bailey's Ranch on the North Fork of the South Platte. The prolonged battle between the Rio Grande & Santa Fé roads also goaded Evans and his staff in the hope of reaching Leadville ahead of the competing larger roads—an advantage which all realized would be of vital importance.

of the financial limitations of their company, were not concerned with finances, but rather with the extension and construction of their road so as to protect the Santa Fe′ trade.

Following a futile attempt by Strong to negotiate an operating agreement, lease, or outright purchase of the narrow gauge road, the Santa Fe′ construction chief, late in January 1878, determined upon a bold stand to outflank the Denver and Rio Grande. On February 26, the evening before the narrow gauge field crews were scheduled to begin construction in the strategic Raton Pass—most favorable route through the mountains into northern New Mexico—Strong sent Robinson and a crew, the latter made up largely of Trinidad residents who thoroughly despised the Rio Grande company, to seize the pass for the Santa Fe′ despite the fact that the terminus of the Atchison roadbed was still more than one hundred miles to the north and that his men had to reach the disputed area in a specially chartered Rio Grande train! Robinson acted with such dispatch that when the Colorado company's men arrived they discovered that their rivals had not only physical possession of the proposed right-of-way, but had completed the purchase of the historic Wootton toll road to use as the basis of their roadbed. There was little Palmer could do; he had been outflanked both in the field and legally for he had failed to file a right-of-way claim—despite thorough surveys made the previous year under the provisions of the special Congressional act of 1872 which permitted him to secure a right-of-way through the public domain. The Colorado company could only abandon the route to the Santa Fé or select a second and less favorable route. A sudden renewal of interest in the upper Arkansas Valley caused the Colorado entrepreneur to adopt the former plan and thereby the Kansas company was left to exploit the New Mexico trade to the fullest.[41]

During the summer of 1877 rich silver strikes were made in California Gulch on the upper Arkansas. A full-blown rush to the area rapidly developed. Leadville became a "metropolis" overnight and the long arduous trail up the Arkansas carried a continuous stream of people, supplies and equipment en route to the new district. The problem of transportation was accentuated by the shortage of teams and wagons which contributed to the high cost of freighting in the 11,000 foot rugged mountain area.

Following a hurried, though thorough, visit to the workings with his chief engineer, General Palmer determined to rush construction of the Rio Grande from its terminus at Canon City through the Royal Gorge (then termed the Grand Canyon of the Arkansas) and up the Arkansas to Leadville—a route envisioned in the original articles of incorporation of the road and actually surveyed several years earlier. Strong and Robinson were also acutely aware of the potentialities of the upper Arkansas excitement and recognized that the company

[41] This did not mean the complete abandonment of the Rio Grande's plan for securing the New Mexico traffic. Palmer still intended to push the narrow gauge southward from the San Luis Valley to Santa Fé and thence down the Rio Grande to Mexico. Expediency had played a large part in this decision; the entire New Mexico traffic currently amounted to $2,000,000, while any sizable "bonanza" in the newly discovered mining area on the upper Arkansas could easily surpass that figure and would require less "pioneering" by the railroad.

which held control of the narrow gorge above Canon City could capture the traffic of the new mining district. Under the aegis of an especially incorporated "local company," The Canon City and San Juan Railway Company, Strong and his field officers hurriedly organized a force of

(Courtesy Santa Fé Railway)

Passenger Train at Raton Pass near Wootton

Canon City residents led by Santa Fe' engineer William R. Morley (who had been a member of the survey party in 1877 which had laid out the proposed Rio Grande line through the Royal Gorge) and seized the mouth of the narrow defile on April 19, 1878—despite the fact that the Colorado company's crews had begun work below the Canon at almost the same moment. The second phase of the so called war with the Santa Fe' was on and soon became known as the "Royal Gorge War."

In the days that followed each side sought to maintain an aggressive tactical position in the field while seeking to outmaneuver the other by legal process. Threats of armed conflict, confused conferences, desertions and "raiding" of each others crews, realignments among the local elements supporting the contestants, injunctions and counter legal maneuverings characterized the dispute. Both sides continued to construct roadbeds—the Canon City company (Santa Fe') within the Gorge, the Rio Grande and a second Santa Fe' subsidiary, the Pueblo and Arkansas Valley Railroad, above the defile. Palmer's crews erected stone barricades to prevent the Kansas company and its subsidiary from grading a continuous roadbed to Leadville. Despite such efforts the Santa Fe' crews succeeded in preparing a roadbed almost the entire distance from Canon City to the bustling mining camp now named Leadville. In the meanwhile the court battles called forth the best efforts of star-studded legal staffs assembled by the contestants. Crux of the dispute was the Rio Grande's claim of a priority to the right-of-way through the Gorge. Conflicting decisions in the state and United States District Courts brought the case on appeal to the Supreme Court of the United States where the priority, though not exclusive right, of the narrow gauge road was recognized.[42]

While the court battles raged without abatement, affairs within the Colorado company took a decided turn for the worse. An attempt to refinance the Rio Grande in New York, England, and France failed.[43] Representatives of the foreign and eastern security holders, fearful that the prolonged struggle with the Santa Fe' might, regardless of the ultimate decision, leave the narrow gauge road in an insolvent condition, forced Palmer to lease the Rio Grande to the Atchison company for thirty years.[44] Reluctantly Palmer surrendered the line to the Santa Fe' on December 13, 1878, under terms of a lease by which the latter organization agreed to protect the interests of the narrow gauge line and not to discriminate against Denver in the matter of freight rates.

Almost at once it became evident that General Manager Strong and his associates had no intention of complying with the latter provision of the contract. Rates between Denver and Pueblo were raised sharply, freight usually brought to Denver over the narrow gauge was deliberately routed eastward without regard for the Denver interest, while Kansas City jobbers and distributing agents were given preferential treatment to the detriment of the enraged Denver commercial houses. Charges of a bold plan to ruin the Denver & Rio Grande Railway filled the state press. Palmer and his colleagues protested, but the Santa Fe' refused to concede the validity of the allegations.

[42] The best published account of the Royal Gorge may be found in Hall, *op. cit.* II, 370-391. This account, however, errs in some important details and omits much that is relevant. It is the purpose here to give only an outline of the affair since the importance of the dispute lay not in the details of the Royal Gorge struggle, but in the long reaching results—not only to the major roads involved, but on the long run development of transportation in Colorado.

[43] It was at this time that a proposed loan of $910,000 by Jay Gould and Russell Sage failed to materialize. Letters, W. J. Palmer to D. C. Dodge, May 24, June 29, August 17, 1878, *D. & R. G. W. Archives.* See also *Minutes,* Board of Directors D. & R. G. Railway I, 308 *et. seq.* Throughout the lease negotiations Palmer opposed the sale or lease of the line to the Santa Fé.

[44] During 1877 and 1878 a considerable amount of Philadelphia-owned stock in the Rio Grande changed hands—a large part of it falling into the possession of New York and Boston interests which also had large holdings in the Santa Fé road. *D. & R. G. W. Archives.*

Backed by Denver civic and commercial leaders, attorneys for the narrow gauge company filed suit against the Santa Fe' charging violation of the lease and demanding the return of the property. Early in June 1879 a court order for the restoration of the property was secured by Palmer, who, on June 9, with surprising rapidity took forcible possession of the entire road, ejecting without ceremony the employees of the Kansas company. Enraged, Strong attempted to meet force with force, but the initiative gained through the surprise action could not be overcome.[45] The lessees appealed to the federal district court, and, on June 24, Judge Hallett issued an order appointing Colonel L. C. Ellsworth of Denver as receiver. Palmer promptly surrendered the line as directed by the court. In the midst of the exhausting struggle (and the disheartening spectacle of two major corporations engaging in private warfare with armed bodies of men violating the peace and security of the community),[46] Jay Gould and his group of railroad speculators and "reorganizers" secured actual control of the Denver and Rio Grande Railway. While trying to acquire control of the Rio Grande, Gould had already taken steps to guarantee control of the Colorado traffic through his interests in the Denver Pacific and Union Pacific, and had taken positive steps to capture the Leadville business. In November 1878 Gould, Russell Sage, Sidney Dillon, Oren Henry, Charles Welch, Loveland, and Berthoud incorporated the Georgetown, Leadville and San Juan Railroad Company, but before any steps towards construction could be taken the eastern clique purchased a controlling interest in Governor Evans' Denver, South Park and Pacific road. This assured Gould a direct connection between the new gold and silver mines and the east.[47]

Following up an agreement made with Palmer on September 15, 1879, the New York capitalist undertook to finance future extensions of the narrow gauge line and also sought a quick solution with the Santa Fe' operators. An agreement between the two feuding companies was quickly reached in Boston on February 2, 1880. The Santa Fe'

[45] Strong secured the services of "Bat" Masterson and endeavored to maintain control over the Pueblo roundhouse and shops. The effort failed when Palmer offered the mercenaries a higher fee for their services.

[46] This was not the first instance of lawlessness and lack of respect for constitutional forms and guarantees in Colorado railroad history. In 1876, during the struggle between Golden and Denver for supremacy, over-enthusiastic Boulder proponents kidnapped Judge Amherst W. Stone in order to prevent his ruling in favor of Denver. Hall, *op. cit.* II, 413-414.

[47] Articles of Incorporation, Office of the Secretary of State, Denver; Denver, South Park and Pacific files in State Historical Society of Colorado. Gould's interest in the South Park line was heightened by the contract between that road and the Santa Fé, signed in 1878. The Boston Company had purchased $700,000 worth of first mortgage bonds of the South Park company in exchange for trackage rights over that line's projected tracks to Leadville, and an agreement to divide the freight from the region. The Santa Fé aid was utilized to extend the long dormant South Park road to Bailey's Ranch. An interesting sidelight on the South Park sale to the Union Pacific group is found in an affidavit of Evans that he had already contracted to sell the South Park road to the Rio Grande when Gould, one of his stockholders, literally "hi-jacked" the sales contract for the Union Pacific interests. *See* John Evans *vs.* The Union Pacific, Denver and Gulf Railway Co., # 3001, U. S. District Court, Denver, "Affidavit of John Evans and Charles Wheeler," filed November 18, 1893, 6-8.

company agreed to abrogate the lease and to return all property and to drop all pending litigation. Palmer and his group readily assented to the purchase from the Boston company of the latter's improvements and graded line from Cañon City to Leadville for $1,400,000. Of particular importance, however, was the specific agreement by the Santa Fe' company not to build north or west of Pueblo (except for a line to the Cañon coal mines), for ten years while the narrow gauge company contracted not to build east of its existing line from Denver to El Moro or south of a point seventy-five miles south of Conejos in the San Luis Valley. Thus the Santa Fe' threat to the Rio Grande's favorable position in regard to the mountain mining traffic was eliminated, and the fear of Palmer building south into New Mexico and thereby threatening the position of the Santa Fe' in that area was ended for at least a decade.[48] The "battle for the passes", or Royal Gorge War, was over, but the Denver Rio Grande had changed its character—it was no longer the "home-owned and operated" north and south line projected in 1870 by General Palmer. By virtue of its control by Gould and the surrender of its right to build south, the Rio Grande had become another of the pawns in the national chess game of creating a through line from the East to the West. Despite its apparent recovery the position of the narrow gauge road remained precarious, and its founders were now but a "front" for the powerful eastern interests.

With the end of the Royal Gorge struggle on April 5, 1880, the Denver & Rio Grande Railway rapidly completed the roadbed which had been prepared by its crews and those of the Santa Fe' company during the long controversy. The long awaited railroad into Leadville was completed on July 20 amid wild and prolonged celebration by the elated—if somewhat inebriated—miners, merchants and assorted citizens of the "highest city in the United States."[49] A few weeks thereafter the first Denver, South Park and Pacific train pulled up noisily alongside the long wooden freight dock and station erected by the Rio Grande company. Gould, in control of both the Rio Grande and the South Park lines, had "negotiated" an agreement by which the latter line acquired trackage rights over the Rio Grande's hard-won roadbed into Leadville from Buena Vista. Palmer and his associates were thus deprived of the full fruits of their "victory", while Gould succeeded in bolstering the precarious condition of his South Park road.

By the end of 1880 Palmer had begun to push his "San Juan Division" beyond Alamosa toward the Conejos range and Durango. Anxious to obtain the traffic from the newly opened mines in the vicinity of Ten Mile Creek and Dillon—and to prevent the South Park company from capturing the traffic he completed an extension during 1880 northwestward over Fremont Pass from Leadville to Grand River, Ten Mile Creek, and Blue River to Robinson. The line south of Alamosa into New Mexico—as far as the Santa Fe' agreement would

[48] *D. & R.G.W. Archives,* and case records #154, 155, 186, U. S. District Court, Denver.
[49] Arthur Ridgway, *Denver and Rio Grande Development of Physical Property in Chronological Narrative,* Denver and Rio Grande Archives, 5205. 1921.

permit—reached Chama and Espanola in December. Some 347 miles of new trackage was added to the Denver & Rio Grande system during 1880.

The decade ended amid confusion, suspicion, and strife among the Colorado carriers. Gone was local control and to some extent local operation, and in place of Evans, Loveland, and Palmer stood the ominous figure of Jay Gould whose manipulations had already brought under control such western lines as the Union Pacific, Kansas Pacific, Denver Pacific, Denver South Park & Pacific, Missouri Pacific and, to a somewhat lesser degree, the Denver & Rio Grande Railway. Of the major roads already operating in Colorado by the end of the decade only the Atchison, Topeka and Santa Fe' was completely independent of the Gould organization, and even it was party to rate and traffic agreements through which it hoped to share in the rich traffic of the mountain mining communities. Gould's ambitions extended far beyond the control of the individual roads and their traffic; behind the maze-like manipulations lay the desire to put together a unified system independent of the Union Pacific which would link the east with the Pacific. Except for a momentary interest in securing the rich mountain traffic—which would assist the larger transcontinental roads—Gould used the local Colorado roads as pawns on his more complicated chessboard.

It was inevitable, perhaps, that the control of even the smaller Colorado railroads would pass into hands other than those who had organized and promoted them. Despite its gold and silver activity the financial resources required to construct and operate railroads did not then exist in Colorado. The quest for such funds had led Evans, Loveland, and Palmer to Philadelphia, New York, Boston, and ultimately to Great Britain (to the flourishing industrial and financial centers of Liverpool, Birmingham, Manchester, London, Edinburgh, Dundee and Aberdeen) and to the continent of Europe and the money markets at Paris, Brussels, Amsterdam, Cologne and Frankfort-on-Main. During the decade the Denver Pacific had marketed in Europe three-quarters of a million dollars worth of its first mortgage bonds, while the Kansas Pacific had found purchasers for its securities in England and on the continent aggregating another million and a quarter dollars. Palmer had also tapped the European sources of investment capital, selling one and a half million dollars worth of bonds in Amsterdam and a quarter of a million in England. So familiar had become Colorado rail securities in the London market that the financial pages and stock exchange lists carried regular reports on those of the Union Pacific, Kansas Pacific, Denver Pacific, Denver South Park & Pacific, Santa Fe', and the Denver & Rio Grande Railway. In addition to the European sales—which were largely of mortgage bonds—substantial investments in common and preferred stock, as well as bonds, were secured in the eastern states. Although in certain instances, notably the Denver & Rio Grande, the foreign investors held the larger proportion of the mortgage bonds, the actual corporate control in each case remained in the United States through the control of the stock by New York, Philadelphia, or Boston investment cliques.

During the period from 1870 and 1880 Congressional land grants were secured in Colorado by the Union Pacific, Kansas Pacific (3,000,000 acres), and Denver Pacific (900,000 acres) railroads. To exploit such lands the latter roads utilized the services of the railroad-organized and operated National Land Company. Tens of thousands of acres of railroad lands were sold to individual settlers, speculators and colony organizations.[50] Although the Denver and Rio Grande Railway had received no land subsidies, its promoters—like those of the larger transcontinental roads—realized that substantial profits were to be gained from the exploitation of the lands and natural resources adjacent to their roadbeds. Palmer, Bell, and former governor A. C. Hunt worked quietly to acquire substantial tracts of lands along the projected narrow gauge route and from such enterprise secured the sites of the future communities of Colorado Springs, South Pueblo, Alamosa, the Labran (Florence) coal fields, and the coal deposits near Trinidad. Substantial profits from these land developments accrued to the venturesome promoters and, of greater importance, resulted in the founding of permanent settlements and the commercial development of an important part of Colorado's vast natural resources.

Numerous advertisements were inserted in the eastern United States and European press describing the advantages of life in the Rockies and the wealth to be there obtained. Land company agents sought to interest minority groups (religious and political) in the formation of colony companies to emigrate to Colorado. Such projects were not for the poverty-stricken and unskilled, but, on the contrary, called for persons with sufficient means to purchase land and finance their operations until firmly established. Railroad subsidiaries, as well as independent organizations founded by officers and directors of the railroad companies, opened and developed coal fields near Boulder, in the Arkansas Valley, and in the vicinity of Trinidad. Timber and tie cutting mills were established in various forested areas including the Black Forest near Colorado Springs, in South Park, the upper Arkansas and along the Big Thompson River. General Palmer and his associates established the Colorado Coal and Iron Company in Pueblo and opened iron mines to supply the new mill with the raw material to manufacture the mine and smelter supplies and equipment needed in the gold and silver camps, as well as for farm and industrial materials.[51]

In accord with the general practice throughout the country, the actual building of Colorado's railroads was the work of specially organized construction companies, promoted largely by the same men who headed the railroad corporations. This device had many advantages, not the least being the relief of the parent company from

[50] Among the more successful of the colony experiments founded on railroad lands was that at Greeley. James F. Willard, *The Union Colony at Greeley, Colorado 1869-1871*. Boulder. 1918. *See* also James F. Willard and Colin B. Goodykoontz, *Experiments in Colorado Colonization 1869-1872*. Boulder. 1926.

[51] Brayer, *op. cit.*

financial liabilities attendant upon the marketing of railroad securities at less than their par value in order to obtain construction funds. Securities were accepted in payment of the construction contracts and then marketed wherever possible, and not infrequently at depreciated values ranging from twenty to as much as forty percent less than the face value.

Such practices were essential where, as in the instance of the Denver and Rio Grande Railway, the promoters at the outset endeavored to market millions of dollars worth of securities secured by a mortgage upon a railroad which had not a foot of completed roadbed, an acre of land, a single piece of rolling stock, or other visible assets. All too frequently the estimated cost of construction per mile (which varied in Colorado from $16,000 to $75,000) was greatly exceeded, and extensions built into areas for "stategic reasons" and from which profitable revenues could not be secured for many years.[52] While substantial profits were realized from construction contracts, net operating profits were small throughout the period—when such profits did exist at all.

During the era a considerable part of the reported revenues were derived from the carriage of construction materials, field crews, and supplies used by the lines. In almost no instance did the revenues anticipated in the widely distributed company prospectuses materialize. The precarious financial position of the local carriers was further affected by the nationwide depression and the poor condition of the transcontinental carriers with which the local companies were so closely allied.

In spite of the critical economic situation during a large part of the 'seventies, railroad construction in Colorado made spectacular progress: In 1870 there was 157 miles of operated road in the state; in 1871, 328; 1872, 483; 1873, 602; 1874, 682; 1875, 807; 1876, 957; 1877, 1045; 1878, 1165; 1879, 1208; 1880, 1570.

During the construction period the labor shortage was always serious and frequently acute. "Raiding" of skilled and experienced field crews, engineers and construction superintendents and foremen was frequent. Large numbers of common laborers were recruited from the northern New Mexico villages, while others were recruited from the crews used on the transcontinental extensions. Among the latter workers were large numbers of European immigrants, notably Irish, German, and a considerable representation from Italy and the Slavic countries. A number of Chinese laborers, recently released by the Central Pacific, joined the Colorado construction crews for a brief period, but the Orientals soon found life in the mining camps more to their liking. The shortage of labor plus the illusionary attraction of the mines accounted for the relatively high wages paid the crews assembled by the contractors. For train crews and shopmen the

[52] See the frank statement of this policy in *17th Annual Report of the Board of Directors of the Atchison, Topeka and Santa Fé Railroad Company to the Stockholders for the Year Ending December 31, 1888* (Boston, George H. Ellis, 1889), 16.

Colorado roads depended in large measure upon "boomers"—the itinerant railroaders who "floated" from one state to another and from road to road. Wages and salaries varied widely; construction workers earned from $65.00 to $90.00 per month and keep; those who supplied a wagon and team were paid an additional fifty cents per day. Train engineers received from $100 to $125.00; master mechanics $65.00 to $115.00; ordinary shopmen earned from $40.00 to $55.00 a month.

During the first decade of railroading in Colorado there were few labor disputes and no major strikes, although General Palmer was threatened with that possibility in 1877, when his construction crews on the La Veta-San Luis Valley extension went unpaid for three months because of an acute shortage of operating funds.

Equipment and supplies for the Colorado railroads were expensive. Iron rails, tie plates and rolling stock were purchased in Pennsylvania, the manufacturers frequently accepting bonds of the purchaser in exchange at discounts varying from twenty-five to forty-five percent of their face value. To iron its first division from Denver to Colorado Springs, the Denver & Rio Grande Railway in 1871 purchased thirty-pound iron rails in England and Belgium, and shipped them to Denver by way of New Orleans. The foreign manufacturers accepted bonds in payment. An English manufactured Fairlie locomotive was similarly secured for the narrow gauge road. Ties were secured in the mountains with substantial profits being earned by timber companies especially organized and operated by the railroad promoters and their associates. The carriage of construction crews, materials and equipment used in furthering their own extensions made up a considerable portion of the tonnage and revenue reported by the local roads during this period.

In general the Colorado lines founded during the period were poorly constructed; roadbeds were rough, unpacked, and poorly ballasted; iron rails cracked and were quickly pounded out; untreated timbers in bridges and ties required frequent replacement; washouts were common occurrences while grades and curves were excessive and dangerous throughout the mountain areas.[53]

Despite fear of further machinations by Jay Gould and the precarious financial structure of the local as well as continental lines, the mushroom-like expansion of the Colorado mining districts, the rapid growth of agricultural enterprise, and the spectacular increase in population served to spur existing railroads to renewed efforts to extend their rails, while promoters projected scores of new roads and sought energetically to float new companies. The race for the mountain traffic from the new "gold and silver fields" was on!

---

[53] Material for the foregoing paragraphs was secured by a study of operating reports, annual reports, newspaper files and archival collections of the Denver & Rio Grande Railway (now the Denver & Rio Grande Western Railroad Company), the Denver, South Park and Pacific Railway, and the outstanding collection of railroad materials in the State Historical Society of Colorado. Reference was also had to documents in the Denver Public Library, the library of the University of Colorado at Boulder, and the remarkable library of the American Association of Railroads in Washington, D. C.

COMPLETION AND CHAOS 1881-1900

With the end of the Santa Fe'-Rio Grande controversy and the completion of the latter road to Leadville, the Colorado carriers opened a new era of expansion and conflict characterized by "rate wars",[54] frantic efforts to outbuild competitors to remote mountain areas where reported "strikes" heralded the mushroom growth of new mining districts, and a struggle by the larger and more powerful continental lines to capture and control the east and westbound traffic by domination of the local mountain lines. It was a period of frenzied finance with railroad promoters and operators more interested in the harvest to be reaped from the manipulation of heavily-watered security issues than in sound construction and efficient operation. While in New York stock deals totaling many millions of dollars were not infrequent, in Colorado chief engineers, division superintendents, and shop foremen fought to maintain efficient operations on restricted budgets and with inadequate equipment and rolling stock. The outcry against high fares and abnormal freight tariffs, a local manifestation of the nation-wide agitation to control the "railroad monopolies", resulted in widespread demands for reform which ultimately brought about state regulation. By the end of the century the last vestiges of local control and ownership had disappeared and the mountain lines had become integral parts of the powerful eastern lines tapping the Centennial State.

Continuing the spree which had characterized railroad construction throughout the nation since 1878, the Colorado roads—largely under the impetus exerted by the Gould group—added 616.98 miles of new road in 1881, and 579.41 miles in 1882. In addition to various mine and quarry branches, the rejuvenated Rio Grande completed its line to Gunnison and Crested Butte and rushed work on the extension to the Colorado-Utah border which was formally opened on December 20, 1882. In August the Colorado line had concluded a thirty year contract leasing the Denver & Rio Grande Western, another Palmer built line from Ogden, Utah, to the Colorado border. Palmer's construction crews laid the line to Wagon Wheel Gap, and by ironing the roadbed from Chama, New Mexico, to Durango and on to the end of the Silverton track, finally tapped the San Juan traffic at its source. For General Palmer 1881 and 1882 were years of visible progress, but the precarious "wedding" with Gould was the source of continuous irritation to the Colorado executive who strongly, though not very diplomatically, resisted the former's efforts to control the Rio Grande. The inevitable conflict in 1882 led to the resignation of Gould from the board of directors, but the criticism directed by eastern and foreign bondholders at Palmer made his position an untenable one.

---

[54] The Colorado Railways' Association, formed in 1879 by the Union Pacific, Kansas Pacific, Santa Fé and the controlled local carriers to establish uniform freight rates—and to which the Rio Grande company was admitted after it came out of receivership—was an unstable alliance which actually operated to exclude non-members from sharing in the traffic by refusing to interchange freight or equipment. Actually, it failed to prevent rate wars such as that between the Rio Grande and the South Park companies. The Burlington was later admitted to the Association.

In the meanwhile the Denver, South Park and Pacific under Gould's active direction was further extending its roadbed into the territory preempted by the Denver & Rio Grande Railway. In addition to challenging Palmer for the Leadville trade by completing an independent line to the carbonate city,[55] the South Park operators laid their tracks to Gunnison and announced intentions to build westward.

Denver, South Park and Pacific Railway, Pine Grove, 1895

While Palmer and the Union Pacific combine under Gould were waging war for control of the mountain traffic,[56] the rails of other railroads in Colorado were rapidly lacing the state into a pattern which spread north and south as well as east and west. Cognizant of the material saving on freight costs from the east and Europe to be gained by using water transport, former Governor John Evans and his colleague Walter Cheesman projected a road from Denver southwards to the Gulf of Mexico. The original plan called for tapping the water-borne traffic at Galveston or at New Orleans, by means of an interchange agreement with the Texas lines. By thus taking advantage of the more favorable water rates from New York or other shiping points to the Gulf, Evans hoped to be able to reduce

[55] The South Park line was in a favorable position to compete with the Denver and Rio Grande as its run to Denver was considerably shorter than that of the Palmer company. Throughout the 'eighties the battle for the Leadville traffic led to slashing rate wars and "incentive" offers to shippers.

[56] The Union Pacific at this time, 1882, controlled in addition to the Denver, South Park & Pacific, the Colorado Central (330.40 miles), Denver & Boulder Valley (27 miles), Golden, Boulder & Caribou Railway (6 miles), the Greeley, Salt Lake & Pacific (Greeley to Longmont 18.5 miles), in addition to the former Kansas Pacific and Denver Pacific lines (289.12 miles).

the overall freight cost of goods sent to Denver. In June 1882 the promoters completed their standard gauged Denver & New Orleans Railway from Denver to Pueblo and rushed plans to connect at the Canadian River with General Grenville M. Dodge's Fort Worth & Denver City Railroad then being extended northward. The Denver, Utah & Pacific, in which H. A. W. Tabor and Henry R. Wollcott were interested, constructed some twenty-three miles of road from Denver to Hallack Junction and Mitchell in addition to leasing eleven miles of trackage from the Denver, Longmont & Western Railroad. During 1882 the Union Pacific added an additional 151 miles to its Colorado lines by the construction of the Julesburg Branch from La Salle to Denver Junction, Nebraska.

Of outstanding importance during 1882 was the completion on May 29 of the 175 mile line of the Chicago, Burlington & Quincy subsidiary, the Burlington & Missouri River in Nebraska, from Wray to Denver. Colorado now had four outlets to the industrial East and agricultural Midwest, two by way of the Union Pacific system (over the former Denver Pacific and Kansas Pacific tracks), the Santa Fe' and the newly completed Burlington extension. The Illinois company left little doubt of its future intentions; Burlington survey parties began a systematic search for a suitable pass through the mountains to the West.

By the end of 1882 it was evident that the nation's railroads were in serious trouble. Despite the phenomenal expansion since 1878—much of it into mountain areas where population was sparse and where years would be required to develop sufficient traffic to pay even operating expenses—the astounding expansion of fictitious capital had caused an increasing suspicion among investors of almost all railroad securities, particularly western offerings.[57] The inability of many roads to pay dividends or to meet their fixed charges brought a sharp reaction throughout the country. Construction dropped to its lowest level in five years, while in Colorado it plunged to its lowest level since 1870. Only sixty miles of new trackage were built during 1883—thirty-five by the Rio Grande, seven by the Greeley, Salt Lake & Pacific and twenty-four miles by the Denver, South Park & Pacific. In April at the annual meeting of the Rio Grande stock holders, General Palmer faced an overwhelming barrage from disgruntled eastern and foreign security holders (skillfully organized by the vengeance-seeking Gould interests in New York), whose vigorous attack on his stewardship centered about the non-profitable extensions built during the preceding five years. The pressure was too great and the pioneer Western railroad promoter and executive resigned and was succeeded as president by the New York capitalist Frederick Lovejoy. The stock of the company dropped on the New York stock exchange to a new low of 21¼. Despite the reorganization the Rio Grande was unable to meet the interest on its bonds the following spring and autumn and

[57] The situation nationally had reached the point where securities in the amount of $80,000 a mile of constructed line were offered in place of the actual average cost of $30,000 per mile.

the defaulted company was placed in receivership. As receiver Judge Hallack appointed William S. Jackson, former treasurer of the road and one of Palmer's closest associates.

Cattle in Colorado Mountain Pasture

Other Colorado roads were similarly embarrassed. The Denver, Utah & Pacific defaulted in July 1883 and was sold and reorganized the following April. The gloom was further heightened by the depressing announcement of the default of Governor Evans' Denver & New Orleans Railroad. The extent of the "crash" became painfully apparent a few months later when the Union Pacific announced that it was "compelled to forego dividends."[58] One national railroad authority commented,

> . . . a few years ago there was, in public estimation, no more inviting field for railroad enterprises than the State of Colorado. A vast system of railroads, covering the whole State, was constructed with very great rapidity, involving a nominal expenditure of nearly $100,000,000, almost the whole of which is unproductive.

[58] Dividends paid by the Union Pacific following 1878 were: five percent, 1878; six percent, 1879; six percent, 1880; six and three-quarters percent, 1881; seven percent, 1882; six and three-quarters percent, 1883; four and one-half percent, 1884, and nothing in 1885.

The worst was yet to come. In 1884 less than twenty-nine miles of new railroad were constructed in Colorado—8.3 miles by the Georgetown, Breckenridge & Leadville from Georgetown to Graymont, and approximately twenty miles from Kokomo to Leadville by the South Park company. In 1885 new construction amounted to the depressing figure of but twelve miles. Dividends continued to decline sharply or were passed completely as the earnings of the nation's rail carriers dipped to new lows. In 1884 Colorado's railroads recorded a net deficit of $452,410. Common stock of the Rio Grande reached a record low of 4⅜ on the New York exchange in June 1885. In the midst of this economic catastrophe the long smoldering demand for railroad regulation and reform broke into flames throughout the East and Midwest. Investigations were undertaken and regulatory measures and commissions established in a number of states.

Heated protests over high freight tariffs and passenger rates, discriminatory practices, negligence and inefficiency arose throughout Colorado. Demands for legislative action to correct such abuses had been heard in ever-increasing volume since 1881, but a powerful and not overly scrupulous railroad lobby effectively blocked the passage of remedial or regulatory measures until 1885, when the General Assembly could no longer ignore the popular will.[59] In April the Assembly completed action on an emergency act establishing a state railroad commissioner with authority to investigate, advise, and partially regulate (although such regulatory power was well watered down) the Colorado carriers. Commissioner W. B. Felker endeavored energetically, if not too brilliantly, to carry out the spirit of the act. After one year, however, he found himself impotent and without adequate organized support due to the intransigence of carrier officials and the reluctance of the General Assembly, under effective pressure from the bitterly opposed railroad lobby, to provide funds with which to carry out his duties.[60]

During 1885 and 1886 the reorganization of the Colorado railroads continued. Receiver Jackson continued to reduce operation costs and effect much needed economies throughout the Denver & Rio Grande system. Following the default and appointment of the receiver the Colorado company had abandoned its thirty-year operating contract with Palmer's Denver & Rio Grande Western and a receiver took over control of the Utah line. A working agreement between the two roads made possible the operation of through trains despite this separation of operating organizations. At the same time Gould temporarily lost control of the Union Pacific Consolidated System and the conservative,

[59] William A. Hamill, *Biennial Report of the Railroad Commissioner of the State of Colorado for the Years 1891 and 1892* (Denver, Smith-Brooks Printing Co., 1893), 4-5. The Granger movement in the 'seventies had had a decided effect in Colorado and upon the constitution adopted in 1876, but the prosperity of the last years of the decade had militated against the success of the reform movement until the critical situation in the 'eighties forced action upon the Assembly.

[60] W. B. Felker, *Report of the Railroad Commissioner of the State of Colorado, for the Year ending June 30, 1885* (Denver, 1886), passim. Hamill, *loc. cit.* Journals of the House of Representatives, General Assembly, 1885, *State Archives,* Denver.

though innocuous, Bostonian, Charles Francis Adams, Jr., became president. Serious difficulties soon confronted both Jackson and Adams.

Charging unfair and illegal practices, Governor Evans, as president of the Denver, Texas and Gulf Railroad, filed formal complaints

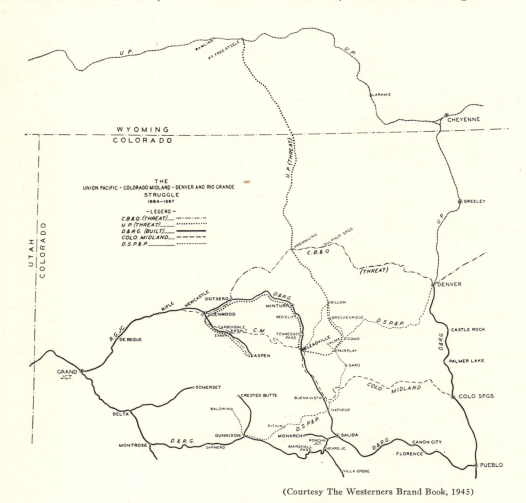

(Courtesy The Westerners Brand Book, 1945)

Railway Conflicts in the Rockies, 1884-1887

against the Rio Grande, Union Pacific, and Santa Fé alleging that a "tripartite agreement" between the three carriers for the interchange and division of traffic operated to exclude the Gulf road from its share of the Colorado business.[61] Evans' difficulties mounted as the Burling-

---

[61] The Denver & New Orleans Railroad had been foreclosed and sold in March 1885. It was reorganized under the name Denver, Texas & Gulf Railroad by the bondholders with the same officers and directors as those of the defunct organization. It is interesting to note that in 1885 this was the only major road in Colorado the majority stock of which was owned within the state. Felker, *ibid.,* "Table I-Capital Stock," 71.

ton & Missouri River Railroad (C. B. & Q.) joined the "blockade" and refused to receive or accept freight for or from the Denver, Texas & Gulf company, to interchange equipment, or provide for through passenger tickets or passenger baggage. Commissioner Felker upheld the right of the defendant companies to refuse to do business with the Gulf company.

An increase in traffic during the latter part of 1886 brought about a mild revival of interest by the eastern financial directors. Only twenty-three miles of new construction were recorded during the year, but plans for extensive building were approved and announced by a number of companies and construction crews recruited to take the field with the arrival of spring.

Despite the uneasiness resulting from Presidential approval on February 4, 1887, of the Interstate Commerce Act, the Colorado companies early in 1887 undertook to construct new roadbeds to the flourishing mountain mining districts. For many months Receiver Jackson of the Denver & Rio Grande had urged the directors of the company to approve a plan for the immediate extension of that company's lines to the newly opened Aspen mining district in order to prevent the loss of not only the traffic of the district, but to protect the strategic position of the company against the threat interposed by the contemplated construction of a new company, the Colorado Midland Railway. This new competitor had been charactered in November 1883, and in April 1886 had begun construction of a roadbed projected from Colorado Springs to the Leadville-Aspen mining districts.

While Jackson was endeavoring to secure the mountain traffic, Governor Evans was still trying to bring to fruition his plan to link Denver with the Gulf of Mexico. In April 1887 his recognized line, the Denver, Texas & Gulf Railroad, was bogged down at Pueblo, a gap of about two hundred and twenty-five miles still separating his tracks from those of Dodge's Fort Worth & Denver City Railway. Evans was in financial difficulties and no solution was in sight. Dodge, however, was pushing his line slowly northward to the Texas state line. Early in 1887 Dodge and Evans devised a plan to unite the two roads and on April 12 they incorporated the Denver, Texas & Fort Worth Railroad Company to construct the line linking the tracks of their separate lines. Evans also contracted with the Rio Grande for joint operation over that company's tracks between Pueblo, Walsenburg and Trinidad. A third rail was laid to provide for operation of standard gauge equipment over this division.

Jackson also looked with considerable uneasiness upon the activities of Burlington survey and grading parties who now appeared in the Grand River Valley. It was not until after the foreclosure sale and reorganization of the Denver & Rio Grande in July 1886, and the election of Jackson as president of the new company, that the crisis developed. Jackson soon found that he faced not only a race with the Colorado Midland and the Burlington, but also a third threat from the powerful Union Pacific. President Adams of the latter company had two strings to his bow and threatened to use both. He could strengthen the subsidiary Denver, South Park & Pacific and extend its sphere of activity to the areas of the new mining excitement, or, he might well—he announced—divert the entire traffic northward and away from Colorado by constructing a new road from the Union Pacific main line at Fort Steele, Wyoming, to Dillon, South Park, Leadville and Aspen! Jackson was quick to recognize that in either case the matter was a serious one for the Rio Grande, but that a possible linking up of the Union Pacific and the Midland would be a major disaster.

The race was a close one but the Rio Grande won, completing a narrow gauge line to Aspen on November 7, 1887. Before the end of the year the broad gauge tracks of the Midland Company—the first of standard width to cross the Rockies in Colorado—crossed Hagerman Pass and reached the booming Aspen camp.

Despite the victory it was a needlessly costly affair for the Rio Grande. Because of the failure to construct the line when originally urged by Receiver Jackson, the directors and shareholders of the company permitted the Colorado Midland promoters to believe they might outstrip the older company. Having once started their construction it was too late to stop them merely by outbuilding them. The result was that the Rio Grande was now forced to share the Aspen trade with the Midland, and the Leadville traffic with both the Denver, South Park and Pacific and the Colorado Midland. Of greater importance, it now placed the Midland company in position to further challenge the Denver company by threatening to build a line to Grand Junction and Utah parallel to one contemplated by the Rio Grande.[62]

Construction figures for 1887 showed a new record for railroad extension in Colorado. Of the 872.47 miles of road built during the year the Denver & Rio Grande and Colorado Midland accounted for over a third; the former's new trackage running from Redcliffe to Glenwood Springs and Aspen, and from Montrose to Ouray, while the Midland's line was extended from Colorado Springs by way of Buena Vista, Leadville (completed on September 3), Glenwood Springs, and Aspen (finished on December 18). While the mountain roads were engaged in the struggle for the Aspen traffic, the Atchison, Topeka and Santa Fe', through its subsidiary, the Denver & Santa Fe' Railway Company, constructed a new line between South Pueblo and Denver, completing this vital link on October 9, 1887.[63] The years' most ominous development was the completion of the Pueblo & State Line Railroad, subsidiary of the Missouri Pacific Railroad, to Pueblo on December 15. Jay Gould, as president of the Missouri Company, emerged once again as a potent force in the railroad development of Colorado.

Railroad mileage within the state had risen to 3773.14 miles by December 31, 1887, but the pace of construction slowed perceptibly in

---

[62] For an excellent account of this struggle see William S. Jackson, "The Record vs. Reminiscence," *The Westerners Brand Book 1945* (Denver, 1946), 59-89; the Midland's case may be found in the same volume, pages 219-231, Percy Hagerman, "The Colorado Midland."

[63] The Atchison company was able to secure access to the Denver terminal through its purchase of the Denver Circle Railroad and its facilities. The latter was a six mile local line operating within Denver and its southern suburbs.

1888 when 270.64 miles of new trackage was laid down. Of major significance was the completion of the Denver, Texas & Fort Worth Railway to the Texas state line, thereby completing a through line from Denver to Fort Worth by closing the gap between the Denver, Texas & Gulf road and the Fort Worth & Denver City Railway. By means of interchange agreements, Evans and Dodge secured a profitable traffic from the ports of Galveston and New Orleans. While the freight rates from New York and other eastern and European ports to Denver by way of the Gulf ports and the newly completed railroad were somewhat lower than by way of the continental rail lines, the elapsed time of the water-rail shipment was appreciably longer than by the all-rail route. Other important construction in 1888 included that of the Colorado Midland, which reached New Castle on October 15. To avoid a costly construction race the Midland operators entered into a contract with the Rio Grande by which both companies transferred their interests down the Grand River from Rifle to Grand Junction to a jointly owned third organization, the Rio Grande Junction Railway Company. With the completion of this extension on November 16, 1890, a through standard gauge road from Denver to Ogden, Utah,[64] over the Rio Grande Junction and Rio Grande Western Railways, was opened by the Denver & Rio Grande Railroad Company.

Last of the great transcontinental roads to enter the state was the Chicago, Rock Island & Colorado Railway Company (part of the C. R. I. & P. System) which opened its line from the Kansas border to Colorado Springs in 1888. By an agreement with the Union Pacific the Rock Island company secured trackage rights from Limon to Denver over the former's tracks, and reached Pueblo by means of a similar agreement with the Denver & Rio Grande Railroad Company. Interest in the potential traffic of the San Juan mining districts led to the completion in 1888, by the energetic Otto Mears, of the "Rainbow Route" line of the Silverton Railroad from Silverton over Sheridan Pass to Red Mountain and Ironton. The Denver & Rio Grande opened its extension to Lake City in June 1889 and that bustling community added its mining traffic to the mounting tonnage carried over the road.

By the end of 1890 the railroad picture in Colorado was again in a state of flux. In April 1887 President Jackson resigned from the board and direction of the Denver & Rio Grande Railroad, and was succeeded by David H. Moffat who was closely aligned at that moment with the reemerging Gould railroad empire. In 1890 Gould summarily removed Charles Francis Adams as president of the Union Pacific and took over the active direction of that great system. The Denver, Leadville & Gunnison Railway, incorporated by Union Pacific interests on July 6, 1889, secured control of the financially embarrassed Denver, South Park & Pacific Railroad Company on August 29, and the new company became an integral part of the Union Pacific system. Com-

---

[64] The Denver & Rio Grande had standard gauged its roadbed from Cañon City to Leadville during 1889 and 1890 and during the winter of 1889 used over one thousand men to rush completion of its road to Rifle.

petition with the reorganized mountain lines took a new turn in October 1890 when the Atchison, Topeka & Santa Fe' company, long desirous of tapping the Leadville traffic and foreseeing the possibility of a Pacific connection through Utah, acquired control of the Colorado Midland Railway. This not wholly unexpected development—a traffic agreement had existed between the two roads for several years—gave the Gould interests considerable concern. What if the Santa Fe' linked up with Palmer's Rio Grande Western at Grand Junction or some other line determined to push on to the Pacific? The threat to Gould's dream of forming a through transcontinental route by linking the Wabash, Missouri Pacific, and Denver & Rio Grande with a Pacific connection was quite real. Only Palmer's distrust of the eastern promoter and the specter of a new business depression prevented the immediate realization of this program.

Another profound change in the Colorado railroad structure was in the making by the end of 1889. For some months General Dodge, who, in addition to being head of the Fort Worth & Denver City Railway, was also a large stockholder and former officer of the Union Pacific, had urged the consolidation of his line and that of the Denver, Texas & Fort Worth (which had absorbed the Denver, Texas & Gulf Company) with the Union Pacific. Governor Evans agreed to the merger with some reservations, and in February 1890 the consolidation was approved. In order to streamline the operation of its short lines, most of which were in Colorado, the Union Pacific operators on April 1, 1890 formed the Union Pacific, Denver & Gulf Railway by consolidating the Colorado Central Railroad Company, Georgetown Breckenridge & Leadville Railway Company, Denver, Marshall & Boulder Railway Company, Denver & Middle Park Railroad Company, Greeley, Salt Lake & Pacific Railway Company, Denver, Texas & Gulf Railroad Company, Denver, Texas & Fort Worth Railroad Company, Road Cañon Railroad Company, Chicosa Cañon Railway Company, Cañon d'Agua Railroad Company, Colorado Central Railroad Company of Wyoming and the Cheyenne & Northern Railroad Company—a system amounting to 1463.23 miles of operated roadbed. The new Gulf system was a precarious union from the outset. Many of its corporate parts were seriously over-capitalized and earnings were frequently insufficient to service fixed charges, leave alone paying dividends on millions of dollars of common and preferred shares.

With almost every new gold or silver discovery, shanty mining camps in narrow mountain valleys below barren serrated peaks of the Rockies mushroomed into major communities. The rapid erection of general stores, mine supply houses, the ubiquitous saloons and gambling "parlors", the bustling newspaper plant, and the neat little clapboard churches and schools, were followed almost immediately by loud and persistent demands for railroad service. When the traffic hungry Rio Grande, Denver South Park & Pacific, Colorado Midland or other existing mountain carrier was either too distant or too dilatory, local promoters founded new companies and energetically—though frequently unwisely—undertook to construct independent roads. Construction figures from 1887, after the revival following the disastrous depression, to 1899 show the effect not only of the new "strikes" upon the extension of the Colorado rail network but also of the depression of 1891 and the subsequent silver controversy which ended in a major catastrophe for a large part of the Colorado mining industry upon which the carriers depended so largely:

Date	Total State Mileage	Constructed During Year	Major Extensions and Notes
1887	3773.14	872.47	*Denver & Rio Grande Railroad Co.,* Redcliffe to Glenwood Springs, Aspen; Montrose to Ouray.
			Colorado Midland Railway Company, Colorado Springs to Buena Vista, Leadville, Glenwood Springs, Aspen.
			Denver & Santa Fé Railway Co. (A. T. & S. F.), South Pueblo to Denver.
			Pueblo & State Line Railroad Co. (Missouri Pacific), Kansas State Line to Pueblo.
			Gilpin County Tramway Co., Central City and Black Hawk mining districts.
			Burlington & Colorado Railroad Co. (C. B. & Q.), Kansas border to Sterling and Colorado-Wyoming border.
1888	4038.04	270.64	*Colorado Midland Railway Co.,* Glenwood Springs to New Castle.
			Chicago, Kansas & Nebraska Railway Co. (C. R. I. & P.) Kansas border to Colorado Springs with trackage agreements over Union Pacific from Limon to Denver, and with Rio Grande from Colorado Springs to Pueblo.
			Denver, Texas & Fort Worth Railroad Co., Trinidad to New Mexico border.
			Colorado & Eastern Railroad Co., Denver to Scranton.
1889	4097.37	160.31	*Aspen Short Line Railway,* leased by Colorado Midland.
			Silverton Railroad Company, built by Otto Mears through San Juan mining area, Silverton over Sheridan Pass to Red Mountain and Ironton.
			Denver & Rio Grande Railroad Co., Lake Fork Branch; Glenwood Springs to Rifle Creek; branch to Aberdeen granite quarry in Gunnison to secure stone for the new state capitol building in Denver.
1890	4291.11	191.11	*Burlington & Colorado Railroad Co.,* Colorado to Montana cutoff from Brush.
			Rio Grande Southern Railroad Co., backed by Rio Grande interests constructed from Ridgeway to Telluride by Otto Mears.
			Manitou & Pike's Peak Railway Co., cog road up Pike's Peak.
			Denver & Rio Grande Railroad Co., Villa Grove to Alamosa; completion of standard gauge road Denver to Ogden over Rio Grande Junction Railroad and Denver & Rio Grande Western Railroad tracks.
			Rio Grande Junction Company, Rifle to Grand Junction; jointly built and used by Denver & Rio Grande Railroad and Colorado Midland.
1891	4441.33	160.86	*Denver & Rio Grande Railroad Co.,* Wagon Wheel Gap to site of new mining boom at Creede.
			Rio Grande Southern Railroad Co., Telluride to Durango.
			Denver, Lakewood & Golden Railroad Co., Denver to Golden.
1892	4451.52	15.88	
1893	4488.22	47.19	*Florence & Cripple Creek Railroad Co.,* Florence to Cañon City and Divide.

Date	Total State Mileage	Constructed During Year	
1894	4538.86	65.57	*Florence & Cripple Creek Railroad Co.,* Divide to Cripple Creek. *Midland Terminal Railroad Co.,* built to Victor. *Silverton Northern Railroad Co.,* Silverton to Eureka.
1895	4503.19	41.94	*Denver, Texas & Gulf Railroad Co.,* Trinidad to Walsenburg. *Midland Terminal Railroad Co.,* Divide to Cripple Creek.
1896	4509.46	20.75	
1897	4575.86	60.10	
1898	4608.85	30.75	*Colorado & Northwestern Railroad Company* (later renamed Denver, Boulder & Western Railroad Co.), Boulder to Ward.
1899	4616.51	36.36	

While the condition of the Colorado carriers was closely geared to both the national economy and to the overall railroad situation, local

Cog Road of the Manitou and Pike's Peak Railway, circa 1890

conditions—new silver and gold discoveries (at Leadville, Aspen, Silverton, Creede, Cripple Creek and a score of other camps), fluctuations in the demand and price of minerals, heavy traffic in mining supplies, equipment, ore and matte, as well as construction supplies for new rail extensions—influenced the development of the expanding network of rails. With the resumption of specie payments on January 1, 1879, the long period of depression was ended and the nation again entered upon a period of industrial expansion. The spectacular development of the Colorado rail system from 1880 to 1882 corresponded in part with the greatest years of railroad construction in American history. The reaction to this unprecedented growth and expenditure—much of the latter, as in Colorado, being frozen in over-extended and over-capitalized roads—was not long in coming.

During 1883, 1884 and 1885 the money markets at home and abroad were generally closed to railroad promoters, and, as in the case of Receiver Jackson and the Denver & Rio Grande, over-cautious directors refused to take risks even to the extent of losing the initiative to competing companies and jeopardizing preempted markets. No railroad enterprise of major importance was begun in the entire nation during this period, while in Colorado new construction and extension reached the lowest point since 1870. Characteristically, the succeeding three or four years (1887-1890) were again ones of rapid expansion, especially in the West, where the long projected transcontinental lines from the Southern Pacific on the south to the Great Northern in the north completed the parallel ties linking the Mississippi Valley with the entire Pacific coast. The monopoly of the Union Pacific-Central Pacific was ended forever. In Colorado the five year construction spurt, which ended with resounding repercussions in 1891, witnessed the completion of the state's rail network with only one major and a few minor exceptions.

Defaults, failures and foreclosures—the fruit reaped from years of speculation, unwarranted over-capitalization and the construction of unremunerative extensions—which had not been unknown in Colorado up to 1891 reached disaster proportions after the silver crisis of that year. The list included:

Railroad	Receiver Appointed	Sold at Foreclosure
1. Denver & Rio Grande Railway Co.	1884	1886
2. Denver & Rio Grande Western Railway Co.	1884	—
3. Denver Circle Railway Co.	1885	1887
4. Denver Western & Pacific Railway Co.	—	1885
5. Denver & New Orleans Railroad Co.	—	1886
6. Denver, South Park & Pacific Railway Co.	—	1889
7. Denver, Leadville & Gunnison Railroad Co.	1893	1898
8. Fort Worth & Denver City Railway Co.	1893	1898
9. Rio Grande Southern Railroad Co.	1893	—
10. Brighton & Boulder Branch (U. P. R. R.)	1893	—
11. Union Pacific, Denver & Gulf Railroad Co.	1893	1898
12. Atchison, Topeka & Santa Fé Railroad Co.	1894	1895
13. Colorado Midland Railway Co.	1894	1897
14. Colorado Eastern Railroad Co.	1894	—
15. Denver, Lakewood & Golden Railroad Co.	1896	—
16. Crystal River Railroad Co.	1896	1896
17. Denver Pacific Railway Co. (U. P. R. R.)	—	1898
18. Silverton Railroad Co.	1899	—

Such failure was part of the national scene. The number of railroad receiverships in the United States in 1892 was almost double that of any year from 1886 to 1891. Added to such local causes as the rapid decline in the value of silver, the failure of the huge international banking house of Baring Brothers in 1890, and the panic caused by the Venezuela incident had been contributory factors to the financial catastrophe. One hundred and nineteen companies were forced under court protection in 1893. No return was paid on sixty-five percent of the railroad share capital in the United States in 1894.

A further contributory element to the difficulties experienced by the Colorado carriers was the rugged character of railroading in the Rockies: steep four percent gradients and sharp curves, heavy construction and maintenance costs, problems resulting from mountainous operation at altitudes consistently above 7,500 feet (and up to 12,000 feet), fluctuating and seasonal traffic patterns, a high proportion of low revenue freight, and hundreds of miles of line traversing areas averaging less than three persons per square mile. There were too many eggs in one basket; if veins of silver or gold petered out after a few years (frequently all too short a period to return even the costs of railroad construction to the camps), or if, as in 1891, the value and market of the white metal plummeted, with them into the depths went the fortunes of the mountain carriers. In a similar manner the fluctuation in the price of livestock adversely affected those roads which annually carried heavy loads of both cattle and sheep. It was clearly evident that even the traffic of so rich a ''strike'' as Leadville could not, by itself, support a railroad; the success of the Colorado mountain carriers depended more and more upon firm links with one or more of the great transcontinental lines—and even then success was not always assured.

Efforts to regulate the carriers to prevent gross inequalities and discrimination, and to promote a safe and more efficient operation among the Colorado railroads continued despite the failure of the legislative act of 1885. When the legislature at the behest of a powerful railroad lobby failed to appropriate funds to continue the work of the railroad commissioner, that official ceased to function. Five years later, in May 1891, over the vigorous opposition of the railroads, the office was reactivated by a Populist administration and a pioneer Coloradan, William A. Hamill, appointed commissioner. Although he approached the problem with tact and understanding, the new commissioner lacked authority and funds to compel the carriers to abandon objectionable practices and to comply with his orders. The inevitable result was failure, but before completing his term the commissioner urged upon the legislature the passage of ''a wise, conservative and liberal railroad law,'' and the creation of a board of three commissioners which would include one member selected upon the recommendation of the railroad companies, and one member who was a competent railroad engineer.[65]

Before the end of the century conditions of railroad labor and employment had changed materially. From a chronic scarcity of skilled as well as unskilled labor up to 1880, there now appeared to be a surplus of both classes of employees. During heavy construction years (1881-2, 1887-1891) skilled labor was at a premium, but in the era following the panic of 1893 labor surpluses resulted in lower salary and wage scales, increased labor disputes within the industry,

[65] William A. Hamill, *Biennial Report of the Railroad Commissioner of the State of Colorado for the Years 1891 and 1892* (Smith-Brooks Printing Co., Denver, 1893), 4-5, 23-24.

and the transfer of many skilled as well as unskilled railroad workers to other types of employment. Considering the high cost of living in Colorado during the mineral era, the average salaries officially reported in 1885 by the Colorado companies give graphic reason for the unattractiveness of railroad employment at that date:[66]

Position	Average Monthly Salary
Division and Assistant Superintendents	$244.70
Road Masters	112.81
Clerks	77.31
Master and assistant mechanics	$55—$168.46
Helpers in shops	56.15
Dispatchers	103.96
Conductors	88.85
Engineers	116.77
Firemen and wipers	55.76
Brakemen	57.82
Baggagemen	58.76
Flagmen, switch-tenders, gate-keepers and watchmen	56.49
Station agents	63.09
Telegraph operators	54.55
Section foremen	59.06
Section laborers	35.49
Misc. employees	45.50

While Colorado was relatively free from the railroad labor strife which plagued other states, agitation for wage adjustments, abolition of the practice of reducing wages and raising hours of labor—or increasing duties—without notice was widespread. The state railroad commissioner in 1892 called for correction of these as well as unfair practices by labor, and for arbitration of disputes by a state created board of arbitration.[67]

The nineteenth century ended with the Colorado carriers almost completely in the control of the larger transcontinental lines, with the problem of regulation in the public interest still unsolved, with a very weakened financial structure still unrecovered from the panic and crash of 1893, and still laboring under crushing security burdens. The new century found 4,587 miles of railroad in operation in the state.

Consolidation and Reorganization 1900-1947

With the default of the Rio Grande Southern line in 1893, actually always a feeder line for the Denver & Rio Grande Railroad which had assisted materially in its promotion, the president of the Rio Grande was designated by the federal court as receiver—the first to hold that position in the fifty-five years of unbroken receivership up to 1948. Most serious Colorado casualty of the "Panic of 1893" was the delicately organized Union Pacific, Denver & Gulf Railroad Com-

---

[66] Figures given are computed from totals reported in W. B. Felker, *First Annual Report of the Railroad Commissioner of the State of Colorado, for the Year ending June 30, 1885* (Collier & Cleaveland, Denver, 1886), tables, 71-512.

[67] Hamill, *op. cit.*, 25.

pany which had been established less than three years before by the
Union Pacific. After considerable wrangling by security holders and
creditors the system was turned over to Frank Trumbull as receiver.
Under a reorganization plan adopted in 1898 the Julesburg-La Salle
cut-off was awarded to the reorganized Union Pacific company and
all the rest sold under foreclosure. The bondholders of the old company purchased the assets and placed them under a newly organized
company, the Colorado & Southern Railroad Company. On December 21, 1908, Great Northern and Northern Pacific interests, who since
1901 had also control of the Burlington system, purchased equally
control of the more than 1800 miles of road operated by the Colorado
& Southern and its various subsidiaries including the Fort Worth &
Denver City (plus the Wichita Valley lines), and the Denver, Leadville & Gunnison Railroad (successor to the historic South Park company). By this one transaction the Burlington System acquired a
through line from Cheyenne and Denver southward to Fort Worth
and Dallas with connections to Houston and Galveston, and therewith
created a new short route from the Pacific Northwest to the Gulf.[68]

On December 2, 1892 Jay Gould died, leaving his twenty-eight
year old son George Jay Gould as head of the family and overseer of
his vast estate. It was soon found that the great railroad manipulator
had kept actual control over four lines, the Missouri Pacific, Texas &
Pacific, International & Great Northern, and the Wabash railroad
companies. George Gould shared his father's long ambition to create
a single transcontinental road from the Atlantic to the Pacific and
without much delay began to develop a program which would bring
the dream to fruition.[69] An outlet to the Atlantic for the Wabash was
projected via Pittsburgh and Baltimore. At the same time Gould and
his colleagues turned their attention to securing a Pacific connection
for the Missouri Pacific west of Pueblo. George Gould was well aware
of his father's earlier experience with Palmer and the Denver & Rio
Grande, but he also recognized the potential advantage of the already
completed standard gauge line to Ogden, Utah, by way of the Denver
& Rio Grande Western over any new construction project. For several
years the Missouri Pacific had had a transfer agreement affecting
freight and passengers with the Colorado company at Pueblo, but it
was not until 1900 that the Missouri Pacific directors moved to secure
control of the Denver & Rio Grande.

As Palmer and his successors had foreseen since 1883, the physical
union of the Denver & Rio Grande and the Rio Grande Western was
essential to any plan to tap the Pacific traffic by a central route west
of Pueblo or Denver. Provision for such consolidation had been provided in the Colorado company's reorganization program of 1886, but
circumstances had prevented realization of the project. Both the

---

68 Richard C. Overton, *Burlington West* (Harvard Univ. Press, 1941), 480.

69 As today, the great "gateways", Chicago, St. Louis, and New Orleans, were termini
for both eastern and western continental lines, no single company operating through a
gateway. Many others besides Gould had dreamed of forming one company linking both
Pacific and Atlantic, but none had been able to forge the chain of roads necessary to the
success of the plan.

Colorado company and the Utah corporation had made a number of preliminary field surveys of routes to the Pacific or explored possibilities of connections with existing California carriers. It was not until the autumn of 1900, however, that serious negotiations were opened looking toward consolidation of the two lines. Progress was rapid. A plan for the purchase of the Utah line was approved by both boards of directors. George Gould was elected a director of the Denver & Rio Grande in mid-February, 1901, and soon thereafter joined the directorate of the Utah company. Physical consolidation of the two lines was effected in June and July 1901, but the final unification did not take place until July 23, 1908.

Fired by his quick success Gould, who had already purchased through the Missouri Pacific a controlling interest in the Denver & Rio Grande, now sought a Pacific connection which would leave him free of dependence upon the Union Pacific west of Ogden.[70] His very real fear of the Harriman system (despite the fact that both Harriman and Jacob H. Schiff of the Union Pacific directorate were also members of the Denver & Rio Grande board), was that the Union Pacific company—which had recently acquired the old Central Pacific line from Ogden to California—would close the Ogden gateway, thereby leaving the consolidated Rio Grande roads without a link to the Pacific. This was precisely what did happen. Independence was the only answer and with utmost dispatch Gould, in 1906, began the construction of a new route from Salt Lake City to Oakland. As finally approved, the California connection, incorporated as the Western Pacific, was completed from Ogden to Oakland via Beckwith Pass and the Feather River Canon and opened August 22, 1910.

Financing the new system upon a sound basis proved a difficult, if not impossible, task for Gould and his colleagues. The Atlantic gateway via the Wabash from St. Louis hinged on the entrance to Pittsburgh, and Gould secured this position only by resorting to unorthodox financing. The strain of this arrangement made expedient the use of equally dubious means to finance the western outlet. To guarantee the securities of the Western Pacific, Gould pledged the earnings of the Denver & Rio Grande Western company. By 1915 the Rio Grande had advanced $52,000,000 to pay interest charges and part of the Pacific company's operating expenses. Despite the increased bridge traffic the Colorado company was placed in the unenviable position of guarantor for a line it didn't own, operate, or control. The seeds for a new disaster for the Rio Grande had been planted.[71]

After a number of corporate changes in which Gould found himself attacked from within the organization, the eastern promoter-

[70] Gould's purposes are further illuminated by the fact that he simultaneously concluded a contract with the N. K. K., Japanese shipping line, for interchange at San Francisco of freight to and from the Orient. This arrangement made possible a further incursion into the fields of the Harriman, Huntington and Villard companies.

[71] Material for this and subsequent paragraphs on the evolution of the Denver & Rio Grande Western Railroad—formed through the consolidation of the Colorado and Utah companies—was taken from the original files and records of that company. *Archives,* D. & R. G. W. R. R. 1870-1948.

financier resigned as chairman of the board of the Colorado company in 1912, and was succeeded by Edward F. Jefferey, former president of the company. Despite this change Gould retained a measure of control by virtue of his large security holdings in both the Missouri and the Colorado companies. In November of the same year the Rio Grande purchased the half interest in the Rio Grande Junction Railway owned by the Colorado Midland company, thereby ending—after thirty-five years—the threat to its mountain traffic by the Atchison, Topeka & Santa Fe' Railroad. In the meantime it became increasingly evident that the Western Pacific was facing insurmountable financial difficulties due to the staggering fixed charges resulting from Gould's unorthodox financing during the period of its construction. On March 1, 1915, the new line defaulted on its bonds and the road was placed in receivership four days later.

Following the Western Pacific foreclosure sale, the mortgage trustee brought suit against the Rio Grande for the amount of the defaulted principal and interest on the bonds of the Western Pacific. A deficiency judgment of approximately $38,000,000 awarded by the court against the Colorado company resulted in the seizure of a large part of that company's funds and assets. A receiver was appointed in January 1918, and at the subsequent sale the Rio Grande's properties were purchased on behalf of the Western Pacific and transferred to the newly incorporated (November 15, 1920) Denver & Rio Grande Western Railroad Company. From its outset the company was in financial difficulties which soon culminated in a new default and the appointment of a receiver on July 21, 1922. As a result of an approved reorganization program (which did not materially reduce the crushing indebtedness), and the subsequent sale of the road at public auction on December 20, 1924, the common stock of the Rio Grande became the property—jointly and equally—of the Western Pacific and the Missouri Pacific companies. The "bridge" welded by George Gould was thus maintained intact.

While Gould, Jefferey, and their successors were working out the destiny of the Denver & Rio Grande Western Railroad, the other Colorado carriers were battling for an ever increasing share of the inter-mountain traffic. Although the Spanish-American War and the inflationary period which followed gave some impetus to the Rocky Mountain railroad systems, the effect was temporary. A brief construction revival due to new mineral activity at Cripple Creek occurred in 1900 and 1901, but thereafter new mileage was small until 1907 when the Denver, Northwestern & Pacific Railway, promoted by one of the few remaining pioneer Colorado railroad developers, David H. Moffat, constructed its road to Routt County.

The Denver, Northwestern & Pacific Railway—"The Moffat Road" —was the last major railroad to be constructed in Colorado into undeveloped country.[72] Neither its route nor its purpose of opening a direct line to Utah and the Pacific were new. Railroad surveys up

---

[72] At the time of its completion to Steamboat Springs there were not 10,000 people in all of Grand and Routt counties.

Boulder Cañon and through Gore Cañon had been made in the 'seventies and at least one company, the Burlington, had started to grade a roadbed. The same route had earlier been selected for a Union Pacific extension. A glance at a Colorado railroad map for 1900 will demonstrate the desirability of such a road. Instead of the long trip south to Pueblo and up the Arkansas by the Denver & Rio Grande Western, or the northern run to Cheyenne and thence west over the Union Pacific, the plan envisioned striking due west from Denver by the most practical mountain pass, thereby eliminating approximately 175 miles and some five hours running time between Denver and Ogden. After several false starts David Moffat, Walter Cheesman, and William G. Evans (son of former governor Dr. John Evans) together with a number of other prominent Denverites founded the Denver, Northwestern & Pacific Railway Company in July 1902. At that time all three of the principal promoters were also intimately connected with the Denver Tramway Company which operated the Denver & Northwestern Railroad to the Leyden coal fields, and which thereby furnished a ready entrance to Denver for the projected railroad.

Opposition to the short-cut road quickly developed from the large trunk lines headed by Harriman and Gould. Moffat soon discovered that the money markets had been tightly closed to him and his project. Determined to carry on regardless of this vigorous opposition, the Colorado entrepreneur invested $4,000,000 of his own fortune plus what he was able to raise personally among friends and colleagues in Colorado. Construction of the Denver, Northwestern and Pacific began in the Spring of 1903. Slow but steady progress was made up South Boulder Creek and across the Continental Divide at Rollins Pass and through Gore Cañon. In order to avoid the heavy grade over the 11,000 foot pass Moffat and his engineers had studied several possible tunnel sites under the Divide, but the scarcity of capital made such costly construction impractical at that date. Despite construction problems the road was completed to Steamboat Springs on November 1, 1908, and, under the direction of Newman Erb (late of the Pere Marquette Railroad), to Craig on November 22, 1913.

As Moffat recognized, the key to the success of his precarious venture lay in the construction of a tunnel which would eliminate the tortuous climb over 11,600 feet high Rollins Pass. At the time of his death on March 18, 1911, the promoter had expended most of his fortune in the enterprise, and had failed completely, despite numerous attempts, to find the funds for the tunnel under the divide. William G. Evans succeeded Moffat as president of the road, but the financial position of the company soon forced it into receivership. Seventy-five thousand dollars a mile had been expended on construction to Steamboat Springs and not a dollar of net profit had been realized.[73] The road was reorganized in 1913 under the name Denver & Salt Lake

[73] Edgar C. McMechen, *The Moffat Tunnel of Colorado* . . . (Walgreen Publishing Co., Denver, 1927), 122. This work is the best published account of the development of the Moffat line, and of the tunnel which played such a vital role in its history.

Railroad Company, and the receivers appointed in 1912, Lawrence C. Phipps, Sr. and Charles Boettcher, discharged. The reorganization brought into the company David Child Dodge, one of the principal builders and long time general manager of the Denver & Rio Grande, L. C. Phipps, Sr., Henry M. Porter and Gerald Hughes of Denver. A substantial investment was made by British interests headed by Dr. D. F. S. Pearson, London financier. Newman Erb was employed to manage the company's operations. Pearson's death in the sinking of the *Lusitania* proved a serious blow to the new company as it abruptly terminated the promising plans he had initiated for securing European financial aid for construction of the transmontane tunnel.

Attempts to secure financial support for the project from both the state legislature and the city of Denver failed; in the latter instance in 1914 the Supreme Court invalidated an approved $3,000,000 bond issue to finance the tunnel. The public, security holders, and the operators of the road were thoroughly disheartened by this reversal. On December 15, 1915, the local owners secured control of the company and elected Charles Boettcher as president. The change, however, proved only a temporary respite for the line was again placed in receivership on August 7, 1917. Boettcher and William R. Freeman were appointed receivers, but the outbreak of the war and the seizure of the nation's rail system by the United States Railroad Administration prevented the operation of the receivership.

Federal operation of the Denver & Salt Lake Railroad proved a heaven-sent boon to that road. The Craig extension had sapped the last financial resources of the line and by 1917 the roadbed, rolling stock, and facilities were in deplorable condition. In order to secure the badly needed coal of Routt County for the Pueblo steel mills' war production the War Board purchased a million dollars worth of company bonds so as to provide funds for rehabilitation of the roadbed and equipment. The federal administrator placed the line under control of the Burlington company, whose Colorado & Southern subsidiary carried a heavy traffic in iron ore to Pueblo. William Freeman operated the line and took full advantage of federal assistance to build up the company's property. An additional half million dollars was secured in settlement with the United States government after the war.

With the end of federal control the old problems again became acute. After another attempt to secure tunnel aid had failed, due in no small part to the vigorous opposition of the larger railroad companies, eastern and foreign security holders sought to have the road junked. A combination of events saved the line from abandonment: Receiver Freeman was able to improve operations and reduce the twenty-year string of annual deficits; there was a steady increase in coal production while the discovery and production of petroleum, and the spectacular growth of agriculture (notably lettuce) in Grant, Routt and Moffat counties raised freight traffic to new levels. At almost the same time the long battle to secure a tunnel subsidy reached its climax.

On May 12, 1922, the General Assembly, after prolonged consideration of a paired measure calling for creation of a flood control district for flood-ravaged Pueblo and a Moffat Tunnel Improvement District, gave its assent and the way was cleared for construction of a tunnel under the Divide. The legislative act placed the financial burden of the project upon the lands to be benefited—Denver, Grand, Routt and Moffat, and portions of Jefferson, Adams, Boulder, Eagle, and Gilpin counties. Denver's share was later fixed at eighty-nine percent.

Suits to invalidate the legislative authorization were quickly filed and speedily adjudicated, with the constitutionality of the measure upheld by both state and federal supreme courts. Construction began in mid-1923 on the 6.09 mile tunnel. The return from the original authorized bond issue of $6,720,000 was soon expended and new issues were floated. When completed in 1926 the project had cost more than fifteen million dollars.

With success finally assured the security holders of the Denver & Salt Lake Railroad reorganized the company as the Denver & Salt Lake Western Railroad Company and purchased the line at auction in 1926. Freeman was elected president and a contract with the Moffat Tunnel commissioners for use of the publicly owned tunnel was concluded. On August 26, 1928 the first scheduled train passed through the huge structure and a new era opened for the residents of northeastern Colorado.

During the quarter of a century in which the Moffat line was struggling for existence many changes were taking place in Colorado's railroad system. Rail mileage continued to mount until 1914 when there were 5,814 miles of operated trackage in Colorado.[74] While many small alterations and extensions were made between 1900 and 1914, the principal additions—other than the construction of the Denver, Northwestern & Pacific—were:

Date	Company	Extensions
1900	Chicago, Burlington & Quincy R. R. Co.	From Colorado-Nebraska border near Peetz to Sterling where it connected with the Union Pacific, and from Union to Brush. This construction and lease gave the Burlington a direct route, over the Union Pacific from Union to Sterling, to Alliance, Nebraska.
1903	Colorado & Wyoming Railroad Co.	A subsidiary of the Colorado Fuel & Iron Co., of Pueblo; from Trinidad west along the Las Animas to Cuatro, 32 miles.
1905	Uintah Railroad Company	A narrow gauge line from Mack (on the Rio Grande) to the Gilsonite beds at Dragon, Utah.

[74] There is some disagreement as to this total given by the Interstate Commerce Commission. The State Tax Commission reports agree that 1914 was the peak year of rail mileage in the state but set the figure at 5,739 miles. The difference can be accounted for in the time of the year in which the figures were compiled, reported abandonments, and lines not in operation.

DATE	COMPANY	EXTENSIONS
1906	Argentine Central Railroad Co.	A narrow gauge fifteen mile road from Silver Plume to the summit of Mount McClellan. This scenic line actually reached an altitude of over 14,000 feet, the highest railroad construction in North America.
1906	Colorado & Northwestern Railroad Co.	Extension from Ward to El Dora and Sunset.
1909-10	Denver, Laramie & Northwestern Railroad Co.	Line completed from Denver to Greeley. It was later abandoned and salvaged.
1910	Great Western Railway Co.	Closely linked with Great Western Sugar Company interests, this line by 1910 had constructed 55 miles of railroad through the beet fields north of Denver.
1910	San Luis Southern Railroad Co.	A subsidiary of the Costilla Estates Development Co., owner of the Costilla Estate—southern half of the famed Sangre de Cristo land grant—completed a 32 miles track from Blanca to Garosa.
1911	Laramie, Hahn's Peak & Pacific Railway Co.	This company, which went through several reorganizations and changes of name, constructed a line from Laramie, Wyoming, to Coalmont in North Park. It was later known as the Laramie, North Park & Western Railroad, and became a part of the Union Pacific system.
1913	San Luis Central Railroad Co.	A short line from Monte Vista to Center, where a profitable though seasonable traffic in hauling farm produce — especially potatoes — was secured.

After 1914 railroad mileage in Colorado began to shrink. The rapid decline in the mining industry following the silver debacle of 1893 led to the closing of scores of Colorado mines and the abandonment of thousands of claims. Once bustling mountain communities became ghost towns, and their need for rail service passed almost as quickly as it had begun. Small mine extensions were abandoned first. On August 4, 1918, the Colorado Midland Railroad Company ceased operations.[75] Both the Colorado Springs & Cripple Creek District Railroad and the Florence and Cripple Creek Railroad soon met the same fate. In 1923 the Colorado & Southern began the long process of abandonment of what had once been the Denver, South Park & Pacific—later the Denver, Gunnison & San Juan. By 1939 all

---

[75] The Midland Company was controlled by the Santa Fé railroad from January 1891 until sold under foreclosure on September 8, 1897. Reorganized as the Colorado Midland Railway Co., on October 11, 1897, the new operators forced the bondholders of the Busk Tunnel Railway Co., to sell the tunnel property to the Midland, whereupon the line over Hagerman Pass was finally abandoned. In May 1900, the Denver & Rio Grande and the Colorado & Southern each purchased half of the capital stock of the Midland. Difficulties arose in 1912 and on December 13, at the request of the bondholders committee, a receiver was appointed by the federal court. A foreclosure sale on April 21, 1917 resulted in the purchase of the property by A. E. Carlton and associates. Within a short while, however, the line was again thrown into receivership. Five months after the line ceased operations, on January 17, 1919, the Public Utilities Commission assented to the junking of the road. By April 21, 1923, stockholders had received one hundred and twenty-three percent on their investment. The company was formally dissolved on May 20, 1922.

that remained of that spectacular road was an isolated, though profitable, piece of line between Climax and Leadville. The Denver & Rio Grande Western Railroad also divested itself of various pieces of unprofitable mountain mileage. In 1924 the Blue River branch from Leadville to Dillon was abandoned. The Silverton Northern Railroad in the once booming San Juan mining district passed into oblivion when the road was closed to Genesee in 1922 and to Las Animas and Gladstone in 1935. During the depression and pre-World War II years from 1930 to 1940 more than six-hundred miles of trackage were abandoned throughout the state. The long unprofitable "Chile Line" between Antonito and Santa Fe' was abandoned by the Denver & Rio Grande Western in September 1941. Opposition to abandonments was vigorous and in some instances local political pressure prevented the closing of branches which were no longer economically sound.

The long battle to regulate Colorado's rail carriers, begun in 1876 with the drafting of the state constitution, had met with repeated failures despite the passage of regulatory measures in 1881 and 1883, and the establishment of the office of state railroad commissioner in 1885. The vehement opposition by the politically powerful carriers to such legislative action continued without abatement after the turn of the century. Faced with the questionable tactics employed by certain railroad corporations, the General Assembly, in March 1907, passed a regulatory act which provided for a state railroad commission of three members, and granted them authority to compel compliance with the terms of the new statute. As expected, the carriers promptly brought suit in the United States District Court attacking the constitutionality of the measure. On April 9, 1910, after the new commission had ordered a material reduction in freight rates, the law was declared unconstitutional by the federal district court. While a commission appeal to the United States Supreme Court was pending, the General Assembly at a special session amended and then reenacted the law of 1907, eliminating some of the features objected to as unconstitutional, including the right to adjust freight rates.[76] The long struggle to secure an enforceable statute ended in 1912 when the Supreme Court declared the Colorado law constitutional and recognized the right of the state body to fix freight tariffs for intra-state roads. Based upon this decision, and the recommendations of the railroad commission in its biennial report,[77] the Assembly in 1913 created the Public Utilities Commisssion and delegated authority to it to regulate the carriers and to enforce the statutes. In the more than three decades since it was established, and despite repeated attempts to exert political pressure upon it, the Public Utilities Commission has compiled an excellent record of accomplishment and cooperation.

Two world wars have materially affected the Colorado railroad system. As already shown the establishment of federal control over

---

[76] *Second Report of the State Railroad Commission of Colorado from January 1, 1909 to January 1, 1911* (Smith Brooks Printing Co., Denver, 1911), 3-5.

[77] *Third Report of the State Railroad Commission of Colorado from January 1, 1911 to January 1, 1913* (Smith Brooks Printing Co., Denver, 1913), 3-7.

the carriers by the United States Railroad Administration in the first great struggle temporarily prevented the liquidation of both the Denver & Salt Lake and the Denver & Rio Grande Western until those lines were returned to their companies and receivers. In the interim

The Royal Gorge and Suspension Bridge

federal funds were used to improve roadbeds, purchase new equipment needed during the war, and to pay fixed charges. A number of companies demanded and received large sums in compensation from the government following the return of the roads to private ownership and operation. In general, however, the record of operations under the federal agency was not an efficient one. Red tape, conflicting directives, and inexperienced officials at various levels contributed to the chaotic situation brought about by the unpreparedness of the nation and the carriers. It was this experience which led to the drafting by the carriers themselves in the period between the wars, of definite plans for operation of the railroads in the event of future conflagrations. The result was clearly evident in the record established by the companies during World War II when the Colorado carriers were faced with the task of hauling more freight than ever before in their history with less equipment, and fewer experienced personnel than was used in the first world war.

The depression from 1930 to 1938 had left in its wake a broad trail of defaults, receiverships and trusteeships, and the outbreak of hostilities in 1941 found the Colorado railroads recovering but still shaky. Between the two wars, bus and truck lines had made marked inroads upon certain classes of local passenger and freight traffic, once carried almost exclusively by the railroads. Concerted efforts by the railroad companies in Colorado to limit the operations of the motor carriers by securing passage of restrictive legislation failed. Unable to "whip 'em" the roads adopted a policy of "joinin' 'em", and during the 'thirties the Union Pacific, Burlington, Rock Island, Santa Fé and the Rio Grande founded or purchased and operated bus and truck lines throughout the state. A decade of experience taught the companies the advantage of coordinated service utilizing all three forms of land transport—rail, truck, and bus. In a number of instances the Rio Grande "discovered" that it could offer the public better and cheaper service by replacing part of its narrow gauge lines with modern motor equipment. The abandonment of inefficient branches and their replacement with gasoline and diesel powered highway units proved beneficial to both the general public and the rail carrier. This coordinated operation proved highly advantageous during the war period when the carriers found it more and more necessary to restrict civilian rail travel and to conserve power and rolling stock for operations connected directly with the transport of war supplies, equipment, troops and essential civilian personnel.

War time operations in Colorado from 1941-45 strained rail facilities to almost the breaking point. The shortsighted policy of drafting highly skilled and experienced men for service in non-transport military units, where their training and experience went unused, resulted in the employment of inexperienced car and shop men to handle the greatest traffic load in history. Confusion and inexcusable inefficiency in the War Production Board and allocations agencies resulted in prolonged delays in the delivery of replacement parts and supplies essential to the maximum operation demanded by military authorities. Despite these handicaps the Colorado carriers established a record for operations and efficiency far beyond that recorded by the same companies under federal control during the first world struggle.

New factories, mills, mines, and military establishments established throughout the state during the second world war presented the carriers with unprecedented freight problems. For the first time since their construction the railroads were faced with a swelling westbound freight traffic which to their astonishment caught up with and then surpassed eastbound traffic. This resulted in acute power problems as well as passing difficulties. Lines built and planned to handle a well defined number of train units per day suddenly found their tracks jammed with more than twice that number. The guns, tanks, planes, and other supplies and equipment, in addition to entire armies of men, went through without the prolonged delays, numerous accidents, and terminal chaos which so characterized operations in 1917 and 1918. The pre-war planning, combined with decentralized operations control made the difference despite the irritations, faulty judgments, and short-sightedness which are a part of war.

Although considerable portions of the power and rolling stock required major repairs or replacement after the cessation of hostilities, and roadbeds were sadly in need of the maintenance which war-time shortages of supplies and men had prevented, the Colorado railroad system is today (1948) more efficient, better staffed and equipped than in any period in its history. Profits resulting from the heavy war-time traffic, as well as that since the end of the conflict, made possible the retirement of a substantial part of the indebtedness which had plagued the carriers throughout the twentieth century.

One major alteration in the railroad structure of Colorado has taken place since the end of the war, the reorganization of the Denver & Rio Grande Western Railroad Company. After the ineffective reorganization of 1924, Rio Grande officials—who had opposed the Moffat tunnel scheme from its beginning—watched the construction of the tunnel with increased interest. They objected vigorously to an announced plan by the Denver & Salt Lake Western to construct a spur from its line to Dotsero on the Rio Grande. Owing to the withdrawal of public lands bordering on the Colorado River, it was not until 1927 that the Moffat company was able to secure a right-of-way for the branch. This delay, combined with the active resistance of the Rio Grande, postponed the completion of this important connecting link for over six years.

The matter was finally resolved through an agreement between the two companies and the Reconstruction Finance Corporation by which the charter for the construction and operation of the proposed connection passed into the possession of the Rio Grande company. Work was started on November 11, 1932 and the thirty-eight mile line completed linking the Rio Grande at Dotsero with the Moffat track at Orestod (Dotsero spelled backwards!) on June 15, 1934. Denver's dream of a direct transcontinental railroad was realized at long last. The 606.9 mile direct line from Denver to Ogden completed a central route which served not only the westbound Missouri Pacific but also the Rock Island and the Chicago, Burlington & Quincy railroads. The

Denver & Rio Grande Western Railroad had become a vital "bridge" in the nation's transcontinental rail system.

Jubilation over this success, however, was tempered by the effects of the depression. Despite sharp reductions in operating budgets, curtailment of maintenance and replacement, and reductions in personnel (frequently to the detriment of efficient operations) the Rio Grande company found itself in financial difficulties. Unable to pay the interest on its securities the company was forced on November 1, 1935 to petition the United States District Court for reorganization. Judge J. Foster Symes, on November 18, formally granted the petition and appointed Judge Wilson McCarthy, president of the Denver & Salt Lake Western Railroad and formerly a member of the Reconstruction Finance Corporation, and Henry Swan, vice-president of the United States National Bank of Denver, as co-trustees.

McCarthy and Swan were not in any real sense railroad administrators, but each brought to the job long experience in business and finance plus an acute awareness of modern trends and techniques. The result was nothing short of a revolution in Rio Grande operations. Traditional but long antiquated office procedures were modernized; motive power was completely overhauled and modern steam and diesel equipment purchased; existing rolling stock—some seventy per cent of which was over twenty years of age when the trustees took charge—was rebuilt or retired and almost 5,000 new freight cars constructed or purchased; transportation service and operating efficiency reached the highest point in the road's history; steps were taken to increase traffic; the fiscal setup was completely renovated; personnel and employee relations were markedly improved; safety programs were instituted and a better than fifty percent decrease in employee casualties was recorded in the eleven year trusteeship period; the establishment of both a technical laboratory and a bureau of research and statistics resulted in significant developments and improvements in equipment, roadbed, maintenance and operations, as well as a better understanding of traffic trends, the effects of the new improvements and the coordination of rail and truck service as well as the significance of current economic trends upon the company and its program. War time operations proved the wisdom of these innovations. When the trustees turned the road over to the reorganized company on April 11, 1947, their eleven and one-half year program of rejuvenation had placed the Denver & Rio Grande Western Railroad on its firmest footing since its founding seventy-six years earlier.

As finally approved the plan of reorganization reduced the staggering indebtedness of the company by 33.5 per cent, and placed control of the company in a board made up almost wholly of Colorado and Utah directors headed by John Evans—grandson of Governor John Evans and the third member of his family to play an important role in Colorado's railroad development. Former trustee Judge Wilson McCarthy ascended to the post of president, while his co-trustee Henry Swan joined the directorate and accepted the post of chairman of the finance committee of the board. The long contemplated consolidation of the Denver & Salt Lake Western Railroad Company with the Rio Grande became a reality, thereby making the new company a composite of forty-six different organizations founded in Colorado, New Mexico and Utah over a period of three quarters of a century. Under the new program the Western Pacific-Missouri Pacific joint ownership of the Rio Grande stock was terminated. In their place were some four thousand stockholders. For the first time since 1883 the Denver & Rio Grande Western Railroad Company, still mainly composed of the two unique mountain roads created by General Palmer, the Denver & Rio Grande Railway Company and the Rio Grande Western Railway Company—returned to western direction and operation.

With the reorganization of the Rio Grande in 1947, the Colorado railroads entered a new era. The great continental lines which enter the state have reached a new peak in performance and service. From the flashy diesel stream-liners which link Colorado with the Pacific and the east to the heavy diesel-powered freight trains, the steam-driven limiteds and locals, and the still unique narrow gauge units which breach the mountain passes and cut through the scenic wonders of the Rockies, the increased efficiency is clearly evident. The day of the purely local carriers has largely gone and in their place, tieing Colorado inextricably with the economy of the nation, stand the powerful monuments to the foresight and ability of American enterprise, the Atchison, Topeka & Santa Fé, the Burlington, Rock Island, Rio Grande, Missouri Pacific, and Union Pacific. The post war period brought many problems as yet unsolved. While it is patently true that bridge traffic must continue to play the major role in the success of the carriers, it is also clearly evident that originated traffic will play an ever more important role in their future operations. The trend toward decentralization of industry, the founding of new enterprises in Colorado, and the development of new uses for as yet vast natural resources, will lead inevitably to the growth of population and increased production with a correspondingly greater demand for goods. The result will be an appreciable increase in traffic for the railroads in the commonwealth. Their immediate as well as long run corporate health as private enterprises must depend, however, upon a number of imponderables: improved and continued efficient operation with the reduction of indebtedness; an increasing regard for public sentiment combined with a policy of freight tariff and passenger fare adjustments in line with income and operations costs; modernization and adaptation of new types of equipment; elimination of unprofitable branches and divisions; the elimination of costly featherbedding practices; a more effective co-ordination of bus, truck and rail transport; development of a sound labor-management relations program based upon mutual welfare and the responsibility of both parties to the general public.

APPENDIX
(See Chapter XVIII, Vol. II)

COMPARATIVE CHART OF MINERAL PRODUCTION IN COLORADO FROM 1858 TO 1943

Year	GOLD (121) Fine Ozs.	Value	SILVER (121) Fine Ozs.	Value	COPPER (121) Pounds	Value
1858-67		$25,021,784	302,829	$406,139		
1868		2,010,000	200,716	266,150	50,000	$11,500
1869		3,180,000	475,472	630,000	102,000	24,735
1870		3,015,000	496,988	660,000	182,500	38,654
1871		3,633,951	776,648	1,029,059	183,000	44,140
1872		2,646,463	1,524,206	2,015,000	204,000	72,542
1873		2,018,931	1,543,047	2,001,331	379,493	106,258
1874		2,152,487	2,348,174	3,000,966	475,541	104,619
1875		2,224,568	2,330,291	2,889,560	280,815	63,745
1876		2,726,311	2,564,403	2,974,707	333,333	70,000
1877		3,148,708	2,882,121	3,458,546	493,664	93,796
1878		3,240,348	4,672,961	5,373,904	536,145	89,000
1879		3,193,500	11,899,335	13,327,257	704,301	131,000
1880		3,252,514	14,397,539	16,557,170	859,000	183,826
1881		3,300,000	13,272,188	14,997,572	884,000	160,868
1882		3,360,000	12,761,719	14,548,359	1,494,000	285,354
1883		4,100,000	13,434,610	14,912,417	1,152,652	190,188
1884		4,300,000	12,375,000	13,736,251	2,013,125	261,706
1885		4,203,425	12,220,982	13,076,451	1,146,460	123,818
1886		4,450,000	12,375,000	12,251,250	1,146,460	127,257
1887		4,000,000	11,601,563	11,369,534	2,012,027	277,660
1888		3,758,099	14,695,313	13,813,596	1,621,100	272,345
1889		3,883,859	18,375,136	17,272,629	1,170,063	157,956
1890		4,151,132	18,800,000	19,740,000	3,585,691	559,368
1891		4,600,000	21,160,000	20,948,401	6,336,878	811,121
1892		5,300,000	24,000,000	20,880,000	7,593,674	880,866
1893		7,527,000	25,838,600	20,154,107	7,695,826	831,149
1894		9,491,514	23,281,398	14,667,281	6,461,413	615,734
1895		13,209,601	23,398,500	15,209,024	6,079,243	650,479
1896		14,911,000	22,573,000	15,349,642	6,022,176	650,395
1897		19,579,433	21,278,202	12,766,919	9,149,967	1,097,995
1898		23,534,532	23,502,601	13,866,532	10,870,701	1,347,965
1899		26,508,675	23,111,688	13,868,811	7,356,970	1,258,041
1900		28,762,036	20,336,512	12,608,637	7,826,815	1,299,251
1901		27,679,443	18,492,563	11,095,538	7,872,529	1,314,712
1902		28,516,914	15,941,523	8,449,008	8,463,928	1,132,601
1903		21,605,357	13,245,438	7,152,536	7,809,920	1,069,958
1904		24,242,485	12,960,792	7,517,260	9,412,707	1,204,828
1905		25,295,222	12,339,435	7,527,056	9,661,546	1,507,201
1906		22,905,671	12,339,052	8,390,553	6,618,332	1,277,338
1907		20,307,648	11,599,514	7,655,679	8,826,254	1,765,251
1908		22,595,571	9,002,316	4,771,227	10,201,123	1,346,547
1909		21,984,008	8,904,701	4,630,444	10,916,191	1,419,105
1910		20,505,614	8,508,942	4,594,829	8,359,307	1,061,632
1911		19,001,975	7,330,168	3,884,989	8,024,488	1,003,061
1912		18,588,562	8,212,070	5,050,423	7,107,303	1,172,705
1913		18,146,916	9,325,255	5,632,454	7,227,826	1,120,313
1914		19,883,105	8,796,065	4,864,224	6,639,173	883,010
1915		22,414,944	7,027,972	3,563,182	7,112,537	1,244,694
1916		19,153,821	7,656,544	5,038,006	8,624,081	2,121,524
1917		15,729,224	7,304,353	6,018,787	8,122,004	2,217,307
1918		12,751,718	7,063,554	7,063,554	6,277,332	1,550,501
1919		9,886,627	5,758,010	6,448,971	3,560,207	662,198
1920	366,504.43	7,576,319	5,409,335	5,896,175	4,043,734	744,047
1921	330,658.99	6,835,328	5,631,657	5,631,657	4,153,442	535,794
1922	308,314.15	6,373,419	5,855,911	5,855,911	3,373,454	455,416
1923	318,870.05	6,591,629	5,334,488	4,374,280	4,248,109	624,472
1924	415,691.98	8,593,116	3,254,370	2,108,428	2,713,219	355,432
1925	349,607.20	7,227,022	4,506,940	3,127,816	2,360,500	335,191
1926	342,399.84	7,078,033	4,704,122	2,935,372	3,403,850	476,539
1927	255,400.00	5,279,118	3,784,605	2,145,871	5,670,581	742,846
1928	256,646.20	5,304,876	4,052,253	2,370,568	8,594,646	1,237,629
1929	213,708.17	4,417,358	4,397,377	2,343,802	8,905,074	1,567,293
1930	218,539.82	4,517,619	4,382,852	1,687,398	10,514,000	1,366,820
1931	233,299.75	4,822,734	2,195,914	636,815	8,165,000	743,015
1932	317,927.95	6,572,154	1,860,408	524,635	7,398,000	466,074
1933	242,827.70	6,206,676	2,186,140	765,149	9,667,000	618,688
1934	324,923.32	11,356,070	3,475,661	2,246,892	11,294,000	903,520
1935	340,280.80	12,224,828	4,696,064	3,375,296	14,654,000	1,216,282
1936	366,607	12,831,245	5,902,776	4,571,700	17,730,000	1,631,160
1937	368,905	12,911,675	6,260,693	4,842,646	21,868,000	2,646,028
1938	367,468	12,861,380	7,932,095	5,127,819	28,342,000	2,777,516
1939	366,852	12,839,820	8,496,488	5,767,313	26,430,000	2,748,720
1940	367,336	12,856,760	9,710,709	6,905,393	24,304,000	2,746,352
1941	380,029	13,301,015	7,301,697	5,192,318	13,496,000	1,592,528
1942	268,627	9,401,945	3,096,211	2,201,750	2,204,000	266,684
1943	137,558	4,814,530	2,664,142	1,894,501	2,056,000	267,280

COMPARATIVE CHART OF MINERAL PRODUCTION IN COLORADO FROM 1858 TO 1943

| Year | LEAD | | ZINC | | TUNGSTEN | |
| | (121) | | (121) | | (122) | |
	Pounds	Value	Pounds	Value	Short Tons	Value
1858-67						
1868						
1869	150,000	$9,000				
1870	250,000	15,000		—		
1871	555,000	33,300				
1872	1,150,000	73,600		—		
1873	1,236,400	74,184				
1874	1,277,933	76,676		—		
1875	1,636,000	94,888				
1876	1,334,020	81,375		—		
1877	4,286,364	235,750		—		
1878	13,722,222	494,000				
1879	47,348,000	1,941,268		—		
1880	71,348,000	3,567,400				
1881	81,094,000	3,892,512		—		
1882	110,000,000	5,390,000				
1883	141,114,000	6,067,902		—		
1884	126,330,000	4,674,209				
1885	106,692,000	4,160,989	100,000	$4,300		
1886	118,000,000	5,428,000	100,000	4,400		
1887	126,000,000	5,670,000	100,000	4,600		
1888	128,404,000	5,649,777	300,000	14,700		
1889	133,940,000	5,223,660	300,000	15,000		
1890	109,192,000	4,913,639	300,000	16,500		
1891	126,256,000	5,429,009	300,000	15,000		
1892	120,000,000	4,800,001	1,125,000	51,750		
1893	110,000,000	4,070,000	1,650,000	66,000		
1894	101,226,000	3,340,458	1,500,000	52,500		
1895	93,968,000	3,006,976	1,671,000	60,156		
1896	89,606,000	2,688,178	1,292,000	50,388		
1897	80,794,286	2,908,592	2,683,989	110,044		
1898	113,416,138	4,309,813	3,900,656	179,430		
1899	138,048,446	6,212,178	11,300,656	655,438		
1900	164,274,762	7,228,090	16,282,055	716,410	40	$ 9,600
1901	148,111,020	6,368,772	26,843,731	1,100,593	65	10,062
1902	106,296,827	4,358,169	52,582,510	2,523,963	166	30,677
1903	101,513,414	4,263,566	80,616,000	4,353,263	243	36,304
1904	107,498,864	4,622,453	66,771,590	3,405,353	375	92,700
1905	115,746,777	5,440,098	83,561,396	4,930,123	642	214,556
1906	106,646,506	6,078,850	86,012,903	5,246,787	789	296,348
1907	89,065,232	4,720,457	85,048,564	5,017,865	1,146	573,643
1908	61,645,671	2,589,118	30,130,002	1,416,110	584	204,465
1909	72,162,326	3,102,980	51,210,260	2,765,354	993	391,160
1910	76,058,775	3,346,586	77,089,648	4,162,841	1,221	535,567
1911	69,679,289	3,135,568	94,607,456	5,392,625	730	234,513
1912	75,242,267	3,385,902	132,222,812	9,123,374	812	305,474
1913	87,897,773	3,867,502	119,346,429	6,683,400	953	428,760
1914	74,211,898	2,894,264	96,774,960	4,935,523	467	182,013
1915	68,810,597	3,234,098	104,594,994	12,969,779	963	2,311,200
1916	70,914,087	4,893,072	134,285,463	17,994,252	2,401	4,666,301
1917	67,990,012	5,847,141	120,315,775	12,272,209	2,707	2,994,000
1918	65,960,760	4,683,214	89,133,901	8,111,185	1,910	2,595,800
1919	37,070,241	1,964,722	37,220,493	2,717,096	130	78,334
1920	46,629,788	3,730,383	48,790,742	3,952,050	216	101,800
1921	19,660,466	884,721	2,360,000	118,000	none	none
1922	23,477,200	1,291,246	23,258,000	1,207,706	none	none
1923	45,698,185	3,198,873	54,152,000	3,682,336	241	144,000
1924	47,557,061	3,804,565	56,727,000	3,687,255	123	62,519
1925	62,966,000	5,478,042	61,621,000	4,683,196	201	127,474
1926	68,987,800	5,519,024	65,000,000	4,875,000	232	148,200
1927	66,772,557	4,206,671	71,729,000	4,590,656	332	209,007
1928	53,501,723	3,103,100	71,462,000	4,359,182	229	149,423
1929	48,889,906	3,080,064	58,861,000	3,884,826	152	124,416
1930	44,260,000	2,213,000	72,518,000	3,480,864	47	37,050
1931	13,768,000	509,416	32,373,000	1,230,174	98	73,563
1932	4,299,000	128,970	218,000	6,540	a few	-------
1933	4,803,000	177,711	2,569,000	107,898	86	49,371
1934	8,435,000	312,095	1,544,000	66,392	342	298,063
1935	11,345,000	453,800	2,403,000	105,732	390	312,858
1936	14,534,000	668,564	2,344,000	117,200	180	154,431
1937	19,572,000	1,154,748	8,494,000	552,110	219	246,260
1938	18,910,000	869,860	9,106,000	437,088	240	249,020
1939	16,444,000	772,868	3,660,000	190,320	479	488,628
1940	22,952,000	1,147,600	10,120,000	637,560	693	822,988
1941	25,148,000	1,433,436	31,444,000	2,358,300	631	928,508
1942	30,362,000	2,034,254	64,430,000	5,991,990	380	548,177
1943	36,064,000	2,704,800	88,188,000	9,524,304	342	514,486

COMPARATIVE CHART OF MINERAL PRODUCTION IN COLORADO FROM 1858 TO 1943

Year	MOLYBDENUM (123) Pounds	Value	COAL (125) Tons	Value	PETROLEUM (126) Barrels	Value
1858-67			25,100	$50,200		
1868			10,500	21,000		
1869			8,000	16,000		
1870			13,500	27,000		
1871			15,860	31,720		
1872			68,540	137,080		
1873			69,997	139,980		
1874			77,372	154,744		
1875			98,838	197,676		
1876			117,666	235,332		
1877			160,000	320,000		
1878			200,630	401,260		
1879			322,732	645,464		
1880			462,747	1,041,181		
1881			706,744	1,590,174		
1882			1,061,479	2,388,328		
1883			1,229,593	2,766,584		
1884			1,130,024	2,542,554		
1885			1,356,062	3,051,589		
1886			1,368,338	3,215,594		
1887			1,791,735	3,941,817	76,000	$ 76,295
1888			2,185,477	4,808,049	298,000	267,851
1889			2,597,181	3,993,768	317,000	280,240
1890			3,077,003	4,344,196	369,000	309,827
1891			3,512,632	4,800,000	666,000	559,005
1892			3,510,830	5,685,112	824,000	692,160
1893			4,102,389	5,104,602	594,000	497,581
1894			2,831,409	3,516,340	516,000	303,652
1895			3,082,982	3,675,185	438,000	336,010
1896			3,112,402	3,606,642	361,000	318,977
1897			3,361,703	3,947,186	385,000	332,122
1898			4,076,347	4,686,081	444,000	367,447
1899			4,776,224	5,363,667	390,000	404,110
1900			5,244,364	5,858,036	317,000	323,434
1901			5,700,015	6,441,891	461,000	461,031
1902			7,401,343	8,397,812	397,000	484,683
1903			7,423,602	9,150,943	484,000	431,723
1904			6,658,355	8,751,821	501,000	578,035
1905			8,826,429	10,810,978	376,000	337,606
1906			10,111,218	12,735,616	328,000	262,675
1907			10,790,236	15,079,449	332,000	272,813
1908			9,634,973	13,586,988	380,000	346,403
1909			10,716,936	14,296,012	311,000	318,162
1910			11,973,736	17,026,934	240,000	263,402
1911			10,157,383	14,747,764	227,000	228,104
1912			10,977,824	16,345,336	206,000	199,661
1913			9,232,510	14,035,090	189,000	174,779
1914			8,170,559	13,601,718	223,000	200,894
1915			8,624,980	13,599,264	208,000	183,485
1916			10,484,237	16,964,104	197,000	217,139
1917			12,483,336	27,669,129	121,000	128,100
1918	663,386	$995,695	12,407,571	33,404,743	143,000	188,472
1919	296,813	340,444	10,323,420	28,748,534	121,000	183,000
1920	none	none	12,278,225	42,829,000	111,000	199,000
1921	none	none	9,122,760	32,377,000	108,000	132,000
1922	none	none	10,019,597	31,701,000	97,000	114,000
1923	none	none	10,346,218	33,299,000	86,000	102,000
1924	156,935	(124)	10,444,098	31,863,000	445,000	490,000
1925	821,757		10,310,551	30,322,000	1,226,000	1,810,000
1926	1,057,367		10,637,225	29,529,000	2,768,000	5,100,000
1927	1,858,228		9,724,075	27,044,000	2,831,000	3,400,000
1928	2,957,845		9,847,707	27,613,000	2,774,000	2,750,000
1929	3,529,741		9,920,741	26,254,000	2,358,000	2,380,000
1930	3,083,000		8,196,910	21,485,000	1,656,000	1,480,000
1931	2,644,399		6,604,369	15,944,000	1,545,000	825,000
1932	1,913,395		5,598,721	12,237,000	1,136,000	880,000
1933	5,028,695		5,229,767	11,350,000	919,000	540,000
1934	8,378,683		5,210,933	12,063,000	1,139,000	1,060,000
1935	9,558,120		5,910,511	13,675,000	1,560,000	1,420,000
1936	16,001,816		6,811,802	16,277,000	1,650,000	1,660,000
1937	23,566,481		7,187,211	18,327,000	1,605,000	1,800,000
1938	20,763,884		5,663,144	14,828,000	1,412,000	1,540,000
1939	25,437,893		5,923,210	14,620,726	1,404,000	1,330,000
1940	18,600,897		6,588,742	16,644,265	1,626,000	1,480,000
1941	24,942,003		6,948,532	19,654,459	2,150,000	2,300,000
1942	41,852,136	29,000,000	8,085,680	23,163,270	2,199,000	2,440,000
1943	46,133,715	33,000,000	8,250,000	26,978,000	2,320,000	2,600,000

INDEX

Schoolhouse, first in Colorado, especially built for that purpose, was at Boulder, and Abner Brown was the instructor, II, 160

School libraries, II, 551

Schools, administration of city systems, II, 177-82; affected by depression years, II, 355; conducted in rented quarters previous to 1872 and in 1864 public schools were closed for a time for lack of tax money, I, 257-58; disturbed by mining excitement, II, 166; early administration of; in state, county and district, II, 175-77; first one, opened in Denver in 1859, was housed in a log cabin, it became known as the Denver Union School, II, 160; funds discussed, I, 348-49; having classes for the handicapped, II, 179; progress reported, II, 163-67, 170-72, 186-87; public, started in 1861, I, 428; II, 161; statistics of, II, 162-63; threatened by Indians, II, 165; were established at Mount Vernon, Golden and Boulder, I, 193

Schram, J. E., the first mayor of Glenwood Springs, I, 409

Schram, Joe, opened a store in Glenwood Springs, I, 407

Schurz, Carl (Secretary of the Interior), appointed a commission to investigate Indian troubles, I, 386-87; spoke in tribute to Chief Ouray, I, 390-91

Schwayder Brothers, II, 607

Schwayder, Jesse, II, 607

Schweiker, Frederick W., II, 465

Science Gossip (British), II, 22

Scotch settlers in Colorado, II, 102

Scott (Bishop), II, 201

Scott, Tully (Judge), II, 378

Scott's lode at Gold Hill, II, 487, 489

Scout's Rest Ranch, I, 494

Scouten, D. G., II, 255

Scrip issued by banks and express companies during the currency shortage of 1873-74, II, 284

Scudder, Edwin, member of the Colorado House of Representatives, I, 283

Sculptors, non-resident, represented in Denver, II, 435

Sears, J. P., established a wholesale provision house; became a gold buyer and banker, II, 292

Seasons in Colorado, I, 4

Seckner, H., had a mercantile store in Windsor, I, 426

Second Colorado Cavalry in the Civil War, The (by Adams, Blanche V., in the *Colorado Magazine*, VIII, 95-106), I, 307

Second Colorado Infantry, I, 302, 307

Second Regiment of Colorado Cavalry Volunteers, I, 308

Secondary education in Colorado, II, 188

Sects and Cults, II, 224

Securities and Exchange Commission, I, 562-63

Sedgwick post office established in 1880 and the town site surveyed and laid off in April, 1887, by Hiram Sapp and John Casey; incorporation took place on Jan. 28, 1918, I, 433

Sedgwick, John (Major) (for whom Sedgwick County was named), led four companies of cavalry in the campaign against the Cheyennes, I, 135-36; met a Missouri party of gold seekers, I, 141

See Bar See Land and Cattle Company, I, 435

Seed industry in Colorado, II, 144

Seep, Albert, II, 589

Seep, Herman F., II, 589

Seep, Joseph, II, 588

Seerie, David, II, 606

Segregation of Negroes in Colorado, II, 119

Segundo, I, 450

Seibert, named for Henry Seibert, a New York official of the Rock Island Railroad, I, 438

Select Choir, directed by Dr. Gower, II, 467

Selective draft system adopted by the United States in 1917, I, 539

Selig, Joseph, principal founder of the town of Montrose, I, 401

Seltzer, C. C., *Racial Prehistory in the Southwest and the Hawikuh Zunis* (in, *Papers of the Peabody Museum of American Archaeology and Ethnology, Harvard University*, XXIII, no. 1), II, 42

Semi-Centennial History of the State of Colorado (by Smiley, Jerome C.), I, 50

Sen, Sun Yat (Dr.), II, 117

Senate Executive Document, number 26, of the 39th Congress, second session, gives a 228 page report on the Battle of Sand Creek, I, 317

Sentinel, started in 1871, next year became the *Longmont Press*, II, 258

Serums, II, 579-80

Settle, Pierre, claimed land in Cedaredge, I, 400

Settlements in America, early, I, 8, 21; Colorado, 1819 to 1848, I, 100-4; Jamestown, Va., by the English, 1607, I, 21; on the Arkansas in 1853, I, 106; Quebec, Canada, by the French, 1608, I, 21; San Luis Valley, II, 96; West Indies, first towns by Spain, 1493, I, 21

Settlers Protective Association of Grand Junction, I, 396

Seventh Day Adventist Denomination, II, 216

Sevier River, in Utah, I, 96

Sewall, Eunice D. (Mrs.), II, 568

Sewall, Henry (Dr.), organized the Colorado Medical Library Association, II, 394, 398

Sexton (Captain), with Captain Backus, formed the Second Colorado Infantry Volunteers, I, 307

Seymour, Samuel, landscape painter with the Long Expedition of 1820, I, 57; II, 419

S. and H. Supply Company, II, 592

Swift and Company, II, 572

Swink, George W., father of the Arkansas Valley melon industry, II, 143; partner of A. Russell at Rocky Ford, I, 422; sugar beet industry promoter, II, 146-47

Swits, Charles, pugilist, I, 250

Symes, George G., elected Congressman in 1884, I, 456

Symes, George S., comments favorably on the national banks of Colorado, II, 301

Symphony Club, founded by Florence Taussig, II, 467

Synod of the Reformed Presbyterian Church of North America, II, 210

Synopsis of the Flora of Colorado (1874) (by Porter, T. C., and Coulter, J. M.), II, 20

Tabehuachio Mountains, II, 6

Tabernash, named for the Ute Indian killed near there, became a town with the coming of the Moffat railroad, I, 403

Table Mountain, I, 163

Tabor, Augusta, with her husband and son Maxcy left their Kansas farm for "the Pikes Peak country" but finding the hardships too great opened a boarding house in Auraria. She conducted placer mining operations of her own nearby and, so far as known, was the first woman to have done so, II, 560

Tabor, Baby Doe, II, 454

Tabor Grand Opera House in Denver, I, 366-67; II, 441, 452-53, 456

Tabor, H. A. W., chosen mayor of Leadville, I, 361, II, 424, 588, 590; opened a store in Leadville, I, 361; purchased the Tam O'Shanter group of mines, I, 445; shared in the profits of the "Little Pittsburgh" mine of August Rische and George T. Hook, 1, 362; "Silver King", II, 441; succeeded Senator Chilcott in 1882, I, 456; President of the First National Bank of Leadville, II, 298-99

Tabor Opera House in Leadville, II, 472

Tabor's Silver Circuit, II, 450, 462-63

Taft, Arthur N. (Rev.), II, 439

Taft, Robert, *The Pictorial Record of the West, I, Frenzeny and Tavernier, (in Rocky Mountain News, Feb. 17, 1874),* II, 422

Talbot, Freeman H., II, 470

Talbot, Joseph C. (Bishop), II, 205

Tale of Men who Knew not Fear, A (by Gertrude Harris), I, 302

Tall stories, I, 276

Tammen, Harry H., II, 272-73

Tam-O-Shanter Mine in Pitkin County, II, 588

Taos, I, 16-17; a supply base for trappers, I, 71; settlers from, establish new home in San Luis Valley, I, 118

Taos Massacre, I, 108

Taos Pueblos, II, 54

"Taos Trail," I, 70

Taos Valley, I, 125

Tappan, S. F. (Lieutenant Colonel), on military commission to investigate conduct of Colonel Chivington, I, 301, 317

Tarbell, Fanny, famous portrait painter, II, 426

Tarima, bench of adobe in early Spanish pioneer homes, I, 120

Tarvernier, J., illustrator for Harper's Weekly, II, 422

Tasty Food Company, II, 575

Tax returns for individuals in 1941, II, 90

Taylor (General), in the Mexican War, I, 113

Taylor, Bayard, II, 564; commented on life in the mining camps, II, 241; described his stagecoach trip to the Pikes Peak country, I, 230-31

Taylor, Cyrus, II, 492

Taylor, Dave, took land near Fortification Creek, I, 405

Taylor, Donald, took land near Fortification Creek, I, 405

Taylor, F. M. P. (Mrs.), art patron, II, 440-41

Taylor, Paul S., *Mexican Labor in the United States Valley of the South Platte Colorado,* II, 99

Taylor and Wallace carpenter shop, in Sterling, I, 429

Teachers, qualifications of, II, 172-75

Telegraph lines, completed to Durango in 1881, and the first telegram sent out to the press of the country on July 30, 1881, I, 294, 297, 415

Telephone development, I, 582-86

Telephone service in Colorado, I, 374-76; II, 157, 537

Telephone trans-Atlantic service began in 1927, I, 584

Teller, Henry M. (Senator), became Secretary of the Interior in President Arthur's cabinet, I, 455-56; retired in 1909, I, 510; leader of the Colorado delegation, walked out of the National Republican Convention with thirty-four other delegates, I, 469, II, 287; served in the United States Senate, I, 359, 473; II, 302-4

Teller House, II, 459, 496

Teller, Willard, II, 376

Teller City, founded in Illinois Creek in 1879, became the center of the mining activity, I, 406

Telluride, started in 1878, became the county seat of San Miguel County, I, 444

Telluride Power Transmission Company, II, 502-3

Tellurium discovered, II, 496

Temple Emanuel, best known Jewish synagogue in Colorado, II, 114, 223; congregation organized in 1864, I, 257

Temple, Oscar, II, 606

Templeton, Josie (Miss), taught the first school in Wray in 1886, I, 435

Templeton Opera Company, II, 463

Tenney, R. Q. of Fort Collins, established his Victory Dairy about 1871, II, 142; master of the Clear Creek Valley Grange, II, 155

Tenth Federal Reserve District, formation of the, II, 305-10

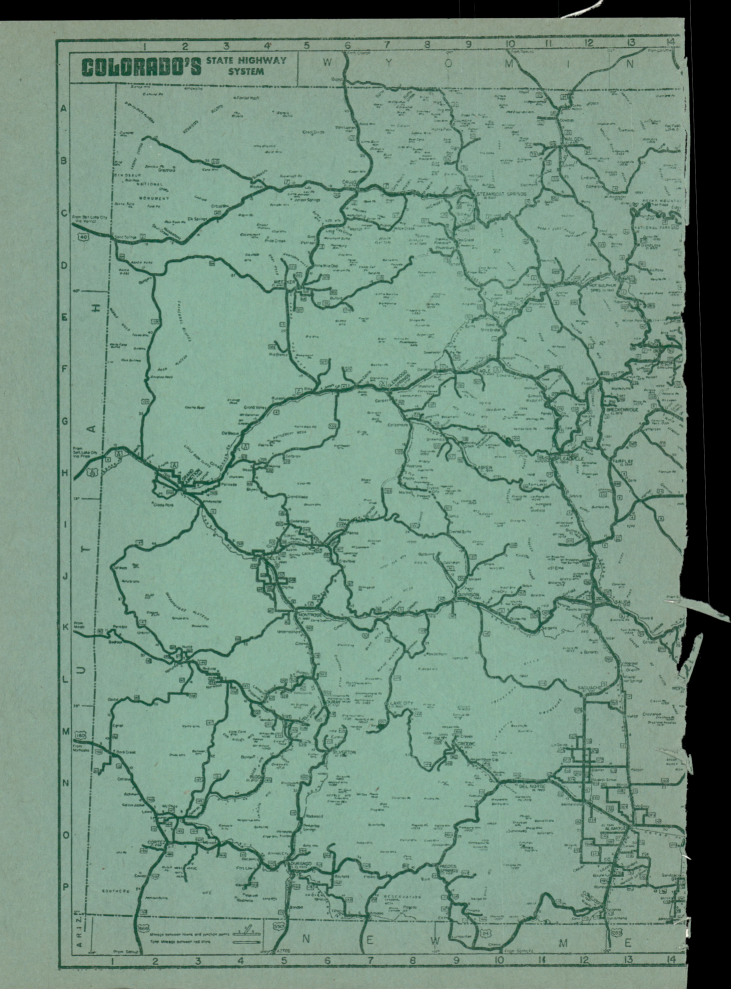

COLORADO'S STATE HIGHWAY SYSTEM